ALEXANDER OF APHRODISIAS
ON FATE

D1614573

ALEXANDER OF APHRODISIAS ON FATE

Text, translation and commentary

R.W. Sharples

Duckworth

To my parents

First published in 1983 by
Gerald Duckworth & Co. Ltd.
The Old Piano Factory
43 Gloucester Crescent, London NW1

© 1983 by R.W. Sharples

All rights reserved. No part of this publication may be reproduced,
stored in a retrieval system, or transmitted, in any form or by
any means, electronic, mechanical, photocopying, recording
or other wise, without the prior permission of the publisher.

ISBN 0 7156 1589 0 (cased)
ISBN 0 7156 1739 7 (paper)

British Library Cataloguing in Publication Data

Alexander of Aphrodisias
  Alexander of Aphrodisias on fate.
  1. Fate and fatalism
  I. Title   II. Sharples, R.W.
  123'.0938   BD411

  ISBN 0-7156-1589-0

Photoset in North Wales by
Derek Doyle & Associates, Mold, Clwyd
Printed in Great Britain by
Redwood Burn Ltd, Trowbridge

Contents

Preface

My principal concern in this book has been to make Alexander's treatise *On Fate and Responsibility* more accessible than hithero to those interested in the history of the philosophical issues with which it is concerned. I have accordingly provided an English translation, accompanied by a commentary, of this treatise and of a number of shorter discussions attributed to Alexander (cf. below, p. 16). To make the details of Alexander's argument accessible to those who have little or no Greek, and to avoid the introduction of misleading nuances, the translation is close to the Greek, even when this has meant sacrificing a more natural English expression. The Commentary, which should be read together with the Introduction and Analysis, is devoted not so much to elucidation of Alexander's argument – which is, with certain exceptions, relatively clear – as to indication of the main issues and problems that it raises, where appropriate referring those who are particularly interested to more detailed studies of specific points by myself or by others. No attempt has been made to give a full commentary on the texts included here other than the *de fato*, as this would involve much duplication; but discussion of points made in these passages may be located in the commentary on the *de fato* with the aid of the Index of Passages Cited.

For the convenience of those readers who do not have easy access to the Greek texts of the works here translated, edited by I. Bruns in *Supplementum Aristotelicum* 2.1-2 (Berlin, 1887 and 1892), a photographic reprint of these texts has been provided (located after the Commentary). Asterisks in the margin indicate places where I prefer a different reading, and have based my translation on it; details of these variations may be found in the 'Notes on the Text', *Adnotationes ad Textum*, which follow the Greek text. (Cf. also below, Introduction, section 3.) It has not been possible to alter Bruns' text where my translation reflects a different reading, and for this reason text and translation have not been placed facing each other.

The Introduction and Commentary draw much material from my 1977 Cambridge Ph.D. thesis *Studies in the De Fato of Alexander of Aphrodisias*. I am grateful for advice and encouragement to my supervisors for the thesis, the late Professor W.K.C. Guthrie, Professor J.D.G. Evans and Dr G.E.R. Lloyd, to its examiners, Professors A.A. Long and F.H. Sandbach, and to many others, in particular Mr Myles Burnyeat, Ms Jean Christensen, Dr Walter Cockle, Professor Terence Irwin, Professor Anthony Preus, Dr Hans-Jochen Ruland, Dr Malcolm Schofield, Dr David Sedley, Professor Richard Sorabji, Professor Robert B. Todd, Professor Michael J. White and Dr Fritz Zimmermann. Various parts of this book reflect papers which I have read at meetings in Oxford, Cambridge and London, and I am grateful to all who contributed to discussion of them. I am also grateful for help in checking MSS readings to Drs Adam Bülow-Jacobsen and David McKie, and to the staff of the following libraries: Biblioteca Nacional, Madrid; Bayerische Staatsbibliothek, Munich; Biblioteca Nazionale Marciana, Venice; Osterreichische Nationalsbibliothek, Vienna; Herzog August Bibliothek, Wolfenbüttel. I have been greatly helped by two microfilms of MS V in the library of the Institute of Classical Studies of the University of London, one of them purchased from the Joyce Southan Memorial Fund; and I am grateful to the Librarian, Miss Ana Healey, for advice in various respects. Professor A.A. Long has kindly read through the translation of the *de fato*, and contributed numerous suggestions. The translation of *Mantissa* XXII is a revision of that which appeared in the *Bulletin of the Institute of Classical Studies* 22 (1975) 37ff.; I am grateful to the Editor for permission to use it here, and to incorporate outher material from the article of which it formed part. The Departments of Greek and Latin at University College London have provided a most stimulating and encouraging environment in which to work, and the library facilities in London are of course second to none.

I am most grateful to Gerald Duckworth and Co., and especially to Mr Colin Haycraft, for undertaking the publication of this book on an author who has been less well-known than his importance deserves.

The writing of this book was completed before the appearance of Richard Sorabji's *Necessity, Cause and Blame: Aspects of Aristotle's Theory* (London 1980), which contains much that is relevant to the themes here discussed, as also does Sarah Waterlow's *Passage and Possibility; a*

Study of Aristotle's Modal Concepts, Oxford, 1982.

My thanks are above all due to my wife Grace, née Nevard, who has read the whole book in typescript and has provided unfailing encouragement and advice throughout its preparation. The responsibility for the views here expressed, and for any remaining errors, is of course entirely my own.

I have completed the proof reading and indexing of this book at a time when there has seemed to be little public sympathy for, or understanding of, any but the most narrowly vocational aspects of higher education in this country. Politicians who are tempted to portray as 'necessary in the circumstances' policies which in fact reflect their own choices would do well to ponder what Alexander has to say on p. 93 below; conversely, scholars may take comfort in the fact that we are not, at least, liable to attack for reasons quite as ignorant and foolish as Caracalla's (p. 125).

University College London
December 1982.   R.W.S.

Note on Abbreviations

References to Alexander's writings are throughout given by page and line number of the following editions. *De anima* and *de anima libri mantissa* (= *m*): I. Bruns, *Supplementum Aristotelicum* 2.1 (Berlin, 1887). *Quaestiones* (= *q*), 'Problems in Ethics' (= *p*), *de fato* (= *f*) and *de mixtione*: id. 2.2 (1892). *On Providence* (= *de prov.*): Ruland (cf. Bibliography p.287). *On the Principles of the Universe* (= *de princ.*): Badawi (cf. Bibliography p.286). Bruns' line numbers appear in the left-hand margin of the text and his page numbers in the outer margin of each page. The page and line numbers in the right-hand margin of the text are those of the editions of Orelli (*f*), a¹ (*m*) and Spengel (*q*). Details of works cited by the author's name only will be found in the Bibliography (or, in the case of works cited in the textual apparatus and critical appendix, in the Sigla); editions of other ancient editions according to which references have been given are listed, where there is any possibility of doubt, in the Bibliography. The following abbreviations have been used:

> *Dox.* H. Diels, ed., *Doxographi Graeci*, ed. iterata, Berlin and Leipzig, 1929.
>
> *PG* *Patrologia Graeca*, ed. J-P. Migne, Paris 1857-1904.
>
> *SVF* H. von Arnim, ed., *Stoicorum Veterum Fragmenta*, Leipzig 1903-1905; vol. IV, index, by M. Adler, 1924.
>
> Calcidius = Calcidius *in Platonis Timaeum Commentarius* (cf. Bibliography).
>
> [Plutarch] = [Plutarch] *de fato* (Plutarch *Moralia* 568B – 574F).

Introduction

Alexander of Aphrodisias' treatise *To the Emperors on Fate and Responsibility*[1] (*de fato*) is perhaps the most comprehensive treatment surviving from classical antiquity of the problem of responsibility and determinism – a problem which is still of great philosophical interest, and one where many of the points made by Alexander are still relevant. This in itself would justify making more accessible a work that has only once before been translated into English (by A. FitzGerald; London, 1931) and that scarcely adequately. However, an almost equally important reason for interest in Alexander's treatise is his criticism of what is above all a Stoic position[2] from an Aristotelian standpoint;[3] consideration of his arguments thus illuminates the differences between Aristotelian and Stoic approaches to the question, and so throws light on each individually. Moreover, the earlier Stoics' own writings have not survived, and Alexander's treatise is a major secondary source for their doctrine, though one which must be used with caution. The present work should make it easier to consider passages from the treatise which provide evidence for the Stoic position not in isolation but in the context of Alexander's argument as a whole.

1. The problem before Alexander[4]

The problem of determinism and responsibility was not realised, in the form in which it was eventually passed on to post-classical thinkers, until relatively late in the history of Greek thought.

---

[1] On 'responsibility' as a rendering of *tò eph' hēmin* cf. p. 9.

[2] Cf. pp. 19-21.

[3] Cf. *f.* I.164.13, 165.3, VI 171.16f., XXXIX 212.5, 17; and pp. 22-25.

[4] For reasons of space I have not given full references to secondary literature in this Introduction; the reader is advised to consult the Select Bibliography.

Although there are passages in which it is recognised that there is something problematic in holding someone responsible for an action that a god has foretold he will perform,[5] it is generally misleading in the interpretation of the literature of the fifth century B.C. and earlier to assume that the difficulty is always as obvious or as important as it seems to us.[6] The mechanistic atomism of Democritus (born 460-457 B.C.) may well seem to *us* to raise difficulties for human responsibility, and it seemed to do so to Epicurus,[7] but Democritus himself apparently felt no such problem.[8] The question of the relation between destiny and human choice is raised, in mythical form, at the end of the *Republic* of Plato (*c.* 429-347 B.C.), in a passage that was to be important for later discussion;[9] but it only attains its full significance in the context of a theory claiming that *all* events in the physical world are governed by a rigid determinism, and this is not present in Plato, for whom what admits of absolute regularity with no exceptions is to be found among the Ideas rather than in sensible phenomena.[10]

The classic notion of determinism – of a system in which every state of affairs is a necessary consequence of any and every preceding state of affairs – is almost entirely absent from the approach to the physical world of Aristotle (384-322 B.C.) also; more important for him is the contrast between, on the one hand, the absolute necessity and invariance which applies to the motions of the heavenly bodies, to mathematical truths, and to certain attributes of beings in the sublunary world – the mortality of all men, for example – and, on the other hand, the irregularity and variation of many aspects of the

[5] Cf. Sophocles *Oedipus at Colonus* 969ff., and, for comic effect, Aristophanes *Frogs* 1183.

[6] E.R. Dodds, *The Greeks and the Irrational* (Berkeley 1951) 3ff., and 'On misunderstanding the *Oedipus Rex*', *Greece and Rome* 13 (1966) 42f.; N.G.L. Hammond, 'Personal freedom and its limitations in the *Oresteia*', *JHS* 85 (1965) 552f.; A.W.H. Adkins, *Merit and Responsibility* (Oxford 1960) 118ff., 324; cf. Huby 345-7.

[7] Epicurus On Nature 31.30.7ff. Arrighetti; cf. Diogenes of Oenoanda fr. 32 Chilton.

[8] Bailey 186ff. (cf. however L. Edmunds, 'Necessity, chance and freedom in the early atomists', *Phoenix* 26 (1972) 357). It is not certain how far Democritus, in reducing everything to the movements and collisions of atoms, had consciously formulated the idea of a deterministic nexus extending over all time (cf. Huby (1967) 359-61; *contra*, Balme (1941)); whether he had or not, his position was of interest to Plato (*Laws* X 889b ff.) and to Aristotle (*phys.* 2.4 196a24 ff.) not as deterministic but as denying providence (cf. W.K.C. Guthrie, *History of Greek Philosophy* II (Cambridge, 1965) 416ff.; Edmunds op. cit. 305f.).

[9] Cf. p. 13.

[10] Cf. G.R. Morrow, 'Necessity and persuasion in Plato's *Timaeus*', *Philos. Rev.* 59 (1950) 160f.

sublunary world, where the most that can be said of many things is
that they happen for the most part but not always, and where there
are many accidental connections that fall outside the scope of
scientific knowledge – concerned with what is always or usually the
case – altogether.[11] Aristotle's picture of the consequences of an
event is not one of chains of cause and effect interwoven in a nexus
extending to infinity, but rather, in Professor Balme's analogy,[12] one
resembling the ripples caused by the throwing of a stone into a
pond, which spread out and combine with the ripples caused by
other stones, but eventually die away and came to nothing. And
conversely, Aristotle can assert that there are fresh beginnings
(*archai*), not confined to human agency, without supposing that
there is a deterministic causal nexus occasionally interrupted by
undetermined events; he simply does not see the question in these
terms.[13] He does discuss the question whether all events are
determined by necessary chains of causation at *Metaphyisics* E 3
1027a30 – b14, and there denies this possibility insisting that not
everything is necessary;[14] but here as elsewhere it is not clear that he
distinguishes between (i) the claim that there are events which are
not predetermined, and (ii) the lesser claim that there are some
things that do not always happen in the same way – which does not
exclude their being predetermined by different factors on each
occasion.[15] He certainly holds that there are events which result
from chance rather than necessity;[16] but as has often been pointed
out his treatment of chance events in terms of coincidence is not
incompatible with determinism.[17] He is in fact interested in a
different question, that of *explanation*; it may well be that chance
events have no scientific explanation,[18] without their thereby

[11] *de gen. et corr.* 2.11 334b13; *de part.an.* 1.1 639b24 ff.; *metaph.* E 2 1026b3 ff., 27 ff.,
1027a19 ff., Θ 8 1050b16 ff.; *eth. Nic.* 3.3 1112a23 ff. Cf. S. Sambursky, 'On the possible
and the probable in Ancient Greece', *Osiris* 12 (1956) 39, 46-48; Sharples (1975,1) 259-
64.
[12] Balme (1939) 137f.
[13] Cf. especially *de gen. an.* 4.10 778a5, and below p. 136; Balme (1939) 132, (1972)
76-84.
[14] Cf. *metaph.* E 2 1026b29, *de int.* 9. 19a7-22. Cf. Huby 36f.; Hintikka (1977) 107 ff.
[15] Cf. Sharples (1975,1) 250, 259-66, Hintikka (1977) 21f., 31f., 43-8, 111 ff.
[16] *metaph.* E 3 loc. cit.; *phys.* 2.5 196b10-17.
[17] E.g. W.D. Ross, *Aristotle*[5] (London 1949) 77f. (but on *metaph.* E 2 1027a23 ff. cf.
Sharples (1975,1) 263f.).
[18] Cf. *metaph.* E 2 1026b3 ff., 1027a19 ff.

involving indeterminism.[19] It would indeed be rash to claim that there are *no* passages where Aristotle intends to assert freedom from determinism as later philosophers would understand it;[20] but this is not, in dealing with the universe as a whole, his main concern. And Aristotle's emphasis on other questions, particularly that of the presence or absence of a variation which may well be entirely predetermined, was highly influential on later thinkers, Alexander among them, who *were* concerned with the problem of determinism.[21]

Aristotle did however discuss the issue of the analysis of responsible human action in a way which, although it does not form part of a treatment of determinism in the world as a whole, was nevertheless to be influential when this topic was later discussed. In *Nicomachean Ethics* III.1 he defines voluntary (*hekousion*) action as that where there is no external compulsion, so that the source (*archē*) of the action is in the agent, and where the agent is not ignorant of the particular details of what he is doing.[22] In *this* chapter he is concerned with the practical, quasi-legal problem of the imputability of actions to their agents, rather than with a philosophical analysis of freedom of choice,[23] but the question of the presence or absence of external compulsion was to be important in later discussion.[24]

In *Nicomachean Ethics* III.5 Aristotle asserts that responsible actions – those which 'depend on us' (cf. below) – involve the possibility of choosing otherwise (1113b7). He then meets the objection that a man's character may be such that he *cannot* choose other than actions of a particular sort by arguing that, since dispositions develop as a result of actions,[25] even if a man cannot *now* choose not to act in a certain way, it is his responsibility that he came to be like this in the first place (1114a3-31). This argument, however, only pushes the problem back into the past, till one comes

[19] Cf. p. 131.
[20] Cf. Sharples (1975,1) 264-7.
[21] Cf. Sharples (1975,1) 264f. and nn. 45, 48, also 249 n.5; (1978) 252 and n.20. On the features of Aristotle's position discussed in the above paragraph cf. the subtle and sensitive analysis of E. Hartman, *Substance, Body and Soul* (Princeton 1977) 51-6.
[22] 1109b35 – 1111a24; cf. Alexander *p.* 9 139.13ff.; 11 and 12 *passim*; 29 158.23ff.
[23] H.D.P. Lee, 'The legal background of two passages in the *Nicomachean Ethics*', *CQ.* 31 (1937) 140; Huby 354f.
[24] Cf. below, nn. 45 and p. 146; and, in the context of modern discussion, Taylor 366ff. and O'Connor 72ff.
[25] Cf. *eth. Nic.* 2.1 1103a31 ff.

to influences in our childhood – natural endowment, training and education – for which we can hardly be regarded as responsible.[26]

Aristotle is not indeed arguing against the background of a determist system, and it would be a mistake to press his argument too closely so as to extract deterministic implications from it.[27] It seems that he is operating with basically libertarian assumptions, starting from the position that responsibility involves freedom to choose between different courses of action, and dealing with difficulties arising from the determination of action by character only as a subordinate issue.[28] It is true that 'the possibility of choosing otherwise' *could* be interpreted in a qualified sense which would make it acceptable to a determinist,[29] but there is no explicit indication of this in Aristotle's text, and it seems likely that such attempts to reconcile determinism and responsibility only arose later as a reaction to the explicit assertion of the necessity of choosing between determinism and indeterminism.[30] However, Aristotle's treatment is not entirely satisfactory,[31] and its limitations and difficulties do become apparent when later thinkers, and above all Alexander, use it as a basis from which to argue against determinism.[32]

It is with Epicurus and the Stoics that clearly indeterministic and deterministic positions are first formulated. Epicurus (341-270 B.C.)

[26] At *eth. Nic.* 10.9 1179b20 ff. Aristotle comments that our natural endowment does not depend on us, but does *not* make the same observation concerning our education. – R. Foley, 'Compatibilism', *Mind* 87 (1978) 427f., argues that the power of free choice could be preserved if in our moral development from childood we *first* became able to influence our choice of ends and *then* as a result became able to act freely; but there is no sign of such a theory in Aristotle, who rather suggests that our conception of the end is formed by the way we act (cf. *eth. Nic.* 2.1 1103b13-23 with 3.5 1114b22 ff.). Alexander clearly both recognises the regress suggested in my text and attempts to escape it (cf. below, pp. 160-4).

[27] That even a settled disposition *can* be changed is suggested by *Cat.* 10 13a23-31, *eth. Nic.* 7.10 1152a29 ff. (but cf., for a different emphasis which should not however be pressed, ibid. 7.8 1150b31-5). Furley 190f.; W. Bondeson, 'Aristotle on responsibility for one's character and the possibility of character change', *Phronesis* 19 (1974) 59-65. And cf. below p. 161.

[28] Contrast, however, Furley 189f., 215-25.

[29] Cf. G.E. Moore, *Ethics* (Oxford 1912) 102-15; J. Austin, 'If's and can's', *Proc. Br. Acad.* 42 (1956) 109-32.

[30] Cf. Huby 354-7. Contrast, however, H.H. Joachim, Aristotle, *The Nicomachean Ethics* (Oxford 1951) 107-11, and D.J. Allan, 'The practical syllogism', in *Autour d'Aristote* (Festschrift Mansion, Louvain, 1955), 335f.

[31] Cf. Hardie, 174ff.

[32] Cf. below, pp. 148-9, 160-4.

8 *Introduction*

claimed that human freedom could only be maintained in the atomist system by the unpredetermined swerve of certain atoms from the paths which they would otherwise follow.[33] The problems of this position, which seems to reduce responsible human choice to pure randomness, have often been pointed out;[34] however, analogous problems seem involved in *any* attempt to treat responsibility in terms of the possibility of choosing otherwise, if this is to be combined with a rational explanation of why men do, or should, choose in a particular way.[35]

The Stoic position, given definitive expression by Chrysippus (*c.* 280-207 B.C.), the third head of the school, represents not the opposite extreme from that of Epicurus but an attempt to compromise, to combine determinism and responsibility. Their theory of the universe is indeed a completely deterministic one; everything is governed by fate, identified with the sequence of causes;[36] nothing could happen otherwise than it does, and in any given set of circumstances one and only one result can follow – otherwise an uncaused motion would occur.[37] Fate is also identified with providence[38] and with god,[39] and thus with *pneuma* or spirit, the divine active principle – or perhaps better the instrument or vehicle of the divine will – which penetrates the entire universe, bringing about and governing all processes within it and giving each thing its character.[40]

Chrysippus was however concerned to preserve human responsibility in the context of his determinist system. His position

---

[33] Lucretius 2.251-93; Cicero *de fato* 22f., 46ff.; Diogenes of Oenoanda fr. 32 Chilton.

[34] E.g. Bailey 435 ff., Furley 163f., 232f. (but cf. Long (1974) 61).

[35] Cf. pp. 149, 163-4.

[36] *SVF* 2.917f., 921, 933, 946, 1024; cf. also 2.528 fin., 913-915 (deriving *heimarmene* from *eiro*), 916.

[37] This position is indeed given some of its most telling expressions by Alexander himself and even later authors (cf. Alexander *f.* XV 185.7-10, XXII 192.22ff., *m.* 170.2-7, 174.3f.; also *f.* X 176.19-22, *q.* I.4 9.10-17, and *SVF* 2.946 p.273.41, 2.986 p.287.19 (Plotinus), 2.991 p.290.36 (Nemesius). For the Stoics as Alexander's opponents cf. below p. 19). But it is clearly implied by earlier statements in some cases going back to Chrysippus himself; cf. especially *SVF* 2.1000 p. 293.29-32, also '*SVF* 2.921f. and Cicero *de fato* 19-21. For the denial of uncaused motion cf. also Cicero *de fato* 23 ff., 34; *SVF* 2.912, 973 (Samburksy (1959) 56). Below p. 147.

[38] *SVF* 1.176, 2.528, 937, cf. 933.

[39] *SVF* 1.160, 2.528, 580 (= 1.102), 931, 937, 1076f.; cf. 2.929.

[40] *SVF* 2.913, cf. *SVF* 1.159, 2.300, 310, 323a, 416, 441f., 473, 475, 546, 1027, 1033-1048, 1051, 3.370. Cf. Sandbach 73f.; R.B. Todd, 'Monism and immanence', in J.M. Rist (ed.), *The Stoics* (Berkeley 1978) 137-160.

was thus one of 'soft determinism', as opposed on the one hand to
that of the 'hard determinist' who claims that determinism excludes
responsibility, and on the other to that of the libertarian who agrees
on the incompatibility but preserves responsibility by rejecting
determinism.[41] The Greek *to eph' hēmin*, 'what depends on us', like
the English 'responsibility', was used both by libertarians and by
soft determinists, though they differed as to what it involved; thus
the occurrence of the expression is not a safe guide to the type of
position involved. The situation is complicated by the fact that the
debate is in Greek philosophy conducted entirely in terms of
responsibility (*to eph' hēmin*) rather than of freedom or free will;[42]
nevertheless it can be shown that some thinkers, Alexander among
them, have a libertarian rather than a soft-determinist conception of
responsibility, and in such cases I have not hesitated to use
expressions like 'freedom'.[43] The expression 'free will' *is* employed in
discussions of the problem in ancient *Latin* writers.[44]

Chrysippus argued that we are responsible for those actions
which, even though they are predetermined, depend chiefly on
ourselves rather than on external factors.[45] (Epicurus, by contrast,
insisted that free actions must be free not only from external
necessity but also from necessitation by factors internal to the
agent.)[46] This is the force of Chrysippus' famous analogy of the
cylinder; just as the fact that a cylinder and cone roll, and do so in
different ways, when pushed on a slope depends primarily not on the
person who pushes them, who is only an auxiliary or initiating
cause, but on their shape in each case, the principal cause, so the
way in which different men react to the same stimulus depends

[41] For the terminology, originated by William James, cf. Taylor 368.

[42] 'Freedom' is indeed a favourite term of the Stoics, but it is used rather to express
the freedom of the wise man whose desires are such that they cannot be hindered by
outside interference (*SVF* 3.355-364, 544; Seneca *vit. beat.* 15.7; Epictetus *diss.* 1.12.9-
15. Long (1971) 189ff. and nn.; Sharples (1982,1) 50. Responsibility for actions
however, is something shared by all men, not just by the wise; cf. Stough 224 and n.46.

[43] Cf. pp. 21-2, 146. Even *to autoexousion*, used by Alexander at *f.* XIV 182.24 to
emphasise the contrast between his libertarian position and the soft-determinist one,
does not in itself necessarily have libertarian connotations; cf. *f.* XVIII 188.21,
Epictetus *diss.* 2.2.3, 4.1.62, 68, 100. Voelke 145 n.8; G. Pfligersdorffer, 'Fatum und
Fortuna', *Literaturwiss. Jahrb.* n.f. 2 (1961) 14f. and n.44.

[44] Cicero *de fato* 39, Augustine *SVF* 2.995; cf. Lucretius 2.256f.

[45] Cf. above n.24; Long (1971) 174f.

[46] Lucretius 2.288f., cf. Epicurus *On Nature* 31.27.4-9 Arrighetti; Furley 178-82,
186f., 194.

primarily on their own characters.[47] This raises the question of responsibility for character, rather as in Aristotle *Nicomachean Ethics* III.5; the Stoics certainly discussed men's initial natural endowment and its development in some detail,[48] but their general determinist position clearly precluded their giving any account of our responsibility for our character that would satisfy a libertarian.

Chrysippus also defended human responsibility by his doctrine of 'co-fated' events, advanced to counter the 'Lazy Argument' (*argos logos*) – 'if it is fated that you will recover, you will recover whether you call in a doctor or not; if it is fated that you will not recover, you will not recover whether you call in a doctor or not; and one or the other is fated; so (either way) there is no point in calling in a doctor.' Against this Chrysippus argued that, even if all events are predetermined, that does not mean that our action has no part to play and that subsequent events do not depend on it, for certain consequences cannot follow without certain actions on our part; if it is fated that Laius will have a son, it is also fated that he will sleep with a woman.[49] Determinism is not an excuse for fatalism[50] (though this does not prevent Alexander from repeatedly treating it as if it were).[51]

Certain ancient authors put forward arguments for praise, blame, punishment and reward in a determinist system with no appeal to responsbility – arguments which may therefore be classified as *hard*-determinist.[52] The wrongdoer should be punished for the protection of others whether or not he is responsible for his actions, just as noxious plants or animals are destroyed.[53] A Stoic source for these

[47] *SVF* 2.974, cf. 2.1000; also 2.994, 997. (However, *SVF* 2.974, from Cicero's *de fato* 39ff. and probably deriving from Antiochus of Ascalon, appears to distort Chrysippus' position in certain respects; cf. Donini (1974,1) 1-27, Sharples (1981) 84-5.

[48] *SVF* 1.518, 2.943 (applying to education the doctrine of 'co-fated' events, below n.49), 951, 1000 p.294.5ff. (cf. Long (1971) 187 and n.48), 3.188, 217, 223, 228-35. Long (1971) 184, 193; Reesor (1978) 191ff., and 'The 'Indifferents' in the Old and Middle Stoa', *Trans. Amer. Philol. Assoc.* 82 (1951) 104-106; Stough 212f., 225 and nn. 48f. Cf. Alexander *f.* XVIII and below n.104.

[49] *SVF* 2.956f., cf. 2.998. Cf. Aristotle *de interpretatione* 9 (below, n.55) 18b31, and below p. 166).

[50] Fatalism may be defined as the belief that the fortune cannot be affected by any of our actions; determinism does not claim this, but only that it is already predetermined which actions we will choose to perform. Taylor 368; O'Connor 13ff.

[51] Cf. pp. 141, 150, 171.

[52] Cf. e.g. H. Ofstad, 'Recent work on the free-will problem', *Amer. Philos. Quart.* 4 (1967) 182.

[53] Manilius 4.107-16 (cf. especially 117: *nec refert scelus unde cadat, scelus esse fatendum*)

arguments cannot be ruled out, for the Stoics may well have reinforced soft-determinist arguments justifying praise, blame, punishment and reward by others not referring to responsibility.[54]

In addition to physical, causal determinism one may also speak of 'logical' determinism. In chapter 9 of his *De Interpretatione*, the famous 'Sea-Battle' passage, Aristotle poses the problem that, if a prediction is either true or false, it seems that what is predicted must in the one case necessarily occur and in the other necessarily not occur. Aristotle's own solution to the problem is obscure.[55] Both Epicurus and the Stoics accepted a connection between the truth or falsity of the prediction and the eventual outcome's being predetermined, Epicurus rejecting determinism and consequently denying that all future-tense propositions *are* true or false,[56] the Stoics arguing that all propositions are true or false and using this as an argument to support determinism.[57] Carneades (214/3-129/8 B.C.), the founder of the sceptical New Academy, argued against both schools that the necessary connection between the truth of the prediction and the occurence of the event is simply an indication of what is meant by describing a proposition as true, and does not have any deterministic implications.[58] The predominant interpretation of Aristotle's own position in later antiquity was that a prediction of a future contingent event does have a truth value – it is true or false – but not a 'definite' one;[59] this position first appears in the last

---

and Galen *quod animi mores* 73.13ff. Müller, especially 74.9f. Theiler 56 and n.2; Donini (1974,2) 146f. and n.35. For the general attitude cf. K.J. Dover, *Greek Popular Morality* (Oxford 1974) 149.

[54] Cf. below p. 150, and the arguments at Alexander *f.* XXXV 207.5ff., XXXVI 210.8ff. (Responsibility is not mentioned in that at *f.* XXXIV 205.24ff., either, but is clearly implied by the references to right and wrong actions.)

[55] The literature on the chapter is vast; for summaries of the controversy cf. J. Ackrill, *Aristotle, Categories and De Interpretatione* (Oxford 1963) 132-42, and V.R. McKim, 'Fatalism and the future: Aristotle's way out', *Rev. of Metaphysics* 25 (1972) 80-111, and for bibliography cf. Hintikka 178-8. (Throughout this paragraph I use 'prediction' simply to refer to a future-tense statement, *not* implying that it is one based on some evidence about the future course of events; the problems of future truth and of foreknowledge are distinct.)

[56] Cicero *de fato* 21, 28 (*SVF* 2.952f.), 37; cf. id. *Acad. pr.* 2.97 (*SVF* 2.219), *de natura deorum* 1.70.

[57] *SVF* 2.912, 952f.

[58] Cicero *de fato* 19f., 27f.; cf. Long (1974) 102f.

[59] Ammonius *in de int. CAG* 4.5.138.16f., 139.14f., etc.; Boethius *in de int.*[1] 123.8ff., etc.,[2] 191.5, 208.11 ff. etc. Cf. J. Lukasiewicz, 'Philosophical remarks on many-valued systems of propositional logic', in S. McCall, ed., *Polish Logic 1920-1939* (Oxford 1967) 64.

section of *quaestio* I.4 attributed to Alexander,[60] but is not found in the *de fato*. It was probably advanced as a defence against those who attacked Aristotle as denying that predictions of contingent events had any truth value at all; Cicero indeed attributes this position to Epicurus and *not* to Aristotle (whom he regards as a determinist),[61] but we know that both Stoics and others had attacked Aristotle for holding such a view.[62]

A form of logical determinism which the Stoics however found less acceptable was that involved in the Master Argument of Diodorus Cronus (*fl. c.* 315-284 B.C.), a member of the Dialectical school.[63] From the premisses 'all that is past and true is necessary' and 'what is impossible does not follow from what is possible' Diodorus claimed to infer that only what is, or will be, true is possible.[64] Both Chrysippus and his predecessor Cleanthes (331-232 B.C.), however, rejected this conclusion, Cleanthes rejecting the first premiss, Chrysippus the second.[65] For the Stoics there are things that are possible even though they will not happen and even though it is predetermined that they will not.[66] Nevertheless, Cicero (106-43 B.C.), in his *de fato*, and other anti-determinist critics of the Stoics claimed that this was not compatible with their determinist position, and that they were committed to Diodorus' definition of the possible whether they liked it or not.[67] The issue is really one of the point of view taken. Even in a determinist system it may be useful to distinguish between things which *could* happen (given certain circumstances) but may or may not actually do so, depending on factors which may be obscure to us, and others which cannot happen at all. But those who are opposed to determinism are likely to find all such distinctions beside the point as long as it is still admitted that the actual outcome in each case is predetermined.[68]

[60] *q*. I.4 12.13ff.   [61] Cicero *de fato* 39. Cf. Verbeke, 75f.

[62] Boethius in de int.[2] 208.1ff., cf. 215.16ff. On Alexander's own position cf. below p. 138, and on the whole question cf. Sharples (1978) 263-4.

[63] D. Sedley, 'Diodorus Cronus and Hellenistic philosophy', *Proc. Cambridge Philol. Soc.* n.s. 23 (1977) 74-80, 82.

[64] *SVF* 2.283; Alexander *in an pr. CAG* 2.1.183.34-184.6. On the argument cf. A.N. Prior, 'Diodorean modalities', *Philos. Quart.* 5 (1955) 209-11, Hintikka 179-213, Sedley (op. cit. in n.63) 97-101.

[65] *SVF* 2.283, cf. 2.202a (below pp. 137-8), 2.954 (below p. 170).

[66] *SVF* 2.202, 2.954.13; Boethius *in de int.*[2] 235.4ff. Cf. below p. 134; Sharples (1981) 81-3.

[67] Cicero *de fato* 12-16 (*SVF* 2.954), Plutarch *de Stoic. rep.* 46 (*SVF* 2.202), Boethius loc. cit.; Alexander *f*. X 176.14 ff., *q*. I.4 9.30 etc.

[68] Cf. p. 135-6.

Cicero's treatise, of which unfortunately only the later part is extant, apart from a few fragments, is of particular importance for its presentation of the arguments advanced by Carneades, from whom the greater part of the treatise seems ultimately to derive.[69] Just as in the case of the problem of the truth of predictions Carneades endeavoured to show that both the Stoic and the Epicurean position rested on a common misconception, so in the case of physical determinism he argued that there was a middle ground between universal determinism on the one hand, and the occurrence of uncaused events on the other. Chance events are caused, in that they have accidental causes, but not predetermined;[70] human actions are not uncaused because their cause is in the nature of voluntary motion itself.[71] Both these claims are similar to ones made by Alexander, and will be discussed in the appropriate parts of the Commentary.[72]

It was probably Carneades, too, who made popular a series of arguments from the alleged practical consequences of determinism, reflected in later authors and among them Alexander (*f*.XVI-XX).[73] Our information on the place of Carneades in this tradition would probably be much better if we still possessed the lost part of Cicero's *de fato*.[74]

The last major development in the debate before Alexander was the elaboration by certain Middle-Platonists of a doctrine of conditional fate, based on Plato's teaching in *Republic* X where the souls, before their reincarnation, are themselves responsible for the choice of their subsequent lives.[75] This was adapted to apply within the course of an individual's earthly life; fate does not determine our choices, but it does decree that certain consequences will follow from those choices. The doctrine is referred to in Tacitus' *Annals*, probably from the second decade of the second century A.D.,[76] and appears in the *Didascalicus* ascribed to Alcinous (otherwise unknown) but perhaps by Albinus (*fl. c.* 150 A.D.)[77], and in a more

---

[69] Cf. Yon xl-xlvi; Dillon 85.

[70] Cicero *de fato* 19, 26ff.

[71] ibid. 23-5.

[72] pp. 131, 147 respectively.

[73] Cf. Amand *passim*, especially 62-8, 136-56, 571-86.

[74] Cf. Amand 78-80. On Carneades cf. further Long (1974) 101-4.

[75] Plato *Republic* X 617e. Cf. also *Laws* X 904b6ff.

[76] *Annals* 6.22.4; cf. Theiler 67ff., Pfligersdorffer (op. cit., above n.43) 22 n.68.

[77] 26 179.1ff. Hermann. Cf. J. Whittaker, 'Parisinus Graecus 1962 and the writings of Albinus', *Phoenix* 28 (1974) 450-6.

developed form in the treatise *de fato* falsely ascribed to Plutarch[78] and in two later works, the commentary on Plato's *Timaeus* by Calcidius (fourth century A.D.)[79] and the treatise *On the nature of Man* by Nemesius of Emesa (*fl. c.* 400 A.D.)[80]

This doctrine of 'conditional fate' is in some respects reminiscent of the Stoic doctrine of co-fated events, with the crucial difference that for the Platonists, while the initial choice is 'in fate' in that it is referred to in the conditional law which constitutes fate, it is not itself determined by fate.[81] However, the accounts given of how the initial free choices fit into an overall pattern of causation are not very adequate; these authors are content to repeat standard analyses of chance, possibility and the contingent which ultimately rest on Aristotelian foundations and are consequently of limited use in a discussion of determinism.[82] And, unlike Alexander, the *Didascalicus* and pseudo-Plutarch do not concern themselves with problems relating to the analysis of human action in particular; though it should be stressed that the *Didascalicus* is only a summary and that pseudo-Plutarch's treatise explicitly does not claim to be a full treatment.[83]

Pseudo-Plutarch's treatise can probably be dated to the latter half of the second century A.D.;[84] and it seems likely that the conditional-fate doctrine was known to Alexander, though he disregards it in the *de fato*, as indeed he disregards the Stoic doctrine of co-fated events.[85] His neglect of the Platonist doctrine perhaps reflects a reluctance, in what is after all a work inaugurating his appointment as teacher of Aristotelian philosophy, to make use of too distinctive a doctrine from another school.[86]

---

[78] 570a-e. Cf. D. Babut, *Plutarque et le stoïcisme* (Paris 1969) 157-61.

[79] CL ff., 186.13ff. Waszink.

[80] XXXVIII, *PG* 40.753b ff. (cf. also XXXVII 749b; Theiler, 79 and n.1). On the origin of the developed doctrine cf. Dillon, 295-8, 320-38, 406f.

[81] Albinus 26 179.2f., [Plutarch] *de fato* 570ce.

[82] Above, pp. 4-6, Sharples (1978) 252f.

[83] [Plutarch] *de fato* 574f; cf. Babut (op. cit. in n.78) 160 and n.67. Calcidius does consider this aspect, but he does not really face the problem of the causation of human actions in the way that Alexander, for all the shortcomings of his treatment, does; Nemesius only refers to the Middle-Platonist doctrine in passing.

[84] Cf. Valgiglio (1964) xxxv f.; Dillon, 320.

[85] Above, n.51; cf. Long (1970) 260.

[86] On inter-school hostility cf. Dillon 248-50. For Alexander's familiarity with contemporary Platonism cf. *q.* II.21 70.34 (below n.173); fr. 2 in G. Vitelli, 'Due Frammenti di Alessandro di Afrodisia', *Festschrift Theodor Gomperz* (Vienna 1902) 90-3 (cf. [Plutarch] *de fato* 568cd, 573d, Albinus *didasc.* 10 164.16ff.); and, perhaps, below

2. Alexander and the De Fato

Our knowledge of Alexander's life is very limited; the dedication of the *de fato* to Septimius Severus and Caracalla (I 164.3) itself provides the chief indication of his date, showing that the work was written between 198 and 209 A.D.[87] Alexander had probably been appointed to the post of teacher of Aristotelian philosophy established in Athens, along with similar posts in Platonic, Stoic and Epicurean philosophy, by Marcus Aurelius in 176 A.D.[88] – though there were similar posts elsewhere, and that Alexander's was in Athens is not firmly attested.[89] He was probably not, in any case, a head of the actual school founded by Aristotle, the Lyceum, for it is likely that it had ceased to exist as an institution at Sulla's capture of Athens in 86 B.C.[90]

Alexander occupies a key position in the long tradition of ancient commentators on Aristotle; he is the first from whom a substantial number of commentaries survives[91] and the last to write as a Peripatetic rather than as a Neoplatonist. For his ancient successors he was 'The Commentator' *par excellence*.[92] His commentaries, including some now lost, were extensively studied and cited by his successors, both Greek and Arabic;[93] in particular, his

---

n.176. There is little evidence for Alexander's sharing any specific anti-determinist common source with the Middle-Platonist writers, as opposed to his simply drawing on a common polemical tradition; cf. Sharples (1978) 245-53.

[87] Todd 1 n.3.

[88] Dio Cassius 72.31, cf. Philostratus *vit. soph.* 566, Lucian *Eun.* 3.8. Zeller-Alleyne 192 n.1, Todd 1 n.2, 6 n.29.

[89] *Historia Augusta*, Antoninus Pius 11.6; J.P. Lynch, *Aristotle's School* (Berkeley 1972) 193, 214. Cf. however the reference to Aristotle's statue in Athens, Alexander *in metaph.* CAG 1.415.29-31; Todd 1 n.2.

[90] Lynch op. cit. 192-207.

[91] For Alexander's commentaries cf. Todd 14f. The only earlier extant commentaries are those of Aspasius *in eth. Nic.* (*CAG* 19.1) and, probably, *Anon. in eth. Nic.* 2-5 (*CAG* 20; cf. A. Kenny, *The Aristotelian Ethics* (Oxford 1978) 37 n.3, who suggests it may be by Adrastus of Aphrodisias.

[92] Simplicius *in phys. CAG* 10.1170.13, 1176.32; Olympiodorus *in meteor. CAG* 12.2.263.21. Zeller-Alleyne 318 n.3; G. Théry, 'Autour du décret de 1210: II, Alexandre d'Aphrodise, Aperçu sur l'influence de sa noétique', *Bibliothèque Thomiste* 7 (1926) 14 and nn.1-2.

[93] Cf. Théry op. cit. 13-27; P. Kraus, *Jabir ibn Hayyan, II, Jabir et la science grecque* (Cairo 1942; *Mémoires présentés àl'Inst. d'Egypte*, 45) 324f.; S. Pines, '*Omne quod movetur necesse est ab aliquo moveri*: a refutation of Galen by Alexander of Aphrodisias and the

interpretation of Aristotle's theory of the intellect in the *de anima* influenced that of Averroes, which in turn became the centre of a major controversy in Western Europe in the Middle Ages.[94] In addition to his commentaries Alexander wrote a number of treatises, of which the *de fato* is one, in which he speaks in his own right rather than as a commentator on Aristotle – though the latter's influence is everywhere apparent, and the polemic against Stoicism which is a marked feature of the treatises is also present in the commentaries.[95] There are also many shorter discussions of varied length and character ascribed to Alexander; those surviving in Greek are collected in the so-called second book of Alexander's treatise *de anima*, renamed *mantissa* (meaning 'supplement', 'makeweight') by Bruns,[96] and in the *quaestiones naturales* (three books) and 'Problems in Ethics' (the fourth book of the *quaestiones*)[97] A number of texts, some corresponding with some of those preserved in Greek but many different, are also preserved in Arabic translation.[98] It seems probable that these shorter texts are not all Alexander's own work, but they do seem to reflect the activity of his school. Some may be records of his exegesis of Aristotelian texts and

theory of motion', *Isis* 52 (1961) 48-54; A. Badawī, *La transmission de la philosophie grecque en monde arabe* (Paris 1968; *Etudes de philosophie médiévale*, 56) 95-9; H.V.B. Brown, 'Avicenna and the Christian philosophers in Bagdhad', in *Islamic philosophy and the classical tradition, Studies presented to Richard Walzer* (Oxford, Cassirer, 1973) 35-48; and below pp. 28-9. For Alexander's influence on Plotinus in particular cf. Porphyry, *vit. Plot.* 14; P. Merlan, 'Plotinus *Enneads* 2.2', *Trans. Amer. Philol. Assoc.* 74 (1943) 179-91; J.M. Rist, 'On tracking Alexander of Aphrodisias', *Arch. Gesch. Philos.* 48 (1966) 82-90; and *Entretiens Hardt* V, 'Les Sources de Plotin' (Vandoeuvres-Genève, 1960) 414-49.

[94] Cf. Théry (op. cit. in n.93) 34-67, 105-16.

[95] Moraux xvi and 28; Todd 17, 21ff. On the sources of Alexander's knowledge of Stoicism cf. Todd 23f.

[96] *Supplementum Aristotelicum* 2.1 (1887) 100-86. The last four sections are here numbered XXII-XXV, following the division into sections in Bruns' edition; in MS V (see below) the sections are numbered from 1 to 27, new sections beginning at 107.21 and 107.29 (cf. Bruns' apparatus ad locc.).

[97] *Suppl. Ar.* 2.2 (1892) 1-163. The *Iatrika aporēmata kai phusika problēmata* are spurious, as is the *de febribus*; cf. Cranz (1960) 125-35.

[98] Listed by A. Dietrich, 'Die arabische Version einer unbekannten Schrift des Alexander von Aphrodisias über die Differentia specifica', *Nachr. Akad. Wiss. Göttingen*, phil.-hist. kl., 1974, 42-100, and J. van Ess. 'Uber eininge neue Fragmente des Alexander von Aphrodisias und des Proklos in arabische Ubersetzung', *Der Islam* 42 (1966) 149-54; cf. also H. Gaetje, 'Zur Arabischen Uberlieferung des Alexander von Aphrodisias', *Zeitschr. des Deutschen Morgenländischen Gesellschaft* 106 (1966) 255-78, and F.W. Zimmermann and H.V.B. Brown, 'Neue arabischen Ubersetzungstexte aus dem Bereich der spätantiken griechischen Philosophie', *Der Islam* 50 (1973) 313-24.

doctrines, others perhaps exercises written by his pupils.[99] (In the case of these shorter texts references to 'the author' or, for the sake of brevity, to 'Alexander' should not be taken as necessarily implying that the text in question either definitely is or definitely is not by Alexander.)

Alexander's *de fato* falls into two very unequal main parts. After the introduction in ch. I, chs. II-VI are concerned with establishing Alexander's own, non-deterministic theory of fate, while chs. VII-XXXVIII are devoted to polemic against the determinist position. This polemic is in turn divided into two main parts, chs. VII-XXI attacking the determinist position by pointing to its allegedly absurd consequences, while chs. XXII-XXXVIII rebut various arguments advanced in support of the determinist position; but this division is not rigidly observed (thus ch. XV is really a defence of Alexander's own position against a determinist objection), and some topics are discussed, rather awkwardly, in both sections (cf. ch. XXXIII with ch. XIV).

The rhetorical, even sophistical flourishes of the opening and closing sections of the *de fato* should not deceive us as to the true character of the work;[100] its approach is basically philosophical. The references to the alleged consequences for men's conduct of belief in determinism,[101] though a regular part of discussion on this topic,[102] may well be intended to appeal to the imperial dedicatees by stressing the practical relevance of Alexander's treatment, just as it is probably not accidental that he stresses the bad influence of upholders of the rival view on their pupils.[103] Nevertheless, the alleged implications for practical conduct of a belief in determinism do have a legitimate place in philosophical discussion of the issue; the determinists must either show that their thesis *is* in fact consistent with present human behaviour or argue that the latter

[99] On the whole question cf. Bruns, *Suppl. Ar.* 2.2 i-xiv; Moraux 19-28, 132-42 (and 'Le *de anima* dans la tradition grecque', *Aristotle on Mind and the Senses* (ed. G.E.R. Lloyd and G.E.L. Owen, Cambridge 1978) 296-305); Todd 12-19; Sharples (1975,2) 41f., and (1980).

[100] Cf. especially I. 164.11ff., 165.7-9, XXXIX 212.9ff.; Sharples (1978) 253.

[101] I.164.17, VII,171.27, XVI-XXI passim (cf. 186.18), XXXIX 212.6ff. Cf. *m*.180.14ff. Alexander's assessment of this type of argument is shown by passage 4 from his commentary on the *Topics* (below, p. 120); cf. also passage 2, ibid.

[102] Above, n.73; below, p. 150.

[103] VII 171.25, XVI 187.8-12, 30f., XIX 190.5 ff., XXI 191.23-5; cf. XVIII 188.22-189.8.

should be changed. Alexander repeatedly stresses that his opponents' practice fails to accord with their precepts;[104] that many of the consequences that he claims follow from a belief in determinism do not in fact do so[105] is a separate point, and does not render this whole type of argument any less relevant. The opening chapters of the treatise are marked by a somewhat pedagogic air,[106] but parts of it are highly technical;[107] Alexander's claim that his intention is examination of the problems rather than display (I 165.5-7) does appear legitimate.[108]

Alexander's argument in the *de fato* is characterised by appeals to the obvious[109] and to common opinion[110] (which sometimes means: to standard Aristotelian doctrine);[111] such arguments are in accordance with Aristotelian practice,[112] though the terminology in which they are expressed is often Stoic.[113] He repeatedly complains that his opponents do not use terms in their normal sense.[114]

There is a marked absence of superstitious elements in the treatise; astrology is nowhere mentioned[115] and references to prophecy are either sceptical[116] or dialectical, Alexander claiming that his own position is more compatible with it than is his

---

[104] XII 180.23f., XVI 186.20-3, XVIII 188.19ff., XIX 190.11, XX 190.23; *m.* 182.21. In accusing his opponents of self-contradiction Alexander assumes that they understand certain key concepts in the way that he himself does; cf. below, ch. X comm. pp. 136, 139, ch. XXXIII comm. p. 168, and passage 3 from the commentary on the *Topics* (below, p. 120).

[105] Above, n.51.

[106] Cf. III 166.19-22, 26-9, IV 167.16.

[107] Cf. e.g. ch. X and commentary.

[108] Cf. Alexander *de mixtione* II.215.30; Todd, 20 and n.95, 186.

[109] VII 172.1-3, IX 175.8, XII 180.23, XVI 186.22, XXII 191.28f., XXVI 196.13-21, XXX 201.6, 26, XXXVIII 212.3; *m.* 175.1, 183.7, 24.

[110] III 166.16, VII 172.4, VIII 172.17 ff., 174.7, XI 178.17 (and cf. 179.24), XII 180.24, XIV 182.20, XIX 189.11, XIX 190.4, XXVI 196.13, XXXII 204.25; *m.* 179.26, 182.6, 183.1, 5, 186.4.

[111] Cf. below, commentary on ch. VIII; Long (1970) 250ff.

[112] Cf. Aristotle *eth. Nic.* 1.8 1098b27, 7.1 1145b2-7, 10.2 1172b36.

[113] (*koinē*) *prolēpsis* II 165.15, 25, XIV 182.21, XXVI 196.14 (cf. also XI 178.25); *koinai te kai phusikai ennoiai*, VIII 172.17. Verbeke, 78 and n.16, 99 and n.99; Todd, 185, 195, and id. 'The Stoic Common Notions: a re-examination and re-interpretation', *Symbolae Osloenses* 48 (1973) 60ff. and n.83.

[114] VII 172.9ff., VIII 173.20ff., XIII 181.10, XIV 182.20ff., XXIV 194.23-25, XXXVIII 211.30; cf. X 177.5, XII 180.4.

[115] As is noted by Amand, 154f. Cf. below, comm. on VI 169.26.

[116] XXX 200.4ff., *m.* 180.14-33; cf. *f.* VIII 174.22, XVII 188.2. Alexander attacks his opponents for credulous belief in myths, XXXI 203.29ff.; incorporation of such traditional material into their position was characteristic of the Stoics, cf. e.g. *SVF* 2.1076ff. and Philodemus *de signis* 38. Long (1974) 149f.

opponents', without necessarily indicating his own acceptance of it.[117] Possibly the absence of references to astrology was to avoid offending the emperors by criticizing it;[118] it certainly brings out the essentially academic concerns of Alexander's treatise, which rests to a considerable extent on Aristotle's own discussions[119] and makes no particular reference to contemporary issues.

Alexander nowhere in the *de fato* names his determinist opponents – this contrasting with his practice, for example, in the treatise *on mixture*.[120] However, there seems no doubt that those he attacks are primarily to be identified with the Stoics;[121] this is shown by their identification of fate with god,[122] their belief that nature is predominantly purposive,[123] their emphasis on the unity of the universe,[124] their claim that virtue alone is good and that almost all men are bad,[125] their appeals to divine foreknowledge[126] and prophecy,[127] their use of the argument from the impossibility of uncaused motion[128] and their explanation of chance as 'a cause obscure to human reasoning'.[129]

However, two qualifications are necessary. First, Alexander is concerned with determinism as a philosophical thesis in itself, not in

---

[117] VI 171.7, XVII 188.11, XXXI 201.28; *m.* 179.16, 182.28, 185.33, 186.8. (*m.* 184.1 seems more positive in its tone, but the significance of the first person plural verb should not perhaps be pressed; Alexander's authorship of this text is in any case doubtful.)

[118] Cf. N.-I. Boussoulas, 'Notes sur la pensée antique II', *Analekta: (etesia) ekdosis ton Institouton ton Anatolikon spoudon tes patriarchikes bibliothekes Alexandreias*, ed. Th. D. Moschonas, 9 (1960) 200 (or at *Epistemonike epeteris tes philosophikas scholes tou Aristoteleiou panepistemiov Thessalonikes* 12 (1973) 290); and for the devotion of Alexander's dedicatees to astrology cf. Dio Cassius 77.11, 79.2, and *Historia Augusta* Severus 3.9, 4.3. On the whole question cf. I. Bruns, *Interpretationes variae* (Kiel, 1893) 14-17.

[119] Cf. Long (1970) 247.3, and below p. 21.

[120] *de mixt.* I 213.7 (*SVF* 2.481), II 214.18, 28, III 2156.5ff. (*SVF* 2,470) etc.; cf. also *de an.* 17.16, 26.16f., *m.* 150.28ff. (*SVF* 3.183), etc.

[121] Gercke (1885) 694; Long (1970) 247.

[122] XXII 192.25ff., cf. 191.31f.; XXXI 203.12. Cf. n.39.

[123] XI 179.24, XXIII 193.26-8, XXVIII 199.11, XXXI 203.12ff. Above, n.38. The belief is shared by Alexander himself and almost all philosophers (XI 179.24-6); however, it rules out the possibility of Alexander's attack being directed against Atomism.

[124] XXII 192.8-14 (cf. Commentary ad loc.), XXXVII 210.15ff.

[125] XXIX 199.14; cf. Commentary ad loc.

[126] XXX 200.12; cf. Commentary ad loc.

[127] XXXI 201.32; cf. Commentary ad loc.

[128] XV 185.7ff., XXII 192.11ff., 22, XXV 195.4. Above, n. 37.

[129] VIII 174.1. (Admittedly, this definition was not only used by the Stoics.) Cf. Commentary ad loc.

the context of the Stoic system as a whole; thus, though he occasionally mentions such features as the identification of fate with god and its providential nature, and exploits them in his polemic when it is his interest to do so,[130] he does not lay the emphasis on them that the Stoics would have done; and this concern with determinism in itself may well, as Long has pointed out, suggest why he does not identify his opponents by name.[131] Such isolation of a philosophical thesis from its original context and treatment of it for its own sake are found elsewhere in Alexander's work too.[132] And, secondly, Alexander does not regard himself as obliged to present the Stoic position in the terms that they themselves would have used when, from his hostile standpoint, to do so would simply obscure the issue. Thus he often speaks as if the agent, in the determinist view, is entirely at the mercy of external factors.[133] This the Stoics would not have accepted, for the agent's contribution is, they claim, *more* important; but since the eventual outcome is *ex hypothesi* predetermined (even if the response of a human agent is far more complex than that of a cylinder when pushed)[134] it is legitimate from Alexander's libertarian point of view (see below) to stress that, for the determinists, given the character a man has, he must act in one way in one set of circumstances and in another in another. For the determinists cannot, consistently with their basic position, show that the agent can be responsible for his character in any way that would satisfy a libertarian; rather, as Alexander points out, every action must ultimately be traceable back to determining causes outside the agent.[135] Similarly, Alexander throughout speaks as if fate and necessity, for the determinists, were identical;[136] the Stoics may indeed have been prepared in certain contexts to say that all things were necessary, but it does not seem that they laid such emphasis on the necessity of all things as does Alexander in stating his opponents' position.[137] But since Alexander finds his opponents' attempts to separate fate and necessity trivial,[138] from his own point

---

[130] Cf. the passages cited in n.123, and XII 180.24; also *q.* I.4 10.24, 32 (*SVF* 2.962).
[131] Long (1970) 247 and n.3, 266ff.
[132] Cf. Todd 25ff. and n.22, 73ff., 82ff., and my comments at *Phoenix* 31 (1977) 88.
[133] XII 180.5-7, XXXIV 206.19, XXXVI 208.9; *m.* 174.4. Long (1970) 259. Cf. however below n.135.
[134] Long (1970) 262. Compare O'Connor, 91f.
[135] XXXVI 207.27ff.; cf. XVI 187.22.
[136] Cf. VII 171.20, 26, 172.8; VIII 173.17, 22, 24; XXXI 202.2, 5; XXXVI 209.15f. Sharples (1975,1) 248 n.2; Donini (1977) 189 n.26.
[137] Long (1970) 248f.; Sharples (1981) 183-4.
[138] X 176.23f., 177.5ff., 15, 178.6. Cf. XXXIV 206.9ff.

of view his presentation of the determinist position is legitimate. It follows, however, that his statements must be used with considerable caution as evidence for the Stoic position.[139]

Professor Donini has indeed recently argued that Alexander in the *de fato* is attacking not a single consistent determinist position, but rather a variety of positions known to him largely from Aristotle's objections to them; in particular, he claims that ch. IX is directed against the Megarian denial of possibility in Aristotle *Metaphysics* Θ 3 1047a10-17[140]. He is right to stress the influence of Aristotle's discussions on Alexander; but the latter cetainly gives his reader the impression that he is attacking a single set of opponents. It is true that only necessity, not fate, is mentioned in ch. IX; but formulations of the determinist position in terms of necessity and of fate are elsewhere regarded as equivalent.[141]

Alexander's own position becomes apparent not only in the constructive argument of *de fato* II-VI, but also in his polemic against the determinists, though the structure of his treatise has the consequence that his own position is not always clear – his arguments against the determinists are often dialectical, and he is concerned to refute them on diverse topics rather than to construct a systematic position of his own. The last section of the *mantissa* appears to be an attempt, whether by Alexander himself or a follower, to cast material from the *de fato* into a more constructive and systematic form, though its advances in this direction are relatively superficial;[142] *mantissa* XXIII, too, brings together points from different sections of the *de fato*, and *mantissa* XXII takes further issues that the *de fato* leaves unclear, though it arrives at a highly paradoxical position as a consequence.[143]

One crucial point that is however clear is that Alexander's own conception of responsibility is a libertarian one. He objects not just to determination of our actions by external causes alone, but to that resulting from a combination of internal and external factors;[144] it is not enough that an individual contributes something to the result, if

---

[139] Long (1970) 247f. and n.4, Todd 22ff., against von Arnim *SVF* I p. xvii.

[140] Donini (1977) 183ff., taking up my *per impossibile* suggestion at Sharples (1975,1) 253 n.14.

[141] Above, n. 136.

[142] Cf. Sharples (1980) 84-5.

[143] Cf. Merlan (1969) 85-8, Sharples (1975,2) passim.

[144] Cf. XIX 190.8, XXXIV 206.22, XXXVI 207.27; above, n.135. He opposes his own conception of responsible action to the soft-determinist interpretation of it as what comes about through us (XIII 181.14, XXXVIII 211.30) and finds the determinist

that contribution is predetermined. This shows that his repeated descriptions of responsbility in terms of the power or capacity for opposite courses of action[145] are to be understood in terms of an unqualified, unrestricted possibility. At the same time, like Carneades, he claims to avoid the Stoic charge of introducing uncaused motion.[146] Epicurus is nowhere mentioned in the *de fato* in connection with determinism, but only with reference to his denial of divine providence;[147] possibly consideration of the Epicurean atomic swerve would have exposed difficulties in Alexander's own position.[148] He stresses the connection between responsbility and reason, which shows that his libertarian conception of responsbility is not just one of arbitrary caprice;[149] at the same time, he faces very real difficulties in combining his libertarian position with an account of the rational element in human behaviour, and does not really solve it.[150] This problem is perhaps most acute when human action is seen in the context of the universe as an ordered whole; this is so in *mantissa* XXII, with bizarre consequences – responsibility being identified with human weakness – but not, because of its piecemeal approach, in the *de fato*.[151] (For the Stoics and Neoplatonists, on the other hand, freedom is located not in the possibility for alternatives but precisely in choosing the most rational course of action.)[152]

The concept of fate does not play any appreciable part in

---

accounts of chance and responsibility inadequate *because they are determinist* (VII 172.8, VIII 173.16ff., XIII 181.7ff.) Cf. also pp. 160-4.

[145] Cf. II 166.12f., V 169.7ff., 14f., XII 180.5ff., 20f., 26f., 181.5f., XIII 181.3f., XX 190.25, XXVIII 199.9, XXXVI 206.19, XXXVIII 211.32. The forms of expression used here may be compared with those applied to contingency (IX 175.3, 7, 16, 176.1); for explicit connection between the two concepts cf. *m.* 172.3-7, 173.4-6, 184.7-13.

[146] XV 185.7f., XXIV 193.31, 194.22; cf. above nn.70f., and contrast the position of the author of *m.* XXII (above n.143; *m.* 170.7, 171.14, 22, 172.9).

[147] XXXI 203.10, XXXVII 211.7.

[148] Cf. however above n.86. In fact the only philosophers other than Aristotle mentioned by name in the *de fato*, very much in passing, are Anaxagoras (II 165.19), Heraclitus (VI 170.19), Socrates (VI 171.12, 14, and, as an example, at XXIV 194.10), and Zeno (of Elea – not the Stoic Zeno of Citium; XXVI 196.19).

[149] Cf. XI 178.17, XIV 183.21-184.20 and Commentary, XXXIII 205.15ff. Verbeke 90 n.57.

[150] Below, pp. 149, 163-4.

[151] Cf. Pack 433f., Sharples (1975,2) 42 and nn. It is perhaps in this context that den Boeft's contrast between the logical approach of Alexander and the metaphysical one of the Platonists is most strikingly marked (den Boeft, 54, 82, 134).

[152] Cf. above n.42; St. Augustine *de civ. dei* 22.30, Boethius *cons. phil.* 5 pr. 2.16, 21, and, of *responsible* action, Plotinus 3.1.9.5, 3.1.10.4, 3.2.10. Taylor, 359.

Aristotle's writings; there are only a very few passing references.[153] Alexander however presents the theory of fate as individual nature that he puts forward in chs. II-VI as 'the opinion of Aristotle'; clearly, it represents not so much Aristotle's own consciously held view as an attempt to formulate, on the basis of Aristotle's writings, an opinion on a question which he had not himself considered.

It seems probable that Peripatetic interest in the concept of fate was largely stimulated by its central place in Stoicism. The Stoics had identified fate and nature[154] – though their position on these topics was very different from Alexander's;[155] Alexander's concern to oppose Stoicism shows its influence on him, and he was certainly prepared to borrow Stoic terminology.[156] (None of this, however, is to suggest that Alexander's doctrine of fate does not rest on a central Aristotelian concept, that of the natural as what occurs for the most part but not always,[157] or that the argument by which it is established in II-VI is not, as Donini has stressed, purely Aristotelian in character.)[158]

Alexander does not however appear to have been the first Peripatetic to take an interest in fate. There is an awkward transition in *de fato* VI from consideration of (i) the fact that creatures reproduce themselves for the most part, but not always, to (ii) the observation that an individual's nature determines his life generally but admits of exceptions; (ii) includes in fate characteristics peculiar to the individual and coming below the level of species, while (i) does not. (ii) also appears in *mantissa* XXV; Donini has tentatively suggested that it reflects an earlier Peripatetic doctrine of fate, and that Alexander's distinctive contribution in *de fato* VI was to introduce the motion of the heavenly bodies as the cause of fate, this

[153] Apart from *phys.* 5.6 230 a 32 and *meteor.* 1.14 352 a 28 (cf. *m.* 186.13ff.; the adjective *heimarmenos* rather than the noun *heimarmene* is used in these passages) cf. *poet.* 16 1455 a 11 (Valgiglio (1967) 310 n.8) – but this is not evidence for Aristotle's own view.

[154] *SVF* 1.176, 2.913, 937, 1024, 1076f.; cf. Alexander *f.* XXXIV 205.24, XXXVI 208.3ff., and especially XXII 192.27 (referring to individual nature; but cf. below p. 129).

[155] Below, pp. 128-9, 152 (However, the idea of exceptions to a regular order *does* appear in Stoicism; cf. below, p. 159.)

[156] Cf. above n.113, below pp. 139, 142; Moraux 196, Todd 226. In general for Stoic influence on Alexander cf. Pohlenz (1967) 2.169 and n.17, Todd 27f. and n.32.

[157] Cf. phys. 2.8 199b18, 25, *de part. an.* 1.1 641b25; Verbeke 81f. And compare Alexander *in an. pr., CAG* 2.1.162.2-9 (on 1.13 32b6ff.) with *f.* VI 169.27-30.

[158] Donini (1977) 174-83.

there appearing in (i) but not in (ii).[159] It may well be that (ii) is an earlier doctrine imperfectly assimilated in the *de fato*; though as far as *mantissa* XXV is concerned it should be stressed that, on other grounds, it seems later than the *de fato*, and that a similar tension between fate as concerned with the peculiar characteristics of individuals and fate as concerned with the reproduction of species appears in *mantissa* XXV too – which may indeed be seen as attempting to resolve it.[160] It should also be stressed that the reference to the heavenly bodies in *de fato* VI is very much in passing and for the sake of a particular argument.

Mantissa XXV, unlike the *de fato*, supports the doctrine of fate as individual nature by appealing to earlier authorities – not only to two Aristotelian passages but also to the *Callicles* of Aristotle's pupil Theophrastus and to an otherwise unknown Polyzelus.[161] That Theophrastus did at least say something that could be interpreted as identifying fate with the nature of the individual is also attested by the doxographer Aëtius (? second century A.D.);[162] however, as Donini observes, such statements may, at least where Theophrastus is observed, reflect somewhat anachronistic later interpretation.[163] Certainly the identification of fate with individual nature admitting of exceptions – the last point implying that it is the nature of *sublunary* creatures[164] – was not the *only* Peripatetic theory of fate put forward in the period before Alexander; for the Platonist Atticus (*c.* 150-200 A.D.) attacks Peripatetics for whom fate, governing the motion of the heavens, is distinct from nature which is concerned with the sublunary.[165] The pseudo-Aristotelian treatise *de mundo* (which Alexander appears to have known and referred to),[166] while

[159] *f.* VI 169.23; Donini (1977) 182 n. 16.
[160] Cf. *m.* 185.8 ff.; Sharples (1980) 81.
[161] *m.* 186.13-31.
[162] Aëtius 1.29.4. Cf. W. Fortenbaugh, 'Theophrastus on fate and character', in *Arctouros, Hellenic Studies presented to Bernard M.W. Knox* (Berlin 1979) 372ff., and, in more detail, the commentary on the passage in his forthcoming edition of the ethical fragments of Theophrastus. (I am most grateful to Professor Fortenburgh for having let me see drafts of his commentary in advance of publication.) For Theophrastus' holding that not everything is fated, cf. [Plutarch] *de vita et poesi Homeri* 2.120.
[163] Donini (1977) 182 n.16 fin.
[164] This point is not explicit in *f.* VI; it *is* asserted at *m* 182.9ff., though this passage is problematic (below, p. 176).
[165] fr.8.8ff. des Places.
[166] P. Moraux, 'Alexander von Aphrodisias *Quaest.* 2.3', *Hermes* 95 (1967) 160 n.2, 163 init.

applying the term 'fate' to the divine influence which extends from the heavens to the sublunary, takes over Stoic etymologies, with their implication that it admits of no variation.[167] However, for the anonymous commentator on Aristotle *Nicomachean Ethics* II-V, who is probably earlier than Alexander,[168] fate according to the Peripatetics falls under nature and admits of exceptions.[169]

There is an instructive parallel between Alexander's treatment of fate and his theory of providence;[170] here too Aristotle had not explicitly discussed, in his esoteric works at least, a topic that became of much interest later.[171] The standard position attributed to Aristotle in the first two centuries A.D. was that divine providence has the heavenly bodies as its objects, but is not concerned with the sublunary region.[172] Probably as a response to Platonist attacks on this position,[173] Alexander argued that providence has as its object

---

[167] [Aristotle] *de mundo* 7, 401 b 9 (*aniketos*), 13 (*anapodrastos*); cf. *SVF* 2.202, 528, 997.

[168] Above, n.91.

[169] *CAG* 20.150.2-4. Cf. also Gellius *noct. Att.* 13.1 (below p. 129).

[170] For which cf., in addition to the *de providentia* (above p. xi), *q.* I.25, II.3, 19, 21, and Maimonides *Guide of the Perplexed* 3.15-17 (trans. R. Friedländer, London 1885); I. Bruns, 'Studien zu Alexander von Aphrodisias – II. *Quaestiones* II.3', *Rheinisches Museum* 45 (1890) 138-45, and 'III. Lehre von der Vorsehung', ibid. 223-35; Moraux 195-202, and also art. cit. in n.166 above; P. Thillet, 'Un traité inconnu d'Alexandre d'Aphrodise sur la providence dans une version arabe inédite', in *L'homme et son destin* ..., *Actes du 1er congrès internat. de philos. médiévale*, Louvain, 1960, 313-24; H. Happ, 'Weltbild und Seinslehre bei Aristoteles', *Antike und Abendland* 14 (1968) 72-91; Hager 172-5, 179; Todd 213 ff.; Ruland 133 ff.; Sharples, 'Alexander of Aphrodisias on divine providence: Two problems', *Class Quart.* 32 (1982) 198-211.

[171] In *metaph. A* God, the Unmoved Mover, has no knowledge of the world (9 1074b33-8). Cf. however Aristotle *de philosophia* fr.26 Ross (Ruland 133f.; also *de prov.* 33.1ff. and Ruland's n.), and [Aristotle] *de mundo* 6 (above n.166).

[172] Aëtius 2.3.4, Diogenes Laertius 5.32, Atticus fr. 3.56f., 69ff. des Places, Epiphanius *Dox.* 592.10 + 20 (= Critolaus fr. 15 p. 52 Wehrli); cf. Arius Didymus *fr. phys.* 9 (*Dox.* 450.16), Aspasius *in eth. Nic. CAG* 19.1.71.25ff. Aëtius loc. cit. allows that the heavens have an *accidental* providential effect on the sublunary (cf. Adrastus of Aphrodisias ap. Theon of Smyrna *expositio* 149.14f. Hiller); but for Alexander *accidental* providence is a *contradictio in adiecto* (*de prov.* 63.2ff., *q.*II.21 65.25ff.). Cf. A.-J. Festugière, *L'idéal religieux des grecs et l'Evangile* (Paris 1932) 224-62; P. Moraux, 'L'exposé de la philosophie d'Aristote chez Diogène Laërce', *Rev. philos. de Louvain* 47 (1949) 33f., and *D'Aristote à Bessarion* (Laval 1970) 54ff' Pfligersdorffer (op. cit., above n.43) 9ff.; and compare above, pp. 4-5 and n.11.

[173] *q.*II.21 70.33ff.; Merlan 90f. Alexander may not however have been the first Peripatetic to put forward a theory of (non-accidental) providential concern with the sublunary; cf. *m.* (*de intellectu*) 113.6ff., *q.*II.3 48.19-22. Moraux, op. cit. in n. 166, 163f. n.2, 'Aristoteles, der Lehrer Alexanders von Aphrodisias', *Arch. Gesch. Philos.* 49 (1967) 169-82, especially 174f., and op. cit. in n.99, 294-6; Donini (1974,2) 51f. n.115, cf. 59-62.

not the heavenly bodies but the sublunary;[174] it is exercised by the
souls of the heavenly spheres (rather than by the Unmoved Mover(s)
themselves)[175] through the medium of the heavenly rotations, which
ensure the preservation of species[176] – the connection between the
heavenly rotations and the continuity of sublunary coming-to-be
being a central idea in Aristotle.[177] Providence is not however
concerned with the fortunes of individuals – this meeting the
objection that the undeserved misfortunes of individuals seem
incompatible with divine providence,[178] and also that concern with a
multiplicity of details is neither possible for the gods[179] nor in
accordance with their dignity.[180] With providence, as with fate,
Alexander is concerned to present his theory as Aristotelian.[181]

Since the influence of the heavenly bodies is identified with
sublunary nature[182] and hence with fate, it is natural to suppose
either that fate and providence are identical for Alexander or that
the former is the outworking of the latter.[183] There is no direct
reference to Alexander's doctrine of providence in the *de fato*, but the
picture it presents is generally consistent with it; the notion of

[174] *de prov.* 59.6ff., *q.*II.19 63.15ff.; cf. *q.*I.25 41.4-19.

[175] This is suggested, though not absolutely required, by fr.2 Vitelli (above, n.86) and by Alexander *in meteor. CAG* 3.2.6.5ff.; so Bruns (op. cit. in n.170) 230, Hager 179 n.34. Cf. above, n.171. For the plurality of Unmoved Movers cf. Donini (1974,2) 31ff.; also Moraux, op. cit. in n.99, 300, and at *Gnomon* 50 (1978) 532f.

[176] *de prov.* 31.15ff., 33.1ff. (= fr. 3b Grant), 87.5ff.; *q.*I.25 41.12ff., II.19 63.22ff. Cf. Alexander fr.36 Freudenthal and Maimonides pp. 67f. Friedländer (above n.170). For [Plutarch] *de fato* 573a secondary providence is concerned with the preservation of species, tertiary with the actions of individuals.

[177] Aristotle *de gen. et corr.* 2.10 336b31ff., 2.11 338a18ff., *meteor.* 1.2 339a21; [Aristotle] *de mundo* 6 398a3, b8, Alexander *in meteor.* 6.15, *de princ.* 138.24ff., and ap. Philoponus *in de gen. et corr. CAG* 14.2.291.18ff. Moraux, 199 n.8.

[178] *de prov.* 11.6ff., cf. fr.36 Freudenthal and Maimonides p.67 Friedl. However, though the problem of evil is taken up at *de prov.* 101.3ff., neither in this case nor in that of the problems in the next two nn. is the way in which the connection of providence with species can provide a solution really spelled out explicitly in *de prov.* Cf. below, n.188.

[179] *de prov.* 15.15 (contrast the view, rejected by Alexander, at 7.18 = fr.1 Grant); cf. fr.36 Freudenthal, Maimonides p. 64 Friedl. Contrast the Neoplatonic position (below n.196).

[180] *de prov.* 19.3ff, 25.1ff, 31.16, 53.1ff., 63.11ff.; *q.*II.21 68.19ff.; *m* 113.12ff. (*SVF* 2.1038). Cf. below p. 156, Todd 226f., and [Aristotle] *de mundo* 6 397b20ff., 398a5ff.

[181] *de prov.* 31.19, 33.1ff. (= fr. 3b Grant, cf. his n. (f)), 91.5ff.; *q.*I.25 41.10, II.21 65.19ff., 70.24ff. Thillet, op. cit. in n.170, 318.

[182] Cf., in addition to *f.* VI.169.23 (above n.159), *m.* 172.17ff., *q.*II.3 47.30ff., 49.29, *in meteor. CAG*3.2.7.9, *de prov.* 77.12; cf. ibid. 87.5, 95.16ff., *de princ.* 137.15. Moraux 198.

[183] The former view at Zeller-Alleyne 330 and Moraux loc. cit.; the latter, by implication, at Todd 224.

exceptions to an overall pattern caused by the heavenly motions occurs not only in VI but at the end of XXV, and the limitation of divine foreknowledge in XXX is in general accord with the view that providence does not extend to everything that happens to individuals.[184] Both fate and providence, by admitting of exceptions, leave scope for human freedom.[185] However, Alexander's argument in the *de fato* that his opponents' determinist position leaves no scope for the exercise of divine providence[186] must be taken as purely dialectical; for Alexander's own theory of providence, in view of its somewhat mechanistic nature,[187] might seem open to similar objections. A more serious discrepancy is that, while the doctrine of providence as concerned with species accords well enough with the first part of *de fato* VI, it is easy to reconcile it with the subsequent identification of fate with the peculiar characteristics of *individuals* (even if these too do not always have their natural consequences). This may further support the suggestion that the latter part of *de fato* VI represents an earlier and imperfectly assimilated theory; at the same time, the identification of fate and providence for Alexander is an inference, not something he explicitly states, and he may well never have fully formulated an entirely coherent and systematic position on these topics. As argued above, the *de fato* itself does not give a systematic statement of Alexander's own position; and in the *de providentia*, too, it does not seem that every problem was explicitly resolved.[188]

Alexander's positive theory of fate is perhaps a less significant contribution to philosophical discussion than is his consideration of various issues in the later, polemical part of the *de fato*. It seems a less philosophically fertile notion than does, at least potentially, the Platonist theory of conditional fate;[189] and it is with some justice

[184] Below, p. 165. Providence implies knowledge a fortiori; cf. fr.36 112.17-113.2 Freudenthal, *de prov.* 17.7.

[185] Moraux 199. The Stoics themselves argued that divine providence was not concerned with every detail in the universe; below, p. 159.

[186] *f.*XVII 188.1-6, XXXIX 212.8f.; determinism is incompatible with prayer, XX 190.27, *m.* 175.6, 182.4, 184.10, 186.3.

[187] Remarked by Moraux 200.

[188] Above, n.178. The concern of providence with species may also provide the answer to the problem that nature can be neither a primary concern of the gods (*de prov.* 63.8 ff., *q.*II.21 68.12ff., 70.9ff.; above n. 180) nor accidental (above n. 172); cf. *q.* II.21 68.5-11. But such a solution is not clearly indicated in *de providentia*; *q.*II.21 is regrettably incomplete. Cf. my article cited in n. 170 above.

[189] Cf. Sharples (1978) 250.

that Proclus criticised Alexander's view for making fate 'too weak'[190]
– that is, presumably, by allowing exceptions to fate it does not do
justice to the usual force of the term.[191] It is significant that
Alexander sometimes seems to speak as if the term 'fate' in itself does
have deterministic implications.[192]

There is no space here to do more than provide a few indications
of the influence of the *de fato* on later writers.[193] Its influence is
clearly apparent in the early treatise *On Fate* (*Enneads* 3.1) by
Plotinus (205-269/70 A.D.)[194] It also seems probable that the
doctrine of divine foreknowledge of Plotinus' pupil Porphyry (232/3
– *c.* 305 A.D.) was influenced by Alexander's discussion in *de fato*
XXX.[195] Proclus (410/412-485 A.D.) formulated his view that the
gods have definite foreknowledge of what is indefinite and
contingent, the nature of knowledge being determined by that of the
knower rather than that of the known,[196] in conscious opposition to a
'Peripatetic' view, that of Alexander, on the one hand and to that of
the Stoics on the other.[197] Proclus' view was immensely

[190] *in Tim.* 3.272.7ff. Diehl; he distinguishes between this and the position he ascribes
to Aristotle, that fate is *ten taxin tōn kosmikōn penodōn* (cf. Aristotle *meteor.* 1.14 352 a 28;
Alexander *m.* 186.13 ff.). Proclus holds that for Aristotle too fate admits of exceptions;
272.12f., cf. Proclus *de prov.* 11.16ff. and Boese ad loc.

[191] For this criticism cf. Valgiglio (1967) 310. Alexander however has an answer to
this; cf. *f.*II.165.24f., *m.* 176.4, 182.18, 186.9ff.,

[192] Cf. *f.*XXXVII 211.1-4 and Commentary. (At *f.*XXXIV 206.4, however, *tēn
hiemarmenēn te kai tēn anankēn* may be a hendiadys, equivalent to '*necessitating* fate', and at
XXXVII 211.25 Alexander may be using an abbreviated expression in the light of
earlier argument.)

[193] Cf. Sharples (1978) 253-66, and, in addition to discussions cited in the following
nn., H. Langerbeck, 'The philosophy of Ammonius Saccas', *JHS.* 77 (1957) 70-4, and
id. *Aufsätze zur Gnosis* (Göttingen 1967) 156, 159, 165f.

[194] 2.30ff. (*SVF* 2.946, above n.37), cf. Alexander *f.*XXII 192.1ff.; 7.14ff., cf.
Alexander *f.*XIIIf. Sharples (1978) 254, 256 and n.147.

[195] Proclus *in Tim.* 1.352.12 Diehl; cf. Calcidius *in Tim.* CLXII, 195.2ff. Waszink.
Den Boeft, 53ff.

[196] Proclus *Elements of Theology* 124; *de decem dubitationibus circa providentiam*, quaestio 2;
de providentia 63.5ff. Boese. Cf. Iamblichus ap. Ammonius *in de int. CAG* 4.5.135.12ff.
(Proclus' concern, however, is generally as much with the problem of the gods'
knowing what is indefinite and changeable *at all* as it is with that of their
*fore*knowledge.) Cf. R.T. Wallis, *Neoplatonism* (London 1972) 29f., 149f.; Sharples
(1978) 260-2.

[197] Proclus *de providentia* 63.1-5 (*SVF* 2.942), cf. *de dec. dub.* quaest.2, 6.3ff. Theiler
51f. n.4, Hager 177. Proclus is thus rejecting the principle, which as Alexander stresses
(*f.*XXX 200.28-201.6) is common to himself and his opponents, that there can be
(definite) foreknowledge only of what is predetermined; cf. also Carneades at Cicero *de
fato* 33 (*SVF* 2.955).

influential, occurring notably, with developments,[198] in the
Consolation of Philosophy of Boethius (*c.* 480-524 A.D.)[199] and in
Aquinas (1226-1274 A.D.).[200]

A considerable proportion of the earlier part of the *de fato* was
quoted or summarised by Eusebius (*c.* 260-340 A.D.) in the sixth
book of his *praeparatio evangelica*;[201] there are marked similarities
between Alexander's treatise and Calcidius' commentary on Plato's
Timaeus (fourth century A.D.).[202] Arguments from the *de fato*, possibly
transmitted through Porphyry, occur in the commentaries on
Aristotle *de interpretatione* 9 (the 'Sea-Battle') by Ammonius (fifth
century A.D.) and Boethius.[203] The treatise influenced Islamic and
Jewish philosophers[204] and was translated into Latin, possibly by
William of Moerbeke in the thirteenth century.[205] It formed the most
substantial part of the collection of translations by Hugo Grotius
(1583-1645), *Philosophorum veterum sententiae de fato.*[206]

3. The text (cf. also below, pp. 231-4)

In Bruns' view all the extent Greek MSS of Alexander's works other
than the commentaries (and the *de mixtione*, which was transmitted
separately from the rest) derive from the earliest MS extant, Venetus
Marcianus gr. 258 (V; 10th century cf. P. Thiller in *Miscellanea
Marciana di studi Bessarionei*, Padua, 1976, 387-406). The two earliest

[198] Cf. P. Hüber, *Die Vereinbarkeit von göttlicher Vorsehung und menschlicher Freiheit in der Consolatio Philosophiae des Boethius* (Zürich, 1976) 20-59.

[199] 5.3-6.

[200] *summa theologia, pars prima*, quaest. 14 art. 13.

[201] VI.9; he cites or summarises 166.22-171.6, 172.19-173.10, 174.20-25, 175.2-27, 178.8-179.2, 180.28-181.5, 188.19-189.16.

[202] Cf. B.W. Switalski, 'Des Chalcidius Kommentar zu Plato's *Timaeus*', *Beiträge zur Geschichte der Philosophie des Mittelaters*, ed. C. Bäumker and G.F. von Hertling (Münster, 1902) 94-6, and Sharples (1978) 265 and nn.225f.

[203] Cf. Sharples (1978) 254-60, and below p. 139.

[204] Cf. J. Guttmann, 'Das Problem der Willensfreiheit bei Crescas, etc.', in *Jewish Studies in Memory of G.A. Kohut*, ed. S.W. Baron etc. (New York 1935) 330 n.9, 341 n.21, and 346-9; Wallis (op. cit. in n.196) 165.

[205] The translation is attributed to William on stylistic grounds by Thillet (below, p. 231) 19-27. There is however a complication in that, while Thillet convincingly shows that the translation is independent of MS V (below, p. 31; Thillet, 17-19), William actually owned this MS; it must thus be supposed that he translated the *de fato* before he acquired MS V (Thillet, 62; cf. Fr. Masai, 'Le *de fato* d'Alexandre d'Aphrodise attribué à Pléthon', *Byzantion* 33 (1963) 253.

[206] For this and the sixteenth-century editions and translations cf. below pp. 232-3, and Cranz (1960) 107-11, (1971) 415-17.

editions, a[1] and a[2], did not seem to him to rest directly on any extant MS, though a[1] appeared closest in the *de fato* to A, while a[2] seemed to combine features of K and of ES. Similarly the translations by the Bagolini (which I have cited only rarely) did not appear to Bruns to rest on any extant MS. The emendations of B[2] have only conjectural value, but I have often accepted them as the best yet suggested.

Independent evidence for the *de fato* is provided by the extensive citations in Eusebius *Praep. Ev.* 6.9 (above, p. 29), which preserve a superior text at a number of points and fill at least one lacuna in all the MSS.[207] Many of his variants may however be due to carelessness or abbreviation, and I have not recorded them all. Bruns, using Gaisford's edition, recorded a number of variants from what are, according to Mras, MSS of Eusebius with no independent value.[208] Minor variations in Cyril of Alexandria's citation of *f*.198.19-26 (cf. p. 232) may be due to careless quotation or to the use of an inferior text;[209] cf., however, my note on 198.23.

Evidence independent of the Greek MSS is also provided by an Arabic translation (via Syriac) of *mantissa* XXIII, and by the medieval Latin translation (above, p. 29) of the *de fato* and of *mantissa* XXV; neither of these was used by Bruns. My knowledge of the Latin text is entirely derived from the edition by Thillet, and of the Arabic from the German translation by Ruland, though I am grateful to Drs Ruland and Zimmermann for checking my inferences against the Arabic text. The German and English translations of the Arabic that I have cited are those of Drs Ruland and Zimmermann respectively. Many of the statements I have made as to the Greek readings implied by the Latin or by the Arabic reflect points made by Thillet and Ruland in their notes (and in Thillet's preface); to acknowledge this on every occasion seemed excessive, but I would like to make this general acknowledgement here. For reasons of space I have frequently cited the Arabic and Latin versions as supporting the Greek text that can be inferred from them; this is *not* to be interpreted as a claim that this was what the translators

---

[207] Cf. *f*.III 166.28f., 167.11, IV 167.24, 168.20, VIII 174.22. On IV 168.18 cf. Comm. p. 127.

[208] So *prohairesin* in cod. S of Eusebius at *f*. IV 167.22 (presumably a gloss); and cf. reading of cod. C of Eusebius at 168.20. Cf. E.R. Dodds, ed., *Plato: Gorgias* (Oxford 1959) 64f.

[209] Cf. Grant, cited below p. 232.

actually found in their Greek texts.[210] The rendering of the Latin translator may often reflect his own conjectural emendations[211] or result from simple error.[212] Thillet has shown that the Latin translation is independent of V, and, by the evidence of certain words left in Greek by the translator who failed to understand them, that it was based on a Greek MS in uncials.[213] The Latin translation is closer to V than it is to Eusebius.[214] I have been greatly helped by Thillet's *indices verborum*, Latin-Greek and Greek-Latin; these, when used together, do much to supplement the inadequacies of Bruns' index to the Greek text.

Caselius' edition was based on a², the anonymous London edition of 1658 on a¹ and Eusebius. Orelli's edition was based on Ha¹² Lond.; there are a number of places where Bruns misrepresents Orelli through neglect of his *Emendanda* (Orelli, p. 359).[215] Some of the pencilled marginal suggestions of y (cf. p. 232) are foolish (cf. e.g. *f.* 169.29), but I have recorded a number that are of interest. The relation of y's conjectures to O is unclear, but he is certainly not entirely dependent on him.

As explained in the Preface, Bruns' text is reprinted here essentially as an accompaniment to the translation. In doubtful passages I have normally incorporated into the translation (and indicated in the 'Notes on the Text') what seemed the best of the alternative conjectures, even where emendation is only possible *exempli gratia*, rather than leaving lacunae. My reports in the 'Notes on the Text' of the Greek MSS and of editions before that of Orelli are for the most part derived from Bruns' apparatus, though I have endeavoured to check his reports where it seemed particularly important to do so. I have generally passed over in silence errors in

[210] For example, both the Arabic and the Latin translations have been cited as supporting *hauton* rather than *auton*, even though they may well have been guided by the sense rather than either reading *auton* in their Greek text or consciously intending to emend.

[211] Cf. e.g. *f.* I 164.13, 20, and in general Donini (1969) 298ff. This is the most likely explanation of cases where L agrees with B².

[212] Cf. Thillet 56-9. Thus *cursus* at *f.*XXXI 202.22 may reflect ignorance of the meaning of *drama* and a guess that it derived from *didrasko* rather than a variant reading; and at 203.23 it would perhaps be rash to infer from *alicui* that the translator read *tini* rather than *tíni*.

[213] Thillet, 14-19, 57f.

[214] Masai, loc cit. in n. 205.

[215] *f.* 171.20, 174.12, 175.8, 179.7, 184.32,189.25 (*tinos*), 191.11, 194.11, 196.13, 197.19, 201.2, 16, 27, 209.24.

the early printed editions where the MSS text is clearly correct, and also places where a reading of V^1 is corrected by V^1 himself or the *vetus corrector* and the correction is confirmed by the medieval Latin translator – provided that there is no reason to suspect anything more than an error on the part of V^1 (since the agreement of the Latin translation with the corrected reading *could* simply reflect the same conjectural emendation; cf. above). Nor have I recorded all cases where V expresses doubt by adding dots or omitting breathings and accents (cf. Bruns *Suppl. Ar.* 2.2 xvi f.) but the Latin translation confirms the reading. Omissions in later MSS, including those than can clearly be explained by homoioteleuton, have not been recorded; neither have minor variations in orthography or word order.

Analysis of the Argument

(I) This treatise contains the opinion of Aristotle concerning fate and responsibility, and criticism of those who had adopted a different position. (II) The existence of fate is established by men's common conception; but they disagree as to its nature and sphere of activity, whether all things happen in accordance with it or whether it admits of exceptions. (III) It is agreed that fate is a cause, and, of the four types of cause distinguished by Aristotle – efficient, material, formal and final – fate is among the efficient causes. (IV) Some things come to be for the sake of something and others not; of the former, some are brought about by nature, some by reason – that is, by skill or by choice – some by luck or the fortuitous. (V) Fate cannot be located either in the things that do not come to be for the sake of anything or in those that are brought about by skill or choice; (VI) so, by elimination, it is to be identified with nature, and, as with nature so with fate the things that come about in accordance with it do so far the most part but not always. Fate is the individual nature of each thing; as with men's bodies in disease, so their way of life and its ending is in accordance with the nature of each individual for the most part but not always – which may explain why the predictions of prophets are not always accurate, any more than are those of physiognomists.

(VII-VIII) The doctrine that all things come to be in accordance with fate conflicts with what is evident and generally accepted. It is incompatible with the occurrence of things as results of 'luck' and 'the fortuitous', at least if these words are used in their accepted sense – to define luck as 'a cause obscure to human reasoning' is not in accordance with the normal usage of the term. (IX) That all things come to be of necessity is also incompatible with the observed fact that some things are contingent and not necessary, some things being receptive of opposites and others not. (X) The arguments by which the determinists endeavour to reconcile possibility and contingency with the coming-to-be of all things of necessity – first on the grounds that *we* are ignorant of the factors that prevent the occurrence of the opposite of what is fated, and secondly on the grounds that 'there will be a sea-battle tomorrow' is not necessary because it becomes false after the event – are absurd.

(XI) Moreover, determinism renders deliberation useless, since it is of use only when we have a choice between alternative courses of action and if we need not follow the first impression that we receive, as the irrational animals do. But man's having the power of deliberation is a primary product of nature, and none of the primary products of nature is in vain. (XII) Responsibility and choice are similarly excluded by determinism. That we have the power of choosing between opposed courses of action is shown by regret and by criticism of others for not judging well. (XIII) Realising the difficulty, the determinists try to redefine responsible action as that which is brought about by fate through living creatures in accordance with their nature as living creatures – that is, through impulse – these actions being just as much necessitated as everything else. (XIV) But, first, there is nothing that is true of living creatures in this argument that justifies the claim that they are responsible for their behaviour while inanimate objects are not responsible for theirs; and, secondly, it is not action in accordance with impulse but action in accordance with *rational* impulse, which is peculiar to man, that is constitutive of responsibility. (The determinists however, who argue that the actions of living creatures necessarily involve impulse, could not similarly argue that those of men necessarily involve deliberation, for we do not always deliberate.) (XV) The power to choose between opposites does not involve 'motion without a cause', for not all causes are external ones; man is himself the cause of his actions. We can choose in different ways because there is more than one end we can pursue. And that all assent is to what 'appears' does not mean that men follow 'appearances' from outside in the way that irrational animals do, for things may also 'appear' as the result of reasoning.

(XVI) The argument that all things come to be in accordance with fate throws human life into confusion; if all men believed it, they would take no pains over what requires effort, and they could not be blamed for this by the determinists, for determinism renders all blame unreasonable. (XVII) It also does away with divine providence, with piety, and with the usefulness of prophecy. (XVIII) Not even the supporters of determinism behave consistently with it in practice. (XIX) Blame and punishment would be undeserved; but the determinists would not accept this consequence. (XX) They would be convinced of the wrongness of their thesis if they tried to live even for a short time on the assumption that it is true. (XXI) It would be less dangerous for men to believe wrongly that they had the power of choice when all was in fact in accordance with fate, than for them to believe that all is determined when in fact it is not.

(XXII) The determinists claim that Nature, which is identical with Fate, is a divine force which organises the whole universe in a coherent system; everything is preceded by some cause and is itself the cause of something else, and the same result must always follow on the same cause in the same circumstances, because the unity of the universe would be disrupted if any motion without a cause were to occur. (XXIII) But it is false to claim that everything is followed by some effect; (XXIV) while everything that comes to be must have a cause preceding it, it is not the case that everything is necessarily the cause of something after it. And some things have only an accidental, not a proper cause. (XXV) It is not the case that whatever is preceded by something else is caused by it; rather, the continuity of the universe is preserved by the motion of the heavens. The infinite succession of causes postulated by the determinists in fact destroys causation by denying the existence of any first cause. Minor exceptions to the order of the universe do not mean that that order as a whole is destroyed.

(XXVI) Even if there are difficulties in the accepted notion of responsible action, it is not reasonable on account of these difficulties to deny what is obviously the case. They argue that, if we are responsible for those things of which we can also do the opposite, the virtuous man will not be responsible for his virtues, since he can no longer act wrongly, nor the wicked man for his vices. (XXVII) However, they are responsible for the dispositions they now have, in that they were responsible for acquiring them. If we possessed virtue by nature it would not be praiseworthy, but what we receive from nature is the capacity for virtue; and it does not develop naturally in the way that certain bodily faculties do, for if it did most of us would possess the virtues, and possession of them would not be praiseworthy. Rather, men's character develops by habituation; we become virtuous by performing virtuous actions. (XXVIII) Those who say that we develop our character of necessity, and also assert that wickedness is the only bad thing and that almost all men are wicked, must admit that nature has made man the worst of all living creatures. (**XXIX**) The virtuous man no longer has the power of not being virtuous, but there is a range of virtuous actions he may perform, and he may also refrain from particular actions, for instance in order to refute those who predict how he will act.

(**XXX**) It is wrong to argue that the gods have foreknowledge of all things and hence that all things are necessary; rather, if things that are contingent cannot be foreknown (definitely), the gods would only have foreknowledge of them *as contingent*. (**XXXI**) The determinist position renders prophecy useless; to say, not that Apollo warned Laius not to beget a child in ignorance as to whether he would obey or disobey, but that if he had not so warned him none of what subsequently occurred would have done so, makes Apollo responsible for all that followed, which is impious. The terrible events related in the myths are in no way conducive to the preservation of the universe. (**XXXII**) While men have the power to become wiser or not, even if they cannot be foolish once they have become wise, the gods do not have the power to be otherwise than they are, and for this reason they are honoured rather than praised; but where individual actions are concerned both the wise man and the gods have the power of doing them or not.

(**XXXIII**) It is wrong to say that responsibility is preserved if action in accordance with impulse is; for, while all responsible action is in accordance with impulse, it is only action in accordance with *rational* impulse that is responsible. (**XXXIV**) To claim that it is natural, and hence in accordance with fate, for some individuals to act rightly and others wrongly is impossible for those who claim that all our actions are necessary, for an action is right or wrong only if the agent also has the power of doing the opposite. (**XXXV-XXXVI**) The long argument of which the basic points are that fate implies law and law implies wrong and right action, an argument which the determinists put forward assuming that the preservation of action in accordance with impulse preserves responsibility, is false; for if all action is predetermined law is useless. Even if law itself is among the factors that determine our actions, it will still be predetermined whether we obey it or not. Consequently if fate is as the determinists claim law is excluded, and so are rewards and punishments; and as they themselves argue, if there are no rewards and punishments there is no virtue or wickedness and no gods. (**XXXVII**) Similarly, it is false to argue that if everything is in accordance with fate the organisation of the universe is unimpeded; but even granted this, and that if the universe exists there are gods and the gods are virtuous, it does not follow that practical wisdom exists and that consequently right and wrong actions and praise, blame, punishment and reward do. For practical wisdom is a virtue of men, not of gods; and if all is fated practical wisdom is useless. (**XXXVIII**) The preservation of movement in accordance with impulse does not preserve responsibility, unless responsible action is understood in a way different from the accepted one, which turns on our having the power to choose between opposite courses of action.

(**XXXIX**) These are the chief points of Aristotle's position concerning fate and responsibility, which is conducive to piety, to gratitude towards rulers like yourselves, and to concern about virtue.

TRANSLATION

De Fato

Introduction

I. It was my desire, great emperors Severus and Antoninus, that I
might myself come into your presence and see you and speak to you,
and give expression | to my thanks for the benefits I have received from
you on many occasions, always obtaining everything I requested,
together with a testimonial that I deserved to receive such things
when I asked for them. But even if we cannot sacrifice to the gods by
being present at their sacred rites, [we are] commanded to sacrifice to
them everywhere and from every place, and to send votive offerings
which we cannot bring ourselves; [and so] I have ventured to follow in
your case the example of what is allowed in the case of the divine, so as
to | send to you, as a votive offering, some offering of my first-fruits, the
most appropriate for you of all offerings.

For what could be a more appropriate offering to those who
genuinely honour and promote philosophy than a book that
undertakes philosophical speculation? The book contains the opinion
concerning fate and responsibility held by Aristotle, of whose
philosophical teaching I am the principal exponent, having been |
publicly declared teacher of it by your testimonial. This part of
philosophical doctrine is second to no other; for its usefulness extends
everywhere and to all things. For there is a difference, where their
actions are concerned, between those who believe that all things come
to be of necessity and in accordance with fate, and those who suppose
that some things come to be that do not have causes of their existing
with no alternative | laid down beforehand. And the discovery of the
truth in this matter is most difficult, for both positions seem to be
opposed by many evident facts. | But since some doctrines become
more clearly established by argument against those who do not hold a
similar position (and I think that this applies especially to this present
one), when I have spoken in accordance with the position of Aristotle
I will argue against those who have adopted a different position from

vol. 2.2
p. 164.3
Bruns

10

15

20

165.1

---

* Asterisks indicate points in the translation where reference should be
made to the Commentary.

5   him on these matters, so that in the comparison of the | positions the
truth may become clearer to you.

     The intention of my arguments is not for display, but for a more
exact examination and explanation of the issues; this it can be seen
you also zealously pursue in all that you do. For indeed no action of
yours can be found which makes appearance, rather than truth, its
10   goal. If, when you persue the book | at your leisure, it seems that
anything needs to be put more clearly, I request that you should also
grant me the honour of writing to me about your questions. For it is
not easy to make clear in their entirety, in a single book, both the
actual issues and the points which are used in the explanation of
them.

The Peripatetic doctrine of fate

II-VI

165.14   II. That there is such a thing as fate, and that it is the cause of some
15   things' | coming to be in accordance with itself, is sufficiently
established by men's conception. For the common nature of men is
not vain and does not aim wide of the truth, [that common nature] in
accordance with which they hold the same opinions as one another on
certain topics – those of them, at least, who are not compelled to adopt
a different position on account of some opinions already laid down,
through their desire to preserve their own self-consistency. It is for
20   this reason that, although Anaxagoras | of Clazomenae is in other
respects not negligible among exponents of natural philosophy, he
does not deserve credence when he testifies against the common belief
of men concerning fate; for *he* says that nothing that comes to be does
so in accorance with fate, and that this term is an empty one.

25   But as to *what* fate is and where it is located, the common |
conception of men is no longer sufficient to indicate this. For not only
do they not all agree with each other, but even the same individual
does not always hold the same opinions about it. For they change
166.1   their opinion concerning fate | with the times and present
circumstances. As many of them as say that all things happen in
accordance with fate understand by fate some cause that is
unalterable and inescapable. But there are some who do not think
that all the things that come to be do so in accordance with fate, and
5   suppose that there are | also certain other causes of things that come to

be; nor do they regard fate itself as being firm and unalterable, but
suppose that some even of the things that naturally come to be in
accordance with fate come to be not in accordance with it, but
'contrary to destiny', as the poets say, and contrary to fate. And there
are some who sometimes think that all the things that come to be so do
so in accordance with fate, and especially if the things that are
[matters] of luck go against them, | but when they are successful in   10
their enterprises suppose that they are themselves the causes of their
successes, on the grounds that things that happened would not have
happened if they had not themselves done certain things rather than
others, regarding themselves as having the power also *not* to do them.
On account of this disagreement it is necessary for philosophers to
enquire concerning fate, not whether it exists, but what it is and in
which of the things that come to be, and are, a thing of such a nature is
located.

III. That all those who speak about fate at all say that it is a cause for   166.15
things that come to be is familiar; for it is this that they give in
explanation and say is the cause of the things that come to be coming
to be in the way that they do. But since 'cause' is an expression used in
many ways, it is necessary for those who deal with the problem in
order first | to apprehend under which type of cause fate should be   20
placed; for no expression which is used in many ways is clear if it is
uttered without the proper distinctions.

Well, the causes of the things that come to be are divided into four
types of cause, as Aristotle showed. For some causes are efficient,
some have the rôle of matter, and also among [the causes]* is the
formal cause; | and besides these three causes the end, too, for the sake   25
of which what comes to be does so, is a cause among [the causes]*.
And this is the total of distinctions between causes; for whatever is a
cause of anything will be found to fall under one of these causes, and,
even if not everything that comes to be needs so many causes, at any
rate those that need most do not exceed the stated number.

The distinction | between them will become easier to understand if   167.1
it is seen in the case of some example of the things that come to be. Let
us then display the distinction between the causes in the case of a
statue. The cause of the statue in the sense of the efficient cause is the
craftsman who made it, whom we call a sculptor; in the sense of the
material, the underlying bronze or stone | or whatever it is that is   5
shaped by the craftsman in accordance with his craft, for this too is a

cause of the statue's having come to be and being. The form, too, which is brought into being in this underlying [material] by the craftsman is itself a cause of the statue, and it is on account of this form that it is a discus-thrower or a javelin-thrower or in conformity with some other definite shape. But these are not the only causes of

10 the coming to be | of the statue; for second to none of the causes of its coming to be is the end, for the sake of which it came to be – honour to someone or some reverence towards the gods. For without such a cause the statue would not even have come to be in the first place. There being, then, this number of causes and the distinction between them being clear, we would be right to count fate among efficient

15 causes, for it preserves | a parallel, in relation to the things that come to be in accordance with it, to the craftsman who fashions the statue.

167.16 IV. This being so, the next point is to discuss efficient causes; for thus it will be clear, whether fate should be regarded as the cause of all the things that come to be, or whether one should also admit other [causes], apart from this one, as efficient causes of certain things.

20 Well, Aristotle, | distinguishing between all the things that come to be, says that some of them come to be for the sake of something, since he who brings them about has before him a certain goal and end of the things that come to be, but others [for the sake] of nothing. For as many things as are not brought about by the agent* in accordance with any purpose and cannot be referred to a definite end (such as

25 clutching and twiddling toothpicks and touching and pulling | one's hair, and as many things as come about in a similar way to these) – that such things happen is familiar, but nevertheless they do not have a cause in the sense of an end and 'for the sake of what?'

168.1 | Well, there is no reasonable way of dividing up the things that come to be in this way, coming to be without a goal and independently; but, of the things that *may* be referred to something [as their end] and come to be for the sake of something, some come to be in accordance with nature, and others in accordance with reason. For those things which have nature as the cause of their coming to be

5 progress, according to a certain definite | and numbered order, to some end, and cease from coming to be when they arrive at it; unless something obstructs them and prevents them from following the natural path to the end before them.

Moreover, the things that come to be according to reason, too, have some end. For none of the things that comes to be in accordance with reason comes to be just as it happens, but all of them are referred to some goal. Things that come to be in accordance with reason are all those that are brought about | by agents who reason about them and contrive how they may come to be. This is how all the things that come to be in accordance with skill (craft) and choice do so, differing from the things that come to be by nature. For the things that come to be by nature have the beginning and cause of such coming-to-be in themselves (for this is what nature is like; and they come to be in accordance with a certain order, but without the nature | that brings them about employing reasoning about them in the same way as the crafts); but the things that come to be in accordance with skill and choice have their beginning of movement and their efficient cause outside and not in themselves, and the cause of their coming to be is the reasoning of the agent concerning them.

And thirdly there are among the things that come to be for the sake of something the things which are believed to come to be from luck | and the fortuitous; these differ from those which come to be for the sake of something in a primary way, in that in the case of the latter everything that comes to be before the end does so for the sake of the end, while in the case of the former the things that come to be before the end do so for the sake of something else; but, while they come to be for the sake of something else, that which is said to come to be fortuitously and from luck meets with them as their end.

V. These things being so, and all the things that | come to be having been distributed into these types, the next point after this is to see in which sort of efficient cause fate should be located. Is it to be located in the things that do not come to be for the sake of anything? No, this is completely unreasonable; for we always | use the term 'fate' of some end, saying that it came to be in accordance with fate. So fate must necessarily be located in the things that come to be for the sake of something; and since of the things that come to be for the sake of something some come to be in accordance with reason and other in accordance with nature, fate must necessarily | be located either in both of them, so that we say that all the things that come to be do so in accordance with fate, or in one or the other.

But the things that come to be in accordance with reason seem to come to be in accordance with reason in virtue of the agent's having the power also not to bring them about; for the things that are made to come to be by craftsmen in accordance with skill do not seem to be

10

20

168.25

169.1

5

made to come to be by them of necessity – at any rate, they bring each
10   of them about in the manner of those who have | equal power not to
bring them about; besides, how is it not absurd to say that a house or a
bed came to be in accordance with fate? And the things over which
choice has control, too (that is, all actions that are in conformity with
virtue or vice) are also thought to depend on us. If those things depend
15   on us over which we seem to have control | both of their being done and
of their not being done, and [if] it is not possible to say that fate is the
cause of these things, or that there are certain (beginnings) and
causes, laid down beforehand eternally, of some one of these things
coming to be or not coming to be with no alternative (for none of these
69.18 things would any longer depend on us, if it came to be in this way); | –
[VI] [then] we are left with saying that fate is in the things that come to
be by nature, so that fate and nature are the same thing.
20 | For what is fated is in accordance with nature and what is in
accordance with nature is fated. For it is not the case that man comes
to be from man, and horse from horse, in accordance with nature but
not in accordance with fate; rather, these causes accompany each
other as if differing only in name. It is for this reason, too, that men
say that the first causes of the coming-to-be of each thing in
25   accordance with nature (that is, the heavenly bodies and their |
orderly revolution) are also causes of fate. For the beginning of all
coming-to-be is the heavenly bodies', in their motion, being in one
type of position or another in relation to things on earth.
As fate is located in these things and is of such a nature, it
is necessary that, as are the things that come to be in accordance
with nature, so should those be too that come to be in accordance with
fate But the things that come to be in accordance with nature do not
30   do so of necessity, but the coming to be of | the things that come to be in
this way is sometimes hindered; for which reason the things that come
to be in accordance with nature come to be for the most part, but not
170.1 of necessity. For that which is contrary to nature, | too, has a place in
them, and comes to be when nature is hindered in its proper working
by some external cause. It is for this reason that man does not come
from man of necessity but for the most part, and neither does each of
the things that come to be in accordance with nature always come to
be in accordance with the fixed time that seems to be laid down for the
5   things | that come to be in this way.
If there is in the things that come to be in accordance with nature
that too which is contrary to nature, as also in the things in

accordance with craft [that which is contrary to craft], what is contrary to fate will also have a place in the things that come to be in accordance with fate, so that if what is contrary to nature has a place and is not an empty expression, what is contrary to fate, too, will have a place in the things that come to be. And for this reason one might reasonably say, too, that it is the proper|nature of each thing that is its 10 beginning and cause of the ordered pattern of the things that come to be in it in accordance with nature. For it is from this, for the most part, that the lives of men and their deaths derive their pattern.

At any rate we see that the body, through being like this or like that in nature, is affected both in disease and in death in accordance with its natural constitution, but not of necessity; for treatments and changes|of climate and doctors' orders and advice from the gods are 15 sufficient to break such a pattern. And in the same way in the case of the soul too one would find the choices and actions and way of life of each individual differing from, and contrary to, his natural constitution. For 'men's character is their guardian spirit' according to Heraclitus, that is, their nature.

For men's actions and lives|and endings can for the most part be 20 seen to be in accordance with their natural constitutions and dispositions. The man who loves danger and is by nature bold meets some violent death for the most part (for this is the fate in [his*] nature). For the man who is licentious in nature what is in accordance with fate* is spending his life in licentious pleasures and the life of the incontinent, unless something better comes to be|in him and shakes 25 him out of the life that is in accordance with [his] nature; and for the man who is of an enduring [nature], again, it is putting up with troubles, and persistence, and ending life|in such circumstances. And 171.1 for those who are illiberal by nature and insatiable in the acquisition of goods the results of fate, too, are in accord; they spend their life for the most part in wrong-doing, and the end of life for those who act in this way is in accordance with this. And people are accustomed|to 5 reproach such men, when they are in the circumstances that follow on their way of life and are in accordance with fate, as being themselves the causes of their present troubles.

Moreover, someone who wanted to come to the aid of those who profess the art of prophecy might give this as the cause of their not always hitting the mark: while the nature and fate of each individual does not have a free passage in all things, but some things come to be| 10 contrary to it as well, the prophets reveal the things that come to be in

accordance with fate, as indeed do the physiognomists. At any rate, when Zopyrus the physiognomist said certain extraordinary things about the philosopher Socrates which were very far removed from his chosen manner of life, and was ridiculed for this by Socrates'
15   associates, Socrates said that Zopyrus had not been at all mistaken; | for he would have been like that as far as his nature was concerned, if he had not, through the discipline that comes from philosophy, become better than his nature. – And this is, to state it in a summary fashion, the opinion concerning fate of the Peripatetic school.

Difficulties of the determinist position
(i) VII-VIII Luck and the fortuitous

171.18   VII. What has been stated will be more clearly established if, alongside the preceding demonstrations of the established position,
20   we place the absurdities that follow for those who say that | all things come to be in accordance with fate. For by this discussion we will both make the truth more easily understood, by the placing of the doctrines beside each other, and in addition to this we will not find it necessary to mention the same subjects on many occasions.

One might reasonably be bewildered as to how certain people, who say that they practise philosophy and pursue the truth in the things that are, and suppose that they have the advantage over the rest of
25   men | in this respect and for this reason encourage others to do this, have surrendered themselves to the doctrine that asserts that all things come to be of necessity and in accordance with fate, [a doctrine] in which we see only those among ordinary people* taking refuge who are conscious of nothing successful in their lives, trans-
172.1   ferring from themselves | to fate the responsibility for their bad circumstances. This doctrine is not in harmony with what is evident, nor are there any convincing demonstrations that this is how matters are. Moreover, it does away with there being anything which depends on us; and if *this* is believed, what greater penalty than this could come from argument?
5   That [this doctrine] is contrary to what is evident is clear | from [the following]. Almost all philosophers and ordinary people believe that some things come to be fortuitously and from luck, and that some of the things that come to be do so contingently, and that there is a place

in the things that are for 'no more this than that'.* But none of these
points is preserved according to those who say that all things come to
be of necessity, if at least they are preserved by not altering the
meanings | to which these terms are accepted as applying; for to   10
substitute other things for the terms to signify and to think that,
because the latter remain, the things mentioned above do so as well, is
not the action of those who preserve what is accepted. For the coming-
to-be of some things from luck is not preserved if one does away with
the real nature of the things that come to be in this way and makes
luck a name for things that come to be of necessity, but if | one shows 15
that those things can be preserved to which the term 'luck' is accepted
as applying.

VIII. Well, all men who adhere to common and natural conceptions   172.17
describe as coming to be from luck and the fortuitous those things that
supervene on causes which are productive of something else
primarily.* For whenever there happens to something, that comes to
be for the sake of something else, not that for the sake of which it came
to be, but something else which was | not even expected at the   20
beginning, this is said to have come to be from luck; having *per se* come
to be without a cause, but having as a cause *per accidens* that which
came to be for the coming-to-be of something else. And that it is
something like this that everyone refers to as coming to be from luck is
clear from their meaning when they say that things come to be from
luck.* | 25
    For they say that someone has found a treasure from luck, if,
when digging for the sake of something else and not for that of
finding treasure, he chances on a treasure. For the man who dug for
this reason [*sc.* that of finding treasure] did not [find the treasure]
from luck; there happened to him that for the sake of which he dug.
But the man whom all describe as having found the treasure from
luck is the man who had no concern with finding the treasure, but to
whom, when he was acting for the sake of something else, | the finding 30
of the treasure happened as the [accidental] end of that [action].
And they describe | someone as having recovered money from luck   173.1
when he goes to the market-place for the sake of something else,
chances on his debtor who has money with him, and recovers what
was owing to him. For his coming to the market-place had some
other primary end, but the collection of what was owed happened to
it, coming to be as an end for it *per accidens*. For one | would no longer   5

be described as having recovered a debt 'from luck' if one went to the market-place for the sake of this, for one's going would have the end that was set before it. And a horse is described as having been saved for certain people 'fortuitously' when it flees from its captors in the hope of food or for the sake of something else, but it happens to it in
10   its|flight [*literally*: 'it happens to its flight and course'] that it chances upon its owners. And what need is there to accumulate more examples for you or to split hairs about what has been said already? For it is sufficient for the purpose in hand to show to what things – signified the terms mentioned are applied.

Well, if the things that come to be from luck and fortuitously are like this, so as not to come to be in accordance with a primary*
15   cause| (for it is to things that rarely happen to those that have come to be before them that luck and the spontaneous relate), how would anything of what has been stated above be preserved according to those who maintain that everything that is or comes to be does so of necessity by certain antecedent and primary* causes, each of the things that comes to be having some cause laid down beforehand, [such that] if this is or has come to be it is necessary for the thing itself either to be or to come to be?
20 |To preserve nothing of what has been stated above, but decree that the term 'luck' should apply to something else, and to say that, because that [something else] is not done away with by him who holds that all things come to be of necessity, neither is luck done away⸍with, is the action of those who deceive themselves and their hearers alike by fallacious argument; for on this basis nothing will prevent one from saying that luck and fate are the same thing, and
25   [thus] to be| so far from doing away with luck as to say that *all* the things that come to be do so from luck. But they were not blamed on the issue of the preservation of the *term* luck, but on that of doing away with the coming to be of some things in this way, things to
174.1   which 'coming to be|from luck and fortuitously' is applied.

For what else do those do who define luck and the fortuitous as 'a cause obscure to human reasoning', than introduce by decree some private signification of 'luck'? For to employ, to establish this, the
5   fact that some people say that they are ill 'fortuitously', when| the cause of the illness is obscure to them, is false. For it is not on the ground that there *is* some cause, though it is obscure to them, that they speak thus, but they apply 'fortuitously' to those things that they persuade themselves have come to be *without* a cause. At any

rate, no-one says that the thing for which they seek the cause and assume it to exist has come to be fortuitously, and one does not look for the cause of that which one is persuaded has come to be fortuitously. It is for this reason that the doctors | at least do not   10
speak about these things in this way, even when they admit that they still do not know the causes of them. Such an account of luck would be more properly applied, *not* to the cases mentioned above as being said by everyone to come to be from luck, but [rather] to other things which no-one ever described as coming to be from luck.

For the causes of the discovery of the treasure and of the collecting of the debt are not | obscure to human reasoning, but clear and   15
obvious; [the cause] of the finding is the digging, and of the collecting of the debt the going to the market place. For neither would the former person have found [the treasure] if he had not dug, nor would the latter have collected the debt if he had not gone [there]; but since the aforementioned things are not primary* causes of these [results] but came to be for the sake of something else, for this reason [the results] are supposed | to come to be from   20
luck. 'Obscure to human reasoning' are rather the causes of those things which are believed to come to be in accordance with certain reactions, the cause through which they come to be being unknown, in the way that certain amulets are employed which have no reasonable and credible cause [or: explanation] for their acting in this way, also spells and certain trickeries of that sort. For all agree that the cause of these [acting as they do] is obscure, | which is why   25
they say that they are things for which no cause can be assigned, but no-one says that any of these things acts from luck, because they are believed to act as they do in accordance with some definite cause. For the things that are from luck are not said to come to be in this way [*sc.* from luck] because of the obscurity of their cause, but because of the absence of causation by the cause in the primary* and proper sense.

Difficulties of the determinist position

(ii) IX-X. Contingency and possibility

IX. Such are the things they say about luck, and this is how they   174.29
are in accord with what is accepted [i.e.: not at all]. And the contingent and the coming-to-be of some things 'in whichever way | 175.1
it happens' are also done away with by those who say that all things

come to be of necessity. This is immediately obvious. For those
things are said to come to be contingently, in the proper sense, in the
case of which there is also room for their being able *not* to come to be
(as the very expression 'in whichever way it happens' makes clear);
5 but the things that come to be of necessity|cannot not come to be. (I
am not applying 'the necessary' to what comes to be by force, nor
should anyone censure the term with reference to this [meaning],
but [I am applying it rather] to those things that are naturally made
to come to be by certain things and of which the opposites could not
possibly come to be).

And indeed, how is it not absurd, and contrary to what is obvious,
to say that necessity extends so far that no-one can suffer movement
10 in any respect, or move | any of his parts, in a way in which it was
also possible for him not to move at that time, but that a chance
turning of the neck or extension of a finger or raising of the eyebrows
or anything like this follows on certain primary* causes and could at
no time be made by us to come about otherwise, and this too when
they see that there is a great difference in the things that are and
15 come to be, | from which it was easy to learn that not everything is
enmeshed in such causes?

We do at any rate see that some of the things which are have no
capacity for change to the opposite of the state in which they are, but
others of them are no more* able to be in the opposite state than in
that in which they are. Fire is not able to admit cold, which is the
20 opposite of its natural heat,|and neither could snow admit heat and
remain snow; but it is not impossible for water, even if it is cold, to
lose this [property] and admit its contrary, heat. And in a similar
way both this is possible, and [it is possible] for him who is sitting to
stand and for him who is moving to be still and for him who is
speaking to be silent, and in countless other cases one would find
that there is present some capacity admitting of opposites; and if
25 things that are of | necessity in the one state do *not* have the capacity
of admitting the opposite of the state in which they are, things which
do also admit the opposite of the states in which they are will not be
in those states of necessity. But if not of necessity, contingently.

Moreover, the things which are in a certain state contingently are
in it in this way, [namely,] that they have come to be in it not of
176.1 necessity but | contingently; and what has come to be in a certain
state contingently was able also *not* to have come to be in it. For each
of these things is in the state in which it happens to be because it was

possible for it to be in one or other [of the] opposed states; but, because of its capacity for the opposed states, it is not of necessity simply in the state in which it now is. But | the things which are in 5 certain states in this way are not in them on account of certain causes laid down beforehand and leading to these states of necessity. So that, if all the things that can alike admit [either of two] opposed states are contingently in the states in which they are, and not in those in which they are not, the things which are and come to be contingently will be countless.

For it is absurd to speak in a similar way of 'being in a certain state of necessity' both in the case of those things which cannot admit | of the opposites of the states in which they are, and in that of 10 those which are no more at any time whatsoever able to admit these than [to admit] their opposites. For if the things which are of necessity in a certain state cannot admit its opposite, the things which *can* admit the opposite will not be in the state in which they are of necessity.

X. [Consider the following argument*]: 'The possible and 176.14 contingent is not done away with if all things | come to be according 15 to fate, on these grounds. [i] It is possible for that to come to be which is not prevented from coming to be by anything, even if it does not come to be. [ii] The opposites of the things that come to be in accordance with fate have not been prevented from coming to be (for which reason they are still possible even though they do not come to be). [iii] That they have not been prevented from coming to be is shown by the fact that the things that prevent them are unknown to us, although there certainly *are* some.' (For | the causes of the coming 20 to be of the opposites of these things in accordance with fate are also the causes of these things' *not* coming to be, if, as they say, it is impossible for opposites to come to be in the same circumstances. However, because certain things that exist are not known to us, for this reason they say that the coming to be [of the opposites of the things that are in accordance with fate] is not prevented.) – Well, how is saying this not the action of those who jest in arguments where jesting is not what is needed? | For our ignorance makes no 25 difference to the existence or non-existence of the facts. It is clear, when people speak like this, that the possible will according to them exist in virtue of our [degree of] knowledge. For those things will not be possible, for those who can know their causes (and these would

177.1   be | the prophets), that *are* possible for those who know that they
have been prevented but do not know by what they are prevented.

Preserving the nature of the possible in the way we have
described, they say that even the things that come to be in
accordance with fate, although they come to be unalterably, do not
5   come to be of necessity, for this reason, that it is possible | for their
opposite too to come to be – possible in the sense described above.
But these are, as I have said, the arguments of those who jest rather
than of those who are supporting a position.

And similar to this is the argument that the proposition* 'there
will be a sea-battle tomorrow' can be true but not also necessary; for
what is necessary is what is always true, but this [proposition] no
10   longer remains true when the sea-battle comes to be; | but if this is
not necessary, neither is what is signified by it of necessity,
[namely] that there will be a sea-battle. But if there will be a sea-
battle, but not of necessity (since it *is* true that there will be a sea-
battle, but not [true that there will be a sea-battle] of necessity),
clearly [there will be a sea-battle] contingently; and if contingently,
the coming-to-be of some things contingently is not done away with
by the coming-to-be of all things in accordance with fate.

15   But this [argument] too is again like that stated previously; | [it is
the argument] of those who both jest and do not know what they are
talking about. For neither is everything that comes to be *of necessity*
necessary, if what is *necessary* is the eternal, but what comes to be *of*
necessity has been prevented from being like this by its very coming-
to-be; nor is the proposition that asserts this [*sc.* what comes to be of
necessity] necessary, if what is signified by it is not of this sort [*sc.*
necessary]. (For we do not describe every proposition, in which
20   what is necessary is contained, as *ipso facto* | necessary; for it is not in
this way that it is judged that a proposition is necessary, but by its
not being able to change from being true to being false.)

If then [the proposition that asserts what comes to be of
necessity*] is not *necessary*, it has not at all been prevented from
being *true*, just as 'there will be a sea-battle tomorrow'. For, [even]
if [when] stated as [something] necessary it is not true because
of the addition of the necessary, if it does not become necessary by the
25   addition of '*of necessity*' it will still be true | in the same way as [the
proposition] uttered without this addition. But if this is true, when
the next day arrives the proposition that 'a sea-battle came to be of
necessity' will be true; and if of necessity, not contingently.

And indeed, if 'there will be a sea-battle tomorrow' is true, it will always be the case that a sea-battle came to be in accordance with fate, if indeed | all the things that come to be are in accordance with fate. But if in accordance with fate, unalterably, and if unalterably, it cannot not come to be, and it is impossible for that not to come to be which cannot come to be; and how can we say that that for which it is impossible not to come to be can also not come to be, since it is necessary for that to come to be | for which it is impossible not to come to be? So all the things that come to be in accordance with fate will be of necessity, according to them,* and not also contingently, as they say in jest.

178.1

5

Difficulties of the determinist position
(iii) XI-XV. Deliberation and responsbility

XI. Moreover the consequence, if all the things that come to be follow on some causes that have been laid down beforehand and are definite and exist beforehand, is that men | deliberate in vain about the things that they have to do. And if deliberating were in vain, man would have the power of deliberation in vain. (And yet, if nature does nothing of what is primary in vain, and man's being a living creature with the power of deliberation is a primary product of nature (and not something that [merely] accompanies and happens along with the primary products), the conclusion would be drawn that men do | not have the power of deliberation in vain.)

178.8

10

15

That deliberating is in vain if everything comes to be of necessity can easily be realised by those who know the use of deliberating. It is agreed by everyone that man has this advantage from nature over the other living creatures, that he does not follow appearances in the same way as them, but has reason from her as a judge of | the appearances that impinge on him concerning certain things as deserving to be chosen. Using this, if, when they are examined, the things that appeared *are* indeed as they initially appeared, he assents to the appearance and so goes in pursuit of them; but if they appear different or something else [appears] more deserving to be chosen, he chooses that, leaving behind what initially appeared to him as deserving of choice. At any rate [there are] many things [which], having seemed different to us in their first appearances [from what they appeared to us subsequently], no longer | remained as in our previous notion when reason put them to the test; and so, though

20

25

they would have been done as far as concerned the appearance of them, on account of [our] deliberating about them they were not done – we being in control of the deliberating and of the choice of the things that resulted from the deliberation.

It is, at any rate, for this reason that we do not deliberate about the eternal things or about the things which are agreed to come to be
30 of necessity – because | no advantage would come to us from deliberating about them. And neither do we deliberate about the things which do not come to be of necessity but depend on some other people, because there is not any advantage to us from deliberation about these things either. Nor yet do we deliberate about the things which
179.1 were able to be done by us but are past, because | no advantage comes to us by deliberation about these things either. But we deliberate only about the things which are both done by us and future,* clearly on the grounds that we will gain something from this [deliberating] for the choice and doing of them.

For if we do not deliberate in those matters in which no advantage
5 comes to us from deliberating | beyond the fact of having deliberated itself, it is clear that, in those matters where we *do* deliberate, we deliberate about them [because] we will gain some advantage from deliberating besides the fact of having deliberated. For the fact of having deliberated itself, at any rate, is a consequence enjoyed also by those who deliberate about the other things of which we have spoken earlier.

What then is the advantage from deliberation? That we, having power over the choice of the things that are to be done, choose and
10 do what | we would not have done if we had not deliberated, because we would have done something else on account of yielding to the impression that impinged [on us; we choose and do] the former rather than the latter when it has appeared through reason to be more deserving of choice. And this will happen if we do not do everything compulsorily. But if we should do everything we do through some causes laid down beforehand, so as to have no power
15 to do this particular thing or not, but [only] to do precisely | each of the things that we do, in the same way as the fire that heats and the stone that is carried downwards and the cylinder that rolls down the slope – what advantage comes to us, as far as action is concerned, from deliberating about what will be done? For [on this view] it is necessary for us, even after deliberating, to do what we would have
20 done if we had not deliberated, so that no advantage comes to us |

from the deliberating beyond the fact of having deliberated itself. But in fact, [although] we could do this even in the case of those things that do not depend on us, we declined to do it on the grounds that it was useless. So [on our opponents' hypothesis] deliberating will be useless even in those cases in which we use it on the grounds that it provides something useful to us.

From this it followed that nature's gift to us of having the power of deliberation is in vain; and if to this there were added the view held by these men themselves | and in common by nearly all philosophers,   25
that nothing is brought about by nature in vain, that [premiss] would be refuted from which it followed that our having the power of deliberation was in vain. | But this followed on our not having such   180.1
power over the things done by us as to be able to do their opposites.

XII. Deliberating is done away with according to them, as has been   180.3
shown, and so clearly is what depends on us. For this is what all those who are not defending some | position accept as depending on   5
us – that over which we have control both to do it and not to do it, not following some causes which surround us from outside or giving in to them [and following] in the way in which they lead us. And choice, the peculiar activity of man, is concerned with the same things; for choice is the impulse with desire towards what has been preferred as a result of deliberation. And for this reason choice does not apply to the things | that come to be necessarily, nor to those that   10
do so not necessarily but not through us, nor even in the case of all the things that do so through us; but in the case of those things that come to be through us over which we have control both to do and not to do them.

For the person who deliberates about something either (i) deliberates about whether he should do it or not, or (ii) he enquires earnestly by what means he might attain some good; | and if in his   15
enquiry he comes upon something impossible, he leaves that aside, and similarly he leaves aside the things that are possible but do not depend on him, but persists in his enquiry concerning the proposed [end], until he comes upon something of which he is persuaded he himself has the power; and after this he ceases from deliberating, since he has brought back the enquiry to that which is the principle of actions [*i.e.* himself; but cf. Commentary], and begins on the action | leading to what is proposed. But his enquiry [in case (ii)] too   20
is carried out on the assumption that he has the power also to do the

opposite things [to what he in fact does]. For concerning each of the things that fall under the deliberation the deliberator's enquiry is 'whether this or its opposite should be done by me' – even if he says that all things come to be in accordance with fate.

For the truth [displayed] in the things that are to be done refutes the erroneous opinions concerning them; and how it is not absurd to say|that this mistake [*sc.* of supposing that they *do* have the power to do the opposite] is one that all men in common have made by nature? For we assume that we have this power in actions, that we can choose the opposite, and not that everything which we choose has causes laid down beforehand, on account of which it is not possible for us not to choose it; this is sufficiently shown also by the regret that often occurs in relation to what has been chosen. For it is on the grounds that it was possible|for us also not to have chosen and not to have done this that we feel regret and blame ourselves for our neglect of deliberation. But also, when we see others|not judging well about the things that they have to do, we reproach them too as going wrong, and we think that these people should make use of advisers – on the grounds that it depends on us to call in advisers for ourselves or not and to do, on account of the presence of such people, other things too and not those|which we [in fact] do.

It is clear even in itself that 'what depends on us' is applied to those things over which we have the power of also choosing the opposite things; [but] this is also adequately called to mind by what has been said.

181.7   **XIII.** This being what [that which depends on us] is like, they do not even begin to try to show that this is preserved according to those* who say that all things come to be in accordance with fate (for they know that they will be attempting the impossible); but, as in the case of luck they substitute another meaning for the term | 'luck' and try to mislead their hearers into thinking that they themselves, too, preserve the coming-to-be of some things from luck – so they do also in the case of what depends on us. For, doing away with men's possession of the power of choosing and doing opposites, they say that what depends on us is what comes about through us.

|For since, they say, the natures of the things that are and come to be are various and different (for those of animate and inanimate things are not the same, nor even, again, are those of all animate things the same; for the differences in species of the things that are

show the differences in their natures), and the things that are
brought about by each thing come about in accordance with its
proper nature – those by a stone in accordance with that of | a stone,   20
those by fire in accordance with that of fire and those by a living
creature in accordance with that of a living creature – nothing of the
things which are brought about by each thing in accordance with its
proper nature, they say, can be otherwise, but each of the things
brought about by them comes about compulsorily, in accordance
not with the necessity that results from force but [with that]
resulting from its being impossible for that which has a nature of
that sort to be moved at that time in some other way and not in this, | 25
when the circumstances are such as could not possibly not have been
present to it. For it is not possible for the stone, if it is released
from some height, not to be carried downwards, if nothing hinders. Because it has weight in itself, and this is the natural cause of such a
motion, whenever the external causes which contribute to the natural
movement of the stone are also present, | of necessity the stone is   30
moved in the way in which it is its nature to be moved; and certainly
it is of necessity | that those causes are present to it on account of   182.1
which it is then moved. Not only can it not fail to be moved when
these [causes] are present, but it is moved then of necessity, and
such movement is brought about by fate through the stone. And the
same account [applies] in the case of other things, too. And as it is in
the case of inanimate | things, so it is also, they say, in that of living   5
creatures. For there is a certain movement that is in accordance with
nature for living creatures too, and this is movement in accordance
with impulse; for every living creature that moves *qua* living creature
is moved in a movement according to impulse brought about by fate
through the creature.

These things being so, and fate bringing about movements and
activities in the world, some | through earth, if it so happens, some   10
through air, some through fire, some through something else, and
some also being brought about through living creatures (and such
are the movements in accordance with impulse), they say that those
brought about by fate through the living creatures "depend on" the
living creatures – coming about in a similar way, as far as necessity
is concerned, to all the others; because for these too [*i.e.* the living
creatures] the external causes must of necessity be present | then, so   15
that of necessity they perform the movement which is from themselves and in accordance with impulse in some such way. But because

[the movements of living creatures] come about through impulse and assent, [the others] in some cases on account of weight, in others on account of heat, in others in accordance with some other cause, [for this reason] they say that this [movement] depends on the living creatures, but not that each of the others depends, in one case on the stone, in another on the fire. – And such, to state it
20 briefly, is|their opinion about what depends on us.

182.20 XIV. It is possible to see whether, saying these things, they preserve the common conceptions of all men about what depends on us. For those who ask them how it is possible for what depends on us to be preserved if all things are in accordance with fate do not ask this putting forward only the *name* of what depends on us, but also that
25 thing which it signifies, that which is in our own power.|For it is on account of their conviction that this is what that which depends on us is like that they censure those who say that all things come to be of necessity. These ought straight away to have said that it was not preserved, and to have sought for and presented the reasons for its not being preserved; but since they saw that this was something altogether paradoxical and that many of their doctrines would suffer the same as what depends on us, they showed that [what depends on us] was in accord with the doctrine of fate, thinking | that by
30 misleading their hearers through the ambiguity they would escape the absurdities that follow for those who say that nothing depends on us.

But when they say these things, first of all one might reasonably
183.1 ask them why, when different things are brought about | through different things by fate, and fate acts through the proper nature of each of the things that are, they do not apply 'what depends on them' to any of the other things, but only to living creatures. For the reasons why they say that the things that come about through the living creatures depend on the living creatures can be asserted also
5 in the case of each|of the other things. For since the things that come about through the living creature would not come about if the living creature had not exercised impulse, but they come about through the living creature's assenting and exercising impulse and do not come about if it does not assent – for this reason they say that these things depend on the living creature. They will be brought about by it of necessity (for it is not possible [that they should come about] in another way); but they think that they depend on the living creature

because they cannot come about through | anything else, or through   10
it in any other way.

But this can be asserted also concerning each of the other things.
For what comes about through the fire could neither come about
through anything else, nor through the fire in any other way than
through its heating; so that, since the things that come about
through the fire could not come about in any other way than if the
fire heats, and will come about if the fire heats | but not if it does not,   15
these things would depend on the fire. And it will be possible to say
the same in the case of each of the other things. What need is there
to make a long story of it when what is said is obvious? [We] do not
begrudge [their use] of *names*; but it is their thinking that they are
according more to living creatures in the things that come about
through them than to the other things too through which something
comes about, when they are preserving nothing more for them than
the *name* | of what depends on them -- this is what is blameworthy,   20
because they themselves are deceived through the *name* being
common [to their position and ours], or because they choose to
deceive others.

And in addition to this one might wonder at them over this point,
why on earth they say that what depends on us is [to be found] in
impulse and assent (for which reason they preserve it in all living
creatures alike). For what depends on us is not [to be found] in
[creatures'] yielding of their own accord | to an appearance when it   25
impinges on them and exercising impulse towards what has
appeared, but this perhaps is what constitutes and indicates the
voluntary. But the voluntary and what depends on us are not indeed
the same thing. For it is what comes about from an assent that is not
enforced that is voluntary; but it is what comes about with an assent
that is in accordance with reason and judgement that depends on us.
And for this reason, if something depends on us it is | also voluntary,   30
but not everything that is voluntary depends on us. For the
irrational living creatures too, which act in accordance with the
impulse and assent in them, act voluntarily; but it is peculiar to man
that something of the things that are brought about by him depends
on him. For this is what his being rational is, having in himself
reason which is a judge and discoverer of the appearances that
impinge and generally of the things that are and are not | to be done.   184.1
And for this reason the other living creatures, which yield to
appearances alone, have the causes of their assents and of their

impulses to actions in accordance with these; but man has reason as
a judge of the appearances which impinge on him from outside
concerning things that are to be done, and using this he examines
each of them, | not only as to whether it *appears* of the kind it appears
[to be] but whether it also *is* [of the kind it appears to be]. And if he
finds in his reasoned enquiry that its reality is different from the
appearance, he does not concede to it because it *appears* of a certain
kind, but resists it because it *is* not also of that kind. In this way, at
least, he often refrains from things that appear pleasant, although he
has a desire for them, because his reason is not | in accord with what
appears; and similarly he passes over some things that seem
advantageous, since this is the judgement of reason [i.e. that he
should pass over them].

If what depends on us is [to be found] in rational assent, which
comes about through deliberating, and they say that it is [to be
found] in assent and impulse, because it also comes about
irrationally, it is clear from what they say that they consider it in too
lazy a fashion, since they do not say either what | it is or in what it
comes to be. For to be rational is nothing other than to be a
beginning of actions. For as the being of different things is [to be
found] in different things, that of a living creature in being a living
creature with impulse, that of fire in being hot and a thing with the
power to heat, and that of other things in other things, so that of
man is [to be found] in being rational, which is equivalent to having
in oneself a principle (beginning) of both choosing something and
not; and both are the same thing, so that the person who | does away
with this does away with man.

But they seem to have passed over reason and to locate what
depends on us in impulse because, if they say that it is [to be found]
in deliberation, their sophistical argument no longer goes forward.
For in the case of impulse they are able to say that what comes about
in accordance with impulse depends on the living creatures, because
it is not possible for [the living creatures] to do the things that come
about through them without impulse; but if what depends on us |
were [to be found] in deliberation, then it would no longer follow for
them that the things that come about through man cannot come
about in any other way. For [although] man has the power of
deliberating, he does not do all the things that come about through
him by deliberating. For we do not do all the things that we do after
deliberating, but often, when the right moment for doing the things

that need doing does not allow time for deliberating, we do some
things | also without having deliberated; and often on account of   30
laziness or some other cause. But if some things come about when
we have deliberated and some also when we have not, there is no
longer any room to say that the things that come about through
deliberating | depend on man because nothing can come about   185.1
through him in any other way.

So, if we do some things after deliberating and some not after
deliberating, no longer do the things that come to be through us
come about simply in the way that the things [do] that come about
through [the other] living creatures or through fire or through the
two heavy bodies [i.e. earth and water]. And if we have from | nature   5
the power of doing something after deliberating, it is clear that we
would also have the power of doing something else through having
deliberated, and not [doing], with no alternative, what [we would
have done] even if we had not deliberated. For [otherwise] we would
deliberate in vain.

XV. To rely on the argument that 'if in the same circumstances   185.7
someone acts now in this way and now in another, motion without a
cause is introduced', and for this reason to say that no-one can | do   10
the opposite of what he will do – may this too not be an oversight like
those already mentioned? For the things that come to be in
accordance with a cause do not always and in every case have the
cause of their coming to be outside [themselves]. For it is on account
of a power of this sort that something depends on us, [namely,] that
we [ourselves] are in control of the things that come about in this
way, and not some cause from outside. And for this reason the
things that come about in this way do not come about without a
cause, having | their cause from us. For man is the beginning and   15
cause of the actions that come about through him, and this is what
being is for a man, [i.e. it is] to have the beginnings of his acting in
himself in this way, as for a sphere it is to be carried rolling down a slope.
And for this reason each of the other things follows the causes that
surround it from outside, but man does not, because for him being is [to
be found] in | having a beginning and cause for himself, so as not to   20
follow the things that surround him from outside, with no alternative.

For indeed, if our judgement about what is to be done took place
with reference to a single goal, perhaps there would be some reason

for our judgements about the same things always being similar; but since it is not so (for we choose the things that we choose, sometimes something on account of what is noble, sometimes on account of
25   what is pleasant, sometimes | on account of what is advantageous, and it is not the same things that bring these about), it is possible for us at one time to prefer certain of the things that surround us, being attracted to what is noble, and at another time [to prefer] others, referring our judgement to the pleasant or the advantageous.

For as we do not look for any other cause, on account of which earth is carried downwards in accordance with the heaviness in it, or
30   on account of which a living creature does what it does | in accordance with impulse, because each of them contributes this cause from itself to the things that come about, being like this in nature; so neither in the case of the things that are brought about in
186.1   different ways | at different times by us in identical circumstances should any other cause be demanded besides man himself. For this is what being was for a man; for [it was] to be a beginning and cause of the actions that come about through oneself.

To say that those who have deliberated, too, assent to what
5   'appears' [to them to be best], and for this | reason follow 'appearances' in the same way as the other living creatures, is not true. For not everything that 'appears' is an 'appearance'. For an 'appearance' is simple and is brought about without reasoning by the things that impinge from outside, being like the activities of perception, and for this reason it has power above all in the irrational living creatures; but some things also 'appear' that take
10   the cause of their appearing through reason | and from reasoning, and these no-one would still call 'appearances'. For the person who assents to something, on account of the reasoning which comes about in him in deliberating, is himself the cause to himself of the assent.

Difficulties of the determinist position
(iv) XVI-XXI. Practical consequences

186.13   XVI. Now it is clear from what has been said that neither do those who say that all things come to be in accordance with fate preserve what depends on us (for they do not preserve that about which we
15   are enquiring whether it is preserved | according to them, rather, they even try to give a reason for the thing's not even being possible

in the first place), nor is the reason that they give for doing away with such a power true, since there is nothing reasonable in it. But indeed the consequence for those who do away with anything's depending on us in this way is that, as far as is in their power, they confound and overturn human life.

| For suppose that, when things are as they are (for it is not even 20 possible to persuade any of *them* not to do those things which they do in the manner of those who have the power both to do them and not to do them, let alone [to persuade] anyone else; such great strength, and clear evidence from the things that come to be, does the truth have) – suppose that, when things are like this their opinion should become so strong that all | men believed that we are in control of 25 nothing, but always follow the circumstances about us, giving in to them and assenting to them, and do the things that we do through being altogether obliged to do them (for it is not possible, [they say], when the circumstances are of such a sort, to do anything else), and again in a similar way do not do [what we do not do] on account of our inability to go against the circumstances which | are of a certain 30 sort. What else will happen other than that all men, on account of such a belief, will say goodbye to all the things that come about with any | toil and concern, and choose the pleasures that are 187.1 accompanied by ease, on the grounds that the things that must come about will certainly come about, even if they themselves do nothing noble concerning them? When they are so disposed and their actions are in accordance with their choices (for it is not indeed the case that, on account of their false belief, things | will be any different 5 from the way they are), what else will happen but that all men will think little of the things that are fine (for the acquisition and possession of all such things involves labour) and will choose the things that are bad because they are brought about with ease and pleasure?

What could those whose doctrines had persuaded these people to do these things say against them? For if they *were* | to blame them, 10 they could justifiably say that it was not possible for them to do anything else, the circumstances being of such a sort. How will it be reasonable for those who have been their teachers, through such doctrines, to reproach them? Rather, neither reproaches nor punishments nor exhortation nor honour nor any other of such things will preserve its proper nature according to [the determinists], but each of these things too | will come to be 15

compulsorily, in the same way as will also those things to which they
apply.

    For how could Alexander [Paris] the son of Priam still be blamed
for having done wrong concerning the rape of Helen? How would it
be reasonable for Agamemnon to condemn himself saying 'not even
I myself deny it' [*Iliad* IX.116]? For if indeed either Alexander had
had the power to ignore the circumstances that were then
20 surrounding him and inviting him | to the rape, (or Menelaus the
things that urged him to anger*), or Agamemnon the things
concerning which he criticises himself as having done wrong, [then]
it would be reasonable for them to be blamed. But if long
beforehand, and even before that, and before any of them ever came
to be in the first place, it was true to predict of each of them that
thing which they are censured for having done, how could they still
themselves be blamed for the actual things that came to be? And
25 how | will anyone [be able to] explain how virtues and vices, too,
depend on us? For if it is because we are in such a state, how will it
still be reasonable for some to be praised and others blamed? This
doctrine does nothing other than afford a defence to the wicked. At
any rate we do not see anyone blaming fate or necessity for good and
30 fine deeds, but [rather] the wicked saying | that it is on account of
this that they are like that; and if they are confident that the
philosophers too say this, how will they not quite openly turn to
188.1 [wicked deeds] themselves | and turn others to them?

188.1 XVII. And how, saying such things, could [the determinists]
preserve the providential concern of the gods for mortals? For if the
manifestations of the gods, which they say happen to certain people,
come about in accordance with some cause laid down beforehand,
so that before any of [these people] came to be it was true that the
5 gods would show some concern | for this man but not for this [other]
one, how would it still be right for anyone to call this providence,
when it comes about not in accordance with [men's] deserving but
in accordance with some necessity laid down beforehand? And how
too would the piety towards the gods of those who are thought to be
pious be preserved, since it was not in their power [did not depend
on them] not to act in the way that they did? And those people, too,
who receive something more from the gods than others do, would do
10 so | because the beginnings of these things were laid down even
before these people existed.

And how would they not do away with prophecy as well, when the usefulness of prophecy is done away with? For what would anyone either [take pains to] learn [from the prophets] or guard against as a result of having learned from the prophets, if we are only able to learn, and they to reveal, those things which it was necessitated even before our birth | we should learn and do or not do in each case, and 15 [if] it is not we who are in control of our abiding by what the gods foretell, since the causes of the things that will occur by our agency have been laid down beforehand?

XVIII. But that this doctrine causes an overthrowing of the whole of human life is easy, I suppose, for everyone to understand; and there is sufficient evidence that it is also false in the fact that not even its champions | are able to comply with what they themselves say. 20 For in all that they say they preserve what is free and in our own power, as if they had never heard of such a doctrine [as determinism] from anyone else. On the one hand, they try to persuade people, in the manner of those who themselves have the power both to do this | or not to do it, and on the assumption that 189.1 those who are being persuaded are able, on account of what they say, to choose [to do] certain things of which they would have done the opposites if these men had remained silent; on the other hand, they reproach and rebuke people for not doing what they should do. And they compose and leave behind them many writings | through 5 which they expect to educate the young, not as having been prevented from *not* writing this on account of the circumstances being of such a sort, but as choosing to write, when it depends on them both to write and not to, through love of their fellow men.

XIX. They would have ceased from their combativeness in argument and would have conceded that | what depends on us is free 10 and in our own power and in control of the choice and doing of opposites in the same circumstances, if they had paid attention to what is agreed by all. For there is a law that is believed to be just by men, both by private individuals and by lawgivers; and this is that those deserve to be pardoned who do something of such a sort [as to required pardon] *involuntarily*, punishment being laid down with reference not to the deed that is brought about but to | the manner of 15 the doing; and this neither anyone else nor these men themselves blame as not being right. And yet, [this being so], why should those

men who do wrong through ignorance of the things they are doing or through force be more deserving of pardon than those who know what they are doing, but do not have in themselves, when the circumstances surrounding them are those that must at all events and necessarily surround them, the power of doing anything other
20   and what they | do? For [they argue] their nature is of a certain sort, and what is in accordance with their proper nature is to do each of the things that they do in accordance with fate, as for heavy things [what is in accordance with their proper nature is] to be carried downwards when they are thrown* from above, and for round things [it is] to move down a slope, if they are thrown*, of their own accord. For it is like thinking it right to punish a horse, because it is not a man, and
25   each of the other | animals, because they received this lot and not some better one. But no Phalaris is so savage and stupid as to punish the doer for anything that comes about in this way. For what things, then, are punishments reasonable? For no others than those which come
190.1 about through the doers' own wicked choice. | For it is in matters where they themselves have the power of choice, and neglect to make what is noble and the law the aim of their actions, but for the sake of some gain or pleasure take no notice of these and do what is base – it is
5   those [who act thus] that all men think deserve punishment, giving | pardon to those who do wrong in some other way.

It is indeed time for all the wicked, having learned this amazing doctrine from the philosophers, to teach their teachers that they too themselves [*sc.* the wicked] are deserving of pardon, no less than those who do wrong involuntarily. For it is not by something external compelling them, of a sort against which they would perhaps even be able to take precautions, that they do what they do; but it is not
10   possible | for them to be freed from the nature in themselves in anything that they do, and nothing is deserving of blame even in the very things that they do wrong. But if neither anyone else nor even those whose doctrine this [*sc.* determinism] is would pardon anyone who gave this explanation of his wrongdoings, on the grounds that he was uttering a falsehood, it is clear that both these men and everyone
15   else similarly believe that what depends on us | is not as these men feign it to be, when they speak with concern for the issue, but rather that it is as both these men themselves and all men bear witness through their deeds. For if they believed that it was [as they say it is], they would pardon all those who do wrong, on the grounds that they do not have the power of not doing all [the things that they do].

XX. But that it is possible to call something 'what depends on us',   190.19
and that nothing | comes to be without a cause because of this power,   20
because man is the cause of the things that come to be in this way,
being himself the begining of the things that are brought about
by himself – this is sufficiently shown by what has been said, and
even those who try to argue against it would have been sufficiently
persuaded, if they had persisted even for a short time in doing
everything that they do on the assumption that they are speaking
truly about the matters of which they speak – believing that none of
the things that | are brought about by anyone is brought about in   25
such a way that he then has the power also of not doing it. For he
who believes this cannot reproach anyone or praise or advise or
exhort anyone or pray to the gods or give them thanks for anything
or do any of the things which ought reasonably to be done by those
who are confident that they have the power | also of not doing each of   191.1
the things that they do. But indeed without these things the life of
men would be unlivable and would not even any longer be [the life]
of *men* in the first place [at all].

XXI. And let not the following point, too, be left aside unexamined   191.2
by us. If someone supposed that it was no more true that there is
something that depends on us, in the way that we maintain and that
the nature of the facts | bears witness it does, than that all things   5
come to be of necessity and in accordance with fate, but that each of
these [beliefs] was equally either credible or unclear, which belief
would it be safer and less dangerous for men to obey, and which
false [judgement] would be preferable; [i] to suppose, if all things *do*
come to be in accordance with fate, that that is not the case but that
we too are in control of doing something | or not doing it; or [ii], if   10
there *is* something that depends on us in the way that we have
previously stated, to be persuaded that this is false and that even all
the things that are done by us in accordance with our power come
about compulsorily?
     – Or is it clear that [i], if all things came to be in accordance with
fate, those who persuaded themselves that they have power over
certain things both to do them and not would not at all go wrong | in   15
what they do by this belief, because they would not even be in
control of any of the things that are brought about by them in the
first place; so that the danger from erring in *this* way extends only to
words [and not to deeds]. But if [ii], when there *is* something that

depends on us and all things do not come to be of necessity, we are
going to be persuaded that we are not in control of anything, [then]
we will leave aside many of the things that ought to be done by us
20   both | on account of having deliberated about them and on account of
eagerly undertaking the efforts involved in what is done; we will have
become lazy with regard to doing anything of our own accord, on
account of the belief that what ought to come about *would* come about,
even if we did not exert ourselves about what needed to be done. And
since these things are so it is clear that it is preferable for those who
25   engage in philosophy both to choose the less dangerous road |
themselves and to lead others on it.

Arguments for the determinist position
(i) XXII-XXV. Causation and the unity of the universe

191.26   XXII. Now that we have first considered these points, it would not
be a bad idea to set alongside them those which they actually make
concerning fate, and to see whether there is any such force in the
latter as to make it reasonable, on account of their closeness to the
truth, to disregard in this way even the clear facts of the matter. But
30   our discussion of these points will only be to the extent | to which it is
useful for the purpose before us.

Well then, they say that this universe, which is one and contains
in itself all that exists, and is organised by a Nature which is alive,
192.1   rational and intelligent, possesses the organisation | of the things that
are*, which is eternal and progresses according to a certain
sequence and order; the things which come to be first are causes for
those after them, and in this way all things are bound together with
one another. Nothing comes to be in the universe in such a way that
there is not something else which follows it with no alternative and is
attached to it as to a cause; nor, on the other hand, can any of the
5   things | which come to be subsequently be disconnected from the
things which have come to be previously, so as not to follow some
one of them as if bound to it. But everything which has come to be is
followed by something else which of necessity depends on it as a
cause, and everything which comes to be has something preceding it
to which it is connected as a cause. For nothing either is or comes to
10   be in the universe without a cause, because there is nothing | of the
things in it that is separated and disconnected from all the things
that have preceded. For the universe would be torn apart and

divided and not remain single for ever, organised according to a single order and organisation, if any causeless motion were introduced; and it would be introduced, if all the things that are and come to be did not have causes* which have come to be beforehand [and] which they follow of necessity. And they say that for something to come to be without a cause | is similar to, and as 15 impossible as, the coming to be of something from what is not. The organisation of the whole, which is like this, goes on from infinity to infinity evidently and unceasingly.

There is a certain difference among the causes, in expounding which they speak of a swarm of causes, some initiating, some contributory, some sustaining, some constitutive, and so on (for [our] need is not | at all to prolong the argument by bringing in 20 everything they say, but to show the point of their opinion concerning fate). – There are, then, several sorts of cause, and they say that it is equally true of all of them that it is impossible that, when all the circumstances surrounding both the cause and that for which it is a cause are the same, the matter should sometimes *not* turn out in a particular way and sometimes should. For if this | 25 happens there will be some motion without a cause.

Fate itself, Nature, and the reason according to which the whole is organised, they assert to be God; it is present in all that is and comes to be, and in this way employs the individual nature of every thing for the organisation of the whole. And such, | to put it briefly, is the 193.1 opinion they lay down concerning fate.

XXIII. The falsity of what they say needs no arguments or 193.2 refutations from elsewhere, but is evident from the statements themselves. For what clearer refutation of a statement could there be than that it does not fit the things about which it is made? The first | 5 statement, at any rate, that all the things that are become causes of some of the things after them, and that in this way things are connected to one another by the later being attached to the earlier in the manner of a chain, this being what they propose as the essence as if it were of fate – how is this not clearly in conflict with the facts? For if fathers are causes of their children, and enquiry after causes should be governed by considerations of affinity, | so that the cause of 10 a man is a man, and of a horse a horse, of which of those after them are those who never even married in the first place the causes? Of whom are those children that die before maturity the causes? For

many of the things that come to be, because of their falling short in
size, either are not roused or perish too early,* and so do not succeed
in becoming the causes of anything in accordance with the potential
15   that they possess. What will they say is caused by | the superfluities
that grow on certain parts of the body? What by monstrosities and
things which come to be in a way contrary to nature, which cannot
even survive in the first place? But if the outer husk in plants is for
the sake of the inner husk and the inner husk for the sake of the fruit,
and if they are watered so that they may be nourished and nourished
so that they may bear fruit – even so, one can find many things in
20   them which do not come to be in this | way. For of what subsequent
things would one say that those fruits which have rotted or dried up
are the causes? Of what the fact that certain leaves are double?
From these points it is obvious to those who want to see the truth
and are able [to do so] that, just as not all that has potential
exercises it, so not everything that might become a cause either is
already a cause or has become one or will become one; indeed, it is
not the case that everything that has come to be is at once, in virtue
25   of its | being, already the cause of something that will be in the
future.

To say on the one hand, in engaging with their opponents, that
these things too are causes, but retreat to the claim that it is not
clear of what they are the causes (as, indeed, they are often
compelled to do in connection with the Providence of which they
speak, too) is the tactic of those who are trying to find an easy way
out of their difficulties. For by using this argument it will be possible
to say of all the most absurd things that they both exist and have
30   causes | which are in accordance with reason, though still obscure to
us.

193.30   XXIV. Is it then the case that, if this is how these things are,
something will come to be without a cause, and does our argument
194.1   give support to this? Or is it possible | to preserve [the thesis] that
nothing comes to be without a cause, even though matters are as we
state? For if we abandon the chain of causes and cease saying that,
when certain things have first come to be, it follows of necessity that
they must by nature become causes, as if [being] causes were
5   included | in their essence, and [if instead we] assign causes starting
from the things that are coming to be and are subsequent, and,
further, look for the causes in the proper sense of the things that are

coming to be, we will find *both* that nothing that comes to be comes to be without a cause, *and* that it is not, on account of this, the case that everything that comes to be will be of necessity, in accordance with the sort of fate described.

| For it does not follow of necessity that, just because   10
Sophroniscus exists, he must therefore be a father and the cause of some one of those after him. If however Socrates is to exist, of necessity Sophroniscus is the cause of his coming-to-be. If a foundation exists, it is not necessary for a house to come to be, but if a house exists the foundation must necessarily have been laid first; and it is in this way that one must understand that the causes are of necessity in the things that come to be by nature too, not that it follows of necessity that the things that are first should be causes of something, but that those that come to be | subsequently must of   15
necessity have one of the things preceding them as a cause.

And there are some things among those that come to be that are of such a sort as to have a cause, indeed, not however one that is proper to them and primary*, but [rather], as we are accustomed to say, [one that is] accidental. The finding of treasure by someone who was digging in order to plant has the digging as a cause, indeed, but it is not [a cause] proper to it and did not come to be on account of it. For causes | in the strict sense are followed by what is caused   20
either of necessity, as our opponents think, or for the most part; but causes that are accidental in this way rarely become causes of such things.

So if one argues in this way it follows that one *both* says that nothing comes to be without a cause *and* preserves the coming-to-be of some things as a result of luck and fortuitously, and the existence of what depends on us and the contingent, | in the realm of facts and   25
not just as expressions.*

XXV. For how is it not clearly false to say that everything that   194.25
follows something derives the cause of its being from it, and that everything that precedes something is its cause? For we see that not all the things which succeed one another in time come to be because of those which have come to be earlier and before them. Walking is not caused by standing up, nor night | by day, nor the Isthmian   30
games by the Olympian, | nor yet summer by winter. And for this   195.1
reason one might wonder at their making the assignment of causes in such a way that they always regard what has come to be first as

the cause of what follows it and construct a successive connection
and continuity of the causes, and [at their] giving this as the
explanation for nothing's coming to be without a cause.

5 | For we see that in many cases the same thing is the cause both
for the things that come to be first and for those that come to be
later. At any rate, the cause of standing up and of walking about is
the same; for standing up is not the cause of walking about, but the
cause of both is the [man] who stands up and walks about and his
choice. And we see that night and day, too, which have a certain
order in relation to each other, have one and the same cause, as does
10 similarly | the changing of the seasons. Winter is not the cause of
summer, but both the former things [night and day] and the latter
things [winter and summer] are caused by the motion and rotation
of the divine body* and the inclination along the ecliptic; the sun,
moving along this, is the cause of all alike of the things mentioned
above.

Nor indeed does it follow that, because night is not the cause of
day nor winter of summer, and these things are not intertwined with
15 one another in the manner | of a chain, they therefore come to be
without a cause, or that if they did not come to be in this way [*sc.* in
the manner of a chain] the unity of the universe and of the things
that are and come to be in it will be torn apart. For the heavenly
bodies and their rotation are sufficient to preserve the continuity of
the things that come to be in the universe. Nor indeed is walking
without a cause, [just] because it does not derive its cause from
standing up.

20 | So the sequence of causes of which they speak would not be a
reasonable explanation to give of nothing's coming to be without a
cause. For as motions and times have some cause indeed, though the
cause of a motion is not the previous motion nor of a time the
previous time, so it is with the things that come to be in them and
through them. For the continuity of the things that come to be has a
cause, and it is on account of this that the universe is one and
25 eternal, | always organised in one and the same way; and one should
look for this and not leave the cause aside. But one should not
suppose that it is of such a sort as this, [namely] that what is
younger comes to be from what is older, as we see is the case with
the coming-to-be of living creatures.

It is reasonable, too, to say that there is some first beginning
among the causes, which has no other beginning or cause before it.

For it is not the case that, if | all things that come to be have causes, 30
therefore all things must necessarily have causes. For | not everything 196.1
that is comes to be. How is it not absurd to say that the causes and
the sequence and successive connection of them extend to infinity, so
that there is nothing that is first or last? For to say that there is no
first cause is to do away with cause; for if the first beginning is done
away with it is necessary that what follows | it be done away with. 5
And knowledge too would be done away with by this argument, if
knowledge in the proper sense is acquaintance with the first causes,
but according to them there is no first cause among causes.

Nor does every transgression of an established order do away with
the things in which it occurs: for it is not impossible that
some things should come to pass in a way that conflicts with the
monarch's order, but not therefore be altogether destructive of his
monarchy. | Nor, if something of the sort happens in the universe, 10
does it at once follow that it altogether destroys the happy state of
the universe, just as that of the house and its master is not
[altogether destroyed] by some negligence or other on the part of the
servants.

Arguments for the determinist position
(ii) XXVI-XXIX, XXXII. Action and character

XXVI. The difficulties that they raise with regard to what depends 196.13
on us being such as the common conception of men believes it to be
are not unreasonable difficulties; | but to rely on the difficulties as 15
agreed, and to do away with things that are so evident and to represent the life of men as some illusion and jest, struggling [against what
is evident*] in support of the difficulties raised by themselves – how is
this not totally unreasonable? For it is not the case that the person
who cannot solve some one of Zeno [the Eleatic]'s arguments
against motion should therefore deny motion; the | clear evidence of 20
the thing is a more adequate reason for assent than all the
persuasiveness that seeks to do away with it through arguments.

Perhaps however it is not a bad idea for us too to consider those of
the difficulties raised by them in which they place most confidence,
and to examine how [the matter] stands; for perhaps they will not
appear too difficult to resolve. Well, one of the difficulties they raise
is like this. 'If,' they say, 'those things depend on | us of which we are 25

able [to do] the opposites too, and it is to such as these that praise
and blame and exhortation and dissuasion and punishments and
honours apply, being wise* and possessing the virtues will not
depend on those who possess them, because they can no longer
admit the vices which are opposed to the virtues. And similarly
vices, too, will no longer depend on those who are vicious; for it does
not depend on them [is not in their power] not to be bad any longer.

197.1   But | its is absurd to deny that virtues and vices depend on us and are
the objects of praise and blame; so what depends on us is not like this
[*sc.* that of which we are also able to do the opposite].'

197.3   XXVII. Granting to them that virtues and vices cannot be lost, we
might perhaps take [the point] in a more obvious way by saying that

5   it is in this respect that dispositions | depend on those who possess
them, [namely] in so far as, before they acquired them, it was in
their power [depended on them] also not to acquire them. For those
who possess the virtues have, by choosing what was better instead of
neglecting it, become the causes of their own acquisition of virtue;
and similarly with those who possess the vices. And the same
argument also applies to skills; for in the case of craftsmen, too, each

10   one, before he possessed the | skill, possessed the power also of not
becoming someone of such a kind, but when he has [so] become he
will no longer be in control over his not having come to be, and
being, someone of such a kind. For the coming to be of such things
depends on us; and on account of this what is true is not similar in
the case of the things that are about to come to be and in that of
those that are and have come to be. For what is and has come to be
cannot either not be or not have come to be; but what is about to

15   come to be can | also not come to be. For which reason, before some
particular person possessed virtue, it was true that he could also not
come to be someone of such a kind, but of what does come to be of
such a kind, when it has actually come to be, it is true to say that it
has come to be in this way.

        If then the wise man were of such a kind from his birth, and
possessed [his wisdom] having received it from nature in addition to

20   the other gifts given to him by her, it would not at all depend on him |
to be of such a kind, just as it would not [depend on him] to be two-
footed or rational either; nor would he any longer be praised for
being like this, but rather wondered at as having received so great a
gift from divine nature.* For in the case of those who are healthy,

those of them who are weak by nature but are [healthy] through
their own care, these we praise on the grounds that they show
proper concern for themselves, and on account of this concern | do   25
not suffer sickness; but those who are healthy, and not sick, as a result
of their nature without trouble and attention, these we no longer
praise but congratulate, as possessing without effort that which
others welcome even if its presence comes about with effort. And we
would behave in the same way, or even more so, in the case of the
virtures, if they were present in some people by nature – as indeed
we do | in the case of the gods. But since this is impossible for us, and   30
we ought not to ask anything impossible of nature (for [nature] is
the measure of the possible and the impossible; | virtue is the   198.1
perfection and culmination of the proper nature of each thing, but it
is impossible that anything incomplete should be in a state of
perfection, and what has come to be is incomplete immediately it
has come to be*), it is not possible for man to be born possessing
virtue.

Nature does not indeed make no contribution to the acquisition of
[virtue], but [man] has from her | a capacity and fitness that admits   5
of [virtue], which none of the other living creatures has. And it is on
account of this capacity that man surpasses the other living
creatures in [his] nature, though he falls short of many creatures in
bodily advantages. If then we had the capacity that admits of the
virtues from [nature] in such a way that, as we progressed and were
perfected we acquired this too, as [we acquire the ability of]
walking, | and the growing of teeth and beard and any other of the   10
things that we acquire in accordance with nature – not in this way
either would the virtues depend on us, just as none of the afore-
mentioned things does. But we do not acquire [the virtues] in this
way. For if wisdom and virtue were inborn in man in the same way
as the other things, all or at any rate most of us would possess from
[nature] not only the capacity that | admits of the virtues but also the   15
virtues themselves, just as [we possess] the other things that are in
accordance with nature for us; and neither in this way would there
be any need for praise or blame or any such thing in connection with
virtues and vices, as we would have a more divine reason for and
reality (?*) of their presence. However, it is not like this. For we do
not see everyone or even the majority possessing | the virtues, this   20
being a sign of the things that come to be in accordance with nature,
but we are content if we find one such person, who through practice

and instruction displays the natural superiority of men to the other living creatures, through himself adding what is necessarily lacking to our nature.* So the acquisition of the virtues depends on us, and
25   neither praise nor blame is useless or | in vain, nor exhortations to [do] what is better, nor training in better habits in accordance with the laws.

For none of the natural characteristics of things can become different through any habituation (what is heavy cannot be thrown upwards so many times that it will become accustomed to be carried upwards in accordance with its own nature); but the characters of
199.1   men become of this sort or that through their differing habits.| In the case of the things that are by nature we first possess the dispositions and then act in accordance with them (for we do not acquire the disposition of seeing by seeing many times, but we possess it and see accordingly); but in the case of the things that are not by nature we acquire the dispositions from the activities. For no-one could become a carpenter in any other way than by having frequently
5   performed | the activities of a carpenter in accordance with the instructions of his teacher. So, since we acquire the virtues too in this way (for it is by acting in a temperate way that we become temperate), they cannot be present in us by nature.

XXVIII.   Those who say that it is of necessity that we are and come to be of a certain kind, and do not leave us the power of both doing and not doing those things through which we might come to be of
10   such a kind, | and on account of this [assert] that it is not possible either for those who come to be bad not to do those things by doing which they come to be of a certain kind, nor for the good – how will they avoid admitting that nature has made man the worst of all living creatures, [man] on account of whom they say everything else came to be, as contributing to his preservation? According to them
15   virtue and vice are the only things that are, in the one case, good,| in the other, bad, and none of the other living creatures is able to admit of either; and of men the greatest number are bad, or rather there are one or two whom they speak of as having become good men as in a fable, a sort of incredible creature as it were and contrary to nature and rarer than the Ethiopian phoenix; and the others are all wicked and are so to an equal extent, so that there is no difference between
20   one and another, | and all who are not wise are alike mad. [If this is so,] how will man not be the most wretched creature of all, having

wickedness and madness innate in him and allotted to him? But the examination of the paradoxes in their doctrines, through which they disagree with the truth, must for the most part be excused for the present, and we must go back to where we turned aside.

XXIX. We showed that | it is in this way that it depends on the wise   199.25
man himself to be someone of such a kind, that he is himself
responsible for [= is himself the cause of] such a disposition and the
acquisition of it, because he previously had the power also not to
become like this. He does not then possess the *disposition* any longer
as [something that] depends on him (just as [it is no longer in the
power of, depends on] the person who had thrown himself from a
height to stop, though he did have the power both to throw himself
off and not to); but it *is* in his power also not to perform some of the
activities | which he performs through possessing the disposition. For   30
even if it is pre-eminently reasonable that the wise man should
perform the activities which are in accordance with reason and
wisdom, firstly [it is not a question of] definitely performing
particular [actions] of such a sort [and not others] and doing so to a
certain extent, but | all the things that come to be in this way admit   200.1
of a certain breadth, and a slight difference in these matters does not
do away with what was proposed. Next, it is not by compulsion that
the wise man does any one of the things which he chooses, but as
himself having control also over not doing any one of them. For it
might also sometimes seem reasonable to the wise man | *not* to do on   5
some occasion what would reasonably have been brought about by
him – in order to show the freedom in his actions, if some prophet
predicted to him that he would of necessity do this very thing. This
indeed those who claim to be prophets [actually] suspect, and
avoiding immediate refutations do not make any such predictions to
those who could refute them; but just as they avoid laying down the
times | [when] the things, which they predict are going to occur, [will   10
do so], so they also avoid saying and prophesying anything to those
who can immediately do the opposite of what is prophesied.

Arguments for the determinist position
XXX-XXXI. Digression: Divine foreknowledge and prophecy

200.12   XXX. To say that it is reasonable that the gods should have foreknowledge of the things that will be, because it is absurd to say that they fail to know anything of the things that will be, and,

15   assuming this, to try to establish by means of it that all things | come to be of necessity and in accordance with fate – [this] is neither true nor reasonable. For if the nature of the things admits of this, there is non-one for whom it would be more reasonable to know the things that are going to be than [it would be] for the gods [to do so]; but when [the nature of the things] is not able to admit of such prediction and foreknowledge, it is no longer reasonable even for the gods to know anything that is impossible.* For the things that are

20   impossible in their own nature | preserve the same nature even where the gods are concerned. For it is impossible even for the gods either to make the diagonal commensurable with the side [of a square], or twice two five, or any of the things that have happened not to have happened. Nor do they even want to [do so] in the first place in the case of things that are impossible in this way [i.e. in their own nature]; for the difficulty is present in the very statement of them. And it is similarly impossible for them, in the case of that which has

25   in its proper nature the possibility | of both coming to be and not, to have foreknowledge that at all events it *will* be or that at all events* it *will not* be. For if foreknowledge about these things before they [occur] does away with what is contingent in them, it is clear that, if this were to be preserved, foreknowledge concerning them would be impossible.

And that this is so according to [the determinists] too is clear from their assuming that the gods have foreknowledge of the things that

30   are going to be and establishing by means of this | that they come to be of necessity, on the grounds that, if they did *not* come to be in this way, [the gods] would not have foreknowledge of them. But if even according to them necessity follows on the gods' foreknowledge and prediction, [then], if necessity were *not* present in the things that

201.1   come to be, not even according to | them would the gods have foreknowledge of the things that are going to be. So they too themselves preserve the same lack of power for the gods – if indeed one should say that it is through lack of power and weakness that it comes about that one is unable to do things that are impossible.

They do not indeed ascribe greater power to the divine through [the power of] prediction, but, on account of their | assuming [that the 5 gods have this power] they introduce the view of things [that they do].* saying things that are in no way consistent and harmonious with the things that come to be and are evident.

For by applying this [argument] it will be possible to show that all the things that are impossible are possible, since it is not reasonable that the gods should fail to know them. For someone could assume that it is absurd that the gods should not know the measure of the infinite, | and, laying this down, go on to suppose that it is possible to 10 know the measure of the infinite, and that, if this is so*, it is possible for there to be a certain definite measure of the infinite; for if it were not [possible], not even the gods would have known the measure of it.

But since to have foreknowledge of the things that are going to be is to have cognizance of them *as being such as they are* (for having foreknowledge is different from bringing about), it is clear | that he 15 who has foreknowledge of things that are contingent will have foreknowledge of them *as such*. For it is not foreknowledge to say that what is contingent will be in the manner of [what] will be necessarily. So the gods too would have foreknowledge of the things that are contingent *as contingent*, and necessity will not at all follow on this on account of foreknowledge of *this* sort. And it is in this way that we actually listen to those who make predictions. For those who make predictions along with advising someone | to choose and do 20 what he should, do not speak about the things they predict as things that will be of necessity.

And in general, if [i] they say that *all* things are possible for the gods, and even impossible things will be possible for them, it will not indeed be shown through their foreknowledge concerning the things that are going to be that all the things that come to be do so of necessity. But if [ii] they concede that the things that are impossible are so also for the gods, they | should first show that this sort of 25 foreknowledge [i.e. the sort that they assert – as opposed to foreknowledge of the contingent as contingent] is possible, and *then* attribute it to the gods. For it is neither evident nor in agreement with the things that [actually] come to be that it is this sort of foreknowledge concerning the things that are going to be that the gods exercise.

We therefore do not do away either with prophecy or with the gods'

foreknowledge by saying that they make predictions about things in
201.30   accordance with | the way the things naturally are; | XXXI but
neither do we take away from men the usefulness of prophecy, which
comes about through someone's being able actually to take
precautions against something, when he would not have done so if the
202.1   god had not advised him. But those who sing the praises of prophecy |
and say that it is preserved only by their own account, and use it as a
proof that all things come to be in accordance with fate, not only say
nothing that is true but in addition have the effrontery, what is more,
to say things about the gods that are absurd and altogether alien from
5   them. For how are the things that they say about these matters not |
absurd? Certain people raise the difficulty against them why indeed,
if all the things that come to be do so of necessity, the prophecies that
come from the gods resemble pieces of advice, as if those who had
heard them could both take precautions against something and do
something on account of what they had heard. Moreover, [the
objectors] bring forward the oracle given to Laius, in which Pythian
[Apollo] says to him, concerning the fact that he ought not to beget
10   children, | 'If you beget a child, the one who is born will slay you, and
all your house will wade in blood' [Euripides *Phoenissae* 19-20]. But, as
their writings proclaim, [the determinists] do not say that [Apollo]
prophesied in this way because he did not know that [Laius] would
not obey (for he knew this above all). Rather, [they say] that* if he
had not made any such prophecy, none of the things that came about
15   in the | tragic reversal concerning Laius and Oedipus would have done
so. For neither would Laius have exposed the son that was born to
him in the way that he did, nor would the child have been taken up by
the herdsman and given for adoption to the Corinthian Polybus, and,
when he grew up and met Laius on the road, slain him without
recognising him or being recognised. For if he had been brought up as
20   a son in his parents' house, | he would never have failed to recognise
them, and so killed one of them and married the other. So, in order
that [the occurrence of] all these things should be preserved and the
drama of fate fulfilled, the god gave Laius the impression through the
oracle that he could take precautions against what was said; and
when he had become drunk and begotten a child, he exposed the child
25   that had been born in order to destroy it; and it was this exposure | that
became the cause of the unholy stories.
     Well, if someone says these things, how does he either preserve
prophecy, or teach pious conceptions concerning the gods, or show

that prophecy has any usefulness? For prophecy is thought to be
prediction | of the things that are going to happen, but they make   203.1
Apollo the author of the things he predicts. For that which would
not have happened thus if the god had not prophesied in this way
(and he prophesied in this way for this very reason, that the things
that came about concerning them* should come about) – how is this
not the deed of him who prophesied, rather than revelation of the
things that were going to be? But even if the gods | must have some   5
advantage over the other prophets, so that they assist the things that
are going to be, it is reasonable that they should contribute to the
coming about of what is good (for the poets constantly sing this
about the gods, that they are 'givers of good things'). Yet according
to what [the determinists] say, at least, Apollo does not contribute
to anything good for Laius, but strives and does all he can with a
view to his house escaping nothing | of [all] that is most unholy and   10
impious. Who, when he heard these things, would not say that the
absence of [divine] providence asserted by the followers of Epicurus
was more pious than this sort of providential care?

And how is it consistent both to say that fate is god and employs
the things that are and come to be in the universe for the
preservation both of the universe itself and of the ordering of the
things within it, and [also] | to say such things about it as that it   15
employs even Apollo as an accomplice in the most unholy deeds on
account of its eagerness that they [should happen]? What will they
say fate preserves by its employment of the killing of a father by his
son and the unholy marriage of a mother and her son and the birth
of children who are also the brothers of their father? What [aspect]
of the organisation of the universe is it reasonable [to suppose] has
its preservation from these things, | so that even Apollo should fear   20
that any of them might be left undone? If they had not come about,
would it have hindered the dwelling of men in cities and according
to laws? Or the preservation of the elements of the universe? Or the
orderly and eternal revolution of the heavenly bodies? Or which of
the things out of which the universe comes to be constituted and
organised in accordance with reason? It is clear that, if again they
hear | any other story from one of the tragic poets whose concern is   25
fictions of this sort – either some woman who through jealousy
plotted against someone else's children but slew her own, or some
unfortunate old Thyestes eating the flesh of his own children when
some Atreus his brother has put such a meal before him – they

30   believe such stories as things that happened, and establish | fate and
204.1 providence through them, as if making it their business | to do away
with what they want to establish through the very [arguments that
they use to] establish it. And yet it would be far better and more
sensible to do away with their assumptions on account of the
absurdity of their consequences, [rather] than to defend such
absurdities on account of the assumptions. But they both find it easy
5   to believe in the most absurd things, and do not | shrink from stating
explanations of how their coming about is in accordance with reason.

204.5 **XXXII.** But enough of such matters (for it is sufficient in each case
to display the absurdity of [their] opinion). And I think it has been
sufficiently shown how it is said that being wise depends on the wise
man even though he cannot now not be wise; for [it is] not because
now, when he is wise, it depends on him to be like this (for he would
10   also have control over | not now being wise), but [it is] because,
before coming to be like this, just as he had the power of coming to
be [like this], so he also [had the power] of not coming to be like
this, and [because], for the reason which we stated before*, he
contributed to his own coming to be like this.

In the case of the gods being such [as they are*] will no longer
depend on them (which indeed was also itself among the difficulties
raised by [the determinists*]), because being like this is present in
15   their nature, and none | of the things that are present in this way
depends on oneself. It is for this reason that the good things that [the
gods] have are the objects of honour and blessing, possessing
something greater than [do] those good things that are the objects of
praise, because [the gods'] nature cannot admit in the first place
what is less good*; but we are praised for the acquisition of the
virtues, because, although our nature admits also of what is worse,
we did not shrink from [pursuing] the better – when, moreover, the
20   worse | seems to be acquired without sweat and toil, virtue with
labour and toil and much sweat. However, the wise man has, in the
case of individual actions, the power of also not doing them; and the
gods too have this power, if indeed they too perform some actions
concerning the things that can also be otherwise. For Apollo is not
25   deprived of the power of both prophesying to the same person and |
not, nor Asclepius of that of helping [and not]. At any rate almost all
men have recourse to him, where he is most fully manifested,
believing that he bestows his [aid] more on those who are eager to

have him as their doctor than on those who are not eager.

Arguments for the determinist position
(iii) XXXIII-XXXVIII. Miscellaneous

XXXIII. [Consider the following argument*]: 'Those who do not think that the preservation of the activity of living creatures according to impulse already preserves what depends on us are mistaken; for everything that come to be according to impulse depends on those who exercise the impulse* For is not what depends on us an activity? And, again, this being agreed, | do not some activities seem to be according to impulse and some not? And, again, this being so, [is it not true that] none of those things that are activities indeed, but *not* according to impulse, depends on us? So, if this too is conceded, it follows on the basis of these [assertions] that all that comes to be according to impulse depends on those who act thus; for [what depends on us] is not [to be found] in any of those activities that are of *another* sort [i.e., *not* according to impulse]. | Therefore what depends on us, [in the sense of] what can both be brought about by us and not, is preserved in our position; for the things that come to be in this way, too, are [to be found*] in those that come to be according to impulse.' – How is this not [the argument] of those who are totally ignorant of the matters they are discussing? For [even] if it has been conceded that what depends on us is [to be found] in activities according to impulse, it does not yet follow on account of this argument that all activity that is | according to impulse depends on us. For 'what depends on us' is only present in those of the things that come to be according to impulse that are activities in accordance with *rational* impulse. And rational impulse is that which comes about in [creatures] endowed with deliberation and choice; that is, the [impulse] of men, when it comes about in relation to [deliberation and choice]. For the activities according to impulse of other creatures are not like this, because with them it is no longer the case that they possess the power | of also *not* performing the activity that is according to impulse. – And for this reason what depends on us is [to be found] in activities according to impulse, but it is not indeed, on account of this, the case that *every* activity that comes about according to impulse involves 'what depends on us'.

205.1

5

10

15

20

205.22 **XXXIV.** And how is it not [the action] of those who do not know
the things that are brought about by themselves to use the truth of
the things that are brought about*, which they do away with
through their doctrine, in establishing the doctrine that does away
25 with it? For | taking it that each of the things constituted by nature is
such as it is according to fate, 'by nature' and 'according to fate'
being the same*, they add 'Therefore it is in accordance with fate
that living creatures will have perception and exercise impulse, and
that some living creatures will merely act and others will act
rationally, and some will act rightly and some wrongly; for this is in
accordance with nature for them. But if right and wrong actions
206.1 remain and such | natures and qualities are not done away with,
praise too remains and blame and punishments and rewards. For
such is the sequence and order of these things.' But it does not
indeed still follow that these things come about in this way for those
who transfer nature, and the things that come to be according to
5 nature, to fate and necessity. | For it *is* according to nature for living
creatures that are capable of action and rational that they are able to
act both wrongly and rightly, because they do neither of these
compulsorily; and this is true and this is how it is. But it does not
follow for those who say that we do all the things that we do of
necessity that some of those who act rationally act rightly and others
10 wrongly; and we *do* do | all things of necessity according to those
who maintain that it is impossible for us not to do [them] in these
particular circumstances, and that the circumstances on account of
which we do [them] will of necessity always be present to us. For it
is not the man who does something pleasing in just *any* way that one
says acts rightly, nor the man who does something base in just any
way that [one says] acts wrongly; but if in any way someone who
15 has the power [to do] what is worse chooses and does | what is better,
it is this man whom we says acts rightly. At any rate, we no longer
say that the man who has done these same things from chance acts
rightly, since acting rightly is judged not only from the things that
are done, but much more from the disposition* and capacity from
which what is done [has its origin]. And the same argument applies
to wrong actions.

But those whose power of doing some other things besides those
20 which they do | has been taken away by the circumstances, and who
do not themselves contribute anything to those circumstances
surrounding them on account of which they do [these things] – how

could anyone still say that these act wrongly or rightly? For the man himself has power neither over [his having] this kind of disposition, from which, when these particular circumstances surround him, the impulse to do these particular things comes about, nor over the circumstances being of the kind they are. For it is on account of this that none | of these [expressions – *sc.* 'acting wrongly' or 'acting   25 rightly'] is applied to the irrational living creatures. Being led to do [what he does] by his disposition and particular circumstances, and not himself having control over his not being in this condition, [the agent] would no longer be said to act wrongly or rightly in the case of things that are done in this way. But since praise and blame, punishments and rewards apply to wrong and right actions, as they themselves too say, | it is clear that if the latter are done away with   30 each of the former will be too.

Acting rightly would not be applied to the gods in the strict sense, but as equivalent to 'doing | what is good', if those who have [the   207.1 power of] acting rightly also have that of acting wrongly, but the divine cannot admit of wrong action. For it is on account of this that we do not praise the gods, because they are superior to praise and to the right actions to which praises apply.

XXXV. And let us not pass over that argument, either, in which   207.4 they place | confidence as being able to prove something of the points   5 at issue. They say: 'it is not the case that fate is of this sort but Destiny does not exist; or that Destiny exists but Apportionment does not; or that Apportionment exists but Retribution does not; or that Retribution exists but law does not; or that law exists but right reason enjoining what should be done and forbidding what should not be done does not. But | it is wrong actions that are forbidden and   10 right actions that are enjoined. So it is not then the case that fate is of this sort but wrong and right actions do not exist. But if there are wrong and right actions, virtue and vice exist, and if these exist, the noble and the base exist. But the noble is praiseworthy, the base blameworthy. So it is not then the case that fate is of this | sort but   15 there does not exist what is praiseworthy or blameworthy. But praiseworthy things deserve reward and blameworthy things deserve punishment. So it is not then the case that fate is of this sort but there are not reward and punishment. But reward is a deeming worthy of privilege, and punishment is correction. So it is not then the case that fate is of this sort but there is not deeming worthy of

privilege and correction. But if these things are so, all the things that
20   were mentioned remain even when all things come to be | according
to fate – right and wrong actions and rewards and punishments and
deemings worthy of privilege and praise and blame.'

207.21   XXXVI. Well, if they are compelled to say these things in this way
as an effect of their circumstances*, it is right to pardon them, and
there is no need either for us greatly to bother ourselves about the
things which they say in accordance with necessity, or for them
[greatly to bother themselves] about those who do not speak in a
25   similar way to them | (for it is the power of the circumstances that is
the cause of what is said, and of the opinions that are held, by each
party); and there is no need to blame those who speak, as they
contribute nothing [themselves] towards their speaking in this way,
if indeed they do not have the cause in themselves either of the
circumstances nor of the disposition in accordance with which it
came about that they were moved in this way by the circumstances.
208.1   But if we do have the power to speak worse or better, who would | not
be amazed at the way in which their argument is put together, for its
simplicity and [the way in which] it reaches its conclusion from
admitted and evident premisses?

    Or have they gained no benefit at all, then, from all their long
labour over syllogisms?* They posit that fate employs all the things
that have come to be and are coming to be in accordance with itself
5   for the unimpeded | realisation of the things that it brings about,
according as each of them has come to be and is by nature,
[employing] the stone as a stone, the plant as a plant, the living
creature as a living creature, and if as a living creature also as
possessing impulse; and when they posit that [fate] employs the
living creature as a living creature and possessed of impulse and that
the things which are brought about by [fate]* through the creatures
come about according to the impulse of the creatures (these too
10   following the causes | which of necessity surround them at that time,
whatever these are), [they do so] thinking that, by preserving the
activity of living creatures according to impulse when all things
come to be in accordance with fate, they also preserve the existence
of something that depends on us. [It is thinking thus] that they put
forward their other arguments and in particular the one just stated –
not, it seems to me, so much trusting in it as true, as thinking that
through its length and the number of terms and the unclear way

[they] are put together, they will|mislead their listeners.   15
But let us see what it is that it says, for the present passing over the
majority of the terms that are laid down; and, taking away Destiny
and Apportionment and Retribution, terms that they use to signify
what they themselves decide, let us examine [what it says] in respect
of the other [terms involved]. For it would be worth finding out the
necessity of the consequence 'it is not the case that fate is of this|sort   20
but law does not exist'. For if the things that come about in
accordance with fate follow the causes which of necessity surround
them, and it is not possible for the person who acts according to
impulse not to follow these causes, joining the cause from himself to
them whatever happens, as [it is not possible] for the stone thrown*
from a height not to be carried downwards or from the sphere not to
roll down the slope when it is | thrown* down it, what use is there   25
any longer for laws? For as the stone would never be prevented
[from being carried downwards] by a person who said that it should
not be carried downwards, because it is itself like this by nature and
has the external causes assisting to bring this about; so none|even of   209.1
us would ever be persuaded by an argument or a law which said that
he should act contrary to the necessity of the circumstances. For
there is no advantage to us from knowing what is enjoined by the
laws, if there are* causes laid down beforehand which our impulse
must necessarily follow when they surround [us]. And in this way | 5
the usefulness of the laws would be done away with – if at least the
laws enjoin the things that should be done and forbid those that
should not, but the laws' command is not followed by our action
according to impulse when the causes which surround us of necessity
move and carry us to some other [course of action]. And if the
usefulness of the laws were done away with through fate of this sort,
so would the|laws be. For what is the advantage of laws when we are   10
deprived by fate of the power of obeying them?
    It does not then follow that, if fate is of this sort, law exists. For
fate and law are opposed, if the law enjoins what should be done and
what should not, on the assumption that those who act can obey it
when it gives commands (and for this reason it punishes those who
do not obey for|acting wrongly, rewarding those who obey for acting   15
rightly); but fate says that all the things that come to be do so
necessarily and on account of causes of a similar sort, and of things
that come about on account of causes of a similar sort it is not
possible to say that some are wrong actions and some right actions.

If someone were to say that the law too is among the causes which
20   are necessary and laid down beforehand by fate, it is clear that, | for
those who do according to impulse the things that are in accordance
with it, it will itself necessarily be among the causes that surround
them, and that it will not be present* to those who do the things that
are not in accordance with it. But it is clear that those who have this
cause of their not doing the things in accordance with [the law]
would not be blamed. For how are they deserving of blame, if the
cause from the laws was not among the causes which surrounded
25   them according to necessity | [and] which their impulse could not
but follow, [but, rather, it was] prevented from being present by
some necessity and fate? But in this way at least it would no longer
be law, since those who obeyed it (if this should be called 'obeying')
would follow of necessity, and those who disobeyed it would have
been prevented from obeying it by some necessity. So a much truer
30   consequence would be, 'if fate is of this sort, | law does not exist'. And
if law is done away with, and with it wrong and right action, [then]
210.1   as they themselves too assumed in the consequence in their |
argument, virtue and vice would be done away with, [as would]
there being something in men that is shameful or noble and
praiseworthy or blameworthy or deserving of reward or punishment.

Nothing then is left of what was established by the argument
which was advanced with such skill, and that consequence will
5   follow for them, beginning | in its later stages, that they say follows
for those who try to do away with there being anything that depends
on us; as though it were agreed that they themselves preserve it
through having taken the initiative in criticising others, thinking
that they [themselves] escape through not seeming to be involved [in
the difficulties] themselves*. For if there are no rewards or
punishments, [they argue,] neither [is there] praise or blame; if not
these, nor [are there] right and wrong actions; if not these, nor [are
10   there] | virtue and vice; and if not these, they say, nor are there even
gods. But the first, [namely] that there are no rewards or
punishments, follows on [the assertion] that all things come to be in
accordance with fate, as has been shown. So the last [proposition
follows] too; but this is absurd and impossible. So we must reject
[the assertion] that all things come to be in accordance with fate, on
which this followed.

XXXVII. But let us see whether the argument advanced after this   210.14
does not involve | similar necessary [consequences].   15
It runs as
follows: 'It is not the case [both] that all things are in accordance
with fate, and that the organisation of the universe is hindered or
impeded*; nor [that it is unhindered and unimpeded] but that there
is not an (ordered) universe; nor that there is a universe but that
there are not gods. But if there are gods, the gods are good; but if
this is so, virtue exists; but if virtue exists, practical wisdom exists;
but if this is so, knowledge of what should be done and of what
should | not be done exists. But right actions should be done and   20
wrong actions should not be done. So it is not the case that
everything comes to be in accordance with fate but wrong and right
actions do not exist. But right actions are noble, wrong actions base,
and noble things are praiseworthy, base things blameworthy. So it is
not the case that all things are in accordance with fate but that there
are not things that are praiseworthy and blameworthy. But | if this is   25
so, praise and blame exist. But we reward what we praise and
punish what we blame; and he who gives a reward gives a privilege,
he who punishes corrects. So it is not the case that all things come to
be in accordance with fate but giving privilege and correcting do not
exist*.'

   This argument too, indeed, comes from the same wrestling-school
and may clearly be refuted as being false through the same points. For
first, who will readily | concede 'it is not the case both that all things   30
are in accordance with fate and that the | organisation of the universe   211.1
is hindered or impeded'*? For some things come to be of necessity,
some contingently, and of these some in accordance with nature,
some in accordance with choice and reason, some according to
impulse, some from luck and fortuitously. But all the others are done
away with by fate; so it is not | the case that the organisation of the   5
universe would remain unhindered and unimpeded* [if all things
were in accordance with fate]. But even if this were conceded, and
that the universe exists and that if the universe exists the gods do –
although according to Epicurus they are outside it – and that the gods
are good, and [even if] it followed from [the existence of] the gods that
virtue exists too, how would it follow from the existence of the virtue of
the *gods* that practical wisdom exists? What is the necessity of | this   10
consequence? For if the supposition was that the virtue of *men* existed,
[the existence of] practical wisdom too would follow from this, but
since from what had been laid down it was supposed that the virtue of

the *gods* existed, how would [the existence of] practical wisdom still follow from [that of] the virture of the gods, when [practical wisdom] is a virtue of men? For it is not possible to say that the virtues of men and of gods are the same. For neither is it in other respects true to say

15 that the | same perfections and virtues belong to those who are so far removed from each other in nature, nor are the arguments that they state concerning these matters in any reasonable. Practical wisdom is a virtue of *men*; it is, as they say, the knowledge of what should be done and of what should not be done. For it is in cases where it is possible for something to be done also of those things that should not be done

20 that the knowledge of what should be done and of | what should not be done has its place; but if all things come to be in accordance with fate the knowledge of what should be done and of what should not be done is useless. For what is the advantage of such knowledge to those who cannot guard against any of the things that they do? But if the knowledge of these things were in no way useful, practical wisdom would be done away with, so that the consequence is more true [that]

25 'if fate exists, practical wisdom does not'. For | by the argument by which law was done away with when fate was laid down*, (by this argument) practical wisdom too will be done away with. And if this is done away with it is clear that each one of the other things too which were posited in the sequence which followed on practical wisdom will be done away with.

211.27 **XXXVIII.** It has already many times been stated and shown in the earlier parts [of this work] that they do not preserve what depends on us even by showing that movement according to impulse is preserved for living creatures when all things come about in

30 accordance with fate | – unless someone wants simply to say that what is brought about by something in accordance with its own nature depends on it, introducing another meaning of 'what depends on us' besides that which is accepted and [in accordance with] our conception [of it], which we say is on account of our

212.1 having the power for opposite [courses of] action. | And all the other arguments that they put forward to establish this doctrine are like these, for the most part being ingenious as far as the *words* are concerned, but not gaining credibility from agreement with the facts concerning which they are stated.

Conclusion

XXXIX. These are, O most divine emperors, the chief points, in my   212.5
view, of the opinion of Aristotle concerning fate and what depends
on us. If we hold this opinion we will, first, be pious towards the
gods, giving them thanks for the benefits we have already received
from them and asking things from them on the grounds that they are
in control both of giving and of not giving. And we shall also feel
gratitude concerning both you [yourselves] and rulers | like you,   10
since you act concerning us as your own choice leads you, doing
what you do through choice of what is better and by taking thought
concerning the judgement of it, but not following certain causes laid
down beforehand, which it is necessary to follow wherever they
lead. And we will also be concerned about virtue, as being ourselves
in control of becoming better or worse. | For a man is only in control   15
of those things over which he himself has the power also not to do
them. And, [as] I have tried to present to you throughout my
account, we will only seem to do the other things that we do in life*
reasonably if we assign their causes in accordance with the opinion
of Aristotle concerning them.

De Anima libri mantissa, XXII-XXV

Mantissa XXII
From the [teachings] of Aristotle
concerning what depends on us

About what depends on us an opinion such as the following was also put forward. If the nature of all men | is not alike, but differs (for by nature some are well-endowed and others ill-endowed), and nature exercises the greatest influence towards men's coming to be of one sort or another, and after nature habits, choice too coming to be of a certain sort as a result of both of these, one might be altogether at a loss as to how choice will still depend on us. For indeed, even if one were to regard education too as a cause* [of our choices], not even learning depends on us (I describe | that sort of thing as 'depending on us' of which the opposite too is both possible and depends on us)*. And this would be a matter of even greater difficulty, if it were to be the case that nothing comes to be without a cause; and this too is what all supposed.* For it is necessary that the cause of the things which are brought about by us at the present should exist beforehand, and it is impossible | that the same cause should be [the cause] of opposites; but if this [is so], all things that come to be come to be of necessity, for their causes have been laid down beforehand. That this then should be so is necessary, unless some motion without a cause is discovered.

But it is discovered and it does exist; and when this is shown both what depends on us will be preserved, and the fortuitous and the things that depend on luck. Aristotle too thinks that there is some motion | without a cause, as is stated in the fifth book of the *Metaphysics* [E 2 1026b13ff.*]. The existence of motion without a cause is established, if it should be shown that there is not-being [*literally*: what is not] in the things that are, diffused somehow among them and accompanying them. For if there is somehow not-being in the things that are (and there is, for there is *per accidens* being in the things that are; for what is not, if it attaches as an accident to anything, is described as being something *per accidens*)

there would be some motion without a cause, | and if this existed the   15
point set before us would have been shown. And that not-being is
somehow in the things that are in actuality one could easily learn
from considering them.

For if some of the things that are are eternal, and others perish,
the difference between these would not be present in them as a result
of any other cause than their sharing in not-being. For it is as a
result of the mixture and blending and presence of this that | 20
slackness and weakness come to be in the things that are not eternal
and prevent them from always | existing and always being in the   170.1
same state. For if there were not any not-being in the things that are,
they would not desire the good [?]. But if it is as a result of the
mixture of not-being that perishable things are such [as they are],
and in addition to them things that are false, and if there are some
things among the things that are that are perishable and perish and
are false, [then] there is some not-being in them. | And this is sound   5
when taken conversely, too; if there is not not-being in the things
that are, it will not be the case that certain of the things that are are
perishable. So there is not-being.

If then not-being is diffused among the things that are subject to
coming-to-be, and mixed with them, and things that come to be are
preceded* by certain causes which are not themselves eternal either,
there is some not-being in causes too, and this is what we call a
cause *per accidens*. | For what is *per accidens* when it is present in the   10
same things *qua* causes, would be a cause *per accidens*. For when
anything follows on a certain cause, the cause not existing for the
sake of this thing's coming about, then what precedes* is called the
cause *per accidens* of this thing that followed on it, that is, not a cause.
So what followed on this cause came about without a cause, for it
did not do so on account of a proper cause of its own. This, | when it   15
occurs in external causes, creates luck and the fortuitous; when in
the [causes] in us, what depends on us.

For nature and habit seem to be cause[s] in us of choice; but, to
the extent to which there is not-being in these, to this extent (there is
not-being) also in choice. And for this reason we sometimes choose
those things of which the cause has not been laid down in us
beforehand, on account of the weakness and slackness | of mortal   20
nature; for [otherwise*] we would always be moved in a similar way
in the same situations*. But the nature of not-being, as I said,
removes eternity and perpetual activity in the same manner* from

those things in which it is present. So it is those choices that we
make without a cause and with no cause existing beforehand that
are said to depend on us; and the opposites of these, too, are
25   possible, as that cause has not been laid down beforehand that, | if it
had existed beforehand, would certainly have rendered it necessary
that this should come to be. For this reason it often happens that
some who are similar in nature and have been brought up in the
same habits become different from each other, as a result of the
choices that have no cause.

Not-being is neither mixed with many of the things that are, nor is
there much of it in those things in which it *is* present, but [it is] in
30   few of the things which are and in a small amount. For it is in those |
of the the things that are in which there is non-eternity; that is, the
region around the earth. And this region is very small in relation to
the whole universe. For if the earth has the ratio of a point to the
whole heaven, according to the astronomers, and not-being is
concerned with this and the things in it, it would be concerned with
a very small [part]. – And it is in even these things in an obscure sort
35   of way and not to any great extent. For in the things which | are
subject to coming-to-be there is on the one hand that which is for the
172.1   most part, of which nature is the cause, but as much as is | released
from nature and its power for making the things that come to be
according to it come to be of necessity – that is, what is for the least
part, in which is situated that which can also be otherwise* – it is
with this that the weakness that results from not-being, too, is
concerned: So not-being is not in the things that are of necessity
5   (and for this reason neither is the contingent*), nor | is it in those
things in which there is being-for-the-most-part, to the extent that
they are like this, but in the the things that are opposed to these, that
is, in those that are for the least part; and it is in these that things
due to luck and fortuitous things are located, and those which are
said to depend on us in the proper sense.

For those choices of which nature or training or habit is the cause
are said to depend on us in the sense that they come about through
us; but those which come to be without a cause and in accordance
10   with not-being, (these) in this way preserve | what is said to depend
on us in the proper sense, coming to be through weakness of nature;
and that which depends on us is this, of which the opposite too could
have been chosen by the one who chose this. So what depends on us
is a matter of* that which through the existence of not-being has

weakened the continuity of the causes in us; and it occupies this position, becoming a cause in cases where the necessary cause has failed on account of | the mixing and interweaving of not-being in   15 what is.

Mantissa XXIII
From the [teachings] of Aristotle
concerning what depends on us

Of the things that are brought about and put together by the divine   172.17 power that comes to be in that body that is subject to coming to be, as a result of its proximity to the divine* – and this [power] we also call 'nature' – the most honourable is man. For he alone of things | 20 here [on earth] has a share in the most perfect of the powers of soul, and this is mind, and he alone has rational soul, in respect of which he is able to deliberate and enquire about the things he should do, and is not like the other living creatures; these, in virtue of their not sharing in such a power, we call irrational, following and assenting to the appearances that impinge on them and doing | each of the   25 things that they do without examination. For man alone of the other living creatures is able, after an appearance has impinged on him that something should be done, to enquire about it and deliberate, whether he should assent to what appeared or not. And when he has deliberated and decided, accordingly he sets out [exercises impulse] either to do or not to do either [alternative]; and he goes for whichever [alternative] he preferred | as a result of the deliberation.   30 And on account of this [man] alone of all living creatures has his acting depending on himself, because he has the power also of not doing this same thing. For the choice of the things that should be done depends on himself, if deliberating and deciding | depend on   173.1 himself. For [having these things] depending on himself is the same as being a beginning and efficient cause of those things which we say depend on himself.

   What depends on us is located in those things with which deliberation, too, is concerned. And we deliberate neither about things that have come to be [already] nor about those which are already, but about those which are in the future and are able | to come   5 to be and not to come to be, and of which the cause is intelligence. For these things can both be done by us and not. So it is in these that what depends on us, too, is located, and man is a beginning and

cause of the things that are done through him, having this as a special [gift] from nature as compared with all the other things that are brought about by her, because he alone is also rational by nature
10   and has the power of deliberation. For it is in this | that being rational consists.

But if the cause is the beginning of those things of which it is the cause, and man is the beginning of the things that are done by him[self], he will also be the cause of these things. If then it is absurd to enquire after and speak of the beginning of a beginning (for that thing is not simply a beginning, of which there is some other beginning), there will not, either, be some efficient cause [of the things done by a man] laid down beforehand, other than [his]
15   choice and will and | decision of a certain sort and [in short] the man [himself]* (for [otherwise] he would no longer remain a beginning); but the cause of the things that are done by him is himself and his decision and choice and the efficient cause of these*, but of these things themselves there is no longer anything else [that is the cause]. For if these things are a beginning, and there is no beginning and cause of what is called a beginning in the proper sense (there is a
20   cause of the man's being and coming to be, | but not of his choosing these things or these; for this [is what] being [is] for him, that is, [it is] to have a power like this in himself), [man's power and capacity of action depend on himself*].

For how would deliberating even be useful any longer, if we had causes of our actions laid down beforehand? And how would man any longer be more honourable than the other living creatures, if deliberating were shown to be useless? And [it would be] useless if
25   preferring something as a result of deliberation | and choosing that which we preferred did not depend on us. To say that the 'appearance' is the cause of [our] deliberating about what appeared is in no way absurd; but to regard not the deliberation but the appearance as the cause also of [our] doing a certain thing is to do away with deliberation, and [so] with [the appearance's being a] cause, as we hold it to be; [for we hold it to be] the cause of something that *exists**. So, if what appeared is the cause of the
30   deliberating, the deliberation of the decision, | the decision of the impulse, and the impulse of the action, nothing among these will be without a cause.

And just as deliberating shows that something depends on us, so does repenting of certain things that have been done and blaming

ourselves and our own choice; for such blame is evidence that we are
responsible for having then done what has been done. But to look for
some other cause|of [our] having preferred a certain course of action   35
as a result of the deliberation is to do away with deliberation. For| 174.1
the essence of deliberating is in being able to decide and choose what
appears best as a result of the deliberation. The person who takes
this away from deliberation leaves only the name of deliberation.

   To say that, when all the external circumstances are similar, *either*
[i] someone will choose, or even do, the same things *or* [ii] something
will be without a cause, and that|of these [ii], that something should   5
come to be without a cause, is impossible, while [i], that [someone]
chooses the same things when the circumstances are the same,
shows that the external causes have control over the things that we
do – this is not sound. For neither is it necessary for a man always to
choose the same things when all the circumstances are the same, nor
is the action without a cause, if it does not come about in the same
way. For the deliberation and the choice|and the decision and the   10
man are the cause of action of this sort, [and the man], having in
himself the power of deliberating about the circumstances, has also
the ability not to make the same choice from the same things.

   And this is not asserted unreasonably, nor is what is said special
pleading. For if [the agent] had one goal to which he referred his
decision, it would be reasonable that he should always choose|the   15
same thing from among the same things, if at least he had and
preserved the same position in relation to the goal set before him,
towards which he looked in making his judgement of them. But
since there are several ends, looking towards which he makes his
judgement and choice of the things he should do (for he has both the
pleasant and the advantageous and the noble before his eyes), and
these are different from each other, and not all | the things   20
surrounding [him] are in the same position in relation to each of
these, he makes his judgement between them and choice from
among them at one time with regard to the pleasant, at another with
regard to the noble, at another with regard to the advantageous,
[and] will not always do or choose the same things when all the
circumstances are the same, but on each occasion those things
which seem to him most conducive to the goal on which he has
decided. And by means of this | one might resolve the argument   25
which attributes responsibility for [*or*: the cause of] the actions to
the 'appearance', on the grounds that no-one would ever do

anything contrary to what appears better to him. For there are several goals with regard to which the 'appearance' is judged.

Moreover, even if someone chooses the same things when the circumstances are the same, it does not at once follow that he chooses the same things necessarily and that the external things are the causes of the | decision. For in the case of each choice it is possible to show that before doing and preferring something he was also able to choose the opposite; for he does not choose these things because he is not able to do their opposites, but because they seem more reasonable to him. At any rate it is possible for him, desiring on some occasion to show that his choice is not necessitated, and being contentious about this, | to choose also what does not seem reasonable.

Moreover, if the disposition in accordance with which we deliberate is not always the same*, we will not always choose the same things from the things that surround us, [even though they] are the same. But if, in the same circumstances, people who are not alike do not choose the same things, it is clear that the cause even of the choice of similar things is not the circumstances being alike but the person to whom they are present being in a similar [disposition].

And in general, | to try to show by argument that there is something that depends on us, when it is so evident, is [the action] of those who do not know how to distinguish between what is clear and what is not. For this is apparent, as we said, from many things: from deliberating, from repenting, from giving advice, from condemning certain people, from exhorting, from praising, | from blaming, from rewarding, from punishing, from teaching, from commanding, from seeking prophecies, from praying, from habituating, from legislating. For in general the whole of human life, making use of these [activities] and those like them, bears witness that nothing is so peculiar to man, as compared with the other living creatures, as what depends on us.

And that the beginning of our coming to be of a certain sort in character | – on account of which we make choices of different sorts – rests with ourselves*, [this] is clear from the fact that it is through habit that we come to be of a certain sort, and that most of our habits depend on us. For even if someone became accustomed to bad habits in the beginning when he was still a child, by nature all men, when they are fully developed, are capable of perceiving the things that are noble. At any rate no one who is in a natural state lacks the

conception of which things are just and which | unjust, which noble   15
and which base. And neither do they fail to realise that it is from
developing habits of a certain sort that they become capable of
choosing and of doing either the things that are noble or those that
are base. At any rate those who want to practise and learn
something turn to advancing themselves to the [goal] set before
them through habituation, since they are not ignorant of the
strength of habit for achieving the [goal] set before one. | For to   20
whom is it not clear, that it is through doing things that are
temperate that temperance comes about? But if the things that are
noble are well known to those who are still in a natural state and not
yet incapacitated by wickedness, and the route to them depends on
us and is clear, it will depend on us both to come to be of a certain
sort in character and to acquire the dispositions as a result of which
we will choose and do these things or those. | Good or bad   25
endowments by nature for certain things, as long as they do not
destroy man's own proper nature*, contribute only to the easier or
more difficult acquisition of the things for which [people] are well or
badly endowed by nature. For it is possible for all men who are in a
natural state and not perverted in their judgement and choice to
acquire virtue, and possible [to do so] through one's own [agency].
And for this reason | some people who are less well endowed by   30
nature often become better than many who are well endowed by
nature for virtue, remedying the shortcomings of their nature by the
power that comes from themselves.

Mantissa XXIV
On luck

Sufficient evidence that luck and the fortuitous are among the things   176.2
that are is provided by the common conception of men; but what
each of them is and with which of the things that are it is concerned,
[these are questions where] the majority are no longer the masters of
| teaching the opinions that have been established. For they do not   5
agree either with themselves or with each other about these things,
though they agree in the belief that each of them exists. It is worth
while, then, considering what their nature is and with which of the
things that are their coming-to-be is concerned.

Well, these too seem to be numbered among causes; for luck
seems to be the cause of the things that come to be from luck, and

10   the fortuitous of things of | that sort*. Since then there are four
causes, about which it is our custom often to speak, the material
[cause] and that in accordance with the form and the efficient
[cause] and the end, it is necessary that each of these things too
should be among these, if indeed they *are* causes.

Well, no one would give luck and the fortuitous as the causes *as
matter* of the things that come to be as a result of them; for luck is not
15   something which underlies and is shaped and | formed by something
as matter. For [matter] persists when it receives the form, and is a
cause of the things that come to be by being present in the things
that have come to be from it; but luck and the fortuitous are not
present in the things that come to be on account of them. For the
thing that comes to be in accordance with luck does not itself have
luck in itself. But on account of this it is not as form and essence that
20   these things are causes of the things that are | on account of them,
either; for the form is present in that of which it is the cause, coming
to be in the matter and remaining, but neither of these [is present in
this way]. But neither are luck and the fortuitous cause[s] as the end
and 'that for the sake of which'; for luck is not the goal of any of the
things that come to be, as the goal of each of the things that come to
be for the sake of something is definite, but each of these [luck and
the fortuitous] is indefinite.

25   But if luck is not | among any of these three causes, either it is not
the cause of anything, or it will be among the efficient [causes].
Now, it is for the sake of something that the efficient causes bring
about the things that come about through them, and they have some
definite end set before them, as [with] nature and skill and choice,
but neither luck nor the fortuitous is the same as any of these. For
each of [luck and the fortuitous] seems to be something other
30   besides these, and | these on the one hand are definite and lead to
177.1   something definite, but what is [a matter] of luck is unstable | and
indefinite.

If then luck and the fortuitous seem to be causes of certain things,
but are not the same as any of the [types of] cause, it would seem
that either they do not exist at all, or else some other manner of
cause must be sought. Well, to say that they do not exist at all is
absurd, when they are things believed to have such great power
5   among the things that are; but what other manner | of cause could
there are besides those that have been mentioned already? – Perhaps
then, since of causes some are *per se* and others *per accidens* – for there

are some causes that are *per accidens*; for that which attaches as an accident to what is a cause *per se* and in the proper sense is [itself] a cause *per accidens*, and that very thing itself to which this attached was a cause in the primary sense. The doctor is *per se* the cause of | 10 health, the pale man *per accidens*, if this [*sc.* being pale] should be an accidental attribute of the doctor; for what attaches as an accident to the agent is [itself] an efficient cause *per accidens*. Moreover, the doctor is the efficient cause *per accidens* of, for example, thinness, if this should attach as an accident to the man who is being cured. – Since then of causes some are *per se* and others *per accidens*, and luck cannot be placed among | *per se* causes, it will be among [causes that 15 are] *per accidens*. For the things that are definite would not be *per accidens*, but those that are *per accidens* are indefinite and unstable, just as that which is a matter of luck is accustomed to be; for the things which can attach as accidents to what is a cause *per se* and in the proper sense are indefinite [in their variety*], and all these themselves become causes *per accidens*.

But if luck is a cause *per accidens*, it must | attach as an accident to 20 some one of what we speak of as causes in the proper sense. Since then luck seems to bring something about (for we say that the things that are in accordance with luck come to be and have come to be 'from luck'), [luck and the fortuitous] must necessarily attach to some one of the efficient causes, if they are to keep their place among the causes. But the efficient causes in the proper sense are nature and skill and choice. All those things, which bring [something] about | in the proper sense and definitely, bring about the things 25 which are brought about by them for the sake of some end, and we see that all the things that come about for the sake of something are brought about by some one of these; so luck attaches as an accident to some one of these.

But since it seems that the things that are in accordance with luck are among the things that are matters of choice (for the things that we say come to be from luck are those for the sake of which we would also have chosen to do something, in order to obtain those of them in the case of which we speak of | 'good luck', and in order not to obtain 30 those to which we apply 'bad luck'), luck will be [something that] accompanies the things that come to be in accordance with choice, and among these it will be a cause *per accidens*. For when we do something in accordance with choice, but there happens to us not the end that was intended in accordance with the choice, but

something else accidentally, the action that came about in
35   accordance with choice is the cause of what happened | but was not
intended; and we say that this has come about from luck. If, to the
178.1 person | who digs in accordance with choice for the sake of planting,
there happens as a result of the digging the finding of some treasure,
we say that the finding of the treasure came about from luck; but [it
would] not [have done so] from luck if he had dug for the sake of
this. For then the digging would have been the cause of the finding
5   *not per accidens*, just as it is not | [the cause] of the planting [*per
accidens*]; but as it is [it is the cause of the finding] *per accidens*, for it
was not for the sake of this that it came about. – So luck is that
which comes about in accordance with choice, when it becomes the
cause of something *per accidens*; and what comes about for the sake of
something will always come to be an *indefinite* cause in this way, and
luck will be a cause *per accidens* – not simply, however, but among the
efficient [causes] that come to be for the sake of something, and of
10   these among those in accordance with | choice. For we do not speak
of what is from luck in the case of the things that come to be in
accordance with nature, when something else comes to be that is not
in accordance with the goal of nature, as with monstrosities. Of
these too what comes to be by nature is the cause *per accidens*, but this
is not [a matter] of luck. [So too] in the case of those things of which
the things that come to be in accordance with skill become causes *per
accidens*, for example things that are misshapen*; luck is not
15   responsible | in the case of these things either. So [luck] is [to be
found] among the things that are in accordance with choice, as we
said.
When, therefore, that which comes to be in accordance with
choice becomes the cause *per accidens* of some success, we call this
'good luck'; when of something bad, 'bad luck' – for example, if
someone digging were bitten by some serpent, when the place was
20   not otherwise | suited to serpents of that sort; for if there was a
multitude of serpents [there] and the man dug without care, it was
not luck that was the cause of his being bitten, but a certain lack of
consideration and foresight of his own.
What is of luck is like this and is a cause in this way; 'the
fortuitous' is customarily applied also to the things that come to be
from luck, but nevertheless to a greater extent in the case of the
25   things that are by nature. For when something else follows on | what
comes to be by nature, and not that for the sake of which it came to

be, we say that this has come to be 'fortuitously', as with monstrosities. For when that end, for the sake of which something comes to be by nature*, does not [itself] come to be, we say that [that which comes to be by nature] has itself come to be 'in vain', and (we say) that what followed upon it has come to be 'fortuitously'*, because what has come to be in vain is a cause *per accidens*. And, in a word, everything that follows on what comes to be| in accordance with nature, [but] is not that for the sake of which it came to be, is said to have come to be| fortuitously. Thus the stone which was carried downwards and fell in such a way that one can sit on it acquired this position fortuitously, [the position] following on the natural downwards motion of the stone on account of its weight. In the same way, too, the horse which went to a particular place on account of food, but was on account of this saved| from the enemy; for [the horse] too the natural desire for food was the cause of its being saved, [though] it did not go in order to be saved.

30

179.1

5

To say that luck is 'a cause obscure to human reasoning' is not [the assertion] of those who are laying down some [real] nature that luck has, but of those who are saying that luck consists in men's being in a certain state in relation to the causes; in this way the same thing will be from luck for one man but not for another, when the one| knows its cause and the other does not. Moreover, since there are several causes of the same thing, if there are [causes] of four types, and it is possible that some people should know some of these but not others, the same thing will at the same time be from luck and not from luck for the same person, if he knows some of the causes but does not know the others; for the distinction has not been made, from ignorance concerning *which* of the causes luck [arises]. If they say that luck is not| the cause which is obscure to *some* men, but that which is obscure to all men, they would not even admit that luck exists at all, [since] they grant that the art of prophecy exists and assert that it brings knowledge of the things which seem to be obscure to others. And if wanting to make this distinction* they say that luck is the cause which is obscure to those lacking knowledge, according to this argument the things that come to be| in accordance with knowledge and skill will, for those who lack knowledge and skill, be from luck; for neither does the man who is not a carpenter know the cause (explanation) of the things that are matters of carpentry, nor the man who is not a musician that of things musical, nor any other person who does not possess a skill the things that are

10

15

20

[matters] of that skill; for it is in knowing the causes (explanations) of the things that come to be in accordance with skill that skill [consists].

Mantissa XXV
On fate

[A – Statement of the Problem]

179.25　Concerning fate it is worth considering what it is and in which of the things that are [it is located]. That fate is something is sufficiently established by the common conception of men (for nature is not vain and does not aim wide [*sc.* of the truth]. Anaxagoras is not deserving of credence when he testifies against the common belief; for he says that fate is not anything at all, but that this term is an empty one.)

30　But | as to what it is and in what [it is located], the common conception of men is no longer sufficient to indicate this. For they cannot agree either with each other or with themselves about this. For they change their opinion concerning fate with the times and the

180.1　|circumstances. At one time they posit fate as something unalterable and inescapable, and place all the things that are and come to be under it; at another one can hear them often speaking of what is contrary to fate and of what is contrary to destiny. And for the most

5　part those for whom | those things that are matters of luck do not go successfully, and those that are matters of judgement and of their own choice are not any more healthy either, flee to fate as to some refuge, transferring from themselves to it the cause of [responsibility for,] the things that have not been done, or are not being done, as they should be. And at these times these people say that all things come to be in accordance with fate; but when their luck changes for

10　the | better, they no longer abide by the same opinion. But those for whom the things that are a matter of their own judgement go successfully, and all those that come from luck are in harmony, [these] assign the cause of [responsibility for] the things that come to be to themselves rather than to fate. Others again hold either themselves or the divine responsible for everything that goes successfully, but in the case of what [goes] less well call upon [the name of] fate.

15　　And there are certain religious charlatans, who | observe the weakness of the majority [of men] in judgement concerning fate and the things that come to be in accordance with it, and their readiness, on account of their love of self and their consciousness that they

themselves have [achieved] nothing successful, to believe that fate is
responsible for all the things in which they go wrong. [So the
charlatans] declare that everything that comes to be does so in
accordance with fate, and profess some art according to which | they   20
say they are able to foreknow and to declare beforehand [all] the
things that will be in any way at all, since none of them comes to be
without a certain necessity, which they call fate. And taking as their
supporters those who are responsible for their having this art,* they
persuade the majority of men, assailing them in [difficult]
circumstances and misfortunes when they are all but praying that it
should be shown [to them] that this is how | this matter is. In   25
accordance with a sort of experience and understanding of such
matters, and observation of the sequence in them, they foretell with
a sure aim certain of the things that will ensue for those in such a
condition; and, saying that they are able to do this as a result of their
art concerning fate, they collect no small rewards for such
malpractice, those who experience [their success in prediction]
gladly rewarding them as being supporters | and defenders [of   30
themselves] concerning the things in which they themselves go
wrong. And these people have persuaded the majority of mankind –
who have on account of idleness not concerned themselves with
considering how these matters [really] are, and what is the position
of fate in the things that are – to say that all the things that come to
be do so in accordance with fate.

But since not even those who call upon [the name of] fate to a
considerable extent appear to entrust everything to it in the | conduct   181.1
of life (for the truth is sufficient to show that those who are believed
to speak falsely are inconsistent with themselves*), it is worth our
while to begin from [the point made] above and see, what is the
nature of fate and in what things [it is located] and how far its power
extends.

[B – Where Fate is located]

And first let us consider with which of the things that are it is   181.4
reasonable to say | [fate] is concerned; for when this becomes clear it   5
will be useful also with respect to our other enquiries concerning it.
Well, to place it over all the things that are and to say that all the
things that are are in accordance with fate, in a similar way both
those that are eternal and those that are not, is not reasonable,
especially when it is not agreed [even] by those who most of all sing

the praises of fate as the cause of all the things that come to be. For it
10   is not | reasonable to say that the eternal things are in accordance
with a fate of this sort; it is ridiculous to say that the diagonal is
incommensurable with the side in accordance with fate, or that it is
on account of this that the internal angles of a triangle are equal to
two right angles, and in general it is in no way reasonable to say that
those things which are always the same and in the same state are so
in accordance with fate.

But neither [is it reasonable to say that] all the things that come
15   to be [do so in accordance with fate]. For as many of these | too as
have a coming-to-be which is orderly and definite, these too fall
outside fate. For it is not in accordance with fate that the sun comes
to be at the winter or the summer solstice, nor yet does each of the
heavenly bodies* have fate as the cause of its proper motion, but just
as it is free in respect of its being and substance from a cause of this
20   sort, so it is in respect of its proper | activities. And for this reason fate
is not the cause of any of the things that are eternal or that come to
be always in the same way, but the activity of fate seems to be in the
things that are subject to coming-to-be and passing away. For it is in
the things that are fitted for opposites as far as their natural
endowment is concerned that the power of fate seems to be located,
holding them in one of the opposite states and keeping them in it
according to a certain ordered | sequence. For it is those things that
25   would not be as they are without fate that seem to be kept in their
present ordering by fate; and such are none other of the things that
are than those subject to coming-to-be and passing away, so it is
somewhere here that what is a matter of fate too [is located].

But since of these things also some come to be in accordance with
skill and some reasoning of the type involved in skill, others in
30   accordance with choice, others in accordance | with nature, we must
consider in which of these what is a matter of fate [is located], if it
cannot be in them all. Well, to say that the things that come to be in
accordance with skill come to be and are in accordance with fate is
in no way in harmony with [men's] opinions concerning fate. For it
is absurd to say that a bed or a bench came to be in accordance with
35   fate; for in this way we shall call | every skill fate. But neither will the
things of which choice is the cause be in accordance with fate; for the
182.1   source of these things is in us and not outside, | but fate is not in us.
Even if fate is concerned with the same things with which what
depends on us is concerned, it is [something] other than what

depends on us. So we must remove from fate those of the things subject to coming-to-be, too, that come to be in accordance with skill and choice. And when these are removed there are left remaining those things for which | nature is the cause of [their]   5
coming-to-be; and it is in these things, too, that what is a matter of fate is thought to have power. For if someone wished to examine closely the opinions that have been laid down concerning fate, he will not find that they place fate in any other things or concerning any other things than those that come to be by nature, and of these most of all in the [nature]* of living creatures and of those things that result from combinations of the things subject to coming-to-be. For it is not | very usual to say that the changing of the elements into   10
each other comes about in accordance with fate.

[C – Does Fate admit of exceptions?]
What is in accordance with fate, then, being located in the things we   182.11
have stated, and this having become clear, it [naturally] follows after this to enquire whether [what is in accordance with fate] is such as to be necessary and unalterable, in accordance with the poet who says

| 'I say that no man has escaped his destiny,   15
  Whether base or noble, when he has once been born'

[Homer, *Iliad* VI.488], or whether it is such that one can go against it and that it does not in every way have necessity in itself.

Well, from the common judgement of men concerning this we have neither of these [positions] firmly laid down; for at one time they sing the praises of what is | a matter of fate as [being] necessary,   20
at another they do not believe that it preserves its continuity in every way. For even those who exercise themselves greatly in their arguments on its behalf, and attribute everything to it, do not seem to believe in it in the conduct of life; for they often call on [the name of] luck, admitting that this is some cause other than fate, and | they   25
do not cease from praying to the gods, on the assumption that something can be brought about by [the gods] on account of the prayers even contrary to fate, and they deliberate about the things they should do, although they say that these too are in accordance with fate, and they call in advisers and do not hesitate to make use of prophecies, on the assumption that it is possible for them to guard

against some one of the things that are fated if they learn [of it] in
30   advance. But since these people | turn out to be in obvious
disagreement with themselves in this way concerning the most
important matters (for their ingenious arguments to show that these
things are consistent are certainly most unpersuasive), and since it is
thought that in the things that are subject to coming-to-be and
passing away there is also the contingent, which is the cause of
nothing coming to be necessarily in the things in which it is, it is
worth considering whether [the contingent] exists or not. For if this
naturally-existing-thing is defined | it [will] greatly contribute
towards our finding the essence of fate.

183.1 | Well, common usage is sufficient to establish [the existence of]
the nature of the contingent*. For none even of those who say that
all things come to be from necessity does not bear witness in living
and in the activities of life to the fact that some of the things that
come to be can not come to be and [some] of the things that do not
5   come to be [can] come to be. Moreover, | this is also easy to show by
argument. For many of the things that come to be are believed to
come to be, some from luck, some from the fortuitous; and that there
is also something that depends on us is so clear that not even those
who try to give the things that are matters of fate such force that they
are altogether necessary can resist this belief. But if there is
something that depends on us, and this is concerned with the same
10   things that | it was concluded fate is concerned with, it is ruled out
that fate should be unalterable and unable to be impeded and
necessary; for it is impossible to say that those things, the choice or
not of which begins with us*, are necessitated.

But it *is* necessary for those who say that fate exists to say that it is
concerned with the same things with which what depends on us, too,
is concerned. For whether they were to say [i] that it is the ends [of
15   action] alone that are in accordance with | fate, or whether [ii] they
say that it is the actions too which the ends follow, either way it
follows that they say that fate is concerned with the same things with
which what depends on us is also concerned. If [ii] someone were to
say that the actions too are in accordance with fate, what was
posited is at once clear, for it is in these that what depends on us,
too, is located. But if [i] [he were to say] that the ends, for the sake of
which the actions [are performed, are in accordance with fate], and
20   ends of a certain sort follow on actions | of a certain sort (for it is not
indeed the case that the same end follows for those who act in

whatever way at all), it is necessary to say that the actions too, which ends of this sort follow, are fated. For the end that is in accordance with fate will not follow if the actions that lead to it have not preceded. And it is with these that what depends on us is concerned.

That there is something that depends on us will also be clear from the following points – if indeed one needs to use demonstrative arguments | concerning things that are clearly apparent: none of the 25 things that are brought about by nature as its primary [ends] comes about in vain, and deliberating, which is in man by nature and is a primary work of nature (if indeed it is by this most of all that man is thought to differ from the other living creatures) comes about in vain if he who deliberates is not in control of choosing anything as a result of deliberating. | But it is as having power over this that we 30 deliberate by ourselves concerning the things we should do, and do not yield to the irrational appearances [that] the other living creatures [experience]* and follow them in a similar way; and that we call in as advisers whoever we see are more able than ourselves, to assist in the judgement and choice | of the courses that are set 184.1 before us. And when [we are] concerned with greater and more difficult matters, at this point we do not hesitate to call in the gods too as advisers, asking that we should be told by them, either through oracles or through counsels or through certain dreams, which we should choose of the things about which we enquire. Sufficient to | establish [that there is something that depends on us] 5 are the codes of law, too, in which it is commanded that certain things should be taught and the things that should be done are enjoined, and those who obey these are rewarded, those who do not are punished.

But indeed if there is something that depends on us the contingent too, exists, if at least it depends on us both to do something and not to. And if this exists it is impossible that what is a matter of fate should be necessary in the case of those things in which, what depends|on us too 10 has a place. Prayers to the gods, too, are sufficient to establish that there are certain things which are contingent, some people asking them to avert certain things, others [asking them] to give things, on the assumption that there are some things which can both be brought about by the gods and not [be brought about by them] on account of our request.

And moreover it is possible to learn this also from the natural

15 constitution of each of the things that are. For nature | itself has given
to those things which are and come to be of necessity no fitness for
the opposite, but unfitness for the [states] that are impossible; for
they would have fitness for change into these in vain, [since] they
cannot be otherwise [than they are]. For we see that neither does fire
have the capacity for coldness in itself, nor snow that for blackness,
20 nor the things that are heavy that for lightness, | at least while they
remain what they are, nor [does] any of the eternal things [have the
capacity] for being destroyed. But those things for which it is not
necessary that they should be and remain definitely in *one* of the
opposite [states], these have from nature readiness also for change to
the opposite [state]. Such are most of the things subject to coming-
to-be and passing away, with which one of the opposites is not
25 cognate; for each of them is able both to undergo | the opposites and
not, that is, it can both undergo [them] and not. But what can
change into the opposite [state] is not of necessity in that one of [the
opposite states] in which it is already.

That not everything that comes to be does so of necessity is
established both by what depends on us, as we said, and by luck,
which is capable of interrupting the continuity of the things that are
30 thought to come to be in a certain order. But if it is no less | clear
than [that] fate [exists] that there is something that depends on us,
and that many things come to be both from luck and from the
fortuitous, and altogether that in the things that are subject to
coming-to-be, in which fate too is located, there is also the nature of
the contingent, and this excludes what is necessary, it is impossible
185.1 that fate should be something which is necessary and | which one
cannot go against.

[D – Fate as individual nature]

185.1 But it is agreed that all the things that come to be in accordance
with fate come to be in accordance with a certain order and
sequence and have a certain succession in themselves. For it is not
indeed the case that the things that are matters of fate are like the
things that [result] from luck; for the latter are unstable and come to
5 be infrequently and are almost without a cause [explanation], but |
that which is in accordance with fate is entirely the opposite; for
they say that [fate] is a chain of causes. But neither does fate seem to
be the same as what is in accordance with choice; for the continuity
of [Fate] is often broken by us and our choice.

However, we see that there are the following causes in the things that come to be and pass away besides the nature which puts them together and fashions them: choice and the | fortuitous and luck (for that which is in accordance with *skill* is not [present] in these). But that which is a matter of fate does not seem to be the same as any of these. We are left, then, with fate being nothing other than the proper nature of each thing. For that which is a matter of fate is not in what is universal and common, for example simply [in] living creature or man, but in the individuals, Socrates and Callias. And in these the nature that is particular to them is, [through] being | of a certain sort, the beginning and cause of the ordered pattern that comes to be in accordance with it. For it is from this, in general, that [men's] lives and their endings [result], when it is not impeded by anything.

At any rate we see that the body, through being like this or like that as a result of nature, is affected both in disease and in death in accordance with its natural constitution. But not of necessity; for treatments and changes | of climate and doctors' orders and advice from the gods are sufficient to break such a pattern. And in the same way in the case of the soul too one could find the actions and choices and way of life of each individual differing from, and contrary to, his natural constitution. For 'men's character is their guardian spirit' according to Heraclitus, that is, their nature.

For men's actions and lives | and the endings of their lives turn out for the most part to be in accordance with their natural constitutions and dispositions. Men who are eager for battle and love danger for the most part meet some violent death, for this is their fate and nature; and the man who is licentious and spends his life in pleasure [for the most part meets death] in immoderate behaviour, he who is of an enduring [nature] that through excess of troubles and persistence in them, |the man who is illiberal that from eagerness over what is indifferent*, on account of which they act unjustly and neglect themselves and toil beyond their power. It is on this account, at any rate, that people are accustomed to reproach such men, [saying that] the man was himself the cause of his own death.

If that which is in accordance with fate is like this, we shall not say any longer that prophecy is useless, either, [as] it foresees what will result in accordance with | nature and assists us through advising and commanding us to resist the natural sequence [when it inclines to] the worse. Neither will the nature of luck be done | away with, but

10

15

20

25

30

35

186.1

it will be responsible for certain things, coinciding with the things that come to be in accordance with choice. And still more will the divine and the assistance that comes from it, and prayers and entreaties from us, preserve their proper place, when that which is a matter of fate is like this. And in agreement with these things, too, is
5 the saying that | many things come to be contrary to destiny and contrary to fate, as the poet somewhere shows saying

'Lest you come to the house of Hades even before it is destined.'

[*Iliad* XX.336]. And this opinion might also be established by the fact that the prophets do not hit the mark in everything that they foretell.
10 It is in no way surprising that | men do not hold this opinion concerning fate. For the majority do not aim badly concerning things in their outline, but [when it comes to] the particular details and defining [them] and making [them] exact they make many errors. For the former is the work of nature, the latter of understanding.

Aristotle already mentions the name of fate in the first book of the
15 *Meteorologica* [1.14 352a28] as follows: | 'but the cause of all these things must be supposed to be that at fated times there comes about, just as winter does in the seasons of the year, a Great Winter in some great cycle.' And it seems that in these words he is saying that fate is nature (for the fated times, the winter and [that] of the other things*, are those whose reciprocal succession is natural, but
20 not unalterable and | necessitated). And in the fifth book of the *Physics* [5.6 230a32], too, he again mentions fate as follows: 'are there then comings-to-be which are forcible and not fated, to which those that are in accordance with nature are opposite?'; through which it is again clear that he employs the name of fate in connection with the things that come to be in accordance with nature. For if he says that what is in accordance with nature is
25 opposite to what is not fated, and what is contrary|to fate is opposite to what is in accordance with fate, what is in accordance with fate will be the same as what is in accordance with nature. For it is not possible to say that several things are opposite to what is not in accordance with fate, [if] this last is one thing; [firstly] what *is* in accordance with fate, which clearly *is* opposite to it, and [secondly] what is in accordance with nature, [this] being other than what is in accordance with fate. And Theophrastus very clearly shows in his

Callisthenes that what is in accordance with fate is the same as | what   30
is in accordance with nature, [as does] also Polyzelus in the book
that is entitled *Concerning Fate*.

Quaestiones II.4, II.5, III.13, and passages from Alexander's commentary on Aristotle's *Topics*

QUAESTIO II.4

That, if the opposite of what depends on us does not depend on us, not even what depends on us, itself, will depend on us

If that depends on us of which the opposite depends on us, that of which the opposite does not depend on us does not depend on us.

51.1 But the opposite of what depends|on us does not depend on us; for it is what does not depend on us that is opposite to what depends on us. So not even what depends on us, then, [depends on us]. But if what depends on us does not depend on us, nothing depends on us. So – according to those who maintain that what depends on us is that of which the opposite too depends on us – nothing depends on us. –

5 Or else it is false that, if it|does not depend on us that something depends on us, nothing depends on us. For that something depends on us is in our nature and essence and does not depend on us, just as being rational does not either; but the matters that we deal with in a manner that depends on us, (these) do depend on us. For the opposites of these too depend on us. That something depends on us

10 does not depend on us; but walking about depends on us, because| not walking about [does so] too. And if [what depends on us] depends on us on the [same] grounds on which the opposite of what depends on us depends on us, it is clear that those things of which the opposites depend on us do also themselves depend on us, because the things that depend on us are among things that are matters of action. But that something depends on us among things that are objects of deliberation and can also be otherwise is not [itself] a matter of action. And [since] that something depends on us

15 is not among [matters of action],| it is reasonable that the power, according to which something depends on us, does not [itself] depend on us, but the the things in relation to which we use the power of having something depending on us do depend on us; just as

the use [we make] of reason depends on us, but [our possessing] the power to use it does not depend on us.

QUAESTIO II.5
Concerning the [claim] that what depends on us, too, is in accordance with fate

The opposite of something's depending on us is for nothing to depend on us. But for nothing to depend on us is impossible; so the opposite of something's depending on us is impossible*. However, that of which the opposite is impossible is in accordance with fate, if indeed those things come to be in accordance with fate of which it is impossible for the opposites either to be or to come to be. So that something depends on us is in accordance with fate; and, by the fact that something depends on us in accordance with | fate*, the depending of something on us will be preserved according to those who say that all things come to be in accordance with fate.

Or else it is not true that that of which the opposite is impossible is in accordance with fate. For if that which is of necessity were the same as that which is in accordance with fate, [then], just as 'that of which the opposite is impossible' *is* the definition of that which is of necessity, so it would be of that which is in accordance with fate. But that which is of necessity | is wider than that which is in accordance with fate; for not everything which is of necessity is in accordance with fate. | At any rate, twice two are four of necessity, but not in accordance with fate, if that which is in accordance with fate is located in things which come to be; so the formula saying 'that of which the opposite is impossible' will no longer be the definition of that which is in accordance with fate. Although this too* will indeed apply to the things that are in accordance with fate, since they too* are necessary, | nevertheless it will *not* do so so as to have the same extension as them. And if it does not have the same extension, it will not be convertible. It is not the case that that of which the opposite is impossible is always and at all events in accordance with fate; [rather], this is [what is] *necessary*, and it is of *this* that the formula stated is the definition. What depends on us*, indeed, is necessary, because everything that is in the essence of something applies to it | necessarily; but [it is] *not* in accordance with fate. For it is those things, of which the opposite is impossible, that come to be in accordance with a sequence of causes that will be in accordance with fate.

51.20

25

30

52.1

5

10

QUAESTIO III.13
Some points concerning that which depends on us

That which depends on us is located in rational assent; it is on
account of this that it is only in man that what depends on us [is
found], because man is also, alone of living creatures, rational and
capable of deliberation. The irrational living creatures assent too,
but they follow the appearances that come to be in them from
10 objects of perception | through their senses, and the affection that
comes to be in them from these, and make their assents being led by
these wheresoever they lead. But man, when he makes his assents
qua man, needs reason in addition to the appearances; it is [by]
having this from nature for the judgement of such things that he is a
man, and through this reason he judges the appearances. And for
15 this reason | if, when he deliberates about the impression that
impinged upon him, it does not seem as it appeared at first, he does
not assent to it, [though] he would have assented as far as the
affection [that results] from the appearance is concerned; and it is
this sort of assent which is choice, being a deliberative desire. For it
is the decision, resulting from deliberation, about that which
[comes] from what is perceived and before oneself that is choice.*
20 If | then even when we deliberated it followed that we always*
assented to the appearance, not even assent accompanied by
deliberation would depend on us; but since having deliberated often
makes our assent that follows on the appearance different from [that
which would be produced by] the affection [that results] from it, it
would no longer be reasonable to say that we 'assent to
appearances'. Since we do not assent to appearances, and [our
25 doing so] would | do away with what depends on us, neither will
there being something that depends on us be done away with*.
If indeed it followed without qualification [on every impression]
that we deliberated upon it, perhaps it would seem that
[deliberating] itself did not depend on us but was some attribute of
the impression brought about by it; and if [the deliberating] had
derived its being from [the appearance] it would have seemed that
the assent that follows on [the deliberating], too, came about in
accordance with [the appearance], in accordance with which the
30 deliberation too, | on which the assent followed, [came about]. But if
the appearance is not in control of man's deliberating, but
deliberating and not [doing so] depend on him ([for] we do at any

rate assent to many appearances without deliberating, in a similar way to the irrational living creatures), not even such assent [*sc.* that *not* preceded by deliberation] will be the product of the appearance, since [assent] resists [the impression] in many cases and in many ways.

That | we are in control of deliberating about the appearances is   35 clear from what has already been said, that we have the power of deliberating and not, and that the appearance is not in control of this. For if it were not the appearance, what else | could be posited as in   108.1 control of this besides ourselves? It is not the case that, [just] because we say in a more general way that what is discovered and approved in accordance with reason, too, 'appears' to us, therefore we should say that such assent is 'an appearance' and 'to an appearance', if at least an 'appearance' in the proper sense is a movement produced by the actual perception.

Moreover, the fact that those | who deliberate are praised and   5 those who do not are blamed is a sign that deliberating depends on us and is not the product of the appearance. For praise and blame are for the things that depend on us, and it is for this reason that we are neither praised nor blamed for the appearances [that we experience], unless we are ourselves responsible for some of them;* but both of these [praise and blame] *do* apply to the assents that follow on [the appearances]. We *are* blamed for those | appearances   10 that come to be of such a sort for us on account of our failure to practise [virtue, where] the practice is [something] of which we are in control.*

[And] since to call in advisers, and these rather than or instead of those, depends on us, it is clear that deliberating in the first place, too, depends on us. [And] since the punishments for misdeeds | 15 resulting from forethought are greater, on the grounds that [the agents] acted in accordance with deliberate choice, it is clear that everything that comes about as a result of forethought, too, depends on us.

*

Fate is mentioned as a topic of discussion in four passages from Alexander's commentary on Aristotle's Topics; *it is of interest to compare these passages with the* de fato:

1. Alexander *in top.*, *CAG* 2.2 76.26-77.3 Wallies; on Aristotle *Topics* 1.11 104b5. Cf. *de fato* ch. II.

And 'each group' [*sc.* the wise and the majority] disagree among themselves'. Among the wise [there are disagreements] concerning fate, the immortality of the soul, the infinite, the void and such matters; the majority [disagree] with one another in the cases where some of them say that health is preferable to wealth, others the opposite, and some prefer strength to handsomeness, others handsomeness to strength, and so on.

2. Ibid. 95.7-12 (Aristotle 1.14 105b25). Cf. *de fato* I 164.17, and XI.

Among physical problems and propositions, too, there are some which relate 'to choice and avoidance'. For 'whether all things come to be in accordance with fate and necessarily' is a physical [question], but relates 'to choice and avoidance'; for it is on this that it depends whether it seems right to deliberate about the things that are or are not to be done.

3. Ibid. 566.18-23 (Aristotle 8.11 161b11). Cf. *de fato* XVIII; *mantissa* 181.1f., 182.30.

He says that errors in arguments come about in dialectical argument itself as a result of ignorance and because it has not been determined when [people are assuming] the contrary [of the assertions from which they started] and 'when they are assuming what [was asserted] at the beginning'. For it is on account of ignorance of this that people often go wrong in argument. And this happens both when they are speaking on their own account, and when they are answering [questions]; for the person who says that all things are in accordance with fate, and that some things are contingent and depend on us, does not realise that he is contradicting himself.

4. Ibid. 570.4-11 (Aristotle 8.11 161b38). Cf. *de fato* XVI-XXI; Introduction p. 17.

For the [argument] that does away with the coming to be of all things in accordance with fate and reason, on account of the fact that praise and blame are [then] in vain, would not seem to deserve criticism if it is examined in itself. If however someone examined it in relation to the question at issue, it would seem inadequate; for what is at issue can be shown through more, and more generally accepted, arguments – through the fact that everything that is contingent is done away with [by the assertion that all things come to be in accordance with fate], as is also what depends on us; so that deliberating, too, is in vain. And thus [the contention] that virtue and vice do not depend on us is done away with, too.

COMMENTARY

Commentary

De fato

I. (Cf. Introduction, pp. 15, 17.) 164. 18-19 is the position of Alexander's determinist opponents, 19-20 his own, as later becomes clear (see below on II). For the statement of the determinist position in terms of necessity as well as of fate (164.18) cf. Introduction, p. 20. Throughout the treatise difficulty in translation is caused by the fact that the Greek *panta gignetai* covers both 'all things come to be' and 'all events happen'; cf. further below, p. 154.

164.21-165.1 is at first surprising, in view of Alexander's repeated insistence that his own position is in accord with what is obvious (above, p. 18 n. 109); the reference is probably to the determinist arguments countered in chs. XXII-XXXVIII. Cf. XXVI 196.14.

With the elaborate rhetorical flattery of this introduction one may compare that to book I of Pollux's *Onomasticon*, dedicated to Commodus (I am grateful to Dr M.W. Haslam for this reference.) Caracalla, the second of Alexander's dedicatees, was scarcely sympathetic to Peripatetic philosophy; believing the tradition that blamed Aristotle for the death of Alexander the Great, whom he greatly admired, he abolished the common meals of the Peripatetics at Alexandria and threatened to burn their books (Dio Cassius 78.7.3, ?212 A.D.; Lynch, op. cit. p. 15 n. 89 above, 195).

II. (Cf. Introduction, p. 18; *m*, 179.25-181.4.) The distinction between the question whether fate exists and that of its nature is Aristotelian; cf. Aristotle *an. post.* 2.1 89b31-5, *phys.* 3.4 202b35f.; also Cicero *de natura deorum* 2.13 and R.B. Todd, 'The Stoic common notions', *Symbolae Osloenses* 48 (1973), 73 n. 83. Cf. Alexander *m.* 176.1ff., 179.25ff. The claim that Anaxagoras denied that anything came to be in accordance with fate is unique (hence Orelli's deletion); contrast the other passages collected with the present one in H. Diels – W. Kranz, *Die Fragmente der Vorsokratiker*[6] (Berlin, 1951)

59A66. Anaxagoras' doctrine of cosmogonic *nous* might be held to be incompatible with determinism (cf. Verbeke, 78 n. 15); but a similar point might be made with regard to Stoicism, and, on Anaxagoras' *nous* cf. the complaints of Plato, Phaedo 98b, and Aristotle *metaph.* *A* 4 985a18ff.

166.3-8 is in fact Alexander's own position, as is indicated in VI; for fate as *aparabatos* and *anapodrastos* (166.2-3) cf. *SVF* 2.528, 917, 918, 1000; above p. 25 n. 167, and Sharples (1981) p. 84 and n. 28. The parallel drawn by Long (1970) 266 between the classification of views here and those in Tacitus *Annals* 6.22 and Josephus *ant. Jud.* 13.172f. (cf. ibid. 18.13f., *bell. Jud.* 2.16ff.; also Calcidius CXLII 181.16ff., CXC 214.1-16. Theiler, *passim*) is not all that close; there is no reference in these other texts to a group who change their view (166.8-13). Moreover, it is not clear whether the references in Tacitus and Josephus to a view that combines human responsibility and fate are to be understood in a libertarian or in a soft-determinist manner; but they cannot *both* be accurate representations of the Stoic position *and* introduce responsibility in a sense that would satisfy Alexander (cf. Long (1970) 266 n. 47). The Stoics could certainly accept that certain things would not have happened if the agents had acted otherwise (166.11-12); but not that they had a power of acting otherwise (166.12-13) in a categorical, unqualified sense. Cf. Introduction, pp. 21-2; and further below, p. 145.

The present survey of views may be compared with that of views on *eudaimonia* at Aristotle *eth. Nic.* 1.4 1095a20-8. With 166.7 cf. *m.* 186.7; also *m.* 180.4.

III. For the fourfold classification of 'causes' cf. Aristotle *phys.* 2.3 194b23ff., also 2.7 198a14ff.; *metaph.* A3 983 a 26ff., *Δ* 2 1013a24ff. *aitia* might be better rendered 'explanation'; but after this chapter the term is almost entirely used of efficient *aitiai*, and I have therefore retained 'cause' as the translation. (Cf. M. Hocutt, 'Aristotle's four becauses', *Philosophy* 49 (1974) 385-99.) Alexander's concentration on the efficient cause in what follows seems acceptable, in spite of Pack's complaint (420); that fate is *purposive* is recognised at V 168.27ff., and though Stoic fate is in some ways analogous to the Aristotelian *formal* cause (above, Introduction p. 8) it is as an active, 'efficient' principle that it is so. In any case Alexander is still concerned with common opinion (cf. 166.15-18) rather than with specifically Stoic doctrine (cf. above, Introduction p. 23 and n. 158).

The use of the single example of the statue to illustrate all four 'causes' is not found in Aristotle himself; cf. Seneca *ep. mor.* 65.4-6, Clement of Alexandria *strom.* 8.9, *PG* 9.596ab. (R.B. Todd, 'The four causes: Aristotle's exposition and the ancients', *Journ. Hist. Ideas* 37 (1976) 319-22). For the claim that not everything has all four causes (166.28) cf. Aristotle *metaph.* Z 17 1041a28-32, *H* 4 1044b7-15. In both 166.24 and 166.25 'among [the causes]' might alternatively be rendered 'in the case of [the things that come to be]'.

IV. For the division into things for the sake of something and those that are not cf. Aristotle *phys.* 2.4 196b17. With the subdivision of the former cf. (without the subsuming of craft and choice under reason) *m.* 176.27, 181.28ff.; also (though in no case is the correspondence exact) Aristotle *phys.* 2.5 196b21, *metaph.* Z 7 1032a20, b23, and *eth. Nic.* 3.3 1112a31ff.; Aëtius 1.29.2, Nemesius *de nat. hom.* XXXIX, *PG* 40.761b. That the principle (*archē*) of coming-to-be is internal in the products of nature, external in those of reason is asserted at Aristotle *phys.* 2.1 192b13ff., 2.8 199b28, *metaph.* Θ 7 1049a5-18; for nature not deliberating cf. *phys.* 2.8 199a20, b26, and W.D. Ross (*Aristotle's Physics*, Oxford 1936) on the latter passage. For natural coming-to-be proceeding to its goal unless hindered (168.5) cf. Aristotle *phys.* 2.8 199b15ff., *part. an.* 1.1 641b25ff.

The products of 'chance' (which I have throughout used to cover both *Tuchē*, translated 'luck', and *to automaton*, translated 'the fortuitous'; cf. ch. VIII and comm.) are introduced here as something of an afterthought; they are in a somewhat anomalous position, being 'for the sake of something' only in the sense that they *could* have been brought about purposefully though in fact they were not (cf. Aristotle *phys.* 2.5 196b21f.; Ross op. cit. 517f.; W. Charlton, *Aristotle's Physics I, II* (Oxford 1970) 106). Cf. *proēgoumenōs*, 168.20, and apparatus ad loc. *triton de* at 168.18, it may be noted, occurs only in Eusebius. Cf. further below, on ch. V.

At 167.22-3, 'are not brought about by the agent'] literally: 'do not come to be by the agency of the doer'. With the examples in 167.24f. compose *SVF* 3.118 and 495; also below, IX 175.11. At 167.26 a^2's *tinòs* 'for the sake of something', would make the sentence run more easily; L however supports *tinòs*. (I am grateful to Professor Long for drawing my attention to this question.)

V. For the connection between reason and the possibility for alternatives (169.9f., 13-15) cf. Aristotle *metaph.* Θ 2 1046b4ff., Θ

5 1048a8ff.; on the sense of possibility for alternatives in Alexander, cf. Introduction p. 21-2, and in Aristotle, p. 7 and the discussions cited in n. 30. Such possibility *is* incompatible with determinism if it is understood in Alexander's libertarian sense, but not if it is taken in a qualified soft-determinist one; nor would the appeal to common usage (169.10-12) necessarily be regarded by a Stoic as finally settling the matter (Long (1970) 250-3). For the Stoics fate, identified with universal nature (Introduction, n. 154) *included* the products of reason; Verbeke, 80 n. 23.

With the arguments of the present chapter may be compared those at *m.* 181.31-182.7. The products of chance (IV 168.18ff.) are neglected in the elimination argument of V-VI; either there is a slide in the sense of 'natural' between 169.4f. and 169.30f., or, more probably, it is already in the former passage confined to what is usual, in which case the claim there made is simply erroneous. Alexander may well neglect chance as a candidate for identification with fate because for him (unlike the Stoics; cf. below, ch. VIII comm.) it is irreducibly disorderly; the point *is* argued at *m.* 184.3, but it is omitted here. Cf. Sharples (1980) 84.

VI. Cf. above, Introduction pp. 22-8, *m.* 185.11-33.)
The observation that the heavenly bodies are called the causes of fate (169.23-5) is surely an allusion to astrology, but the argument is not to be taken as an endorsement of astrology by Alexander himself. (Orelli 268 n. 3 appears to take *schesis* at 169.26 in the technical sense of *constellatio*, but the reference is probably to the effect of the obliquity of the ecliptic on natural coming-to-be; cf. *q.* II 3 50.6, II. 19 63.26, Alex. *de mixt.* X 223.12, XI 225.33.) With 169.23-4 cf. Aristotle *phys.* 2.2 194b13, *metaph. Λ* 5 1071a15, Alex. *de prov.* 59.11, and above, Introduction p. 26 n. 177. For the standard Aristotelian example 'man begets man' (169.21, 170.2) cf. XXIII 193.8-10 and comm., XXV 195.26, *de prov.* 59.11; Aristotle *phys.* loc. cit., *metaph. Z* 7 1032a25 etc., *Λ* 4 1070b34.

For the shift of emphasis in this chapter and the introduction at 170.9 of the notion of fate as the peculiar nature of each individual cf. Introduction pp. 23-4; *hekastois* at 169.24 is hardly comparable. The point is apparently (*dio*, 170.9) presented as an *inference* from the fact that nature admits of exceptions. The Stoics held that the nature of an individual could be impeded but that of the universe could not (*SVF* 2.935, cf. 937), and identified fate with the latter rather than with the former; Alexander does indeed cite his opponents as connecting fate with the nature of the individual (cf. the passages cited in Introduction n. 154), but for the Stoics this is only correct with the addition that, even when the individual's nature is impeded, that is part of the overall plan of fate. Alexander has disregarded – rather than argued against – the possibility that what is unnatural in the context of the part may nevertheless be natural in the context of the whole; this *is* claimed by Philoponus *in phys. CAG* 17.201.10, but contrast Themistius *in phys. CAG* 5.2.37.9, Simplicius *in phys.* 9.271.10 (S. Sambursky, *The Physical World of Late Antiquity*, London 1962, 93-8, and 'Conceptual developments and modes of explanation in late Greek scientific thought', in A.C. Crombie (ed.), *Scientific Change*, London 1963, 70-3). Cf. also Aristotle *metaph. E* 2 1027a25, and my comments at Sharples (1975,1) 263f.

A contrast between men's general character, which may be predetermined, and their particular actions which are not, is drawn by Cicero *de fato* 7ff. (*SVF* 2.950; cf. further below); cf. also, on Epicurus, Huby 362. Gellius *noct. Att.* 13.1 connects fate with natural, as opposed to violent, death, and allows that there may be exceptions to fate. Cf. also below, pp. 158-9.

Alexander apparently intends his theory of fate as a rejection of determinism; but there is no reason why the unusual events cited in 170.14ff. should not result from factors themselves predetermined – though they will only be predetermined for all time beforehand given the notion of a universal causal nexus, and this Alexander like Aristotle lacks (cf. Introduction p. 5, and below p. 136). It seems unlikely that Alexander intends to confine his argument here entirely to cases of human volition (cf. 170.5ff., and, perhaps, *aerōn hupallagai* in 170.15), though it is with these that it is chiefly concerned from 170.9 onwards. Characteristically, there is no clear analysis of the causes of the exceptions to fate, and no attempt is made to link the present discussion to the subsequent treatments of human agency and of chance. At 170.17 *para* makes the more forceful point and gives a better connection between 16-18 and what precedes; Eusebius' addition in 170.18, almost certainly his own paraphrase of what follows (quotation only being resumed in 171.11) shows that he read *para*. Cf. also *m.* 185.22. The notion of natural endowment admitting of exceptions is also utilised in *m.* 171.16ff., 35ff.; but where in *f*.VI most of the examples are of men *transcending* their nature, in *m.* 171f. it is rather a question of their falling short (cf. Sharples (1975,2) 49ff.). '[his]' at 170.23 is explicit at *m.* 185.27; in what follows *eisi kath' heimarmenēn* (171.1) is to be taken with 170.23-5 as well as with 170.25-171.1 (so Donini (1969) 303, noting *palin* in 171.1).

Whereas Alexander here operates with the notion of a natural endowment that may be resisted but not, apparently, changed (cf. 171.16), in XXVII (q.v. Comm.) he uses the more familiar Aristotelian notion of an initial natural endowment that may be developed in alternative directions (Donini (1974,2) 161-5, 169-73. Cf., however, Aristotle *eth. Nic.* 6.13 1144b4ff.; A.W.H. Adkins, *From the Many to the One* (London 1970) 183f.). Donini has suggested that in the present passage Alexander has in mind particularly the physiological determinism advanced by Galen (Donini, op. cit. 127-56, 163-5; above, Introduction p. 10 and n. 53. On Alexander and Galen cf. Todd (1976) 3-5). For differences in men's natural constitutions cf. also *de prov.* 85.3ff. On Alexander's interpretation of the quotation from Heraclitus at 170.18 (22B119 Diels-Kranz, above p. 125), cf. H. Gomperz, 'Über die ursprünglich Reihenfolge einiger Bruchstücke Heraklits', *Hermes* 58 (1923), 42.

The anecdote of Zopyrus and Socrates (171.11ff.) is used to make a similar point against determinism in Cicero *de fato* 10; it also appears at Cicero *Tusc. disp.* 4.80. For further references, and its probable origin in a fourth-century B.C. Socratic dialogue by Phaedo of Elis, cf. P.R. Foerster, *Scriptores Physiognomici Graeci* (Leipzig, Teubner, 1893) I vii-xiii; L. Rosetti, 'Ricerche sui "Dialoghi Socratici" di Fedone e di Euclide', *Hermes* 108 (1980) 183-99. It seems likely that the story was originally simply a protreptic to philosophy, and that its connection with the issue of determinism was secondary – perhaps due to Carneades; the context in Cicero's *de fato* is in part concerned with astrology. Cf. above, introduction p. 13 and nn.; Amand, 49ff., 63f. and 64 n. 3. For Aristotle's interest in physiognomy cf. *an.pr.* 2.27 70b7ff. and Foerster op. cit. I. xvi f.; however, the supposition that Alexander wrote a commentary on [Aristotle] *Physiognomonica* results from an error (Foerster, I. xxxiii) and the passages cited by Foerster II p. 283, nos. 86f., are not from a genuine work of Alexander's (above, Introduction n. 97).

The *Stoic* explanation of the failures of prophecy (171.7-11) was rather in terms of the shortcomings of its practitioners (*SVF* 2.1210; cf. Tacitus *Annals* 6.22.6).

VII. For belief in determinism as an excuse for misfortune (rather than for moral shortcomings, as argued by Pack 419, 436 n. 68; cf. II 166.9, VII 172.1, *m.* 180.4f., 24; but contrast XVI 187.28-30) cf. II 166.8-10, *m.* 180.4ff., 23ff., 29ff. This would hardly be a legitimate motive to attribute to the Stoics, for whom wickedness is the only evil thing and external circumstances are indifferent (Long, 1970, 249f.); and Alexander does not indeed attribute it to his opponents themselves – cf. 171.23 with 171.28, though the former is itself two-edged. Cf. also *m.* 180.22 and Commentary. 'Ordinary people' in 171.28 = non-philosophers, as 172.5 shows.

Only chance and the contingent are mentioned in 172.4ff., not responsibility, discussed in XII; contrast XXIV 194.23, XXXVII 211.1-4, *m.* 184.29ff. Sharples (1980) 77. 'No more this than that' (172.7f.): i.e., there are things that do not happen in one way any more [often] than in another, that may equally well happen in either. Cf. ch. IX below, and Sharples (1975,1) 264f. and n. 48, (1978) 250f. and n. 79.

VIII. (On terminology cf. above, comm. on ch. IV.) Alexander's analysis of chance follows Aristotle very closely (cf. Aristotle *phys.* 2.5-6, *metaph.* Δ 30) as do his distinction between luck (*tuchē*) and the fortuitous (*to automaton*), the former involving human agency (cf. Aristotle *phys.* 2.6 197a36-b22), and the examples he uses (cf. Aristotle *phys.* 2.5 196b33, 2.6 197b15; *metaph.* Δ 30 1025a15; *eth. Nic.* 3.3 1112a27. Sharples (1975,2) 46 and nn. 87-9). However, there is nothing in chance so analysed that is necessarily incompatible with determinism (cf. Introduction, p. 5). There may be no *explanation* (*aitia*) of the coincidence of A's digging for another purpose in the very spot where B had buried his treasure, over and above the separate explanations of A's and B's each digging where they did (I am grateful to Professor Sorabji for this point); none the less, assuming that each of these separate events was predetermined (which is legitimate, as the question is whether or not chance *in itself* introduces freedom from determinism), B's chance finding of A's treasure is inevitable, even though inexplicable. (Cf. further below, p. 158.)

Alexander's analysis of chance events does however differ from the determinists'. Chance for him is closely connected with what is irregular and exceptional (cf. 173.13, XXIV 194.21, *m.* 185.4, *de prov.* 5.10; Sharples (1975,2) 45f. and n. 74), while the determinist position implies that in the last analysis all that happens can be subsumed under regular laws (cf. 173.16ff., and above, p. 8), thus making chance a purely subjective matter (cf. *m.* 179.6ff. The definition of luck as 'a cause obscure to human reasoning', *f.*174.2, was adopted by the Stoics – *SVF* 2.965f., 971, cf. 973 –, though it was not originated by them; cf. Aristotle *phys.* 2.4 196b5ff.). For the Peripatetic, however, the accidental cannot be reduced entirely to regular laws (cf. Introduction p. 5, and Sharples (1975,2) 59 n. 105).

Moreover, Alexander does not here emphasise the notion of chance as a coincidence of two causes – an analysis which is implied by Aristotle *metaph.* *Δ* 30 1025a27 and his own comment, *CAG* 1.438.22ff., and explicit at [Plutarch] 572c, Calcidius CLIX 192.17ff., Nemesius XXXIX *PG* 40.761bf. Rather, he concentrates on just one of the causes involved – the digging, rather than the original burying of the treasure – and stresses the fact that this in itself does not regularly produce the chance result. This emphasis on the question of regularity or its absence explains the close connection that he is able to draw between chance, the contingent and responsbility (VII 172.6ff., XXIV 194.23ff. Cf. Sharples (1975,1) 250, 259-64, 267; (1975,2) 47 and nn.).

Difficulties arise in Alexander's criticisms of the formula 'a cause obscure to human reasoning'. Luck and the fortuitous should presumably be treated analogously; but whereas in the case of the latter Alexander insists that there is believed to be no cause (or explanation), in that of the former he maintains that there is a cause but not one that in itself necessitates the result. The digging is not of course a cause of the finding of the treasure in the sense that it can provide an explanation of the generalised type with which science is concerned; that it is a cause of the finding of the treasure is only apparent in the particular case and after the event. Alexander's treatment of the fortuitous here may reflect a general tendency to assimilate accidental causes, indefinite in that they cannot be brought under any general rule, to absence of cause (cf. Sharples (1975,2) 48 and nn., and Alexander *in metaph.* *Δ* 30, *CAG* 1.483.6-17). In the present chapter the phrasing at 174.28 may be intended to mitigate the difficulty; cf. also 172.21f. and *m.* 185.4. However, the point is one on which Alexander might well have been clearer; for that chance events are not uncaused is an essential point in his argument against the determinists in XXIV 194.15ff.

The term *proēgoumenos* can be used either in the sense of 'antecedent in time' or in that of 'primary', as opposed to 'secondary' or 'accidental', this being the regular sense of the adverb *proēgoumenōs*. Both these uses are found in the *de fato*, at XXV 194.27 and XI 178.12 respectively. It is true that at VIII 173.3 the 'primary end' could be interpreted as one *envisaged in advance* (I am grateful to Professor Michael J. White for independently suggesting this), and that the application of *proēgoumenos* to intended *ends could* perhaps always be explained in this way. But it would seem misleading to interpret Alexander as claiming *just* that chance events do not have *antecedent* causes. Such a claim would not indeed be impossible (cf., perhaps, Aristotle *metaph.* *E* 3 1027a29; Sharples (1975,2) 49). But Alexander's language in the present chapter seems clearly to suggest that the central contrast is between *proēgoumena* causes and accidental ones; *proēgoumena* could only be taken to refer to *antecedent* causes in this context in the light of an established doctrine that accidental causes were not antecedent, and it might be expected that so crucial a point would be made explicit. On the whole question cf., in more detail, Sharples loc. cit.; and on the topics discussed in the present chapter cf. ibid. 46-9.

At 172.19 V's –ōs is supported by L; the double dative would be awkward, and *allōn tinōn poiētikais* seems to require qualification. 172.25: literally, 'from the significations that they supply for the things which they say come to be from luck'. At 173.17, on the above interpretation of *proēgoumenōs*, there seems to be a sort of word-play; L evades the difficulty by translating only one of the terms. The claim at 173.22 that the determinists deceive *both* themselves *and* their hearers is illogical, if interpreted in terms of *deliberate* deception (and contrast XIV 183.20); but cf. below on X 178.6. The reference back at 174.11-12 is not to 174.9-11, but to the standard examples of chance events at 172.25-173.10.

IX. Alexander appears not to distinguish between (i) examples of events which might indeed not be predetermined, and (ii) examples of alterations in things which might well be predetermined and can certainly be admitted by the Stoic theory. As I have argued at length in Sharples (1975,1) 247-67, this seems to be due to Alexander's characteristic concentration, following Aristotle, on the presence or absence of variation rather than on the question whether a particular state of affairs is necessary when *all* the relevant factors are considered. (Cf. Introduction pp. 4-6, also p. 14). An analogous argument occurs at *m.* 184.13-27; on differences in terminology between this and the present chapter cf. Sharples (1980) 86.

On *proēgoumenais aitiais* (175.12) cf. above, comm. on ch. VIII, and on *ouden mallon* (175.17) cf. the apparatus. 175.22 might alternatively be rendered 'in a similar way this too is possible, [*viz.*] both for him who is sitting ... and ...' (I am grateful to Professor Long for this point). At 176.2f. L's *impossible erat* is clearly wrong, going against the whole argument of the chapter. In 176.4 *haplōs* should be taken with *estin* rather than with *ex anankēs*; the distinction between absolute and conditional necessity has been obscured, rather than stressed, in what has preceded, and if recognised would weaken the force of Alexander's argument as an objection to a Stoic type of determinism. For Alexander's argument depends on treating the necessity of the determinist position as absolute necessity admitting of no variation. (Cf. Sharples (1975,1) 250f. n. 7). Similarly, in 176.9 *homoiōs* should be taken with *legein* rather than with *ex anankēs*.

For the argument that fate is not concerned with trivial things (175.11) cf. Cicero *de fato* 7-9 (*SVF* 2.950) and Gellius *noctes Atticae* 14.1.3f., 23ff. (of astrology). With the present chapter should be compared the more complex treatments of the contingent in the Middle-Platonists (Sharples (1978) 250f.) and in Ammonius and Boethius (R.W. Sharples, 'Temporally qualified necessity and impossibility', *Liverpool Classical Monthly* 3 (1978) 89-91).

X. (Cf. Bibliography, p. 285, under 'Stoics: possibility'.) The Stoic definitions of 'necessary' and 'possible' (*SVF* 2.201) may be interpreted in terms of a distinction between, first, what is necessary or impossible because of the nature of the thing involved, and, secondly, what is possible as far as the nature of the thing involved is concerned, but is either necessitated or rendered impossible by external factors. The definitions thus support the principle [i] attributed by Alexander to his opponents, that for a thing to be possible it must not be prevented (it must also be compatible with the nature of the thing involved, but Alexander either intends 'not prevented' to cover this too, or more probably takes this point for granted). It is also clear that the Stoics did indeed assert that some things were possible even if they would not happen (above, p. 12 and n. 66). What is however controversial is the basis on which the Stoics claimed that such things were not prevented in their determinist system. The apparent suggestion here that their theory of possibility was a purely subjective, epistemic one, basing possibility on our ignorance, is unique (Boethius *in de int.*.[2] 197.13 relates possibility to our *power*, not to our knowledge or ignorance; cf. however the epistemic Stoic theory of *chance*, above p. 132. Beothius' repeated insistence that the contingency he himself is asserting is objective and not epistemic may relate to the Stoic theory of chance; his account of the Stoic view of possibility in SVF 2.201 nowhere suggests that it depends on our ignorance.) Some critics have argued that possibility for the Stoics depended rather on the claim that the outcome has not been prevented until the preventing factors have actually come into operation – this being an objective, not a subjective, matter – even if it is predetermined that they will do so. (Cf. Reesor (1965) 293, 296, and 292 n. 20; (1978) 194; Rist 121ff.; Stough 228 n. 9.) And it has recently been emphasises that Alexander at 176.18 only refers to our ignorance as *showing* that the events in question are not prevented, not as itself constituting the absence of prevention; the point will then be that our ignorance of the preventing factors is a sign that external factors are involved, so that the outcome in question is not impossible until they come into operation. (So Reesor (1978) 194; and V. Celluprica, 'L'argomento dominatore di Diodoro Crono e il concetto di possibile di Crisippo', in G. Giannantoni (ed.), *Scuole socratiche minori e filosofia ellenistica*, Bologna, 1977, 72f.) It is true that at 177.5 Alexander does speak rather as if our ignorance *was* constitutive of possibility in the Stoic view (cf. 176.22ff.), but this may be his misrepresentation (cf. Reesor loc. cit.). It does at any rate seem that the present passage should be treated with some caution as evidence for an epistemic Stoic theory of possibility, whether Alexander himself is sincere in adopting such an interpretation or has deliberately distorted a position with which he does not sympathise. It is easier to see a connection – which seems *prima facie* likely – between an *objective* theory of possibility and human responsibility than it is in the case of epistemic possibility; a connection may indeed be drawn between human responsibility and our ignorance of factors *internal to us* (cf. Gould (1970) 152 n. 1, Donini (1974,1) 42 n. 1, both citing Spinoza); but there seems no ancient evidence for such an argument.

Alexander's objection to this first argument in X amounts to little more than restatement of his own belief in real, objective possibility (Long (1970) 256f.); but the *de fato* is a work of polemic, and if the determinist system excludes any other than subjective possibility – as Alexander presents it – so much the worse, he may well argue, for the determinist system. Ancient commentators, including Alexander, regularly represent Aristotle himself as holding (1), against Philo of Megara, that what is prevented is not possible, but also (2), against Diodorus Cronus, that things may be possible even if they will not in fact happen. (Alexander *in an pr., CAG* 2.1 184.10ff.; cf. Simplicius *in cat., CAG* 8.196.2-4, Philoponus *in an pr., CAG* 13.2.169.21, and *in de gen. et corr., CAG* 14.2.302.30ff. Cf. Aristotle *de int.* 9 19a12ff., *metaph.* Θ 5 1048a16, Θ 7 1049a6, 13.) Hintikka has argued ((1973) 201ff., cf. (1977) 36ff.) that the combination of (1) with Aristotle's view that possibilities are realised unless they are prevented (*phys.* 8.4 255a34-b11, *metaph.* Θ 5 1048a5-7) in fact implies, against (2), that what will not in fact happen is impossible; but this only follows, as Dr Schofield has pointed out to me, if one, assumes that it is already decided whether a possible future event will be prevented or not. This is not however Aristotle's way of thinking about these matters (above, p. 5; cf. especially *metaph. E* 3 1027b11f.) or Alexander's; indeed from a Peripatetic point of view the fact that the realisation of possibilities can be impeded is an argument *against*, rather than for, determinism (cf. above on IV 168.5 and on VI; Valgiglio (1967) 310 n. 8, Verbeke 82 n. 89).

In the translation I have broken up the long sentence at 176.14-24 and given the determinist argument in direct rather than reported speech. Bruns' parenthesis at 176.16-18 is perhaps intended to show that Alexander would himself accept [i] but reject [ii] (so Long (1970) 255); however true though this is, with *kekōlusthai* in 17 – more natural as parallel to *einai* in 15 – it seems more natural to place only   *dio … dunata* in parenthesis. The contrast between prevention at the time of the event and absence of prevention previously is implied by the perfect *kekōlusthai* in 17, but it can only be understood in the light of 18ff.; Long's supplement at 16 (cf. Notes on the Text, below) would therefore be obscure (and he himself tells me how he would not now propose it). 177.1-2 is not to be taken as suggesting that the determinists actually call things possible which they know are prevented; rather, since their position does, as Alexander presents it, imply that what will not happen is in fact prevented even if we do not know it, he characteristically treats the claim that things are possible, even if they will not happen, as a claim that we can call things possible even when we *know* they are prevented. (Cf. below on 178.6.) It may be noted that the suggestion at 176.27f. that, for Alexander's opponents, prophets know the causes of certain things not happening (cf. also *m.* 179.14-18) conflicts with the interpretation of Chrysippus' argument in *SVF* 2.954 as turning on the fact that divination gives information as to what will happen but *not* as to the underlying causes (below, p. 170).

The second determinist argument in X has little in common with the first (though both alike would tend to confine necessity in the future to the more obvious regularities in the world). Mignucci, 330-5, suggests a connection between this argument and that of *SVF* 2.954; but cf. id. pp. 335ff. Sorabji (1980, 1) 84 suggests that the present determinist argument may be *ad hominem* against Diodorus, who defined the necessary as what is true and will not be false (Boethius, *in de int.*² 234.25; cf. O. Becker, 'Zur Rekonstruktion des Kyrieuon Logos des Diodoros Kronos', in *Erkenntnis und Verantwortung, Festschrift für Theodor Litt*, Dusseldorf 1960) 254f).

The definition of 'necessary' as 'always true' (177.9) seems particularly appropriate when applied to sentences which refer to states of affairs at the time of utterance and are regarded as changing in truth-value with changes in the state of affairs (cf. Aristotle *cat.* 5 4a23ff., *metaph.* Θ 19 1051b13ff.; Kneale 49 n. 1, 153ff., Hintikka (1973) 63-76, 149-53). The determinist argument here turns not only on the application of this definition to sentences referring to a single, specified sea-battle, but also on the assumption that future- and past-tense sentences referring to the same event constitute different *axiōmata* the truth-values of which may be discussed separately (cf. Kneale 153ff., Hintikka (1973) 85, 152 and n. 10; my translation of *axiōma* by 'sentence' is not exact, but does not lead to any serious distortion in the present argument).

Although a parallel argument could be constructed for the non-necessity of some past events, from the fact that past-tense statements about them are false *before* the event occurs, there is no hint of this in the text – rather the reverse (cf. 177.20f.); this supports Rist's attribution of the argument to Chrysippus, who accepted the necessity of all that is past (Rist, 117), against its attribution by P.-M. Schuhl (*Le Dominateur et les Possibles*, Paris 1960, 124) and M. Frede (117) to Cleanthes, who rejected it. Cf. *SVF* 2.283, and *SVF* 2.954 p. 276.42f. with Becker loc. cit. Bruns' parallels ((1889) 613f.) between this argument and that by Chrysippus recorded by Alexander *in an. pr. CAG* 2.1.177.19ff. (*SVF*

2.202a; cf. Mignucci 317-25, Sorabji (1980, 1) 72) are not, in fact, with Chrysippus' argument but with Alexander's refutation of it (cf. *f.*177.9 with *in an. pr.* 178.19ff.; also *f.*177.16f. – from Alexander's reply – with *in an. pr.* 178.31).

SVF's emendations in 177.10f. have the advantage that 'necessary' is applied only to the propositon and 'of necessity' only to the event – the inference from the former to the latter being challenged in Alexander's reply; anticipation of this may have influenced the form in which he presents the determinist argument, the distinction between 'necessary' and 'of necessity' then being his own rather than his opponents'. (There does not seem to be any connection with the contrast between *anankaiōs* and *ex anankēs* at *q.* I.4 10.11ff.; cf. Sharples (1981) 89.) The translation given of *ouk ex anankēs de* in 177.12, rather than the alternative 'it is of necessity true that there will be a sea-battle', is supported by the application of 'of necessity' elsewhere in the chapter to events rather than to sentences.

Many details of Alexander's reply are obscure; but it seems clear, even with Bruns' *tot'* in 177.25, that Alexander *accepts* that the future-tense sentence becomes false after the event, while insisting that its consequent non-necessity does not mean that the event does not occur of necessity. *menoi* in 24 thus does not have a temporal sense. *homoiōs - legomenoi* in 25 seems to require that the sentence which *is* true before the event is not just the simple 'there will be a sea-battle' (so Bruns (1889) 616), but 'there will be a sea-battle of necessity' (177.23-4 in itself being ambiguous). The whole discussion is in any case conducted on the assumption that the sea-battle is predetermined; consequently it does not provide any direct evidence for Alexander's own position on the question whether the truth of the simple prediction 'there will be a sea-battle' is compatible with the contingency of the event (cf. Introduction, pp. 11-12), though if Alexander had held this one might have expected him to indicate the *ad homines* nature of his present argument rather more clearly. (The same applies at XVI 187.22ff., XVII 188.3; cf. also XXVII 197.12ff. and comm., *q.* I.4 11.10, 17, 12.8ff., and Sharples (1978) 264.) In the present passage *alēthes men einai dunasthai* at 177.7-8 may express Alexander's caveat; himself holding that events like sea-battles are contingent, he would himself reject the truth of the prediction.

The transition to the time after the event at 177.25ff. is probably motivated by the fact that the necessity of the past is less controversial than that of the future; admittedly it has more point if the occurrence of the sea-battle of necessity has *not* already been referred to in 22-5, but this does not seem to outweigh the considerations mentioned above. The suspicion cannot however be disregarded that at 28 Alexander, disregarding his own earlier distinctions, is appealing to the principle that it will *always* be true (after the event), and hence necessary, that the sea-battle occurred of necessity (cf. Aristotle *de int.* 9 18b10, 19a6, with the comments of C. Strang, 'Aristotle and the Sea Battle', *Mind* 69 (1960), 451; Hintikka (1973) 105, 167; D. Frede, 'Aristoteles und die "Seeschlacht" ', Göttingen 1970 (*Hypomnemata*, 27) 38-40, 49-52, 100, 103). The argument up to 177.27 shows only that an event *can* be necessary in spite of the prediction being false after the event (*ouden kekōlutai* 21f.); from 27 onwards it is argued that, if the event is predetermined, it *will* be necessary. (I am grateful to Dr Schofield for this point.) At 178.6 that the event occurs necessarily is of course (*pace* Fitzgerald) not what the determinists actually say, but Alexander's view of the implications of their position; cf. above on 177.1-2.

At 177.19, 'in which what is *necessary* is contained', one would rather expect 'what is *of necessity*'. At 177.15-16 what comes to be *of necessity* appears to *include* what is necessary, rather than being contrasted with it as in 177.16-17.

XI. The argument at 178.8-15 is repeated at *m.* 182.25ff. and by Ammonius, *in de int. CAG* 4.5.148.11ff.; cf. *m.* 173.21-5 and Boethius *in de int.*² 220.8ff. Sharples (1978) 259. For the thesis that nature does nothing in vain cf. Aristotle *de cael.* 1.4 271a33, 2.11 291b14; *de part. an.* 2.13 658a9, 3.1 661b24; *de gen. an.* 2.5 741b5, 2.6 744a36; *Politics* 1.2 1253a9, 1.8 1256b20. For the distinction here drawn in this connection between primary and secondary ends cf. *m.* 183.26, Boethius *in de int.*² 236.16, Euesbius *praep. ev.* 6.6, *PG* 21.417c; Alexander allows that there are some things with no purpose, cf. *f.* IV 167.22ff. and the doubling of leaves at XXIII 193.21. Cf. Verbeke, 87 n. 47. The terminology in which the distinction is drawn is Stoic; cf. *SVF* 2.1156-7, Epictetus *diss.* 2.8.6, and *kata parakolouthesin* in *SVF* 2.1170; also *SVF* 3.280 and Alexander *q* III. 4.87.8ff.

For the claim that reason and deliberation, the latter analysed as the power to reject first impressions or appearances (*phantasiai*, rendered 'appearances' for the sake of the argument at XV 186.6ff.) are the distinguishing characteristics of man as opposed to other living creatures (178.17-28) cf. XIV 183.30-184.11, *m.* 172.19-28, *q.*

III.13 107.6-17; compare also XXXIII 205.16ff., *q.* III.13 107.32, Alexander *de an.* 71.22ff., Aristotle *de an.*3.11 434a5ff., Ammonius *in de int.* 4.5.142.17-20. It is clear that in speaking thus of deliberation Alexander does have in mind a process that involves value judgements (cf. XIV 184.8-11 with Aristotle *eth. Nic.* 7.3 1147a5, 32; XI 178.23, 179.9, XII 180.13, 22; *m.* 172.22f.), but the emphasis is rather different from that in Aristotle's analysis of deliberation as the choice of means to an end (*eth. Nic.* 3.3 1112b15ff., *eth. Eud.* 2.10ˊ1227a12ff.; this appears only as the second alternative in the description of deliberation at XII 180.12ff.). Alexander has doubtless been influenced by Stoic emphasis on the question of our reaction to impressions (cf. below, and especially *SVF* 2.879 p. 236.3ff.; Voelke 43 and n. 4). He has certainly borrowed the terms *horme* and *sunkatathesis* from them; cf. XII 180.9, XIV 183.30ff., etc.; also Alexander *de an.* 72.14ff., 73.17ff.; *SVF* 2.72-4, 896, 3.169, 171, 175; Cicero *de fato* 40. Verbeke 88f., 100; Long (1970) 259; Todd (1976) 28, and id. 'Lexicographical notes on Alexander of Aphrodisias' philosophical terminology', *Glotta* 52 (1974) 209f.; A. Preus, 'Aristotle and the Stoics on Action and Impulse.' *Apeiron* 15 (1981) 48-56. (I am very grateful to Professor Preus for letting me see a copy of this paper in advance of publication.)

The Stoics certainly allowed, contrary to the impression that Alexander here gives of his opponents' position, that it is men's responsibility whether they assent to impressions or not (*SVF* 1.61, 2.91, 115, 974 p. 283.26ff., 992, 994, 3.177; Epictetus *ench.* 1.5, 19.1, fr. 9 (= Gellius *noct. Att.* 19.1.15f.), cf. *diss.* 1.1.7ff., 1.12.34, 1.17.21ff., 3.24.69, 4.1.69, 74; Long (1970) 259, 264, (1971) 190 and nn.; W. Görler, 'Zur Stoischen Erkenntnistheorie', *Würzburger Jahrb f. Altertumswiss.* n.f. 3 (1977) 83-92, especially 90ff.). Only, of course, this responsibility cannot be understood in a libertarian sense and hence cannot satisfy Alexander. (Cf. F.H. Sandbach, '*Phantasia katalēptikē*', in A.A. Long (ed.), *Problems in Stoicism* (London 1971) 14f.) The Stoics also stressed the difference in this respect between men and animals (below, p. 144). It is true that they did not lay great emphasis on choice between alternative courses of action – to have to consider how to act is a sign of weakness, alien to the sage (Rist 15, Long (1976) 91f., Lloyd 245). They did however allow for the formation of impressions by mental processes; *SVF* 2.61, 83, 87, 223 p. 74.6f. (I am grateful to Professor Todd for this reference), 3.72; Seneca *ep.* 120.4, *de ira* 2.3f.; Epictetus *diss.* 1.6.10. Voelke 61-65; A.

Graeser, *Plotinus and the Stoics* (Leiden 1972) 49. Alexander therefore misrepresents their position by his emphasis on *external sense*-impressions (*prospiptousai exōthen*, XIV 184.3, XV 186.7; cf. XI 178.19, XV 185.18ff.), as had Cicero (cf. *extrinsecus* at *SVF* 2.974 p. 283.20, and his rendering of *phantasia* by *visum* (*SVF* 1.55)). Cf. also *SVF* 2.988 p. 288.2ff. and Long (1976) 81; and below p. 149.

More generally, Alexander is wrong to assume that determinism implies that deliberation will make no difference to our actions (179.17-23, cf. XII 181.3-5); it is perfectly compatible with determinism that deliberation should lead us to decide against the course of action that initially appeared favourable, only it will be predetermined that it should do so. The classification at 178.28ff. is based on that at Aristotle *eth. Nic.* 3.3 1112a21ff. (cf. also *p.* XXIX 160.5ff.; Sharples (1978) 265 n. 229); there as elsewhere Alexander is concerned with freedom of *action* rather than with freedom of choice, and Alexander's dependence on Aristotle here may, as Dr Lloyd has pointed out to me, have reinforced his tendency to assume that if the outcome is predetermined our deliberation must be irrelevant to it. Deliberation is concerned with what admits of being otherwise (Aristotle *eth. Nic.* 3.3 1112b2, 6.1 1139b7ff., 6.5 1140a31ff.; Alexander *p.* XXIX 160.15) as is choice (below XII 180.7ff.; Aristotle *eth. Nic.* 3.2 1111b31ff., cf. 6.2 1139b5). At *de int.* 9 18b31 Aristotle argues that, if predictions are true or false before the event, there is no need for deliberation; this is a relevant point as far as the paradox of future truth with its allegedly *fatalistic* implications is concerned, but does not necessarily apply in the context of a non-fatalistic causal determinism. Cf. G.E.M. Anscombe, 'Aristotle and the Sea Battle', in J.M.E. Moravcsik (ed.), *Aristotle* (London 1968) 22; above p. 10 and nn. 50f.

At 179.2 'both being done by us and future' might be rendered 'both being done by us and will be done'; but it seems probable that deliberation, like possibility, applies only to the future and not also to the present. Cf. *m.* 173.3ff., *f.* XXVII 197.12ff., Aristotle *de int.* 9 18a28, 19a23, and *rhet.* 3.17 1418a2-5 (but contrast *de cael.* 1.12 283b13f.); cf. also *eth. Nic.* 6.2 1139b7f. Hintikka (1973) 183. Cf. also [Plutarch] 571d with the comments of de Lacy – Einarson, 334 n. (a), and Valgiglio (1964) 38.). At 179.24ff. the obvious exceptions are the Epicureans. Bruns' doubts about 179.23-180.2 probable stem from its repeating (178.8-15; but cf. the rather pedantic presentation of the parallel argument at *m.* 183.25-9.

XII. The definition of choice at 180.8f. is based on Aristotle's at *eth. Nic.* 3.3 1113a10 (cf. 6.2 1139b4), but cast in terminology borrowed from the Stoics (above p. 23). 180.14-20 echoes *eth. Nic.* 3.3 1112b23f., 180.19 probably refers to the starting point of the action as the last point reached in the deliberation (cf. Aristotle *eth. Nic.* 3.3 1112b23f., *eth. Eud.* 2.11 1227b23f.) rather than to the agent as initiating the action (cf. XIV 184.16, XV 185.15, and below p. 146). The latter idea would be introduced very abruptly; the neuter would be awkward (though less so without *hauto*); and the reference to *tēn zētēsin* in 18f. tends to support the former view (Donini (1969) 305f.). With the former interpretation one might rather, as Dr Lloyd has pointed out to me, expect *praxeōs*. Verbeke 89 n. 53 takes the reference to be to that *in* man which is the starting point of action (cf. *eth. Nic.* 3.3 1113a6, *magna moralia* 1.11 1187b5); for this, as Donini points out, *eph 'hautou ho* would be more natural.

That a deterministic analysis of deliberation does not do justice to our intuitions (180.20, 26; cf. Nemesius *de nat. hom.* XXXVII, *PG* 40.753a) is perhaps Alexander's strongest argument (though not one that his opponents would accept); cf. *m.* 174.39f., Origen in *SVF* 2.989 p. 289.13ff., Oenomaus ap. Eusebius *praep. ev.* 6.7, *PG* 21.436cff. (Zeller-Alleyne, 296 and n. 2); M.Y. Henry, 'Cicero's treatment of the free will problem', *Trans. Amer. Philol. Assoc.* 58 (1927) 32-42. The argument at 180.24f. that it is strange that nature should have caused the majority of men to err on this question, gains its force from the Stoics' belief in a *providential* determinism (G.L. Fonsegrive, *Libre arbitre* (Paris 1887) 76; cf. Ammonius *in de int. CAG* 4.5.137.25-138.10. A further argument used by Ammonius, but not by Alexander, is to question the point of our being made to go through a predetermined process of deliberation; ibid. 148.24ff.). With the reference to advisers at 181.2ff. cf. *m.* 182.28f., 183.32ff., *q.* III.13 108.11ff.; Aristotle *eth. Nic.* 3.3 1112b10f. Mras interprets Eusebius' *toisde* at 181.2 in the sense of 'certain particular advisers (rather than others)' (n. ad loc.).

XIII. This determinist account of responsibility is very similar to one attributed by Nemesius (*SVF* 2.991) to Chrysippus and Philopator (a Stoic of the second century A.D.; Theiler 66f.). For other parallel arguments in later authors cf. Sharples (1978) 253-8. The examples of the natural behaviour of various types of thing used here (182.8ff.; cf. XIV 183.11ff., 184.16ff., 185.3f.) are used by Alexander to characterise the determinist position elsewhere in the

treatise too (cf. XI 179.15ff., XIX 189.21f., XXXVI 208.6f., 23ff.;
Sharples (1978) 253 n. 109, 255 n. 131) and are coupled at XI
179.15ff. with the familiar Chrysippean example of the cylinder
(above p. 9; cf. also XIX 189.22, 208.24). Though there are
affinities between the present argument and the cylinder argument
(cf. Sharples (1978) 253 n. 112), the present argument differs on the
face of it by stressing the *difference* between the behaviour of living
creatures in accordance with impulse and that of inanimate objects,
whereas the cylinder argument rather turns on an *analogy* between
the two. It may indeed be that it is Alexander who has laid
particular emphasis on the contrast between living creatures and
inanimate objects in the present argument, since this is the first
point he will attack in ch. XIV; it is rather less prominent in
Nemesius' account of the Stoic position. Nevertheless, it seems likely
that the present argument and the cylinder-argument were
originally distinct, though related. Cf. further below, XXXIV
205.24ff., and Sharples (1978) 253-6.

For impulse (*hormē*) as characteristic of living creatures cf. *SVF*
2.714, 844, 988, 3.178; cf. the classifications of different types of
motion at *SVF* 2.499, 714, 988f., and compare also *SVF* 1.158, 2.458,
716, and 1013 p. 302.36ff. The subjects of *epicheirousin* in 181.9 are
identified in 10-12 with those described in ch. VIII as holding that all
things are in accordance with fate (cf. 173.20ff., especially 24; above
pp. 20-1 and n. 136); they are presumably therefore either identical
with, or a group among, *tous ... legontas* in 181.8, though the
expression is odd. The Stoics do of course allow the power of choice
between opposites (181.7-14); what they do not allow is free choice
as a libertarian would understand it. The expression *di' hēmōn* at
181.14 is probably not the determinists' own (Theiler, 66, suggested
it was Philopator's), but rather a reflection of libertarian criticism;
cf. Long (1970) 268 and n. 54, Sharples (1970) 254f. and nn. 124,
134. At 182.2 the first *mē* might be deleted rather than the second
(for the sense so given cf. *SVF* 2.974 p. 283.17-23); but this gives a
less forceful sense. 182.14, too, probably refers not to the external
factors' being necessary conditions for the outcome, but rather to
the inevitability of their being present; cf. 181.24, 30f., XXXIV
206.11, XXXVI 208.21. This gives a more natural sense to *hōste*. 'The
things brought about through living creatures' probably include not
only their actions but also the consequences of those actions (cf. XIV
183.11-15).

XIV. Alexander's first objection, that the determinist argument allows no real difference between living creatures and inanimate objects, would be rejected by his opponents, but is valid enough from his own libertarian standpoint; for him all other differences are insignificant besides the fact that in a determinist system the behaviour of living creatures and inanimate objects alike is predetermined (above, p. 20). Secondly, he objects that the determinists do not locate responsibility in *rational* assent. The Stoics certainly emphasised that men, unlike irrational animals, have the power of refusing assent to initial impressions (cf. above p. 140, and, for the contrast with animals, Epictetus *diss.* 1.6.12ff., 2.8.7f., Marcus Aurelius 3.16, and *SVF* 2.714, 2.988 p. 288.8ff. Gould (1974) 22, 26; G.B. Kerferd, 'The origin of evil in Stoic thought', *Bull. John Rylands Lib.* (Manchester) 60 (1978) 488). Reason is characteristic of man (*SVF* 2.879 p. 236.10, 2.1153; O. Rieth, *Grundbegriffe der Stoischen Ethik* (*Problemata*, 9; Berlin 1933) 160); indeed for the Stoics *all* human impulse and action is rational (*SVF* 3.169, 175; Alexander *m.* 118.6 (*SVF* 2.823); cf. J. Brunschwig, 'Le modèle conjonctif', in *Les stoiciens et leur logique, actes du colloque de Chantilly* (Paris 1978) 70-2). Alexander seems at the least guilty of a certain distortion in the present passage, by his neglect of the Stoics' emphasis on human reason (cf. Long (1970) 264f. and n. 45, and contrast XXXIV 205.28); if indeed the Stoics did regard man's power of reasoned witholding of assent as constitutive of his responsibility, Alexander has grossly misrepresented their position.

Professor Terence Irwin has pointed out to me that emphasis is laid on this power in the account of responsbility in *SVF* 2.974 (p.283.27). It is not however stressed in *SVF* 2.991 (on which cf. above p. 142 and Sharples (1978) 255) or *SVF* 2.1000. The Stoics do indeed hold that the giving or refusing of assent depends on us (above p. 140); but this is rather different from asserting that it is this that *constitutes* responsibility. Alexander has a clear motive for confining responsibility to rational human beings, in that he associates reason closely with the power of choosing between alternatives (XI 178.17ff., XIV 183.30ff., 184.18f., XXXIII 205.16-20; Sharples (1978) 259 n. 173; above, pp. 22, 127-8); but it is not clear that the Stoics would have the same motive. Possibly they did regard the actions of animals as depending on them, but in a different sense from that in which the actions of men depend on *them*; so that only rational action (and all human action is rational, cf. above) depends

on, or 'is attributable to', men *as men*; this is suggested by Stough
229 n. 21. If so, Alexander has not *totally* misrepresented the Stoic
position, though he has given a very incomplete and partial account
of it. Cf. Long (1970) 263f.

Alexander throughout speaks as if irrational animals, both in the
Stoic view and in his own, have the power of giving assent (cf.
183.31, and *q*. III.13 107.8ff.); what they lack is the power of
withholding it. That animals do indeed assent for the Stoics is
suggested by *SVF* 2.115 and by *SVF* 2.991 p. 290.28 (cf. above), and
less certainly by the definitions of perception in *SVF* 2.72, 74 (since
it may here only be human perception that is in question). That
assent is confined to man, however, is suggested by *SVF* 2.714 and
3.169 (ii).

Alexander's contrast between responsible and voluntary action at
183.24ff. (cf. *p*. XXIX 159.33f., *tōn hekousiōn tauta to eph' hēmin echei, hosa
esti prohaireta*; also *f*. XXXIII 205.15f., *q*. III.13 107.6-8) is at first sight
reminiscent of that drawn by Aristotle between deliberate choice and
voluntary action (*eth. Nic.* 3.2 1111b8, *eth. Eud.* 2.8 1223b38, 2.10
1226b34, *magna moralia* 1.17 1189b1; cf. Preus, above p. 140); in each
case the latter includes, but is wider than, the former. However,
Aristotle regards men as responsible for all their actions, not just
those resulting from deliberate choice, and links responsibility (*to eph'
hēmin*) and voluntary action, connecting both with possibility for
opposites (cf. *eth. Nic.* 3.1 1111a17, 3.5 1113b7, 21; and cf. Nemesius
de nat. hom. XL, *PG* 40.768a). J.M. Rist suggests that Alexander
connects responsibility with *reason* because he regards the reason as
the truly human self (cf. above pp. 127-8; J.M. Rist, 'Prohairesis:
Proclus, Plotinus et alii', in *De Jamblique à Proclus, Entretiens Hardt* 21
(Geneva 1975) 107); cf. also Verbeke, 90 and n. 57. Alexander indeed
probably wishes to argue, not that responsibility is confined to cases
where we do in fact deliberate, but rather that the fact that we are
rational and can deliberate shows that we are responsible for all our
actions, whether or not we actually deliberate on any particular
occasion. The difference between his position and Aristotle's, as far as
the responsibility of human beings (as opposed to that of irrational
animals and children) is concerned, is thus one of emphasis and
presentation rather than of substance. That animals and children, as
well as adults, are responsible for their behaviour in Aristotle's view is
suggested by *eth. Nic.* 3.1 1111a25f. (though, as Professor Irwin has
pointed out to me, in *eth. Eud.* voluntary action is analysed in terms of

146 *Commentary*

'thought', *dianoia*, which suggests the contrary; *eth. Eud.* 2.8 1224a5ff., 2.9 1225a37ff.). Alexander's position in the present chapter certainly seems to imply that animals and children are *not* responsible; but this point should not perhaps be pressed. Nor can 183.24-6 be pressed to the point of suggesting that the determinist position *can* provide an accurate account of *voluntary* as opposed to responsible, action; for this would undermine the first objection, at 182.31-183.21. Alexander is probably influenced at 183.27f. by Aristotle's emphasis on absence of external compulsion as a criterion for voluntary action (cf. p. 6 and n. 22); but Aristotle was not arguing in the context of a discussion of determinism, as Alexander is, and by the distinction that he draws between voluntary and responsible action Alexander puts himself in a position which risks being paradoxical if pressed.

ex anankēs ... autou at 183.8 probably refers, not to the impulse's being a necessary condition of the action, but to the action's occurring of necessity (cf. XIII 182.13-16); this gives a better force to *men ... de*. At 183.21 Hackforth's *<ou> koinōnian* refers to the determinists' restriction of responsibility to living creatures, regarded by Alexander as arbitrary in the context of their system; but the MSS reading can be taken to refer to the fact that the determinist position shares the *term* with the popular view, while not sharing its interpretation. At 185.5 the point is probably not that, since we have the power to deliberate or not, *a fortiori* we have the power to deliberate in a certain way (cf. *q.* III.13 107.25-37), but rather that, if all were determined, the power of deliberation would be useless (cf. Schwartz's reading in 185.7, and above pp. 141-2).

XV. The claim that man is the starting-point of his actions picks up XIV 184.15ff.; hence the somewhat anomalous introduction here of what is a defence of Alexander's own position rather than an attack on his opponents (cf. Introduction, p. 17). The doctrine is Aristotelian (*eth. Nic.* 3.3 1112b31, cf. 1113a5; 3.5 1113b18; *eth. Eud.* 2.6 1222b15ff.; cf. *eth. Nic.* 6.2 1139b5, *de int.* 9 19a8. That the starting-point of the action is in the agent is a criterion for voluntary action; cf. above p. 6 and n. 22; *eth. Nic* 3.1 1110a17, b4; *eth. Eud.* 2.8 1224b10; Alexander *p.* XI 131.1, XII *passim*, XXIX 159.12-28). From Alexander's general position it seems clear that the claim here is to be understood in a libertarian rather than in a soft-determinist way, as it probably is in Aristotle too (above, p. 7; cf. further below).

It may however be questioned how far this argument really provides any escape from the dilemma of determinism or uncaused motion (above, p. 22. No distinction appears to be drawn between 'the occurrence of *something* without a cause' and 'the occurrence of *motion* without a cause'; cf. 185.9 with 185.14, *m*. 170.3 with *m*. 170.7). The determinist thesis, in the classical form in which it is advanced by the Stoics, claims that the state of the world at any time is necessitated by its state at any and every other time (the position of Laplace; cf. *SVF* 2.921, 944; Sambursky, 56). Accordingly, either there must at some point be an occurrence not entirely determined by what has preceded, the causal chain being broken (cf. *m*. 185.6-8), or else there will be no possibility of real freedom of action in the sense that would satisfy a libertarian; and, since in the latter case the outcome is determined by the state of the world at *any* time beforehand, the dilemma applies even if we cannot identify all the alleged causal connections, particularly where mental processes are involved. It is none the less the case, either that the outcome is determined by the state of the universe at any time beforehand, or that it is not. The only way of resolving the dilemma would be to attack the whole approach to causation on which the determinist position is based; both in the present context and elsewhere the position of Aristotle and Alexander may be held to contain the beginnings of such an alternative approach (above, p. 5), but it can hardly be said that Alexander gives adequate attention in the *de fato* to the analysis of causation as such – even in chs. XXII-XXV, between which and the present chapter no explicit link is drawn – or that he is fully conscious of the significance of the difference between his approach and his opponents'; the impression gives is rather of an uncritical acceptance of Aristotelian positions, and of a series of debating points rather than a detailed examination of the issue. Cf. O'Connor, 81-109; and on the Aristotelian notion of 'cause' cf. further below, pp. 154, 157; D.J. Furley, 'Self movers', in G.E.R. Lloyd and G.E.L. Owen (eds.), *Aristotle on Mind and the Senses* (Cambridge 1978) 165-79.

The present discussion is very similar to one attributed to Carneades in Cicero *de fato* (23-5). In each case however the analogies used follow naturally from the preceding discussion – Cicero's from criticism of the Epicurean atomic swerve (22f.), Alexander's from criticism of the determinist argument in XIII (cf. 185.28-31 with XIII 181.26ff., 182.16ff.; also 185.17 with XI 179.16,

XIX 189.22, XXXVI 208.24). Moreover, for Cicero the cause is the nature of voluntary action, rather than the agent (25). Alexander may have known of Carneades' argument (cf. also below on 185.11); but if so either he or Cicero's source, or perhaps both, has considerably re-worked it. And Alexander's argument is also inspired by Aristotle (cf. above).

Comparison with XIV 184.16ff. shows that Hackforth's supplement in 185.17 is unnecessary; Alexander is drawing an *analogy* between the sphere's rolling and the human agent's being a starting-point of actions, even though the latter is free and the former is not (so Rodier 67, Valgiglio (1967) 312 n. 12). Both in the present chapter (185.11) and in Cicero *de fato* 24 the point is made that human action does not have an external cause; this *could* be taken to imply merely that internal factors are decisive rather than external ones, the outcome still being predetermined, and this the Stoics could accept (above, p. 9). However, it seems that in both cases more than this is intended; Cicero denies that human choices have *antecedent* causes (23 fin.), and it may well be argued that in a determinist system all causes are ultimately external (above, p. 20 and n. 135). For Cicero's opposition to determinism cf. his *de fato* 19, 28, 33ff. Alexander's stress on freedom from external causes here picks up his complaint that, according to his opponents, men follow external impressions like the animals (XI 178.18f., XII 180.5-7, XIV 183.21-184.11, XV 186.5); cf. above p. 20 and n. 133. At 186.1 *autois* gives better force to *gar* in 185.28; *allois* would imply only that we act differently in different circumstances, which would be compatible with determinism (It does however seem to be no more than this that is claimed in *m.* 174.35ff.) It is doubtful whether 185.18-21 should be taken to imply that human agency is the *only* exception to determinism in Alexander's view (Amand, 140-3); cf. pp. 129, 156, 158. It follows on closely from the connection of possibility for alternatives with reason at XIV 184.18f. (above, p. 144).

At 185.21-8 Alexander discusses the problem of the determination of action by its end. This may seem a totally different matter from determination by antecedent causes; however, our conceptions of the ends of action may be regarded as antecedent, efficient causes of our actions even though the ends themselves are not (cf. Hocutt (op. cit, on p. 126) 398), and for Aristotle it is our character that determines our conception of the end (*eth. Nic.* 3.5 1114b1, 6.12 1144a7, 7.8 1151a15; Alexander *m.* 175.9ff., 183.14ff., *p.* IX 129.31ff.,

XXIX 158.20ff., 161.3-4). Nor is much achieved by arguing that our actions are determined under their description as physical events though free under their description as actions. Cf. O'Connor 99-109. Alexander's introduction of the noble, the pleasant and the advantageous as ends of action has an Aristotelian basis (cf. *eth. Nic.* 2.3 1104b30). It may also be Aristotelian to hold that these are irreducible alternatives which cannot be measured against each other in terms of some further end (that such a view is Aristotelian is denied by Donini (1974,2) 176-9; but see now M.F. Burnyeat, 'Aristotle on learning to be good', in *Essays on Aristotle's Ethics*, ed. A.O. Rorty (Berkeley, 1981), 86ff. and nn.; cf. also D. Wiggins, 'Weakness of will, commensurability, and the objects of deliberation and desire', *Proc. Ar. Soc.* 1978-9, 266ff. and nn.). But it is not clear how any *rational* account of a man's choosing to pursue one of these ends rather than another could be given, except in terms of his view of them in relation to some further end superior to them all – 'happiness', *eudaimonia* – which simply reintroduces the problem of the determination of action by its end, or else in terms of earlier conditioning (cf. Burnyeat, 85), which raises the problem of the regress discussed below in connection with ch. XXVII.

Finally (186.3-12) Alexander argues that the claim that all assent is to 'what appears' does not mean that all assent is to external 'appearances'. For the distinction here drawn one may compare Alexander *de anima* 73.7ff. (I am grateful to Professor Todd for this reference); *q.* III.13 108.1ff.; *p.* XXIX 161.3ff. (where read *host'<ei>* *alēthes* in 3 and delete *ei* in 4; *alēthes ... autos aitios* (3-4) and *alēthes de ... heautōi* (5) are the two premisses leading to *alēthes estai* etc. (5ff.), the argument being an application of Chrysippus' 'first undemonstrated argument', *modus ponendo ponens; SVF* 2.242 p. 80.28-81.1). However, the Stoics themselves allowed a distinction between 'appearances' (*phantasiai*) directly resulting from sense-perception and those produced by operations of the mind (above p. 140; cf. especially with the present passage *SVF* 2.223 p. 74.6f. I am grateful to Professor Todd for this reference.) The present passage is a defence of Alexander's own position rather than an attack on the determinist one; nevertheless, the impression given here and in what has preceded (above p. 141) that the distinction here drawn is one that the Stoics failed to recognise is scarcely a fair one. Alexander might wish to claim that the mind is free in formulating *phainomena* in a way that it cannot be for the Stoics; but he gives no account of how this is so. And since his defence here draws a distinction that the Stoics already recognised, the objection at 186.3-5 is probably not an authentic Stoic argument but may be one formulated by Alexander himself for the sake of his reply (cf. below, p. 159).

XVI. For the general character of Alexander's arguments in chs. XVI-XXI cf. Introduction p. 17, also p. 13 and n. 73. They frequently involve the erroneous assumption that determinism implies that our actions cannot affect the course of events (cf. Introduction p. 10); so at XVI 186.30ff., XVII 181.1-11, XIX 198.1-2, XXI 191.16f., 21ff.; n.b. especially *argoteroi* in 191.21 (above, p. 10). This might be explained by Alexander's having taken over arguments of Carneades directed against *astrological* determinism, which does have fatalistic imperfections; but one may compare similar assumptions made by Alexander elsewhere too (cf. pp. 141, 171). Alexander's arguments also depend for their force in the interpretation of responsibility in a libertarian, rather than a soft-determinist sense; cf. XVIII 188.22-189.4, 189.6f., XIX 189.16ff., XX 190.25ff.

The incompatibility of praise, blame, punishment and reward with determinism (XVI 187.8-30, XVIII 188.22-189.4, XIX 189.11-190.19, XX 190.26ff.) was a standard anti-determinist argument, no doubt popularised by Carneades but going back even earlier: cf. Epicurus *ad Menoeceum* 133 (and compare id. *On Nature*, 31.22.1ff., 31.27.2ff.), Cicero *de fato* 40 (attributed to Epicurus by P.M. Huby, *Phronesis* 15, 1970, 83-5), and *SVF* 2.1000 p. 294.30ff., which suggests Chrysippus already had to meet the argument; cf. ibid. 293.34ff. Praise and blame are connected with responsible action by Aristotle *eth. Nic.* 3.1 1109b31, 3.5 1113b23ff., *magna moralia* 1.9 1187a19ff.; and compare Plato *Protagoras* 323cff. The Stoics did indeed insist, on the basis of their soft-determinist notion of responsibility, that praise, blame, punishment and reward were compatible with determinism (cf. SVF loc. cit., and below XXXIV 206.1f.; also Introduction pp. 8-9), but this Alexander rejects. The point that punishment will itself be predetermined (XVI 187.12ff.) was made by Zeno, who must have been asserting its compatibility with determinism (*SVF* 1.298; cf. Eusebius *praep. ev.* 6.6, *PG* 21.416a, and, for comic effect, Plautus *Aulularia* 743. I am grateful to Professors Richard Sorabji and E.W. Handley for these references.)

With 186.18 cf. Eusebius *praep. ev. PG* 21.413b, St. John Chrysostom *hom.* VIII, *PG* 63.510.33ff., and Ammonius *in de int. CAG*

4.5.150.23f.; Amand, 573f. At 186.21 the MSS *echontas*, followed by Rodier, would suggest that the determinists' actual possession of freedom (as opposed to what they *say*) makes it impossible to persuade them to act otherwise than they do; with Bruns' *echontes* the meaning is rather that they cannot be persuaded to act in any way other than one which, in Alexander's view, can only rest on their assuming that they are in fact free, contrary to what they say. (On either view the reference is probably to such behaviour as that described at XVII 188.20ff.; cf. Introduction p. 18 and n. 104, and, for Alexander's readiness to speak as if his opponents shared assumptions which are in fact only his own, cf. above on X 177.1-2, 178.6.) The sense with Bruns' reading seems clearer and more to the point; but on either view there is no close connection between 20-3 and what follows after 23. Rather, 23ff. takes up *echonton ... echei* in 20, and 20-3 offers a purely incidental argument in support of that. *kalon* in 187.2 is supported by 186.31-187.1. (The belief that our *actions* are predetermined would *not* of course be a logical reason for our failing to act on the grounds that the *outcome* is predetermined whatever our action; on Alexander's confusion here see above.) The reference to Menelaus at 187.20 is unsupported by anything in 16-18. On *prolegomenon* in 187.23 cf. above, p. 138. At 187.26 Bruns' suggestion involves an idea introduced already (XIII 181.14), Amand's one only introduced later (XXXIV 205.29 init.); in Apelt's version the 'if'-clause seems redundant. 187.28-30 is unfair as an objection against the Stoics themselves (see above); cf. XIX 190.17, where it is stressed that the determinists do not themselves regard this as an excuse.

XVII. For the incompatibility of determinism with prayer cf. [Plutarch] 574d fin., Nemesius *de nat. hom.* XXXVIII *PG* 40.756a-757a, Theiler 46n.1; with providence, Nemesius loc. cit. and Calcidius CLXXV 203.9ff. Alexander here interprets both prayer and providence in terms of the gods' intervening in the course events would otherwise take; Valgiglio (1967) 312 n. 13 well contrasts Cleanthes' view of prayer as submission to the divine will (*SVF* 1.527). Cf. above, Introduction pp. 21, 27, for the dialectical nature of Alexander's argument here.

Prophecy itself only implies that we have no freedom to act (188.11ff.) when the prophecy is categorical, not when it is conditional (cf. below, XXXI comm.). But here as elsewhere Alexander is probably confusing determinism and fatalism (above,

XVI comm.). At 188.12 Rodier and Donini object to Schwartz that it is not the possibility, but the utility of learning from prophets that is in question; but *mathoi* seems a possible way of expressing this.

XVIII. Cf. above, XVI comm., and p. 17. That the Stoics did themselves apply the doctrine of co-fated events (p. 10) in the context of education (cf. 189.2) is suggested by Caldidius (*SVF* 2.943).

XIX. Cf. XVI comm. With 189.16f. cf. Introduction p. 6 and n. 22; for 189.21ff. cf. XIII comm., and for the rendering 'thrown' cf. *SVF* 2.1000 p. 294.17 and [Aristotle] *de mundo* 6 398b28. Phalaris (189.26) was tyrant of Acragas in Sicily and a by-word for cruelty; cf. Aristotle *eth. Nic.* 7.5 1148b24, *SVF* 3.535, 586. At 190.9 the suggestion that the external factors could be evaded is purely rhetorical; contrast 189.19, XIII 181.24, 182.14, XXXIV 206.21-24.

XX-XXI. Ch. XX summarises the argument of XVI-XIX; XXI is added, not so much as an afterthought but as a *tour de force*. With XXI may be compared Pascal's wager concerning the existence of God (Boussoulas, op. cit. in p. 19 n. 118, 206 n. 1).

XXII. For Stoic emphasis on the unity of the universe cf. *SVF* 2.441, 470, 473, 475 (all from Alexander's *de mixtione*), also 2.447f., 533, 546, 1013; for its connection with determinism cf. [Plutarch] 574e (*SVF* 2.912). Cf. also below XXXVII 210.15ff.; and for Stoic denial of causeless motion cf. Introduction p. 8 n. 37 fin. That nothing can come from nothing (192.15) is a familiar principle in Greek philosophy; cf. Parmenides, fr. 8 (28B8 Diels-Kranz) 7ff., Aristotle *physics* 1.8 191a30, Lucretius 1.146ff. The identification of fate with god at 192.25ff. (cf. also 191.31f.) is authentically Stoic (cf. Introduction p. 8 n. 39), as is the presence of god in each thing (192.26f.; above p. 8 n. 40); this latter point is prominent in *de mixtione* XI (below, p. 156) but is not stressed in the *de fato*. Cf. Introduction, p. 20. For fate's employing of each thing (192.27f.) cf. XXXI 203.12ff., XXXVI 208.3ff.; and for the subordination of the part to the whole (ibid.) cf. *SVF* 2.1176. *echein ten ... dioikesin* at 191.32f. is probably, in spite of *SVF* 2.528, p. 169.33, to be interpreted not as equivalent to *dioikein* (active) but rather in the sense of 'has in itself the organisation'; though indeed for the Stoics the active and passive principles in the universe are always inseparable in fact. For the term cf. 191.31f., 192.12, 16, XXXI 203.19, 24, XXXVII 210.15; *SVF* 2.416, 534, 912f. For fate as a *heirmos*

(192.1) cf. XXV 195.19, 196.2, *m.* 185.5; *SVF* 2.917f., 921 (*series*), 946. Alexander is justified from his own point of view in passing over his opponents' distinctions between different types of cause (192.17ff.), for, even though such distinctions are central to the Stoics' soft-determinist defence of responsibility (above, p. 9), from Alexander's libertarian point of view the important feature of the determinist position is that it is still true of every type of cause that, if all the other factors involved are the same, the same result must always follow. (At *m.* 174.3 the reference is rather to 'similar' circumstances; Long (1971) 188 and n. 51 relates the mention of 'the same' circumstances to the Stoic doctrine of the cyclical recurrence of events, but even if this is correct and it is not just a loose way of speaking it does not seem that the deterministic implications of the thesis are in any way diminished. Cf. *SVF* 1.109, 2.596-632; J. Barnes, 'La doctrine du retour éternel', in *Les stoïciens et leur logique* (Actes du colloque de Chantilly, Paris 1978, 3-20; Sorabji, (1980, 1) 119). For *hoi estin aition* (192.23) cf. *SVF* 2.349; the knife is the cause *to* the flesh *of* being cut.

Alexander's list of causes at 192.18f. is identical, except for the presence of *hektika* rather than *sunerga*, to lists at [Galen] *hist. philos.* 19 (*Dox.* 611.8ff.) and Clement of Alexandria *strom.* 8.9, *PG* 9.600c (*SVF* 2.351); cf. also id. 592c (*SVF* 2.346: *prokatarktika, sunektika, sunerga, hōn ouk aneu*) and [Basil] *spir. sanct. PG* 32.76ab (the same but with *sunaitia* not *sunektika*). These lists are themselves, according to Pohlenz , the result of a conflation of two classifications: (i) into *prokatarktika* and *sunektika* causes (cf. the Stoic distinction between *prokatarktika* and *autotele* causes – Chrysippus' cylinder argument, *SVF* 2.974, and *SVF* 2.994, 997, Seneca *epist.* 87.31 (Posidonius); *sunektika* and *autotelē* causes are identified, Clement *strom.* 8.9, *PG* 9.592c, 600d (*SVF* 2.346, 351)); and (ii) one into *sunektika, sunaitia* and *sunerga* (Sextus Empiricus *Pyrrh. hyp.* 3.15; cf. Clement *strom.* 1.20, *PG* 8.816bc (*SVF* 2.352)). In general, for ancient classifications of causes cf. also Galen *De causis pulsuum* 1.1, IX.1ff. Kühn, [Galen] *def. med.* XIX 392f. Kühn (*SVF* 2.354); O. Rieth (op. cit. on p. 144) 134-55; Pohlenz 1.209ff. and n. 11, and id. 'Grundfragen der Stoischen Philosophie', *Abh. Göttingen* phil.-hist. kl. 3.26 (1940) 104-12; J. Kollesch, *Untersuchungen zu den Pseudogalenischen Definitiones medicae* (Berlin 1973) 119-24; M. Frede, 'The original notion of cause', in *Doubt and Dogmatism: Studies in Hellenistic Epistemology,* eds. M. Schofield, M. Burnyeat, J. Barnes, Oxford 1980, 215-49, especially 234ff.

Alexander's reference here to *hektika* causes is however apparently unique. Rieth 67ff. discusses uses of the term *hektikos*, suggesting that air and fire are *sunektika aitia* for the other elements but *hektika aitia* for themselves. His argument here is based in particular on *SVF* 2.444 p. 146.35; however, Pohlenz there read *sunektika* not *hektika*, and a comparable distinction does not always seem to be observed (cf. *SVF* 2.440 p. 145.2; 2.444 p. 146.32; 2.716 p. 205.20; Galen *caus. cont.*, *Corp. Med. Graec.* suppl. orient. 2.137.16f.). Cf. also, with Rieth loc. cit., *SVF* 2.392 (*hektikas* Kalbfleisch for *hektas*), 3.510; in the latter passage *hektikos* has the force of 'habitual', 'settled' (cf. Liddell-Scott-Jones, *A Greek-English Lexicon*, s.v.). In connection with the rendering 'sustaining' it may be noted that medical writers stress that the growth and decline of the *sunektikon* cause is contemporaneous with that of the disease it causes: cf. [Galen], *Dox.* 611.9-11, [Galen] *def. med.* XIX 393.5f. Kühn, and Pohlenz 'Grundfragen' 108 n. 2.

At 192.14 a more accurate translation would be 'did not have certain (i.e. some, not here specified, as opposed to none) causes'; but I have omitted 'certain' to avoid ambiguity.

XXIII. Alexander interprets the production of effects in a peculiarly Aristotelian way, the prime example being the production of one living creature by another (above, p. 128). The determinists do, according to Alexander, say that everything is the cause of some*thing* after it (*ti*, 192.4, 7), which seems to rule out the defence that they are only claiming that everything must be *taken into account* in inferring a later state of affairs from an earlier (but cf. XXII 192.9-11, 18ff, for factors which have no effect on an outcome, XXXVI 209.18ff. and comm., *q.* I.4 10.29f.). However, for the Stoics a body is the cause of an incorporeal predicate to another body (*SVF* 2.341, 349; cf. Reesor (1965) 287 n. 4), and it might seem that Alexander's objections could be met by the argument that the effect of a fruit drying up is (e.g.) the greater opportunity for other plants to grow in a particular place. There may indeed be *some* cases where there is no detectable result whatsoever; but one does suspect Alexander finds his objections too easily. The Stoics do describe fate as a sequence of *things* (*SVF* 2.919, 1000), but more often as a sequence of causes (Introduction, p. 8 and n. 36). Cf. G. Verbeke, 'La philosophie du signe chez les Stoïciens', *Les Stoïciens et leur logique* (above, p. 153) 420 n. 22; and, on Aristotle, Hartman (op. cit. in p. 6 n. 21) 51f.

For Aristotle some residues (193.15) are useful, others not; cf. in general A.L. Peck, *Aristotle: Generation of Animals* (Loeb Classical Library, 1942) lxv f. However, of those naturally described as *growing* (*phuomena* 193.15) hair *is* useful for Aristotle (*part. an.* 2.8 653b32, 2.14 658b2ff.); Alexander may have in mind such things as warts (Dr Lloyd's suggestion). Cf. also Theophrastus *metaph.* 28ff., especially 10b7ff. With the example of husk and fruit (193.17f.) compare Aristotle *de an.* 2.1 412b2, *phys.* 2.8 199a25; and with that of rain and crops (193.18) contrast the view attacked by Aristotle *phys.* 2.8 198b11 (cf. Simplicius *in phys.*, *CAG* 9.374.18ff.; but contrast Themistius *in phys.*, *CAG* 5.2.60.9ff.). At 193.12ff. the sense *might* rather be '[that, either] because ... in size, or [because] they are not roused ... early, do not succeed ...'. *to(i) einai* in 193.24f. means '(simply) in virtue of its being', essentially as opposed to accidentally (I am grateful to Dr Lloyd for pointing this out); cf. XXIV 194.9, also 194.4f., 13f. With 193.26-8 cf. XXXI 204.4f.; *SVF* 2.1172, also 1152, 1154, 1163, 1166 and, of causes, *SVF* 2,973.

XXIV. The examples of father and child, foundation and house probably come from Aristotle *de gen. et corr.* 2.11 338b9-11, 337b14-18, 31-2; cf. also *an. post.* 2.12 95b3ff., *rhet.* 2.19 1392a19ff., 1393a6ff., Cicero *Topics* 60. *De gen. et corr.* 2.11 is discussed in *q.* II. 22, III. 5; here the emphasis on necessity *a fronte* ('If B is to occur, A must necessarily occur first') as opposed to that *a tergo* ('If A occurs, B necessarily follows') which is characteristic of Aristotle (cf. *phys.* 2.9 199b34ff., *de part. an.* 1.1 639b24ff., 642a5ff.; D.M. Balme, *Aristotle's de partibus animalium I*, etc. (Oxford 1972) 76-84; Sharples (1975,1) 260 n. 30) is taken to the point of claiming that there cannot even be conditional *a tergo* necessity except where the consequent is in any case necessary independently on the antecedent – a position rightly attacked by Philoponus *in de gen. et corr.*, *CAG* 14.2.308.13ff. Cf. Sharples, ' "If what is earlier, then of necessity what is later"?: some ancient discussions of Aristotle *de gen. et corr.* 2.11', *Bull. Inst. Class. Stud.* (London) 26 (1979) 27-44.

Alexander's point in the present passage is not that we should consider final rather than efficient causation (for not everything has a final cause, IV 167.22ff.), but rather that, while everything that does occur has an efficient cause, some things are not themselves the efficient causes of anything. (*kuriōs* in 194.6 probably refers back to XXIII 193.8ff.) This appears to be intended as an answer to determinism (cf. 194.7ff.), but is a poor one; first it does not allow for alternative outcomes, only for the absence of an outcome, and secondly the absence of an effect may well itself be the necessary result of certain factors (cf. XXIII 193.12f., 20, but also above p. 133). In spite of the examples used, Alexander's point is explicitly a general one not restricted to human actions; cf. 194.12ff. The deletion of *ex anankēs* is required either in 194.10 or in 194.10-11; it is true that the existence of Sophroniscus is only *absolutely*, as opposed to conditionally, necessary if that of Socrates is itself necessary, but neither Aristotle nor Alexander would allow that the existence of a particular individual *is* absolutely necessary (Donini (1969) 309). *houtōs* in 194.12 qualifies *ex anankēs* in 13; *this* is the way in which necessity applies to these cases. Bruns' addition in 13 is not therefore needed.

On the second part of the chapter, and 'primary' in 194.17, cf. above, comm. on ch. VIII. With Hackforth's reading in 194.19-20 cf. *SVF* 2.963. The reference to responsibility at 194.24 is presumably justified by ch. XV; nevertheless, it seems abrupt in the present context. Certainly no attempt has been made to discuss whether the *contingent* involves uncaused motion or not. On 194.25 cf. Introduction p. 18 and n. 114.

XXV. That the unity of the universe is preserved by the rotation of the heavens is similarly argued against the Stoics by Alexander in *de mixtione* X 223.9ff.; there however his objection is rather to the Stoic doctrine of the divine *pneuma* penetrating all things (ibid. 223.6ff.) and, among other points, to its degrading of God by his presence in unworthy things (ibid. XI 226.24ff. (*SVF* 2.1048)). Cf. above, p. 8 and n. 40, 26 and n. 180; Todd 212-28. A similar argument to that here is presented, more briefly, in *de prov.* 95.4-19, also taking up the point of ch. XXIII that not everything is followed by an effect (for this seems to be the force of 95.11; cf. *matēn* in Ruland p. 96 n. 13. I am grateful to Drs Ruland and Zimmermann for advice on this point). *tou theiou sōmatos* at 195.11 probably refers to the whole system of heavenly spheres (so at *q.* I. 25 40.24, Alexander *in metaph. CAG* 1.310.28, *in meteor. CAG* 3.2.6.13), rather than just to the *primum mobile*; cf. S. Pines, '*Omne quod movetur necesse est ab aliquo moveri:* A refutation of Galen by Alexander of Aphrodisias and the theory of motion', *Isis* 52 (1961) 44 n. 106. Cf. also *ta theia* at *f.* VI 169.24, XXV 195.17, XXXI 203.22.

That not everything is caused by what precedes it is argued with similar examples at Cicero *de fato* 34; however, the Stoics themselves attributed the seasons to the movements of the sun (*SVF* 2.693, though admittedly *aition* is not there used; Sambursky, 154f.). For the example of the Olympian and Isthmian games cf. Aristotle *metaph. a* 2. 994a22. For Aristotle as for Alexander the notion of cause is not primarily one of the causation of what is later by what is earlier; the sequences discussed in *phys.* 8.5 256a4ff. and *metaph. Λ* 7 1072a23-6 are rather sequences *in space* – in the cosmic context, causation proceeds from the circumference of the universe where the Unmoved Mover is situated (*phys.* 8.10 267b5ff., cf. Alexander ap. Simplicius *in phys. CAG* 10.1354.22) to the sublunary realm. Cf. P. Brown, 'Infinite causal regression', *Philos. Rev.* 75 (1966) 514f., 523; A. Kenny, *The Five Ways: St. Thomas Aquinas' proofs of God's existence* (London 1969) 12f.

At 195.13ff., in Hackforth's version one might expect *alla* rather than *ē*. It is slightly difficult that in Bruns' and *SVF*'s suggestions *houtōs* in 195.15 has to refer back to *haluseōs dikēn* rather than to *anaitiōs*; but cf. perhaps XXIV 194.21.

Alexander's insistence that there is a cause of the sequence of changes in the sublunary world that is itself outside that sequence (195.20ff., 25f.) leads up to the argument that the infinite succession of causes does away with any first cause and so with causation altogether (195.27-196.7). This is reminiscent of Aristotle *metaph. a* 2 (cf. especially 994a16-19, also 994b20 with 196.5 here); cf. also *phys. 8.5 256a13-b3, metaph. Λ* 7 1072a23-6, and Aquinas *summ. theol.* la q.2 art. 3, *secunda via*. (At Aristotle *de gen. et corr.* 2.11 337b25ff. it is necessity, rather than causation, that is in question). For the connection of *knowledge* with first causes (196.5ff.) cf. Aristotle *phys.* 1.1 184a13, 2.3 194b20, *metaph. Γ* 1 1003a31. Cf. Valgiglio (1967) 314 n. 17.

Alexander's argument here might seem open to the objection brought against that of Aquinas cited above, that in arguing that the absence of a first cause does away with causation it assumes what it sets out to prove, that there *is* a first cause (cf. Brown op. cit. 512f., Kenny op. cit. 25-7). However, Aristotle's conception of causation, on which these arguments are based, is not one of succession in time (cf. above); moreover, he is concerned with cause as that to which *responsibility* can be attached (cf. the meaning of *aitios*), and an infinite regress of causes is rather an evasion of responsibility. (Cf. Brown op. cit. 516ff., 522ff.; C.J.F. Williams, 'Hoc autem non est procedure in infinitum', *Mind* 69 (1969) 494f.; Hocutt (op. cit. on p. 126) 394.) An infinite temporal succession of causes is insufficient to explain the continuity of motion, because it is not necessary (cf. Aristotle *phys.* 8.6 258b29ff., Alexander *q.* I. 1 3.2ff.).

The absence of a first cause, and the existence rather of an infinite regress of causes in time, would not in itself do away with determinism; provided that the world as a whole is a closed system (which the Stoics explicitly held; *SVF* 2.935) *either* each state of it is necessitated by every other, even if there is no ultimate explanation why any state is as it is, only an infinite regress, or else there must be some indeterministic breach of the causal nexus. But in fact it is not clear that the Stoics *did* deny the existence of a first cause; for God is described as the first cause from whom all other causes depend (Seneca *de benef.* 4.7.2 (*SVF* 2.1024), Augustine *de civ. dei* 5.8 202.16f. Dombart; cf. also Seneca *nat. quaest.* 2.45.2, Marcus Aurelius 4.40, 5.8.2, 9.39, *SVF* 2.986 p. 287.15), either with reference to his identity with fate or with reference to his containing the 'seminal reasons' of all things in himself at the beginning of each world-cycle (*SVF* 2.1027, cf. 1.98; Marcus Aurelius 9.1.5; cf. Seneca *nat. quaest.* 3.29.3 and *SVF* 2.620 p. 188.38; above, p. 153). Cf. Theiler 44-48. (Theiler 44 connects *ta prōta* at *f.* XXII 192.1 and XXIII 193.7, with this idea; this may be correct, but the arguments of those chapters in fact apply to sequences of causes quite generally.

It is not clear whether Alexander actually wishes to claim at 196.7-12 that the exceptions for which his position allows are cases of indeterminism, or what he would say the cause of these exceptions is. The most likely candidate is matter; cf. *de prov.* 103.2ff. (and 83.9ff.; Ruland, 138f.); *q.* III. 5 89.15; Aristotle *de gen. an* 4.10 778a5ff.; Sharples (1975,2) 59 n. 113. Other possible explanations are distance from the first cause (cf. *q.* II. 3 49.5ff., Aristotle *de gen. et corr.*2.10 336b31, [Aristotle] *de mundo* 6 397b28); the multiplicity of causes involved (*q.* III. 5 89.18-20); and the interference of one cause with another (*de gen. an.,* loc. cit.). These explanations are not mutually exclusive. Characteristically, the connection between these exceptions and human agency, chance and the contingent remains obscure (cf. above, p. 21). The passage is indeed introduced by abruptly (196.7); little attempt seems to have been made to integrate it into the argument as a whole.

The analogy of the household (196.11) recalls Aristotle *metaph.* *Λ* 10 1075a19ff., paraphrased by Alexander *de princ.* 137.18f.; cf. also *taxis* (196.7, 9) with *metaph.* 1075a14-16. On the alleged implications of the *metaph.* passage for *Aristotle's* view of human

freedom cf. Sharples (1975,2) 51 and id. 'Responsibility and the
possibility of more than one course of action', *Bull. Inst. Class. Stud.*
(London) 23 (1976) 69. Alexander also uses the analogy of the
household, in attacking the concern of Stoic providence with even
trivial details, at *de prov.* 25.3ff. Chrysippus had himself used it to
argue that there could be occasional exceptions to providence (*SVF*
2.1178, cf. Cicero *de nat. deorum* 2.167), though it is difficult to see
how this could be reconciled with his normal position, or to suppose
that such occurrences were not for him predetermined by fate. Cf.
Babut (op. cit. in p. 14 n. 78) 292; Pfligersdorffer (op. cit. in p. 9
n. 43) 9ff., 16f. n. 53, 25f.; and my discussion in 'Nemesius of Emesa
and some theories of divine providence', forthcoming in *Vigiliae
Christianae*.

XXVI. The argument here attributed to the determinists serves to
introduce a discussion by Alexander, in XXVII, which is based on
Aristotle's own treatment of a difficulty of which he was already
aware. (Cf. below on ch. XXVII, and Introduction p. 6.) It may
be that the Stoics had drawn for polemical purposes on a point
already raised by Aristotle; but it also seems possible that Alexander
may, to introduce his subsequent discussion, have placed in his
opponents' mouths an argument which he has himself formulated.
(Cf. below, comm. on *q.* II. 4-5; Donini (1977) 194; and cf. Verbeke's
paraphrase of the present passage (94).) The argument is directed
against a libertarian notion of responsibility defined in terms of the
possibility of pursuing an opposite course of action (196.24f.); this is
already present in Aristotle (above, p. 6) and is implied in
Epicurus' treatment of the topic, but in extant literature at any rate
it is only in Alexander himself that it becomes particularly
prominent (above, p. 22 n. 145) – though in view of the inadequacy
of our information on earlier inter-school polemic this may not be as
significant as it at first appears.

If however the argument *is* an authentic Stoic one, it seems that
Alexander may have distorted its point. For in the subsequent
chapter he takes this to be that both good and bad character, once
established, determine a man's actions – as in Aristotle's discussion
in *eth. Nic.* III. 5; admittedly, the extent to which Aristotle there
intends to imply that character, once established, cannot be
changed should not be overstated (cf. above, p. 7 n. 27), but
Alexander's argument in ch. XXVII does not seem to envisage

change of character once established. But, while the Stoics did regard settled dispositions (*hexeis*) as important in morality (cf. *SVF* 3.384, 510; M.E. Reesor, 'The indifferents in the Old and Middle Stoa', *Trans. Amer. Philol. Assoc.* 82 (1951) 104f.), they certainly held that wicked men could become virtuous (above, p. 10 n. 48) – even if they could not, given their determinist position, provide an analysis of this process that would satisfy a libertarian conception of responsibility – and regarded the question of whether virtue, once possessed, could be lost as at least a topic for debate (*SVF* 3.237f.; Rist, 16ff.). (The argument at 196.24ff., on the other hand, treats virtue and vice exactly alike.) It may therefore be that, as suggested by Stough 208ff., Alexander has misrepresented, as concerned with the question whether character can change, an argument that was only intended by its Stoic authors to relate to the question whether men can act against their character *now* (which is Alexander's concern, too, in ch. XXIX, q.v. Cf. also Long (1971) 183ff. and n. 35; Gould (1974) 25f.). Alternatively, *if* the argument *is* an authentic Stoic one, they could have adopted Peripatetic assumptions in arguing *ad homines* against Peripatetic opponents. (196.24ff. is not of course evidence for the Stoics' themselves having defined responsibility in terms of the possibility of doing the opposite (A. Graeser, *Plotinus and the Stoics*, Leiden, 1972, 117 n. 6; cf. Pack 427); they are represented as assuming it only for the sake of the argument that rejects it.)

The Stoics would not themselves have accepted that their soft-determinist position makes life an 'illusion and jest' (196.16), and would have recognised no ultimate discrepancy between arguments and physical facts, both being aspects of the one universal Reason (*Logos*). My supplement in the translation of 196.17 follows Boussoulas. On the force of 'wise' (*phronimos*) cf. below XXXVII comm. ad fin.

XXVII. Alexander's initial reply to the difficulty raised in XXVI is based on that of Aristotle in *eth. Nic.* III. 5 (above, p. 6); we are responsible for having acquired our character even if we cannot act against it now. (Cf. also below XXIX 199.27-9, and *p.* IX 129.24ff., XXIX 158.20ff., 160.25ff. Donini (1974,2) 169-73.) However, this simply leads to a regress (above, p. 7); and that Alexander is well aware of this is shown both by his reference at XXVIII 199.9ff. to the actions through which we acquire the moral disposition, and also by his further arguments in ch. XXIX. (Cf. Donini (1974,2) 181ff.)

The contrast between natural endowment and moral character as a disposition acquired by practice is Aristotelian (*eth. Nic.* 2.1 1103a18ff.), as is the point that weights cannot be trained by throwing upwards (198.27; *eth. Nic.* 2.1 1103a20ff.). For the analogy between virtue and practical skills (197.8-11, 199.4-7; cf. *p.* XXIX 160.32ff., 161.22ff.) cf. *eth. Nic.* 2.1 1103a32ff., and for the point that praise and blame do not apply to natural endowment and the contrast between physical conditions that are natural and those that are not (197.22ff.) cf. *eth. Nic.* 3.5 1114a23ff., *magna moralia* 1.9 1187a23ff. (though there it is a question of *poor* physical condition, not as here of good). Cf. also *Plato* Protagoras 323Cff. and above p. 150. The argument is here modified by the further point that virtue would not be praiseworthy even if, though we do not possess it at birth, it developed naturally in the same way as teeth and beard (198.8ff.). The relation between natural endowment and what we ourselves contribute is discussed in more detail at *m.* 175.12ff., 25ff. (cf. *p.* XXIX 160.32ff.); there it is argued that, though natural endowment may affect the ease with which we acquire virtue, its influence is never so great, provided we are in a natural state, as to prevent us doing so altogether; cf. Origen at *SVF* 2.990 p. 290.9ff., and contrast Galen *de moribus* (J.N. Mattock, 'The Arabic epitome of Galen's book *peri ethōn*', *Islamic Philosophy and the Classical Tradition: Studies presented to Richard Walzer*, Oxford 1973, p. 239 ad init.). Cf. Donini (1974,2) 168-70, and R.B. Todd, 'Alexander of Aphrodisias on *de interpretatione* 16a26-29', *Hermes* 104 (1976), 144 n. 19. Alexander's approach in the present chapter may be contrasted with that in ch. VI (above, p. 130; Donini (1974,2) 161-5, 169-73); the passages cited from *m* and *p* may represent an attempt to reconcile these two approaches. (198.26 here need not imply that our *moral* nature cannot be changed even though we may act against it (Valgiglio (1967) 309 n. 7); that is rather the position of ch. VI, above p. 130.) That the *capacity* for virtue is natural (198.3ff.) is argued at *eth. Nic.* 2.1 1103a23ff.; cf. 2.5 1106a9. The contrast between initial natural endowment and the way in which it is developed is stressed by Alexander in other contexts too; cf. q. III. 11 100.30ff., *de an.* 82.3-5, and Ammonius *in de int. CAG* 4.5.39.17-32; Todd, op. cit., 140-6.

In 197.3 *legoimen* must be read rather than *legoien*, for, in Alexander's view at least, his opponents do not regard men as responsible for the development of their dispositions; cf. XXVIII 199.7ff. and comm. In 197.12-17 the emphasis is on the presence of *possibility* before the event but not after it, rather than on the question of the truth-value of the *categorical* prediction 'X will become virtuous'; however, it may be doubted whether Alexander would have expressed himself in exactly this way if he had held that the truth of a prediction was compatible with contingency (cf. above p. 138). 197.21f., 'from divine nature': i.e., probably, 'from the divine nature that he would then have'; cf. 197.29f., XXXII 204.14. For the connection of blessing rather than praise with the gods (197.26-30) cf., in a different connection, *eth. Nic.* 1.12 1101b18ff.; and for the reference to the gods as not responsible for their nature cf. 198.17 and XXXII 204.12ff. Cf. R.W. Sharples, 'Responsibility and the possibility of more than one course of action: a note on Aristotle *de caelo* II. 12', *Bull. Inst. Class. Stud.* (London) 23 (1976) 71 n. 10.

198.2-3 might more naturally be rendered, as Professor Long has pointed out to me, 'what comes to be is incomplete at once by its having come to be' (i.e., just because it is a thing that is subject to coming-to-be? cf. Alexander fr.1 92.5 Vitelli (above, p. 14 n. 86); also X 177.16f., XXIII 193.24f., XXIV 194.8f.). However, this seems to go too far in the present context, by excluding even the possibility of a later perfection. With 198.6ff. cf. Alexander *de prov.* 99.4ff. At 198.18, for the MSS 'reality of', Gercke's emendation would give 'cause for'; Caspar Orelli explains his *hosian* as equivalent to *dikaiosin* 'justification', but this scarcely seems to the point. The rarity of good men (198.19) is a Stoic doctrine (cf. ch. XXVIII comm.) but is also Aristotelian (cf. *eth. Nic.* 10.9 1179b7ff.). At 198.23 V's *anankaion* might be rendered 'what is necessary [but] lacking to our nature'; so, approximately, Grotius and Boussoulas. The emphasis at 198.24 on the question of the *utility* of praise and blame rather than, as more usually, on that of its *justification* involves Alexander in the false view that determinism implies that external factors cannot affect a man's course of action; cf. below, ch. XXXVII comm.

XXVIII. For Stoic belief in the rarity of good men cf. *SVF* 3.662, 666, 668, and 3 Diog. 32; and further below. For the claim that virtue is the only good (199.14) cf. *SVF* 3.29-37, and for the equation of badness, folly and madness (implied at 199.18ff.) cf. *SVF* 3.657, 659, 662-6, 668. For the claim that all is arranged for man's benefit (199.12ff.) cf. *SVF* 2.1152f., 1156f., 1162.

The Stoics would not accept that their position takes away from men the responsibility for their character (199.7-9); nevertheless, there is a problem in reconciling the rareness of good men with the *providential* ordering of the universe, though it is in no way incompatible with determinism as such (above, p. 20). A similar objection is raised by Cicero, *de nat. deorum* 3.79, and Plutarch, *de Stoic. rep.* 1048ef, *comm. not.* 1076b.; cf. Philodemus in *SVF* 2.1183 p. 340.15, and the related argument at Cicero *de nat. deorum* 1.23 and 3.70, that it is strange that the gods should design everything for the sake of men (cf. supr.) when there are so few good men. Cf. P.H. De Lacy, 'Lucretius and the history of Epicureanism', *Trans. Amer. Philiol. Assoc.* 79 (1948) 16f. At *q.* I. 14 (*SVF* 3.32) Alexander argues that, if we are responsible for our actions and virtue is the only good, the gods cannot bestow any good on men; cf. *q.* II.21 70.2ff. (*SVF* 2.1118), *de prov.* 29.3ff., and Plutarch *de Stoic. rep.* 1048ce (*SVF* 3.215).

XXIX. Still allowing that a man cannot change his *disposition* once it has developed (199.27-9; cf. the rather less forceful image at Aristotle *eth. Nic.* 3.5 1114a17, and Pack 427 on the implausibility of such a 'headlong descent to virtue'), Alexander argues that a man's disposition does not determine his actions in every detail (199.31-200.2; cf. *eth. Nic.* 2.9 1109b18ff.; D. Frede, *Aristoteles und die "Seeschlacht"*, Göttingen 1970 (*Hypomnemata*, 27) 119. Cf. also above ch. VI; but character was there regarded as natural endowment, while in XXVII ff. it is not moral character but the capacity for acquiring it that is regarded as natural; see above.) Alexander's point in the present passage may plausibly be interpreted as the claim that, though a courageous man (for example) must perform courageous rather than cowardly actions, it does not therefore follow that he must perform *this* particular courageous action rather than that (cf. D. Frede loc. cit., and, of the Stoics, Long (1971) 184 – but *their* general position does imply that more than just the moral quality of the action is predetermined). This however still leaves the difficulty that it is precisely the moral character of actions that is most important where responsibility is concerned, both generally and in particular in the context of character development. Secondly, Alexander argues that a wise man may (at least) *refrain* from a certain course of action (200.2-9, cf. 199.29f.); the negative nature of this argument clearly shows the difficulty that he is in (cf. Donini (1974,2) 182ff., and above ch. XV comm. p. 148). In *m.* 174.27-35 a distinction is drawn between an action's being reasonable (*eulogon*) and its being necessitated; cf.

199.30, 200.4, 6, here. However, the point does not appear as a separate one here as it does in the *mantissa*. A distinction between *possible* courses of action and the rational course of action could indeed resolve the problem that man's potentiality for opposites may, in the context of a metaphysical analysis of the universe as a whole, seem a sign of inferiority; for it may be argued that man's acting rightly is the more praiseworthy because he can do otherwise. But Alexander does not seem to adopt such a position here – man is indeed praised whereas the gods are not (XXXII 204.15ff., cf. XXVII 198.14ff., XXXIV 207.2), but the emphasis is on his inferiority to the gods rather than, in this context at least, on his potentiality for opposites raising him *above* the rest of sublunary nature. (But cf. above p. 145). And in any case this would not solve the more immediate problem of analysing actions which *are* contrary to what is reasonable (though not necessary) in such a way that they are neither the result of factors for which the agent is not responsible, nor yet totally random and inexplicable. Neither here nor in ch. XV (by contrast with *m.* XXII) is any attempt made to set the question of human responsibility in the context of the ordering of the universe as a whole. Cf. above, p. 22 and nn. 151f.; Sharples (op. cit. at p. 159 above) 69 and nn. 7-10; Epiphanius *Panarion* 1.1 *haeres.* 16.4, *PG* 41.253B.

With *en platei* (200.1) compare Alexander's answer to the *sorites* argument in fr. 1 Vitelli (above, p. 14 n. 86), especially 91.25, 92.1. On the reference to prophecy (200.7ff.) cf. Introduction p. 18 and n. 116.

XXX. This and the following chapter form a digression resulting from the mention of prophecy in XXIX 200.7ff. (Greene, 375); XXXII returns to the topic of XXVI-XXIX. For Stoic use of divine foreknowledge as an argument for determinism cf. *SVF* 2.943, and compare *SVF* 2.944 and Cicero *de div.* 2.18. For the principle that the impossible is impossible even for the gods (200.19) cf. Alexander *de prov.* 15.8 (in a context closely parallel to the present; cf. Thillet, op. cit. at p. 25 n. 170, p. 323), *de princ.* 138.9f., *q.* I. 18 32.3ff., 14ff., and Alexander ap. Simplicius *in de caelo, CAG* 7.359.20ff. (cf. M. Baltes, *Die Weltenstehung des Platonischen Timaios*, etc., Leiden 1976, 77ff.); Galen, *De usu partium* 11.14, III. 906.6 Kühn (t.2 p. 158.17ff. Helmreich); R. Walzer, *Galen on Jews and Christians* (London 1949) 28ff. *SVF* 2.1183 shows the Stoics themselves as accepting this principle and allowing that the gods cannot know everything (cf.

Gercke 699, Rist 48 n. 5); however, it seems that the reference may be
to logical impossibilities rather than to there being actual occurences
which escape divine notice – Rist's connection of this passage with
SVF 2.1178 (above p. 159) may be misleading. If so, Alexander's
argument at 201.7ff., suggesting that the Stoics did not distinguish
between the gods' knowing everything that happens and their
knowing logical impossibilities, is disingenuous; though his
complaint about the order of their argument at 201.24ff. still applies.
Walzer loc. cit. takes *SVF* 2.1107 as showing that the Stoics held that
all is possible for the gods; but this seems overstated. The
incommensurability of the diagonal (200.21) is a standard example of
what is impossible: Aristotle *metaph.* *Δ* 12 1019b24, *Θ* 4 1047b6,
Alexander *de prov.* 15.1, *m.* 181.10, *q.* I. 18 31.13, and ap. Simplicius op.
cit. 359.10.

Alexander allows (though only hypothetically, 210.17; cf. above
p. 21) that the gods might have foreknowledge of the contingent *as
contingent* (201.13ff.). The expression is in itself ambiguous, for the
matter is put in similar terms by later writers who hold that the gods
have definite foreknowledge of what is in itself indefinite (Proclus *de
dec. dub.* q. 2 8.10ff., cf. Boethius *in de int.*[2] 226.1ff., *cons. phil.* 5 pr.
6.93; above p. 28, and Sharples (1978) 261 and n. 193). However,
Alexander's position here is clearly not, as in Proclus, that the gods
know how I will choose but also that I will do so freely rather than of
necessity; rather, the foreknowledge that he is prepared to allow to
the gods extends only to the fact that I will be free to choose in this
way or that, *not* also to knowledge of the way in which I will in fact
choose. Cf. Sharples (1978) 260-62; if this were not Alexander's
position, he would be open to the objection that he brings against his
opponents' view of prophecy in ch. XXXI (cf. 202.12f.). *pantōs* at
200.25 is probably Alexander's way of referring to what later writers
will call definite, as opposed to indefinite, foreknowledge (Proclus *de
prov.* 63.1ff (*SVF* 2.942), cf. *de dec. dub.* q. 2 7.28, 8.9; Iamblichus ap.
Ammonius *in de int.* 4.5.136.25ff.). Cf. also Origen at *SVF* 2.957
p. 278.36ff., 2.964.

200.17ff. might also be rendered 'if the nature of the things
admitted ... than [it would be] for the gods ... but since [the nature
...]'; Alexander may be allowing that there are *some* things (those
that are *not* contingent) of which the gods may have (definite)
foreknowledge, or he may be concentrating attention on those
things which *are* contingent and of which even the gods cannot

therefore, in his view, have such foreknowledge. At 200.25 my 'at all events' renders *houtōs*, referring back to *pantōs* (cf. above). L. appears to have read *pantōs houtōs*; with this reading *houtōs* seems redundant, though not impossibly so. At 200.32 Donini argues that the omission of *kai* is compensated for by reading *oud'*; however, good sense may be obtained with both included. 201.5, 'the view of things [that they do]'; literally, 'such a nature of things'. At 201.11 Grotius and Orelli punctuate *after dunaton*; but the conclusion originally envisaged was that the absurdity is possible, not that it actually occurs.

For the subsequent influence of this chapter cf. Sharples (1978) 260-2, and above p. 28.

XXXI. For Stoic use of prophecy as an argument to support determinism cf. *SVF* 2.912, 939, 943, and for Alexander's own attitude cf. above pp. 18-19. The appeal to oracles conditional in form, where the outcome depends upon the action of the recipient, provides an escape from the fatalistic implications of categorical oracles (*SVF* 2.958, Boethius *in de int.*[2] 225.4; cf. Seneca *nat. quaest.* 2.37). Alexander does not here argue that, if all is predetermined, prophecy cannot affect the course of events (cf. above, XVII 188.11ff.); rather, he questions the motive of Apollo in giving the oracle when he knew what the outcome would be. There is nothing here that is incompatible with determinism as such, as opposed to *providential* determinism (above, p. 20; I am grateful to Dr Lloyd for pointing this out).

It seems probable that Chrysippus had himself used the story of Laius and Oedipus to show that oracles could affect the course of events in a determinist system, stressing Laius' inability to escape the consequences once he had disobeyed the oracle, but also stressing, as his soft-determinist position allowed, that the disobedience was Laius' own responsibility, even though it was predetermined how he would act and Apollo knew it (cf. *SVF* 2.939, 956, 978; Sharples (1978) 246f.; Reesor (1978) 199f.). That for a soft determinist Laius' disobedience is his own responsibility is a point that Alexander characteristically ignores (203.1). As for Apollo's original motive in giving the oracle. Chrysippus may well have followed the story according to which it was a punishment for Laius' rape of Chrysippus son of Pelops (cf. H. Lloyd-Jones, *The Justice of Zeus*, Berkeley 1971, 120f.).

Alexander represents the example as being introduced by opponents of determinism (202.8f.); this seems strange, in that it seems so well suited to a defence of oracles and of human responsibility from a soft-determinist point of view. (Reading *paradechomenōn* in 202.8f. gives a less natural connection with what precedes; and, if the determinists used the example before their critics, they probably used it to make the very point raised in the critics' question, that in the case of conditional oracles the outcome depends on our response – in which case the critics' question seems odd.) At the very least, Alexander seems guilty of failing to indicate to his readers the *positive* use that Chrysippus made of the example. The example was used by the Middle Platonists to illustrate their doctrine of conditional fate (above, p. 13; Albinus 26 179.13ff., Calcidius CLIII 188.9f.), but it is unlikely that this is alluded to here, being ignored elsewhere in the treatise. Certainly it cannot be the Middle Platonists that Alexander is here *attacking*, for their whole position depends on its not being predetermined, and hence not foreknown, whether Laius will obey or not. The example may originally have been used against the Stoics by the authors of the 'Lazy Argument' (above, p. 10).

Alexander's claim that his own position preserves divination (201.30) does not seem coherently thought out; it is difficult to see how Laius' murder could have been inevitable even once he had disobeyed, given that Oedipus was *not*, presumably, inevitably constrained by his character to kill him (cf. chs. VI, XXIX). A possible solution is indicated at *m.* 185.33ff. (cf. Pack 428f. and n. 34), but the point is not made here.

Whether the determinists are represented as themselves explicitly asserting that Apollo knew that Laius would disobey will in part depend upon the reading adopted in 202.12 (though Bruns' <*ou*> *phasin* is itself ambiguous in this respect); in any case this is a legitimate deduction from their position (cf. XXX 200.12f.). The example of Oedipus was used by Carneades in arguing that only what is predetermined can be foreknown (*SVF* 2.955). At 203.3 *ep' autois* might be rendered 'depending on them'; but to preserve the argument this would have to be taken as referring to a claim by the determinists that predetermined events are still the responsibility of the agents involved, a claim not endorsed by Alexander himself. This is not impossible, but, as there has been no previous reference in this chapter to a determinist claim that such events *are* the responsibility of those involved, the interpretation in the translation seems preferable. For the gods as *dōtēres eaōn* (cf. 207.7) cf. Homer

Odyssey 8.325, 335, Hesiod *Theogony* 46, 111, 633, 664; Plutarch *comm. not.* 14 1065e, 32 1075e, and Cherniss' note on 1065e (*Plutarch's Moralia*, Loeb ed., vol. 13.2, 1976). On 203.24ff. cf. above p. 18 n. 116. Orelli takes the reference at 203.26 to be to Medea, but Alexander's expression seems more apt to a woman who killed her own children *in mistake for* someone else's; Mr A.H. Griffiths has drawn my attention to the story of Aëdon, wife of Zethus, who plotted to kill the child of Niobe but slew her own son Itylus by mistake (schol. *Odyssey* 19.518; H.J. Rose, *A Handbook of Greek Mythology*[6] (London 1964) p. 340B)..

XXXII. Cf. above, XXVII-XXIX comm. The reference at 204.11f. is probably not to XIV (so Orelli, 314 n. 2) but to XXVII. My supplement to the translation in 204.13 follows Nourrisson, Hackforth, Boussoulas, Valgiglio (1967) 316; *SVF* 2.985's *'toioutois* (scil. *phronimois)'* is impossible, for *phronēsis* is not a divine virtue (cf. XXXVII 211.8ff.). The attribution at 204.13 of the argument of 204.12ff. to the determinists is odd; no such point was made in XXVI, and it is difficult to see why it should be supposed natural to hold that the gods' nature *should* depend on themselves; Alexander's response is simply to deny that they are. Cf. above, XXVII 198.17 and comm; XXXIV 206.30ff. At 204.17 (cf. app. crit.) Caspar Orelli, following Grotius, understands the MSS text in the sense of 'cannot admit of *anything*, good or bad (over and above what is already present); with O's reading cf. *SVF* 2.1021 (Gercke, no. 132, ad loc.). 204.19ff. alludes to Hesiod *Works and Days* 287ff. (ibid.). With 204.21ff. cf. XXIX 200.2ff., and, concerning the gods, XVII 188.2-6, 8-11.

XXXIII. The point at issue is essentially the same as in XIV 183.21ff.; Alexander presents his opponents' position as turning on an error of logic (205.13ff.), but it may be suspected that he has misrepresented their intentions in attributing to them his own, libertarian notion of responsibility (205.10f.). On the question of the relation between responsibility and *rational* impulse in the *Stoic* view cf. above, p. 144.

As in ch. X 176.14ff., for the sake of clarity in the translation I have broken up the long sentence 205.1-13 and given the argument Alexander attributes to the determinists in direct, rather than in indirect speech. At 205.2, if *mē* is retained (cf. Notes on the Text, below), the sense will be '... depends on us, because [they claim] not everything that comes to be ... who exercise the impulse, are mistaken.' The argument at 205.8-9 is illogical, since, from the fact that activities not according to impulse do not depend on us, it follows at most that *some* activities according to impulse depend on us (and even this only if we rule out the possibility that no activities depend on us at all), but not that they *all* do. At 205.11f. *einai en* might be translated 'consists in'; but this rendering would be impossible at 204.13-15. Cf. XIV 183.22f.

XXXIV. The determinist argument at 205.24-206.2 is similar to that in ch. XIII, but while it was there argued that it is in accordance with fate for living creatures to act according to impulse, here the argument is that it is in accordance with fate for some men to act virtuously and others viciously. (Cf. *SVF* 2.1000 p. 294.7ff., Marcus Aurelius 5.17, 9.42.3; Long (1971) 197 n. 48. And cf. above, p. 11 and n. 54). At 205.23 'of the things that are brought about' might be rendered 'of the things that come to be', simply, not referring back to 'brought about by themselves'.

Alexander objects that the determinists cannot use such an argument because their own position excludes men's acting virtuously or viciously; this objection is valid enough from a libertarian point of view, but not from a soft-determinist one. (As Dr Lloyd points out, Alexander only says in 206.2-4 that the conclusion *does not follow* for the determinists, but it is clear from elsewhere that he regards it as *incompatible* with their position.) Cf. also below, comm. on *q*. II. 5. On 296.4 cf. p. 28 n. 192; it is because of the ambiguity here that I have not rendered 205.26 'since "by nature" and "according to fate" *are* the same'.

206.17f. should be taken as a reference to the agent's having the power to act otherwise, as the sequel suggests, rather than to the doctrine that an action is only virtuous if it proceeds from a virtuous disposition (Aristotle *eth. Nic.* 2.4 1105a32, 5.6 1134a17, 5.8 1135b22, 5.9 1137a21), as that would be difficult to reconcile with the view that virtuous and vicious action involve the possibility of acting otherwise (206.14f.; cf. XXVIIIff. comm.). Cf. Verbeke, 98 n. 95. On 206.22 cf. Introduction p. 21 and n. 144. With 206.30ff. cf. XXXII 204.12ff., XXVII 198.17, and comm.

XXXV. With the form of the determinist argument here compare

XXXVI 210.5ff. (but cf. comm.), XXXVII 210.15-28, and *SVF* 3.362;
Frede 200. Alexander's criticism at XXXVI 208.14f. appears quite
justified. It seems likely that the arguments here and in XXXVII,
which in general show no obvious signs of rewording by Alexander,
are reasonably accurate representations of original Stoic arguments.
(However, though *toiaute* in 207.6 *may* have been in place in an
original Stoic context, it may have been introduced by Alexander. It
appears to mean here 'necessitating' or 'universal'; cf. 207.19f.,
XXXVI 210.15, and Sharples (1975, 1) 248 n. 2, (1981) 84). The
definition of law at 207.8f. is given as Chrysippus' at *SVF* 3.314f.,
323, 332; for the Stoics the universal law is identified with divine
reason (*SVF* 3.316) and hence with fate (cf. Gercke (1885) 694,
Rieth, above p. 144, 136, Valgiglio (1967) 316 n. 21). Characteristically, Alexander completely ignores this connection between law and
fate in the Stoic view in his criticisms (XXXVI 208.18ff.).

It is clear that the formula '*ouk esti men* X, *ouk esti* Y' is to be
taken as 'not: X exists and Y does not'. Chrysippus drew a
distinction between this form of statement and the conditional 'if X
exists then Y exists' (*SVF* 2.954); it has been suggested that this
reflected the distinction between cases where X is the *cause* of Y,
where the conditional would be appropriate, and the type of
connection observed by diviners, where the occurrence of Y can be
inferred from that of X but is not directly caused by it. (Donini
(1973) 343ff. Cf. also Samburský 78f.; Gould (1970) 75-82; Frede
85ff.; I. Mueller, 'An introduction to Stoic logic', in J.M. Rist (ed.),
The Stoics, Berkeley 1978, 18ff., 24f.; Mignucci 330-41; Moreau; G.
Verbeke, 'La philosophie du signe chez les Stoïciens', *Les Stoïciens et
leur logique, actes du colloque de Chantilly* (Paris 1978) 405-17; F.
Caujolle-Zaslawsky, 'Le style stoïcien et la "paremphasis"', ibid.
432.4; and Sorabji (1980, 1) 74-8. Above, p. 137.) However, as
Sorabji observes (78 n. 33), it is difficult to see any principle
underlying the use of the different forms in different stages of the
present argument. The formula can*not* have the sense 'if X does not
exist Y does not exist' (Valgiglio (1967) 316, Verbeke 98), for some
links in the chain *are* of the constructive form 'if X then Y'. The
argument is not therefore a reductive one; rather, it claims to
establish the positive conclusion 'if fate exists praise and blame do'
(this justifying Hackforth's emendation at 207.19), and hence, *a
fortiori*, the compatibility of praise and blame with fate. For the
formula 'not: X and not-Y' cf. further *SVF* 2.274, 665, 1192

(p. 343.11), 3.471; Gercke (1885) 704, Frede 86).

XXXVI. That the determinists cannot, on their own premisses, be blamed for asserting what they do is argued by Oenomaus, ap. Eusebius *praep. ev.* 6.7 *PG* 21.444c, and Calcidius CLXXV 204.1; that they cannot blame those who disagree with them by Epicurus, *sent. Vat.* 40 (cf. also *On Nature* 31.28; D.N. Sedley, 'Epicurus *On Nature* book XXVIII', *Cronache Ercolanesi* 73 (1973) 27 and n. 170, M.F. Burnyeat, 'Protagoras and self-refutation in later Greek philosophy', *Philos. Rev.* 85 (1976) 57 and n. 22; O'Connor 35ff.). Cf. also above, XII 180.24f. 'As an effect of their circumstances' (207.21f.): literally, 'by some causes that surround them'. On 207.25ff. cf. Introduction p. 21 and n. 144.

The claim at 208.3ff. that the argument of XXXV depends on the soft-determinist analysis of responsibility (the exposition of which here is closely parallel to that in XIII) seems odd at first sight, since there is no explicit reference to responsibility in XXXV itself. However, Alexander does at 208.18ff. reject the inference from fate to law by claiming that law is only compatible with a libertarian view of responsibility; and his point may be, not that the argument of XXXV in particular involves a soft-determinist view of responsibility, but that his opponents' position as a whole does and that this is the main issue between himself and them (cf. XXXVIII below). On 'thrown' (208.25) cf. above p. 152. At 208.1ff. the sense might rather be (cf. Notes on the Text, below) '... reaches, from accepted and evident premisses, the conclusion that there is no need after all of that which was the object of all their long labour over syllogisms'; at 208.8, with the reading of V. 'brought about by the creatures through themselves.' 'There are' (209.4): literally, 'we have'.

208.18-209.18 involves the erroneous assumption that determinism implies that law cannot affect our actions; this is however corrected at 209.18ff. (where, it may be noted, Alexander argues, not as previously that law will be *useless* in a determinist system, but that censure will be *unjustified* (209.23) and that the very concept of law will be meaningless (209.26ff.). Law and punishment may indeed still be *useful* in a determinist system, by deterring some offenders if not all.). At 209.19-22 and 25 law is only regarded as a cause of our action if the action is in accordance with it (so, rightly, Boussoulas; Grotius has *efficientia* for *aitia* at 209.25). Law will presumably still be among the factors involved, however, even if it is predetermined that it will not be obeyed and so will not be a cause; 209.21 seems to deny this, but should probably be taken as an abbreviation for *ou peristēsetai hōs aitia*. What fails to prevent is not a cause; cf. Clement of Alexandria *Strom*. 1.17, *PG* 8.797a ff. (*SVF* 2.353), 4.12 *PG* 8.1293d-1296a, 8.9 *PG* 9.59a.

210.6ff., with *SVF*'s text (cf. Notes on the Text, below), would run: '... preserve it; namely that, deriving another proposition through the first, they then bring up the absurdities which seem to follow on this, and with these attack the first premiss'. The argument at 210.8-10 is in some respects similar to those of XXXV (q.v. comm.) and XXXVII 210.15-28; however, it is much shorter, and, unlike those arguments, *is* cast in the form of a *reductio*.

XXXVII. On the form of the determinist argument cf. above, XXXV comm.; for the definition of 'practical wisdom', *phronēsis* (210.19, 211.18) cf. *SVF* 1.375, 3.262, 268. '... and that the organisation of the universe is hindered or impeded' (210.15f., 30f.): literally, 'but that ... is not unhindered and unimpeded'; The initial premiss at 210.15f. is approximately equivalent to 'if all things are in accordance with fate, the organisation of the universe is unhindered and unimpeded'; but cf. above XXXV comm. Cf. *SVF* 2.935, 937. *esti* at 210.27 might alternatively be rendered 'it is not possible to give privilege ...'. At 210.29 the interrogative *tis* clearly gives the better force. L's omission of *an* is not decisive (cf. Thillet loc. cit.), but, with the interrogative, *an* if retained must be transposed after *tís*, and the indicative without *an* gives the better force.

At 211.4 'all the rest' might at first sight mean either 'other than fate' (which *must* be the meaning of O's conjectured *tauta*) or 'other than necessity'. However, while fate as *Alexander* understands it *might* be supposed to exclude necessity (though in fact he holds that *some* things are necessary), it certainly does not exclude nature. Therefore he must be referring to fate as the determinsts understand it; and it must be the items other than *necessity* that are excluded (thought the Stoics certainly would not accept this). Cf. Introduction, p. 28 and n. 192. At 211.5 the sense *without* Diels' addition of *ouk* seems more to the point than that obtained with it. ('it is not the case that the organisation ... would be hindered' 'would not be unhindered' [*sc*. if all things were not in accordance with fato]); for the determinists had not been represented as claiming that it would be, in XXXVI at least (but cf. XXV). *ouk ar'an*, simply, therefore seems to give the best sense.

211.20ff. wrongly assumes that determinism implies that our being wise or otherwise will have no effect on our actions (above, p. 10). For 'practical wisdom' as a purely human virtue and its concern with things that can be otherwise cf. Aristotle *eth. Nic.* 6.5 1140b2, 6.7 1141a20, b8. 211.25 refers back to XXXVI 208.18-209.30, 211.26-8 to 210.19-28.

XXXVIII. Cf. above, chs. XIIIf., XXXIII; also XXXVI 208.3-13 and comm., *m.* 172.8 with Sharples (1975,2) 41 and n. 35.

XXXIX. Cf. above, Introduction p. 17. The reference of *ta alla* at 212.16 is probably not to those actions *for which we are not responsible* (so Rodier), but to such features of human life as praise, blame, exhortation, punishment, deliberation and the rest, which Alexander has repeatedly claimed are incompatible with determinism. If Alexander has *throughout* being concerned to explain the *causes* of what we do (so Bruns' text), he has hardly done so systematically (cf. Introduction p. 21).

Mantissa XXII: 'From the [teachings] of Aristotle concerning what depends on us.'

Cf. Introduction 21-2, and commentary on *f.* ch. VIII; also Sharples (1975,2) *passim*.

169.36. Or, perhaps, 'regard education as *the* cause'; Donini (1974,2) 166.

170.2. The MSS add 'which is the sort of thing we maintain what depends on us to be', bracketed by Bruns as an interpolation.

170.4, 'what all supposed'; apparently referring to a school-discussion. Cf. references in Notes on the Text, below.

170.9ff. For the connection between the accidental and not-being, based on Aristotle *metaph. E* 2 1026b21, and for that between accidental causation and absence of a cause cf. Sharples (1975,2) 48 and n. 111.

171.8 *proēgeitai*, 171.13 *proēgoumenon*: cf. comm. on *f.* ch. VIII, above p. 132-3.

171.20. 'Otherwise' supplied by Caninius and by Nourrisson (p. 64).

171.20, 22. Or 'for the same ends' in both places (so Nourrisson loc. cit.); but this seems less to the point in the context. (Cf. however *f.*

XV 185.21ff., and comm., *m.* 174.13ff.).

172.4. 'The contingent': *to endechomenon,* picking up *to endechomenon kai allōs echein* in 172.2f. (on which cf. Sharples (1975,2) 48f.).

172.13. 'Is a matter of': literally, 'that which has weakened ... *katechei* what depends on us'; *katechei* most naturally would have the stronger sense 'restrain', as Dr Lloyd points out to me. I have taken *to ... exesthenēkos* as subject of both *katechei* and *echei.* Cf. Sharples (1975,2) 52 and n. 188.

Mantissa XXIII: 'From the [teachings] of Aristotle concerning what depends on us'.
This discussion is not marked by the radical divergences from the positions of *f.* found in *m.* XXII, and may for the most part be seen as a development and bringing together of certain points from *f.*; cf. especially *f.* chs. XI, XV, XXVII and XXIX with comm.

172.18. 'The divine', i.e. the heavens; cf. *f.* XXV 195.11 and above p. 156.

173.14. Cf., with Bruns, 173.16 and 174.9f.; the placing of 'the man' at the end of the sequence is odd at first sight, but is repeated in 174.10 and seems intended to produce a climax.

173.17. 'The efficient cause of these' is perhaps best taken as referring to deliberation (cf. 174.9); but the expression is very obscure. (It would be less so if we followed arab. in reading *bouleuseōs* in 173.14; but Alexander's usual word is *boulē,* and the sandwiching of 'deliberation' *between* 'choice' and 'decision' would be odd.)

173.20. I have translated Ruland's conjectural supplement, based on *m.* 172.30f. above (cf. Apparatus).

173.25ff. should probably not be taken as indicating that the 'appearance' *necessitates* our deliberating (let alone *how* we deliberate and what decision we reach); cf. *q.* III. 13 107.25-37. The argument of 173.25-31 regards true causation as a *non-transitive* relation; cf. above, p. 157. From this point of view, if a chain of *transitive* causation can be traced back further, the true cause of the thing in question has not yet been found; to be the cause of C, B must itself be uncaused, or at least not have a cause which can itself be regarded as the cause of C. Cf. C.J.F. Williams, loc. cit. at p. 157; above 173.17ff.; and *f.* ch. XV and comm. (One may compare here Aristotle's analogy between man's initiating action and one animal's begetting another – *eth. Eud.* 2.6 1222b 16, *magna moralia* 1.11 1187a29ff.; even if there were factors by which it was necessarily predetermined that a creature should beget offspring, they would scarcely be *causes* of the offspring in the same way that its parent is.) Cf. also Sharples (1975,2) 46.

173.28. I.e., if deliberation does not exist, 'appearance' cannot be its cause (so Bruns ad loc.).

On 174.13ff. cf. above p. 149; 174.27ff., p. 163-4; and 174.35ff., p. 148. At 174.27, Dr. Ruland informs me, the literal translation of the Arabic would be *oud' eti* (or *kai*) *ei*; he compares its rendering at 174.34. Cf. *hoti* E for *eti* at *f.* 174.20.

174.35. Literally, 'if we are not always alike with respect to the disposition ...'.

175.10. Literally, 'we ourselves possess the beginning'.

For the point at 175.12ff., that everyone is naturally able to tell right from wrong and is aware of the effect of action upon character, cf. Bondeson, op. cit. at p. 7 n. 27 above, 61ff.

175.25f. Literally (but cf. App. Crit.): 'as long as they preserve the man in his own proper (i.e., human) nature'. For *mē pepērōmenois* (175.22) cf. *p.* XXIX 160.34; Aristotle *eth. Nic.* 1.9 1099b19.

175.28. For *adiastrophos* cf. Diogenes Laertius 7.89 (*SVF* 3.228); Sextus Empiricus *Purrh. hyp.* 3.194; Anon, *in eth. Nic., CAG* 20.232.10, Eustratius *in eth. Nic., CAG* 20.259.3, 403.11, and Michael of Ephesus *in eth. Nic., CAG* 22.3.46.10, 47.6.

Mantissa XXIV: 'On Luck'.

Cf. Introduction pp. 16-17; comm. on *f.* VIII; and Sharples (1975,2) 46-9.

176.10. 'of that sort': i.e. 'such as come to be fortuitously'.

177.17. Cf. Aristotle *physics* 2.5 197a8, 14ff.

178.15. Bruns takes the reference to be to the artificial production of misshapen monsters, but what is wanted is a case where skill leads to a result which is *not* intended; probably there is a quite general reference to cases where products of skill or craft turn out misshapen though the maker did not intend this.

178.26ff. The author is attempting to derive *automatōs* 'fortuitously' from *auto* 'itself' and *matēn* 'in vain'; cf. Aristotle *physics* 2.6 197b22-32. 'for the sake of which something comes to be by nature': literally, 'for the sake of which that, which comes to be by nature, comes to be'.

170.16ff. Cf. above, pp. 18-19.

179.18. 'this distinction': i.e. that ruled out at the beginning of the previous sentence, 'not ... *some* men, but ... all men'.

Mantissa XXV: 'On Fate'.
Cf. Introduction pp. 21, 23-4, and comm. pp. 128-130, 134, 139, 167, Sharples (1980) *passim*.
180.14-34: cf. Introduction pp. 18-19 and nn. 'those who are responsible ... art': i.e. the determinists whose doctrine of fate justifies the diviners' claims; Bruns, *Interpretationes variae* (Kiel 1893) 17. Above, p. 166.
181.1f.; the sense seems odd, but cf. *f*. XVI 186.20-3.
181.17. 'heavenly bodies': especially the planets, as the following reference to proper, peculiar motions shows.
181.22-28. This passage is difficult to reconcile with the treatment of exceptions to fate, and of contingency, in *f*. VI, IX, and *m*. 184.13-27, 185.15ff.; cf. Sharples (1975, 1) 271-4.
182.9. '[nature]' is suggested also, as a possibility, by Donini (1977; cf. p. 23) 182 n. 16; the expression is as he says tortuous, but does not seem impossibly so. Cf. Sharples (1980) 81 and n. 65.
183.1. Literally: 'the nature that is contingent.'
183.11. Literally: 'of which we are the beginnings to choose them or not.'
183.31. 'that the other living creatures [experience]': for *alogoi phantasiai* as the *phantasiai* of irrational animals cf. *SVF* 2.61. It is true that the passage as here translated is not strictly logical (how *could* men follow *other creatures'* impressions?) and that other Alexandrian texts speak as if men and irrational animals reacted differently to initial impressions which are themselves similar. However, *tois alogois tōn allōn zōōn* does not make sense. L's rendering supports *tais*; but the genitive with *paraplesiōs* as he takes it is rare, and Alexander regularly uses the dative (cf. *m*. 144.37, *q*. 89.1, 107.13, *f*. 179.15).
185.31. 'What is indifferent'; i.e. external, material goods (Stoic technical term).
186.1. Cf. *m*. 178.15, and for *echein aitian* = 'be responsible for', *f*. XVI 187.24. One might expect the nominative *sumpiptousa*; L indeed has the nominative, but this is not good evidence unless one also regards his *causa* and *erit* as directly reflecting the Greek.
186.7. Also cited at Gellius *noctes Atticae* 13.1.2.
186.18. 'that of the other things': i.e., the Great Winter as a fated time in the great cycle.

Quaestiones II.4, II.5
The problems and solutions of these *quaestiones* turn on relatively

superficial points of dubious logic. It is possible that the arguments that set up the problems have been constructed as logical exercises purely in the context of Alexander's school; cf. *f.* XXVI and commentary, though the issues raised there are more serious, and Introduction *p.* 20 and n. 132, *q.* II. 5 51.24-26, cited by von Arnim as part of *SVF* 2.1007, is clearly Alexander's own comment.

The problem in *q.* II. 4 is diagnosed as turning on a confusion between the faculty (*dunamis*, 51.15) of responsible action and the actions performed with it (*pragmata*, 51.7, cf. 51.14ff.; cf. Sharples (1975,2) 45f. and n. 78, 50 and n. 151, and, for the thesis that reason and responsible action are characteristic of men (51.5ff., 15ff.), *f.* XIV 183.30-184.20, XV 185.15ff., *m.* 172.19ff., *q.* II. 5 52.8. There is a slide in the statement of the paradox at 50.31-51.2 from 'the opposite of what depends on us is *what* does not depend on us' to 'the opposite of what depends on us does not depend on us'.

With Bruns' text at the beginning of II. 5, giving 'the opposite of something's depending on us is for nothing to depend on us and be possible; so the opposite of something's depending on us is impossible', the argument turns on a slide; but with *SVF*'s text, followed in the translation, there is simply an assertion that responsible action is a necessary property of man. For the distinction between necessity and fate, the latter being confined to the chain of causes, compare *m.* 181.9, 12, 22ff.; and cf. above p. 20. It does perhaps provide an adequate dialectical answer to a determinist position stated in terms of *fate* (51.25f.); but it would provide no answer to a claim that responsible action is preserved if all things come to be of *necessity*. More to the point would be an argument that action which is predetermined *cannot be* responsible action in the first place; cf., of right and wrong action, *f.* XXXIV 206.2ff.

At 51.25 one would rather expect 'by the fact that the dependence of something on us is in accordance with fate'; the expression may be inexact. Cf. Notes on the Text, below. At 52.7, similarly, one would expect 'the fact that something depends on us'. 'This too' (52.4): *sc.* as well as the definition that is *peculiar* to things in accordance with fate, and distinguishes them from those that are necessary but not fated (hence 'they too' in the following clause).

Quaestio III.13, 'Some points concerning that which depends on us'. This discussion covers similar ground to *f.* XI 178.17-28, XII, XIV

183.21-185.7, XV 186.3-12, *m.* 172.17-174.3; q.v. comm. At 107.19 omission of *ek tou* (cf. Notes on the Text) would give simply '... about what is perceived ...'. At 107.20 'always' is required by the argument, for deliberation without an appearance is certainly *sometimes* followed by assent to the initial appearance cf. *pollakis* in 107.22. To be formally valid the argument at 107.24-25 would require 'our assenting to appearances is the *only* thing that could do away with what depends on us'. On 107.25ff. cf. above p. 146. The reference at 180.1, 9-11 to appearances for which we are responsible is to our conception of the moral end, determined by our character, for which we are responsible as it is, at least in part, the result of our actions (above, pp. 148, 160; cf. *p.* IX 129.24 – 130.2, and Aristotle *eth. Nic.* 3.5 1114a31 – b25, with Hardie 176-80).

GREEK TEXT

ΑΛΕΞΑΝΔΡΟΥ ΑΦΡΟΔΙΣΙΕΩΣ ΠΡΟΣ ΤΟΥΣ ΑΥΤΟΚΡΑΤΟΡΑΣ ΠΕΡΙ ΕΙΜΑΡΜΕΝΗΣ.

Ed.
Orelli
p. 2

* vol. 2
p. 164
Bruns

Ἦν μὲν δι' εὐχῆς μοι, μέγιστοι αὐτοκράτορες Σεβῆρε καὶ 'Αντωνῖνε, I
αὐτῷ γενομένῳ παρ' ὑμῖν ἰδεῖν τε ὑμᾶς καὶ προσειπεῖν καὶ καθομολογῆσαι
5 χάριν ἀνθ' ὧν ἔπαθον εὖ παρ' ὑμῶν πολλάκις, αἰεὶ τυχὼν πάντων ὧν 5
ἠξίωσα μετὰ μαρτυρίας † ἧς δίκαιος εἶναι τυγχάνειν τοιαῦτα αἰτούμενος. ἐπεὶ *
δὲ ἐφεῖται, καὶ εἰ μὴ παρών τις τοῖς ἱεροῖς θύειν δύναται, τὸ θύειν αὐτοῖς *
πανταχόθεν τε καὶ πανταχοῦ καὶ πέμπειν ἀναθήματα, ἃ μὴ κομίζειν αὐτὸς οἷόν τε, ἐθάρσησα πρὸς ὑμᾶς τῇ πρὸς τὸ θεῖον ἐξουσίᾳ, καί τινα 10
10 ἀπαρχὴν ὑμῖν τῶν ἡμετέρων καρπῶν ἀνάθημα πέμψαι οἰκειότατον ὑμῖν ἀνα-
θημάτων ἁπάντων. τί γὰρ ἂν οἰκειότερον τοῖς γνησίως φιλοσοφίαν τιμῶ-
σίν τε καὶ προάγουσιν ἀνάθημα γένοιτο βιβλίου ὑπισχνουμένου θεωρίαν φιλό- 15
σοφον; περιέχει τε τὸ βιβλίον τὴν δόξαν τὴν 'Αριστοτέλους, ἣν ἔχει περί
τε εἱμαρμένης καὶ τοῦ ἐφ' ἡμῖν, οὗ τῆς φιλοσοφίας προΐσταμαι ὑπὸ τῆς
5 ὑμετέρας μαρτυρίας διδάσκαλος αὐτῆς κεκηρυγμένος. ἔστι δὲ οὐδενὸς δεύ- 20
τερον τῶν κατὰ φιλοσοφίαν δογμάτων τουτὶ τὸ δόγμα· ἥ τε γὰρ ἀπ' αὐ-
τοῦ χρεία πανταχοῦ | τε καὶ ἐπὶ πάντα διατείνει (οὐ γὰρ ὁμοίως περὶ τὰς 4
πράξεις ἔχουσιν οἵ τε πάντα ἐξ ἀνάγκης καὶ καθ' εἱμαρμένη γίγνεσθαι πεπιστευκότες καὶ οἷς δοκεῖ γίνεσθαί τινα καὶ μὴ τοῦ πάντως ἔσεσθαι προ- 5
) καταβεβλημένας αἰτίας ἔχοντα), ἥ τε εὕρεσις τῆς ἀληθείας τῆς ἐν αὐτῇ *
χαλεπωτάτη τῷ δοκεῖν τῶν δοξῶν ἑκατέρᾳ πολλὰ ἀντιμαρτυρεῖν τῶν ἐναργῶν. ἐπεὶ δὲ ἐνίων δογμάτων ⟨ἡ⟩ κατασκευὴ διὰ τὴν πρὸς τοὺς μὴ ὁμοίως 165
λέγοντας ἀντιλογίαν γίνεται φανερωτέρα (ὧν ἐν τοῖς μάλιστα κατ' αὐτοῦ * * 10 *
τε εἶεν μείζω ἢ κατὰ τὴν 'Αριστοτέλους δόξαν εἰπεῖν), ποιήσομαι τὸν λόγον
πρὸς τοὺς οὐχ ὁμοίως ἐκείνῳ περὶ τούτων εἰρηκότας, ὅπως ἐν τῇ τῶν λε-
5 γομένων παραθέσει φανερώτερον ὑμῖν τἀληθὲς γένηται. ἔστι δὲ ἡ τῶν λόγων 15
τῶν ἡμετέρων προαίρεσις οὐ πρὸς ἐπίδειξιν νενευκυῖα, ἀλλὰ πρὸς ἐξέτασίν τε
καὶ διδασκαλίαν τῶν προκειμένων ἀκριβεστέραν, ἣν καὶ ὑμᾶς πᾶσιν οἷς
πράσσετε ὁρᾶν ἔνεστιν ἐζηλωκότας. οὐδεμίαν γοῦν πρᾶξιν ὑμῶν ἔστιν εὑρεῖν,
ἣ τὴν φαντασίαν πρὸ τῆς ἀληθείας σκοπὸν πεποίηται. εἰ δέ τι κατὰ σχο- 20
10 λὴν ἐντυγχάνουσιν ὑμῖν τῷ βιβλίῳ δεῖσθαι δόξει ῥηθῆναι γνωριμώτερον,
ἀξιῶ τιμηθῆναι καὶ ταύτῃ τῇ τιμῇ πρὸς ὑμῶν καὶ γραφῆναί μοι περὶ τῶν
ζητουμένων· οὐδὲ γὰρ ῥᾴδιον πάντα γνώριμα ποιῆσαι δι' ἑνὸς βιβλίου αὐτά 25
τε τὰ προχείμενα καὶ οἷς τις χρῆται πρὸς τὴν μήνυσιν αὐτῶν.

Τὸ μὲν οὖν εἶναί τι τὴν εἱμαρμένην καὶ αἰτίαν εἶναι τοῦ γίνεσθαί II
15 τινα κατ᾽ αὐτὴν ἱκανῶς ἡ τῶν ἀνθρώπων συνίστησιν πρόληψις (οὐ γὰρ 30
κενὸν οὐδ᾽ ἄστοχον τἀληθοῦς ἡ κοινὴ τῶν ἀνθρώπων φύσις, καθ᾽ ἣν περί
τινων ὁμοδοξοῦσιν ἀλλήλοις, ὅσοι γε αὐτῶν μὴ διά τινας προκαταβεβλημέ-
νας δόξας ὑφ᾽ | αὐτῶν διὰ τὸ σώζειν βούλεσθαι τὴν πρὸς αὐτὰς ἀκολου- 6
θίαν ἄλλως ἀναγκάζονται λέγειν· δι᾽ ἣν αἰτίαν οὐδὲ Ἀναξαγόρας ὁ Κλα-
20 ζομένιος, καίτοι τἆλλα ὢν ἐν τοῖς τὴν φυσικὴν φιλοσοφίαν φιλοσοφήσασιν 5
οὐκ ἀπερριμμένος, οὐκ ἀξιόπιστος ἀντιμαρτυρῶν τῇ κοινῇ τῶν ἀνθρώπων
πίστει περὶ εἱμαρμένης· λέγει γὰρ οὗτός γε μηδὲν τῶν γινομένων γίνεσθαι
καθ᾽ εἱμαρμένην, ἀλλ᾽ εἶναι κενὸν τοῦτο τοὔνομα), τί δέ ποτ᾽ ἐστὶν ἡ εἱμαρμένη καὶ ἐν τίσιν, οὐκέθ᾽ [οὐ γὰρ μόνον οὐκ ἀλλήλοις ἅπαντες, ἀλλ᾽ 10
25 οὐδὲ] ἡ τῶν ἀνθρώπων κοινὴ πρόληψις ἱκανὴ τοῦτο μηνῦσαι. οὔτε γὰρ
ἀλλήλοις ἅπαντες, ἀλλ᾽ οὐδὲ αὐτὸς αὑτῷ τις περὶ αὐτῆς αἰεὶ [αὑτῷ] τὰ
αὐτὰ δοξάζει. πρὸς γὰρ τοὺς καιρούς τε καὶ τὰς περιεστώσας τύχας καὶ
τὴν περὶ τῆς εἱμαρμένης δόξαν μεταφέρουσιν. ὅσοι μὲν γὰρ αὐτῶν πάντα 15
καθ᾽ εἱμαρμένην γίνεσθαι λέγουσιν, τὴν εἱμαρμένην ὑπολαμβάνουσιν ἀπαράβατόν τινα αἰτίαν εἶναι καὶ ἀναπόδραστον, εἰσὶ δ᾽ οἷς οὐ πάντα τὰ γινόμενα γίνεσθαι δοκεῖ καθ᾽ εἱμαρμένην, ἀλλ᾽ εἶναί τινας ὑπολαμβάνουσιν τῶν 20
5 γινομένων καὶ ἄλλας αἰτίας· ἀλλ᾽ οὐδὲ τὴν εἱμαρμένην αὐτὴν τὸ πάγιόν τε
καὶ ἀπαράβατον ἔχειν τίθενται, ἀλλὰ γίνεσθαί τινα καὶ τῶν καθ᾽ εἱμαρμένην γίνεσθαι πεφυκότων οὐ κατ᾽ αὐτήν, ἀλλὰ παρὰ μοῖραν, ὡς οἱ ποιηταί
φασιν, καὶ παρὰ τὴν εἱμαρμένην. ἔστι δ᾽ οἷς ποτὲ πάντα γίνεσθαι τὰ γινό- 25
μενα δοκεῖ καθ᾽ εἱμαρμένην καὶ μάλιστ᾽ ἂν αὐτοῖς τὰ τῆς τύχης ἀντι-
10 πίπτῃ, κατορθοῦντες δὲ ἐν τοῖς προκειμένοις αὑτοὺς αἰτίους εἶναι τῶν κατορθωμάτων ὑπολαμβάνουσιν, ὡς οὐκ ἂν ἀπαντησάντων τῶν ἀπηντηκότων, 30
εἰ μὴ αὐτοὶ τάδε μᾶλλον ἔπραξαν ἀντὶ τῶνδε, ὡς ἔχοντες καὶ τοῦ μὴ πράττειν αὐτὰ τὴν ἐξουσίαν. δι᾽ ἣν διαφωνίαν ἀναγκαία τοῖς φιλοσοφοῦσιν ἡ
ζήτησις ἡ περὶ τῆς εἱμαρμένης, οὐκ εἰ ἔστιν, ἀλλὰ τί ποτ᾽ ἐστὶν καὶ ἐν
15 τίσιν τῶν γινομένων τε καὶ ὄντων ἐστὶν ἡ τοιαύτη φύσις. ὅτι μὲν οὖν 8 III
αἰτίαν τινὰ τὴν εἱμαρμένην τοῖς γινομένοις [ὧν] εἶναι λέγουσιν πάντες οἱ
περὶ εἱμαρμένης λέγοντές τι, γνώριμον (ταύτην γὰρ ἀποδιδόασίν τε καί φασιν
αἰτίαν εἶναι τοῦ γίνεσθαι τὰ γινόμενα ὃν τρόπον γίνεται), ἐπεὶ δὲ πλεοναχῶς 5
λέγεται τὰ αἴτια, ἀναγκαῖον τοῖς ἐν τάξει τὸ πρόβλημα μετιοῦσιν πρῶτον
20 λαβεῖν, ὑπὸ τίνα τρόπον τῶν αἰτίων χρὴ τιθέναι τὴν εἱμαρμένην· οὐδὲν
γὰρ τῶν πολλαχῶς λεγομένων γνώριμον χωρὶς τῆς οἰκείας διαιρέσεως λεγόμενον. διαιρεῖται δὴ τὰ τῶν γινομένων αἴτια εἰς τρόπους αἰτίων τέσσαρας, 10
καθὼς [αἰτίας] Ἀριστοτέλης δέδειχεν. τῶν γὰρ αἰτίων τὰ μέν ἐστι ποιητικά,
τὰ δὲ ὕλης ἐπέχει λόγον, ἔστι δέ τις ἐν αὐτοῖς καὶ ἡ κατὰ τὸ εἶδος αἰτία·
25 παρὰ δὲ τὰς τρεῖς ταύτας αἰτίας ἐστὶν αἴτιον ἐν αὐτοῖς καὶ τὸ τέλος, οὗ 15
χάριν καὶ τὸ γινόμενον γίνεται. καὶ τοσαῦται μὲν αἱ τῶν αἰτίων διαφοραί.
ὅτι γὰρ ἂν αἴτιον ᾖ τινος, ὑπὸ τούτων τι τῶν αἰτίων ὂν εὑρεθήσεται.
καὶ γὰρ εἰ μὴ πάντα τὰ γινόμενα τοσούτων αἰτίων δεῖται, ἀλλὰ τά γε
πλείστων δεόμενα οὐχ ὑπερβαίνει τὸν ἀριθμὸν τὸν εἰρημένον. γνωριμωτέρα 20

δ' ἂν αὐτῶν ἡ διαφορὰ γίγνοιτο, εἰ ἐπὶ παραδείγματός τινος τῶν γινο- 167
μένων ὁραθείη. ἔστω δὴ ἐπ' ἀνδριάντος ἡμῖν ἡ τῶν αἰτίων δεικνυμένη
διαίρεσις. τοῦ δὲ ἀνδριάντος ὡς μὲν ποιητικὸν αἴτιον ὁ ποιήσας τεχνίτης, 25
ὃν ἀνδριαντοποιὸν καλοῦμεν, ὡς δὲ ἡ ὕλη ὁ ὑποκείμενος χαλκὸς ἢ λίθος
5 ἢ ὅτι ἂν ᾖ τὸ ὑπὸ τοῦ τεχνίτου σχηματιζόμενον κατὰ τὴν τέχνην· αἴτιον
γὰρ καὶ τοῦτο τοῦ γεγονέναι τε καὶ εἶναι τὸν ἀνδριάντα. ἔστι δὲ καὶ τὸ
εἶδος τὸ ἐν τῷ ὑποκειμένῳ τούτῳ γενόμενον ὑπὸ τοῦ τεχνίτου καὶ αὐτὸ 30
τοῦ ἀνδριάντος αἴτιον, δι' ὅ ἐστιν εἶδος δισκεύων ἢ ἀκοντίζων ἢ ἐπ' ἄλλου
τινὸς ὡρισμένου σχήματος. οὐ μόνα δὲ ταῦτα τῆς τοῦ ἀνδριάντος γενέσεως
10 αἴτιά ἐστιν· οὐδενὸς γὰρ τῶν αἰτίων τῆς γενέσεως αὐτοῦ δεύτερον τὸ τέ- 10
λος, οὗ χάριν γεγονός ἐστι, ἢ τιμή τινος ἢ εἰς θεοὺς εὐσέβειά τις. ἄνευ
γὰρ τοιαύτης αἰτίας οὐδ' ἂν τὴν ἀρχὴν ὁ ἀνδριὰς ἐγένετο. ὄντων τοίνυν
τοσούτων τῶν αἰτίων καὶ τὴν πρὸς ἄλληλα διαφορὰν ἐχόντων γνώριμον 5
τὴν εἱμαρμένην ἐν τοῖς ποιητικοῖς αἰτίοις δικαίως ἂν καταριθμοῖμεν ἀναλο-
15 γίαν σώζουσαν πρὸς τὰ γινόμενα κατ' αὐτὴν τῷ τοῦ ἀνδριάντος δημιουργῷ
τεχνίτῃ. τούτου δ' οὕτως ἔχοντος ἀκόλουθον ἂν εἴη περὶ τῶν ποιητικῶν 10 IV
αἰτίων ποιήσασθαι τὸν λόγον. οὕτως γὰρ ἔσται γνώριμον, εἴ τε πάντων τῶν
γινομένων χρὴ τὴν εἱμαρμένην αἰτιᾶσθαι, εἴ τε δεῖ καὶ ἄλλοις τισὶν παρὰ
τήνδε συγχωρεῖν ὡς οὖσιν ποιητικοῖς τινων αἰτίοις. ἁπάντων δὴ τῶν
20 γινομένων Ἀριστοτέλης ποιούμενος τὴν διαίρεσιν τὰ μὲν αὐτῶν τινος χάριν 15
γίνεσθαι λέγει σκοπόν τινα καὶ τέλος τῶν γινομένων προκείμενον ἔχοντος
τοῦ ποιοῦντος αὐτά, τὰ δὲ οὐδενός. ὅσα γὰρ οὐ κατὰ πρόθεσίν τινα ὑπὸ
τοῦ ποιοῦντος γίνεται οὐδ' ἐπὶ τέλος ὡρισμένον ἔχει τὴν ἀναφοράν, τοιαῦτα 20
(ὁποῖά ἐστι χαρφῶν τέ τινων διακρατήσεις καὶ περιστροφαὶ καὶ τριχῶν ἐπα-
25 φαί τε καὶ ἐκτάσεις καὶ ὅσα τούτοις ὁμοίως γίνεται), [ἃ] ὅτι μὲν γίνεται
καὶ αὐτὰ γνώριμον, οὐ μὴν ἔχει τὴν κατὰ τὸ τέλος καὶ τίνος χάριν αἰτίαν. 25
τὰ μὲν οὖν οὕτως γινόμενα ἀσκόπως τε καὶ ἁπλῶς γινόμενα οὐδεμίαν εὔ- 168
λογον ἔχει διαίρεσιν, τῶν δὲ ἐπί τι τὴν ἀναφορὰν ἐχόντων καί τινος γινομένων χάριν τὰ μὲν κατὰ τὴν φύσιν, τὰ δὲ κατὰ τὸν λόγον γίνεται. τά
τε γὰρ φύσιν αἰτίαν ἔχοντα τῆς γενέσεως κατά τινας ἀριθμοὺς καὶ τάξιν 30
5 ὡρισμένην πρόεισιν εἴς τι τέλος, ἐν ᾧ γενόμενα τοῦ γίνεσθαι παύεται, εἰ
μή τι αὐτοῖς ἐνστὰν ἐμποδῶν γένοιτο τῇ κατὰ φύσιν αὐτῶν ἐπὶ τὸ προκεί- 12
μενον τέλος ὁδῷ, ἀλλὰ καὶ τὰ κατὰ λόγον γινόμενα ἔχει τι τέλος. οὐδὲν
γὰρ ὡς ἔτυχεν τῶν κατὰ λόγον γινομένων γίνεται, ἀλλ' ἐπί τινα σκοπὸν
ἡ ἀναφορὰ πᾶσιν αὐτοῖς. ἔστι δὲ κατὰ λόγον γινόμενα, ὅσα ὑπὸ τῶν ποι- 5
10 ούντων αὐτὰ γίνεται λογιζομένων τε περὶ αὐτῶν καὶ συντιθέντων καθ' ὃν
ἂν τρόπον γένοιντο. οὕτως γίνεται τά τε κατὰ τὰς τέχνας γινόμενα πάντα
καὶ κατὰ προαίρεσιν, ἃ διαφέρει τῶν γινομένων φύσει τῷ τὰ μὲν φύσει ✱
γινόμενα ἐν αὐτοῖς ἔχειν τὴν ἀρχήν τε καὶ αἰτίαν τῆς τοιαύτης γενέσεως 10
(τοιοῦτον γὰρ ἡ φύσις· καὶ γίνεται μὲν κατὰ τάξιν τινά, οὐ μὴν τῆς ποι-
15 ούσης αὐτὰ φύσεως ὁμοίως ταῖς τέχναις λογισμῷ περὶ αὐτῶν χρωμένης),
τὰ δὲ γινόμενα κατὰ τέχνην τε καὶ προαίρεσιν ἔξωθεν ἔχει τὴν ἀρχὴν τῆς 15
κινήσεως καὶ τὴν αἰτίαν τὴν ποιοῦσαν, ἀλλ' οὐκ ἐν αὐτοῖς καὶ τῆς γενέ- ✱

* σεως αὐτῶν τοῦ ποιοῦντος γίνεται περὶ αὐτῶν λογισμός. τρίτον δέ ἐστιν
ἐν τοῖς ἕνεκά του γινομένοις καὶ τὰ ἀπὸ τύχης τε καὶ ταὐτομάτου γίνεσθαι
20 πεπιστευμένα ταύτῃ τῶν προηγουμένως ἕνεκά του γινομένων διαφέροντα, 20
ᾗ ἐπ᾽ ἐκείνων μὲν πᾶν τὸ πρὸ τοῦ τέλους γινόμενον τοῦ τέλους χάριν γίνεται, ἐπὶ δὲ τούτων τὰ μὲν γινόμενα πρὸ τοῦ τέλους ἄλλου χάριν γίνεται,
ἀπαντᾷ δ᾽ αὐτοῖς ἄλλου χάριν γινομένοις ὡς τέλος τὸ αὐτομάτως τε καὶ 25
ἀπὸ τύχης γίνεσθαι λεγόμενον. τούτων δ᾽ οὕτως ἐχόντων καὶ πάντων τῶν V
25 γινομένων εἰς τούτους τοὺς τρόπους νενεμημένων ἀκόλουθον ἐπὶ τούτοις
ἰδεῖν, ἐν ποίῳ τῶν ποιητικῶν αἰτίων χρὴ τιθέναι τὴν εἱμαρμένην. ἆρά
γε ἐν τοῖς οὐδενὸς γινομένοις χάριν; ἢ τοῦτο μὲν παντάπασιν ἄλογον· αἰεὶ 30
169   γὰρ ἐπὶ τέλους τινὸς τῷ τῆς εἱμαρμένης ὀνόματι χρώμεθα καθ᾽ εἱμαρμένην
αὐτὸ λέγοντες γεγονέναι. διὸ ἐν τοῖς ἕνεκά του γινομένοις ἀναγκαῖον τιθέναι 14
τὴν εἱμαρμένην· καὶ ἐπεὶ τῶν ἕνεκά του γινομένων τὰ μὲν γίνεται κατὰ
λόγον, τὰ δὲ κατὰ φύσιν, ἢ ἐν ἀμφοτέροις αὐτοῖς τὴν εἱμαρμένην ἀναγκαῖον
5 εἶναι τίθεσθαι, ὡς πάντα τὰ γιγνόμενα καθ᾽ εἱμαρμένην γίνεσθαι λέγειν, 5
ἢ ἐν θατέρῳ. ἀλλὰ τὰ μὲν κατὰ λόγον γινόμενα τούτῳ δοκεῖ γίνεσθαι κατὰ
λόγον τῷ τὸν ποιοῦντα αὐτὰ καὶ τοῦ μὴ ποιεῖν ἔχειν ἐξουσίαν. τά τε γὰρ
ὑπὸ τῶν τεχνιτῶν γινόμενα κατὰ τέχνην οὐκ ἐξ ἀνάγκης ὑπ᾽ αὐτῶν γίνεσθαι δοκεῖ (οὕτως γοῦν ἕκαστον ποιοῦσιν αὐτῶν ὡς καὶ τοῦ μὴ ποιεῖν 10
10 αὐτὰ τὴν ἴσην ἔχοντες ἐξουσίαν· ἔτι τε πῶς οὐκ ἄτοπον τὴν οἰκίαν καὶ τὴν
κλίνην καθ᾽ εἱμαρμένην λέγειν γεγονέναι ἢ τὴν λύραν ἡρμόσθαι καθ᾽ εἱμαρμένην;), ἀλλὰ μὴν καὶ ὧν προαίρεσις κυρία (ταῦτα δ᾽ ἐστὶν ὅσα κατ᾽
ἀρετήν τε καὶ κακίαν πράττεται) καὶ ταῦτα ἐφ᾽ ἡμῖν εἶναι δοκεῖ. εἰ ἐφ᾽ 15
ἡμῖν δὲ ταῦτα, ὧν καὶ τοῦ πραχθῆναι καὶ τοῦ μὴ πραχθῆναι ἡμεῖς εἶναι
15 δοκοῦμεν κύριοι, τούτων δὲ οὐχ οἷόν τε λέγειν αἰτίαν τὴν εἱμαρμένην οὐδὲ
ἀρχὰς εἶναί τινας καὶ αἰτίας ἔξωθεν προκαταβεβλημένας τοῦ ¯πάντως ἢ 20
γενέσθαι τι αὐτῶν ἢ μὴ γενέσθαι (οὐκέτι γὰρ ἂν εἴη τι τούτων ἐφ᾽ ἡμῖν,
εἰ γένοιτο τοῦτον τὸν τρόπον), λείπεται δὴ λοιπὸν τὴν εἱμαρμένην ἐν τοῖς VI
φύσει γινομένοις εἶναι λέγειν, ὡς εἶναι ταὐτὸν εἱμαρμένην τε καὶ φύσιν.
20 τό τε γὰρ εἱμαρμένον κατὰ φύσιν καὶ τὸ κατὰ φύσιν εἱμαρμένον. οὐ γὰρ 25
κατὰ φύσιν μέν ἐστιν ἄνθρωπον ἐξ ἀνθρώπου καὶ ἵππον ἐξ ἵππου γίνεσθαι,
οὐ καθ᾽ εἱμαρμένην δέ, ἀλλὰ συνοδεύει τὰ αἴτια ταῦτα ἀλλήλοις ὡς ἂν
ἔχοντα κατὰ τοὔνομα μόνον τὴν διαφοράν. διὸ καὶ τὰ πρῶτα τῆς κατὰ
φύσιν ἑκάστοις γενέσεως αἴτια (ἔστιν δὲ ταῦτα ⟨τὰ⟩ θεῖα καὶ ἡ τούτων 30
25 εὔτακτος περιφορὰ) καὶ τῆς εἱμαρμένης αἴτια λέγουσιν. πάσης γὰρ γενέσεως ἀρχὴ ἡ τῶν θείων κατὰ τὴν κίνησιν ποιὰ σχέσις πρὸς τὰ τῇδε. οὔσης δὲ τῆς εἱμαρμένης ἐν τούτοις τε καὶ τοιαύτης ἀναγκαῖον ὡς ἂν ἔχῃ 16
τὰ γινόμενα κατὰ φύσιν οὕτως ἔχειν καὶ τὰ καθ᾽ εἱμαρμένην. ἀλλὰ μὴν
* τὰ γινόμενα κατὰ φύσιν οὐκ ἐξ ἀνάγκης γίνεται, ἀλλ᾽ ἔστιν ἡ γένεσις τῶν
30 οὕτω γινομένων ἐμποδιζομένη † διὸ ποτὲ μὲν ὡς ἐπὶ τὸ πλεῖστον μὲν γι- 5
νεται τὰ γινόμενα κατὰ φύσιν, οὐ μὴν ἐξ ἀνάγκης [ἔχει]. χώραν γὰρ ἐν
170   αὐτοῖς ἔχει καὶ τὸ παρὰ φύσιν καὶ γίνεται, ὑπό τινος αἰτίας ἔξωθεν ἐμποδισθείσης τῆς φύσεως εἰς τὸ ἔργον τὸ ἑαυτῆς. διὸ οὔτε ἐξ ἀνάγκης ἄν-

θρωπος ἐξ ἀνθρώπου ἀλλ' ὡς ἐπὶ τὸ πλεῖστον, ὥστε καὶ κατὰ τὴν ὡρίσθαι 10   *
δοκοῦσαν προθεσμίαν τοῖς γινομένοις κατὰ φύσιν ἕκαστον τῶν οὕτως γινο-
5 μένων ἀεὶ γίνεται. ὄντος δὲ ἐν τοῖς γινομένοις κατὰ φύσιν καὶ ⟨τοῦ⟩ παρὰ
φύσιν, ὥσπερ καὶ ἐν τοῖς κατὰ τέχνην, χώραν ἂν ἔχοι καὶ ἐν τοῖς κατὰ
τὴν εἱμαρμένην γινομένοις τὸ παρὰ τὴν εἱμαρμένην, ὥστ' εἰ χώραν ἔχει 15
τὸ παρὰ φύσιν καὶ μὴ κενόν ἐστιν ὄνομα, ἔχοι ἂν ἐν τοῖς γινομένοις χώραν
καὶ τὸ παρὰ τὴν εἱμαρμένην. διὸ καὶ λέγοι τις ἂν εὐλόγως τὴν οἰκείαν
10 φύσιν ἀρχὴν ἑκάστου καὶ αἰτίαν εἶναι τῆς τῶν γινομένων ἐν αὐτῷ κατὰ φύσιν 20
τάξεως. ἀπὸ ταύτης γὰρ ὡς ἐπὶ τὸ πλεῖστον οἵ τε βίοι τῶν ἀνθρώπων
τὴν τάξιν καὶ αἱ καταστροφαὶ λαμβάνουσιν. ὁρῶμεν γοῦν ὅτι καὶ τὸ σῶμα
τῷ τοῖον ἢ τοῖον εἶναι τὴν φύσιν καὶ ἐν νόσοις καὶ ἐν φθοραῖς ἀκολούθως
τῇ φυσικῇ συστάσει γίνεται, οὐ μὴν ἐξ ἀνάγκης· ἱκαναὶ γὰρ ἐκκροῦσαι 25
15 τὴν τοιάνδε τάξιν ἐπιμέλειαί τε καὶ ἀέρων ὑπαλλαγαὶ καὶ προστάξεις
ἰατρῶν καὶ συμβουλαὶ θεῶν. κατὰ δὲ τὸν αὐτὸν τρόπον καὶ ἐπὶ τῆς ψυχῆς
εὕροι τις ἂν παρὰ τὴν φυσικὴν κατασκευὴν διαφόρους γινομένας ἑκάστῳ τάς 30
τε προαιρέσεις καὶ τὰς πράξεις καὶ τοὺς βίους. ἦθος γὰρ ἀνθρώπων δαί-
μων κατὰ τὸν Ἡράκλειτον, τουτέστι φύσις. ὡς ἐπὶ τὸ πλεῖστον γὰρ ταῖς
20 φυσικαῖς κατασκευαῖς τε καὶ διαθέσεσιν τάς τε πράξεις καὶ τοὺς βίους καὶ
τὰς καταστροφὰς αὐτῶν ἀκολούθως ἰδεῖν ἔστι. τῷ μὲν γὰρ φιλοκινδύνῳ 18   *
καὶ θρασεῖ φύσει βίαιός τις καὶ ὁ θάνατος ὡς ἐπὶ τὸ πλεῖστον (αὕτη γὰρ
ἡ τῆς φύσεως εἱμαρμένη), τῷ δέ γε ἀκολάστῳ τὴν φύσιν τό τε ἐν ἡδοναῖς τοιαύταις καταζῆν καὶ ὁ τῶν ἀκρατῶν βίος, ἂν μή τι κάλλιον ἐν αὐτῷ 5
25 γενόμενον ἐμποδίζῃ, ⟨τῷ δὲ καρτερικῷ⟩ κατὰ φύσιν αἱ τῶν πόνων ὑπομο-   *
ναὶ καὶ αἱ κακοπάθειαι καὶ ⟨αἱ⟩ ἐν τοῖς τοιούτοις τοῦ βίου καταστροφαὶ
πάλιν εἰσὶ καθ' εἱμαρμένην. καὶ τοῖς ἀνελευθέροις δὲ τὴν φύσιν καὶ   171
ἀπλήστοις περὶ κτῆσιν χρημάτων καὶ τὰ τῆς εἱμαρμένης συνῳδά· ἐν ἀδι- 10
κίαις γὰρ ὡς ἐπὶ τὸ πλεῖστον ὁ τῶν τοιούτων βίος, καὶ ἡ τοῦ βίου δὲ κατα-
στροφὴ τοῖς κατ' αὐτὰ πράττουσιν ἀκόλουθος τούτοις. καὶ ἐπιλέγειν   *
5 εἰώθασιν τοῖς τοιούτοις, ὅταν ἐν ταῖς ἀκολούθοις τε τοῦ βίου ⟨καὶ⟩ καθ' εἱ- 15
μαρμένην περιστάσεσιν ὦσιν, ὡς ἑαυτοῖς γεγονόσιν αἰτίοις τῶν παρόντων
αὐτοῖς κακῶν. καὶ τοῦτ' ἄν τις παρίστασθαι βουλόμενος τοῖς τὰς μαντείας
ἐπαγγελλομένοις τοῦ μὴ πάντως αὐτοὺς ἐπιτυγχάνειν φέροι τὸ αἴτιον, μὴ
πάντα τὴν φύσιν ἑκάστου καὶ τὴν εἱμαρμένην εὐοδεῖν, ἀλλὰ γίνεσθαί τινα 20
10 καὶ παρ' αὐτήν, εἶναι δὲ τοὺς μάντεις μηνυτὰς τῶν γινομένων καθ' εἱμαρμένην, ὥσπερ οὖν καὶ τοὺς φυσιογνώμονας. εἰπόντος γοῦν Ζωπύρου τοῦ
φυσιογνώμονος περὶ Σωκράτους τοῦ φιλοσόφου ἄτοπά τινα καὶ πλεῖστον
ἀφεστῶτα τῆς προαιρέσεως αὐτοῦ τῆς κατὰ τὸν βίον καὶ ἐπὶ τούτοις ὑπὸ τῶν 25
περὶ τὸν Σωκράτη καταγελωμένου οὐδὲν εἶπεν ὁ Σωκράτης ἐψεῦσθαι τὸν Ζώ-
15 πυρον· ἦν γὰρ ἂν τοιοῦτος ὅσον ἐπὶ τῇ φύσει, εἰ μὴ διὰ τὴν ἐκ φιλοσοφίας ἄσκησιν ἀμείνων τῆς φύσεως ἐγένετο. καὶ αὕτη μὲν ἡ περὶ εἱμαρμένης 30
ὡς ἐπὶ κεφαλαίων εἰπεῖν κατὰ τοὺς ἀπὸ τοῦ Περιπάτου δόξα.

Ἡ δὲ κατασκευὴ τῶν εἰρημένων ἔσται φανερωτέρα παρατιθέντων ἡμῶν VII
ταῖς προηγουμέναις τῶν κειμένων ἀποδείξεσιν τὰ ἑπόμενα ἄτοπα τοῖς πάντα 20

* 20 καθ' εἱμαρμένην γίνεσθαι λέγουσιν· μιγνύντες γὰρ οὕτω τὸν λόγον τῇ [τε]
τῶν δοξῶν παρ' ἀλλήλας θέσει γνωριμώτερον τἀληθὲς ποιήσομεν καὶ πρὸς
τούτῳ οὐχ ἕξομεν ἀνάγκην μεμνῆσθαι τῶν αὐτῶν πολλάκις. εὐλόγως γὰρ 5
ἄν τις ἀπορήσαι, πῶς φιλοσοφεῖν τινες λέγοντες καὶ τὴν ἀλήθειαν τὴν ἐν
τοῖς οὖσιν μετέρχεσθαι καὶ ταύτην τῶν ἄλλων ἀνθρώπων πλέον ἔχειν [τοὺς
25 φιλοσοφοῦντας] ὑπολαμβάνοντες καὶ διὰ τοῦτο καὶ τοὺς ἄλλους ἐπὶ τοῦτο
προτρέποντες ἐπέδοσαν αὐτοὺς τῇ δόξῃ τῇ πάντα ἐξ ἀνάγκης τε καὶ καθ' 10
εἱμαρμένην γίνεσθαι λεγούσῃ, ἐφ' ἣν μόνους ὁρῶμεν καταφεύγοντας τῶν
ἰδιωτῶν τοὺς οὐδὲ αὐτοῖς συνειδότας δεξιὸν ἐπὶ τὴν εἱμαρμένην ἀφ' αὑ-
172 τῶν τὴν αἰτίαν τῶν περιεστώτων αὐτοὺς κακῶν. μεταφέροντας; δόξῃ οὔτε
τοῖς ἐναργέσι συναδούσῃ οὔτε τινὰς πιστὰς ἀποδείξεις τοῦ οὕτως ἔχειν 15
ἐχούσῃ· προσέτι τε ἀναιρούσῃ τὸ εἶναί τι ἐφ' ἡμῖν, οὗ πιστευθέντος τίς ἂν
ἄλλη μείζων ἐκ λόγων γένοιτο ζημία; ὅτι μὲν γὰρ παρὰ τὰ ἐναργῆ, δῆλον
5 ἐκ τοῦ πεπιστεῦσθαι μὲν σχεδὸν ὑπὸ πάντων ἰδιωτῶν τε καὶ φιλοσόφων 20
τὸ γίνεσθαί τινα καὶ αὐτομάτως καὶ ἀπὸ τύχης, εἶναι δέ τινα τῶν γινομένων καὶ ἐνδεχομένως· γινόμενα καὶ ἔχειν τινὰ χώραν ἐν τοῖς οὖσιν καὶ τὸ
μηδὲν μᾶλλον τόδε τοῦδε, τούτων δὲ μηδὲν σώζεσθαι κατὰ τοὺς ἐξ ἀναγ-
κης πάντα γίνεσθαι λέγοντας, εἴ γε σώζει μὲν αὐτὰ τὸ ἐφ' οἷς σημαινομέ- 25
10 νοις τὰ ὀνόματα ταῦτα κεῖσθαι πεπίστευται, ταῦτα μὴ κινεῖν· οὐ γὰρ τὸ
ἄλλα τινὰ ὑποβάλλοντα σημαινόμενα τοῖς ὀνόμασιν διὰ τοῦ μένειν ἐκεῖνα
μένειν ἡγεῖσθαι καὶ τὰ προειρημένα σωζόντων ἐστὶ τὰ κείμενα. οὐ γὰρ
σώζεται τὸ γίνεσθαί τινα ἀπὸ τύχης, ⟨ἂν⟩ ἀνελών τις τὴν τῶν οὕτως γινο- 30
μένων φύσιν ὄνομα θῆται τοῖς γινομένοις ἐξ ἀνάγκης τὴν τύχην, ἀλλ' αὐτὰ
* 15 δεῖξαι δυνάμενα σώζεσθαι, ἐφ' ὧν τὸ τῆς τύχης ὄνομα κατηγορεῖσθαι πεπίστευται.   22

Λέγεται δὴ πρὸς ἁπάντων ἀνθρώπων κοιναῖς τε καὶ φυσικαῖς ἐννοίαις VIII
ἐμμενόντων ταῦτα ἀπὸ τύχης τε καὶ τοῦ αὐτομάτου γίνεσθαι, ἃ αἰτίαις
* ἄλλων τινῶν ποιητικαῖς προηγουμέναις ἐπιγίνεται. ὅταν γὰρ ἄλλου τινὸς 5
20 χάριν γινομένῳ τινὶ μὴ τοῦτο ἀπαντήσῃ οὗ χάριν ἐγένετο, ἄλλο δέ, ὃ τὴν
ἀρχὴν μηδὲ ἠλπίζετο, τοῦτ' ἀπὸ τύχης λέγεται γεγονέναι καθ' αὑτὸ μὲν
γεγονὸς ἀναιτίως, κατὰ συμβεβηκὸς δ' ἐσχηκὸς αἴτιον τὸ γενόμενον ἐπ' ἄλλου
γενέσει τινός. καὶ ὅτι τοιοῦτόν τι λέγουσιν πάντες τὸ γινόμενον ἀπὸ τύ- 10
χης δῆλον ἐξ ὧν ὑποβάλλουσιν σημαινομένων οἷς ἀπὸ τύχης φασὶν γίνε-
* 25 σθαι. θησαυρόν τε γάρ φασιν ἀπὸ τύχης εὑρηκέναι τινά, κἂν ἄλλου χάριν ὀρύσσων τίς τινος, ἀλλ' οὐ τοῦ θησαυρὸν εὑρεῖν θησαυρῷ περιπέσῃ
(ὁ μὲν γὰρ τούτου χάριν ὀρύσσων οὐκ ἀπὸ τύχης· οὐ γὰρ χάριν ὤρυσσεν, 15
τοῦτο ἀπήντησεν αὐτῷ, ᾧ δὲ μηδὲ τῆς εὑρέσεως τοῦ θησαυροῦ ἔμελε,
ποιοῦντι δὲ ἄλλου τινὸς χάριν ἡ εὕρεσις ἀπήντησεν ὡς τέλος ἐκείνου, τοῦ-
30 τον ἀπὸ τύχης τὸν θησαυρὸν εὑρηκέναι πάντες λέγουσιν), ἀλλὰ καὶ τὸ ἀργύ-
173 ριον ἀπὸ τύχης κεκομίσθαι τινὰ λέγουσιν, ὅταν εἰς τὴν ἀγορὰν προελθὼν 20
ἄλλου τινὸς χάριν ἀργύριον ἔχοντι περιπεσὼν τῷ χρεώστῃ τὸ ὀφειλόμενον
αὑτῷ λάβῃ. τῷ γὰρ ⟨τοῦ⟩ προελθεῖν εἰς τὴν ἀγορὰν ἄλλο τι προηγούμενον τέλος ἔχοντι τὸ τὸ προοφειλόμενον λαβεῖν ἀπήντησεν ὡς τέλος κατὰ συμβε- 25

5 βηχὸς αὐτῷ γενόμενον· [τὸ μὲν ποιητικὸν αἴτιον τὸ δὲ τούτου τέλος·] οὐ γὰρ
ἀπὸ τύχης ἔτι λέγεταί τις τὸ ὀφειλόμενον εἰληφέναι, εἰ τούτου χάριν εἰς
τὴν ἀγορὰν προῆλθεν, ὅτι τὸ προκείμενον αὐτῷ τέλος ἡ πρόοδος ἔσχεν.
καὶ ὁ ἵππος δὲ αὐτομάτως τισὶν λέγεται σεσῶσθαι, ὅταν τροφῆς μὲν ἐλπίδι 30
ἢ ἄλλου τινὸς χάριν ἀποφύγῃ τοὺς κατέχοντας αὐτόν, ἀπαντήσῃ δὲ αὐτοῦ
10 τῇ φυγῇ καὶ τῷ δρόμῳ τὸ τοῖς δεσπόταις περιπεσεῖν. καὶ τί δεῖ ὑμῖν
πλείω παραδείγματα κατατίθεσθαι ἢ ἀκριβολογεῖσθαι περὶ τῶν προειρημέ- 24
νων; ἱκανὸν γὰρ ὡς πρὸς τὰ προκείμενα τὸ δεῖξαι ἐφ᾽ ὧν σημαινομένων
τὰ ὀνόματα κατηγορεῖται τὰ εἰρημένα. ὄντων δὴ τῶν ἀπὸ τύχης τε καὶ
αὐτομάτως γινομένων τοιούτων, ὡς μὴ γίνεσθαι κατὰ προηγουμένην αἰτίαν 5
15 (τῶν γὰρ σπανίως ἐπὶ τοῖς πρὸ αὐτῶν γεγονόσιν ἀπαντώντων τό τε αὐτόματον καὶ ἡ τύχη), πῶς ἂν σώζοιτό τι τῶν προειρημένων καθ᾽ οὓς πάντα
προγγησαμένοις τισὶν αἰτίοις καὶ προηγουμένοις ἐξ ἀνάγκης ἔστι τε τὰ ὄντα
καὶ τὰ γινόμενα γίνεται ἑκάστου τῶν γινομένων αἴτιόν τι προκαταβεβλημέ- 10
νον ἔχοντος, οὗ ὄντος ἢ γεγονότος ἀνάγκη καὶ αὐτὸ ἢ εἶναι ἢ γενέσθαι,   *
20 [τὸ] μηδὲν μὲν σώζοντας τῶν προειρημένων, κατ᾽ ἄλλου δέ τινος τὸ τῆς   *
τύχης νομοθετήσαντας ὄνομα; ⟨τὸ⟩ γὰρ τῷ μὴ ἀναιρεῖσθαι ἐκεῖνο ὑπὸ τοῦ πάντα 15   *
ἐξ ἀνάγκης γίνεσθαι τιθεμένου μηδὲ τὴν τύχην ἀναιρεῖσθαι λέγειν, σοφιζο-
μένων ἐστὶν ὁμοίως αὐτούς τε καὶ τοὺς ἀκούοντας αὐτῶν· οὕτως μὲν γὰρ
οὐδὲν κωλύσει λέγειν ταὐτὸν εἱμαρμένην τε εἶναι καὶ τύχην καὶ τοσοῦτον
25 ἀποδεῖν τοῦ τὴν τύχην ἀναιρεῖν, ὡς καὶ πάντα τὰ γινόμενα γίνεσθαι λέγειν 20
[οὐκ] ἀπὸ τύχης. ἀλλ᾽ οὐκ ἐπὶ τῷ τοὔνομα σώζειν τὸ τῆς τύχης εἶχον
τὴν αἰτίαν, ἀλλ᾽ ἐπὶ τῷ ἀναιρεῖν τὸ οὕτως γίνεσθαί τινα, ὧν τὸ ἀπὸ τύχης
τε καὶ τὸ αὐτόματον γίνεσθαι κατηγορεῖται. τί γὰρ ἄλλο ποιοῦσιν οἱ τὴν 25   *174
τύχην καὶ τὸ αὐτόματον ὁριζόμενοι αἰτίαν ἄδηλον ἀνθρωπίνῳ λογισμῷ, ⟨ἢ⟩
τύχης τι σημαινόμενον ἴδιον εἰσάγουσίν τε καὶ νομοθετοῦσιν; τὸ γὰρ εἰς
τὴν τούτου σύστασιν χρήσασθαι τῷ λέγειν τινὰς αὐτομάτως νοσεῖν, ὅταν
5 ἄδηλος ᾖ αὐτοῖς ἡ αἰτία τῆς νόσου, ψεῦδός· οὐ γὰρ ὡς οὔσης μέν τινος 30
αἰτίας, ἀδήλου δὲ αὐτοῖς οὕτω λέγουσιν, ἀλλ᾽ ἐφ᾽ ὧν ἀναιτίως γεγονέναι πείθουσιν αὐτούς, ἐπὶ τούτων τὸ αὐτόματον κατηγοροῦσιν· οὐδεὶς γοῦν, ἐφ᾽ οὗ
ζητοῦσιν τὴν αἰτίαν ὡς οὔσης, αὐτομάτως αὐτὸ γεγονέναι λέγει, ἀλλ᾽ οὐδ᾽
ὃ πέπεισταί τις αὐτομάτως γεγονέναι τούτου ζητεῖ τὴν αἰτίαν. διὸ οὐκέθ᾽ 26
10 οἱ ἰατροὶ περὶ τούτων οὕτω λέγουσιν, κἂν τυγχάνωσιν αὐτῶν ἔτι τὰς αἰτίας
ἀγνοοῦντες. οὐ γὰρ ἐφ᾽ ὧν προειρήκαμεν ὡς ἐπὶ πάντων ἀπὸ τύχης γίνε-   *
σθαι λεγομένων, ἀλλ᾽ ἐπ᾽ ἄλλων τινῶν κυριώτερος ὁ τοιοῦτος λόγος τῆς 5
τύχης ἂν κατηγοροῖτο, περὶ ὧν οὐδεὶς ὡς ἀπὸ τύχης γινομένων εἰπέν ποτε.
τῆς μὲν γὰρ εὑρέσεως τοῦ θησαυροῦ καὶ τοῦ τὸ ὀφειλόμενον λαβεῖν οὐκ
15 ἄδηλα ἀνθρωπίνῳ λογισμῷ τὰ αἴτια, ἀλλὰ φανερὰ καὶ πρόδηλα. τῆς μὲν 10
γὰρ εὑρέσεως τὸ ὀρύξαι, τοῦ δὲ τὸ ὀφειλόμενον λαβεῖν τὸ εἰς τὴν ἀγορὰν
προελθεῖν. οὔτε γὰρ ἂν ἐκεῖνος μὴ ὀρύσσων εὗρεν οὔτε οὗτος μὴ προελθὼν τὸ ὀφειλόμενον ἔλαβεν, ἀλλ᾽ ὅτι μὴ προηγούμενα τούτων αἴτια ⟨τὰ⟩
προειρημένα, ἀλλὰ ἄλλου τινὸς χάριν ἐγίνετο, διὰ τοῦτο ἀπὸ τύχης γίνε- 15
20 σθαι προείληπται. ἄδηλα δὲ τὰ αἴτια ἀνθρωπίνῳ λογισμῷ ἐκείνων μᾶλλον

186   De Fato IX

ἃ κατά τινας ἀντιπαθείας γίνεσθαι πεπίστευται ἀγνοουμένης τῆς αἰτίας δι'
ἣν γίνεται, ὁποῖα περίαπτά τέ τινα προσείληπται οὐδεμίαν εὔλογον καὶ πιθα-
νὴν αἰτίαν τοῦ ταῦτα ποιεῖν ἔχοντα, ἔτι δὲ ἐπαοιδαὶ καί τινες τοιαῦται 20
μαγγανεῖαι. τούτων γὰρ ὁμολογεῖται μὲν ὑπὸ πάντων ἄδηλος εἶναι ἡ αἰ-
25 τία, διὸ καὶ ἀναιτιολόγητα λέγουσιν αὐτά. οὐδεὶς δὲ ἀπὸ τύχης τούτων ⟨τι⟩
ποιεῖν λέγει, ὅτι πεπίστευται κατά τινα ὡρισμένην αἰτίαν ἃ ποιεῖ ποιεῖν, 25
ὡς τῶν ἀπὸ τύχης οὐ διὰ τὸ τῆς αἰτίας ἄδηλον οὕτως γίνεσθαι λεγομένων, ἀλλὰ διὰ τὸ ἀναίτιον τῆς προηγουμένης τε καὶ κυρίως αἰτίας.
Καὶ τοιαῦτα μὲν τὰ περὶ τῆς τύχης ὑπ' αὐτῶν λεγόμενα καὶ οὕτως IX
30 τοῖς κειμένοις συνᾴδοντα· ὅτι δὲ καὶ τὸ ἐνδεχόμενόν τε καὶ τὸ ὁπότερ' 30
175   ἔτυχεν γίνεσθαί τινα ὑπὸ τῶν πάντα ἐξ ἀνάγκης γίνεσθαι λεγόντων ἀναιρεῖται, αὐτόθεν πρόδηλον, εἴ γε ταῦτα μὲν κυρίως ἐνδεχομένως γίνεσθαι λέγεται, ἐφ' ὧν καὶ τὸ ἐνδέχεσθαι μὴ γενέσθαι χώραν ἔχει, ὡς καὶ αὐτὸ 28
τὸ ὁπότερ' ἔτυχεν λεγόμενον ποιεῖ γνώριμον, τὰ δ' ἐξ ἀνάγκης γινόμενα
5 οὐκ ἐνδέχεται μὴ γενέσθαι. λέγω δὲ τὸ ἀναγκαῖον οὐκ ἐπὶ τοῦ βίᾳ γινομένου μηδὲ κατὰ τούτου τις εὐθυνέτω τοὔνομα, ἀλλ' ἐπὶ τῶν φύσει γινο- 5
μένων ὑπό τινων, ὧν τὰ ἀντικείμενα ἀδύνατον ⟨ἂν⟩ εἴη γίνεσθαι. καίτοι πῶς
οὐκ ἄτοπα καὶ παρὰ τὰ ἐναργῆ καὶ μέχρι τούτων τὴν ἀνάγκην προεληλυ-
θέναι λέγειν, ὡς μήτε κινηθῆναί τινα δύνασθαι κίνησίν τινα μήτε κινῆσαί
10 τι τῶν αὑτοῦ μερῶν, ἣν κίνησιν καὶ μὴ κινεῖσθαι τότε οἷόν τε ἦν, ἀλλὰ 10
τὴν τυχοῦσαν τοῦ τραχήλου περιστροφὴν καὶ τὴν δακτύλου τινὸς ἔκτασιν
καὶ τὸ ἐπᾶραι τὰ βλέφαρα ἤ τι τῶν τοιούτων προηγουμέναις τισὶν αἰτίαις
ἑπόμενον ἄλλως ὑφ' ἡμῶν μὴ δύνασθαι γίνεσθαί ποτε, καὶ ταῦτα ὁρῶν-
τας ἐν τοῖς οὖσίν τε καὶ γινομένοις πολλὴν οὖσαν διαφορὰν τῶν πραγμά- 15
15 των, ἐξ ἧς ῥᾴδιον ἦν μαθεῖν ὅτι μὴ πάντα ἐνδέδεται ταῖς τοιαύταις αἰτίαις; ὁρῶμεν γοῦν τῶν ὄντων τὰ μέν τινα οὐδεμίαν ἔχοντα δύναμιν τῆς εἰς
τὸ ἀντικείμενον τοῦ ἐν ᾧ ἐστι μεταβολῆς, τὰ δ' οὐδὲν μᾶλλον αὐτῶν ἐν 20
τῷ ἀντικειμένῳ ἢ ἐν ᾧ ἐστιν εἶναι δυνάμενα. πῦρ μὲν γὰρ οὐχ οἷόν τε
δέξασθαι ψυχρότητα, ἥτις ἐστὶν ἐναντία αὐτοῦ τῇ συμφύτῳ θερμότητι,
20 ἀλλ' οὐδὲ χιὼν δέξαιτ' ἂν θερμότητα χιὼν μένουσα, ὕδωρ δὲ κἂν ᾖ ψυχρὸν
οὐκ ἀδύνατον ἀποβαλὸν ταύτην δέξασθαι τὴν ἐναντίαν αὐτῇ θερμότητα· 25
*   ὁμοίως δὲ καὶ τούτῳ δυνατὸν καὶ τὸν καθεζόμενον στῆναι καὶ τὸν κινούμενον ἠρεμῆσαι καὶ τὸν λαλοῦντα σιγῆσαι καὶ ἐπὶ μυρίων εὕροι τις ἂν
δύναμίν τινα ἐνυπάρχουσαν τῶν ἐναντίων δεκτικήν, ὧν, εἰ τὰ ἐξ ἀνάγκης
25 ὄντα ἐν θατέρῳ οὐκ ἔχει δύναμιν τοῦ δέξασθαι τοῦ ἐν ᾧ ἐστι τὸ ἐναν- 30
τίον, οὐκ ἐξ ἀνάγκης ἂν εἴη ἐν οἷς ἐστι τὰ καὶ τοῦ ἐναντίου αὐτοῖς
δεκτικά. εἰ δὲ μὴ ἐξ ἀνάγκης, ἐνδεχομένως. τὰ δὲ ἐνδεχομένως ἔν τινι
176   οὕτως ἐστὶν ἐν αὐτῷ ὡς οὐκ ἐξ ἀνάγκης ἀλλ' ὡς ἐνδεχομένως ἐν αὐτῷ
*   γεγονότα. τὸ δὲ ἐνδεχομένως γεγονὸς ἔν τινι καὶ μὴ γεγονέναι ἐν αὐτῷ 30
οἷόν τε ἦν. ἔστι μὲν γὰρ ἕκαστον καὶ τούτων ἐν ᾧ ὂν τυγχάνει, διότι
ἦν ἐν θατέρῳ αὐτῷ ἀντικειμένῳ εἶναι, ἐν ᾧ δ' ἐστὶ νῦν, οὐκ ἐξ ἀνάγκης 5
ἁπλῶς ἐστιν ἐν τούτῳ διὰ τὴν πρὸς τὰ ἀντικείμενα δύναμιν. ἀλλὰ μὴν
5 τὰ οὕτως ὄντα ἔν τισιν οὐ δι' αἰτίας τινὰς προκαταβεβλημένας [τε] ἐξ

ἀνάγκης εἰς ταῦτα ἀγούσας ἐστὶν ἐν αὐτοῖς. ὥστ' εἰ πάντα τὰ ὁμοίως
τῶν ἀντικειμένων ὄντα δεκτικὰ ἐνδεχομένως τέ ἐστιν ἐν οἷς ἐστιν καὶ 10
οὐκ ἔστιν ἐν οἷς οὐκ ἔστι, μυρία ἂν εἴη τὰ ἐνδεχομένως ὄντα τε καὶ γινόμενα. ἄτοπον γὰρ ὁμοίως ἐξ ἀνάγκης εἶναι λέγειν ἔν τινι τά τε ἀνεπί-
10 δεκτα τῶν ἐναντίων τούτοις ἐν οἷς ἐστι καὶ τὰ μηδὲν μᾶλλον, καθ' ὁντιν-
οῦν χρόνον τούτων ἢ τῶν ἐναντίων αὐτοῖς δεκτικά. εἰ γὰρ τὰ ἐξ ἀνάγκης 15
ὄντα ἔν τινι ἀνεπίδεκτα τοῦ ἐναντίου αὐτῷ, τὰ ἐπιδεκτικὰ τοῦ ἐναντίου οὐκ
ἐξ ἀνάγκης ἂν ἐν ᾧ ἐστιν εἴη.

Τὸ δὲ λέγειν μὴ ἀναιρεῖσθαι πάντων γινομένων καθ' εἱμαρμένην τὸ X
15 δυνατόν τε καὶ ἐνδεχόμενον τῷ δυνατὸν μὲν εἶναι γενέσθαι τοῦτο ὃ ὑπ' 20
οὐδενὸς κωλύεται γενέσθαι, κἂν μὴ γένηται (τῶν δὲ καθ' εἱμαρμένην γι-   *
νομένων οὐ κεκωλῦσθαι τὰ ἀντικείμενα γενέσθαι· διὸ καίτοι μὴ γινόμενα   *
ὅμως ἐστὶ δυνατά), καὶ τοῦ μὴ κεκωλῦσθαι γενέσθαι αὐτὰ ἀπόδειξιν φέρειν
τὸ ἡμῖν τὰ κωλύοντα αὐτὰ [ἂν] ἄγνωστα εἶναι πάντως μέν τινα ὄντα (ἃ 25
20 γάρ ἐστιν αἴτια τοῦ γίνεσθαι τὰ ἀντικείμενα αὐτοῖς καθ' εἱμαρμένην, ταῦτα
καὶ τοῦ μὴ γίνεσθαι τούτοις αἴτια, εἴ γε ὥς φασιν ἀδύνατον τῶν αὐτῶν
περιεστώτων γίνεσθαι τὰ ἀντικείμενα· ἀλλ' ὅτι μὴ ἡμῖν ἐστι γνώριμά 30
τινα ἅ ἐστι, διὰ τοῦτο ἀκώλυτον αὐτῶν τὸ | [μὴ] γίνεσθαι λέγουσιν), τὸ 32
δὴ ταῦτα λέγειν πῶς οὐ παιζόντων ἐστὶν ἐν οὐ παιδιᾶς λόγοις δεομένοις;
25 τὸ γὰρ ἡμᾶς ἀγνοεῖν, οὐδὲν πρὸς τὸ εἶναι ἢ μὴ εἶναι τὰ πράγματα· δῆλοι
γάρ εἰσιν οἱ λέγοντες οὕτως ὡς τῇ ἡμετέρᾳ γνωρίσει τὸ δυνατὸν ἔσται κατ' 5
αὐτούς. τοῖς γὰρ γνωρίζειν αὐτῶν τὰ αἴτια δυναμένοις (οὗτοι δ' ἂν εἶεν
οἱ μάντεις) οὐκ ἔσται δυνατὰ † ὄντα δυνατοῖς εἰδόσιν μὲν αὐτὰ κεκωλυκέναι   *177
ἀγνοοῦσιν δὲ ὑφ' ἡμῶν κωλύοντες. σώζοντες δὲ τὴν τοῦ δυνατοῦ φύσιν 10   *
οὕτως ὡς εἰρήκαμεν διὰ τοῦτό φασιν μηδὲ τὰ γιγνόμενα καθ' εἱμαρμέ-
5 νην καίτοι ἀπαραβάτως γινόμενα ἐξ ἀνάγκης γίνεσθαι, ὅτι ἐστὶν αὐτοῖς
δυνατὸν γενέσθαι καὶ τὸ ἀντικείμενον, δυνατὸν οὕτως ὡς προείρηται. ἀλλὰ 15
ταῦτα μὲν παιζόντων ὥσπερ εἶπόν ἐστιν, ἀλλ' οὐ παρισταμένων δόγματι.
ὅμοιον δὲ τούτῳ καὶ τὸ λέγειν, τὸ ἀξίωμα τὸ 'ἔσται αὔριον ναυμαχία' ἀληθὲς μὲν εἶναι δύνασθαι, οὐ μέντοι καὶ ἀναγκαῖον. ἀναγκαῖον μὲν γὰρ τὸ
ἀεὶ ἀληθές, τοῦτο δὲ οὐκέτ' ἀληθὲς μένει, ἐπειδὰν ἡ ναυμαχία γένηται. 20
10 εἰ δὲ μὴ τοῦτο ἀναγκαῖον, οὐδὲ τὸ ὑπ' αὐτοῦ σημαινόμενον τὸ ἐξ ἀνάγκης   *
ἔσεσθαι ναυμαχίαν. εἰ δὲ ἔσται μὲν οὐκ ἐξ ἀνάγκης ἀληθές, ἀληθοῦς   *
ὄντος τοῦ ἔσεσθαι ναυμαχίαν, οὐκ ἐξ ἀνάγκης δέ, ἐνδεχομένως δηλονότι.
εἰ δὲ ἐνδεχομένως, οὐκ ἀναιρεῖται τὸ ἐνδεχομένως τινὰ γενέσθαι ὑπὸ τοῦ 25
πάντα γίνεσθαι καθ' εἱμαρμένην. πάλιν γὰρ καὶ τοῦτο (ὅμοιον τῷ προειρημένῳ)·
15 ὁμοῦ γὰρ παιζόντων ὁμοῦ δὲ ἀγνοούντων περὶ ὧν λέγουσιν. οὔτε γὰρ πᾶν τὸ
ἐξ ἀνάγκης γιγνόμενον ἀναγκαῖον, εἴ γε τὸ μὲν ἀναγκαῖον ἀΐδιον, τὸ δὲ ἐξ 30
ἀνάγκης γινόμενον ὑπ' αὐτοῦ τοῦ γίνεσθαι τοιοῦτον εἶναι κεκώλυται, οὔτε
τὸ ἀξίωμα τὸ τοῦτο λέγον ἀναγκαῖον, εἴ γε μὴ τὸ ὑπ' αὐτοῦ σημαινόμενον
τοιοῦτον. οὐ γὰρ πᾶν ἀξίωμα, ἐν ᾧ τὸ ἀναγκαῖον περιέχεται, ἀναγκαῖον
20 ἤδη † εἴ γε μήν· οὐ γὰρ | ταύτῃ τὸ ἀναγκαῖον ἀξίωμα κρίνεται, ἀλλὰ τῷ μὴ 34   *
μεταπίπτειν δύνασθαι εἰς ψεῦδος ἐξ ἀληθοῦς. εἰ τοίνυν μὴ ἀναγκαῖον, οὐδὲν

188   De Fato XI

* κεκώλυται ἀληθὲς εἶναι [ὡς] τὸ 'ἔσται αὔριον ναυμαχία'· εἰ γὰρ ὡς
ἀναγκαῖον λεγόμενον διὰ τὴν τοῦ ἀναγκαίου προσθήκην οὐκ ἀληθές, εἰ 5
* μὴ λέγοιτο ἀναγκαῖον τῇ τοῦ ἐξ ἀνάγκης προσθέσει, ἀληθὲς ἂν μένοι
* 25 ὁμοίως τῷ χωρὶς τῆσδε τῆς προσθήκης λεγομένῳ. ἀλλ' εἰ τότ' ἀληθές,
ἀληθὲς ἔσται, ἐνστάσης τῆς αὔριον, ἀξίωμα τὸ ἐξ ἀνάγκης γεγονέναι ναυ- 10
μαχίαν. εἰ δὲ ἐξ ἀνάγκης, οὐκ ἐνδεχομένως. καὶ γὰρ εἰ ἀληθές ἐστι τὸ
'αὔριον ἔσται ναυμαχία', ἀεὶ γενέσθαι ναυμαχίαν καθ' εἱμαρμένην ἔσται, εἴ γε
178 πάντα τὰ γινόμενα καθ' εἱμαρμένην. ἀλλ' εἰ καθ' εἱμαρμένην, ἀπαραβάτως, εἰ ⟨δ'⟩ ἀπαραβάτως, οὐκ ἐνδέχεται μὴ γενέσθαι, ὃ δὲ οὐκ ἐνδέχεται 15
μὴ γενέσθαι, τοῦτο ἀδύνατον μὴ γενέσθαι, ὃ δὲ ἀδύνατον μὴ γενέσθαι,
πῶς οἷόν τε τοῦτο λέγειν ἐνδέχεσθαι καὶ μὴ γενέσθαι; τὸ γὰρ ἀδύνατον
5 μὴ γενέσθαι ἀναγκαῖον γενέσθαι. πάντα ἄρα τὰ καθ' εἱμαρμένην γινό- 20
* μενα ἐξ ἀνάγκης ἔσται κατ' αὐτούς, ἀλλ' οὐχὶ καὶ ἐνδεχομένως, ὡς παί-
ζοντες λέγουσιν.
Ἀκολουθεῖ δὲ τῷ πάντα τὰ γινόμενα προκαταβεβλημέναις καὶ ὡρισ- XI
μέναις καὶ προυπαρχούσαις τισὶν αἰτίαις ἔσεσθαι τὸ καὶ βουλεύεσθαι τοὺς 25
10 ἀνθρώπους μάτην περὶ τῶν πρακτέων αὐτοῖς. εἰ δὲ τὸ βουλεύεσθαι μάτην, μάτην ⟨ἂν⟩ ἄνθρωπος εἴη βουλευτικός. καίτοι εἰ μηδὲν μάτην ἡ
φύσις ποιεῖ τῶν προηγουμένων, τὸ δὲ βουλευτικὸν εἶναι ζῷον τὸν ἄν-
θρωπον | προηγουμένως ὑπὸ τῆς φύσεως, ἀλλ' οὐ κατ' ἐπακολούθημά 36
τι καὶ σύμπτωμα τοῖς προηγουμένως γινομένοις γίνοιτο, συνάγοιτο ἂν ⟨τὸ⟩ μὴ
15 εἶναι μάτην τοὺς ἀνθρώπους βουλευτικούς. ὅτι δὲ τὸ βουλεύεσθαι μάτην 5
πάντων γινομένων ἐξ ἀνάγκης, ῥάδιον γνῶναι τὴν τοῦ βουλεύεσθαι χρείαν
εἰδόσιν. ὁμολογεῖται δὴ πρὸς ἁπάντων τὸ τῶν ἄλλων ζῴων τὸν ἄνθρωπον τοῦτο παρὰ τῆς φύσεως ἔχειν πλέον τὸ μὴ ὁμοίως ἐκείνοις ταῖς φαντασίαις ἕπεσθαι, ἀλλ' ἔχειν παρ' αὐτῆς κριτὴν τῶν προσπιπτουσῶν φαν- 10
20 τασιῶν περί τινων ὡς αἱρετῶν τὸν λόγον, ᾧ χρώμενος, εἰ μὲν ἐξεταζόμενα
τὰ φαντασθέντα, οἷα τὴν ἀρχὴν ἐφάνη, καὶ ἔστι, συγκατατίθεταί τε τῇ
φαντασίᾳ καὶ οὕτως μέτεισιν αὐτά, εἰ δὲ ἀλλοῖα φαίνεται ἢ ἄλλο τι αὖ
αἱρετώτερον, ἐκεῖνο αἱρεῖται καταλείπων τὸ τὴν ἀρχὴν ὡς αἱρετὸν αὐτῷ 15
φανέν. πολλὰ γοῦν ταῖς πρώταις φαντασίαις ἡμῖν ἀλλοῖα δόξαντα οὐκέτ'
25 ἔμεινεν ἐπὶ τῆς προλήψεως ἐλέγξαντος αὐτὰ τοῦ λόγου. διὸ πραχθέντα
ἂν ὅσον ἐπὶ τῇ αὐτῶν γενομένῃ φαντασίᾳ [γενομένῃ], διὰ τὸ βουλεύσασθαι 20
περὶ αὐτῶν οὐκ ἐπράχθη, ἡμῶν τοῦ τε βουλεύσασθαι καὶ τῆς αἱρέσεως
τῶν ἐκ τῆς βουλῆς ὄντων κυρίων. διὰ τοῦτο γοῦν οὔτε περὶ τῶν ἀιδίων
βουλευόμεθα οὔτε περὶ τῶν ὁμολογουμένως γινομένων ἐξ ἀνάγκης, ὅτι
30 μηδὲν ἡμῖν ἐκ τοῦ περὶ αὐτῶν βουλεύεσθαι περιγίνεται πλέον. ἀλλ' οὐδὲ 25
περὶ τῶν ἐξ ἀνάγκης μὲν μὴ γινομένων, ἐπ' ἄλλοις δέ τισιν ὄντων βουλευόμεθα, ὅτι μηδὲ ἀπὸ τῆς περὶ ἐκείνων βουλῆς ὄφελός τι ἡμῖν· ἀλλ'
οὐδὲ περὶ τῶν ἡμῖν μὲν πρακτῶν, παρεληλυθότων δὲ βουλευόμεθα, ὅτι
179 μηδὲ τῇ περὶ τούτων βουλῇ πλέον τι ἡμῖν γίνεται. βουλευόμεθα δὲ 30
περὶ μόνων τῶν ὑφ' ἡμῶν τε πραττομένων καὶ μελλόντων, δῆλον ὡς
ἐξοντές τι διὰ τούτου πλέον εἰς τὴν αἵρεσίν τε καὶ πρᾶξιν αὐτῶν. εἰ γάρ,

ἐν οἷς οὐδὲν ἡμῖν πλέον ἐκ τοῦ βουλεύεσθαι ⟨τοῦ βουλεύεσθαι⟩ αὐτοῦ μόνου *
5 περιγίνεται, οὐ βουλευόμεθα, | δῆλον ὡς ἐν οἷς βουλευόμεθα πλέον τι ἕξοντες 38 *
ἐκ τοῦ βουλεύεσθαι παρὰ τὸ βουλεύσασθαι βουλευόμεθα περὶ αὐτῶν † ἐπ' αὐτό *
τε τὸ βουλεύσασθαι περιγίνεται καὶ περὶ τῶν ἄλλων βουλευομένοις περὶ *
ὧν προειρήκαμεν. τί ποτ' οὖν τὸ περιγινόμενον ἐκ τῆς βουλῆς; τὸ ἔχον- 5
τας ἡμᾶς ἐξουσίαν τῆς αἱρέσεως τῶν πρακτέων, ὃ οὐκ ἂν ἐπράξαμεν μὴ
10 βουλευσάμενοι τῷ ἄλλο πρᾶξαι ἂν διὰ τὸ εἶξαι τῇ προσπεσούσῃ φαντασίᾳ.
τοῦτο αἱρετώτερον ὑπὸ λόγου φανὲν αἱρεῖσθαί τε καὶ πράττειν πρὸ ἐκεί- 10
νου· ὃ γίνοιτ' ἄν, εἰ μὴ πάντα πράττομεν κατηναγκασμένως. εἰ δὲ εἴη-
μεν πάντα ἃ πράττομεν πράττοντες διά τινας αἰτίας προκαταβεβλημένας ὡς
μηδεμίαν ἔχειν ἐξουσίαν τοῦ πρᾶξαι τόδε τι καὶ μή, ἀλλ' ἀφωρισμένως
15 ἕκαστον πράττειν ὧν πράττομεν, παραπλησίως τῷ θερμαίνοντι πυρὶ καὶ 15
τῷ λίθῳ τῷ κάτω φερομένῳ καὶ τῷ κατὰ τοῦ πρανοῦς κυλιομένῳ κυλίν-
δρῳ, τί πλέον ἡμῖν εἰς τὸ πράττειν ἐκ τοῦ βουλεύσασθαι περὶ τοῦ πρα-
χθησομένου γίνεται; ὃ γὰρ ἂν ἐπράξαμεν μὴ βουλευσάμενοι, τοῦτο καὶ 20
μετὰ τὸ βουλεύσασθαι πράττειν ἀνάγκη, ὥστ' οὐδὲν ἡμῖν πλέον ἐκ τοῦ
20 βουλεύσασθαι αὐτοῦ τοῦ βουλεύσασθαι περιγίνεται. ἀλλὰ μὴν τοῦτο καὶ
ἐπὶ τῶν ⟨οὐκ⟩ ἐφ' ἡμῖν δυνάμενοι ποιεῖν ὡς ἄχρηστον ὃν παρῃτούμεθα.
ἄχρηστον ἄρα τὸ βουλεύσασθαι, καὶ ἐφ' ὧν αὐτῷ ὥς τι χρήσιμον ἡμῖν 25 *
παρεχομένῳ χρώμεθα. ᾧ εἵπετο τὸ μάτην ἡμῖν ὑπὸ τῆς φύσεως τὸ βουλευτικοῖς εἶναι δεδόσθαι. ᾧ προστεθέντος τοῦ αὐτοῖς γε τούτοις καὶ κοι-
25 νῶς πᾶσιν σχεδὸν τοῖς φιλοσοφοῦσιν δοκοῦντος, τοῦ μηδὲν ὑπὸ τῆς φύσεως 30
γίνεσθαι μάτην, ἀναιροῖτο ἄν, ᾧ εἵπετο τὸ μάτην ἡμᾶς εἶναι βουλευτικούς.
εἵπετο δὲ τοῦτο τῷ τῶν πραττομένων ὑφ' ἡμῶν μὴ ἔχειν ἡμᾶς τοιαύτην
ἐξουσίαν, ὡς δύνασθαι τὰ ἀντικείμενα. |					180

Ἀναιρουμένου δὲ ὡς ἐδείχθη τοῦ βουλεύσασθαι κατ' αὐτοὺς ἀναιρεῖ- 40 XII
ται καὶ τὸ ἐφ' ἡμῖν προδήλως. τοῦτο γὰρ ἐφ' ἡμῖν πάντες, ὅσοι μὴ
5 θέσει τινὶ παρίστανται, παρειλήφασιν εἶναι, οὗ ἡμεῖς μὲν καὶ τοῦ πραχθῆ- 5
ναι καὶ τοῦ μὴ πραχθῆναι κύριοι, οὐχ ἑπόμενοί τισιν ἔξωθεν ἡμᾶς περι-
στάσιν αἰτίοις οὐδὲ ἐνδιδόντες αὐτοῖς, ἢ ἐκεῖνα ἄγει, καὶ ἡ προαίρεσις, τὸ *
ἴδιον ἔργον τῶν ἀνθρώπων, περὶ ταὐτό· ἡ γὰρ ἐπὶ τὸ προκριθὲν ἐκ τῆς
βουλῆς μετὰ ὀρέξεως ὁρμὴ προαίρεσις. διὸ οὐδὲ ἐπὶ τοῖς ἀναγκαίοις γινο- 10
10 μένοις ἡ προαίρεσις οὔτε ἐπὶ τοῖς μὴ ἀναγκαίως μὲν μὴ δι' ἡμῶν ⟨δέ⟩,
ἀλλ' οὐδὲ ἐν πᾶσιν τοῖς δι' ἡμῶν, ἀλλ' ἐν τούτοις τοῖς γινομένοις δι'
ἡμῶν, ὧν ἡμεῖς καὶ τοῦ πρᾶξαι καὶ τοῦ μὴ πρᾶξαι κύριοι. ὁ γὰρ βουλευόμενος περί τινος ἤτοι περὶ τοῦ δεῖν αὐτὸ πράττειν ἢ μὴ πράττειν 15
βουλεύεται, ἢ σπουδάζων ὡς περὶ ἀγαθόν τι ζητεῖ, δι' ὧν ἂν τούτου τύ-
15 χοι· κἂν μὲν ἀδυνάτῳ τινὶ ζητῶν ἐντύχῃ, τοῦ μὲν ἀφίσταται, ἀφίσταται δὲ
ὁμοίως καὶ τῶν δυνατῶν μέν, οὐκ ὄντων δὲ ἐπ' αὐτῷ, μένει δὲ ἐν τῇ
περὶ τοῦ προχειμένου ζητήσει, ἕως ἂν ἐντύχῃ τινί, οὗ τὴν ἐξουσίαν αὐτὸς 20
ἔχειν πέπεισται, μεθ' ὃ παυσάμενος τοῦ βουλεύεσθαι ὡς ἀναγαγὼν τὴν
ζήτησιν ἐφ' αὑτό, ὅ ἐστιν ἀρχὴ τῶν πράξεων, ἄρχεται τῆς πρὸς τὸ προ- *
20 κείμενον πράξεως. γίνεται δὲ καὶ ἡ ζήτησις αὐτῷ ὡς ἐξουσίαν ἔχοντι τοῦ

190   De Fato XIII

πράττειν καὶ τὰ ἀντικείμενα. καθ᾽ ἕκαστον γὰρ τῶν ὑπὸ τὴν βουλὴν ἡ 25
ζήτησις βουλευομένῳ γίνεται, πότερον τοῦτο ἢ τὸ ἀντικείμενον αὐτῷ πρα-
κτέον μοι, κἂν πάντα λέγῃ γίνεσθαι καθ᾽ εἱμαρμένην. ἐλέγχει γὰρ ἡ ἐν τοῖς
πρακτοῖς ἀλήθεια τὰς περὶ αὐτῶν ἡμαρτημένας δόξας· ἣν πλάνην κοινῶς πάν-
25 τας ἀνθρώπους ὑπὸ τῆς φύσεως πεπλανῆσθαι πῶς οὐκ ἄτοπον λέγειν; ὅτι 30
γὰρ ταύτην ἔχειν τὴν ἐξουσίαν ἐν τοῖς πρακτοῖς προειλήφαμεν, ὡς δύνα-
* σθαι διαιρεῖσθαι τὸ ἀντικείμενον, καὶ μὴ πᾶν ὃ αἱρούμεθα ἔχειν προκαταβεβλημένας αἰτίας, δι᾽ ἃς οὐχ οἷόν τε ἡμᾶς μὴ τοῦτο αἱρεῖσθαι, ἱκανὴ 42
δεῖξαι καὶ ἡ ἐπὶ τοῖς αἱρεθεῖσιν γινομένη πολλάκις μετάνοια. ὡς γὰρ ἐνὸν
30 ἡμῖν καὶ μὴ ᾑρῆσθαι καὶ μὴ πεπραχέναι τοῦτο μετανοοῦμέν τε καὶ μεμ- 5
φόμεθα αὐτοῖς τῆς περὶ τὴν βουλὴν ὀλιγωρίας. ἀλλὰ κἂν ἄλλους ἴδωμεν
181   μὴ καλῶς περὶ τῶν πρακτέων διαλαμβάνοντας, κἀκείνοις ἐπικαλοῦμεν ὡς
* ἁμαρτάνουσιν, ἀξιοῦμεν δὲ συμβούλοις † τοιοῖσδε χρῆσθαι ὡς ἐφ᾽ ἡμῖν ὂν
* τό τε παραλαμβάνειν αὐτοὺς συμβούλους ὄντας ἢ μὴ παραλαμβάνειν τοὺς 10
* πρᾶξαι ἂν διὰ τὴν τῶν τοιούτων παρουσίαν ἄλλα [καὶ] τινὰ καὶ μὴ ταῦτα
5 ἃ πράσσομεν. ἀλλ᾽ ὅτι μὲν τὸ ἐφ᾽ ἡμῖν ἐπὶ τούτων κατηγορεῖται, ὧν ἐν
* ἡμῖν ἡ ἐξουσία τοῦ ἐλέσθαι καὶ τὰ ἀντικείμενα, γνώριμον ὂν καὶ ἐξ αὐ- 15
τοῦ, ἱκανὰ ὑπομνῆσαι καὶ τὰ προειρημένα. τοιούτου δ᾽ ὄντος αὐτοῦ, τὸ XIII
μὲν δεικνύναι τοῦτο σωζόμενον κατὰ τοὺς πάντα λέγοντας γίνεσθαι καθ᾽
* εἱμαρμένην οὐδὲ ἐπιχειροῦσιν τὴν ἀρχήν (ἴσασιν γὰρ ἐγχειρήσαντες ἀδυνά- 20
10 τοις), ὡς δὲ ἐπὶ τῆς τύχης ἄλλο τι σημαινόμενον ὑποθέντες τῷ τῆς τύχης
ὀνόματι παράγειν πειρῶνται τοὺς ἀκούοντας αὐτῶν ὡς σώζοντες καὶ αὐτοὶ
τὸ ἀπὸ τύχης γίνεσθαί τινα, οὕτως δὲ καὶ ἐπὶ τοῦ ἐφ᾽ ἡμῖν ποιοῦσιν.
ἀναιροῦντες γὰρ τὸ ἐξουσίαν ἔχειν τὸν ἄνθρωπον τῆς αἱρέσεώς τε καὶ πρά- 25
* ξεως τῶν ἀντικειμένων λέγουσιν ἐφ᾽ ἡμῖν εἶναι τὸ γινόμενον καὶ δι᾽ ἡμῶν.
15 ἐπεὶ γάρ, φασίν, τῶν ὄντων τε καὶ γινομένων αἱ φύσεις ἕτεραί τε καὶ
διάφοροι (οὐ γὰρ αἱ αὐταὶ τῶν ἐμψύχων τε καὶ τῶν ἀψύχων, ἀλλ᾽ οὐδὲ
τῶν ἐμψύχων ἁπάντων αἱ αὐταὶ πάλιν· αἱ γὰρ κατ᾽ εἶδος τῶν ὄντων δια- 30
φοραὶ τὰς τῶν φύσεων αὐτῶν διαφορὰς δεικνύουσιν), γίνεται δὲ τὰ ὑφ᾽
20 ἑκάστου γινόμενα κατὰ τὴν οἰκείαν φύσιν, τὰ μὲν ὑπὸ λίθου κατὰ τὴν |
λίθου, τὰ δ᾽ ὑπὸ πυρὸς κατὰ τὴν πυρὸς καὶ τὰ ὑπὸ ζῴου κατὰ τὴν 44
[ὑπὸ] ζῴου, οὐδὲν μὲν τῶν κατὰ τὴν οἰκείαν φύσιν ὑφ᾽ ἑκάστου γινομένων δύνασθαί φασιν ἄλλως ἔχειν, ἀλλ᾽ ἕκαστον τῶν γινομένων ὑπ᾽ αὐτῶν
γίνεσθαι κατηναγκασμένως, κατ᾽ ἀνάγκην οὐ τὴν ἐκ βίας, ἀλλ᾽ ἐκ τοῦ μὴ 5
* δύνασθαι τὸ μὴ πεφυκὸς οὕτως (ὄντων τῶν περιεστώτων τοιούτων ⟨ὡς⟩
25 ἀδύνατον αὐτῷ μὴ περιεστάναι) τότε ἄλλως πως καὶ μὴ οὕτως κινηθῆναι.
μήτε γὰρ τὸν λίθον, εἰ ἀπὸ ὕψους ἀφεθείη τινός, δύνασθαι μὴ φέρεσθαι 10
* κάτω μηδενὸς ἐμποδίζοντος — τῷ βαρύτητα μὲν ἔχειν αὐτὸν ἐν αὐτῷ,
ταύτην δ᾽ εἶναι ⟨τὴν⟩ τῆς τοιαύτης κινήσεως κατὰ φύσιν ⟨αἰτίαν⟩, ὅταν καὶ τὰ
* ἔξωθεν αἴτια τὰ πρὸς τὴν κατὰ φύσιν κίνησιν τῷ λίθῳ συντελοῦντα παρῇ,
30 ἐξ ἀνάγκης τὸν λίθον ὡς πέφυκε φέρεσθαι· πάντως δ᾽ αὐτῷ καὶ ἐξ 15
*182   ἀνάγκης παρεῖναι ταῦτα τὰ αἴτια, δι᾽ ἃ κινεῖται τότε, — οὐ μόνον μὴ
δυνάμενον μὴ κινεῖσθαι τούτων [μὴ] παρόντων, ἀλλὰ καὶ ἐξ ἀνάγκης κι-

νεῖσθαι τότε, καὶ γίνεσθαι τὴν τοιαύτην κίνησιν ὑπὸ τῆς εἱμαρμένης διὰ 20
τοῦ λίθου· ὁ δ' αὐτὸς καὶ ἐπὶ τῶν ἄλλων λόγος. ὡς δὲ ἐπὶ τῶν ἀψύχων
5 ἔχει, οὕτως δὲ καὶ ἐπὶ τῶν ζώων ἔχειν φασίν. εἶναι γάρ τινα καὶ τοῖς
ζώοις κίνησιν κατὰ φύσιν, ταύτην δ' εἶναι τὴν καθ' ὁρμήν· πᾶν γὰρ
ζῷον ὡς ζῷον κινούμενον κινεῖσθαι ⟨τὴν⟩ καθ' ὁρμὴν κίνησιν ὑπὸ τῆς 25
εἱμαρμένης διὰ ζῴου γινομένην. οὕτως δὲ τούτων ἐχόντων, καὶ γινομένων ὑπὸ τῆς εἱμαρμένης κινήσεών τε καὶ ἐνεργειῶν ἐν τῷ κόσμῳ τῶν
10 μὲν διὰ γῆς, ἂν οὕτω τύχῃ, τῶν δὲ δι' ἀέρος, τῶν δὲ διὰ πυρός, τῶν δὲ
δι' ἄλλου τινός, γινομένων δέ τινων καὶ διὰ ζῴων (τοιαῦται δὲ αἱ καθ' 30
ὁρμὴν κινήσεις), τὰς διὰ τῶν ζῴων ὑπὸ τῆς εἱμαρμένης γινομένας ἐπὶ
τοῖς ζῴοις εἶναι λέγουσιν, ὁμοίως δὲ ὡς πρὸς τὸ ἀναγκαῖον τοῖς ἄλλοις *
γινομένας ἅπασιν, τῷ δεῖν καὶ τοῖς ἐξ ἀνάγκης | τὰ ἔξωθεν αἴτια παρεῖναι 46 *
15 τότε, ὥστε αὐτὰ τὴν ἐξ ἑαυτῶν τε καὶ καθ' ὁρμὴν κίνησιν ἐξ ἀνάγκης
οὕτω πως ἐνεργεῖν. ὅτι δὲ αὗται μὲν δι' ὁρμῆς τε καὶ συγκαταθέσεως, *
ἐκείνων δὲ αἱ μὲν διὰ βαρύτητα γίνονται, αἱ δὲ διὰ θερμότητα, αἱ δὲ 5
κατ' ἄλλην τινά * * *, ταύτην μὲν ἐπὶ τοῖς ζῴοις λέγοντες, οὐκέτι δὲ ἐκείνων *
ἑκάστην, τὴν μὲν ἐπὶ τῷ λίθῳ, τὴν δὲ ἐπὶ τῷ πυρί. καὶ τοιαύτη μὲν
20 αὐτῶν ἡ περὶ τοῦ ἐφ' ἡμῖν δόξα ὡς δι' ὀλίγων εἰπεῖν. ἔνεστι δ' ὁρᾶν, 10 XIV
εἰ ταῦτα λέγοντες σώζουσιν τὰς κοινὰς περὶ τοῦ ἐφ' ἡμῖν πάντων ἀνθρώπων προλήψεις. οἱ γὰρ ἀπαιτοῦντες αὐτούς, πῶς οἷόν τε πάντων ὄντων
καθ' εἱμαρμένην τὸ ἐφ' ἡμῖν σώζεσθαι, οὐκ ὄνομα μόνον τοῦ ἐφ' ἡμῖν
τιθέντες τοῦτ' ἀπαιτοῦσιν, ἀλλὰ καὶ σημαινόμενον ἐκεῖνο τὸ αὐτεξούσιον. 15
25 διὰ γὰρ τὸ τοιοῦτον εἶναι τὸ ἐφ' ἡμῖν πεπιστεῦσθαι εὐθύνουσιν τοὺς ἐξ
ἀνάγκης πάντα γίνεσθαι λέγοντας. οἱ δὲ δέον αὐτόθεν μὴ σώζεσθαι λέ- *
γειν καὶ τοῦ μὴ σώζεσθαι ζητεῖν τε καὶ παρέχεσθαι τὰς αἰτίας, ἐπεὶ 20
τοῦτο ἑώρων παντάπασιν ἄδοξόν τε ὂν καὶ πολλὰ τῶν καὶ αὐτοῖς † τοῦ ἐφ' *
ἡμῖν πᾶσάν τε ταὐτὸ δεικνὺς συνοδεῦον τῷ τῆς εἱμαρμένης λόγῳ, ⟨τῷ⟩ διὰ *
30 τῆς ὁμωνυμίας παρακρούεσθαι τοὺς ἀκούοντας ἡγοῦνται φεύγειν τὰ ἄτοπα, *
ὅσα ἕπεται τοῖς μηδὲν ἐφ' ἡμῖν εἶναι λέγουσιν. ταῦτα δὲ λέγοντας αὐ- 25
τοὺς πρῶτον μὲν ἂν ἀπαιτήσαι τις εὐλόγως, τί δή ποτε ἄλλου δι' ἄλλων *
γινομένων ὑπὸ τῆς εἱμαρμένης, καὶ διὰ τῆς οἰκείας φύσεως τῶν ὄντων 183
ἑκάστου τῆς εἱμαρμένης ἐνεργούσης, ἐπὶ μὲν τῶν ἄλλων οὐδενὸς τὸ ἐπ' 30
αὐτοῖς εἶναι κατηγοροῦσιν, ἐπὶ δὲ τῶν ζῴων μόνον. δι' ἃ γὰρ λέγουσιν
ἐπὶ τῶν ζῴων τὰ διὰ τοῦ ζῴου γινόμενα, ταῦτ' ἔνεστι καὶ ἐπὶ τῶν ἄλλων *
5 ἑκάστου λέγειν. ἐπεὶ γὰρ οὐκ ἄλλως· γένοιτο τὰ διὰ τοῦ | ζῴου γινόμενα, 48 *
μὴ ὁρμήσαντος τοῦ ζῴου, ἀλλὰ διὰ τὸ συγκατατίθεσθαι μὲν τὸ ζῷον καὶ *
ὁρμῆσαι γίνεται, μὴ συγκαταθεμένου δὲ οὐ γίνεται, ταῦτα ἐπὶ τῷ ζῴῳ
φασὶν εἶναι, ἐξ ἀνάγκης μὲν ἐσόμενα ὑπ' αὐτοῦ (οὐ γὰρ οἷόν τε ἄλλως), 5
τῷ δὲ μὴ δύνασθαι δι' ἄλλου τινὸς ἢ διὰ τούτου γενέσθαι, μηδ' ἄλλως
10 ἢ οὕτως διὰ τούτου, τὸ εἶναι αὐτὰ ἐπὶ τῷ ζῴῳ οἰηθέντες. ἀλλὰ τοῦτό
γε καὶ ἐπὶ τῶν ἄλλων ἑκάστου λέγειν ἔστιν. οὔτε γὰρ τὸ διὰ τοῦ πυρὸς
γινόμενον ὑπ' ἄλλου τινὸς ἂν γένοιτο οὔτ' ἄλλως διὰ τοῦ πυρὸς ἢ 10
διὰ τοῦ θερμῆναι, ὥστ', ἐπεὶ μηδ' ἄλλως γένοιτο τὰ διὰ τοῦ πυρὸς

γινόμενα ἢ θερμήναντος τοῦ πυρός, καὶ θερμήναντος μὲν αὐτοῦ ἔσται,
15 μὴ θερμήναντος δὲ οὐκ ἔσται, εἴη ἂν ἐπὶ τῷ πυρὶ ταῦτα, τὰ δ᾽ αὐτὰ
καὶ ἐφ᾽ ἑκάστου τῶν ἄλλων ἔσται λέγειν.   τί γὰρ δεῖ μακρολογεῖν γεγο- 15
νότος τοῦ λεγομένου γνωρίμου; ὀνομάτων μὲν οὖν οὐδεὶς φθόνος, τὸ δ᾽
ἡγεῖσθαι πλέον τι τοῖς ζῴοις διδόναι ἐν τοῖς γινομένοις δι᾽ αὐτῶν παρὰ
τἄλλα, δι᾽ ὧν τι καὶ αὐτῶν γίνεται, μηδὲν πλέον τοῦ ἐπ᾽ αὐτοῖς ὀνόματος 20
20 τηροῦντας αὐτοῖς, τοῦτ᾽ αὐτὸ αἰτιατέον, ὡς αὐτῶν ἀπατωμένων διὰ τὴν
* τοῦ ὀνόματος κοινωνίαν, ἢ ὡς τοῦ ἄλλους ἀπατᾶν προαιρουμένων.   ἐπὶ
τούτῳ δὲ ἐκεῖνο ἄν τις αὐτῶν θαυμάσειεν, τί παθόντες ἐν τῇ ὁρμῇ τε
καὶ συγκαταθέσει τὸ ἐφ᾽ ἡμῖν φασιν εἶναι, δι᾽ ὃ καὶ ὁμοίως ἐν πᾶσιν 25
τοῖς ζῴοις τηροῦσιν αὐτό.   οὐ γὰρ τὸ ἐφ᾽ ἡμῖν ἐν τῷ φαντασίας προσπε-
25 σούσης εἶξαί τε ἐξ ἑαυτῶν τῇ φαντασίᾳ καὶ ὁρμῆσαι ἐπὶ τὸ φανέν, ἀλλὰ
τοῦτο μὲν ἂν ἴσως εἴη τοῦ ἑκουσίου κατασκευαστικόν τε καὶ δεικτικόν.   οὐ 30
μὴν ταὐτὸν τό τε ἑκούσιον καὶ τὸ ἐφ᾽ ἡμῖν.   ἑκούσιον μὲν γὰρ τὸ ἐξ
ἀβιάστου γινόμενον συγκαταθέσεως, ἐφ᾽ ἡμῖν δὲ τὸ γινόμενον μετὰ τῆς
κατὰ λόγον τε καὶ κρίσιν συγκαταθέσεως.   διὸ εἴ τι μὲν ἐφ᾽ ἡμῖν, τοῦτο
30 καὶ ἑκούσιον, οὐ μὴν πᾶν τὸ | ἑκούσιον ἐφ᾽ ἡμῖν.   ἑκουσίως μὲν γὰρ καὶ τὰ 50
ἄλογα ζῷα, ὅσα κατὰ τὴν ὁρμήν τε καὶ συγκατάθεσιν τὴν ἐν αὐτοῖς ⟨ποιεῖ⟩,
ποιεῖ, τὸ δὲ ἐπ᾽ αὐτῷ τι εἶναι τῶν γινομένων ὑπ᾽ αὐτοῦ ἴδιον ἀνθρώπου.
* τοῦτο γάρ ἐστιν αὐτῷ τῷ εἶναι λογικῷ τὸ ἔχειν ἐν αὐτῷ λόγον τῶν προσπι- 5
πτουσῶν φαντασιῶν καὶ ὅλως τῶν πρακτέων τε καὶ μὴ κριτήν τε καὶ
184 εὑρετήν.   διὸ τὰ μὲν ἄλλα ζῷα, ἃ εἴκει ταῖς φαντασίαις μόναις, κατ᾽
αὐτὰς ἔχει τῶν συγκαταθέσεών τε καὶ τῶν κατὰ τὰς πράξεις ὁρμῶν αἰ- 10
τίας, ὁ δὲ ἄνθρωπος ἔχει τῶν προσπιπτουσῶν ἔξωθεν φαντασιῶν αὐτῷ
περὶ τῶν πρακτέων κριτὴν τὸν λόγον, ᾧ χρώμενος ἑκάστην αὐτῶν ἐξετά-
5 ζει, μὴ μόνον εἰ φαίνεται τοιαύτη, ὁποία φαίνεται, ἀλλὰ καὶ εἰ ἔστι.   κἂν
εὕρῃ ζητῶν κατὰ τὸν λόγον ἀλλοῖον αὐτῆς τοῦ φαίνεσθαι τὸ εἶναι, οὐ διότι 15
τοιάδε τις φαίνεται συνεχώρησεν αὐτῇ, ἀλλ᾽, ὅτι μὴ καὶ ἔστι τοιαύτη,
ἐνίσταται πρὸς αὐτήν.   οὕτως γοῦν καὶ ἡδέων τινῶν φαινομένων πολλάκις ἀπέχεται, καίτοι ὄρεξιν (ἔχων) αὐτῶν, ὅτι μὴ τὸν λόγον ἔσχεν τῷ
10 φαινομένῳ συνᾴδοντα, ὁμοίως δὲ καὶ συμφέροντα φανέντα τινὰ παρῃτή- 20
σατο, τῷ λόγῳ τοῦτο δόξαν.   εἰ δὲ τὸ ἐφ᾽ ἡμῖν ἐστι ἐν τῇ λογικῇ συγκαταθέσει, ἥτις διὰ τοῦ βουλεύεσθαι γίνεται, οἱ δὲ ἐν τῇ συγκαταθέσει τε
καὶ ὁρμῇ φασιν εἶναι, ὅτι καὶ ἀλόγως γίνεται, δῆλοι δι᾽ ὧν λέγουσιν ῥᾳθυ- 25
μότερον περὶ τοῦ ἐφ᾽ ἡμῖν διαλαμβάνοντες, ⟨ὅτι⟩ οὔτε ὅτι ποτ᾽ ἐστὶν
15 αὐτό, οὔτε ἐν τίνι γίνεται, λέγουσιν.   τὸ γὰρ εἶναι λογικῷ οὐδὲν ἄλλο ἐστίν,
ἢ τὸ ἀρχὴν·πράξεων εἶναι.   ὡς γὰρ ἄλλῳ ἐν ἄλλῳ τὸ εἶναι, τῷ μὲν ζῴῳ
ἐν τῷ ὁρμητικῷ, τῷ δὲ πυρὶ ἐν τῷ θερμῷ τε καὶ θερμαντικῷ, ἄλλῳ δὲ 30
ἐν ἄλλῳ, οὕτως δὲ τῷ ἀνθρώπῳ ἐν τῷ λογικῷ, ὃ ἴσον ἐστὶ τῷ ἐν αὐτῷ
ἀρχὴν ἔχειν τοῦ καὶ ἑλέσθαι τι καὶ μή· καὶ τὸ αὐτὸ ἄμφω, ὥστε ὁ
20 τοῦτο ἀναιρῶν ἀναιρεῖ τὸν ἄνθρωπον.   ἐοί|κασιν δὲ παραλελοιπότες τὸν 52
λόγον ἐν τῇ ὁρμῇ τὸ ἐφ᾽ ἡμῖν τίθεσθαι, ὅτι μηκέτ᾽ ἐν τῷ βουλεύεσθαι
λέγουσιν αὐτοῖς τὸ ἐφ᾽ ἡμῖν εἶναι προχωρεῖ τὸ σόφισμα.   ἐπὶ μὲν γὰρ

τῆς ὁρμῆς ἔχουσιν λέγειν τὸ ἐπὶ τοῖς ζῴοις εἶναι τὰ γινόμενα καθ' ὁρμήν, 5
ὅτι μὴ οἷά τε χωρὶς ὁρμῆς τὰ δι' αὐτῶν γινόμενα ποιεῖν, εἰ δ' ἐν τῷ
25 βουλεύεσθαι τὸ ἐφ' ἡμῖν, ἔνθεν οὐκέτ' αὐτοῖς εἵπετο τὸ μὴ δύνασθαι τὰ
δι' ἀνθρώπου γινόμενα ἄλλως γενέσθαι τῷ τὸν ἄνθρωπον ὄντα βουλευτι- 10
κὸν μὴ πάντα τὰ γινόμενα δι' αὐτοῦ βουλευόμενον ποιεῖν. οὐ γὰρ πάντα,
ἃ ποιοῦμεν, βουλευσάμενοι ποιοῦμεν, ἀλλὰ πολλάκις μέν, οὐ συγχωροῦν-
τος τοῦ καιροῦ τῶν πραχθῆναι δεόντων τῷ βουλεύσασθαι χρόνον, καὶ μὴ
30 βουλευσάμενοί τινα ποιοῦμεν, πολλάκις δὲ καὶ δι' ἀργίαν ἤ τινα ἄλλην 15
αἰτίαν. εἰ δὲ τὰ μὲν βουλευσαμένων ἡμῶν, τὰ δὲ καὶ μὴ βουλευσαμένων
γίνεται, οὐκέτι χώραν ἔχει τὸ λέγειν τὸ τὰ διὰ τοῦ βουλεύεσθαι γινόμενα
ἐπὶ τῷ ἀνθρώπῳ εἶναι τῷ μὴ δύνασθαι ἄλλως τι δι' αὐτοῦ γίνεσθαι. 20   185
ὥστ', εἰ τὰ μὲν βουλευσάμενοι, τὰ δὲ μὴ βουλευσάμενοι ποιοῦμεν, οὐκέθ'
οὕτως τὰ δι' ἡμῶν γινόμενα ἁπλῶς γίνεται, ὡς τὰ γινόμενα διὰ τῶν ζῴων ἢ διὰ τοῦ πυρὸς ἢ διὰ τῶν βαρέων δύο σωμάτων. εἰ δ' ἔχομεν καὶ
5 τοῦ βουλευσάμενοί τι ποιεῖν παρὰ τῆς φύσεως τὴν ἐξουσίαν, δῆλον ὡς 25
ἔχοιμεν ⟨ἂν⟩ ἐξουσίαν καὶ τοῦ διὰ τοῦ βουλεύσασθαι ἄλλο τι πρᾶξαι, καὶ μὴ
πάντως τοῦτο ὃ καὶ βουλευσάμενοι † ἦν ἂν βουλευοίμεθα. | τὸ δ' ἐποχού- 54 XV *
μένους τῷ 'εἰ δὴ τῶν αὐτῶν περιεστώτων ὁτὲ μὲν οὕτως ὁτὲ δὲ ἄλλως
ἐνεργήσει τις, ἀναίτιον κίνησιν εἰσάγεσθαι' διὰ τοῦτο λέγειν μὴ δύνα-
10 σθαι οὐ πράξει τις πρᾶξαι τὸ ἀντικείμενον, μήποτε καὶ αὐτὸ τῶν ὁμοί- 5
ως τοῖς προειρημένοις παρορωμένων. οὐ γὰρ πάντως ἀεὶ τὰ γινόμενα κατὰ
αἰτίαν ἔξωθεν ἔχει τοῦ γίνεσθαι τὴν αἰτίαν. διὰ γὰρ τὴν τοιαύτην ἐξουσίαν ἐστί τι ἐφ' ἡμῖν, ὅτι τῶν οὕτως γινομένων ἡμεῖς ἐσμεν κύριοι, ἀλλ'
οὐκ ἔξωθέν τις αἰτία. διὸ ⟨οὐκ⟩ ἀναιτίως τὰ οὕτω γινόμενα γίνεται, παρ' 10
15 ἡμῶν τὴν αἰτίαν ἔχοντα. ὁ γὰρ ἄνθρωπος ἀρχὴ καὶ αἰτία τῶν δι' αὐτοῦ
γινομένων πράξεων, καὶ τοῦτό ἐστι τὸ εἶναι ἀνθρώπῳ τὸ τοῦ πράττειν οὕτως
τὴν ἀρχὴν ἔχειν ἐν αὐτῷ, ὡς * * * τῇ σφαίρᾳ τὸ κατὰ τοῦ πρανοῦς κυλιομέ- 15   *
νῃ φέρεσθαι. διὸ τῶν μὲν ἄλλων ἕκαστον ἕπεται ταῖς ἔξωθεν αὐτῷ περιεστώσαις αἰτίαις, ὁ δ' ἄνθρωπος οὐχ, ὅτι ἐστὶν αὐτῷ τὸ εἶναι ἐν τῷ
20 ἔχειν ἀρχήν τε καὶ αἰτίαν ἐν αὐτῷ, ⟨ὡς⟩ μὴ πάντως ἕπεσθαι τοῖς περιεστῶσιν
ἔξωθεν αὐτῷ. καὶ γὰρ ⟨εἰ⟩ ἦν ἡμῖν ἡ περὶ τῶν πρακτέων κρίσις πρὸς 20
ἕνα γινομένη σκοπόν, ἴσως ⟨ἂν⟩ εἶχέ τινα λόγον τὸ ἀεὶ περὶ τῶν αὐτῶν
ὁμοίας ἡμῖν γίνεσθαι τὰς κρίσεις. ἐπεὶ δ' οὐχ οὕτως ἔχει (αἱρούμεθα
γάρ, ἃ αἱρούμεθα, ποτὲ μὲν διὰ τὸ καλόν τι, ποτὲ δὲ διὰ τὸ ἡδύ, ποτὲ
25 δὲ διὰ τὸ σύμφορον, καὶ οὐ ταὐτὰ τούτων ποιητικά), ἐνδέχεται νῦν μὲν 25
ἐπὶ τὸ καλὸν κινηθέντας ἡμᾶς * * * τάδε τῶν περιεστώτων προκείμενα, αὖθις   *
δὲ ἄλλα, πρὸς τὸ ἡδύ ἢ τὸ συμφέρον τὴν ἀναφορὰν τῆς κρίσεως ποιουμένους. ὡς γὰρ οὐ ζητοῦμεν ἄλλην τινὰ αἰτίαν, δι' ἣν κατὰ βαρύτητα τὴν 30
ἐν αὐτῇ ἡ γῆ φέρεται κάτω, ἢ δι' ἣν αἰτίαν, ἃ πράσσει τὸ ζῷον, πράσσει
30 καθ' ὁρμήν, τῷ ταύτην ἕκαστον αὐτῶν τὴν αἰτίαν ἐξ αὐτοῦ πρὸς τὰ γι-
νόμενα συντελεῖν, τοιοῦτον | ὂν τὴν φύσιν, οὕτως οὐδ' ἐπὶ τῶν ἄλλοτ' 56
ἄλλως ὑφ' ἡμῶν γινομένων ἐπὶ περιεστῶσι τοῖς ἄλλοις ἄλλην τινὰ αἰτίαν   *186
ἀπαιτητέον παρ' αὐτὸν τὸν ἄνθρωπον. τοῦτο γὰρ ἦν τὸ ἀνθρώπῳ εἶναι.

τὸ γὰρ ἀρχὴ καὶ αἰτία εἶναι τῶν δι' αὐτοῦ γινομένων πράξεων. τὸ δὲ 5
λέγειν καὶ τοὺς βουλευσαμένους τῷ φαινομένῳ συγκατατίθεσθαι, καὶ διὰ
5 τοῦτο καὶ τῇ φαντασίᾳ ὁμοίως τοῖς ἄλλοις ζῴοις ἔπεσθαι, οὐκ ἀληθές.
οὐ γὰρ φαντασία τὸ φαινόμενον πᾶν. ἡ μὲν γὰρ φαντασία ἁπλῆ τε καὶ 10
χωρὶς λόγου ὑπὸ τῶν ἔξωθεν προσπιπτόντων γίνεται, ἐοικυῖα ταῖς αἰσθη-
τικαῖς ἐνεργείαις, διὸ καὶ τὴν ἰσχὺν ἐν τοῖς ἀλόγοις ζῴοις ἔχει μάλιστα,
φαίνεται δέ τινα καὶ διὰ λόγου τε καὶ παρὰ συλλογισμοῦ τὴν αἰτίαν τοῦ
10 φαίνεσθαι λαμβάνοντα, ἃ οὐκέτ' ἄν τις φαντασίας λέγοι. ὁ γὰρ διὰ τὸν 15
γινόμενον παρ' αὐτοῖς ἐν τῷ βουλεύεσθαι συλλογισμὸν συγκαταθέμενός τινι
αὐτὸς αὑτῷ τῆς συγκαταθέσεως αἴτιος.

Ἀλλ' ὅτι μὲν οὔτε σώζουσι τὸ ἐφ' ἡμῖν οἱ λέγοντες πάντα καθ' εἱ- 20 XVI
μαρμένην ⟨γίνεσθαι⟩ (οὐ γὰρ περὶ οὗ ζητοῦμεν, εἰ σώζεται κατ' αὐτούς,
15 τοῦτο σώζεται, οἵ γε καὶ αἰτίαν ἀποδιδόναι πειρῶνται τοῦ μηδὲ τὴν ἀρχὴν
δυνατὸν εἶναι τὸ πρᾶγμα), οὐδὲ ἣν ἀποδιδόασιν αἰτίαν ἐπ' ἀναιρέσει τῆς
τοιαύτης ἐξουσίας, ἀληθής, μὴ ἔχουσά τι εὔλογον, ἐκ τῶν εἰρημένων 25
γνώριμον. ἀλλὰ μὴν τοῖς ἀναιροῦσιν τὸ εἶναί τι οὕτως ἐφ' ἡμῖν ἕπεται
τὸ συγχεῖν τε καὶ ἀνατρέπειν, ὅσον ἐπ' αὐτοῖς, τὸν τῶν ἀνθρώπων βίον.
20 εἰ γάρ, ἐχόντων μὲν οὕτως τῶν πραγμάτων ὡς ἔχει (οὐδὲ γὰρ αὐτῶν τινα
πεῖσαι δυνατὸν μὴ πράττειν, ἃ πράττουσιν ὡς ἔχοντες τοῦ καὶ πράττειν 30
αὐτὰ καὶ μὴ πράττειν τὴν ἐξουσίαν, | μή τι γε τῶν ἄλλων τινά· τοσαύτην 58
ἰσχὺν ἔχει τἀληθὲς καὶ τὴν παρὰ τῶν γινομένων μαρτυρίαν ἐναργῆ), εἰ
δὴ τούτων οὕτως ἐχόντων ἰσχὺν αὐτῶν ἡ δόξα τοσαύτην λάβοι, ὡς πάν-
25 τας ἀνθρώπους πιστεῦσαι, ὅτι ἡμεῖς μὲν οὐδενὸς κύριοι, ἑπόμεθα δὲ τοῖς 5
περιεστῶσιν ἀεί, τούτοις ἐνδιδόντες τε καὶ συγκατατιθέμενοι, καὶ πράττο-
μέν τε ἃ πράττομεν τῷ πάντως ὀφείλειν ταῦτα πράττειν (μὴ γὰρ εἶναι
δυνατὸν ἡμῖν ὄντων τῶν περιεστώτων τοιούτων ἄλλο τι ποιεῖν), οὐ πράττο-
μέν τε πάλιν ὁμοίως διὰ τὸ μὴ δύνασθαι ἀντιβαίνειν τοῖς περιεστῶσιν οὖ- 10
30 σιν τοιούτοις, τί ἄλλο ἢ συμβήσεται, πάντας ἀνθρώπους διὰ τὴν τοιάνδε
πίστιν τὰ μὲν ὅσα μετὰ πόνου τινὸς καὶ φροντίδος γίνεται, τούτοις μὲν
χαίρειν λέγειν, αἱρεῖσθαι δὲ τὰς μετὰ ῥᾳστώνης ἡδονάς; ὡς, πάντως ἐσο- 15
μένων τῶν ὀφειλόντων γενέσθαι, μηδὲν αὐτοὶ περὶ αὐτῶν † ὦσιν καλόν.
οὕτως δ' αὐτῶν διακειμένων καὶ τῶν πραττομένων ἀκολουθούντων ταῖς
αἱρέσεσιν αὐτῶν (οὐ γὰρ δὴ διὰ τὴν περὶ αὐτῶν ἐψευσμένην πίστιν ἄλλως
5 πως ἕξει τὰ πράγματα, ⟨ἢ⟩ ὡς ἔχει) ἄλλο τι ἢ τῶν μὲν καλῶν παρὰ 20
πάντων ὀλιγωρία τις ἔσται (πάντων γὰρ ἡ κτῆσίς τε καὶ παρουσία τῶν
τοιούτων μετὰ καμάτου περιγίνεται), τῶν δὲ κακῶν αἵρεσις ἅτε γινομένων
μετὰ ῥᾳστώνης τε καὶ ἡδονῆς; πρὸς οὓς τίς ἂν ὁ παρὰ τούτων εἴη λόγος,
ὧν πεισθέντες τοῖς δόγμασιν ἦλθον ἐπὶ ταῦτα; λέγοιεν ἂν γὰρ δικαίως 25
10 πρὸς αὐτούς, εἰ αἰτιῷντο αὐτούς, ὅτι μὴ οἷόν τε ἦν αὐτοῖς τῶν περιεστώτων ὄντων τοιούτων ἀλλοῖόν τι πράττειν. οἷς πῶς ἐπιτιμήσουσιν εὐλόγως
οἱ διὰ τῶν δογμάτων τούτων αὐτοῖς διδάσκαλοι γεγονότες; μᾶλλον δὲ οὔτε 30
ἐπιτιμήσεις οὔτε κολάσεις οὔτε προτροπὴ οὔτε τιμὴ οὔτ' ἄλλο τι τῶν
τοιούτων τὴν οἰκείαν σώσει κατ' αὐτοὺς φύσιν, ἀλλ' ἔσται καὶ τούτων

15 ἕκαστον γινόμενον κατηναγκασμένως, ὥσπερ κἀκεῖνα, ἐφ' οἷς ταῦτα γίνε-
ται. | πῶς γὰρ ⟨ἂν⟩ ἔτι Ἀλέξανδρος ὁ Πριάμου ἐν αἰτίᾳ εἴη ὡς διαμαρτὼν 60
περὶ τὴν τῆς Ἑλένης ἁρπαγήν; πῶς δ' ἂν Ἀγαμέμνων εὐλόγως αὑτοῦ
καταψηφίζοιτο λέγων "οὐδ' αὐτὸς ἀναίνομαι"; εἰ μὲν γὰρ εἶχεν ἐξουσίαν 5
ὑπεριδεῖν ἢ Ἀλέξανδρος τῶν τότε περιεστώτων αὐτὸν καὶ παρακαλούντων
20 ἐπὶ τὴν ἁρπαγήν [ἢ Μενέλαος τῶν ἀγανακτεῖν ἐπαιρόντων] ἢ Ἀγαμέμνων, ἐφ' οἷς ὡς ἂν ἁμαρτήσας αὑτοῦ κατατρέχει, εὐλόγως ἂν ἦσαν ἐν
αἰτίᾳ. εἰ δ' ἦν πάλαι καὶ πρόπαλαι καὶ πρὸ τοῦ τὴν ἀρχήν τινα αὐτῶν 10
γενέσθαι ἀληθὲς περὶ ἑκάστου προλεγόμενον τούτων ἕκαστον, ἐφ' οἷς ποιήσας εὐθύνεται, πῶς ἂν ἔτ' αὐτῶν τῶν γενομένων τὴν αἰτίαν ἔχοιεν; πῶς
25 δέ τις ἐξηγήσεται καὶ τὸ ἐφ' ἡμῖν εἶναι τάς τε ἀρετὰς καὶ τὰς κακίας;
εἰ γὰρ οὕτως † ἔτι δι' ἡμῶν, πῶς ἔτ' ἂν εὐλόγως οἱ μὲν εἶεν ἐν ἐπαίνοις, 15   *
οἱ δὲ ἐν ψόγοις; οὐδὲν γὰρ ἀλλ' ἢ συνηγορίαν τοῖς κακοῖς τὸ δόγμα
τοῦτο προξενεῖ. ὁρῶμεν γοῦν τῶν μὲν ἀγαθῶν τε καὶ καλῶν πράξεων
οὐδένα τὴν εἱμαρμένην οὐδὲ τὴν ἀνάγκην αἰτιώμενον, τοὺς δὲ κακοὺς δι' 20
30 ἐκείνην τοιούτους εἶναι λέγοντας. ὁ πιστεύσαντες καὶ τοὺς φιλοσόφους λέγειν πῶς οὐ μετὰ παρρησίας αὐτοί γε ἐπὶ ταῦτα ἐλεύσονται τούς τε ἄλλους   188
προτρέψουσιν; πῶς δ' ἂν σώζοιεν τοιαῦτα λέγοντες τὴν ὑπὸ τῶν θεῶν 25   XVII
γινομένην τῶν θνητῶν πρόνοιαν; εἰ γὰρ αἵ τε τῶν θεῶν ἐπιφάνειαι, ἅς
φασιν γίνεσθαί τισιν, κατά τινα γίνονται προκαταβεβλημένην αἰτίαν, ὡς πρὸ
5 τοῦ γενέσθαι τινὰ αὐτῶν ἀληθὲς εἶναι τὸ τοῦδε μὲν ἔσεσθαί τινα ἐκ θεῶν
κηδεμονίαν, τοῦδε δὲ μή, πῶς ἂν ἔτι τοῦτο πρόνοιά τις δικαίως λέγοι, 30
τὴν οὐ κατ' ἀξίαν γινομένην, ἀλλὰ κατά τινα ἀνάγκην προκαταβεβλημένην;
πῶς δ' ἂν σώζοιτο καὶ ἡ πρὸς τοὺς θεοὺς εὐσέβεια τῶν εὐσεβεῖν δοκούν-
των, διότι μὴ ἐπ' αὐτοῖς | ἦν τὸ τοῦτο μὴ ποιεῖν, οὕτως ποιούντων; γί- 62
νοιτο δ' ἂν καὶ παρὰ τῶν θεῶν, εἰς οὓς γίνεταί τι παρὰ τοὺς ἄλλους
10 πλέον, ὅτι καὶ τούτων ἦσαν αἱ ἀρχαὶ καὶ πρὸ τοῦ τούτους εἶναι προκατα-
βεβλημέναι. πῶς δ' οὐκ ἀναιροῖεν ἂν καὶ μαντικήν, τῆς ἀπὸ μαντικῆς 5
χρείας ἀναιρουμένης; τί γὰρ ἂν ἢ μαθεῖν ἢ διὰ τὸ μαθεῖν παρὰ τῶν
μάντεων φυλάξαιτ' ἄν τις, εἰ μόνα ταῦτα ἡμῖν τε καὶ μαθεῖν ἐκείνοις τε   *
μηνῦσαι δυνατόν, ὧν τοῦ μαθεῖν ἡμᾶς καὶ ποιῆσαι ἢ μὴ ποιῆσαί τι ἕκαστον   *
15 ἦν καὶ πρὸ τῆς ἡμετέρας γενέσεως κατηναγκασμένον, τοῦ τε ἐμμένειν τοῖς 10
ὑπὸ τῶν θεῶν προαγορευομένοις οὐχ ἡμεῖς κύριοι τῷ τῶν ἐσομένων ὑφ'
ἡμῶν προκαταβεβλῆσθαι τὰς αἰτίας. ἀλλ' ὅτι μὲν τὸ δόγμα τοῦτο ἀνα- XVIII   *
τροπῆς αἴτιον παντὸς τοῦ τῶν ἀνθρώπων βίου, παντί που μαθεῖν ῥᾴδιον, 15
ὅτι δὲ καὶ ψεῦδος, ἱκανὸν μαρτύριον τὸ μηδ' αὐτοὺς τοὺς προστάτας
20 αὐτοῦ δύνασθαι πείθεσθαι τοῖς ὑφ' αὑτῶν λεγομένοις. οὕτω γὰρ ἐν πᾶσι
τοῖς λόγοις φυλάσσουσιν τὸ ἐλεύθερόν τε καὶ αὐτεξούσιον, ὡς μὴ ἀκούσαν- 20
τές ποτε παρ' ἄλλου τοιούτου τινὸς δόγματος, τοῦτο μὲν προτρέπειν
τινὰς πειρώμενοι, ὡς τοῦ τε ποιεῖν ἢ μὴ ποιεῖν τοῦτο τὴν ἐξουσίαν
ἔχοντες αὐτοί, καὶ τῶν προτρεπομένων διὰ τοὺς παρ' αὐτῶν λόγους   189
αἱρεῖσθαί τινα δυναμένων ⟨ὧν⟩ ἔπραξαν ἂν τἀναντία αὐτῶν σιωπώντων, 25
τοῦτο δὲ ἐπιτιμῶντες καὶ ἐπιπλήττοντές τισιν ὡς οὐ τὰ προσήκοντα

196   De Fato XIX

πράττουσιν. ἀλλὰ καὶ συγγράμματα πλείω καταλείπουσίν τε καὶ συγγρά-
5 φουσιν, δι' ὧν ἀξιοῦσιν παιδεύεσθαι τοὺς νέους, οὐχ ὡς κεκωλυμένοι 30
* τοῦτο συγγράφειν διὰ τὸ τὰ περιεστῶτα αὐτοῖς εἶναι τοιαῦτα, ἀλλ' ὡς
ὃν μὲν ἐπ' αὐτοῖς συγγράφειν τε καὶ μή, αἱρούμενοι δὲ τὸ γράφειν
διὰ φιλανθρωπίαν.   64 XIX
* Ἐπαύσαντο δ' ἂν τῆς ἐν τοῖς λόγοις φιλοτιμίας καὶ συγχωρησάντων
10 εἶναι τὸ ἐφ' ἡμῖν ἐλεύθερόν τε καὶ αὐτεξούσιον καὶ κύριον τῆς τῶν ἀντι-
* κειμένων αἱρέσεώς τε καὶ πράξεως * * * ἐπὶ περιεστῶσιν ἀνθρώποις δίκαιος
γίνεσθαι πεπιστευμένος ὁμοίως ἰδιώταις τε καὶ νομοθέταις. ἔστι δὲ τοῦτο 5
τὸ συγγινώσκεσθαι μὲν ἀξίους εἶναι τοὺς ἀκουσίως τοιοῦτόν τι πράξαντας,
οὐχ ὡς ἐπὶ τῷ γιγνομένῳ πράγματι τῆς κολάσεως ὁριζομένης, ἀλλ' ἐπὶ
15 τῷ τρόπῳ τῆς πράξεως· ὅπερ οὔτε τῶν ἄλλων τις οὔτε αὐτῶν τούτων 10
* ὡς οὐ καλῶς ἔχον αἰτιᾶται. καίτοι τί τῶν δι' ἄγνοιαν [πραττομένων] ἁμαρτανόντων ἢ βίᾳ ἧττον ἂν εἶεν συγγνώμης ἄξιοι ⟨οἱ⟩ εἰδότες μὲν ἃ πράττουσιν,
οὐκ ἔχοντες δὲ ἐν αὐτοῖς τὴν ἐξουσίαν τοῦ, τούτων αὐτοῖς περιεστώτων, 15
ἃ πάντως αὐτοῖς καὶ ἐξ ἀνάγκης περιεστάναι δεῖ, ἄλλο τι παρ' ἃ πράττου-
20 σιν ⟨πράττειν⟩ τῷ τὴν φύσιν αὐτῶν εἶναι τοιαύτην, καὶ εἶναι τὸ κατὰ τὴν
οἰκείαν αὐτοῖς φύσιν ἕκαστα πράττειν ὧν πράττουσιν καθ' εἱμαρμένην, ὡς
τοῖς βαρέσιν ἀφεθεῖσιν ἄνωθεν τὸ φέρεσθαι κάτω, καὶ τοῖς περιφερέσι τὸ 20
* κατὰ τοῦ πρανοῦς, εἰ ἀφεθεῖεν, ἀφ' αὑτοῦ κινεῖσθαι; ὅμοιον γὰρ τὸ [τοῦ]
τὸν ἵππον κολάζειν ἀξιοῦν, ὅτι μὴ ἔστιν ἄνθρωπος, καὶ τῶν ἄλλων ζῴων
25 ἕκαστον, ὅτι ταύτης τῆς τύχης καὶ μὴ βελτίονος τετυχήκασίν τινος. ἀλλ' 25
οὐδεὶς Φάλαρις οὕτως ὠμός τε καὶ ἀνόητος, ὡς ἐπὶ τινι τῶν οὕτως γινομένων κολάζειν τὸν ποιήσαντα. ἐπὶ τίσιν οὖν αἱ κολάσεις εὔλογοι; οὐκ
ἐπ' ἄλλοις τισίν, ἢ ἐπὶ τοῖς παρὰ τὴν αὐτῶν μοχθηρὰν αἵρεσιν γινομένοις.
190   ἐφ' ὧν γὰρ αὐτοὶ τὴν ἐξουσίαν τῆς αἱρέσεως ἔχοντες, καταλιπόντες τὸν 30
σκοπὸν τῶν πραττομένων ὑφ' αὑτῶν ποιεῖσθαι τό τε καλὸν καὶ τὸν νόμον, κέρδους χάριν ἢ ἡδονῆς τινος, ὑπερορῶντες ἐκείνων, πράττουσι τὰ
φαῦλα, τούτους | ἀξίους ἡγοῦνται κολάσεως πάντες ἄνθρωποι, συγγνώμην 66
* 5 διδόντες τοῖς οὐχ οὕτως ἁμαρτάνουσιν. ὅρα δὴ πᾶσιν τοῖς κακοῖς τὸ
θαυμαστὸν δόγμα τοῦτο παρὰ τῶν φιλοσόφων μαθοῦσιν διδάσκειν τοὺς
διδάσκοντας, ὅτι εἰσὶ καὶ αὐτοὶ συγγνώμης (ἄξιοι), οὐδὲν ἔλαττον τῶν ἀκου- 5
* σίως ἁμαρτανόντων. οὐ γὰρ ὑπό τινος ἔξωθεν καταναγκάζοντος αὐτοὺς
* ποιοῦσιν ἃ ποιοῦσιν, ὧν ἴσως ἐνῆν αὐτοῖς καὶ φυλάξασθαι, ἀλλ' ὑπὸ τῆς
* 10 φύσεως τῆς ἐν αὐτοῖς οὐδὲν οἷόν τ' ἐστὶν λαθόντας ποιῆσαι καὶ τίς οὐκ 10
* ἂν † αὐτοῖς τοῖς ἁμαρτανομένοις αἴτιον. εἰ δ' οὔτ' ἄλλος τις οὔτ' οἱ τοῦ
δόγματος τούτου κύριοι συγγνώμην δοῖέν τινι ταύτην τῶν ἁμαρτανομένων
φέροντι τὴν αἰτίαν ὡς ψευδός τι [καὶ ψευδεῖ] λέγοντι, δῆλον ὡς ὑπὸ τούτων
καὶ ὑπὸ τῶν ἄλλων ἁπάντων ὁμοίως πεπίστευται τὸ εἶναι τὸ ἐφ' ἡμῖν 15
15 οὐχ οἷον ὑπὸ τούτων πλάσσεται, ὅταν εἰς τὸ πρόβλημα μελετῶντες λέγω-
σιν, ἀλλ' οἴῳ εἶναι αὐτῷ [δεῖ] διὰ τῶν ἔργων οὗτοί τε αὐτοὶ καὶ πάντες
ἄνθρωποι μαρτυροῦσιν. εἰ γὰρ ἦσαν οὕτως ἔχειν πεπιστευκότες, συνεγί- 20
γνωσκον ἂν πᾶσιν τοῖς ἁμαρτάνουσιν ὡς οὐκ ἔχουσιν τοῦ μὴ πάντα πράτ-

De Fato XX, XXI, XXII   197

τειν ἐξουσίαν. ἀλλ' ὅτι μὲν καὶ ἔστι τι ἐφ' ἡμῖν ὀνομάσαι, καὶ οὐ διὰ XX
20 τὴν ἐξουσίαν ταύτην ἀναιτίως τι γίνεται, τῷ τῶν οὕτως γινομένων αἴτιον
τὸν ἄνθρωπον εἶναι, ἀρχὴν αὐτὸν ὄντα τῶν γινομένων ὑφ' αὐτοῦ, ἱκανὰ 25
μὲν δεῖξαι καὶ τὰ εἰρημένα, ἱκανῶς δ' ἂν ἐπείσθησαν καὶ οἱ ἀντιλέγειν
πρὸς αὐτὸ πειρώμενοι, εἰ κἂν πρὸς ὀλίγον πάντα ἃ πράττουσιν ὑπέμειναν
πρᾶξαι ὡς ἀληθεύοντες περὶ ὧν λέγουσιν, πιστεύσαντες τῷ μηδὲν τῶν γι- 30
25 νομένων ὑπό τινος οὕτως γίνεσθαι, ὡς καὶ τοῦ μὴ πράττειν αὐτὸ τὴν ἐξουσίαν ἔχοντος τότε. τῷ γὰρ τοῦτο πεπιστευκότι οὐκ ἐπιτιμῆσαί τινι, οὐκ
ἐπαινέσαι τινα, οὐ συμβουλεῦσαί τινι, οὐ προτρέ|ψασθαί τινα, οὐκ εὔξασθαι 68
θεοῖς, οὐ χάριν αὐτοῖς γνῶναι περί τινων, οὐκ ἄλλο τι ποιεῖν οἷόν τε τῶν
ὀφειλομένων εὐλόγως γίνεσθαι ὑπὸ τῶν καὶ τοῦ ποιεῖν ἕκαστον ὧν   *
ποιοῦσιν τὴν ἐξουσίαν πεπιστευκότων. ἀλλὰ μὴν ἔξω τούτων ἀβίωτος ὁ τῶν 5   *191
ἀνθρώπων ⟨βίος⟩ καὶ οὐδὲ τὴν ἀρχὴν ἀνθρώπων ἔτι. μηδὲ ἐκεῖνο δὲ ἡμῖν XXI
ἀνεξέταστον παραλελείφθω, εἴ τις ὑποθοῖτο, μηδὲν μᾶλλον ἀληθῆ εἶναι τὸ
εἶναί τι οὕτως ἐφ' ἡμῖν, ὡς ἡμεῖς τε ἀξιοῦμεν καὶ ἡ τῶν πραγμάτων φύ- 10
5 σις ἔχειν μαρτυρεῖ, τοῦ πάντα ἐξ ἀνάγκης τε γίνεσθαι καὶ καθ' εἱμαρμένην, ἀλλ' εἶναι ἐπ' ἴσης ἑκάτερον ἢ πιστὸν ἢ ἄδηλον αὐτό, ποτέρᾳ δόξῃ   *
πείθεσθαι τοῖς ἀνθρώποις ἀσφαλέστερόν τε καὶ ἀκινδυνότερον, καὶ ποῖον
ψεῦδος αἱρετώτερον, πότερον τὸ πάντων γινομένων καθ' εἱμαρμένην [ἢ] 15
μὴ οὕτως ἔχειν ὑπολαμβάνειν, ἀλλ' εἶναι καὶ ἡμᾶς τοῦ τι πρᾶξαι ἢ μὴ
10 πρᾶξαι κυρίους, ἢ ὄντος τινὸς καὶ ἐφ' ἡμῖν οὕτως, ὡς προειρήκαμεν, πε-
πεῖσθαι τὸ τοῦτο μὲν ψεῦδος εἶναι, πάντα δὲ καὶ τὰ ὑφ' ἡμῶν πραττό-
μενα κατὰ τὴν ἡμετέραν ἐξουσίαν γίνεσθαι κατηναγκασμένως. ἢ γνώριμον 20
ὅτι οἱ μὲν ἁπάντων γινομένων καθ' εἱμαρμένην αὐτοὺς πείθοντες ὡς ἐξουσίαν ἔχοντάς τινων τοῦ τε πράττειν αὐτὰ καὶ μὴ οὐδὲν ἂν παρὰ τήνδε
15 τὴν πίστιν ἐν τοῖς πραττομένοις ἁμάρτοιεν, τῷ μηδὲ τὴν ἀρχὴν τῶν γινο- 25
μένων τινὸς ὑφ' αὐτῶν εἶναι κύριοι, ὥσθ' ὁ κίνδυνος τῆς κατὰ τοῦτο δια-
μαρτίας πρόεισιν μέχρι ῥημάτων. εἰ δέ γε, ὄντος τινὸς καὶ ἐφ' ἡμῖν καὶ
μὴ πάντων γινομένων ἐξ ἀνάγκης, πείθεσθαι μὲν μηδενὸς ἡμᾶς εἶναι κυ-   *
ρίους, πολλὰ παραλείψομεν τῶν δεόντως ἂν πραχθέντων ὑφ' ἡμῶν καὶ 30
20 διὰ τὸ βουλεύσασθαι περὶ αὐτῶν καὶ διὰ τὸ τοὺς ἐπὶ τοῖς πραττομένοις
χαμάτους προθύμως ὑφίστασθαι, ἀργότεροι γενόμενοι πρὸς τὸ δι' αὐτῶν
τι | ποιεῖν διὰ τὴν πίστιν τοῦ, καὶ μηδὲν ἡμῶν πραγματευομένων περὶ 70
τῶν πρακτέων, τὸ ὀφεῖλον ⟨ἂν⟩ γενέσθαι. οὕτως δὲ τούτων ἐχόντων πρόδηλον
ὡς αἱρετώτερον τοῖς φιλοσοφοῦσιν, τὴν ἀκινδυνοτέραν ὁδὸν αὐτούς τε αἱ- 5
25 ρεῖσθαι καὶ τοὺς ἄλλους ἄγειν.
     Οὐ χεῖρον δέ, τούτων προτεθεωρημένων καὶ αὐτὰ τὰ περὶ τῆς εἱ- XXII
μαρμένης ὑπ' αὐτῶν λεγόμενα παραθεμένους ἰδεῖν, εἴ τινα τοιαύτην ἔχει
βίαν, ὡς εὔλογον εἶναι διὰ τὴν πρὸς τὸ ἀληθὲς οἰκειότητα καὶ τῶν ἐναρ- 10
γῶν οὕτως ὑπεροράν. ἔσται δὲ ἡμῖν καὶ ὁ περὶ τούτων λόγος ἐπὶ τοσοῦ-
30 τον, ἐφ' ὅσον ἐστὶ χρήσιμος πρὸς τὰ προχείμενα. φασὶν δὴ τὸν κόσμον
τόνδε, ἕνα ὄντα καὶ πάντα τὰ ὄντα ἐν αὐτῷ περιέχοντα, καὶ ὑπὸ φύσεως
διοικούμενον ζωτικῆς τε καὶ λογικῆς καὶ νοερᾶς, ἔχειν τὴν τῶν ὄντων 15

192 διοίκησιν ἀίδιον κατὰ εἱρμόν τινα καὶ τάξιν προιοῦσαν, τῶν πρώτων τοῖς
μετὰ ταῦτα γινομένοις αἰτίων γινομένων καὶ τούτῳ τῷ τρόπῳ συνδεομένων
ἀλλήλοις ἁπάντων, καὶ μήτε οὕτως τινὸς ἐν αὐτῷ γινομένου, ὡς μὴ πάντως ἐπακολουθεῖν αὐτῷ καὶ συνῆφθαι ὡς αἰτίῳ ἕτερόν τι, μήτ' αὖ τῶν 20
5 ἐπιγινομένων τινὸς ἀπολελύσθαι δυναμένου τῶν προγεγονότων, ὡς μή τινι
ἐξ αὐτῶν ἀκολουθεῖν ὥσπερ συνδεόμενον, ἀλλὰ παντί τε τῷ γενομένῳ
ἕτερόν τι ἐπακολουθεῖν, ἠρτημένον ⟨ἐξ⟩ αὐτοῦ ἐξ ἀνάγκης ὡς αἰτίου, καὶ 25
πᾶν τὸ γινόμενον ἔχειν τι πρὸ αὐτοῦ, ᾧ ὡς αἰτίῳ συνήρτηται. μηδὲν
γὰρ ἀναιτίως μήτε εἶναι μήτε γίνεσθαι τῶν ἐν τῷ κόσμῳ διὰ τὸ μηδὲν
10 εἶναι τῶν ἐν αὐτῷ ἀπολελυμένον τε καὶ κεχωρισμένον τῶν προγεγονότων
ἁπάντων. διασπᾶσθαι γὰρ καὶ διαιρεῖσθαι καὶ μηκέτι τὸν κόσμον ἕνα μέ- 30
νειν αἰεί, κατὰ μίαν τάξιν τε καὶ οἰκονομίαν διοικούμενον, εἰ ἀναίτιός τις
εἰσάγοιτο κίνησις· ἣν εἰσάγεσθαι, εἰ μὴ πάντα τὰ ὄντα τε καὶ γινόμενα
ἔχοι τινὰ αἴτια προγεγονότα, | οἷς ἐξ ἀνάγκης ἕπεται· ὅμοιόν τε εἶναί 72
15 φασιν καὶ ὁμοίως ἀδύνατον τὸ ἀναιτίως τῷ γίνεσθαί τι ἐκ μὴ ὄντος. τοιαύτην δὲ οὖσαν τὴν τοῦ παντὸς διοίκησιν ἐξ ἀπείρου εἰς ἄπειρον ἐναργῶς
τε καὶ ἀκαταστρόφως γίνεσθαι. οὔσης δέ τινος διαφορᾶς ἐν τοῖς αἰτίοις, 5
* ἣν ἐκτιθέντες (σμῆνος γὰρ αἰτίων καταλέγουσιν, τὰ μὲν προκαταρκτικά,
* τὰ δὲ συναίτια, τὰ δὲ ἑκτικά, τὰ δὲ συνεκτικά, τὰ δὲ ἄλλο τι· οὐδὲν γὰρ
* 20 δεῖ τὸν λόγον μηκύνειν πάντα τὰ λεγόμενα παρατιθέμενα τὸ βούλημα αὐ- 10
τῶν δεῖξαι τοῦ περὶ τῆς εἱμαρμένης δόγματος), ὄντων δὴ πλειόνων αἰτίων,
ἐπ' ἴσης ἐπὶ πάντων αὐτῶν ἀληθές φασιν εἶναι τὸ ἀδύνατον εἶναι, τῶν
αὐτῶν ἁπάντων περιεστηκότων περί τε τὸ αἴτιον καὶ ᾧ ἐστιν αἴτιον, ὁτὲ
μὲν δὴ μὴ οὑτωσί πως συμβαίνειν, ὁτὲ δὲ οὕτως. ἔσεσθαι γάρ, εἰ οὕ- 15
25 τως γίνοιτο, ἀναίτιόν τινα κίνησιν. τὴν δὲ εἱμαρμένην αὐτὴν καὶ τὴν φύσιν καὶ τὸν λόγον, καθ' ὃν διοικεῖται τὸ πᾶν, θεὸν εἶναί φασιν, οὖσαν ἐν
τοῖς οὖσίν τε καὶ γινομένοις ἅπασιν καὶ οὕτως χρωμένην ἁπάντων τῶν
ὄντων τῇ οἰκείᾳ φύσει πρὸς τὴν τοῦ παντὸς οἰκονομίαν. καὶ τοιαύτη μὲν
193 ὡς διὰ βραχέων εἰπεῖν ἡ περὶ τῆς εἱμαρμένης ὑπ' αὐτῶν καταβεβλημένη
δόξα. ἔστι δὲ τὸ ψεῦδος τῶν λεγομένων οὐ λόγων τινῶν οὐδὲ ἐλέγχων 25 XXIII
ἔξωθεν δεόμενον, ἀλλ' αὐτόθεν γνώριμον. τίς γὰρ ἔλεγχος λόγου φανερώτερος τοῦ μὴ ἐφαρμόζειν τούτοις περὶ ὧν λέγεται; τὸ γοῦν πρῶτον
5 εἰρημένον ὡς πάντων τῶν ὄντων αἰτίων τινῶν γινομένων τῶν μετὰ ταῦτα
καὶ τοῦτον τὸν τρόπον ἐχομένων ἀλλήλων τῶν πραγμάτων τῷ δίκην ἁλύ- 30
σεως τοῖς πρώτοις συνηρτῆσθαι τὰ δεύτερα, ὃ ὥσπερ οὐσίαν τῆς εἱμαρμένης ὑποτίθενται, πῶς οὐ φανερῶς ἀπᾴδει τῶν πραγμάτων; εἰ γὰρ τῶν
τέκνων οἱ πατέρες αἴτιοι καὶ δεῖ | κατ' οἰκειότητα τὰς αἰτίας ἀπαιτεῖν, 74
10 ὡς ἀνθρώπου μὲν ἄνθρωπον αἴτιον εἶναι, ἵππου δ' ἵππον, τίνος αἴτιοι τῶν
μετ' αὐτοὺς οἱ τὴν ἀρχὴν μηδὲ γήμαντες, τίνος δὲ οἱ παῖδες οἱ πρὸ τῆς
ἡλικίας διαφθαρέντες; πολλὰ γὰρ τῶν γινομένων, ὑπὸ τῆς κατὰ τὸ ποσὸν 5
ἐκλείψεως ἢ μὴ κινηθέντα ἢ φθαρέντα πρότερον, οὐδενὸς ἔφθη γενόμενα
[τῷ] κατὰ τὴν ὑπάρχουσαν δύναμιν αὐτοῖς αἴτια. τίνος δὲ ἐροῦσιν αἴτια
15 τὰ ἔν τισιν μέρεσιν τοῦ σώματος φυόμενα περιττώματα; τίνος δὲ τὰ τέρα- 10

τά τε καὶ γινόμενα παρὰ φύσιν, ἃ τὴν ἀρχὴν οὐδὲ διαμένειν οἷά τε; εἰ
δ' ὁ μὲν [εἰ] φλοιὸς ἐν τοῖς φυτοῖς ἕνεκα τοῦ περικαρπίου, τὸ δὲ περι-
κάρπιον τοῦ καρποῦ χάριν, καὶ ἀρδεύεται μὲν ἵνα τρέφηται, τρέφεται δὲ
ἵνα καρποφορῇ, ἀλλ' ἔστιν γε πολλὰ ἐν αὐτοῖς εὑρεῖν καὶ μὴ τοῦτον γινό- 15
20 μενα τὸν τρόπον. τίνος γὰρ ἄν τις εἴποι τὰ σεσηπότα καὶ τὰ ξηρὰ τῶν
καρπῶν αἴτια τῶν μετὰ ταῦτα; τίνος δὲ τήν τινων φύλλων διδυμότητα;
ἐξ ὧν φανερὸν τοῖς ὁρᾶν τἀληθῆ βουλομένοις τε καὶ δυναμένοις, ὅτι, ὥσπερ 20
οὐ πᾶν τὸ δυνατὸν ἐνεργεῖν ⟨ἐνεργεῖ⟩, οὕτως οὐδὲ πᾶν, ὃ ἂν γένοιτο αἴτιον, καὶ   *
ἔστιν αἴτιον ἤδη ἢ γέγονεν ἢ γενήσεται. ἀλλ' οὐδὲ πᾶν τὸ γεγονὸς εὐθὺς τῷ
25 εἶναι ἤδη καὶ αἴτιόν ἐστιν ἐσομένου τινός. τὸ δ' ὁμόσε χωροῦντας μὲν   *
λέγειν καὶ ταῦτα, καταφεύγειν δὲ ἐπὶ τὸ ἄδηλον εἶναί τινος αἴτια (ὥσπερ 25   *
ἀμέλει καὶ ἐπὶ τῆς προνοίας τῆς κατ' αὐτοὺς ἀναγκάζονται ποιεῖν πολλάκις) εὐπορίαν ἐστὶ τοῖς ἀπόροις μηχανωμένων. τούτῳ γὰρ χρωμένους
ἐνέσται περὶ πάντων τῶν ἀτοπωτάτων λέγειν ὡς καὶ ὄντων καὶ εὐλόγους
30 ἐχόντων τινὰς αἰτίας, ἡμῖν δὲ ἀδήλους ἔτι. ἀρ' οὖν τούτων οὕτως ἐχόν- 30 XXIV
των ἀναιτίως τι γενήσεται καῦ τοῦθ' ἡμῶν ὁ λόγος προξενεῖ; ἢ δύναται | 76
σώζεσθαι τὸ μηδὲν ἀναιτίως τῶν γινομένων γίνεσθαι καὶ τοῦτον τὸν τρό-   194
πον ἐχόντων ὡς ἡμεῖς λέγομεν τῶν πραγμάτων. ἂν γὰρ παυσάμενοι τῆς
ἀλύσεως τῶν αἰτίων καὶ τοῦ τοῖς πρώτοις γενομένοις λέγειν ἐξ ἀνάγκης 5
ἕπεσθαι τὸ αἴτιος φύσει ὀφείλειν γίνεσθαι ὡς ἐν τῇ οὐσίᾳ αὐτῶν τὸ αἴ-
5 τιον περιέχουσι, ἀπὸ τῶν γινομένων τε καὶ ὑστέρων τὴν ἀπόδοσιν τῶν
αἰτίων ποιώμεθα ἔτι τε τῶν γινομένων κυρίως ζητῶμεν τὰς αἰτίας, οὔτε
ἀναιτίως τι τῶν γινομένων γενήσεται οὔτε διὰ τοῦτο ἐξ ἀνάγκης καῦ' εἰ- 10
μαρμένην τοιαύτην πᾶν τὸ γινόμενον ἔσται. οὐκ ἐξ ἀνάγκης μὲν γὰρ ὁ
Σωφρονίσκος τῷ εἶναι ἤδη καὶ πατήρ ἐστι καὶ αἴτιός τινι τῶν μετ' αὐτόν.
10 εἰ μέντοι Σωκράτης εἴη ἐξ ἀνάγκης, αὐτῷ τῆς γενέσεως Σωφρονίσκος ἐξ   *
ἀνάγκης αἴτιος. ὡς γὰρ θεμελίου μὲν ὄντος οὐκ ἀναγκαῖον οἰκίαν γενέ- 15   *
σθαι, οἰκίας δὲ οὔσης προκαταβληθῆσθαι τὸν θεμέλιον, ἀνάγκη οὕτως ἔχειν   *
ὑποληπτέον καὶ ἐν τοῖς γινομένοις φύσει τὰ αἴτια ἐξ ἀνάγκης, οὐ τοῖς
πρώτοις ἐξ ἀνάγκης ἑπόμενον τὸ αἴτιος εἶναί τινων, ἀλλὰ τοῖς ὑστέροις 20
15 γινομένοις τὸ ἐξ ἀνάγκης ἔχειν τι τῶν πρὸ αὐτῶν αἴτιον. ἔστι δέ τινα
τῶν γινομένων καὶ τοιαῦτα, ὡς ἔχειν μὲν αἴτιόν τι, οὐ μὴν οἰκεῖον οὐδὲ
προηγούμενον, ἀλλ' ὡς ἡμῖν ἔθος λέγειν κατὰ συμβεβηκός. ὁ γὰρ εὑ- •
ρεθεὶς θησαυρὸς ὑπὸ τοῦ διὰ τὸ φυτεύειν σκάπτοντος ἔχει μὲν τὸ σκάπτειν 25
αἴτιον, ἀλλ' οὐκ οἰκεῖον οὐδὲ γενόμενον δι' αὐτόν. τὰ μὲν γὰρ κυρίως
20 αἴτια ἢ ἐξ ἀνάγκης μόνον ὡς τούτοις δοκεῖ καὶ ὡς ἐπὶ τὸ πολὺ ἑπόμενον·   *
ἔχει τὸ αἴτιον, τὰ δὲ κατὰ συμβεβηκὸς οὕτως αἴτια σπανίως γίνεται τῶν 30   *
τοιούτων αἴτια. ὥστε τοῖς τοῦτον τὸν τρόπον λέγουσιν ἅμα μὲν ἕπεται
τὸ μηδὲν ἀναιτίως γίνεσθαι λέγειν. ἅμα δὲ τὸ σώζειν τό τε ἀπὸ τύχης καὶ
αὐτομάτως γίνεσθαί τινα καὶ εἶναι καὶ | τὸ ἐφ' ἡμῖν καὶ τὸ ἐνδεχόμενον 78
25 ἐν τοῖς πράγμασιν ἀλλ' οὐ φωνὴν μόνον. πῶς γὰρ οὐ φανερῶς τὸ λέγειν XXV
ψεῦδος πᾶν τὸ ἑπόμενόν τινι ἐξ ἐκείνου τὴν αἰτίαν τοῦ εἶναι ἔχειν καὶ 5   *
πᾶν τὸ προηγούμενόν τινος αἴτιον ὑπάρχειν ἐκείνῳ; ὁρῶμεν γὰρ ὅτι τὰ

ἐφεξῆς ἀλλήλοις ὄντα τῷ χρόνῳ οὐ πάντα διὰ τὰ ἔμπροσθεν καὶ πρὸ αὐτῶν γεγονότα γίνεται. οὔτε γὰρ τὸ βαδίσαι διὰ τὸ ἀναστῆναι, οὔτε νὺξ

30 διὰ τὴν ἡμέραν, οὔτε ὁ τῶν Ἰσθμίων ἀγὼν διὰ τὸν τῶν Ὀλυμπίων, ἀλλ' 10

195 οὐδὲ διὰ τὸν χειμῶνα τὸ θέρος. ὅθεν καὶ θαυμάσειεν ἄν τις αὐτοὺς τὴν τῶν αἰτίων ἀπόδοσιν τοῦτον ποιουμένους τὸν τρόπον ὡς αἰεὶ τὸ πρῶτον γεγονὸς αἰτιᾶσθαι τοῦ μετὰ τοῦτο καὶ ποιεῖν ἐπισύνδεσίν τινα καὶ συνέχειαν 15

* τῶν αἰτίων, καὶ ταύτην τοῦ μηδὲν ἀναιτίως γίνεσθαι φέρονται τὴν αἰτίαν.
5 ὁρῶμεν γὰρ ἐπὶ πολλῶν ⟨τὸ⟩ αὐτὸ καὶ τοῖς πρώτοις καὶ τοῖς ὑστέροις γινομένοις ὂν αἴτιον. τοῦ γοῦν ἀναστῆναι καὶ τοῦ περιπατῆσαι τὸ αὐτὸ αἴτιον, οὐ γὰρ τὸ ἀναστῆναι τοῦ περιπατῆσαι, ἀλλ' ἀμφοτέρων ὁ ἀναστὰς 20 καὶ περιπατῶν αἴτιος καὶ ἡ τούτου προαίρεσις. ὁρῶμεν δ' ὅτι καὶ νυκτὸς καὶ ἡμέρας τάξιν τινὰ ἐχουσῶν πρὸς ἀλλήλας ἓν καὶ ταὐτὸν αἴτιον, ὁμοίως

10 δὲ καὶ τῆς τῶν καιρῶν μεταβολῆς· οὐ γὰρ ὁ χειμὼν αἴτιος τοῦ θέρους, 25

* ἀλλ' ἐκείνων τε καὶ τούτου ⟨ἡ⟩ τοῦ θείου σώματος κίνησίς τε καὶ περιφορὰ καὶ ἡ κατὰ τὸν λοξὸν κύκλον ἔγκλισις, καθ' ἣν ὁ ἥλιος κινούμενος

* ἁπάντων ὁμοίως τῶν προειρημένων αἴτιος. καὶ ὅτι μὴ ⟨ἡ⟩ νὺξ τῆς ἡμέρας αἰτία ἢ ὁ χειμὼν τοῦ θέρους μηδὲ ἐμπέπλεκται ταῦτα ἀλλήλοις ἁλώσεως 30

* 15 δίκην, † ἂν ἕως ταῦτα γίνεται, ἢ εἰ μὴ οὕτως γίνοιτο, διασπασθήσεται ἡ τοῦ κόσμου τε καὶ τῶν ἐν αὐτῷ γινομένων τε καὶ ὄντων ἕνωσις. ἱκανὰ γὰρ τὰ θεῖα καὶ | ἡ τούτου περιφορὰ τὴν τῶν γινομένων ἐν τῷ κόσμῳ συνέ- 80 χειαν φυλάσσειν. ἀλλ' οὐδὲ τὸ περιπατεῖν ἀναίτιον, ἐπεὶ μὴ ἐκ τοῦ ἀνα-

* στῆναι τὴν αἰτίαν ἔχει. ὥστ' οὐχ † οὕτως αἰτίων εἱρμὸς ὑπ' αὐτῶν λε-
20 γόμενος εὐλόγως ἂν τοῦ μηδὲν ἀναιτίως γίνεσθαι φέροιτο τὴν αἰτίαν. ὡς 5 γὰρ αἱ κινήσεις καὶ οἱ χρόνοι ἔχουσι μέν τινα αἰτίαν (οὐ μὴν οὔτε ἡ κίνησις τὴν πρὸ αὐτῆς οὔτε ὁ χρόνος τὸν πρὸ αὐτοῦ χρόνον), οὕτως ἔχει καὶ τὰ ἐν αὐτοῖς τε καὶ τὰ δι' αὐτῶν γινόμενα πράγματα. τῆς μὲν γὰρ 10 συνεχείας τῶν γινομένων ἐστί τις αἰτία, δι' ἣν ὁ κόσμος εἷς τε καὶ ἀίδιος

25 κατὰ τὸ αὐτό τε καὶ ὡσαύτως ἀεὶ διοικούμενος, καὶ δεῖ ταύτην ζητεῖν τε καὶ ⟨μὴ⟩ παραλιπεῖν τὴν αἰτίαν, οὐ μὴν χρὴ τοιαύτην ὑπολαμβάνειν, ὡς ἐκ τοῦ πρεσβυτέρου γίνεσθαι τὸ νεώτερον, ὡς ὁρῶμεν γινόμενον ἐπὶ τῆς 15 τῶν ζῴων γενέσεως. εὔλογον δὲ καὶ ἀρχήν τινα ἐν τοῖς αἰτίοις εἶναι λέγειν, οὐκέτ' ἄλλην πρὸ αὐτῆς ἀρχὴν καὶ αἰτίαν ἔχουσαν. οὐ γὰρ εἰ |πάντα|

30 τὰ γινόμενα πάντα αἴτια ἔχει, ἤδη καὶ πάντων εἶναί τινας αἰτίας ἀνάγκη. οὐ 20

96 γὰρ πάντα τὰ ὄντα γίνεται. πῶς γὰρ οὐκ ἄτοπον τὸ λέγειν ἐπ' ἄπειρον εἶναι τὰ αἴτια καὶ τὸν εἱρμὸν αὐτῶν καὶ τὴν ἐπισύνδεσιν ὡς μήτε πρῶτόν τι εἶναι μήτε ἔσχατον; τὸ γὰρ μηδὲν εἶναι πρῶτον αἴτιον λέγειν ἀναιρεῖν ἐστι τὸ αἴτιον· ἀναιρουμένης γὰρ ἀρχῆς ἀναιρεῖσθαι καὶ τὸ μετ' 25

5 αὐτὴν ἀνάγκη. ἀναιροῖτο δ' ἂν καὶ ἐπιστήμη κατὰ τὸν λόγον τοῦτον, εἴ γε ἐπιστήμη μέν ἐστι κυρίως ἡ τῶν πρώτων αἰτίων γνῶσις, οὐκ ἔστι δὲ

* κατ' αὐτοὺς ἐν τοῖς αἰτίοις τὸ πρῶτον. οὐ πᾶσά τε τάξεως παράβασις 80 ἀναιρετικὴ τῶν ἐν οἷς γίνεται· γίνεσθαι γὰρ ἔνια καὶ παρὰ τὴν τοῦ βασιλέως τάξιν οὐκ ἀδύνατον, ἃ οὐ πάντως τῆς βασιλείας ἤδη γίνεται φθαρτι-

10 κά, οὐδὲ εἴ τι τοιοῦτον ἐν τῷ κόσμῳ γίνοιτο, πάντως ἤδη τοῦτο λύει τὴν

εὐδαιμονίαν τοῦ κόσμου, | καθάπερ οὐδὲ τὴν τοῦ οἴκου καὶ τὴν τοῦ δεσπότου 82
ἡ τυχοῦσα τῶν οἰκετῶν ῥαδιουργία.

Ἃ δὲ ἀποροῦσιν πρὸς τὸ εἶναι τοιοῦτον τὸ ἐφ᾽ ἡμῖν, ὁποῖον ἡ XXVI
κοινὴ πρόληψις τῶν ἀνθρώπων πεπίστευκεν, ἀπορεῖν μὲν οὐκ ἄλογον,
15 τὸ δὲ τοῖς ἀπορουμένοις ἐποχουμένους ὡς ὁμολογουμένοις ἀναιρεῖν μέν, 5
ἃ οὕτως ἐναργῆ, σκιαγραφίαν δέ τινα καὶ παιδιὰν ἀποφαίνειν τὸν τῶν
ἀνθρώπων βίον καὶ συναγωνίζεσθαι τοῖς ἀπορουμένοις καθ᾽ αὑτῶν,
πῶς οὐ παντάπασιν ἄλογον; οὐδὲ γὰρ τῷ μὴ δυναμένῳ λύειν τινὰ τῶν 10
Ζήνωνος λόγων τῶν κατὰ τῆς κινήσεως ἤδη κίνησιν ἀναιρετέον. ἱκα-
20 νωτέρα γὰρ ἡ τοῦ πράγματος ἐνάργεια πρὸς συγκατάθεσιν πάσης τῆς
διὰ λόγων ἀναιρούσης αὐτὸ πιθανότητος. οὐ χεῖρον δὲ ἴσως καὶ ἡμᾶς 15
τῶν ἀπορουμένων ὑπ᾽ αὐτῶν, οἷς μάλιστα θαρροῦσιν, ταῦτα προχειρισαμέ-
νους ἐξετάσαι, πῶς ἔχει. ἴσως γὰρ οὐδὲ ἄγαν φανεῖται † εἰς αὐτά. ἔστι δή   *
τι τῶν ἀπορουμένων ὑπ᾽ αὐτῶν καὶ τοιοῦτον. ῾εἰ, φασίν, ταῦτά ἐστιν ἐφ᾽
25 ἡμῖν, ὧν καὶ τὰ ἀντικείμενα δυνάμεθα, καὶ ἐπὶ τοῖς τοιούτοις οἵ τε ἔπαι- 20
νοι καὶ οἱ ψόγοι, προτροπαί τε καὶ ἀποτροπαί, κολάσεις τε καὶ τιμαί, οὐκ
ἔσται τὸ φρονίμοις εἶναι καὶ τὰς ἀρετὰς ἔχειν ἐπὶ τοῖς ἔχουσιν, ὅτι μηκέτ᾽
εἰσὶν τῶν ἀντικειμένων κακιῶν ταῖς ἀρεταῖς δεκτικοί, ὁμοίως δὲ οὐδὲ αἱ 25
κακίαι ἐπὶ τοῖς κακοῖς· οὐδὲ γὰρ ἐπὶ τούτοις τὸ μηκέτ᾽ εἶναι κακοῖς· ἀλλὰ
μὴν ἄτοπον τὸ μὴ λέγειν τὰς ἀρετὰς καὶ τὰς κακίας ἐφ᾽ ἡμῖν μηδὲ τοὺς   197
ἐπαίνους καὶ τοὺς ψόγους ἐπὶ τούτων γίνεσθαι· οὐκ ἄρα τὸ ἐφ᾽ ἡμῖν τοι- 30
οῦτον. | οἱ συγχωρήσαντες ἀναποβλήτους τὰς ἀρετάς τε καὶ τὰς κακίας εἶ- 84 XXVII *
ναι, ἴσως προχειρότερον λαμβανόμενον λέγοιμεν ἂν κατὰ τοῦτο τὰς ἕξεις
5 ἐπὶ τοῖς ἔχουσιν εἶναι, καθόσον πρὸ τοῦ λαβεῖν αὐτὰς ἐπ᾽ αὐτοῖς ἦν καὶ
μὴ λαβεῖν. οἵ τε γὰρ τὰς ἀρετὰς ἔχοντες καὶ τοῦ τῶν βελτιόνων 5   *
ἀμελεῖν ἑλόμενοι τὰ βελτίω αὐτοῖς αἴτιοι τῆς τῶν ἀρετῶν ἐγένοντο κτήσεως, οἵ τε τὰς κακίας ἔχοντες παραπλησίως. ὁ δ᾽ αὐτὸς καὶ ἐπὶ τῶν
τεχνῶν λόγος· καὶ γὰρ τῶν τεχνιτῶν ἕκαστος πρὸ μὲν τοῦ τὴν τέχνην 10
10 ἔχειν εἶχεν καὶ τοῦ μὴ γενέσθαι τὴν ἐξουσίαν, γενόμενος δὲ οὐκέτ᾽ ἔσται
κύριος τοῦ μὴ γεγονέναι τε καὶ εἶναι τοιοῦτος. αἱ γὰρ γενέσεις τῶν τοιούτων ἐφ᾽ ἡμῖν, καὶ διὰ τοῦτο οὐχ ὅμοιον τὸ ἀληθὲς ἐπί τε τῶν μελλόντων καὶ ἐπὶ τῶν ὄντων τε καὶ γεγονότων, ὅτι ⟨τὸ⟩ μὲν ὄν τε καὶ γεγονὸς 15
οὐχ οἷόν τε ἢ μὴ εἶναι ἢ μὴ γεγονέναι, τὸ δὲ μέλλον γίνεσθαι ἐνδέχεται
15 καὶ μὴ γίνεσθαι. διὸ πρὸ μὲν τοῦ τὴν ἀρετὴν ἔχειν τόνδε τινὰ ἀληθὲς
ἦν τὸ ἐνδέχεσθαι καὶ μὴ γενέσθαι τοιοῦτον, ὃ δὲ τοιοῦτον γίνεται, τοῦτο 20
καὶ γενόμενον ἀληθὲς οὕτως λέγειν γεγονέναι. εἰ μὲν οὖν ἦν ἐκ γενετῆς
ὁ φρόνιμος τοιοῦτος καὶ τοῦτο πρὸς τοῖς ἄλλοις τοῖς ὑπὸ τῆς φύσεως αὐτῷ δεδομένοις εἶχεν παρ᾽ ἐκείνης λαβών, οὐδ᾽ ὅλως ἂν ἦν ἐπ᾽ αὐτῷ τὸ
20 εἶναι τοιούτῳ, ὥσπερ οὐδὲ τὸ εἶναι δίποδι ἢ λογικῷ, οὐδ᾽ ἂν ἐπῃνεῖτο 25
ἔτι ἐπὶ τῷ τοιοῦτος εἶναι, ἀλλ᾽ ἐθαυμάζετο ὡς ἔχων παρὰ τῆς θείας φύσεως δῶρον τηλικοῦτον. ὡς γὰρ τῶν ὑγιαινόντων, ὅσοι μὲν ἀσθενεῖς ὄντες τὴν φύσιν διὰ τῆς οἰκείας ἐπιμελείας εἰσὶ τοιοῦτοι, τούτους μὲν ἐπαινοῦμεν ἐφ᾽ ἑαυτῶν πρόνοιαν τὴν προσήκουσαν ποιουμένους, δι᾽ ἣν πρόνοιαν 30

25 οὐκ εἰσιν ἐν τῷ νοσεῖν, τοὺς δὲ ἐκ φύσεως ὑγιεινοὺς [καὶ τοὺς νοσοῦντας]
ἄνευ πραγματείας καὶ φροντίδων οὐκέτι μὲν ἐπαινοῦμεν, μακαρίζομεν δὲ
ὡς χωρὶς καμάτων | τοῦτο ἔχοντας, ὃ καὶ τοῖς ἄλλοις ἀγαπητόν, εἰ καὶ 86
μετὰ καμάτου παρείη, τὸν αὐτὸν τρόπον ἢ καὶ ἔτι μᾶλλον ἐπὶ τῶν ἀρετῶν ἐποιοῦμεν ἄν, εἰ ἦσαν ἐκ φύσεώς τισιν παροῦσαι, ὅπερ ἀμέλει ποι-
30 οῦμεν ἐπὶ τῶν θεῶν. ἐπεὶ δὲ ἀδύνατον ἡμῖν τοῦτο, καὶ οὐδὲν ἀδύνατον 5
δεῖ παρὰ τῆς φύσεως ἀπαιτεῖν (αὕτη γὰρ δυνατῷ τε καὶ ἀδυνάτῳ μέτρον·
198   τελειότης μὲν γὰρ ἡ ἀρετὴ καὶ [ἡ] ἀκρότης τῆς οἰκείας φύσεως ἑκάστου,
ἀδύνατον δὲ ἀτελές τι ὂν ἐν τελειότητι εἶναι, ἀτελὲς δὲ τὸ γενόμενον εὐθὺ
τῷ γενέσθαι), οὐδὲ τὴν ἀρετὴν οἷόν τε τὸν ἄνθρωπον (ἔχοντα) φῦναι. οὐ 10
μὴν ἀσύμβολος ἡ φύσις αὐτῷ πρὸς τὴν κτῆσιν αὐτῆς, ἀλλ' ἔχει παρ' αὐ-
5 τῆς δύναμίν τε καὶ ἐπιτηδειότητα δεκτικὴν αὐτῆς, ἣν οὐδὲ τῶν ἄλλων
ζῴων ἔχει. καὶ διὰ τήνδε τὴν δύναμιν ὁ ἄνθρωπός τῶν ἄλλων ζῴων 15
φύσει διαφέρει, καίτοι πολλῶν ζῴων ἀπολειπόμενος ἐν τοῖς σωματικοῖς πλεο-
νεκτήμασιν. εἰ μὲν οὖν οὕτως εἴχομεν παρ' αὐτῆς τὴν δύναμιν τὴν τῶν ἀρετῶν
δεκτικήν, ὡς προιόντες καὶ τελειούμενοι καὶ ταύτην λαμβάνειν, ὡς τὸ περιπα-
10 τεῖν, ὡς τὸ ὀδόντας, ὡς τὸ γένεια φύειν, ὡς ἄλλο τι τῶν ἐπιγινομένων ἡμῖν 20
κατὰ φύσιν, οὐδ' οὕτως ἂν ἐφ' ἡμῖν ἦσαν αἱ ἀρεταὶ ὥσπερ οὐδὲ τῶν προειρημένων τι, ἐπεὶ δὲ μὴ τοῦτον τὸν τρόπον αὐτὰς κτώμεθα (εἰ γὰρ ἦν ὥσπερ τὰ
ἄλλα, οὕτως δὲ καὶ φρόνησίς τε καὶ ἀρετὴ τοῖς ἀνθρώποις συγγενῆ, πάντες ἂν 25
*   ἢ οἵ γε πλεῖστοι, ὥσπερ τῶν ἄλλων κατὰ φύσιν αὐτοῖς τυγχάνουσιν, οὕτως
15 οὐ τὴν δύναμιν τὴν τῶν ἀρετῶν δεκτικὴν μόνην, ἀλλὰ καὶ τὰς ἀρετὰς
αὐτὰς παρ' ἐκείνης ἂν εἴχομεν καὶ οὐδὲν οὐδ' οὕτως ἂν ἔδει ἐπαίνων ἢ 30
ψόγων ἢ τινος τῶν τοιούτων ἐπὶ [δὲ] ταῖς ἀρεταῖς τε καὶ κακίαις θειοτέραν
πρόφασίν τε καὶ οὐσίαν τῆς παρουσίας αὐτῶν ἔχουσιν), ἐπεὶ δὴ οὐχ οὕτως ἔχει (οὐ γὰρ τοὺς πάντας οὐδὲ τοὺς πλείστους ὁρῶμεν τὰς ἀρετὰς
20 ἔχοντας, ὃ τῶν κατὰ φύσιν γινομένων σημεῖόν | ἐστιν, ἀλλ' ἀγαπητὸν ἕνα 88
που λαβεῖν τοιοῦτον, ὃς δι' ἀσκήσεώς τε καὶ διδασκαλίας δείκνυσιν τὴν
τῶν ἀνθρώπων πρὸς τὰ ἄλλα ζῷα φυσικὴν πλεονεξίαν, δι' αὐτοῦ προστι-
*   θεὶς τὸ ἀναγκαῖον ἐνδέον ἡμῶν τῇ φύσει), διὰ τοῦτο ἐφ' ἡμῖν τέ ἐστιν 5
ἡ τῶν ἀρετῶν κτῆσις καὶ οὐκ ἄχρηστοι οὐδὲ μάτην οὔτε οἱ ἔπαινοι οὔτε
25 οἱ ψόγοι οὔτε ⟨αἱ⟩ πρὸς βελτίω προτροπαὶ οὔθ' ἡ διὰ τῶν βελτιόνων ἐθῶν
κατὰ τοὺς νόμους ἀγωγή. τῶν μὲν γὰρ φύσει τισὶν ὑπαρχόντων οὐδὲν 10
οἷόν τε ὑπό τινος ἔθους ἀλλοῖον γενέσθαι (οὐχ οὕτως πολλάκις τὸ βάρος
ἔχον ἀνορριφθήσεται, ὡς ἐθισθῆναι κατὰ τὴν αὐτοῦ φύσιν ἄνω φέρεσθαι),
τὰ δὲ ἤθη τῶν ἀνθρώπων τοῖα καὶ τοῖα διὰ τῶν διαφερόντων ἐθῶν γίνε-
199   ται. καὶ ἐπὶ μὲν τῶν φύσει πρώτας τὰς ἕξεις κτησάμενοι οὕτως ἐνεργοῦ- 15
μεν κατ' αὐτάς (οὐ γὰρ ἰδόντες πολλάκις τὴν ὁρατικὴν ἕξιν κτώμεθα, ἀλλ'
ἔχοντες αὐτὴν οὕτως ὁρῶμεν), ἐπὶ δὲ τῶν οὐ φύσει ἐκ τῶν ἐνεργειῶν τὰς
ἕξεις κτώμεθα. οὐ γὰρ ἄλλως τέκτων τις ἂν γένοιτο μὴ πολλάκις ἐνεργή-
5 σας τὰς τοῦ τέκτονος ἐνεργείας κατὰ τὰς ὑποθήκας τοῦ διδάσκοντος. ὥστ' 20
ἐπεὶ καὶ τὰς ἀρετὰς οὕτως κτώμεθα (ἐνεργοῦντες γὰρ καὶ τὰ σωφρονικὰ
γινόμεθα σώφρονες), οὐκ ἂν ἡμῖν ὑπάρχοιεν φύσει. οἱ δὲ φάσκοντες ἐξ XXVIII
ἀνάγκης ἡμᾶς εἶναί τε καὶ γίνεσθαι τοιούτους, καὶ μὴ καταλιπόντες ἡμῖν 25

τὴν ἐξουσίαν τοῦ ταῦτα πράττειν τε καὶ μή, δι' ὧν ἂν τοιοῦτοι γενοίμεθα,

10 καὶ διὰ τοῦτο μήτε τοῖς κακοῖς γινομένοις ἐξεῖναι μὴ ταῦτα πράττειν, ἃ
πράττοντες γίνονται τοιοῦτοι, μήτε τοῖς ἀγαθοῖς, πῶς οὐχ ὁμολογήσουσιν 30
κάκιστον γεγονέναι τῶν ζῴων ἁπάντων ὑπὸ τῆς φύσεως τὸν ἄνθρωπον, δι'
ὃν φασιν πάντα τἆλλα γενέσθαι ὡς συντελέσαντα πρὸς τὴν τούτου σωτη-
ρίαν; εἰ γὰρ ἡ μὲν ἀρετή τε καὶ ἡ κακία μόναι κατ' | αὐτοὺς ἡ μὲν ἀγα- 90
15 θόν, ἡ δὲ κακόν, καὶ οὐδὲν τῶν ἄλλων ζῴων οὐδετέρου τούτων ἐστὶν ἐπι-
δεκτικόν, τῶν δὲ ἀνθρώπων οἱ πλεῖστοι κακοί, μᾶλλον δὲ ἀγαθὸς μὲν εἷς
ἢ δεύτερος ὑπ' αὐτῶν γεγονέναι μυθεύεται, ὥσπερ τι παράδοξον ζῷον καὶ 5
παρὰ φύσιν σπανιώτερον τοῦ φοίνικος τοῦ παρ' Αἰθίοψιν, οἱ δὲ πάντες
κακοὶ καὶ ἐπίσης ἀλλήλοις τοιοῦτοι, ὡς μηδὲν διαφέρειν ἄλλον ἄλλου, μαί-
20 νεσθαι δὲ ὁμοίως πάντας ὅσοι μὴ σοφοί, πῶς οὐκ ἂν ἀθλιώτατον ζῷον
ἁπάντων ὁ ἄνθρωπος εἴη, ἔχων τήν τε κακίαν καὶ τὸ μαίνεσθαι σύμφυτα 10
αὐτῷ καὶ συγκεκληρωμένα; ἀλλὰ τὸ μὲν τὰς παραδοξολογίας αὐτῶν τὰς
ἐν τοῖς δόγμασιν ἐξετάζειν, δι' ὧν πρὸς τἀληθῆ διαφωνοῦσιν, πλεῖστον
παραιτητέον τοῦ νῦν, ἐπανιτέον δὲ ὅθεν ἐξετραπόμεθα. ἐδείξαμεν δὲ ὅτι 15 XXIX
25 οὕτως ἐπ' αὐτῷ τῷ φρονίμῳ τὸ εἶναι τοιούτῳ, ὅτι τῆς τοιαύτης ἕξεως
καὶ τῆς κτήσεως αὐτῆς αὐτὸς αἴτιος τῷ καὶ τοῦ μὴ γενέσθαι τοιοῦτος
ἔχειν πρότερον τὴν ἐξουσίαν. τὴν μὲν οὖν ἕξιν μηκέτ' ἔχει ὡς ἐπ' αὐ- 20
τῷ (ὥσπερ οὐδὲ τῷ αὐτὸν ἀπὸ ὕψους ἀφέντι τὸ στῆναι καίτοι τοῦ ῥῖψαί
τε καὶ μὴ τὴν ἐξουσίαν ἔχοντι), ἐπ' αὐτῷ δὲ τῶν ἐνεργειῶν ὧν τὴν ἕξιν
30 ἔχων ἐνεργεῖ καὶ μὴ ποιῆσαί τινα. καὶ γὰρ εἰ ὅτι μάλιστα εὔλογον τὸ τὸν
φρόνιμον (τὰς) κατὰ τὸν λόγον καὶ τὴν φρόνησιν ἐνεργείᾳ ἐνεργεῖν, πρῶτον 25
μὲν οὐχ ὡρισμένως αἵδε τινὲς τοιαῦται ἢ μέχρι τοῦδε ἐνεργούμεναι, ἀλλ'
ἔστιν ἐν πλάτει τινὶ πάντα τὰ γινόμενα τοῦτον τὸν τρόπον, καὶ τὸ παρὰ   200
μικρὸν ἐν τούτοις οὐκ ἀναιρεῖ τὸ προκείμενον· ἔπειτα δὲ οὐ κατηναγκασμέ- 30
νως ὁ φρόνιμος ὢν αἱρεῖταί τι πράττει, ἀλλ' ὡς καὶ τοῦ μὴ πρᾶξαί τι
τούτων αὐτὸς ὢν κύριος. εὔλογον γὰρ ἂν δόξαι ποτὲ τῷ φρονίμῳ καὶ
5 ὑπὲρ τοῦ δεῖξαι τὸ τῶν ἐνεργειῶν ἐλεύθερον καὶ μὴ ποιῆσαί ποτε τὸ γι- 92
νόμενον ἂν εὐλόγως ὑπ' αὐτοῦ, εἰ προείποι τις αὐτῷ μάντις ἐξ ἀνάγκης
αὐτὸν τοῦτο πράξειν. τοῦτό τοι καὶ οἱ μάντεις εἶναι λέγουσίν γε ὑφορώμενοι φεύγοντες τοὺς παρὰ πόδας ἐλέγχους οὐδὲν τοιοῦτο προλέγουσιν τοῖς 5
ἐλέγξαι δυναμένοις, ἀλλ' ὥσπερ τὸ τοὺς χρόνους ὁρίζειν τῶν προλεγομένων
10 ὑπ' αὐτῶν ὡς ἐσομένων ὡς εὐέλεγκτον φυλάσσονται, οὕτω φεύγουσιν καὶ
τὸ λέγειν τι καὶ μαντεύεσθαι τοῖς δυναμένοις παραχρῆμα τὸ ἀντικείμενον 10
ποιῆσαι τοῦ μαντεύματος. τὸ δὲ λέγειν εὔλογον εἶναι τοὺς θεοὺς τὰ ἐσό- XXX
μενα προειδέναι (ἄτοπον γὰρ τὸ λέγειν ἐκείνους ἀγνοεῖν τι τῶν ἐσομένων)
καὶ τοῦτο λαμβάνοντας κατασκευάζειν πειρᾶσθαι δι' αὐτοῦ τὸ πάντα ἐξ
15 ἀνάγκης τε γίνεσθαι καὶ καθ' εἱμαρμένην οὔτε ἀληθὲς οὔτε εὔλογον. τῆς 15
μὲν γὰρ φύσεως τῆς τῶν πραγμάτων τοῦτο χωρούσης, οὐδένα [μᾶλλον]
εὐλογώτερον εἰδέναι μᾶλλον τῶν θεῶν τὰ μέλλοντα, ἀδυνάτου δ' οὔσης
τὴν τοιαύτην πρόρρησιν καὶ πρόγνωσιν δέχεσθαι, οὐδὲ τοὺς θεοὺς εὔλογον 20
ἔτι γίνεται [τὸ] εἰδέναι τι τῶν ἀδυνάτων. τὰ γὰρ ἀδύνατα τῇ αὐτῶν φύ-
20 σει καὶ παρὰ τοῖς θεοῖς τὴν αὐτὴν φυλάττει φύσιν. ἀδύνατον γὰρ καὶ

τοῖς θεοῖς ἢ τὸ τὴν διάμετρον ποιῆσαι τῇ πλευρᾷ σύμμετρον ἢ τὰ δὶς
δύο πέντε εἶναι ἢ τῶν γεγονότων τι μὴ γεγονέναι. οὐδὲ γὰρ τὴν ἀρχὴν 25
* βούλονται † ἐπὶ τῶν ἀδυνάτων οὕτως γὰρ ἦν ἐν τοῖς λεγομένοις δυσχωρία.
οἷς ὁμοίως ἀδύνατον καὶ τὸ ἐν τῇ οἰκείᾳ φύσει ἔχον τὸ δύνασθαι γενέσθαι
25 τε καὶ μὴ ὡς ἐσόμενον πάντως ἢ ὡς μὴ ἐσόμενον οὕτως προειδέναι. εἰ
γὰρ ἡ περὶ αὐτῶν πρὸ αὐτῶν πρόγνωσις ἀναιρεῖ τὸ ἐν αὐτοῖς ἐνδεχόμενον, 30
δῆλον ὡς, εἰ σώζοιτο τοῦτο, ἀδύνατος ἂν ἡ περὶ αὐτῶν πρόγνωσις εἴη.
ὅτι γὰρ | καὶ [εἰ] κατὰ τούτους τοῦτο οὕτως ἔχει, δῆλον ἐκ τοῦ λαβόντας 94
αὐτούς, ὅτι οἱ θεοὶ προγιγνώσκουσιν τὰ μέλλοντα, δι' αὐτοῦ κατασκευάζειν
30 τὸ ἐξ ἀνάγκης αὐτὰ γίγνεσθαι, ὡς οὐκ ἂν εἰ μὴ οὕτως γίγνοιτο προγνω-
σομένων. εἰ δὲ τῇ τῶν θεῶν προγνώσει τε καὶ προαγορεύσει τὸ ἀναγκαῖον 5
* ἕπεται, καὶ κατ' αὐτούς, εἰ μὴ τὸ ἀναγκαῖον ἐν τοῖς γινομένοις εἴη, οὐκ ἂν κατ'
201 αὐτοὺς οἱ θεοὶ προγινώσκοιεν τὰ μέλλοντα. ὥστε καὶ αὐτοὶ τὴν αὐτὴν
ἀδυναμίαν τοῖς θεοῖς φυλάσσουσιν, εἴ γε κατ' ἀδυναμίαν χρὴ καὶ ἀσθέ- 10
νειαν λέγειν γίνεσθαι τὸ τὰ ἀδύνατα μὴ δύνασθαι. οὐ δὴ τῷ θείῳ
* πλέον τι δύνασθαι διὰ τῆς προρρήσεως ἀνάπτουσιν, ἀλλὰ διὰ τοῦ προσ-
5 λαμβάνειν τοῦτο τὴν φύσιν τὴν τῶν πραγμάτων τοιαύτην εἰσάγουσιν οὐδαμῶς ἀκόλουθα καὶ συνῳδὰ τοῖς γινομένοις τε καὶ ἐναργέσιν λέγοντες. 15
τούτῳ γὰρ προσχρωμένους ἐνέσται πάντα τὰ ἀδύνατα ⟨δυνατὰ⟩ δεικνύναι
τῷ εὔλογον εἶναι μὴ ἀγνοεῖν αὐτὰ τοὺς θεούς. δύναται γάρ τις λαβὼν
τὸ ἄτοπον εἶναι τοὺς θεοὺς μὴ εἰδέναι τὸ ἄπειρον πόσων ἐστὶ μέ-
10 τρων, θέμενος τοῦτο προσλαμβάνειν τὸ δυνατὸν εἶναι γιγνώσκεσθαι τὸ 20
ἄπειρον πόσων ἐστὶ μέτρων. εἰ δὲ τοῦτο, δυνατὸν εἶναι τὸ ἄπειρον ὡρισμέ-
νων τινῶν μέτρων. εἰ γὰρ μὴ ἦν, οὐδ' ἂν οἱ θεοὶ ᾔδεσαν αὐτὸ πόσων
* ἐστὶ μέτρων. ἐπεὶ δέ, εἰ τὸ προγινώσκειν τὰ μέλλοντά ἐστι τὸ ὁποῖά ἐστι 25
τοιαῦτα αὐτὰ γνωρίζειν ὄντα (ἄλλο γὰρ τὸ προγινώσκειν τοῦ ποιεῖν) δῆλον
15 ὅτι ⟨ὁ⟩ τὰ ἐνδεχόμενα προγινώσκων ὡς τοιαῦτα προγνώσεται. οὐ γὰρ
πρόγνωσις τὸ τὸ ἐνδεχόμενον ὡς ἐσόμενον ἀναγκαίως ἔσεσθαι λέγειν. ὥστε καὶ
οἱ θεοὶ τὰ ἐνδεχόμενα ἂν ὡς ἐνδεχόμενα προγιγνώσκοιεν, ᾧ οὐ πάντως ἀκο- 30
λουθήσει τὸ ἀναγκαῖον διὰ τὴν τοιαύτην πρόγνωσιν. οὕτως δὲ καὶ προ-
λεγόντων ἀκούομεν. οἱ γὰρ μετὰ τοῦ συμβουλεύειν τινὰ αἱρεῖσθαί τε καὶ
20 πράττειν ἃ χρὴ προλέγοντες οὐχ ὡς ἐξ ἀνάγκης | ἐσομένων περὶ ὧν προ- 96
λέγουσι ⟨λέγουσιν⟩. καθόλου δὲ εἰ μὲν πάντα τοῖς θεοῖς δυνατά φασιν εἶναι,
ἔσται δὲ καὶ τὰ ἀδύνατα ἐκείνοις δυνατά, οὐ μὴν δειχθήσεται διὰ τῆς ἐκείνων
περὶ τῶν μελλόντων προγνώσεως τὸ πάντα ἐξ ἀνάγκης τὰ γινόμενα γίνε- 5
σθαι. εἰ δὲ συγχωροῦσιν τὰ ἀδύνατα καὶ τοῖς θεοῖς εἶναι τοιαῦτα, πρῶ-
25 τον μὲν αὐτοὺς χρὴ δεικνύναι δυνατὴν εἶναι τὴν τοιάνδε πρόγνωσιν, εἶθ'
οὕτως αὐτὴν ἀνατιθέναι τοῖς θεοῖς. οὔτε γὰρ ἐναργὲς οὔτε ὑπὸ τῶν γινομένων ὁμολογούμενον τὸ τοιαύτην τὴν περὶ τῶν μελλόντων πρόγνωσιν ποι- 10
εῖσθαι τοὺς θεούς. ἡμεῖς μὲν οὖν οὔτε ἀναιροῦμεν μαντικὴν οὔτε τὴν
πρόγνωσιν τῶν θεῶν, ὡς ἔχει φύσεως τὰ πράγματα οὕτως αὐτοὺς περὶ
30 αὐτῶν προλέγειν λέγοντες, ἀλλ' οὐδὲ ἀφαιρούμεθα τῶν ἀνθρώπων τὸ ἀπὸ 15 XXX
μαντικῆς χρήσιμον, ὃ γίνεται τῷ δύνασθαί τινα καὶ φυλάξασθαί τι, μὴ

φυλαξάμενον ἂν μὴ συμβουλεύσαντος τοῦ θεοῦ· οἱ δὲ ὑμνοῦντες τὴν μαντικὴν καὶ κατὰ τὸν αὐτῶν λόγον μόνον σώζεσθαι λέγοντες αὐτήν, καὶ ταύ- 20   202
τῃ ⟨τῇ⟩ πίστει τοῦ πάντα καθ᾽ εἱμαρμένην γίνεσθαι χρώμενοι πρὸς τῷ μηδὲν   *
ἀληθὲς λέγειν προσέτι καὶ ἄτοπά τινα καὶ ἀλλότρια παντάπασιν θεῶν πέρι   *
αὐτῶν τολμῶσι λέγειν. πῶς γὰρ οὐκ ἄτοπα τὰ περὶ τούτων ὑπ᾽ αὐτῶν
5 λεγόμενα; ἀπορούντων γάρ τινων πρὸς αὐτούς, τί δήποτε, εἰ πάντα τὰ γι- 25
νόμενα ἐξ ἀνάγκης γίνεται, αἱ παρὰ τῶν θεῶν μαντεῖαι μὲν γίγνονται συμ-
βουλαῖς ἐοικυῖαι ὡς δυναμένων δι᾽ ὃ ἤκουσαν καὶ φυλάξασθαί τι καὶ ποιῆσαι τῶν ἀκουσάντων, καὶ δὴ καὶ τὸν τῷ Λαΐῳ δοθέντα χρησμὸν παρεχο- 30
μένων, δι᾽ οὗ λέγει πρὸς αὐτὸν ὁ Πύθιος περὶ τοῦ μὴ δεῖν παιδοποιεῖσθαι 98
10   "εἰ γὰρ φυτεύσεις παῖδα, ἀποκτενεῖ σ᾽ ὁ φύς
          καὶ πᾶς σὸς οἶκος βήσεται δι᾽ αἵματος·"
⟨οὗ⟩ φασιν, ὡς κηρύττει τὰ συγγράμματα αὐτῶν, οὕτως αὐτὸν χρῆσαι
ὡς οὐκ εἰδότα ὅτι μὴ πεισθήσεται (παντὸς γὰρ μᾶλλον ᾔδει), ἀλλ᾽ ὅτι 5
μηδὲν μὲν αὐτοῦ τοιοῦτον χρήσαντος οὐδὲν ἔμελλεν τῶν κατὰ τὴν περι-
15 πέτειαν τὴν περὶ τὸν Λαΐόν τε καὶ τὸν Οἰδίπουν γενομένων γίνεσθαι. οὔτε
γὰρ ἂν ἐξέθηκεν ὁ Λάιος τὸν γενόμενον αὐτῷ παῖδα, ὡς ἐξέθηκεν, οὔτ᾽
ἀναιρεθεὶς ὁ παῖς ὑπὸ τοῦ βουκόλου καὶ δοθεὶς πρὸς εἰσποίησιν τῷ Κορίν- 10
θίῳ Πολύβῳ, ἀνδρωθεὶς καὶ περιτυχὼν τῷ Λαΐῳ κατὰ τὴν ὁδὸν ἀγνοῶν
τε καὶ ἀγνοούμενος ἀπέκτεινεν αὐτόν. οὐ γὰρ ἄν ποτε ὡς υἱὸς ἔνδον παρ᾽
20 αὐτῶν τρεφόμενος ἠγνόησε τοὺς γονεῖς, ὡς τὸν μὲν αὐτῶν ἀποκτεῖναι, τὴν 15
δὲ ἀγαγέσθαι πρὸς γάμον. ὅπως οὖν πάντα ταῦτα σωθῇ καὶ πληρωθῇ
τὸ τῆς εἱμαρμένης δρᾶμα, φαντασίαν ὁ θεὸς διὰ τοῦ χρησμοῦ τῷ Λαΐῳ
παρέσχεν ὡς δυναμένῳ φυλάξασθαι τὰ λεγόμενα, καὶ ἐπεὶ μεθυσθεὶς ἐπαι-
δοποιήσατο, ἐξέθηκεν τὸ γενόμενον παιδίον ὡς διαφθερῶν, ἥτις ἔκθεσις 20
25 αἰτία τῶν ἀνοσίων μύθων ἐγένετο. εἶτά τις ταῦτα λέγων πῶς ἢ σώζει
μαντικήν, ἢ περὶ θεῶν εὐσεβεῖς διδάσκει προλήψεις, ἢ χρήσιμόν τι δείκνυσιν ἔχουσαν τὴν μαντικήν; ἡ μὲν γὰρ μαντικὴ δοκεῖ τῶν μελλόντων 25
προαγόρευσις εἶναι, οἱ δὲ τὸν Ἀπόλλω ποιητὴν ὧν προαγορεύει ποιοῦσιν.   203
ὃ γὰρ οὐκ ἂν οὕτως ἐγένετο μὴ τοῦτον τὸν τρόπον χρήσαντος τοῦ θεοῦ,
καὶ διὰ τοῦτο οὕτως ἔχρησεν, ὅπως γένηται τὰ ἐπ᾽ αὐτοῖς γενόμενα, πῶς
οὐκ ἔργα τοῦ χρήσαντος, ἀλλ᾽ οὐ μήνυσις τῶν ἐσομένων; ἀλλ᾽ εἰ καὶ δεῖ 30
5 πλέον τι τῶν ἄλλων μάντεων ἔχειν τοὺς θεούς, ὡς καὶ συμπράσσειν τοῖς
ἐσομένοις πρὸς τὸ γίνεσθαι † συνεργούμενον (καὶ γὰρ οἱ ποιηταὶ τοῦτό γε   *
περὶ θεῶν ὑμνοῦντες διατελοῦσιν, ὅτι ἄρα εἰσὶ δωρητῆρες ἐάων) | κατά γε 100   *
τὰ ὑπὸ τούτων λεγόμενα εἰς ἀγαθὸν μὲν οὐδὲν ὁ Πύθιος τῷ Λαΐῳ συντελεῖ, ἀγωνίζεται δὲ καὶ πάντα πράττει πρὸς τὸ μηδὲν τῶν ἀνοσιωτάτων τε
10 καὶ ἀσεβεστάτων παρελθεῖν τὸν οἶκον αὐτοῦ. ὧν ἀκούσας τίς οὐκ ἂν εὐ- 5
σεβεστέραν εἴποι τὴν λεγομένην ὑπὸ τῶν περὶ Ἐπίκουρον ἀπρονοησίαν τῆς
τοιαύτης προνοίας; πῶς δὲ συνῳδὰ ἀλλήλοις τὸ ὁμοῦ μὲν θεὸν λέγειν τὴν
εἱμαρμένην καὶ χρῆσθαι τοῖς οὖσίν τε καὶ γινομένοις ἐν τῷ κόσμῳ ἐπὶ
σωτηρίᾳ αὐτοῦ τε τοῦ κόσμου καὶ τῆς τῶν ἐν αὐτῷ τάξεως, ὁμοῦ δὲ τοι- 10
15 αῦτα περὶ αὐτῆς. λέγειν ὡς παραλαμβάνειν πρὸς τὰς πράξεις τὰς ἀνοσιω-

τάτας διὸ τὴν περὶ αὐτὰ σπουδὴν καὶ τὸν Πύθιον συνεργόν;- ἐπὶ τίνων
γὰρ σωτηρίᾳ ἐροῦσι χρῆσθαι τὴν εἱμαρμένην πατρὸς ὑπὸ παιδός; ἀναιρέσει 15
καὶ γάμῳ μητρὸς καὶ παιδὸς ἀνοσίῳ καὶ γενέσει παίδων ἀδελφῶν καὶ
πατρί; τί τῆς ἐν κόσμῳ διοικήσεως ἐκ τούτων ἔχειν εὔλογον τὴν σωτηρί-
20 αν, ὡς καὶ τὸν Ἀπόλλω φοβεῖσθαι μή τι παρέλθῃ τούτων ἄπρακτον; πότερον ἐμπόδια μὴ γινόμενα τῇ τῶν ἀνθρώπων κατὰ πόλεις τε καὶ νόμους 20
οἰκήσει, ἢ τῇ τῶν στοιχείων τοῦ κόσμου σωτηρίᾳ, ἢ τῇ τῶν θείων εὐτά-
κτῳ τε καὶ ἀιδίῳ περιφορᾷ ἢ τίνι τῶν ἐξ ὧν τὸν κόσμον συνεστάναι τε
καὶ διοικεῖσθαι κατὰ λόγον συμβέβηκεν; δῆλον δ᾽ ὅτι, κἂν ἄλλον τινὰ μῦ- 25
25 θον πάλιν ἀκούσωσιν παρά τινος τῶν τραγῳδοποιῶν, οἷς ἔργον τὰ τοιαῦτα
πλάσματα, ἢ γυναικά τινα διὰ ζηλοτυπίαν ἐπιβουλεύσασαν μὲν ἀλλοτρίοις
τέκνοις, ἀποκτείνασαν δὲ τὰ ἑαυτῆς, ἢ Θυέστην τινὰ δυστυχῆ γέροντα τῶν
σαρκῶν τῶν παίδων αὐτοῦ ἐσθίοντα Ἀτρέως τινὸς ἀδελφοῦ τοιαύτην παρα- 30
θέντος αὐτῷ τράπεζαν, πιστεύουσί τε τοῖς μύθοις ὡς γεγονόσι καὶ τὴν
30 εἱμαρμένην τε καὶ πρόνοιαν δι᾽ αὐτῶν κατασκευάζουσιν, ὥσπερ ἔργον ποι-
204   ούμενοι ἃ βούλονται κατασκευάζειν δι᾽ αὐτῶν τῶν κατασκευῶν ἀναιρεῖν.
καίτοι μακρῷ βέλτιον ⟨ἂν⟩ ἦν καὶ εὐγνωμονέστερον ἀναιρεῖν τὰς ὑποθέσεις διὰ 102
τὴν τῶν ἑπομένων αὐταῖς ἀτοπίαν, ἢ τοῖς οὕτως ἀτόποις διὰ τὰς ὑποθέσεις παρίστασθαι. οἱ δὲ καὶ πιστεύουσιν τοῖς ἀτοπωτάτοις ῥᾳδίως καὶ τοῦ 5
5 κατὰ λόγον αὐτὰ γενέσθαι αἰτίας τινὰς λέγειν οὐκ ὀκνοῦσιν. ἀλλὰ τῶν XXXII
μὲν τοιούτων ἅλις (ἱκανὸν γὰρ ἐφ᾽ ἑκάστου τὸ ἐνδείξασθαι τὴν τῆς δόξης
ἀτοπίαν), ἱκανῶς δ᾽ οἶμαι δεδηλῶσθαι, πῶς λέγεται τὸ ἐπὶ τῷ φρονίμῳ 10
εἶναι τὸ φρονεῖν καίτοι μὴ δυναμένῳ μὴ φρονεῖν· οὐ γὰρ ὅτι νῦν, ὅτε
ἐστὶ φρόνιμος, ἐπ᾽ αὐτῷ τὸ εἶναι τοιούτῳ (ἦν γὰρ ἂν καὶ τοῦ νῦν μὴ
10 φρονεῖν κύριος), ἀλλ᾽ ὅτι πρὸ τοῦ τοιοῦτος γενέσθαι εἶχεν ὥσπερ [δὲ] τοῦ
*   γενέσθαι οὕτως δὲ καὶ τοῦ μὴ γενέσθαι τοιοῦτος τὴν ἐξουσίαν, δι᾽ ἣν προ- 15
εἰρήκαμεν αἰτίαν πρὸς τὸ γενέσθαι τοιοῦτος συνήργησεν αὐτῷ. ἐπὶ δὲ τῶν
*   θεῶν οὐκ εἴη ἂν τὸ εἶναι τοιούτοις (ὅπερ ἦν καὶ αὐτὸ ἐν τοῖς ὑπ᾽ αὐτῶν
*   ἀπορουμένοις), ὅτι γάρ ἐστιν αὐτῶν ἐν τῇ φύσει ⟨τὸ⟩ τοιοῦτον, οὐδὲν δὲ 20
15 τῶν οὕτως ὑπαρχόντων ἐπ᾽ αὐτῷ. διὰ τοῦτο γὰρ τὰ μὲν ἐκείνων ἀγαθὰ
τίμιά τε καὶ μακαριστά, μεῖζόν τι τῶν ἐπαινετῶν ἀγαθῶν ἔχοντα, ὅτι
τὴν ἀρχὴν ἡ φύσις αὐτῶν ἀνεπιδεκτός ἐστιν, ἡμεῖς δὲ ἐπὶ τῇ κτήσει τῶν
*   ἀρετῶν ἐπαινούμεθα, ὅτι, τῆς φύσεως ἡμῶν ἐπιδεκτικῆς οὔσης καὶ τοῦ 25
20 καὶ χωρὶς καμάτων περιγίνεσθαι δοκούντων, τῆς δὲ ἀρετῆς μετὰ πόνων τε
καὶ μετὰ καμάτων καὶ πολλῶν ἱδρώτων. ἔχει μέντοι καὶ ὁ φρόνιμος ἐπὶ
*   τῶν καθέκαστα πράξεων τοῦ καὶ μὴ πράττειν αὐτὰς τὴν ἐξουσίαν, εἴποτε 30
κἀκείνοις πράξεις τινὲς γίνοιντο περὶ τὰ ἐνδεχόμενα καὶ ἄλλως ἔχειν. οὐ
25 γὰρ ἀφῄρηται τὴν ἐξουσίαν οὔτε ὁ Πύθιος τοῦ τῷ αὐτῷ χρῆσαί τε καὶ 104
μή, οὔτε ὁ Ἀσκληπιὸς τοῦ παρίστασθαι. πάντες γοῦν σχεδὸν ἄνθρωποι
καταφεύγουσιν ἐπ᾽ αὐτόν, ἔνθα ἂν ἐπιφανέστατος ᾖ, πεπιστευκότες ὅτι τοῖς
σπουδάζουσιν αὐτὸν ἔχειν ἰατρὸν μᾶλλον τῶν οὐ σπουδαζόντων ἐπιδίδωσιν 5
αὐτόν.

Τὸ δὲ λέγειν † ἡγεῖσθαι τοὺς οὐχ ἡγουμένους ἐν τῷ σώζεσθαι τὴν XXXIII
καθ' ὁρμὴν τῶν ζῴων ἐνέργειαν ἤδη σώζεσθαι καὶ τὸ ἐφ' ἡμῖν τῷ [μὴ]   *205
πᾶν τὸ καθ' ὁρμὴν γινόμενον ἐπὶ τοῖς ὁρμῶσιν εἶναι καὶ διὰ τοῦτο ἐρω- 10
τᾶν, εἰ μὴ ἐνέργημά τι τὸ ἐφ' ἡμῖν ἐστι, καὶ λαβόντας ἐπὶ τούτῳ πάλιν
5 ἐρωτᾶν, εἰ μὴ τῶν ἐνεργημάτων τὰ μὲν εἶναι δοκεῖ καθ' ὁρμήν, τὰ δ'
οὐ καθ' ὁρμήν, ἃ λαβόντας πάλιν προστιθέναι τούτῳ τὸ μὴ τῶν ἐνεργημάτων μέν, μὴ καθ' ὁρμὴν δὲ εἶναί τι ἐφ' ἡμῖν, οὗ καὶ αὐτοῦ συγχω- 15
ρούμενου ἐπὶ τούτοις λαμβάνειν τὸ πᾶν τὸ καθ' ὁρμὴν γινόμενον ἐπὶ τοῖς
οὕτως ἐνεργοῦσιν εἶναι, ἐπειδὴ ἐν μηδενὶ τῶν ἄλλως ἐνεργουμένων ἐστί,
10 καὶ διὰ τοῦτο λέγειν σώζεσθαι κατ' αὐτοὺς καὶ τὸ τοιοῦτον ἐφ' ἡμῖν, ὃ
δυνατὸν ὑφ' ἡμῶν γενέσθαι τε καὶ μή, εἶναι δὴ καὶ τὰ οὕτως γινόμενα 20   *
ἐν τοῖς καθ' ὁρμὴν γινομένοις [ἔστι], πῶς οὐ παντάπασιν ἀγνοούντων ταῦτα,   *
πρὸς ἃ ποιοῦνται τοὺς λόγους; οὐ γὰρ εἰ ἐν τοῖς καθ' ὁρμὴν ἐνεργουμέ-
νοις τὸ ἐφ' ἡμῖν εἶναι συγκεχώρηται, διὰ τοῦ λόγου ἤδη πᾶν τὸ καθ' 25   *
15 ὁρμὴν ἐνεργούμενον ἐφ' ἡμῖν. ταῦτα γὰρ μόνα τῶν καθ' ὁρμὴν γινομένων τὸ ἐφ' ἡμῖν ἔχει, ὅσα κατὰ λογικὴν ὁρμὴν ἐνεργεῖται. λογικὴ δ'
ἐστὶν ὁρμὴ ⟨ἡ⟩ ἐν τοῖς βουλευτικοῖς τε καὶ προαιρετικοῖς γινομένη, τουτέστιν
ἡ τῶν ἀνθρώπων, ὅταν ἐπὶ τούτοις γίνηται. τῶν γὰρ ἄλλων ζῴων αἱ 30
καθ' ὁρμήν. ἐνέργειαι οὐ τοιαῦται, ὅτι μηκέτ' ἐν ἐκείνοις ἐξουσία τοῦ καὶ
20 μὴ ποιῆσαι τὸ καθ' ὁρμὴν ἐνεργούμενον. διὸ ἐν ταῖς καθ'.ὁρμὴν ἐνεργεί- 106
αις τὸ ἐφ' ἡμῖν, οὐ μὴν διὰ τοῦτο πᾶσα καθ' ὁρμὴν ἐνέργεια γινομένη
τὸ ἐφ' ἡμῖν ἔχει. πῶς δ' οὐκ ἀγνοούντων τὰ ὑφ' αὐτῶν γινόμενα τὸ τῇ 5 XXXIV
ἀληθείᾳ τῶν γινομένων, ἣν ἀναιροῦσιν διὰ τοῦ δόγματος, αὐτῇ [πρὸς τὸ]   *
κεχρῆσθαι πρὸς κατασκευὴν τοῦ ἀναιροῦντος αὐτὴν δόγματος; λαβόντες
25 γὰρ τὸ ἕκαστον τῶν συνεστώτων φύσει καθ' εἱμαρμένη εἶναι τοιοῦτον,
ὁποῖόν ἐστι, ὡς ταὐτοῦ ὄντος τοῦ τε φύσει καὶ τοῦ καθ' εἱμαρμένην, 10
προστιθέασιν τὸ 'οὐκοῦν κατὰ τὴν εἱμαρμένην καὶ αἰσθήσεται τὰ ζῷα καὶ
ὁρμήσει, καὶ τὰ μὲν τῶν ζῴων ἐνεργήσει μόνον τὰ δὲ πράξει τὰ λογικά,
καὶ τὰ μὲν ἁμαρτήσεται τὰ δὲ κατορθώσει. ταῦτα γὰρ τούτοις κατὰ φύ-
30 σιν μέν, ὄντων δὲ καὶ ἁμαρτημάτων καὶ κατορθωμάτων καὶ τῶν τοιούτων 15   *
φύσεων καὶ ποιοτήτων μὴ ἀγνοουμένων, καὶ ἔπαινοι καὶ ψόγοι καὶ κολάσεις   *206
καὶ τιμαί. ταῦτα γὰρ οὕτως ἔχει ἀκολουθίας τε καὶ τάξεως'. οὐ μὴν
ἀκολουθεῖ ταῦτα ἔτι τούτων γίνεσθαι τὸν τρόπον τοῖς τὴν φύσιν τε καὶ τὰ 20
γινόμενα κατὰ φύσιν εἰς τὴν εἱμαρμένην τε καὶ τὴν ἀνάγκην μεταφέρουσιν.
5 κατὰ φύσιν μὲν γὰρ τοῖς πρακτικοῖς τε καὶ λογικοῖς ζῴοις τὸ καὶ ἁμαρτάνειν καὶ κατορθοῦν δύνασθαι τῷ μηδέτερον αὐτῶν ποιεῖν κατηναγκασμένως, καὶ τοῦτ' ἀληθές ἐστι καὶ τοῦτον ἔχει τὸν τρόπον. οὐ μὴν τοῖς 25
πάντα ἃ ποιοῦμεν ἐξ ἀνάγκης ἡμᾶς ποιεῖν λέγουσιν ἕπεται τοὺς μὲν κατορθοῦν τῶν λογικῶς ἐνεργούντων, τοὺς δ' ἁμαρτάνειν. ἐξ ἀνάγκης
10 δὲ πάντα ποιοῦμεν καθ' οὓς ἀδύνατον μὲν τῶνδέ τινων περιεστώ- 30
των μὴ πράσσειν ἡμᾶς, τὰ δ' ἐξ ἀνάγκης | ἡμᾶς ἀεὶ περιστήσεται 108
ταῦτα δι' ἃ πράσσομεν. οὐ γὰρ τὸν ὁπωσοῦν χαρίεν ποιοῦντα καθορ-   *
θοῦν τις λέγει. ἀλλ' οὐδ' ἁμαρτάνειν τὸν ὁπωσοῦν φαῦλόν τι πράττοντα,

208   De Fato XXV-XXXVI

ἀλλ' εἰ ὁπωσοῦν ἐν ἐξουσίᾳ τις ὢν τῶν χειρόνων αἱρεῖται καὶ πράσσει 5
15 [ἢ] τὰ βελτίω τοῦτον λέγομεν κατορθοῦν.   τὸν γοῦν τὰ αὐτὰ ταῦτα ἀπὸ
τύχης ποιήσαντα οὐκέτι λέγομεν κατορθοῦν ὡς τοῦ κατορθοῦν τὴν κρίσιν
οὐκ ἀπὸ τῶν πραττομένων ἔχοντος μόνον, ἀλλὰ πολὺ πρότερον ἀπὸ τῆς
ἕξεώς τε καὶ δυνάμεως ἀφ' ἧς πράσσεται.   καὶ ὁ αὐτὸς λόγος ἐπὶ τῶν 10
ἁμαρτημάτων.   ὧν δὲ ἡ ἐξουσία τοῦ πράττειν ἄλλα τινὰ παρ' ἃ πράττου-
* 20 σιν ὑπὸ τῶν περιεστώτων ἀφῄρηται, οὐδὲν αὐτοὶ συντελοῦσιν εἰς τὸ [τὰ]
* αὐτοῖς περιεστάναι δι' ἃ πράττουσιν.   πῶς ἂν ἔτι τούτους τις ἢ ἁμαρτά- 15
νειν ἢ κατορθοῦν λέγοι; οὔτε γὰρ τῆς τοιαύτης ἕξεως, ἀφ' ἧς τῶνδέ τινων περιεστώτων περὶ τὸ τάδε τινὰ πράττειν ὁρμὴ γίνεται, αὐτός ἐστιν
ἐν ἐξουσίᾳ οὔτε τοῦ τὰ περιεστῶτα τοιαῦτα εἶναι.   διὰ τοῦτο γὰρ τῶν
25 ἀλόγων ζῴων οὐδὲν τούτων κατηγορεῖται.   ἀγόμενος δὴ ἐπὶ τὸ πράττειν 20
* ὑπό τε ἕξεως καὶ περιστάσεών τινων μηδενὸς κύριος αὐτὸς τοῦ μὴ τοῦτον
ἔχειν τὸν τρόπον.   οὐδ' ἂν ἁμαρτάνειν ἔτι ἢ κατορθοῦν ἐπὶ τοῖς οὕτως
πραττομένοις λέγοιτο.   ἐπεὶ δὲ οἵ τε ἔπαινοι καὶ ψόγοι, κολάσεις τε καὶ
τιμαὶ ἐπὶ τοῖς ἁμαρτήμασί τε καὶ κατορθώμασιν, ὡς καὶ αὐτοὶ λέγουσιν, 25
30 δῆλον ὡς ἀναιρουμένων τούτων ἀναιροῖτ' ἂν κἀκείνων ἕκαστον.   τὸ δὲ
κατορθοῦν ἐπὶ τῶν θεῶν οὐ κυρίως ἂν λέγοιτο, ἀλλ' ὡς ἴσον τῶ τὰ ἀγαθὰ
207 ποιεῖν, εἴ γε ἐν οἷς μὲν τὸ κατορθοῦν, ἐν τούτοις καὶ τὸ ἁμαρτάνειν. [ἐν 30
τούτοις] ἀνεπίδεκτον δὲ ἁμαρτημάτων τὸ θεῖον.   διὰ τοῦτο γὰρ οὐδὲ ἐπαινοῦμεν τοὺς θεούς, ὅτι κρείττους εἰσὶν ἢ κατ' ἐπαίνους καὶ τὰ ἐφ' οἷς οἱ
* ἔπαινοι κατορθώματα. | μηδὲ ἐκεῖνον δὲ παραλείπωμεν τὸν λόγον. ᾧ θαρ- 110 XXXV
5 ροῦσιν ὡς δεικνύναι δυναμένου τῶν προκειμένων τι. λέγουσιν γὰρ 'οὐ γὰρ
ἔστι μὲν τοιαύτη ἡ εἱμαρμένη, οὐκ ἔστι δὲ πεπρωμένη, * * * οὐκ ἔστι 5
δὲ αἶσα, οὐδὲ ἔστι μὲν αἶσα, οὐκ ἔστι δὲ νέμεσις, οὐδὲ ἔστι μὲν νέμεσις,
οὐκ ἔστι δὲ νόμος, οὐδ' ἔστι μὲν νόμος, οὐδ' ἔστιν δὲ λόγος ὀρθὸς
προστακτικὸς μὲν ὧν ποιητέον, ἀπαγορευτικὸς δὲ ὧν οὐ ποιητέον.   ἀλλὰ
10 ἀπαγορεύεται μὲν τὰ ἁμαρτανόμενα, προστάττεται δὲ τὰ κατορθώ- 10
ματα.   οὐκ ἄρα ἔστι μὲν τοιαύτη ἡ εἱμαρμένη, οὐκ ἔστι δὲ ἁμαρτήματα
καὶ κατορθώματα.   ἀλλ' εἰ ἔστιν ἁμαρτήματα καὶ κατορθώματα, ἔστιν
ἀρετὴ καὶ κακία, εἰ δὲ ταῦτα, ἔστι καλὸν καὶ αἰσχρόν.   ἀλλὰ τὸ μὲν καλὸν ἐπαινετόν, τὸ δὲ αἰσχρὸν ψεκτόν.   οὐκ ἄρα ἔστι μὲν τοιαύτη ἡ εἱμαρ- 15
15 μένη, οὐκ ἔστι δὲ ἐπαινετὸν καὶ ψεκτόν.   ἀλλὰ τὰ μὲν ἐπαινετὰ τιμῆς
ἄξια, τὰ δὲ ψεκτὰ κολάσεως.   οὐκ ἄρα ἔστι μὲν τοιαύτη ἡ εἱμαρμένη, οὐκ
ἔστι δὲ τιμὴ καὶ κόλασις, ἀλλ' ἔστιν μὲν τιμὴ γέρως ἀξίωσις, ἡ δὲ κόλασις 20
ἐπανόρθωσις.   οὐκ ἄρα ἔστι μὲν τοιαύτη ἡ εἱμαρμένη, οὐκ ἔστι ⟨δὲ⟩ γέρως
* ἀξίωσις καὶ ἐπανόρθωσις.   εἰ δὲ ταῦτα, ⟨οὐκ⟩ ἀπείρηται μὲν εἶναι πάντων γινο-
20 μένων καθ' εἱμαρμένην κατορθώματά τε καὶ ἁμαρτήματα καὶ τιμαὶ καὶ κολάσεις καὶ γέρως ἀξιώσεις καὶ ἔπαινοι καὶ ψόγοι'.   ἀλλὰ ταῦτά γε εἰ μὲν ὑπό τι- 25 XXXVI
νων αἰτίων περιεστώτων αὐτοῖς οὕτως ἀναγκάζονται λέγειν, συγγινώσκειν αὐτοῖς ἄξιον, καὶ οὐδὲν δεῖ οὔθ' ἡμᾶς περὶ τῶν ὑπ' ἐκείνων κατ' ἀνάγκην λεγομένων πολυπραγμονεῖν· οὔτε ἐκείνους περὶ τῶν οὐχ ὁμοίως αὐτοῖς λεγόντων 30
25 (ἑκάστοις γὰρ τῶν λεγομένων τε καὶ δοξαζομένων αἰτία ἡ τῶν περιεστώτων

δύναμις). καὶ οὐδὲν δεῖ τοὺς λέγοντας | αἰτιᾶσθαι οὐδὲν εἰς τὸ οὕτως λέγειν 112
συντελοῦντας. εἴ γε μήτε τῶν περιεστώτων μήτε τῆς ἕξεως, καθ᾿ ἣν ὑπὸ
τῶν περιεστώτων οὕτως αὐτοῖς κινεῖσθαι συμβέβηκεν, τὴν αἰτίαν ἔχουσιν ἐν
αὐτοῖς. εἰ δὲ ἐξουσίαν ἔχομεν καὶ χεῖρόν τι καὶ βέλτιον εἰπεῖν, τίς οὐκ ὂ
ἂν αὐτῶν θαυμάσαι τὴν σύνθεσιν τοῦ λόγου ὡς ἀπέριττον καὶ ἐξ ὁμολο- 208
γουμένων καὶ ἐναργῶν συνάγουσαν τὸ μὴ δεῖν † ὧν ἦν τὸ ἄρα τῆς περὶ *
τοὺς συλλογισμοὺς ἀσχολίας μακρᾶς. θέμενοι γὰρ τὸ τὴν εἱμαρμένην χρῆ- 10 *
σθαι πᾶσιν τοῖς γεγονόσι τε καὶ γινομένοις καθ᾿ εἱμαρμένην πρὸς τὴν ἀκώ-
5 λυτον τῶν ὑπ᾿ αὐτῆς γινομένων ἐνέργειαν οὕτως, ὡς γέγονεν ἕκαστον αὐ- *
τῶν καὶ φύσεως ἔχει, λίθῳ μὲν ὡς λίθῳ, φυτῷ δὲ ὡς φυτῷ, ζῴῳ δὲ ὡς
ζῴῳ, εἰ δὲ ὡς ζῴῳ, καὶ ⟨ὡς⟩ ὁρμητικῷ, ἐν τῷ τιθέναι τὸ χρῆσθαι αὐτὴν τῷ 15
ζῴῳ ὡς ζῴῳ τε καὶ ὁρμητικῷ καὶ γίνεσθαι τὰ ὑφ᾿ αὐτῶν διὰ τῶν ζῴων *
γινόμενα κατὰ τὴν τῶν ζῴων ὁρμὴν ἑπομένων καὶ τούτων τῶν ἐξ ἀνάγ- *
10 κης περιεστώτων αὐτὰ τότε αἰτίοις ἅτινα ἂν * * * ἡγούμενοι διὰ τοῦ τὸ *
καθ᾿ ὁρμὴν ἐνεργεῖν τὰ ζῷα τηρεῖν ἐν τῷ ἅπαντα γίνεσθαι καθ᾿ εἱμαρμένην 20
καὶ τὸ ἐφ᾿ ἡμῖν εἶναί τι τηρεῖν, τούς τε ἄλλους [οὓς] ἐρωτῶσιν λόγους καὶ
δὴ καὶ τὸν προειρημένον ἐμοὶ δοκεῖ ὡς οὐκ ἀληθεῖ πιστεύοντες τοσοῦτον *
αὐτῷ ὅσον διὰ μῆκός τε καὶ πλῆθος ὀνομάτων καὶ ἀσαφῆ σύνθεσιν παρά- 25
15 ξειν ἡγούμενοι τοὺς ἀκούοντας. ἴδωμεν δὲ τὸ λεγόμενον ἡμεῖς δι᾿ αὐτοῦ
τὰ πολλὰ τῶν κειμένων ὀνομάτων παραιτησάμενοι τὸ νῦν, τὴν δὲ πεπρω-
μένην καὶ τὴν αἶσαν καὶ τὴν νέμεσιν ὑφελόντες, οἷς ὀνόμασιν ἐφ᾿ ὧν αὐτοῖς δοκεῖ σημαινομένων χρῶνται, ἐπὶ τῶν ἄλλων ἐξετάσωμεν. ἄξιον γὰρ 30
μαθεῖν τὴν ἀνάγκην τῆς ἀκολουθίας τῆς ʽοὐ γὰρ ἔστι μὲν τοιαύτη ἡ εἱ-
20 μαρμένη, οὐκ ἔστι δὲ νόμοςʼ. εἰ γὰρ τὰ μὲν γινόμενα καθ᾿ εἱμαρμένην
ἕπεται τοῖς ἐξ ἀνάγκης αὐτὰ περιεστῶσιν αἰτίοις καὶ οὐχ | οἷόν τε τὸν καθ᾿ 114
ὁρμὴν ἐνεργοῦντα μὴ ἀκολουθεῖν τούτοις τοῖς αἰτίοις τὴν αἰτίαν τὴν ἐξ αὐτοῦ πάντως ἐκείνοις συνάπτοντα, ὡς οὐδὲ τὸν ἀπὸ ὕψους ἀφεθέντα λίθον
μὴ κάτω φέρεσθαι ἢ τὴν σφαῖραν κατὰ τοῦ πρανοῦς μὴ κυλίεσθαι ἀφε- 5
25 θεῖσαν κατ᾿ αὐτοῦ, τίς ἔτι χρεία νόμων; ὡς γὰρ ὁ λίθος οὐκ ἂν ὑπὸ τοῦ
λέγοντος μὴ δεῖν κάτω φέρεσθαι κωλυθείη ποτ᾿ ἂν τῷ αὐτός τε τὴν φύσιν εἶναι τοιοῦτος τά τε ἔξωθεν ἔχειν αἴτια συνεργὰ πρὸς τοῦτο, οὕτως οὐδὲ

ἡμῶν τις πεισθείη ποτ᾿ ἂν λόγῳ ἢ νόμῳ ἄλλως ἀξιοῦντι πράττειν παρὰ 10
τὴν τῶν περιεστώτων ἀνάγκην. οὐ γὰρ πλέον τι ἡμῖν ἐκ τοῦ συνιέναι
τῶν προστασσομένων ὑπὸ τῶν νόμων ἔχουσιν προκαταβεβλημένας αἰτίας,
αἷς περιεστώσαις ἀκολουθεῖν τὴν ὁρμὴν ἀνάγκη. οὕτως δὲ ἀναιροῖτ᾿ ἂν 15
5 τὸ ἐκ τῶν νόμων χρήσιμον, εἴ γε οἱ μὲν νόμοι προστακτικοὶ μέν εἰσι τῶν
ποιητέων, ἀπαγορευτικοὶ δὲ τῶν οὐ ποιητέων, οὐχ ἕπεται δὲ τῇ τῶν νόμων προστάξει τὸ καθ᾿ ὁρμὴν ἡμᾶς ἐνεργεῖν, ὅταν τὰ περιεστῶτα αἴτια
ἐξ ἀνάγκης ἡμᾶς ἐπ᾿ ἄλλα τινὰ κινῇ τε καὶ φέρῃ. ἀναιρουμένου δὲ διὰ 20
τὴν τοιαύτην εἱμαρμένην τοῦ ἀπὸ τῶν νόμων χρησίμου, ἀναιροῖντ᾿ ἂν καὶ
10 ⟨οἱ⟩ νόμοι. τί γὰρ ὄφελος νόμων, οἷς πείθεσθαι τὴν ἐξουσίαν ὑπὸ τῆς
εἱμαρμένης ἀφῃρήμεθα; οὐκ ἄρα τῷ τοιαύτην εἶναι τὴν εἱμαρμένην ἕπεται 25
τὸ νόμον εἶναι. ἐναντία γὰρ εἱμαρμένη τε καὶ νόμος, εἴ γε ὁ μὲν νόμος

* προστακτικός ἐστι τῶν πρακτέων τε καὶ μή, ὡς τῶν πραττομένων δυναμένων αὐτῷ πείθεσθαι κελεύοντι (διὸ καὶ τοὺς μὴ πειθομένους ὡς ἁμαρτά- 30
15 νοντας ζημιοῖ, τιμῶν τοὺς πειθομένους ὡς κατορθοῦντας), ἡ δὲ εἱμαρμένη
πάντα τὰ γινόμενα ἀναγκαίως τε καὶ δι᾽ ὁμοίας αἰτίας φησὶ γίνεσθαι, τῶν
δὲ δι᾽ ὁμοίας γινομένων αἰτίας οὐχ οἷόν τε τὰ μὲν ἁμαρτήματα λέγειν, τὰ
δὲ κατορθώματα. εἰ γὰρ λέγοι τις καὶ τὸν νόμον ἐν τοῖς | ἀναγκαίοις τε 116
καὶ προκαταβεβλημένοις ὑπὸ τῆς εἱμαρμένης αἰτίοις εἶναι, δῆλον ὡς καὶ
20 τοῖς πράσσουσιν καθ᾽ ὁρμὴν τὰ κατ᾽ αὐτὸν ἐν τοῖς περιεστῶσιν αἰτίοις
καὶ αὐτὸς ἔσται κατηναγκασμένως, οὐ περιστήσεται δὲ τοῖς πράττουσιν τὰ 5
μὴ κατ᾽ αὐτόν. οἱ δὲ ταύτην τοῦ μὴ πράσσειν τὰ κατὰ τοὺς νόμους
* ἔχοντες τὴν αἰτίαν πρόδηλον ὡς οὐκ ἂν ψέγοιντο. πῶς γὰρ ἄξιοι; τὸ γοῦν
ἐν τοῖς περιεστῶσιν κατ᾽ ἀνάγκην αἰτίοις, οἷς μὴ ἕπεσθαι τὴν ὁρμὴν οὐχ
25 οἷόν τε, οὐκ ἦν ἐκ τῶν νόμων αἰτία, κατ᾽ ἀνάγκην τινὰ καὶ εἱμαρμένην 10
* παρεῖναι κεκωλυμένη. ἀλλὰ οὕτως γε οὐδ᾽ ἂν νόμος ἔτι εἴη ἔχων καὶ
* πειθομένους αὐτῷ, εἴ γε χρὴ τούτῳ πείθεσθαι λέγειν ἐξ ἀνάγκης ἑπομένους,
καὶ τοὺς μὴ πειθομένους ὑπὸ ἀνάγκης τινὸς πείθεσθαι κεκωλυμένους. ὥστε 15
* πολὺ ἂν ἀληθέστερον εἴη συνειλημμένον τὸ ʽεἰ ἔστι τοιαύτη εἱμαρμένη,
30 οὐκ ἔστι νόμοςʼ. ἀναιρουμένου δὲ νόμου καὶ σὺν αὐτῷ ἁμαρτήματός τε
καὶ κατορθώματος, ἀναιροῖτ᾽ ἄν, ὡς καὶ αὐτοὶ διὰ τῆς ἀκολουθίας ἐλάμβα-
210 νον τῆς κατὰ τὸν λόγον, ἀρετή τε καὶ κακία καὶ τὸ εἶναί τι ἐν ἀνθρώποις 20
αἰσχρόν τε καὶ καλὸν καὶ ἐπαινετόν τε καὶ ψεκτὸν καὶ τιμῆς τε καὶ κολά-
* σεως ἄξιον. οὐδὲν ἄρα μένει τοῦ ὑπὸ τοῦ μετὰ τοσαύτης τέχνης ἠρωτη-
* μένου λόγου κατεσκευασμένου, ἀκολουθήσει τε αὐτοῖς ἀρξαμένων κάτωθεν
5 ἀκολουθία, ἣν ἕπεσθαι λέγουσιν τοῖς ἀναιρεῖν πειρωμένοις τὸ ἐφ᾽ ἡμῖν 25
* † εἶναι ὡς αὐτοὶ τηροῦντες ὁμολογουμένως αὐτὸ διὰ τοῦ προλαβόντας
* ἄλλοις ἐπιφέρειν αὐτὰ τὸ μὴ δοκεῖν ἔχεσθαι τὸ καὶ τοῖς διαφεύγειν ἡγου-
* μένοις. εἰ γὰρ μή εἰσι τιμαὶ μηδὲ κολάσεις, οὐδὲ ἔπαινοι οὐδὲ ψόγοι, εἰ 30
* δὲ μὴ ταῦτα, οὐδὲ κατορθώματά τε καὶ ἁμαρτήματα, εἰ δὲ μὴ ταῦτα, οὐ-
10 δὲ ἀρετὴ καὶ κακία, εἰ δὲ μὴ ταῦτα, φασίν, ὅτι μηδὲ θεοί. ἀλλὰ μὴν τὸ
πρῶτον τὸ μὴ εἶναι μήτε τιμὰς μήτε κολάσεις ἕπεται τῷ πάντα γίνεσθαι 118
καθ᾽ εἱμαρμένην, ὡς δέδεικται. ⟨καὶ⟩ τὸ τελευταῖον ἄρα, ὃ ἄτοπον καὶ
ἀδύνατον. ἀναιρετέον ⟨ἄρα⟩ τὸ πάντα γίνεσθαι καθ᾽ εἱμαρμένην, ᾧ τοῦτ᾽
εἴπετο. ἴδωμεν δὲ καὶ ⟨τὸν⟩ ἐπὶ τούτῳ λόγον ἠρωτημένον, εἰ μὴ τὰς ὁμοίας 5 XI
15 ἀνάγκας ἔχει. λέγει δὲ οὕτως· ʽοὐ πάντα μὲν ἔστι καθ᾽ εἱμαρμένην, οὐκ
ἔστι δὲ ἀκώλυτος καὶ ἀπαρεμπόδιστος ἡ τοῦ κόσμου διοίκησις. οὐδὲ ἔστι
μὲν τοῦτο, οὐκ ἔστι δὲ κόσμος, οὐδὲ ἔστι μὲν κόσμος, οὐκ εἰσὶν δὲ θεοί.
εἰ δέ εἰσι θεοί, εἰσὶν ἀγαθοὶ οἱ θεοί, ἀλλὰ εἰ τοῦτο, ἔστιν ‾ἀρετή, ἀλλ᾽ εἰ 10
* ἔστιν ἀρετή, ἔστι φρόνησις, ἀλλ᾽ εἰ τοῦτο, ἔστιν ἡ ἐπιστήμη ποιητέων τε
20 καὶ οὐ ποιητέων· ἀλλὰ ποιητέα μέν ἐστι τὰ κατορθώματα, οὐ ποιητέα δὲ
τὰ ἁμαρτήματα. οὐκ ἄρα πᾶν μὲν γίνεται καθ᾽ εἱμαρμένην, οὐκ ἔστι δὲ
ἁμάρτημα καὶ κατόρθωμα. ἀλλὰ τὰ μὲν κατορθώματα καλά, τὰ δὲ ἁμαρ- 15
τήματα αἰσχρά, καὶ τὰ μὲν καλὰ ἐπαινετά, τὰ δὲ κακὰ ψεκτά. οὐκ ἄρα
πάντα μέν ἐστι καθ᾽ εἱμαρμένην, οὐκ ἔστι δὲ ἐπαινετὰ καὶ ψεκτά. ἀλλ᾽

25 εἰ τοῦτο, εἰσὶν ἔπαινοι καὶ ψόγοι· ἀλλ' ἃ μὲν ἐπαινοῦμεν τιμῶμεν, ἃ δὲ 20
ψέγομεν κολάζομεν, καὶ ὁ μὲν τιμῶν γεραίρει, ὁ δὲ κολάζων ἐπανορθοῖ.
οὐκ ἄρα πάντα μὲν γίνεται καθ' εἱμαρμένην, οὐκ ἔστι δὲ γεραίρειν καὶ ἐπα-
νορθοῦν'. καὶ οὗτος δὴ ὁ λόγος ἀπὸ τῆς αὐτῆς παλαίστρας ὢν δῆλον ὡς
διὰ τῶν αὐτῶν ἂν ψευδὴς ὢν ἐλέγχοιτο. πρῶτον μὲν γὰρ ἄν τις συγχω- 25   *
30 ρήσειε προχείρως τῷ ᾿οὐ πάντα μέν ἐστι καθ' εἱμαρμένην, οὐκ ἔστι δὲ
ἀκώλυτος καὶ ἀπαρεμπόδιστος ἡ τοῦ κόσμου διοίκησις᾽ [ἐν] τῷ γίνεσθαι
τὰ μὲν ἐξ ἀνάγκης, τὰ δὲ ἐνδεχομένως, καὶ τούτων τὰ μὲν κατὰ φύσιν,
τὰ δὲ κατὰ προαίρεσίν τε καὶ λόγον, τὰ δὲ καθ' ὁρμήν, τὰ δ' ἀπὸ τύχης 30
τε καὶ αὐτομάτως. ἀναιρεῖται δὲ πάντα τὰ ἄλλα ὑπὸ τῆς εἱμαρμένης. οὐκ   *
5 ἄρα ⟨οὐκ ἂν⟩ ἀπαρεμπόδιστος οὐδὲ ἀκώλυτος ἡ τοῦ κόσμου διοίκησις μένοι. | *
ἀλλ' εἰ καὶ συγχωρηθείη τοῦτό τε καὶ τὸ κόσμος εἶναι καὶ κόσμου ὄντος 120
θεούς, καίτοι κατ' Ἐπίκουρον ἐκτὸς ὄντας αὐτούς, καὶ τοὺς θεοὺς ἀγαθοὺς
εἶναι, εἴη δὲ καὶ τὸ ἀρετὴν εἶναι τοῖς θεοῖς ἑπόμενον, πῶς τῷ τὴν τῶν 5
θεῶν ἀρετὴν εἶναι ἔποιτ' ἂν τὸ εἶναι φρόνησιν; τίς γὰρ ἡ τῆς ἀκολου-
10 θίας ταύτης ἀνάγκη; εἰ μὲν γὰρ ἦν εἰλημμένον τὸ τὴν ἀνθρώπων ἀρετὴν
εἶναι, ἔποιτ' ἂν τούτῳ καὶ ἡ φρόνησις, ἐπεὶ δ' ἐκ τῶν κειμένων εἴληπται
τὸ τὴν τῶν θεῶν ἀρετὴν εἶναι πῶς ἂν ἔτι ἔποιτο τῇ τῶν θεῶν ἀρετῇ 10
φρόνησις, ἀνθρώπων οὖσα ἀρετή; οὐ γὰρ τὰς αὐτὰς ἀρετὰς οἷόν τε λέγειν
εἶναι τῶν τε ἀνθρώπων καὶ τῶν θεῶν. οὔτε γὰρ ἄλλως ἀληθὲς τὸ τὰς
15 τῶν τοσοῦτον ἀλλήλων κατὰ τὴν φύσιν διεστώτων τὰς αὐτὰς τελειότητάς
τε καὶ ἀρετὰς λέγειν, οὔθ' οἱ πρὸς αὐτῶν περὶ αὐτῶν λεγόμενοι λόγοι 15
εὔλογόν τι ἐν αὐτοῖς ἔχουσιν. ἀνθρώπου δὲ ἡ φρόνησις ἀρετή, ἥ ἐστιν,
ὥς φασιν, ἐπιστήμη ποιητέων τε καὶ οὐ ποιητέων. ἐν οἷς γὰρ οἷόν τε ⟨μὴ⟩   *
πραχθῆναί τι καὶ τῶν ποιητέων, ἐν τούτοις ἡ τῶν ποιητέων τε καὶ οὐ ποι-   *
20 ητέων ἐπιστήμη χώραν ἔχει. ἀλλὰ μὴν πάντων γινομένων καθ' εἱμαρμέ- 20
νην ἄχρηστος ἡ γνῶσις τῶν ποιητέων τε καὶ μή. τί γὰρ ὄφελος τῆς τοιαύτης γνώσεως τοῖς μηδὲν ὧν πράττουσι φυλάξασθαι δυναμένοις; εἰ δὲ μηδὲν ἡ τούτων ἐπιστήμη χρήσιμον, ἀναιροῖτ' ἂν ἡ φρόνησις, ὡς εἶναι τὴν 25
ἀκολουθίαν ἀληθεστέραν τὴν εἰ ἔστιν εἱμαρμένη, μὴ εἶναι φρόνησιν. καθ'
25 ὃν γὰρ λόγον ὁ νόμος ἀνῃρεῖτο κειμένης τῆς εἱμαρμένης, κατὰ τοῦτον ἀναι-
ρεθήσεται καὶ ⟨ἡ⟩ φρόνησις, ἧς ἀναιρουμένης δῆλον ὡς καὶ τῶν ἄλλων ἓν
ἕκαστον ἀναιροῖτ' ἂν τῶν κατὰ τὴν ἀκολουθίαν τὴν πρὸς τὴν φρόνησιν τι- 30
θεμένων. ὅτι δὲ μηδὲ [οἱ] ἐκ τοῦ δεικνύναι τὴν καθ' ὁρμὴν κίνησιν τοῖς XXXVIII
ζῴοις μένουσαν πάντων γινομένων καθ' εἱμαρμένην σώζουσιν τὸ ἐφ' ἡμῖν,
30 εἰ μὴ βούλοιτό τις ἁπλῶς | τὸ ὑπό τινος κατὰ τὴν οἰκείαν γινόμενον φύσιν 122
ἐπ' ἐκείνῳ λέγειν ἄλλο τι σημαινόμενον τοῦ ἐφ' ἡμῖν εἰσαγων παρὰ τὸ
πεπιστευμένον τε καὶ προειλημμένον, ὃ φαμεν εἶναι διὰ τὸ ἔχειν ἡμᾶς ἐξουσίαν τῶν ἐν τοῖς πραττομένοις ἀντιχειμένων, φθάνει διὰ τῶν πρώτων 5
πλεονάκις εἰρῆσθαί τε καὶ δεδεῖχθαι. παραπλήσιοι δὲ τούτοις καὶ ὅσους   212
ἄλλους εἰς σύστασιν τοῦδε τοῦ δόγματος λόγους παρατίθενται ἐπὶ πλέον
καὶ μέχρι ῥημάτων τὴν κομψείαν ἔχοντες, ἀλλ' οὐκ ἐκ τῆς πρὸς τὰ πράγμα- 10
τα περὶ ὧν λέγονται συμφωνίας τὴν πίστιν λαμβάνοντες.

5 Ταῦτα ὑμῖν, ὦ θειότατοι αὐτοκράτορες. τῆς Ἀριστοτέλους δόξης περί τε XXXIX
εἱμαρμένης καὶ τοῦ ἐφ' ἡμῖν κατ' ἐμὴν δόξαν τὰ κεφάλαια, καθ' ἣν δοξάζοντες
εἴς τε θεοὺς εὐσεβήσομεν, τὰ μὲν εἰδότες αὐτοῖς χάριν ἀνθ' ὧν φθάνομεν 15
ὑπ' αὐτῶν εὖ πεπονθότες, τὰ δὲ αἰτούμενοι παρ' αὐτῶν ὡς ὄντων καὶ τοῦ
* δοῦναι καὶ τοῦ μὴ κυρίων· ἐσόμεθα δὲ καὶ περὶ τοὺς ἡμῖν ὁμοίους ἄρχοντας
* 10 εὐχάριστοι † ταῦτα πράττεται εἰς ἡμᾶς τε καὶ ἡ περὶ * * * ὑμῶν οἰκεία 20
* προαίρεσις πράττειν ὑμᾶς αἱρέσει τοῦ βελτίονος καὶ τοῦ περὶ τὴν κρίσιν αὐτοῦ
φροντίζειν ποιοῦντας ἃ ποιεῖτε, ἀλλ' οὐ προκαταβεβλημένοις τισὶν αἰτίοις
ἑπομένους, οἷς ἀναγκαῖον ἕπεσθαι ἢ ἂν ἐκεῖνα ἄγῃ. ποιησόμεθα δὲ καὶ
ἀρετῆς ἐπιμέλειαν ὡς ὄντες αὐτοὶ κύριοι τοῦ βελτίους ἢ χείρους γενέσθαι. 25
15 τούτων γὰρ μόνων κύριός τις, ὧν καὶ τοῦ μὴ πράττειν αὐτὸς ἔχει τὴν
* ἐξουσίαν * * * καὶ τὰ ἄλλα δὲ ὅσα πράττομεν κατὰ τὸν βίον ὅτι μόνως
εὐλόγως πράττειν ἂν δοκοῖμεν, εἰ κατὰ τὴν Ἀριστοτέλους δόξαν περὶ αὐ- 30
* τῶν ἀποδιδοίημεν τὰς αἰτίας, ⟨ἃς⟩ διὰ παντὸς ἐπειράθην ὑμῖν παραστῆσαι
τοῦ λόγου.

MANTISSA XXII

vol. 1
p. 169
Bruns

Τῶν παρὰ Ἀριστοτέλους περὶ τοῦ ἐφ' ἡμῖν.   159r

Περὶ τοῦ ἐφ' ἡμῖν ἐλέγετό τις καὶ τοιάδε δόξα. εἰ ἡ μὲν φύσις οὐχ
* 35 ὁμοία πάντων, ἀλλ' ἔχει διαφοράν (φύσει γὰρ εὐφυεῖς τινες, οἱ δ' ἀφυεῖς·
μεγίστην δὲ ἰσχὺν ἡ φύσις ἔχει πρὸς τὸ τοίους ἢ τοίους γίνεσθαι, μετὰ
* δὲ τὴν φύσιν τὰ ἔθη, ἐξ ὧν ἀμφοτέρων καὶ ἡ προαίρεσις ποιά γίνεται), 5
πῶς ἔτι ἔσται ἐφ' ἡμῖν ἡ προαίρεσις, ὅλως ἀπορήσειεν ἄν τις. καὶ γάρ,
εἰ καὶ τὴν διδασκαλίαν αἰτιῷτο, οὐδὲ τὸ μαθεῖν ἐφ' ἡμῖν, λέγω δὲ τὸ
170 τοιοῦτον ἐφ' ἡμῖν, οὗ καὶ τὸ ἀντικείμενον δυνατόν τέ ἐστι καὶ ἐφ' ἡμῖν,
[ὁποῖον ἡμεῖς εἶναι τὸ ἐφ' ἡμῖν ἀξιοῦμεν]. ἔτι δὲ μᾶλλον ἀποροῖτ' ἂν τοῦτο,
* εἰ μηδὲν ἀναιτίως γίνοιτο· καὶ αὐτὸ ἅπασιν ἐδόκει. δεῖ γὰρ τῶν ἐπὶ τοῦ
παρόντος ὑφ' ἡμῶν γιγνομένων προϋπάρχειν τὸ αἴτιον, ἀδύνατον δέ ἐστι
τὴν αὐτὴν αἰτίαν εἶναι τῶν ἀντικειμένων, ἀλλ', εἰ τοῦτο, ἐξ ἀνάγκης πάντα 10
τὰ γιγνόμενα γίγνεται. προκαταβέβληται γὰρ αὐτῶν τὰ αἴτια. τοῦτο δὴ
οὕτως ἔχειν ἀναγκαῖόν ἐστιν, ἐὰν μή τις ἀναίτιος κίνησις εὑρεθῇ. εὑρίσκε-
ται δὲ καὶ ἔστιν. οὗ δειχθέντος καὶ τὸ ἐφ' ἡμῖν σωθήσεται καὶ τὸ αὐτόματον καὶ τὰ ἐπὶ τῇ τύχῃ. δοκεῖ δὲ καὶ Ἀριστοτέλει εἶναί τις ἀναίτιος
10 κίνησις ὡς ἐν τῷ πέμπτῳ λέγεται τῶν Μετὰ τὰ φυσικά. ἡ δὲ κατασκευὴ
τοῦ εἶναι ἀναίτιον κίνησίν ἐστιν, εἰ δειχθείη ἐν τοῖς οὖσιν τὸ μὴ ὂν
παρεσπαρμένον πως αὐτοῖς καὶ συνοδεῦον. εἰ γάρ ἐστίν πως τὸ μὴ ὂν 15
* ἐν τοῖς οὖσιν, ἔστι τὸ κατὰ συμβεβηκὸς ὄν. τὸ γὰρ μὴ ὄν, † συμβέ-
* βηκεν εἶναι λεγόμενον κατὰ συμβεβηκός τι ὄν, εἴη ἄν τις καὶ κίνησις ἀναί-
15 τιος, οὐ ὄντος δεδειγμένον ἂν εἴη τὸ προκείμενον. ὅτι δέ ἐστί πως τὸ μὴ
ὂν ἐν τοῖς οὖσιν ἐνεργείᾳ, εὐκόλως ἄν τις ἐπιστήσας μάθοι. εἰ γὰρ τῶν
ὄντων τὰ μέν ἐστιν ἀΐδια, ἄλλα δὲ φθειρόμενα, οὐ παρ' ἄλλην τινὰ ἂν
αἰτίαν ἡ διαφορὰ τούτων ἐν αὐτοῖς εἴη ἂν ἢ παρὰ τὴν τοῦ μὴ ὄντος με-

τευσίαν. παρὰ γὰρ τὴν τούτου μῖξίν τε καὶ κρᾶσιν καὶ παρουσίαν ἡ 20
20 ἀτονία τε καὶ ἀσθένεια τοῖς μὴ ἀιδίοις ἐγγιγνομένη κωλύει αὐτὰ ἀεί τε
εἶναι καὶ ὁμοίως ἔχειν ἀεί. εἰ γὰρ μὴ ἦν τι τοῦ μὴ ὄντος ἐν τοῖς οὖσιν,   171
οὐδ' ἂν τοῦ εὖ ἐγίγνετο. εἰ δὲ παρὰ μὲν τὴν τοῦ μὴ ὄντος μῖξιν τά τε   *
φθαρτὰ τοιαῦτ' ἐστι, καὶ πρὸς αὐτοῖς τὰ ψευδῆ, ἔστι δέ τινα ἐν τοῖς οὖσιν
φθαρτά τε καὶ φθειρόμενα καὶ ψευδῆ, ἔστιν τι τοῦ μὴ ὄντος ἐν αὐτοῖς.
5 καὶ ἀνάπαλιν δὲ ὑγιές ἐστι ληφθέν· εἰ μή ἐστι τὸ μὴ ὂν ἐν τοῖς οὖσιν,
οὐκ ἔσται τινὰ τῶν ὄντων φθαρτά. ἔστιν ἄρα τὸ μὴ ὄν. εἰ δή ἐστιν τὸ 25
μὴ ὂν ἐν τοῖς ἐν γενέσει παρεσπαρμένον καὶ μεμιγμένον, τῶν δὲ γιγνομένων αἴτιά τινα προηγεῖται οὐδ' αὐτὰ ὄντα ἀίδια, ἔστι καὶ ἐν τοῖς αἰτίοις τι τοῦ μὴ ὄντος καὶ τοῦτ' ἔστιν, ὃ λέγομεν κατὰ συμβεβηκὸς αἴτιον.
10 τὸ γὰρ κατὰ συμβεβηκὸς ὂν ἐν τοῖς αὐτοῖς, ὅταν ὡς αἰτίοις ᾖ, κατὰ συμβεβηκὸς αἴτιον ἂν εἴη. ὅταν γὰρ ἐπί τινι αἰτίᾳ ἐπακολουθήσῃ τι, μὴ τοῦ
τοῦτο γενέσθαι χάριν τῆς αἰτίας οὔσης, τότε τούτου τοῦ ἐπηκολουθηκότος
κατὰ συμβεβηκὸς αἴτιον λέγεται τὸ προηγούμενον, τουτέστιν οὐκ αἴτιον ἄρα. 30   *
ἐπακολουθήσαν τούτῳ ἀναιτίως ἐγένετο· οὐ γὰρ δι' οἰκείαν αἰτίαν. τοῦτο
15 δὲ ἐν μὲν τοῖς ἐκτὸς αἰτίοις γενόμενον τὴν τύχην ἐποίησεν καὶ τὸ αὐτόματον, ἐν δὲ ταῖς ἐν ἡμῖν τὸ ἐφ' ἡμῖν. αἰτία γὰρ ἐν ἡμῖν φύσις δοκεῖ
καὶ ἔθος εἶναι τῆς προαιρέσεως, ἀλλά, καθόσον καὶ ἐν τούτοις ἐστὶ τὸ μὴ
ὄν, κατὰ τοσοῦτον καὶ ἐν τῇ προαιρέσει. διὸ καὶ προαιρούμεθα ἔσθ' ὅτε
ταῦτα, ὧν ἡ αἰτία οὐ προκαταβέβληται ἐν ἡμῖν δι' ἀσθένειαν καὶ ἀτονίαν
20 τῆς θνητῆς φύσεως· ἀεὶ γὰρ ἂν ὁμοίως ἐπὶ τοῖς αὐτοῖς ἐκινούμεθα. ἀλλὰ 35
ἡ τοῦ μὴ ὄντος φύσις, ὡς εἶπον, ἐν οἷς ἂν ᾖ ταῦτα, ἀφαιρεῖται τὴν ἀιδιό-   *
τητα καὶ τὴν κατὰ τὰ αὐτὰ ἀεὶ ἐνέργειαν. ἃ οὖν ἀναιτίως καὶ μὴ προϋπαρ-
χούσης αἰτίας προαιρούμεθα, ταῦτά ἐστιν τὰ λεγόμενα ἐφ' ἡμῖν, ὧν καὶ τὰ
ἀντικείμενά ἐστι δυνατὰ διὰ τὸ τὴν αἰτίαν μὴ προκαταβεβλῆσθαι, ἥτις προ-
25 ϋπάρχουσα πάντως ἂν τοῦ γενέσθαι τοῦτο τὴν ἀνάγκην παρεῖχεν. διὰ
ταῦτα πολλάκις τινὲς καὶ πεφυκότες ὁμοίως καὶ ἐν τοῖς αὐτοῖς ἔθεσιν
ἠγμένοι διαφέροντες ἀλλήλων γίγνονται παρὰ τὰς ἀναιτίους προαιρέσεις. 40
ἔστιν δὲ τὸ μὴ ὂν ἐγκεκραμένον τοῖς οὖσιν οὔτε πολλοῖς, οὔτε, ἐν οἷς
ἔστι, πολύ τι, ἀλλὰ καὶ ἐν ὀλίγοις τῶν ὄντων καὶ ὀλίγον· τῶν τε γὰρ
30 ὄντων ἐν τούτοις, ἐν οἷς τὸ μὴ ἀίδιον (τοῦτο δέ ἐστι τὸ περὶ τὴν γῆν,
καὶ ὁ τόπος οὗτος ἐλάχιστός ἐστιν ὡς πρὸς πάντα τὸν κόσμον· εἰ γὰρ
ἡ γῆ σημείου λόγον ἐπέχει κατὰ τοὺς ἀστρολόγους πρὸς τὸν ἅπαντα
οὐρανόν, περὶ ταύτην δὲ καὶ τὰ ἐν ταύτῃ τὸ μὴ ὄν, περὶ ὀλίγον πάνυ ἂν
εἴη)· καὶ ἐν τούτοις δὲ ἀμυδρῶς πώς ἐστι καὶ οὐκέτι πολύ. ἐν γὰρ τοῖς ἐν 45   *
35 γενέσει οὖσιν τὸ μὲν ἐπὶ πολύ ἐστιν, οὗ ἡ φύσις αἰτία, ὅσον δὲ παραλύε-
ται τῆς φύσεως καὶ τῆς δυνάμεως αὐτῆς πρὸς τὸ ἐξ ἀνάγκης τὰ κατ' αὐ-   172
τὴν γίγνεσθαι γιγνόμενα (τοῦτό ἐστι τὸ ἐπ' ἔλαττον, ἐν ᾧ τὸ ἐνδεχόμενον
καὶ ἄλλως ἔχειν), περὶ τοῦτό ἐστι καὶ ἡ ἀπὸ τοῦ μὴ ὄντος ἀσθένεια. οὔτε
ἄρα ἐν τοῖς ἐξ ἀνάγκης ἐστὶ τὸ μὴ ὄν (διὸ οὐδὲ τὸ ἐνδεχόμενον), οὐδὲ   *
5 τὸ ἐν τοῖς ἐπὶ πολύ, καθόσον οὕτως ἔχει, ἀλλ' ἐν τοῖς ἀντικειμένοις αὐ-   *
τοῖς. ταῦτα δέ ἐστι τὰ ἐπ' ἔλαττον· ἐν τούτοις δέ ἐστι καὶ τὰ τυχηρὰ 50

καὶ αὐτόματα καὶ κυρίως λεγόμενα ἐφ' ἡμῖν. ὧν γὰρ προαιρέσεων ἡ φύσις
ἢ ἀγωγαὶ καὶ ἔθη ἐστὶν αἴτια, αὗται οὕτως ἐφ' ἡμῖν λέγονται ὡς δι' ἡμῶν
* γιγνόμεναι, † ἀναίτιοι ἃς κατὰ τὸ μὴ ὂν αὗται δεῖ τὸ κυρίως λεγόμενον
10 ἐφ' ἡμῖν οὕτως σώζουσιν, γιγνόμεναι διὰ φύσεως ἀσθένειαν καὶ ἔστι τὸ
ἐφ' ἡμῖν τοῦτο, οὗ καὶ τὸ ἀντικείμενον ἐνεδέχετο προελέσθαι τὸν τοῦτο
προῃρημένον. τὸ οὖν διὰ | τὴν τοῦ μὴ ὄντος ὕπαρξιν ἐξῃσθενηκὸς τὴν 159ᵛ
συνέχειαν τῶν αἰτίων τῶν ἐν ἡμῖν τὸ ἐφ' ἡμῖν κατέχει, καὶ ταύτην τὴν
χώραν ἔχει, αἴτιον γιγνόμενον ἐν οἷς τὸ ἀναγκαῖον ἐπιλέλοιπεν αἴτιον διὰ
15 τὴν τοῦ μὴ ὄντος ἐν τῷ ὄντι μῖξίν τε καὶ συμπλοκήν.

MANTISSA XXIII

Τῶν παρὰ Ἀριστοτέλους περὶ τοῦ ἐφ' ἡμῖν.

172.17   Τῶν γιγνομένων τε καὶ συνισταμένων ὑπὸ τῆς θείας δυνάμεως τῆς 5
ἐν τῷ γενητῷ σώματι ἐγγιγνομένης ἀπὸ τῆς πρὸς τὸ θεῖον γειτνιάσεως,
ἣν καὶ φύσιν καλοῦμεν, τιμιώτατον ἄνθρωπός ἐστι· μόνον γὰρ κεκοινώ-
20 νηκεν τοῦτο τῶν τῇδε τῆς τελειοτάτης τῶν ψυχικῶν δυνάμεων, αὕτη δέ
ἐστι νοῦς, καὶ μόνον ψυχὴν λογικὴν ἔχει, καθ' ἣν βουλεύεσθαί τε καὶ
ζητεῖν δύναται περὶ τῶν πρακτέων αὐτῷ, καὶ οὐ παραπλήσιόν ἐστι τοῖς 10
ἄλλοις ζῴοις, ἃ τῷ μὴ κοινωνεῖν τῆς τοιᾶσδε δυνάμεως ἄλογα καλοῦμεν,
ταῖς προσπιπτούσαις φαντασίαις ἑπόμενά τε καὶ συγκατατιθέμενα καὶ ἀνεξε-
25 τάστως ἕκαστον, ὧν πράττει, ποιοῦντα. ὁ γὰρ ἄνθρωπος μόνον τῶν ἄλλων
ζῴων μετὰ τὴν προσπεσοῦσαν αὐτῷ φαντασίαν περί τινος ὡς πρακτέου
οἷός τε ζητεῖν περὶ αὐτοῦ καὶ βουλεύεσθαι, εἴτε χρὴ συγκατατίθεσθαι τῷ
φανέντι, εἴτε καὶ μή. βουλευσάμενος δὲ καὶ κρίνας οὕτως ὁρμᾷ καὶ ἐπὶ
τὸ πράττειν ἢ μὴ πράττειν ὁπότερον· καὶ ὁπότερον προέκρινεν ἐκ τῆς 15
* :0 βουλῆς ἔρχεται. διὰ τοῦτο καὶ μόνον τῶν ζῴων ἁπάντων ἐφ' αὑτῷ τὸ
πράττειν ἔχει, ὅτι καὶ τοῦ μὴ πράττειν τὸ αὐτὸ τοῦτο τὴν ἐξουσίαν ἔχει.
ἐφ' ἑαυτῷ γὰρ ἡ αἵρεσις τῶν πρακτέων, εἴ γε βουλεύεσθαι καὶ κρίνειν
173   ἐφ' ἑαυτῷ. ἔστι γὰρ τὸ ἐφ' αὑτῷ τὸ αὐτὸ ⟨τῷ⟩ ἀρχήν τε καὶ αἴτιον
ποιητικὸν εἶναι τούτων, ἃ φαμεν εἶναι ἐφ' αὑτῷ. ἔστι δὲ τὸ ἐφ' ἡμῖν
ἐν τούτοις, περὶ ἃ καὶ τὸ βουλεύεσθαι. βουλευόμεθα δὲ οὔτε περὶ τῶν
γεγονότων οὔτε περὶ τῶν ὄντων ἤδη, ἀλλὰ περὶ τῶν μελλόντων καὶ ἐνδε-
5 χομένων γενέσθαι καὶ μὴ γενέσθαι, καὶ ὧν αἰτία διάνοια. ταῦτα γὰρ οἷά
τε ὑφ' ἡμῶν πραχθῆναί τε καὶ μή. ἐν τούτοις ἄρα καὶ τὸ ἐφ' ἡμῖν, 20
καὶ ἔστιν ἀρχὴ καὶ αἰτία τῶν δι' αὐτοῦ πραττομένων ὁ ἄνθρωπος, τοῦτο
παρὰ τῆς φύσεως ἐξαίρετον ἔχων παρὰ τὰ ἄλλα πάντα τὰ γιγνόμενα πρὸς
αὐτῆς, ὅτι καὶ μόνον λογικόν ἐστι φύσει καὶ βουλευτικόν. τὸ γὰρ λογικὸν
10 ἐν τούτῳ τὸ εἶναι ἔχει. εἰ δὲ ἀρχὴ μὲν ἡ αἰτία τούτων, ὧν ἐστιν αἰτία,
ὁ δὲ ἄνθρωπος ἀρχὴ τῶν πραττομένων ὑπ' αὐτοῦ, καὶ αἴτιος τούτων ἂν
εἴη. εἴπερ οὖν ἀρχὴν ἀρχῆς ζητεῖν τε καὶ λέγειν ἄτοπον (οὐ γὰρ ἔτι

ἁπλῶς ἀρχὴ τοῦτο, οὗ ἐστιν ἀρχή τις ἄλλη), οὐδ' ἂν τῆς προαιρέσεως 25
καὶ τῆς βουλήσεώς τε καὶ τοιᾶσδε κρίσεως τοῦ τε ἀνθρώπου αἴτιον ἄλλο
15 τι ποιητικὸν προκαταβεβλημένον εἴη (οὐ γὰρ ἂν ἔτι ἀρχὴ μένοι), ἀλλὰ
τῶν μὲν πραττομένων ὑφ' αὑτοῦ αὐτὸς αἴτιος καὶ ἡ κρίσις τε καὶ προαίρεσις καὶ ἡ ποιητικὴ τούτων αἰτία, αὐτῶν δὲ ἐκείνων οὐκέτι ἄλλο τι. εἰ
γὰρ ἀρχὴ μὲν ταῦτα, οὐκ ἔστιν δὲ τῆς κυρίως λεγομένης ἀρχῆς ἀρχή τε
καὶ αἴτιον (τοῦ μὲν γὰρ εἶναι καὶ γενέσθαι τὸν ἄνθρωπόν ἐστί τις ἀρχή,
20 τοῦ δὲ τάδε ἢ τάδε προαιρεῖσθαι οὔ, καὶ τοῦτο γὰρ εἶναι τουτέστιν αὐτῷ 30 *
τὸ τὴν τοιάνδε ἔχειν δύναμιν ἐν αὐτῷ) †. τί γὰρ ἔτι καὶ χρήσιμον ἂν εἴη *
τὸ βουλεύεσθαι, εἰ προκαταβεβλημένας ἔχοιμεν τῶν πραττομένων τὰς αἰτίας;
πῶς δ' ἂν ἔτι τῶν ἄλλων ζῴων τιμιώτερον ἄνθρωπος εἴη ἀχρήστου τοῦ
βουλεύεσθαι φανέντος; ἄχρηστον δέ, εἰ μὴ ἐφ' ἡμῖν εἴη τὸ ἐκ τῆς βουλῆς
25 προκρῖναί τι καὶ τὸ προκριθὲν ἑλέσθαι. τὸ μὲν γὰρ λέγειν αἰτίαν τὴν
φαντασίαν τοῦ βουλεύεσθαι περὶ τοῦ φανέντος οὐδὲν ἄτοπον, τὸ δὲ καὶ 35
τοῦ πράττειν τόδε τι μὴ τὴν βουλήν, ἀλλὰ τὴν φαντασίαν αἰτιᾶσθαι ἀναιρεῖν ἐστι τὴν βουλήν, ἥν τε ἔχομεν ὡς οὔσης τινὸς τὴν φαντασίαν αἰτίαν.
ὥστ' εἰ τοῦ μὲν βουλεύεσθαι τὸ φανὲν αἴτιον, τῆς δὲ κρίσεως ἡ βουλή,
30 τῆς δὲ ὁρμῆς ἡ κρίσις, ἡ δὲ ὁρμὴ τῶν πραττομένων, οὐδὲν ἐν τούτοις
ἐστὶν ἀναίτιον. ὥσπερ δὲ τὸ βουλεύεσθαι τοῦ ἐφ' ἡμῖν εἶναί τι δεικτικόν,
οὕτως καὶ τὸ μεταγινώσκειν ἐπὶ πραχθεῖσίν τισιν καὶ αὐτοὺς καὶ τὴν αὐτῶν
αἵρεσιν αἰτιᾶσθαι· μαρτύριον γὰρ ἡ τοιαύτη αἰτία τοῦ καὶ τοῦ πρᾶξαι
τότε τὸ πεπραγμένον ἡμᾶς τὴν αἰτίαν ἔχειν, τὸ δὲ ἄλλο τι ζητεῖν αἴτιον 40
35 τοῦ τόδε τι ἐκ τῆς βουλῆς προκρῖναι ἀνελεῖν ἐστι τὴν βουλήν. τὸ γὰρ
εἶναι τῷ βουλεύεσθαι ἐν τῷ δύνασθαι κρίνειν τε καὶ αἱρεῖσθαι τὸ φανὲν   174
ἐκ τῆς βουλῆς ἄριστον. ὁ δὴ τοῦτο τῆς βουλῆς ἀφαιρῶν ὄνομα βουλῆς
καταλείπει μόνον. τὸ γὰρ λέγειν πάντων τῶν ἐκτὸς περιεστώτων ὁμοίων
ἢ ταὐτὰ αἱρήσεσθαί τινα, ἢ καὶ πράξειν, ἢ δὴ ἀναιτίως ἔσεσθαί τι, τού-
5 των δὲ τὸ μὲν ἀναιτίως τι γίγνεσθαι ἀδύνατον εἶναι, τὸ δὲ ταὐτὰ αἱρεῖσθαι τῶν αὐτῶν περιεστώτων δεικτικὸν εἶναι τοῦ τὰ ἐκτὸς αἴτια κύρια 45
τῶν ὑφ' ἡμῶν πραττομένων εἶναι, οὐχ ὑγιές. οὔτε γὰρ ἀνάγκη τὰ αὐτὰ
αἱρεῖσθαι τὸν ἄνθρωπον ἀεὶ τῶν αὐτῶν περιεστώτων ἁπάντων, οὔτε ἀναίτιος ἡ πρᾶξις, εἰ μὴ κατὰ τὰ αὐτὰ γίγνοιτο. ἡ γὰρ βουλὴ καὶ ἡ προαί-
10 ρεσις καὶ ἡ κρίσις καὶ ὁ ἄνθρωπος τῆς τοιαύτης πράξεως αἴτιος, ἔχων ἐν
αὑτῷ τὴν ἐξουσίαν τοῦ βουλεύεσθαι περὶ τῶν περιεστώτων, ἔχει καὶ τὸ
δύνασθαι ἐκ τῶν αὐτῶν μὴ τὰ αὐτὰ αἱρεῖσθαι. καὶ τοῦτο οὐκ ἀλόγως τί- 50
θεται, οὐδέ ἐστιν αἴτημα τὸ λεγόμενον. εἰ μὲν γὰρ ἦν εἷς ὁ σκοπὸς αὐτῷ,
πρὸς ὃν τὴν ἀναφορὰν τῆς κρίσεως ἐποιεῖτο, εὔλογον ἦν ἀπὸ τῶν αὐτῶν
15 ἀεὶ ταὐτὸν αὐτὸν αἱρεῖσθαι τὴν αὐτήν γε σχέσιν ἔχοντα ἀεὶ καὶ φυλάτ-
τοντα πρὸς· τὸν προκείμενον αὐτῷ σκοπόν, πρὸς ὃν ὁρῶν ἐποιεῖτο | τὴν 160r
κρίσιν αὐτῶν. ἐπεὶ δέ ἐστι πλείω τὰ τέλη, πρὸς ἃ βλέπων τὴν κρίσιν
καὶ τὴν αἵρεσιν τῶν πρακτέων ποιεῖται (καὶ γὰρ τὸ ἡδὺ καὶ τὸ συμφέρον
καὶ τὸ καλὸν ἔχει πρὸ ὀφθαλμῶν), ταῦτα δὲ ἀλλήλων διαφέρει, οὐ πάντα
20 δὲ τὰ περιεστῶτα ὁμοίαν τὴν σχέσιν ἔχει πρὸς τούτων ἕκαστον, τὴν κρίσιν

αὐτῶν καὶ τὴν ἐξ αὐτῶν αἴρεσιν ποιούμενος ποτὲ μὲν πρὸς τὸ ἡδύ, ποτὲ δὲ πρὸς τὸ καλόν, ἄλλοτε δὲ πρὸς τὸ συμφέρον καὶ οὐκ ἀεὶ ταὐτὰ πράξει 5 οὐδὲ ἀεὶ ταὐτὰ αἱρήσεται τῶν αὐτῶν περιεστώτων ἁπάντων, ἀλλ' ἑκάστοτε ταῦτα τὰ πρὸς τὸν κριθέντα σκοπὸν μάλιστα συντείνειν δοκοῦντα. λύοιτο 25 δ' ἂν διὰ τούτου καὶ ὁ τῇ φαντασίᾳ τὴν αἰτίαν ἀνατιθεὶς τῶν πραττομένων λόγος, διότι παρὰ τὸ φαινόμενον ἄμεινον αὐτῷ οὐδεὶς ἄν τι πράξαι
* ποτέ. πλείους γὰρ οἱ σκοποί, πρὸς οὓς ἡ τῆς φαντασίας κρίσις. ὅτι δὲ οὐδ' εἰ τὰ αὐτὰ αἱροῖτό τις τῶν αὐτῶν περιεστώτων, ἤδη τούτῳ καὶ τὸ
* κατηναγκασμένως αἱρεῖσθαι ταῦτα ἕπεται καὶ τὸ εἶναι τῆς κρίσεως τὰ ἐκτὸς 10 30 αἴτια· ἐφ' ἑκάστης γὰρ αἱρέσεως ἔνεστιν αὐτὸν δεικνύναι πρὸ τοῦ πρᾶξαι καὶ προκρῖναί γέ τι καὶ τὸ ἀντικείμενον ἑλέσθαι δυνάμενον· οὐ γὰρ ὡς οὐ δυνάμενος καὶ τὰ ἀντικείμενα τούτοις ἑλέσθαι αἱρεῖται ταῦτα, ἀλλ' ὡς εὔλογα μᾶλλον αὐτῷ δοκοῦντα. ἔξεστιν γοῦν αὐτῷ αὐτὸ τὸ μὴ κατηναγκασμένην τὴν αἴρεσιν εἶναι βουληθέντι δεῖξαί ποτε καὶ πρὸς τοῦτο φιλονει-
35 κήσαντι καὶ τὸ μὴ δοκοῦν εὔλογον ἑλέσθαι. ἔτι, εἰ μὴ ἀεὶ τὴν ἕξιν ἐσμὲν 15 ὅμοιοι, καθ' ἣν βουλευόμεθα, οὐκ ἀεὶ τὰ αὐτὰ αἱρησόμεθα ἐκ τῶν περιεστώτων ὄντων ὁμοίων. εἰ δὲ τῶν αὐτῶν περιεστώτων τοῖς ἀνομοίοις οὐ τῶν αὐτῶν ἡ αἴρεσις, δῆλον ὡς καὶ τῆς τῶν ὁμοίων αἱρέσεως αἴτια οὐ τὰ περιεστῶτα ὅμοια ὄντα, ἀλλ' ᾧ περιέστηκεν ὢν ὅμοιος αὐτῷ. ὅλως δέ,
175 ὅτι ἐστίν τι ἐφ' ἡμῖν, πειρᾶσθαι δεικνύναι διὰ λόγων οὕτως ἐναργὲς ὄν, οὐκ εἰδότων κρίνειν ἐστὶ τό τε γνώριμον καὶ τὸ μή· δῆλον γὰρ τοῦτο, ὡς ἔφαμεν,. ἐκ πολλῶν, ἐκ τοῦ βουλεύεσθαι, ἐκ τοῦ μετανοεῖν, ἐκ τοῦ συμ- 20 βουλεύεσθαι, ἐκ τοῦ καταγιγνώσκειν τινῶν, ἐκ τοῦ προτρέπειν, ἐκ τοῦ ἐπαι- 5 νεῖν, ἐκ τοῦ ψέγειν, ἐκ τοῦ τιμᾶν, ἐκ τοῦ κολάζειν, ἐκ τοῦ διδάσκειν, ἐκ τοῦ κελεύειν, ἐκ τοῦ μαντεύεσθαι, ἐκ τοῦ εὔχεσθαι, ἐκ τοῦ ἐθίζειν, ἐκ τοῦ νομοθετεῖν. ὅλως γὰρ τούτοις καὶ τοῖς τοιούτοις ὁ πᾶς τῶν ἀνθρώπων βίος χρώμενος μαρτυρεῖ μηδὲν οὕτως ἴδιον εἶναι τοῦ ἀνθρώπου παρὰ τὰ ἄλλα ζῷα ὡς τὸ ἐφ' ἡμῖν. ὅτι δὲ καὶ τοῦ ποιοί γενέσθαι τὸ ἦθος αὐτοὶ 10 τὴν ἀρχὴν ἔχομεν, δι' ἃ καὶ τὰς αἱρέσεις διαφόρους ποιούμεθα, δῆλον ἐκ 25 τοῦ διὰ τῶν ἐθῶν ἡμᾶς ποιοὺς γίγνεσθαι, τῶν δὲ ἐθῶν τὰ πλεῖστα ἐφ' ἡμῖν εἶναι. καὶ γὰρ εἰ τὰ πρῶτά τις μοχθηρῶς ἐθισθείη παῖς ὢν ἔτι, ἀλλὰ φύσει γε πάντες ἄνθρωποι διορατικοὶ τῶν καλῶν εἰσιν τελειούμενοι. οὐδεὶς γοῦν κατὰ φύσιν ἔχων ἀνεννόητός ἐστιν, τίνα μέν ἐστι δίκαια, τίνα 15 δὲ ἄδικα, καὶ τίνα μὲν καλά, τίνα δὲ αἰσχρά. ἀλλ' οὐδ' ὅτι ἐκ τοῦ ἐθίζε- σθαί πως ἢ τῶν καλῶν ἢ τῶν αἰσχρῶν γίγνονται προαιρετικοί τε καὶ πρακτι- κοί, οὐδὲ τοῦτο αὐτοὺς λανθάνει. οἱ γοῦν ἀσκῆσαί τι καὶ μαθεῖν βουλό- 30 μενοι ἐπὶ τὸ διὰ τῶν ἐθῶν αὐτοὺς προάγειν τῷ προκειμένῳ τρέπονται, ὡς οὐκ ἀγνοοῦντες τὴν τῶν ἐθῶν ἰσχὺν πρὸς τὸ τῶν προχειμένων τυγχά- 20 νειν. τίνι γὰρ ἄδηλον, ὅτι διὰ τοῦ τὰ σωφρονικὰ ποιεῖν περιγίνεται τὸ
* σωφρονεῖν; εἰ δὲ μήτε τὰ καλὰ τοῖς κατὰ φύσιν ἔχουσιν ἔτι καὶ μηδέπω
* διὰ κακίαν πεπηρωμένοις † οὐκ ἀγνοεῖται ἥ γε ὁδὸς ἡ ἐφ' αὐτὰ ἐφ' ἡμῖν τε καὶ γνώριμος, ἐφ' ἡμῖν ἂν εἴη καὶ τὸ ποιοῖς γίνεσθαι τὰ ἤθη καὶ τὰς ἕξεις κτήσασθαι, ἀφ' ὧν ἢ τάδε ⟨ἢ τάδε⟩ αἱρησόμεθά τε καὶ πράξο- 35

25 μεν. αἱ δὲ εὐφυΐαι τε πρός τινα καὶ ἀφυΐαι ἔστ' ἂν ἐν τῇ οἰκείᾳ φύσει τηρῶσιν τὸν ἄνθρωπον, πρὸς εὐκολωτέραν ἀνάληψιν τούτων συντελοῦσιν μόνον ἢ χαλεπωτέραν, πρὸς ἃ πεφύκασιν εὖ τε καὶ κακῶς. πᾶσιν γὰρ ἀνθρώποις τοῖς κατὰ φύσιν τε ἔχουσιν καὶ ἀστρόφοις ἐπὶ τὴν κρίσιν τε *
καὶ τὴν αἵρεσιν δυνατὸν ἀρετὴν κτήσασθαι καὶ δυνατὸν δι' αὐτοῦ. διὸ
30 πολλῶν καλῶς πρὸς ἀρετὴν πεφυκότων φαυλότερόν τινες πεφυκότες ἀμείνους γίγνονται πολλάκις τὴν ἔνδειαν τῆς φύσεως ἰασάμενοι τῇ παρ' αὐτῶν 40 ἐξουσίᾳ.

MANTISSA XXIV

Περὶ τύχης.

Ἡ τύχη καὶ τὸ αὐτόματον, ὅτι μέν ἐστιν ἐν τοῖς οὖσιν, ἱκανὴ περὶ αὐτῶν   176.2
ἡ κοινὴ τῶν ἀνθρώπων πρόληψις μαρτυροῦσα, τί δέ ποτέ ἐστιν ἑκάτερον
αὐτῶν καὶ περὶ τίνα τῶν ὄντων, οὐκέθ' οἱ πολλοὶ τῆς τῶν δεδογμένων
5 διδασκαλίας κύριοι. οὔτε γὰρ ἑαυτοῖς οὔτε ἀλλήλοις συμφωνοῦσιν περὶ 45
τῶνδε, συμφωνοῦντες ἐν τῇ περὶ τοῦ εἶναι ἑκάτερον αὐτῶν δόξῃ. ἄξιον
τοίνυν ἐπιστῆσαι, τίς ποθ' ἡ φύσις αὐτῶν καὶ περὶ τίνα τῶν ὄντων γίγνεται. δοκεῖ τοίνυν ἐν τοῖς [αὐτοῖς] αἰτίοις καὶ ταῦτα καταριθμεῖσθαι· καὶ
γὰρ ἡ τύχη αἰτία δοκεῖ τῶν γιγνομένων ἀπὸ τύχης, καὶ τὸ αὐτόματον τῶν
10 τοιούτων. ὄντων τοίνυν αἰτίων τεττάρων, περὶ ὧν πολλάκις ἡμῖν λέγειν
ἔθος, τοῦ τε ὑλικοῦ καὶ τοῦ κατὰ τὸ εἶδος, καὶ τοῦ ποιητικοῦ, καὶ τοῦ
τέλους, ἐν τούτοις ἀνάγκη κἀκείνων ἑκάτερον εἶναι, εἴ γέ ἐστιν αἴτια. ὡς 50
μὲν οὖν ὕλην τὴν τύχην καὶ τὸ αὐτόματον οὐδεὶς ἂν αἰτιάσαιτο τῶν γιγνομένων δι' αὐτά. οὐ γὰρ ὑποκείμενόν τι ἡ τύχη, σχηματιζόμενόν τε καὶ
15 εἰδοποιούμενον ὑπό τινος ὡς ὕλη. ὑπομένουσα γὰρ αὕτη δέχεται τὸ εἶδος
καὶ ἔστιν αἰτία τῶν γιγνομένων ὡς ἐνυπάρχουσα τοῖς ἐξ αὐτῆς γεγονόσιν,
ἡ δὲ τύχη καὶ τὸ αὐτόματον ἐν τοῖς | δι' αὐτὰ γιγνομένοις οὐκ ἔστιν ἐν- 160v
υπάρχον· τὸ γὰρ αὐτὸ τοῦτο γιγνόμενον κατὰ τύχην ἔχει τὴν τύχην ἐν *
αὐτῷ· διὰ ταῦτα δὲ οὐδ' ὡς εἶδός τε καὶ τὸ τί ἦν εἶναι αἴτια ταῦτα τοῖς
20 δι' αὐτά· τὸ μὲν γὰρ εἶδος ἐνυπάρχει τῷ οὗ αἴτιόν ἐστι, γιγνόμενον ἐν
τῇ ὕλῃ καὶ μένον, τούτων δὲ οὐδέτερον. ἀλλὰ μὴν οὐδ' ὡς τέλος καὶ τὸ
οὗ ἕνεχεν αἴτιον ἡ τύχη τε καὶ τὸ αὐτόματον· οὐδενὶ γὰρ τῶν γιγνομένων
ἡ τύχη σκοπός· ἑκάστῳ μὲν γὰρ τῶν γιγνομένων ἕνεκέν τινος ὡρισμένος 5
ὁ σκοπός, ἀόριστον δὲ τούτων ἑκάτερον. ἀλλὰ μὴν εἰ ἐν μηδενὶ τῶν τριῶν
25 αἰτίων τούτων ἐστὶν ἡ τύχη, ἢ οὐδενός ἐστιν αἰτία. ἢ εἴη ἂν ἐν τοῖς ποιητικοῖς. καὶ μὴν τὰ ποιητικὰ αἴτιά τινος ἕνεχεν ποιεῖ τὰ γιγνόμενα πρὸς
αὐτῶν, καὶ ἔστιν αὐτοῖς ὡρισμένον τι τέλος προκείμενον, ὥσπερ ἥ τε φύσις
καὶ ἡ τέχνη καὶ ἡ προαίρεσις, οὐδενὶ δὲ τούτων ταὐτὸν οὔτε τὸ αὐτόματον
οὔτε ἡ τύχη. ἄλλο γάρ τι παρὰ ταῦτα τούτων ἑκάτερον εἶναι δοκεῖ, καὶ 10
30 τὰ μέν ἐστιν ὡρισμένα, καὶ ἐφ' ὡρισμένον ἄγει τι, ἄστατον δὲ καὶ ἀόριστον τὸ τῆς τύχης. εἰ δὴ δοκεῖ μὲν αἴτιά τινων εἶναι, μηδενὶ δέ ἐστι   177
τῶν αἰτίων ταῦτά, κινδυνεύει ἢ μηδ' ὅλως εἶναι, ἢ ἄλλος τις αἰτίων τρό-

πος ζητητέος. μηδὲ ὅλως μὲν οὖν λέγειν εἶναι αὐτὰ ἄτοπον, πράγματα
τοσαύτην ἰσχὺν ἐν τοῖς οὖσιν ἔχειν πεπιστευμένα, ἄλλος δέ τίς ποτ' ἂν
5 εἴη παρὰ τοὺς προειρημένους τρόπους αἰτίων; μήποτ' οὖν, ἐπεὶ τῶν
αἰτίων τὰ μέν ἐστι καθ' αὑτά, τὰ δὲ κατὰ συμβεβηκός (ἔστι γάρ τινα καὶ
κατὰ συμβεβηκὸς αἴτια· τὸ γὰρ τῷ καθ' αὑτὸ καὶ κυρίως αἰτίῳ τινὸς 15
συμβεβηκὸς κατὰ συμβεβηκὸς αἴτιον, καὶ αὐτὸ τοῦτο προηγουμένως ἦν
αἴτιον, ᾧ τοῦτο συμβεβήκει. ὁ μὲν γὰρ ἰατρὸς αἴτιος καθ' αὑτὸ τῆς
10 ὑγιείας, ὁ δὲ λευκὸς κατὰ συμβεβηκός, εἰ εἴη τῷ ἰατρῷ τοῦτο συμβεβηκός·
τὸ γὰρ συμβεβηκὸς τῷ ποιοῦντι ποιητικὸν αἴτιον κατὰ συμβεβηκός· ἔτι
κατὰ συμβεβηκὸς ὁ ἰατρὸς ποιητικὸν αἴτιον, ἰσχνότητος φέρε εἰπεῖν, ἂν τῷ
ὑγιαζομένῳ τοῦτο ἢ συμβεβηκός), ἐπεὶ τοίνυν ἐστὶ τῶν αἰτίων τὰ μὲν
καθ' αὑτά, τὰ δὲ κατὰ συμβεβηκός, καὶ ἐν τοῖς καθ' αὑτὰ αἰτίοις οὐχ 20
15 οἷόν τε τιθέναι τὴν τύχην, ἐν τοῖς κατὰ συμβεβηκὸς ἂν εἴη. τὰ μὲν γὰρ
ὡρισμένα οὐ κατὰ συμβεβηκὸς ἂν εἴη, τὰ δὲ κατὰ συμβεβηκὸς ἀόριστά τε
καὶ ἄστατα, ὁποῖον καὶ τὸ τῆς τύχης εἶναι φιλεῖ· ἀόριστα γὰρ τὰ τῷ καθ'
αὑτὸ καὶ κυρίως αἰτίῳ συμβεβηκέναι δυνάμενα, ἃ πάντα καὶ αὐτὰ κατὰ
συμβεβηκὸς αἴτια γίγνεται. ἀλλ' εἰ κατὰ συμβεβηκὸς αἴτιον ἡ τύχη, δεῖ
20 τινι τῶν κυρίως αἰτίων λεγομένων αὐτὴν συμβεβηκέναι. ἐπεὶ οὖν δοκεῖ
ποιητικὸν εἶναί τινος ἡ τύχη (τὰ γὰρ κατὰ τύχην ἀπὸ τύχης φαμὲν γίγνε- 25
σθαί τε καὶ γεγονέναι), τῶν ποιητικῶν αἰτίων τινὶ ταῦτα ὑπάρχειν ἀνάγκη,
εἴ γε φυλάξει τὴν χώραν τῶν αἰτίων. ἀλλὰ μὴν τὰ κυρίως αἴτια ποιητικὰ φύσις τε καὶ τέχνη καὶ προαίρεσις. πάντα μὲν γὰρ τὰ κυρίως ὡρι-
25 σμένως ποιητικὰ ἕνεκά τινος τέλους τὰ πρὸς αὐτῶν γιγνόμενα ποιεῖ, ὁρῶμεν δὲ πάντα τά τινος ἕνεκεν γιγνόμενα ὑπὸ τούτων γιγνόμενά τινος·
τούτων ἄρα τινὶ συμβέβηκεν ἡ τύχη. ἐπεὶ δὲ δοκεῖ ἐν τοῖς προαιρετικοῖς
εἶναι τὰ κατὰ τύχην, (ταῦτα γὰρ ἀπὸ τύχης γίγνεσθαί φαμεν, ὧν χάριν 30
κἂν προελοίμεθά τι πρᾶξαι πρὸς τὸ τυχεῖν αὐτῶν, ἐφ' ὧν τὴν εὐτυχίαν
30 λέγομεν, ἢ πρὸς τὸ μὴ τυχεῖν, ὧν τὴν δυστυχίαν κατηγοροῦμεν), εἴη ἂν
ἡ τύχη τοῖς κατὰ προαίρεσιν γιγνομένοις ἑπόμενον, καὶ ἐν τούτοις αἰτία
κατὰ συμβεβηκός. ὅταν γὰρ πράττουσί τι κατὰ προαίρεσιν ἡμῖν ἀπαντήσῃ
μὴ τὸ προκείμενον τέλος κατὰ τὴν προαίρεσιν, ἄλλο δέ τι κατὰ συμβεβηκὸς
γένηται, ἡ κατὰ προαίρεσιν γενομένη πρᾶξις αἰτία τοῦ ἀπαντήσαντός μέν, 35
35 οὐ προκειμένου δέ. λέγομεν δὲ τοῦτ' ἀπὸ τύχης γεγονέναι· τῷ [τε] γὰρ
178   σκάπτοντι κατὰ προαίρεσιν τοῦ φυτεῦσαι χάριν ἂν ἀπαντήσῃ ἐκ τοῦ σκάπτειν θησαυροῦ τινος εὕρεσις, ἀπὸ τύχης φαμὲν τὴν εὕρεσιν τοῦ θησαυροῦ
γεγονέναι· οὐκ ἀπὸ τύχης δέ, εἰ τούτου χάριν ἔσκαπτεν. τότε μὲν γὰρ
ἂν ἦν οὐ κατὰ συμβεβηκὸς τὸ σκάπτειν τῆς εὑρέσεως αἴτιον, ὥσπερ οὐδὲ
5 τὸ φυτεῦσαι, νῦν δὲ κατὰ συμβεβηκός, οὐ γὰρ τούτου χάριν ἐγίνετο. ἡ
γοῦν τύχη ἐστὶ τὸ κατὰ προαίρεσιν γινόμενον, ὅταν αἴτιόν τινος γένηται 40
κατὰ συμβεβηκός, ἀόριστον δὲ ἀεὶ αἴτιον οὕτως τό τινος χάριν γιγνόμενον
γίγνοιτο, καὶ εἴη ἂν ἡ τύχη αἰτία κατὰ συμβεβηκός· οὐχ ἁπλῶς δέ, ἀλλ'
ἐν τοῖς ποιητικοῖς τοῖς ἕνεκά του γιγνομένοις, καὶ τούτων ἐν τοῖς κατὰ
10 προαίρεσιν. οὐ γὰρ λέγομεν τὸ ἀπὸ τύχης ἐν τοῖς κατὰ φύσιν γιγνομένοις,

ὅταν ἄλλο τι παρὰ τὸν τῆς φύσεως σκοπὸν γένηται, ὥσπερ τὰ τέρατα·
καὶ γὰρ τούτων ἐστὶ μὲν τὸ φύσει γιγνόμενον κατὰ συμβεβηκὸς αἴτιον· οὐ
μὴν τύχης τοῦτο. ἀλλ' οὐδ' ὧν τὰ κατὰ τέχνην γιγνόμενα κατὰ συμβε- 45
βηκὸς αἴτια γίνεται, ὡς ἐπὶ τῇ τῶν διαστρόφων, οὐδὲ ἐπὶ τούτων ἡ τύχη   *
15 τὴν αἰτίαν ἔχει. ἐν τοῖς κατὰ προαίρεσιν ἄρα, ὡς ἔφαμεν. ὅταν μὲν οὖν
τὸ γιγνόμενον κατὰ προαίρεσιν δεξιοῦ τινος κατὰ συμβεβηκὸς αἴτιον γένηται, ὡς τὸ σκάπτειν τῆς εὑρέσεως τοῦ θησαυροῦ, εὐτυχίαν τοῦτο λέγομεν,
ὅταν δὲ φαύλου, δυστυχίαν· οἷον εἰ σκάπτων ὑπό τινος ἑρπετοῦ δηχθείη
τις ἐν αὐτῷ τῷ σκάπτειν εὑρεθέντος, οὐκ ὄντος ἐπιτηδείου τὴν ἄλλως τοῦ
20 τόπου πρὸς ἑρπετὰ τοιαῦτα· εἰ γὰρ πλήθους ὄντος ἑρπετῶν ὅδε ὤρυττεν 50
ἀπερισκέπτως, οὐ τύχη τούτῳ τῆς πληγῆς αἰτία, ἀλλ' ἀβουλία τις οἰκεία
καὶ ἀπρονοησία. καὶ τὸ μὲν τῆς τύχης τοιοῦτόν τε καὶ οὕτως αἴτιον, τὸ
δὲ αὐτόματον εἴωθεν μὲν καὶ ἐπὶ τῶν ἀπὸ τύχης γιγνομένων κατηγορεῖσθαι, οὐ μὴν ἀλλὰ μᾶλλον ἐπὶ τῶν φύσει. ὅταν γὰρ τῷ γινομένῳ φύσει
25 ἄλλο τι ἐπακολουθήσῃ, ἀλλὰ μὴ τὸ οὗ χάριν ἐγίνετο, αὐτομάτως τοῦτο λέγομεν γεγονέναι, ὥσπερ τὰ τέρατα. ὅταν γὰρ μὴ οὗ χάριν τέλους γίγνε-
ται τὸ γιγνό|μενον φύσει γένηται, μάτην καὶ αὐτὸ λέγομεν γεγονέναι, καὶ 161r
τὸ ἐπακολουθῆσαν αὐτῷ, ὅτι κατὰ συμβεβηκὸς αἴτιον τὸ μάτην γεγονός
ἐστιν, αὐτομάτως φαμὲν γεγονέναι. καὶ ἁπλῶς πᾶν τὸ τῷ κατὰ φύσιν
30 ἐπακολουθῆσαν γιγνομένῳ, οὐκ ὂν οὗ χάριν ἐγίνετο, αὐτομάτως λέγεται
γεγονέναι. οὕτως ὁ κατενεχθεὶς λίθος καὶ οὕτως πως πεσών, ὡς ἐπ' αὐ-   179
τοῦ καθέζεσθαι δύνασθαι, αὐτομάτως τήνδε τὴν θέσιν ἔσχεν ἐπακολουθή- 5
σασαν τῇ φυσικῇ τοῦ λίθου διὰ τὴν βαρύτητα καταφορά. ὁμοίως καὶ ὁ
μὲν διὰ τὴν τροφὴν ἐλθὼν ἐπὶ τόνδε τὸν τόπον ἵππος, σωθεὶς δὲ διὰ τοῦτο
5 ἀπὸ τῶν πολεμίων· καὶ γὰρ τούτῳ ἡ φυσικὴ τῆς τροφῆς ὄρεξις τῆς σω-
τηρίας αἰτία, οὐκ ἐλθόντι τοῦ σωθῆναι χάριν. τὸ δὲ λέγειν τὴν τύχην
αἰτίαν ἄδηλον ἀνθρωπίνῳ λογισμῷ οὐκ ἔστι φύσιν τινὰ τύχης τιθεμένων,
ἀλλ' ἐν τῇ τῶν ἀνθρώπων πρὸς τὰ αἴτια ποιᾷ σχέσει τὴν τύχην εἶναι λεγόντων, ἔσται τε οὕτως τὸ αὐτὸ τῷ μὲν ἀπὸ τύχης, τῷ δ' οὔ, ὅταν ὁ 10
10 μὲν αὐτοῦ γινώσκῃ τὴν αἰτίαν, ὁ δὲ ἀγνοῇ. προσέτι τε ἐπεὶ πλείω τοῦ
αὐτοῦ αἴτια, εἴ γε τετραχῶς, ὧν τὰ μὲν ἐνδέχεταί τινας εἰδέναι, τὰ δὲ μή,
τὸ αὐτό τι ἅμα τῷ αὐτῷ καὶ ἀπὸ τύχης καὶ οὐχὶ ἀπὸ τύχης ἔσται, ἂν τὰ
μέν τινα τῶν αἰτίων αὐτοῦ γνωρίζῃ, τὰ δὲ ἀγνοῇ· οὐ γὰρ διώρισται παρὰ
τὴν ποτέρου τῶν αἰτίων ἄγνοιαν ἡ τύχη. εἰ γὰρ λέγοιεν μὴ τήν τισιν
15 ἀνθρώποις αἰτίαν ἄδηλον εἶναι τὴν τύχην, ἀλλὰ τὴν καθόλου πᾶσιν ἀνθρώποις, οὐδ' ὅλως εἶναί τι συγχωροῖεν ἂν τὴν τύχην, διδόντες τε εἶναι μαν- 15
τικὴν καὶ τῶν ἀδήλων δοκούντων εἶναι τοῖς ἄλλοις γνωστικὴν αὐτὴν τιθέμενοι. εἰ γὰρ τοῦτο διορίζειν βουλόμενοι λέγοιεν τὴν ἄδηλον τοῖς ἀν-
επιστήμοσιν αἰτίαν τύχην, ἔσται κατὰ τοῦτον τὸν λόγον καὶ τὰ κατὰ τὰς
20 ἐπιστήμας τε καὶ τέχνας γινόμενα τοῖς ἀνεπιστήμοσίν τε καὶ ἀτέχνοις ἀπὸ
τύχης. οὔτε γὰρ ὁ μὴ τέκτων οἶδεν τῶν τεκτονικῶν τὴν αἰτίαν, οὐδ' ὁ
μὴ μουσικὸς τῶν μουσικῶν, οὔτε ἄλλος τις ἄτεχνος τὰ τῆς τέχνης· ἐν
γὰρ τῷ τὰς αἰτίας εἰδέναι τῶν γιγνομένων κατὰ τέχνην ἡ τέχνη. 20

MANTISSA XXV

Περὶ εἱμαρμένης.

179 25 Περὶ τῆς εἱμαρμένης ἄξιον ἐπισκέψασθαι, τί τέ ἐστι καὶ ἐν τίνι τῶν ὄντων. τὸ μὲν γὰρ εἶναί τι τὴν εἱμαρμένην, ἱκανῶς ἡ κοινὴ τῶν ἀνθρώπων συνίστησιν πρόληψις (ἡ γὰρ φύσις οὐ κενὸν οὐδὲ ἄστοχον· ὁ γὰρ Ἀναξαγόρας οὐκ ἀξιόπιστος ἀντιμαρτυρῶν τῇ κοινῇ δόξῃ· λέγει γὰρ οὗτός 25 γε, μηδὲν εἶναι τὴν εἱμαρμένην ὅλως, ἀλλ' εἶναι κενὸν τοῦτο τοὔνομα), τί 30 δέ ποτ' ἐστιν καὶ ἐν τίσιν, οὐκέθ' ἡ τῶν ἀνθρώπων πρόληψις ἱκανὴ τοῦτο μηνῦσαι. οὔτε γὰρ ἀλλήλοις οὔτε αὑτοῖς περὶ τοῦδε συμφωνεῖν δύνανται. πρὸς γὰρ τοὺς καιροὺς καὶ τὰς περιστάσεις καὶ τὴν περὶ τῆς εἱμαρμένης

180 μεταβάλλουσι δόξαν. ποτὲ μὲν γὰρ ἀπαράβατόν τι καὶ ἀναπόδραστον τὴν εἱμαρμένην τίθενται, καὶ πάντα γε τά ̔τε ὄντα καὶ τὰ γιγνόμενα ὑποτάσ- 30 σουσιν αὐτῇ, ὁτὲ δὲ ἔστιν αὐτῶν καὶ τὸ παρὰ τὴν εἱμαρμένην ἀκοῦσαι πολλάκις λεγόντων, καὶ τὸ παρὰ μοῖραν. καὶ ὡς ἐπὶ τὸ πλεῖστον οἷς μὲν 5 μήτε τὰ τῆς τύχης εὖ κυρεῖ, μήτε τι μᾶλλον τὰ τῆς γνώμης τε καὶ τῆς οἰκείας προαιρέσεως ἔρρωται, ἐπὶ τὴν εἱμαρμένην τε ὡς χρησφύγετόν τι καταφεύγουσιν, τὴν αἰτίαν τῶν μὴ δεόντως πεπραγμένων ἢ πραττομένων ἑαυτοῖς ἀφ' αὑτῶν ἐπ' ἐκείνην μεταφέροντες, καὶ πάντα γέ φασιν οὗτοι τότε γίνεσθαι καθ' εἱμαρμένην, μεταπεσούσης δὲ τῆς τύχης αὐτοῖς ἐπὶ τὸ 35 10 βέλτιον, οὐκέτι ἐπὶ τῆς αὐτῆς δόξης μένουσιν· οἷς δὲ τὰ τῆς οἰκείας γνώμης δεξιὰ καὶ ταύτῃ συνῳδὰ τὰ παρὰ τῆς τύχης, εἰς ἑαυτοὺς μᾶλλον ἢ τὴν εἱμαρμένην τὴν αἰτίαν τῶν γινομένων ἀνάπτουσιν. ἄλλοι δ' αὖ τῶν μὲν δεξιῶν ἁπάντων ἢ ἑαυτοὺς ἢ τὸ θεῖον αἰτιῶνται, ἐπὶ δὲ τοῖς χείροσιν ἐπιβοῶνται τὴν εἱμαρμένην. εἰσὶ δέ τινες καὶ γόητες ἄνθρωποι, οἵτινες 15 κατανοήσαντες τὴν τῶν πολλῶν ἀσθένειαν περὶ τὴν τῆς εἱμαρμένης καὶ τῶν κατ' αὐτὴν γιγνομένων κρίσιν, καὶ τὸ ῥᾴδιον αὐτῶν διὰ φιλαυτίαν καὶ 40 τὸ μηδὲν αὑτοῖς συνειδέναι δεξιὸν πρὸς πίστιν τοῦ πάντων τῶν ἁμαρτανομένων τὴν εἱμαρμένην αἰτιᾶσθαι ἀποφαίνονται πᾶν τὸ γιγνόμενον γίγνε- σθαι καθ' εἱμαρμένην, καὶ τέχνην ὑποκρίνονταί τινα τοιαύτην, καθ' ἣν 20 φασιν οἷοί τε εἶναι πάντα προγιγνώσκειν τε καὶ προμηνύειν τὰ ὁπωσοῦν ἐσόμενα, τῷ μηδὲν αὐτῶν γίγνεσθαι χωρὶς ἀνάγκης τινός, ἣν εἱμαρμένην λέγουσι· καὶ λαβόντες βοηθοὺς τοὺς καὶ τῆς τέχνης αὐτοῖς αἰτίους, ἀνα- πείθουσιν τοὺς πλείστους τῶν ἀνθρώπων, ἐν ταῖς περιστάσεσιν αὐτοῖς ἐπι- 45 τιθέμενοι καὶ ταῖς συμφοραῖς, μόνον οὐκ εὐχομένοις τοῦθ' οὕτως ἔχον 25 φανῆναι, κατά τινα τριβήν τε καὶ περὶ τὰ τοιαῦτα σύνεσιν καὶ τῆς ἐν τοῖς τοιούτοις ἀκολουθίας θεωρίαν προλέγοντες εὐστόχως τινὰ τῶν τοῖς οὕτως ἔχουσιν ἀκολούθως ἐσομένων, ὡς δὴ τοῦτ' ἐκ τῆς τέχνης τῆς περὶ τὴν εἱμαρμένην ἔχειν λέγοντες μισθοὺς οὐκ ὀλίγους ὑπὲρ τῆς τοιαύτης κακοτε- χνίας ἐκλέγοντες, ἀσμένως αὐτοῖς τῶν πειρωμένων διδόντων ὡς βοηθοῖς 50 30 καὶ συνηγόροις τῶν οἰκείων ἁμαρτημάτων. οἳ καὶ τοὺς πλείστους τῶν ἀν- θρώπων ἀναπεπείκασιν δι' ἀργίαν ἀφεμένους τοῦ σκοπεῖν, ὅπῃ ποτὲ ταῦτα

Mantissa XXV 221

ἔχει, καὶ τίς ἡ τάξις ἐν τοῖς οὖσιν τῆς εἱμαρμένης, πάντα τὰ γιγνόμενα
καθ' εἱμαρμένην γίγνεσθαι λέγειν. ἀλλ' ἐπειδὴ μηδὲ οἱ πάνυ τὴν εἱμαρμένην ἐπιβοώμενοι ἐν ταῖς κατὰ τὸν βίον πράξεσιν ἐκείνῃ φαίνονται πάντα
πεπιστευκέναι, | (ἱκανὸν γὰρ τἀληθὲς μαχομένους αὐτοῖς ἀποφῆναι τοὺς τὰ 161v   181
ψευδῆ πεπιστευμένους λέγειν) ἄξιον ἡμᾶς ἄνωθεν ἀρξαμένους ἰδεῖν, τίς ποτέ
ἐστιν ἡ φύσις τῆς εἱμαρμένης καὶ ἐν τίσιν καὶ μέχρι πόσου τὴν ἰσχὺν
ἔχει. καὶ πρῶτόν γε περὶ τίνα τῶν ὄντων εὔλογον αὐτὴν λέγειν εἶναι,
5 διασκεψώμεθα· τοῦτο γὰρ φανερὸν γενόμενον πρὸ ἔργου γενήσεται καὶ πρὸς
τὰ ἄλλα τὰ ζητούμενα περὶ αὐτῆς. τὸ μὲν οὖν πᾶσιν τοῖς οὖσιν ἐπιτάσσειν 5
αὐτὴν καὶ πάντα λέγειν εἶναι τὰ ὄντα καθ' εἱμαρμένην, ὁμοίως ἀίδιά τε
καὶ μή, οὔτε εὔλογον ἄλλως οὐδ' ὑπὸ τῶν ὑμνούντων μάλιστα τὴν εἱμαρμένην ὡς αἰτίαν τῶν γιγνομένων ἁπάντων ὁμολογούμενον. οὔτε γὰρ τὰ
10 ἀίδια καθ' εἱμαρμένην εἶναι τοιαύτην λέγειν εὔλογον· γελοῖον γὰρ τὸ τὴν
διάμετρον ἀσύμμετρον τῇ πλευρᾷ λέγειν εἶναι καθ' εἱμαρμένην, ἢ τὸ τρί-
γωνον διὰ τοῦτο δυσὶν ὀρθαῖς ἴσας ἔχειν τὰς ἐντὸς γωνίας, καὶ καθόλου
τὰ ἀεὶ κατὰ τὰ αὐτὰ καὶ ὡσαύτως ἔχοντα οὐδαμῶς εὔλογον καθ' εἱμαρ- 10
μένην οὕτως ἔχειν λέγειν. ἀλλ' οὐδὲ τὰ γιγνόμενα πάντα· ὅσα γὰρ καὶ
15 τούτων εὔτακτόν τε καὶ ὡρισμένην ἔχει τὴν γένεσίν τε καὶ κίνησιν, ἔξω
πίπτει καὶ ταῦτα τῆς εἱμαρμένης. οὐ γὰρ καθ' εἱμαρμένην ὁ ἥλιος ἐν
χειμεριναῖς ἢ θεριναῖς τροπαῖς γίγνεται, οὐδὲ ἕκαστον τῶν ἄστρων εἱμαρμένην αἰτίαν ἔχει τῆς οἰκείας φορᾶς, ἀλλ' ἔστιν ὥσπερ κατὰ τὸ εἶναι καὶ
τὴν οὐσίαν ἐλεύθερα τῆς τοιαύτης αἰτίας, οὕτως δὲ καὶ κατὰ τὰς οἰκείας
20 ἐνεργείας. διὸ τῶν μὲν ἀιδίων ἢ κατὰ τὰ αὐτὰ καὶ ὡσαύτως ἀεὶ γιγνο- 15   *
μένων οὐθενὸς αἴτιον ἡ εἱμαρμένη, δοκεῖ δὲ ἐν τοῖς ἐν γενέσει καὶ φθορᾷ
τῆς εἱμαρμένης ἔργον εἶναι. ἐν γὰρ τοῖς ἐπιτηδείοις ὅσον ἐπὶ τῇ φυσικῇ
παρασκευῇ πρὸς τὰ ἀντικείμενα τῆς εἱμαρμένης ἰσχὺς εἶναι δοκεῖ, ἐν θατέρῳ τῶν ἀντικειμένων κατέχουσα αὐτὰ καὶ φυλάττουσα κατά τινα τάξεως
25 ἀκολουθίαν. ἃ γὰρ οὐκ ἂν οὕτως ἔχοι ἄνευ τῆς εἱμαρμένης, ταῦτα παρὰ
τῆς εἱμαρμένης ἐν τῇδε τῇ τάξει φυλάττεσθαι δοκεῖ· τοιαῦτα δέ ἐστιν
οὐκ ἄλλα τινὰ τῶν ὄντων ἢ τὰ ἐν γενέσει καὶ φθορᾷ· ὥστε ἐνταῦθά 20
που καὶ τὸ τῆς εἱμαρμένης. ἐπεὶ δὲ καὶ τούτων τὰ μὲν κατὰ τέχνην
τε καὶ λόγον τεχνικόν τινα, τὰ δὲ κατὰ προαίρεσιν, τὰ δὲ κατὰ φύσιν
30 γίγνεται, σκεπτέον ἐν τίσιν τούτων τὸ τῆς εἱμαρμένης, εἰ μὴ οἷόν τε
ἐν πᾶσιν. τὰ μὲν οὖν κατὰ τέχνην γιγνόμενα καθ' εἱμαρμένην εἶναί
τε καὶ γίγνεσθαι λέγειν οὐδαμῶς ταῖς περὶ τῆς εἱμαρμένης δόξαις συνῳ-
δόν· γελοῖον γὰρ τὸ τὴν κλίνην ἢ τὸ βάθρον καθ' εἱμαρμένην γεγονέναι λέγειν, ἢ τὴν λύραν ἡρμόσθαι καθ' εἱμαρμένην· οὕτω γὰρ ἐροῦμεν 25
35 πᾶσαν τέχνην εἱμαρμένην. ἀλλ' οὐδ' ὧν προαίρεσις αἰτία, ταῦτα καθ'
εἱμαρμένην ἂν εἴη· τούτων γὰρ ἐν ἡμῖν ἡ ἀρχή, ἀλλ' οὐκ ἔξωθεν,
ἡ δὲ εἱμαρμένη οὐκ ἐν ἡμῖν· καὶ γὰρ εἰ καὶ περὶ ταῦτά ἐστιν ἡ εἱμαρ-   182
μένη, περὶ ἃ καὶ τὸ ἐφ' ἡμῖν, ἀλλὰ ἄλλο γέ ἐστι τοῦ ἐφ' ἡμῖν. ἀφαι-
ρετέον ἄρα τῆς εἱμαρμένης καὶ τῶν ἐν γενέσει τὰ γιγνόμενα κατὰ τέχνην
τε καὶ προαίρεσιν. τούτων δ' ἀφῃρημένων λοιπὸν καταλείπεται ταῦτα, οἷς

5 ἡ φύσις τῆς γενέσεως αἰτία, ἐν οἷς δὴ καὶ δοκεῖ δυναστεύειν τὸ τῆς εἱ- 80
μαρμένης. εἰ γάρ τις ἐπιστήσας ἐξετάζειν βούλοιτο τὰς δόξας τὰς περὶ
τῆς εἱμαρμένης καταβεβλημένας, οὐ περὶ ἄλλα τινά, οὐδὲ ἐν ἄλλοις αὐτὰς
εὑρήσει τὴν εἱμαρμένην τιθείσας, ἀλλ᾽ ἐν τοῖς γινομένοις φύσει, καὶ τούτων
μάλιστα ἐν τῇ τῶν ζῴων καὶ τῶν ἐκ συγκρίσεων τῶν ἐν γενέσει· οὐ γὰρ
10 τὸ τὴν τῶν στοιχείων εἰς ἄλληλα μεταβολὴν καθ᾽ εἱμαρμένην γίνεσθαι λέγειν πάνυ τι σύνηθες. ὄντος τοίνυν τοῦ καθ᾽ εἱμαρμένην ἐν οἷς προειρήκαμεν, καὶ τούτου γνωρίμου γεγονότος, ἀκόλουθον ἂν εἴη μετὰ τοῦτο ζη- 35
τῆσαι, πότερον τοιοῦτόν ἐστιν ὡς ἀναγκαῖόν τε καὶ ἀπαράβατον εἶναι κατὰ
τὸν ποιητὴν τὸν λέγοντα·
15 μοῖραν δ᾽ οὔ τινά φημι πεφυγμένον ἔμμεναι ἀνδρῶν,
οὐ κακὸν οὐδὲ μὲν ἐσθλόν, ἐπὴν τὰ πρῶτα γένηται.
ἢ τοιοῦτον οἷον καὶ παραβαίνεσθαι, καὶ μὴ πάντῃ τὸ ἀναγκαῖον ἔχειν ἐν
αὐτῇ. ἐκ μὲν οὖν τῆς κοινῆς τῶν ἀνθρώπων περὶ τοῦδε κρίσεως οὐδέτερον ἔχομεν βεβαίως τούτων τιθέμενον. ποτὲ μὲν γὰρ τὸ τῆς εἱμαρμένης
* 20 ὑμνοῦσιν ὡς ἀναγκαῖον, ποτὲ δὲ οὐ πάντῃ τὴν συνέχειαν αὐτῆς πιστεύουσι 40
σώζειν. καὶ γὰρ οἱ διὰ τῶν λόγων ὑπὲρ αὐτῆς ὡς οὔσης ἀναγκαίας δια-
τεινόμενοι σφόδρα καὶ πάντα ἀνατιθέντες αὐτῇ ἐν ταῖς κατὰ τὸν βίον
πράξεσιν οὐκ ἐοίκασιν αὐτῇ πεπιστευκέναι· τύχην γοῦν πολλάκις ἐπιβοῶνται, ἄλλην ὁμολογοῦντες εἶναι ταύτην αἰτίαν τῆς εἱμαρμένης· ἀλλὰ καὶ
25 τοῖς θεοῖς οὐ διαλείπουσιν εὐχόμενοι, ὡς δυναμένου τινὸς ὑπ᾽ αὐτῶν διὰ
τὰς εὐχὰς γενέσθαι καὶ παρὰ τὴν εἱμαρμένην· ἀλλὰ καὶ βουλεύονται περὶ 45
τῶν πρακτέων αὐτοῖς, καίτοι καὶ ταῦτα καθ᾽ εἱμαρμένην εἶναι λέγοντες,
καὶ συμβούλους παρακαλοῦσιν καὶ μαντείαις οὐκ ὀκνοῦσι χρῆσθαι, ὡς ἐνὸν
αὐτοῖς, εἰ προμάθοιεν, φυλάξασθαί τι τῶν εἱμαρμένων. ἐπεὶ δὲ οὗτοι μὲν
30 αὐτοῖς περιπίπτουσι περὶ τὰ μέγιστα φανερῶς οὕτως διαφωνίαν ἔχοντες
(ἀπιθανώταται γοῦν εἰσιν αὐτῶν αἱ πρὸς τὴν τούτων συμφωνίαν εὑρησιλο-
γίαι), δοκεῖ δὲ ἐν τοῖς ἐν γενέσει καὶ φθορᾷ καὶ τὸ ἐνδεχόμενον εἶναι, ὃ
τοῦ μηδὲν ἀναγκαίως ἐν τούτοις ἐν οἷς ἂν ᾖ γίγνεσθαι αἴτιόν ἐστιν. ἄξιόν 50
ἐστιν ἐπιστῆσαι περὶ τοῦδε, εἴτε ἔστιν εἴτε μή. αὕτη γὰρ ἡ φύσις ὁρι-
35 σθεῖσα πρὸς τὸ τὴν τῆς εἱμαρμένης οὐσίαν εὑρεῖν ἡμῖν τὸ μέγιστον συμ-
183 βάλλεται. ἱκανὴ μὲν οὖν καὶ ἡ χρῆσις ἡ κοινὴ συστῆσαι τὴν ἐνδεχομένην
φύσιν· οὐδεὶς γὰρ οὐδὲ τῶν ἐξ ἀνάγκης πάντα γίγνεσθαι λεγόντων ἐν τῷ
ζῆν καὶ ταῖς κατὰ τὸν βίον ἐνεργείαις οὐ μαρτυρεῖ τῷ δύνασθαί τινα καὶ
τῶν γιγνομένων μὴ γίγνεσθαι καὶ τῶν μὴ γιγνομένων γίγνεσθαι. οὐ μὴν
5 ἀλλὰ καὶ τῷ λόγῳ τοῦτο | δεῖξαι ῥάδιον. πολλὰ γὰρ τῶν γιγνομένων τὰ 162r
μὲν ἀπὸ τύχης, τὰ δὲ ἀπὸ ταὐτομάτου γίγνεσθαι πεπίστευται, τὸ δ᾽ εἶναί
τι καὶ ἐφ᾽ ἡμῖν οὕτως ἐναργές ἐστιν, ὡς μηδὲ τοὺς τὰ τῆς εἱμαρμένης ὡς
ἀναγκαῖα πάνυ κρατύνειν πειρωμένους ἀντιβλέπειν δύνασθαι τῷδε τῷ δόγματι. ἀλλὰ μὴν εἰ ἔστιν ἐφ᾽ ἡμῖν τι, καὶ τοῦτο περὶ ταὐτά ἐστι, περὶ ἃ
10 καὶ τὴν εἱμαρμένην εἶναι συμβέβηκεν, ἀναιρεῖται τὸ τὴν εἱμαρμένην ἀπα- 5
ράβατόν τε καὶ ἀκώλυτον καὶ ἀναγκαῖον εἶναι· ὧν γὰρ ἡμεῖς ἐσμεν ἀρχαὶ
ἑλέσθαι τε καὶ μή, ταῦτα ἀδύνατον κατηναγκάσθαι λέγειν. ἀλλὰ μὴν

ἀνάγκη τοῖς λέγουσιν τὴν εἱμαρμένην εἶναι, περὶ ταῦτα λέγειν εἶναι, περὶ
ἃ καὶ τὰ ἐφ' ἡμῖν. εἴτε γὰρ τὰ τέλη μόνα λέγοιεν καθ' εἱμαρμένην
15 γίγνεσθαι, εἴτε καὶ τὰς πράξεις, αἷς ἕπεσθαι τὰ τέλη συμβέβηκεν, ἀμφο-
τέρως ἀκολουθεῖ περὶ τὰ αὐτὰ λέγειν εἶναι τὴν εἱμαρμένην, περὶ ἃ καὶ τὸ
ἐφ' ἡμῖν. εἰ μὲν οὖν καὶ τὰς πράξεις καθ' εἱμαρμένην λέγοι τις, αὐτόθεν 10
δῆλον τὸ κείμενον· ἐν γὰρ ταύταις ἐστὶ καὶ τὸ ἐφ' ἡμῖν· εἰ δὲ τὰ τέλη
μόνον, ὧν αἱ πράξεις χάριν, ἀκολουθεῖ δὲ ταῖς τοιαῖσδε πράξεσιν τὰ τοιάδε
20 τέλη (οὐ γὰρ δὴ τοῖς ὁπωσοῦν πραχθεῖσιν ἕπεται ταὐτὸν τέλος), ἀνάγκη
καὶ τὰς πράξεις, αἷς ἀκολουθήσει τὰ τοιαῦτα τέλη, καθειμάρθαι λέγειν.
οὐ γὰρ ἀκολουθήσει τὸ καθ' εἱμαρμένην τέλος μὴ προηγησαμένων τῶν ἐπὶ
τοῦτο ἀγουσῶν πράξεων. καὶ τὸ ἐφ' ἡμῖν δὲ περὶ ταῦτα· ὅτι γάρ ἐστί
τι ἐφ' ἡμῖν, δῆλον καὶ ἐκ τῶνδ' ἂν γένοιτο, εἴ γε δεῖ περὶ τῶν ἐναργῶν 15
25 ἀποδείξεσιν χρῆσθαι· ἔκ τε γὰρ τοῦ μηδὲν μὲν ⟨τῶν⟩ ὑπὸ τῆς φύσεως
προηγουμένως γιγνομένων γίγνεσθαι μάτην, ἐν δὲ τοῖς ἀνθρώποις ὂν τὸ
βουλεύεσθαι φύσει, ὃν δὲ καὶ προηγούμενον ἔργον τῆς φύσεως, εἴ γε τούτῳ
δοκεῖ μάλιστα τῶν ἄλλων ζῴων ἄνθρωπος διαφέρειν, μάτην γίγνεσθαι, [γε-
γονότος κενῶς] εἰ μηδὲν ἐκ τῆς βουλῆς ὁ βουλευόμενος ἐλέσθαι κύριος.
30 ἀλλὰ γὰρ ὡς ἔχοντες τοῦδε τὴν ἐξουσίαν αὐτοί γε ἐφ' αὑτῶν βουλευόμεθα
περὶ τῶν πρακτέων ἡμῖν, ἀλλ' οὐκ εἴξαντες ταῖς φαντασίαις τοῖς ἀλόγοις 20 *
τῶν ἄλλων ζῴων παραπλησίως αὐταῖς ἑπόμεθα, συμβούλους τε παρακαλοῦ-
μεν, οὓς ἂν εἰδῶμεν πλέον τι δυναμένους ἡμῶν, εἰς τὴν κρίσιν τῶν προχειμένων, καὶ τὴν αἵρεσιν συνάρασθαι. ἤδη δὲ περὶ τῶν μειζόνων καὶ 184
χαλεπωτέρων οὐκ ὀκνοῦμεν συμβούλους καὶ τοὺς θεοὺς παρακαλεῖν, ἀξιοῦν-
τες παρ' αὐτῶν μαθεῖν ἢ διὰ χρησμῶν ἢ διὰ συμβούλων, ἢ δι' ὀνείρων *
τινῶν, ὁπότερα χρὴ μᾶλλον ἡμᾶς ἑλέσθαι τῶν ζητουμένων. ἱκαναὶ δὲ καὶ
5 αἱ νομοθεσίαι τοῦτο συστῆσαι, ἐν αἷς διδασκαλίαις τέ τινων κελεύονται καὶ 25 *
προστάσσεται τὰ ποιητέα, καὶ τιμῶνται μὲν οἱ πειθόμενοι τούτοις, κολάζον-
ται δὲ οἱ μή. ἀλλὰ μὴν ὄντος γέ τινος ἐφ' ἡμῖν καὶ τὸ ἐνδεχόμενόν
ἐστιν, εἴ γε ἐφ' ἡμῖν ἐστι τό τε πρᾶξαί τι καὶ τὸ μή. τούτου δὲ ὄντος,
ἀδύνατον ἀναγκαῖον εἶναι τὸ τῆς εἱμαρμένης ὂν ἐν τούτοις, ἐν οἷς καὶ τὸ
10 ἐφ' ἡμῖν ἔχει χώραν. ἱκαναὶ δὲ καὶ αἱ πρὸς τοὺς θεοὺς εὐχαί, τῶν μὲν
ἀποτροπήν τινων αἰτουμένων παρ' αὐτῶν, τῶν δὲ δόσιν ἀγαθῶν ὡς ὄντων
τινῶν ἐνδεχομένων καὶ γενέσθαι καὶ μὴ διὰ τὴν ἡμετέραν αἴτησιν ὑπὸ τῶν 30
θεῶν. συστῆσαι τὸ εἶναί τινα ἐνδεχόμενα. ἀλλὰ μὴν καὶ ἐκ τῆς φυσικῆς
συστάσεως τῶν ὄντων ἑκάστου τοῦθ' οἷόν τε καταμαθεῖν. ἡ γὰρ φύσις
15 αὐτὴ τοῖς μὲν ἐξ ἀνάγκης οὖσίν τε καὶ γιγνομένοις οὐδεμίαν ἐπιτηδειότητα
πρὸς ἀντικείμενον ἔδωκεν, τὴν δὲ ἀνεπιτηδειότητα πρὸς ἀδύνατα· μάτην
γὰρ ἕξειν ἤμελλεν τὴν ἐπιτηδειότητα πρὸς τὴν εἰς ταῦτα μεταβολήν, ὄντα
καὶ ἀδύνατα ἄλλως ἔχειν. ὁρῶμεν γὰρ ὅτι οὔτε τὸ πῦρ ἔχει δύναμιν
ψυχρότητος ἐν αὑτῷ, οὔτε ἡ χιὼν μελανίας, οὔτε τὰ βαρέα κουφότητος, 35
20 μένοντά γε ταῦτα ⟨ἃ⟩ ἐστιν, οὔτε ⟨τι⟩ τῶν ἀϊδίων τοῦ φθαρῆναι. οἷς δὲ οὐκ
ἀναγκαῖον ἐν θατέρῳ τῶν ἀντικειμένων ἀφωρισμένως εἶναί τε καὶ μένειν,
ταῦτα καὶ τῆς εἰς τὸ ἀντικείμενον μεταβολῆς ἐκ φύσεως ἔχει τὴν παρα-

224 *Mantissa XXV*

σκευήν. τοιαῦτα τῶν ἐν γενέσει καὶ φθορᾷ πλεῖστα, οἷς μή ἐστι θάτερον
τῶν ἀντικειμένων σύμφυτον· ἕκαστον γὰρ αὐτῶν οἷόν τε τὰ ἀντικείμενα
25 πάσχειν τε καὶ μή, τοῦτ' ἐνδέχεται παθεῖν τε καὶ μὴ παθεῖν. ὃ δὲ ἐν- 40
δέχεται μεταβάλλειν εἰς τὸ ἀντικείμενον, τοῦτο οὐκ ἔστιν ἐξ ἀνάγκης, ἐν
ᾧ φθάσαν ἐστὶν αὐτῶν. συνίστησιν δὲ τὸ μὴ πάντα ἐξ ἀνάγκης γίγνεσθαι
τὰ γιγνόμενα τό τε ἐφ' ἡμῖν, ὡς ἔφαμεν, καὶ ἡ τύχη, ἱκανὴ διακόψαι τὴν
συνέχειαν τῶν ἐν τάξει τινὶ γίγνεσθαι δοκούντων. εἰ δὲ οὐδὲν μὲν ἧττον
30 ἐναργὲς τῆς εἱμαρμένης τὸ εἶναί τι ἐφ' ἡμῖν, καὶ τὸ γίγνεσθαι καὶ ἀπὸ
τύχης πολλὰ καὶ ἀπὸ ταὐτομάτου, καὶ ὅλως ἐν τοῖς ἐν γενέσει, ἐν οἷς
ἐστι καὶ ἡ εἱμαρμένη, εἶναι καὶ τὴν τοῦ ἐνδεχομένου φύσιν, τοῦτο δὲ 45
ἀναιρεῖ τὸ ἀναγκαῖον, ἀδύνατον εἶναι τὴν εἱμαρμένην ἀναγκαῖόν τι καὶ πα-
185 ραβασθῆναι μὴ δυνάμενον. ἀλλὰ μὴν ὁμολογεῖται πάντα τὰ καθ' εἱμαρμένην γιγνόμενα κατὰ τάξιν καὶ ἀκολουθίαν γίγνεσθαί τινα καί τι ἐφεξῆς
ἔχειν ἐν αὐτοῖς. οὐ γὰρ δὴ τοῖς ἀπὸ τύχης ὅμοια τὰ τῆς εἱμαρμένης·
ἐκεῖνα μὲν γὰρ ἄστατά τε καὶ σπανίως γιγνόμενα καὶ σχεδὸν ἀναίτια, τὸ
5 δὲ καθ' εἱμαρμένην πᾶν τοὐναντίον· εἱρμὸν γοῦν αἰτίων αὐτήν φασιν εἶναι.
ἀλλ' οὐδὲ τῷ κατὰ προαίρεσιν ταὐτὸν ἡ εἱμαρμένη δοκεῖ εἶναι· διακόπτε- 50
σθαι γὰρ τὸ συνεχὲς αὐτῆς ὑφ' ἡμῶν καὶ τῆς ἡμετέρας προαιρέσεως πολλάκις. ἀλλὰ μὴν ἐν τοῖς γενητοῖς τε καὶ φθαρτοῖς ταῦτα ὁρῶμεν αἴτια
παρὰ τὴν συνιστᾶσαν φύσιν αὐτὰ καὶ δημιουργοῦσαν, προαίρεσίν τε καὶ τὸ
10 αὐτόματον καὶ τὴν τύχην (οὐ γὰρ ἐν τούτοις τὸ κατὰ τέχνην), ὧν οὐδενὶ
ταὐτὸν τὸ τῆς εἱμαρμένης εἶναι δοκεῖ. λείπεται ἄρα τὴν εἱμαρμένην μηδὲν ἄλλο ἢ τὴν οἰκείαν εἶναι φύσιν ἑκάστου. οὐ γὰρ δὴ ἐν τῷ καθόλου 162v
καὶ κοινῷ τὸ τῆς εἱμαρμένης, οἷον ἁπλῶς ζῴων, ἀνθρώπων, ἀλλ' ἐν τοῖς
καθ' ἕκαστα, Σωκράτῃ τε καὶ Καλλίᾳ. ἐν δὲ τούτοις ἡ ἰδία φύσις ἀρχὴ
15 καὶ αἰτία, τοιάδε οὖσα, τῆς κατὰ ταῦτα γιγνομένης τάξεως. ἀπὸ γὰρ ταύτης ὡς ἐπὶ τὸ πᾶν καὶ οἱ βίοι καὶ αἱ τῶν βίων γίγνονται καταστροφαί, μὴ
ἐμποδισθείσης ὑπό τινων. ὁρῶμεν γάρ, ὅτι καὶ τὸ σῶμα τῷ τοιόνδε ἢ
τοιόνδε ἐκ φύσεως εἶναι καὶ ἐν νόσοις γίγνεται καὶ ἐν φθοραῖς, ἀκολούθως 5
τῇ φυσικῇ συστάσει. οὐ μὴν ἐξ ἀνάγκης· ἱκαναὶ γὰρ ἐκκροῦσαι τήνδε
20 τὴν τάξιν ἐπιμέλειαί τε καὶ ἀέρων ὑπαλλαγαὶ καὶ πρόσταξις ἰατρῶν, καὶ
συμβουλίαι θεῶν. κατὰ δὲ τὸν αὐτὸν τρόπον καὶ ἐπὶ τῆς ψυχῆς εὕροι
τις ἂν παρὰ τὴν φυσικὴν κατασκευὴν διαφόρους γιγνομένας καὶ τὰς πράξεις
καὶ τὰς προαιρέσεις καὶ τοὺς βίους. ἦθος γὰρ ἀνθρώπων κατὰ τὸν Ἡράκλειτον, δαιμών, τουτέστι φύσις. ὡς ἐπὶ τὸ πλεῖστον γὰρ ταῖς φυσικαῖς
25 κατασκευαῖς τε καὶ διαθέσεσιν καὶ τὰς πράξεις καὶ τοὺς βίους καὶ τὰς τῶν 10
βίων καταστροφὰς ἀκολουθεῖν συμβέβηκεν. τῶν μὲν γὰρ ἀψιμάχων καὶ
φιλοκινδύνων φύσει βίαιός τις καὶ ὁ θάνατος ὡς ἐπὶ τὸ πλεῖστον, αὕτη γὰρ
εἱμαρμένη τε καὶ φύσις αὐτῶν, τῷ δὲ ἀκολάστῳ καὶ ἐν ἡδοναῖς ζῶντι ὁ
ἐν ταῖς ἀκρασίαις· καὶ τῷ καρτερικῷ ὁ δι' ὑπερβολῆς πόνων καὶ κακο-
30 παθειῶν, τῷ δὲ ἀνελευθέρῳ ὁ ἐκ τῆς περὶ τὸ ἀδιάφορον σπουδῆς, δι' ἣν
καὶ ἀδικοῦσιν καὶ αὐτῶν ὀλιγωροῦσιν καὶ πονοῦσιν ὑπὲρ τὴν δύναμιν· διὰ
τοῦτο γοῦν εἰώθασιν καὶ ἐπιλέγειν τοῖς τοιούτοις, ὡς αὐτὸς αὑτῷ γέγονεν 15

Quaestio II.4   225

αἴτιος τοῦ θανάτου. τοιούτου δὲ ὄντος τοῦ καθ' εἱμαρμένην οὔτε τὴν
μαντικὴν ἐροῦμεν ἄχρηστον ἔτι, προορωμένην τε τὸ κατὰ φύσιν ἀποβη-
35 σόμενον καὶ βοηθοῦσαν διὰ τοῦ συμβουλεύειν τε καὶ κελεύειν ἐνίστασθαι
τῇ τῆς φύσεως χείρονος ἀκολουθίᾳ. ἀλλ' οὐδ' ἡ τῆς τύχης ἀναιρεθήσε-
ται φύσις, ἀλλ' ἕξει τινῶν αἰτίαν συμπίπτουσαν τοῖς γιγνομένοις κατὰ   186
προαίρεσιν. ἔτι δὲ μᾶλλον τὸ θεῖον καὶ αἱ ἐκ τούτου βοήθειαι, καὶ αἱ
παρ' ἡμῶν εὐχαί τε καὶ δεήσεις τὴν οἰκείαν χώραν φυλάξουσιν, ὄντος τοῦ 20
τῆς εἱμαρμένης τοιούτου. ὁμολογήσει δὲ τούτοις καὶ τὸ λεγόμενον, ὅτι
5 πολλὰ καὶ παρὰ μοῖραν γίγνεται καὶ παρὰ τὴν εἱμαρμένην, ὥς που καὶ ὁ
ποιητὴς ἐμφαίνει λέγων
                μὴ καὶ ὑπὲρ μοῖραν δόμον Ἄιδος εἰσαφίκηαι.
συνίσταιτο δ' ἂν ᾗδε ἡ δόξα καὶ ὑπὸ τοὺς μάντεις, ἐν οἷς προλέγουσιν μὴ   *
πάντα ἐπιτυγχάνειν. εἰ δὲ μὴ τήνδε τὴν δόξαν περὶ τῆς εἱμαρμένης τοὺς
10 ἀνθρώπους ἔχειν συμβέβηκεν, θαυμαστὸν οὐδέν. οἱ γὰρ πολλοὶ τοῖς μὲν 25
τύποις οὐ κακῶς περὶ τῶν πραγμάτων στοχάζονται, ἐν δὲ τοῖς καθ' ἕκαστα
καὶ ἐν τῷ διορίζειν τε καὶ ἐξακριβοῦν πολλὰ διαμαρτάνουσιν. τὸ μὲν γὰρ
φύσεως, τὸ δὲ ἐπιστήμης ἔργον. ἤδη δὲ τοῦ τῆς εἱμαρμένης ὀνόματος
Ἀριστοτέλης μνημονεύει καὶ ἐν τῷ πρώτῳ τῶν Μετεωρολογουμένων οὕτως·
15 "ἀλλὰ πάντων τούτων αἴτιον ὑποληπτέον, ὅτι γίγνεται διὰ χρόνων εἱμαρμένων,· οἷον ἐν ταῖς κατ' ἐνιαυτὸν ὥραις χειμών, οὕτω περιόδου τινὸς
μεγάλης μέγας χειμών." ἔοικεν δὲ διά τε τούτων τὴν ·εἱμαρμένην τὴν 30
φύσιν λέγειν (οὗτοι γὰρ εἱμαρμένοι χρόνοι, χειμών τε καὶ τῶν ἄλλων,
οἳ φυσικὰς τὰς ἀνταποδόσεις ἔχοντες οὐκ ἔχουσιν αὐτὰς ἀπαραβάτους καὶ
20 κατηναγκασμένας), ἀλλὰ καὶ ἐν τῷ πέμπτῳ τῆς Φυσικῆς Ἀκροάσεως οὕτως
πάλιν εἱμαρμένης μνημονεύει· "ἆρ' οὖν καὶ γενέσεις εἰσὶ βίαιοι καὶ οὐχ
εἱμαρμέναι, αἷς ἐναντίαι αἱ κατὰ φύσιν." [ᾗ] δι' ὧν πάλιν, ὅτι τῷ τῆς   *
εἱμαρμένης ὀνόματι ἐπὶ τῶν κατὰ φύσιν γιγνομένων χρῆται, γνώριμον. εἰ
γὰρ μὴ τῷ εἱμαρμένῳ ἐναντίον φησὶν εἶναι τὸ κατὰ φύσιν, τῷ δὲ παρὰ 35   *
25 τὴν εἱμαρμένην τὸ καθ' εἱμαρμένην ἐναντίον, ταὐτὸν ἂν εἴη τῷ κατὰ φύσιν
τὸ καθ' εἱμαρμένην. οὐ γὰρ δὴ πλείω οἷόν τε ἑνὶ ὄντι τῷ μὴ καθ' εἱμαρμένην ἐναντία λέγειν εἶναι, τό τε καθ' εἱμαρμένην, προδήλως ὂν ἐναντίον αὐτῷ, καὶ τὸ κατὰ φύσιν ἄλλο ὂν τοῦ καθ' εἱμαρμένην. φανερώτατα
δὲ Θεόφραστος δείκνυσιν ταὐτὸν ὂν τὸ καθ' εἱμαρμένην τῷ κατὰ φύσιν 40
30 ἐν τῷ Καλλισθένει, καὶ Πολύζηλος δὲ ἐν τῷ οὕτως ἐπιγραφομένῳ Περὶ
εἱμαρμένης συγγράμματι.

                        QUAESTIO II. 4

        Ὅτι, εἰ τοῦ ἐφ' ἡμῖν τὸ ἀντικείμενον μὴ ἐφ' ἡμῖν, οὐδ' αὐτὸ
              [ἐφ' ἡμῖν, οὐδὲ] τὸ ἐφ' ἡμῖν ἐφ' ἡμῖν ἔσται.   vol. 2
                                                                           p. 50
30 Εἰ ἐφ' ἡμῖν ἐστι τοῦτο, οὗ τὸ ἀντικείμενον [μὴ] ἐφ' ἡμῖν, τὸ οὗ τὸ   Bruns
ἀντικείμενον μὴ ἐφ' ἡμῖν, ἐκεῖνο οὐκ ἐφ' ἡμῖν. τοῦ δ' ἐφ' ἡμῖν τὸ ἀν-

51
*
*
τικείμενον οὐκ ἐφ᾽ ἡμῖν, τῷ γὰρ ἐφ᾽ ἡμῖν τὸ οὐκ ἐφ᾽ ἡμῖν ἀντικείμενον. οὐδὲ τὸ ἐφ᾽ ἡμῖν. εἰ δὲ τὸ ἐφ᾽ ἡμῖν μὴ ἐφ᾽ ἡμῖν, οὐδέν ἐστιν ἐφ᾽ ἡμῖν. καθ᾽ ὃ ἐφ᾽ ἡμῖν ἐστιν, οὗ καὶ τὸ ἀντικείμενον 10
ἐφ᾽ ἡμῖν, κατὰ τούτους οὐδέν ἐστιν ἐφ᾽ ἡμῖν. ⟨ἢ⟩ ψεῦδος τὸ εἰ μὴ
*   5 [τὸ] ἐφ᾽ ἡμῖν τὸ εἶναι ἐφ᾽ ἡμῖν, οὐδέν ἐστιν ἐφ᾽ ἡμῖν. τὸ μὲν γὰρ ἐφ᾽
ἡμῖν τι εἶναι ἐν τῇ φύσει ἡμῶν καὶ τῇ οὐσίᾳ ὂν οὐκ ἐφ᾽ ἡμῖν ἐστι, 15
ὥσπερ οὐδὲ τὸ λογικοῖς εἶναι, τὰ μέντοι πράγματα οἷς χρώμεθα κατὰ τὸ
ἐφ᾽ ἡμῖν, ταῦτα ἐφ᾽ ἡμῖν. τούτων γὰρ καὶ τὰ ἀντικείμενα ἐφ᾽ ἡμῖν. τὸ
μὲν γὰρ ἐφ᾽ ἡμῖν τι εἶναι οὐκ ἐφ᾽ ἡμῖν, τὸ δὲ περιπατῆσαι ἐφ᾽ ἡμῖν, ὅτι
* 10 καὶ τὸ μὴ περιπατῆσαι. καὶ γὰρ ἴδιον τὸ ἀντικείμενον τοῦ ἐφ᾽ ἡμῖν οὐκ 20
*   ἐφ᾽ ἡμῖν διὰ τούτου, τὸ δὲ ἐφ᾽ ἡμῖν † δῆλον. ὡς οὖν τὰ ἀντικείμενα ἐφ᾽
*   ἡμῖν, ταῦτα καὶ αὐτὰ ἐφ᾽ ἡμῖν, ὅτι μὴ ἐφ᾽ ἡμῖν ἐν τοῖς πρακτοῖς. οὐ
πρακτὸν | δὲ τὸ εἶναί τι [τὸ] ἐφ᾽ ἡμῖν ἐν τοῖς βουλευτοῖς καὶ τοῖς ἐνδε- 95
χομένοις καὶ ἄλλως ἔχειν. οὐκ ὄντος δὲ ἐν τούτοις τοῦ εἶναί τι ἐφ᾽ ἡμῖν
 15 εἰκότως ἡ μὲν δύναμις, καθ᾽ ἥν ἐστιν ἐφ᾽ ἡμῖν, οὐκ ἐφ᾽ ἡμῖν, πρὸς ⟨ἃ⟩ 5
δὲ χρώμεθα τῇ τοῦ ἐφ᾽ ἡμῖν τι εἶναι δυνάμει, ἐφ᾽ ἡμῖν ταῦτα, ὥσπερ
καὶ ἡ μὲν χρῆσις τοῦ λόγου ἐφ᾽ ἡμῖν, οὐκ ἐφ᾽ ἡμῖν δὲ ἡ δύναμις τῆς
χρήσεως.

QUAESTIO II.5

Περὶ τοῦ ὅτι καὶ τὸ ἐφ᾽ ἡμῖν καθ᾽ εἱμαρμένην.   10

*51. 20   Τῷ ἐφ᾽ ἡμῖν τι εἶναι ἀντίκειται τὸ μηδὲν εἶναι ἐφ᾽ ἡμῖν. †ἀδύνατον
τὸ οὖν τῷ ἐφ᾽ ἡμῖν τι εἶναι [τὸ] ἀντικείμενον ἀδύνατον. ἀλλὰ μὴν ᾧ
τὸ ἀντικείμενον ἀδύνατον, τοῦτο καθ᾽ εἱμαρμένην, εἴ γε ταῦτα καθ᾽ εἱμαρ- 15
μένην γίνεται, οἷς τὰ ἀντικείμενα ἀδύνατόν ἐστιν ἢ εἶναι ἢ γενέσθαι. τὸ
οὖν ἐφ᾽ ἡμῖν τι εἶναι καθ᾽ εἱμαρμένην. τῷ δὲ ἐφ᾽ ἡμῖν τι εἶναι καθ᾽
 25 εἱμαρμένην σώζοιτο ἂν τὸ ἐφ᾽ ἡμῖν τι εἶναι κατὰ τοὺς ἅπαντα γίνεσθαι
καθ᾽ εἱμαρμένην λέγοντας. ἢ οὐκ ἀληθὲς τὸ ᾧ τὸ ἀντικείμενον ἀδύνατον, 20
τοῦτο εἶναι καθ᾽ εἱμαρμένην. εἰ μὲν γὰρ ταὐτὸν ἦν τὸ ἐξ ἀνάγκης τῷ
καθ᾽ εἱμαρμένην, ⟨ἦν⟩ ἂν ὥσπερ τοῦ ἐξ ἀνάγκης ὁρισμὸς τὸ ᾧ τὸ ἀντι-
κείμενον ἀδύνατον, | οὕτως καὶ τοῦ καθ᾽ εἱμαρμένην. ἐπὶ πλέον δὲ τὸ ἐξ 96
 30 ἀνάγκης τοῦ καθ᾽ εἱμαρμένην· οὐ γὰρ πᾶν τὸ ἐξ ἀνάγκης καθ᾽ εἱμαρ-
52   μένην. τέσσαρα γοῦν τὰ δὶς δύο ἐξ ἀνάγκης, οὐ μὴν καθ᾽ εἱμαρμένην,
εἴ γε ἐν τοῖς γινομένοις τὸ καθ᾽ εἱμαρμένην, ὥστ᾽ οὐκέτ᾽ ἂν ὁρισμὸς εἴη 5
τοῦ καθ᾽ εἱμαρμένην ὁ λόγος ὁ λέγων, οὗ τὸ ἀντικείμενον ἀδύνατον, ἀλλ᾽
ὑπάρχοι μὲν ἂν καὶ τοῦτο τοῖς καθ᾽ εἱμαρμένην, ἐπεὶ καὶ αὐτὰ ἀναγκαῖα,
* 5 οὐ μὴν ὡς ἐπ᾽ ἴσης αὐτοῖς εἶναι. εἰ δὲ μὴ ἐπ᾽ ἴσης, οὐκ ἐπιστρέψει. οὐ 10
*   δεῖται πάντως ᾧ τὸ ἀντικείμενον ἀδύνατον, τοῦτο καθ᾽ εἱμαρμένην, ἀλλὰ
ἀναγκαῖον τοῦτο. οὐ γὰρ ὁρισμὸς ὁ προειρημένος λόγος. τὸ ἐφ᾽ ἡμῖν δὴ
ἐστιν ἀναγκαῖον μέν, ὅτι πᾶν τὸ ἐν τῇ οὐσίᾳ τινὸς ὂν ἀναγκαίως αὐτῷ 15
ὑπάρχει, οὐ μὴν καθ᾽ εἱμαρμένην. οἷς γὰρ καθ᾽ εἱρμὸν αἰτίων γινομένοις
 10 τὸ ἀντικείμενον ἀδύνατον, ταῦτα εἴη ἂν καθ᾽ εἱμαρμένην.

QUAESTIO III.13

Περὶ τοῦ ἐφ' ἡμῖν τινα.

Ἐπεὶ τὸ ἐφ' ἡμῖν ἐστι ἐν λογικῇ συγκαταθέσει (διὰ τοῦτο γὰρ ἐν 5
μόνῳ τῷ ἀνθρώπῳ τὸ ἐφ' ἡμῖν, ὅτι καὶ μόνος τῶν ζῴων ἄνθρωπος λο-
γικός τέ ἐστι καὶ βουλευτικός), συγκατατίθεται μὲν γὰρ καὶ τὰ ἄλογα ζῷα,
ἀλλὰ ταῦτα μὲν ταῖς φαντασίαις ταῖς ἀπὸ τῶν αἰσθητῶν διὰ τῶν αἰσθή- 10
10 σεων γινομέναις ἐν αὐτοῖς ἑπόμενα καὶ τῷ ἀπὸ τούτων ἐν αὐτοῖς γινομένῳ πάθει τὰς συγκαταθέσεις ποιεῖται ἀγόμενα ὑπ' αὐτῶν, ᾗ ἂν ἐκεῖνα
ἄγῃ, ὁ δ' ἄνθρωπος, ὅταν ὡς ἄνθρωπος ποιῆται τὰς συγκαταθέσεις, δεῖται 15
πρὸς ταῖς φαντασίαις καὶ λόγου, ὃν ἔχων παρὰ τῆς φύσεως πρὸς τὴν τῶν
τοιούτων κρίσιν ἄνθρωπός ἐστιν, δι' οὗ λόγου κρίνει τὰ φαντάσματα. διὸ
15 κἂν βουλευομένῳ περὶ τῆς προσπεσούσης φαντασίας αὐτῷ μὴ τοιοῦτον 20
δοκῇ, ὁποῖον τὴν ἀρχὴν ἐφαίνετο, οὐ συγκατατίθεται αὐτῇ, συγκατατιθέ-
μενος ἂν τῷ ὅσον ἐπὶ τῷ ἀπὸ τῆς φαντασίας πάθει, καὶ ἔστι προαίρεσις   *
ἡ τοιαύτη συγκατάθεσις ὄρεξις οὖσα βουλευτική. τὸ γὰρ ἐκ τῆς βουλῆς 25
περὶ τοῦ ἐκ τοῦ αἰσθητοῦ [τε] | καὶ πρὸ αὐτοῦ προκριθὲν ἡ προαίρεσις. εἰ 207   *
20 μὲν οὖν καὶ βουλευομένοις ἡμῖν εἵπετο τῇ φαντασίᾳ συγκατατίθεσθαι, οὐκ
ἂν ἦν ἐφ' ἡμῖν οὐδ' ἡ μετὰ τῆς βουλῆς συγκατάθεσις, ἐπεὶ δὲ ἀλλοιο-
τέραν ἡμῖν πολλάκις τὸ βουλεύσασθαι τὴν συγκατάθεσιν ποιεῖ τὴν ἐπὶ φαν- 5
τασίᾳ τοῦ ἀπ' αὐτῆς πάθους, οὐκέτ' ἂν εὐλόγως ταῖς φαντασίαις λεγοίμεθα
συγκατατίθεσθαι. ἐπεὶ μηδὲ ταῖς φαντασίαις συγκατατιθέμεθα, ἣν δὲ τοῦ   *
25 ἐφ' ἡμῖν ἀναιρετικὸν τοῦτο, οὐδ' ἂν τὸ ἐφ' ἡμῖν εἶναί τι ἀναιροῖτο. καὶ 10
γὰρ εἰ μὲν εἵπετο πάντως ἡμῖν τὸ βουλεύεσθαι ἐπὶ πάσῃ φαντασίᾳ, ἴσως
ἂν ἐδόκει καὶ αὐτὸ οὐκ ἐφ' ἡμῖν εἶναι, ἀλλὰ σύμπτωμά τι τῆς φαντασίας
γενόμενον ὑπ' αὐτῆς, οὗ παρ' ἐκείνῃ τὸ εἶναι ἔχοντος ἔδοξεν ἂν καὶ ἡ 15
ἐπ' αὐτῷ συγκατάθεσις κατ' ἐκείνην γίνεσθαι, καθ' ἣν καὶ τὸ βουλεύεσθαι,
30 ἐφ' ᾧ ἡ συγκατάθεσις. εἰ δὲ μὴ ἡ φαντασία τοῦ βουλεύεσθαι τὸν ἄνθρωπον κυρία, ἀλλ' ἔστιν ἐπ' αὐτῷ καὶ τὸ βουλεύσασθαι καὶ τὸ μή 20
(πολλαῖς γοῦν φαντασίαις χωρὶς τοῦ βουλεύσασθαι συγκατατιθέμεθα τοῖς
ἀλόγοις ζῴοις παραπλησίως), οὐδ' ἂν ἡ τοιαύτη συγκατάθεσις τῆς φαντασίας ἔργον εἴη ὑπεναντιουμένη ἐν πολλοῖς τε αὐτῇ καὶ πολλαχῶς. ὅτι δ' 25
35 ἡμεῖς τοῦ βουλεύεσθαι περὶ τῶν φαντασιῶν κύριοι, δῆλον ἔκ τε τοῦ προ-
ειρημένου τοῦ ἡμᾶς ἔχειν τὴν ἐξουσίαν τοῦ βουλεύσασθαί τε καὶ μή, καὶ
μὴ τὴν φαντα|σίαν εἶναι τούτου κυρίαν. εἰ γὰρ μὴ φαντασία, τί ἂν ἄλλο 208
τεθείη παρ' ἡμᾶς τὸ κύριον τοῦδε; οὐ γὰρ ἐπεὶ κοινότερον λέγομεν φαίνε-   108
σθαι ἡμῖν καὶ τὸ κατὰ τὸν λόγον εὑρεθέν τε καὶ δόξαν, ἤδη χρὴ φαντα- 5
σίαν τε καὶ ἐπὶ φαντασίᾳ λέγειν τὴν τοιαύτην συγκατάθεσιν, εἴ γε ἡ κυρίως
φαντασία ἐστὶν κίνησις ὑπὸ τῆς κατ' ἐνέργειαν αἰσθήσεως. ἀλλὰ τὸ ἐπαι-
5 νεῖσθαι μὲν τοὺς βουλευομένους, ψέγεσθαι δὲ τοὺς μή, σημεῖον τοῦ ἐφ'
ἡμῖν εἶναι τὸ βουλεύεσθαι καὶ μὴ τῆς φαντασίας ἔργον. οἱ γὰρ ἔπαινοι 10
καὶ οἱ ψόγοι ἐπὶ τοῖς ἐφ' ἡμῖν, διὸ ἐπὶ ταῖς φαντασίαις οὔτε ἐπαινούμεθα
οὔτε ψεγόμεθα, εἰ μή τισιν αὐτῶν ἡμεῖς αἴτιοι. ἐπὶ δὲ ταῖς ἐπ' αὐταῖς
συγκαταθέσεσιν ἤδη τούτων θάτερον. ψεγόμεθα γὰρ καὶ τῶν φαντασιῶν 15

228   On Aristotle's Topics

10 ἐπ' ἐκείναις, ὅσαι γίνονταί γε δι' ἀνασκησίαν ἡμῖν τοιαῦται, ἧς ἀσκήσεως
* ἡμεῖς ἦμεν κύριοι. ἐπεὶ τὸ συμβούλους παραλαμβάνειν ἢ καὶ τοῦδε μᾶλλον
ἢ ἀντὶ τῶνδε ἐφ' ἡμῖν, δῆλον ὡς ἐφ' ἡμῖν καὶ τὸ βουλεύεσθαι τὴν ἀρχήν. 20
εἰ γὰρ ἐφ' ἡμῖν τὸ τοῖσδε χρήσασθαι συμβούλοις, δι' οὓς ἡ τοιαύτη συγκατάθεσις, ἐφ' ἡμῖν καὶ τὸ βουλεύεσθαι. ἐπεὶ περὶ τῶν ἐκ προνοίας
15 ἁμαρτανομένων μείζους αἱ κολάσεις ὡς κατὰ προαίρεσιν πεποιηκότων, δῆλον 25
ὡς καὶ πᾶν τὸ ἐκ προνοίας γινόμενον ἐφ' ἡμῖν. |

Alexander, in Aristotelis Topicorum libros viii
Commentaria, ed. M. Wallies, Commentaria in
Aristotelem Graeca 2.2 (Berlin, 1891).

1.. 76.26-77.3 (Aristotle 1.11   104 b 5).

ἑ κ α τ ε ρ ο ι δὲ ἑ α υ τ ο ῖ ς ἐναντίως
27 | δοξάζωσιν, ἐν μὲν τοῖς σοφοῖς περὶ τῆς
28 εἱμαρμένης, περὶ τῆς ἀθανασίας | τῆς ψυχῆς, περὶ
ἀπείρου, περὶ κενοῦ, περὶ τῶν τοιούτων, οἱ δὲ
77.1 πολλοὶ πρὸς | ἀλλήλους, ἐν οἷς οἱ μὲν αὐτῶν τὴν
2 ὑγείαν τοῦ πλούτου αἱρετωτέραν οἱ | δὲ ἔμπαλιν
λέγουσι, καὶ οἱ μὲν ἰσχὺν κάλλους οἱ δὲ κάλλος
3 ἰσχύος προτι|μῶσι, καὶ ὅσα τοιαῦτα.

2. 95.7-12 (Aristotle 1.14   105 b 25).

8 ἔστι δέ τινα | προβλήματα καὶ προτάσεις καὶ ἐν
9 τοῖς φυσικοῖς "πρὸς αἵρεσιν καὶ φυγήν" | τὴν
ἀναφορὰν ἔχοντα· τὸ γὰρ 'πότερον πάντα καθ'
10 εἱμαρμένην καὶ | κατηναγκασμένως γίνεται;' φυσικὸν
11 ὂν τὴν ἀναφορὰν ἔχει "πρὸς αἵρεσιν | καὶ φυγήν"·
εἰ γὰρ δοκεῖ βουλεύεσθαι περὶ τῶν πρακτέων ἢ μή,
12 ἐντεῦθεν | ἤρτηται.

3. 566.18-23 (Aristotle 8.11   161 b 11).

19 λέγει γίνεσθαι καὶ ἐν τῷ διαλέγεσθαι καθ' αὑτὸ
ἁμαρτίας ἐν λόγοις | καὶ παρὰ τὴν ἄγνοιαν καὶ ὅτι
οὐ διώρισται πότε τὰ ἀντικείμενα κ α ὶ π ό τ ε
20 | τ ὰ ἐ ν ἀ ρ χ ῇ λ α μ β ά ν ο υ σ ι· διὰ
21 γὰρ τὸ ἀγνοεῖν τοῦτο πολλάκις ἐν τοῖς | λόγοις
ἁμαρτάνουσι. καὶ ταῦτα συμβαίνει καὶ ἐφ' ἑαυτῶν
22 λέγοντας καὶ | ἀποκρινομένους· ὁ γὰρ λέγων πάντα
23 εἶναι καθ' εἱμαρμένην καὶ εἶναί τινα | ἐνδεχόμενα
καὶ ἐφ' ἡμῖν τὰ ἀντικείμενα αὐτῷ λέγων λανθάνει.

4. 570.4-11 (Aristotle 8.11 161 b 38).

5   ὁ γὰρ | ἀναιρῶν τὸ τὰ πάντα καθ' εἱμαρμένην
6   γίνεσθαι καὶ λόγον διὰ τὸ μάτην | εἶναι τούς τε
    ἐπαίνους καὶ τοὺς ψόγους καθ' αὑτὸν μὲν
7   ἐξεταζόμενος οὐκ | ἂν ἄξιος ἐπιτιμήσεως φαίνοιτο.
    εἰ δέ τις αὐτὸν ἐξετάζοι πρὸς τὸ πρόβλημα,
8 | ἐνδεεστέρως ἂν ἔχειν δοκοῖ τῷ διὰ πλειόνων καὶ
9   ἐνδοξοτέρων δύνασθαι τὸ | προκείμενον δείκνυσθαι·
    διὰ γὰρ τοῦ ἀναιρεῖσθαι πᾶν τὸ ἐνδεχόμενον, ἀλλὰ
10 | καὶ τὸ ἐφ' ἡμῖν, ὡς μάτην εἶναι καὶ τὸ
    βουλεύεσθαι· οὕτω δὲ καὶ τὸ μὴ εἶναι τὴν ἀρετὴν
11 καὶ τὴν κακίαν | ἐφ' ἡμῖν ἀναιρεῖται.

Sigla

(cf. also Introduction, pp. 29-32)

A   Parisinus 1868 (f.166.2-end).

B   Venetus Marcianus gr. 261 (16th cent.; all the works included here. On B^2 cf. Bruns *Suppl. Ar.* 2.2 p. xxiii).

C   Parisinus 2049 (f).

E   Mutinensis Estensis III G 6 (15th-16th cent.; q, f. Bruns' G in q).

F   Neapolitanus III D 12 (1523; q).

H   Havniensis BVH 88 8° Fabr. (16th-17th cent.; m 24, 25, f, q2.4, 2.5).

K   Vaticanus Urbanus 54 (16th cent.; all).

P   Matritensis cod. reg. 109 (15th cent.; m 22-25. Bruns' C in m).

S   Venetus Marcianus append. A IV cod. X (16th-17th cent.; q, f. On S^2 cf. Bruns loc. cit. under B^2.)

V   Venetus Marcianus gr. 258 (10th cent.; all).

     v.c.V – vetus corrector (10th cent.; cf. Bruns *Suppl. Ar.* 2.1 vi-viii).

     V^2 – altera manus (12th cent.; cf. ibid. viii ff.).

W   Vindobonensis phil. gr. 110 (16th cent.; m. 181.2 – end. Bruns' K in m.)

lat.   13th cent. Latin translation (above, p. 29 and n. 205), ed. P. Thillet, *Alexandre d'Aphrodise, de fato ad imperatores, Version de Guillaume de Moerbeke* (Paris, 1963). (f, m. 25).

     lat. (E) Scorialensis lat. V III. 6 (end of 13th cent.).

     lat. (G) Parisinus lat. 16 096 (end of 13th cent.).

     lat. (O) Oxoniensis Corp. Christ. Coll. 243 (1423)

arab.	Arabic version of *m*. 23, tr. Abu 'Utman al-Dimasqi; ed. H.-J. Ruland (below, p. 287) 194-210, cf. 227-231.
a¹	V. Trincavellius, ed., *Opera Themistii omnia*, etc., Venice, Aldus, 1534 (*m, f*).
a²	id., *Quaestiones Alexandri Aphrodisiensis naturales*, etc., Venice, Zanetti, 1536 (*q, f*).
Cas.	J. Caselius, ed., *Alexandri Aphrodisiensis de fato*, etc., Rostock 1588 (*f*).
Vict.	Marginalia of P. Victorius in copies in Munich of a¹ (*m, f*), a² (*q*). Cf. O preface (= O's 'Mon.'), Bruns *Suppl. Ar.* 2.1 xiv, 2.2 xxv.
Lond.	*Alexandri Aphrodisiensis de fato*, etc., anon. ed. and trans.; London, typis T. Roycroft, 1658. (*f*). Cf. R.W. Sharples, 'Dr John Fell – editor of Alexander of Aphrodisias?', *Liverpool Classical Monthly* 4 (1979) 9-11.
y	MS notes in copy of Lond. in British Library (shelf-mark 525b2) Cf. p. 31.
O	J. Orelli, ed., *Alexandri Aphrodisiensis de fato quae supersunt*, etc., Zurich, 1824 (*f, m*. 24, 25).
Sp.	L. Spengel, ed., *Alexandri Aphrodisiensis quaestionum naturalium et moralium libri quattuor*, etc., Munich 1842 (*q*).
Bruns	I. Bruns, ed., *Supplementum Aristotelicum* 2.1 (Berlin, 1887; *m*), 2.2 (ibid. 1892; *q, f*).
Eusebius	*Praep. Ev.* 6.9 (*f*, parts; cf. p. 29 and n. 201). Sigla of K. Mras, ed., *Eusebius: Praeparatio Evangelica* (Berlin, 1954; Die griech christ. Schriftsteller, vol. 43.2).
Cyr.	Cyril of Alexandria *contra Julianum* 3, *PG* 76.621c (*f*.XXVII 198.19-26). Cf. R.M. Grant in *Journal of Theological Studies* n.s. 15 (1964) 272.
Bag.¹	*Hieronymi Bagolini Veronensis in interpretationem Alexandri Aphrodisiensis de fato praefatio*, etc., Verona 1516 (*f, m*. 22-25, *q*. 1.4, 2.21, 3.13).
Bag.²	*Alexandri Aphrodisiensis Peripatetici doctissimi Quaestiones naturales et morales et de fato*, Hieronymo Bagolino Veronensi patre et Ioanne Baptista filio interpreibus, Venice, 1541 etc. (*f. q.*)
Bag.	agreement of Bag.¹ and Bag.²

c	*Alexandri Aphrodisiensis ... de anima liber secundus,* Angelo Caninio Anglarensi interprete; with 1546 and subsequent eds. of Bag.[2] (*m*; *m*. 24-25 reprinted in O).
Grotius	H. Grotius, *Philosophorum veterum sententiae de fato,* etc., Paris 1648 / Leiden 1648 (*f*; reprinted in O).
Schulthess	J.G. Schulthess, *Bibliothek der griechischen Philosophie* IV, Zurich 1782 (*f*); also his annotations in his copy of Lond., cited by O.
Nourrisson	F. Nourrisson, *De la liberté et du hasard: Essai sur Alexandre d'Aphrodise suivi du Traité du Destin,* etc., Paris 1870 (*f*; paraphrases of *m*. 22-25 in ch. 3 of the *Essai*.)
Fitzgerald	*Alexander of Aphrodisias on Destiny,* translated into English by Augustine Fitzgerald. London, 1931. (*f*).
Boussoulas	N.-I. Boussoulas, 'Recherches Philosophiques; II, Alexandre d'Aphrodise, Traité du destin et de ce qui dépend de nous', 'Analekta (cf. above, p. 19 n. 118) 10 (1961) 80-135, cf. 144. (*f*).

(There is also a translation of *f*. into Latin, which I have not seen, by G. Hervetus, Lyon, 1544.)

Casp. O. (= J. Caspar Orelli) Bloch	} conjectures cited from O.
Heine	O. Heine, *Stoicorum de fato doctrina,* progr. Naumburg, 1859.
Gercke	A. Gercke, 'Chrysippea', *Jahrb. f. Klass. Phil.* Supplbd. 14 (1885) 689-781.
Schwartz Usener	} conjectures cited from Gercke or Bruns.
Diels	conjectures cited from Bruns.
Apelt	O. Apelt, 'Die kleinen Schriften des Alexander von Aphrodisias', *Rh. Mus.* 49 (1894) 59-71.
von Arnim	H. von Arnim, 'Textkritik zur Alexander von Aphrodisias', *Wiener Studien* 22 (1900) 1-10.
SVF	id., *Stoicorum Veterum Fragmenta* (above, p. xi).
Rodier	G. Rodier, 'Conjectures sur le texte du *de fato* d'Alexandre d'Aphrodise', *Rev. de Philol.* n.s. 25 (1901) 66-71.

Amand   Cf. below, p. 000.

Hackforth   R. Hackforth, 'Notes on some passages of
             Alexander Aphrodisiensis *de fato*', *Class. Quart.* 40
             (1946) 37-44.

Donini   P.L. Donini, 'Note al *Pen heimarmenes* di Alessandro
             di Afrodisia', *Rivista di Filologia* 97 (1969) 298-313.

Notes on the Text

De Fato cap. I

p.164.4 αὐτῷ BSa¹²Lond.O; αὐτῷ V. 6 lege μαρτυρίας
[ἧς] δίκαιος. ἧς delendum coni. Bruns; ἧς VHa¹; ὧν
Ηγρ.a²; ὧν E mg.; ὡς Lond.Diels; τῆς B²; ὡς ὧν
δίκαιος εἴην coni.O; cum testimonio tali quod dignus
est obtinere lat. (Thillet, 17). 6-9 ἐπεὶ δὲ καὶ
[εἰ] μὴ ... δύναται (ἐφεῖται γὰρ θύειν ... οἶόν τε),
ἐθάρσησα coni. Donini. 7 ἐφεῖται] ἐντέλλεται V mg.;
precipitur lat. lege ἱεροῖς <τοῖς θεοῖς> θύειν
(Bag.Cas. Grotius O Donini, sed post θύειν Cas.O).
9 ἐξουσίᾳ] μιμήσει B². τινας Lond. 10 ἀπαρχὴν
HESB²Cas.O; ἀπαρχῆς Va¹²; ἀπ' ἀρχῆς lat.K; ἀπαρχὰς
Lond. καὶ ἀνάθημα B². 13 περιέχει B² lat.;
περιέχειν Va¹². τε] δὲ coni.O; γὰρ Diels.
19 τινα ἃ καὶ a²Cas.O. 20 ἔχοντα V²(?) a¹; ἔχουσιν
V¹a² Cas.O. et non esse omnium prefixas causas lat.,
? ex coniectura (cf. Donini 299). lege αὐτῷ, coni.
Casp.O, Donini; ipso lat., αὐτῇ codd. gr. 21 ἐστιν
(del.) δοκεῖ τῷ δοκεῖν E; δοκεῖ τῷ δοκεῖν a² Cas.O.

p.165.1 <ἡ> add. Diels. μὴ V²a¹²; om. V¹; in lit.
B; οὐχ von Arnim. 2 ἀντιλογια sic V¹; ἀντιλογίαν V²
lat.; ἐν ἀντιλογίαν B. 2-3 lege ἐν τοῖς μάλιστα καὶ
αὐτὸ τοῦτ' εἶναι νομίζω), κατὰ τὴν 'Αριστοτέλους δόξαν
εἰπὼν ποιήσομαι (Hackforth). καὶ Hackforth; κἂν von
Arnim; κατ' cett. αὐτὸ Hackforth, von Arnim; αὐτοῦ
cett. τοῦτ' εἶναι Hackforth; τεὶ εἰεν V (in mg. τι ut
vid. v.c.); τει ειεν B; τί εἶεν HSa²; εἶεν (in mg.
εἰρηκότες) E; τί εἴη? K; τί εἴη ἂν Cas.O; οὐδὲν οἶμαι
a¹Lond.; τοῦτό γ' εἴη von Arnim. νομίζω Hackforth;
μείζω ει VH; μείζω ἢ a¹²; μεῖζον ἢ Cas.; ἅμα τῷ von
Arnim. fort. <τὰ> κατὰ Hackforth. εἰπὼν Hackforth;
εἰπεῖν cett. ... fit manifestior, nos qui
Aristotelis opinionem s e q u i m u r faciemus
sermonem ad eos qui dixerunt de hiis non similiter
illi lat. (cf. Thillet ad loc.), quae ex coniectura

Adnot. ad text.: c.I-III

esse censet Donini, 299f. 5 ἡμῖν lat. a¹²O.
8 πράσσετε] preestis lat. γοῦν] γὰρ lat.O; οὖν E.
10 δόξει V²a¹²; δόξαι V¹ lat.; δόξει <τινὰ> coni. O.

cap.II

p.165.14 τι] τε coni. O. 20 τἄλλα ὧν ἐν τοῖς
V²a¹²O; ἄλλα ων αυτοῖς sic V¹; ἀλλὰ ὧν αὐτοῖς E;
τἄλλα ὧν αὐτοῖς S². 21 οὐκ] ἀλλ᾽ H; del. Casp.O.
24 οὐκέθ᾽] οὐ καθόλου ES. 24-25 οὐ γὰρ - οὐδὲ del.
Freudenthal (cf. Bibliog.) 14f. n.1, Bruns. Ante
ἅπαντες habet lat. concordant; cf. Thillet 17.
26 αὐτῷ om. a²O.

cap.III

p.166.16 ὧν del. V²; pro ὧν εἶναι exh. lat. quorum est
(Thillet, 16). 17 τι V² lat.; τε V¹. 18 γίνεται
V² lat. a¹; γίνεσθαι V¹a². 19 πρῶτον V² lat. a¹;
πρώτην V¹a². 22 αἰτιῶν Euseb.(I) Lond.O. 23 καθὼς
αἰτίας V¹ lat.; καθὼς V²a¹; καθ᾽ ἃς αἰτίας a²; καθὼς
ὁ θεῖος Euseb. Lond.O, 'fort. recte' Bruns.
24,25 inter ipsas (sc. causas), lat. in utroque loco;
cf. Comm. 28-29 τοσούτων - δεόμενα Euseb.; om. V
(sign. in mg. adposito) lat. a¹²; εἰ καὶ πάντα τὰ
γινόμενά τις σκέψαιτο εὑρήσει οὐχ B².

p.167.1 δ᾽ Euseb. B² Lond.O; γὰρ V lat. a¹². 2 δὴ
Euseb.; γὰρ libri. nobis post δεικνυμένη iterat
lat. (Thillet, 17). 3 δὲ Euseb.(I) Cas.; δὴ libri;
igitur lat. 8 εἰδός ἐστιν Euseb. διοκεῦον ἢ
ἀκοντίζον Euseb.(BON)a¹Lond.O; διοκεύων (sic) ἢ
ἀκοντίζων Euseb.(I). 10 δευτερεῦον Euseb.(ON).
11 γεγονός ἐστι] γέγονε τουτέστι Euseb.; factum est,
scilicet lat. (sed scilicet saepe addit, cf. Thillet
147 s.v.). εἰς del. B²; εἰ Cas. θεοὺς Bruns; θεὸν
Euseb.O; τινος libri. 12 οὐδ᾽ ἂν V²lat.; οὐ γὰρ V¹.
14 ποιητικοῖς V¹γρ.a¹²; τοιούτοις V¹ lat. Cf. Thillet
16. 15f. τῇ ... τέχνη Euseb.

Adnot. ad text.: c.IV-V

cap.IV

p.167.18 δεῖ] δὴ Euseb. 21 λέγει V²lat.; λέγειν V¹.
τῶν γινομένων om. lat. 22 γὰρ om. Euseb.; γε coni.
O. ὑπὸ om. Euseb. 24 καρφῶν Euseb. a²; καρπῶν
V lat. a¹. 25 ἃ om. Euseb. a²; ἃ γὰρ ὅτι O; διότι
Diels, cf. Ind. Arist. 260b49, Doxogr. 742. μὲν οὖν
a²; μὲν γὰρ Euseb. 26 τίνος Va¹; τινὸς a² O Long;
τὴν οὗ Euseb.

p.168.5 γινόμενα Euseb. 6 ἐνστὰν Euseb.(ἐνιστᾶν cod.
B) a² Casp.O; ἐστ' ἂν V¹; del. V²; om. a¹O; aliquando
lat. (i.e. ποτε or ποτ' ἂν? Thillet, 17). 7 τέλος
(pr.) om. Euseb. 168.12 lege καὶ <τὰ> κατα; ita Euseb.
(om. ND), lat. (cod. O), Donini; om. libri.
13 αὐτοῖς Gaisford ad Euseb. 14 γίνεται a²Bruns;
γίνεσθαι V lat. Euseb. a¹O; ὡς γίνεσθαι Schwartz.
17 punct. post αὐτοῖς, non post ποιοῦσαν; ita V, lat.,
Donini. 17f. et d e generatione ipsorum faciens
ipsa habet ratiocinationem de ipsis lat.; sed de (pr.)
ex coniectura esse censet Donini. 18 lege <αἴτιον ὁ>
τοῦ ποιοῦντος cum Donini; ὁ exhib. Euseb. Lond.O.
γίνεται] γ in lit. V; ἡγεῖται Euseb. Lond.O. τρίτον
δέ ἐστιν ἐν Euseb. Bag.¹; ἔστιν ἐν V a¹Bag.²; sunt
autem in lat.; ἔστιν οὖν ἐν a²; ἔστιν οὖν Cas.Lond.;
πρόσεστιν οὖν y. 20 προηγουμένως B²Euseb.(vulg.)
Bag²Lond.O; προηγουμένων V lat. (et Euseb. cod. C; sed
cf. introd. n.208); quae principalem alicuius gratia
fiunt sic Bag¹. Cf. Comm. 21 μὲν ὅτι πᾶν τὸ πρὸ a²;
μὲν δῆλον ὅτι πᾶν τὸ πρὸ E; μὲν τὰ πρὸ Euseb.
γινόμενον om. Euseb.

cap. V

p.168.26 ποίῳ] τίνι Euseb.

p.169.3 ἐπεὶ τῶν] in hiis lat. 9 γοῦν] γὰρ Lond.O.
10 τε] δὲ EO; om. lat. 12 ὧν] quomodo lat. (= ὡς?
Thillet 146).

cap.VI

p.169.20 κατὰ φύσιν καὶ τὸ κατὰ φύσιν εἱμαρμένον add.
V² in marg.; om. lat. (Thillet, 16). 22 καθ'
εἱμαρμένην δ' οὖ a²0. 24 αἴτια (ἔστιν δὲ ταῦτα <τὰ>
Bruns; αἰτίας ἔστι ὁδὲ ταῦτα V¹; αἴτια τάτε V²Ba¹;
αἴτια H; αἴτιά ἐστιν· οἱ δὲ (ἤτοι E², οἱ δ' Lond.)
αὐτὰ τὰ KESa²Cas.Lond.; αἴτια τὰ O; causas ...
aliquando (= αἰτίας ἔστιν ὅτε?) lat., cf. Thillet ad
loc. 24f. τὴν ... εὔτακτον περιφορὰν a². 25 καὶ
τῆς εἱμαρμένης δὲ αἴτια λέγουσιν τὰ αὐτά V²a¹0.
27 τούτοις] talibus lat. (= τοιούτοις? Thillet 17).
ὡς] quomodo lat. (= πῶς? Thillet 146). 29 παρὰ y.
30 lege ἐμποδιζομένη ποτέ. διὸ [μὲν] ὡς ἐπὶ (Diels);
ἐμποδιζομένη διὸ ποτὲ μὲν ὡς ἐπὶ libri (ποτε om.
lat.; διόπερ pro διὸ ποτὲ μὲν B). μὲν (alt.) -om. lat.
a²0; post γίνεται coll. H. 31 ἔχει del. V²; exh.
lat.

170.2 οὔτε]fort. οὐδὲ, Bruns in app. 3 punct. etiam
post ἀνθρώπου. ὡς V²lat.a¹²; οὐκ V¹. ὥστε] lege
οὔτε (Apelt, Rodier); ὥστε V lat. a²; ὅθεν a¹Lond.
καὶ del. Diels, om. lat. 5 οὐκ ἀεὶ Schulthess O.
τοῦ add. Lond.O. 6 τέχνην <τοῦ παρὰ τέχνην> coni.0;
subaudiri tamen potest. 12 τὴν καταστροφὴν a²0;
αἱ ἀναστροφαὶ B². Cf. mantissa 185.16. 13 τοῦον
(bís) Bruns, cf. mantissa 169.36; τοιὸν (bis) libri;
τοιόνδε (bis) Euseb. 14 καταστάσει Euseb.(ND) Vict.
ὁμοίως ἐπὶ πάντων οὐδὲ ἐξ ἀνάγκης Euseb. Vict.
ἐκκροῦσαι πολλάκις Euseb. τάξιν] ἕξιν Euseb. (ex
λέξιν corr. Euseb. cod. O). ἀέρων] βίων Euseb.
Vict. 16 συμβουλίαι Euseb.; cf. mant. 185.21.
17 παρὰ] κατὰ Schulthess O; sed cf. mant. 185.22 et
Comm. 18 ἀνθρώπῳ Lond.O. 21 lege ἀκολουθεῖν
(Donini, cf. mant.185.26); ἀκολούθως V lat. a¹²;
ἀκολούθους Lond.Cas.O. 24 ἂν μὴ] ἀλλ' εἰ a²0.
καταζῆν] vita deficere lat. αυτῷ sic V. 25 lege
γενόμενον ἐκσείσῃ τοῦ κατὰ φύσιν <βίου, τῷ δὲ
καρτερικῷ> αἱ τῶν (Donini); factum eiciat ab eo quod
secundum naturam lat.; γενόμενος ἐκπισητης κατὰ φύσιν

Adnot. ad text.: c.VI-VII

etc. V; γενόμενος ἐκ πίσῃ τῆς κ.φ. a¹; γενόμενος ἐκπέσῃ
τῆς κ.φ. H; γενόμενον (γενώμενον a²) ἑκστῇ τῆς κ.φ.
Hγρ.ESKa²Lond.; γενόμενον ἑκστῇ τοῦ κ.φ. Cas.O; καὶ τῷ
καρτερικῷ ante αἱ τῶν πόνων addenda coni. O 271 n.27a
ex mant.185.29; γενόμενον ἐμποδίζῃ, <τῷ δὲ καρτερικῷ>
κ.φ. Bruns; γενόμενον ἐκσείσῃ τῆς <ἀκολασίας, τῷ δὲ
καρτ.> κ.φ. Diels; ἐν αὐτῷ γεννώμενος ἐκπέσῃ τῆς κ.φ.
<ἀκολασίας, τῷ δὲ καρτ.> τὴν φύσιν Apelt. 26 αἱ ἐν
τοῖς ES; ἐν τοῖς a²O; μεν τοις V¹lat.; μεν τι τοῖς V²;
μέντοι τοῖς Ha¹.

p.171.1 πάλιν om. lat. εἰσὶ in lit. V; exh. lat.
4 κατ' αὐτὰ] lege κατὰ ταῦτα (Bruns in app., lat.).
τούτοις ES lat.; τούτοις διὸ a²Cas.; τούτους V¹; διὸ
V²Ha¹Lond.O; τοῦτο οὖν Schwartz. 5 τοιούτοις] istos
lat. (= τούτοις, Thillet 17). τε] γε V². <καὶ>
add. V²a¹²O; om. V¹lat. (Thillet, 16). 5f. εἱμαρμένην
lat. H Lond.O; εἱμαρμέναις V; εἱμαρμένας ES;
εἱμαρμένης a¹²Cas. 6 γεγόνοσιν V; fort. γεγόνασιν,
Sandbach. αἴτιοι a². 8 πάντως αὐτοὺς V lat. a¹;
πάντα αὐτοὺς a²; πάντα αὐτοῖς O. 9 πάντα κατὰ τὴν
φύσιν lat. Donini. 14 ἐσφάλθαι Euseb.

cap.VII

p.171.20 noli τε delere; om. Cas., del. Bruns, sed cf.
Apelt ad loc., qui Platonis Philebum 63e in ius vocat.
21 παραλλήλας Va¹; παράλληλα a²; παραλλήλῳ Cas.Lond.O;
secus invicem lat. 23 ἀπορῆσαι V¹; ἀπορήσειε V²a¹².
λέγοντες Schwartz; λέγονται libri (sine accentu V).
24 ταύτῃ a²Casp.O, 'fort. recte' Bruns. 24 τοὺς
φιλοσοφοῦντας del. Bruns. 25 ὑπολαμβάνοντες a²;
ὑπολαμβάνοντες (supr. ντες: υσιν)V; ὑπολαμβάνουσιν lat.
a¹O.

p.172.1 αὐτοῖς H. ἀναφέροντας in mg. μεταφέροντας H.
δόξῃ del. Diels. 9 σώζει lat. Lond.; σώζειν V;
σώζειν a¹². αὐτὰ V(η supra τὰ V², ut vid.), lat.;
αὐτά ἐστι a¹². 13 σώζεται V²a¹²; σώζεσθαι V¹; salvat
lat. <ἂν> V²lat.a¹O; om. V¹a². 14 interimit
naturam eorum que sic fiunt e t s i m i l i t e r

Adnot. ad text.: c.VII-VIII

nominat lat. (Thillet 17). 14 αὐτὰ δεῖξαι] lege ἂν
αὐτὰ δείξῃ (Rodier); αὐτὰ δεῖξαι V¹a², ἂν αὐτὰ δεῖξαι
V²a¹0, ἂν ἀποδείξῃ Schwartz.   15 δυνάμενα a²;
δυνάμεναϚ V¹; δυνηθῇ V²a¹0. sed quia ipsa ostendere
potest lat.   κατηγορεῖσθαι V²a¹²; κατηγορεῖται V¹
lat.

cap.VIII

p.172.19 lege προηγουμένωϚ cum V¹lat.a²; προηγουμέναι
V²a¹Lond.0. 'Exspectes προηγουμένωϚ ποιητικαῖϚ' Bruns
cf. Comm.   20 γινομένου V¹, corr. v.c.; γενομένῳ
Euseb.   δέ τι ὅπερ Euseb.   24 οἷϚ ... γίνεσθαι]
qui dicunt aliqua a fortuna fieri lat., cf.
Thillet 17.   25 κἂν] lege ὅταν cum Eusebio; κἂν
V¹a²; ἂν V²lat.a¹Lond.0.   28 ἔμελε V²0; ἔμελλε a¹²
Lond.; πάλιν V¹lat.

p.173.3 αὐτῷ V lat. Ha¹²; αὐτῷ Bag.Grotius Lond.0.
<τοῦ> add. Bruns.   precedenti lat. (προελθόντι?).
4 τὸ τὸ lat.(cf. 73.9 Thillet) a¹; το το sic add.
v.c.V; τὸ a²0.   5 αὐτῷ V¹lat.a¹²; αὐτῶν v.c.V.   [τί
... τέλοϚ] del. Bruns: 'aut multa exciderunt ante haec
verba, aut interpretamentum sunt sequentis enuntiati'.
<οὐ> τέλοϚ coni.0; τ in lit. V.   9 ἀπαντήσῃ lat. a¹²
Euseb.; ἀπαντήσει V.   10 δεῖ lat.a²; δεῖν Va¹.
ἡμῖν lat.   15 τῶν lat.a²0; τῶν corr. m¹ ut vid. in τὸν
V; τὸν γρ. τῶν H; τὸ a¹Lond.   τοῖϚ v.c.V lat. a¹²;
τῶν V¹.   ἀπαντώντων τό τε lat. a²; ἀπαντῶν το τε V¹;
ἀπαντῶν, τό, τε V²?; ἀπαντῶν τό τε a¹ (divisim, cf.
181.5, 182.1).   17 προηγησαμένοιϚ ... προηγουμένοιϚ]
precedentibus quibusdam causis tantum lat.; cf. Comm.
19f. lege γενέσθαι; τὸ <δὲ> μηδὲν (von Arnim + SVF
2.968); τὸ del. Bruns, exh. V¹, τωι ut vid. infra
vers. v.c.V, τῷ lat. (cf. Thillet 16) a¹, τοὺϚ a²Lond.
0.   21 lege ὄνομα, τῷ μὴ cum V¹, von Arnim + SVF
2.968; τῷ γὰρ v.c.V a¹²; τὸ γὰρ lat.(?) 0; <τὸ> γὰρ τῷ
Bruns.   23 αὐτοὺϚ lat.Bag.Grotius 0; αὐτοὺϚ Va¹²
Lond.   καὶ om. a².   24 κωλύσει V²a¹; κωλύσαντεϚ
V¹(post υ lit. 1 litt.) lat.a²; κωλύσανταϚ E Cas.

Adnot. ad text.: c.VIII-IX

25 ἀποδεῖν] concedentes lat. 26 οὐκ ἀπὸ V¹lat.; ἀπὸ
V²a¹²O. ἀλλ᾽ οὐκ ἐπὶ τῷ B²a²; ἀλλ᾽ ἐπὶ V¹lat.; ἀλλ᾽
οὐκ ἐπὶ τὸ V²; ἀλλ᾽ οὐκ ἐπὶ B¹a¹; ἀλλὰ ES.

p.174.1 lege τὸ αὐτομάτως (Donini ex lat.); τὸ
αὐτόματον libri (τὸ om. a²Lond.O); τοῦ αὐτομάτου
quoque coni. Donini. 2 <ἢ> add. V², exh. lat.
(Thillet 16) a²Lond.O. 7 αὐτοὺς] αὐτοὺς Va²Lond.;
persuasum habent ipsi lat. οὐδεὶς γοῦν Va¹; οὐ δεῖ
γὰρ a²Lond.O; nullius (G; nullis EO) enim lat. (cf.
Thillet ad loc.). 8 λέγει V lat.a¹; λέγειν a²Lond.
O. οὐδ᾽ om. a². 9 ζητεῖ lat.B²; ζητεῖν Va¹O; μὴ
ζητεῖν a²Lond. 11 lege ὑπὸ (nos); ἐπὶ. 12 ὧν
ἄδηλον ἡ αἰτία λέγεται ὑπό τινων εἶναι V¹(marg.), lat.
(post λεγομένων). Cf. Thillet 17, 73, et Comm.
κυριωτέρως coni.O; principaliter lat. 13 ἂν lat.a²O;
///ν V; ὧν a¹. 18 προηγούμενα V lat.a¹Lond.O;
προηγουμένως a². <τὰ> add. a². 22 ὁποῖα περίαπτά
Euseb., coni.O; οἷα περίαπτα a²Lond.; ὅμοια π|απτά
(supra π: ε/) V; ὅμοια περὶ ἁπτά H; ὅμοια περίαπτά a¹;
que inattingibilia lat. τέ τινα] τινα ποιεῖν
Euseb. προείληπται Euseb.(vulg.; προσείληπται cod.
B); πρὸς ἐπίληψιν y. 25 <τι> add. Cas.(sed ante ἀπὸ)
Lond.O; οὐδὲν ante τούτων add. B². τούτων] haec
lat.Bag.Grotius. 26 ποιεῖν(pr.)] fieri lat.(EG);
sunt lat.(O).

cap.IX

p.174.29 περὶ a²; ἐπὶ Va¹.

p.175.7 οὐκ ἀδύνατον B². <ἂν> εἴη Bruns; εἴη Lond.
O; ειη μη (sed μη del. et, supra ειη, ηει legendum
indicavit) V; erit lat.; εἴη μὴ Ha¹²; μὴ ES (et fort. H
γρ., sed cf. infra; incertum an de εἴη dubitaverit.)
γίνεσθαι VH; γενέσθαι Ηγρ.a¹². 8 fort. ἄτοπον,
Bruns in app. τούτου SVF 2.936. 10 αὐτοῦ V lat.;
αὐτοῦ a¹²O; αὐτῷ Lond. τότε V lat.(GO) a¹O; ποτὲ
a²; πότε Lond. tunc possibile lat.(GO); compossibile
lat.(E). 11 τὴν (alt.) B²Euseb.Cas.Lond.O; τὸ Va¹².

242

δακτύλου τινὸς] τοῦ δακτύλου Euseb. 13 ἄλλως
Schwartz; ἀλλ' ὡς libri. 15 ἐνδέδεται] ἐνδέδοται
a²; data sunt lat.; ἐνδέχεται a¹. 17 exspectes
οὐδὲν ἧττον; cf. Sharples Phronesis 20 (1975) 251 n.8.
18 ἢ V²a¹²; τῷ V¹lat.; τι ES. 22 καὶ (pr.) del. B².
τούτῳ]lege τοῦτο (coni. Bruns); τῷ αὐτῷ Lond.O; τούτῳ
cett. 24 ὧν εἰ τὰ] εἰ οὖν B². 27 fort. <ὄντα>
ἕν τινι, Bruns.

p.176.3 ἦν ἐν θατέρῳ HS; ην ενθ' ατερωι V; ην ἐν
θατέρω B; ἦν ἔν|θατέρῳ E; ἦν ἐνδεχόμενον ἐν θατέρῳ
a¹²; quia impossibile erat in altero lat.
(Thillet 18), sed cf. Comm. αὐτῷ ἀντικειμένῳ] lege
αὐτὸ τῶν ἀντικειμένων(nos); αὐτῶν ἀντικειμένων V lat.;
αὐτῶν καὶ τῶν ἀντικειμένων a²; αὐτῶν καὶ τὸ
ἀντικείμενον a¹; αὐτῷ ἀντικειμένῳ Bruns. Cf. Comm.
5 τε del. V², om. lat.a¹². 6 ἐστιν ἐν αὐτοῖς V
lat.; ἐν αὐτοῖς ἐνδεχόμενόν ἐστιν a¹²; ἐν αὐτοῖς B; ἐν
αὐτοῖς ἐστιν O. 7 τῶν ἀντικειμένων V²lat.a¹; τοῖς
ἀντικειμένοις V¹a². ὄντα V²lat.a¹; ων V¹; ὧν a².
τέ ἐστιν om. V¹ESK, exh. V²lat.(τε om.) a¹². τε
post οἷς exh. ESK. 11 τούτων] contrarii horum lat.

cap.X

p.176.14 μὴ] μ add. v.c.V; corr. ex ἢ E; ἢ lat.S.
16 δὲ supr. vers. v.c.V; exh. lat.a¹; om. a².
... γένηται (<τὰ μὲν γὰρ ἀντικείμενα τοῖς γινομένοις
πάντως κωλύεσθαι ὑπό τινων γενέσθαι>, τῶν δὲ ... et μὲν
(15) delendum coni. Long, AGPh 52 (1970) 255; sed cf.
Comm. 16f. γενομένων O. 17 κεκωλῦσθαι Usener;
κεκώλυται libri. Cf. Comm. Parenthesis a διὸ
incipere debet (ita Gercke 83 et Bruns RhMus 44 (1889)
617f.), non a τῶν δὲ (16). "τῶν δὲ ... δυνατά" SVF
2.959 (qui κεκώλυται legit). Cf. Comm. 19 ἂν V¹
lat.(Thillet 16); del. V²; om. a¹². 20 γενέσθαι a¹.
21 γενέσθαι a¹². τούτοις] οὗτοι Gercke 83. εἴ γε
a¹²; ουει γε V; οὗ εἴ γε ES; non enim si lat.
23 τίνα (interrog.) SVF 2.959. ἃ om. a², SVF 2.959.
[μὴ] del. Bruns; μὴ sic V; μὴ lat.a¹².

Adnot. ad text.: c.X

24 παιζόντων] *ridiculum* lat., cf. Thillet 49 and n.4.
οὐ (alt.) om. lat.   26 γνωρίσει V²lat.a¹²; γνωρίζει
V¹; γνωρίζειν (**supra** ειν: σει) S.

p.177.1-2. Lege οὐκ ἔσται δυνατὰ τὰ ὄντα δυνατὰ τοῖς
εἰδόσιν μὲν αὐτὰ κεκωλῦσθαι, ἀγνοοῦσιν δὲ ὑπὸ τίνων
κωλύονται (**Langerbeck**, *Hermes* 71 (1936) 473f.; **sim.**
Apelt, sed τὰ **om.**, κεκωλυμένα, ὑφ' οἵων, **vel** ὑφ' ὧν
αἰτίων, κωλύεται); ὁ.ἔ.δ. ὄντα δυνατοῖς εἰδόσιν μὲν
αὐτὰ κεκωλυκέναι, ἀ. δὲ ὑφ' ἡμῶν κωλύοντες V, **sim.**
lat. (**sed** *prohibere*, *ignorantes*). Post ὄντα add. οὖσι
μαντέσι AC Bag.¹², cf. **Bruns** p.xxxiv. εἰδόσιν] εἴδοσι
a¹, εἰσι a². ὁ.ἔ.δ. αὐτὰ τοῖς εἰδόσι δυνάμενα αὐτὰ
(αὐτὰ **om.**O) κεκωλυκέναι, ἀ. δὲ ἡμῖν τὰ κωλύοντα δυνατὰ
ἔσται Lond.O. Cf. **Comm.**   4 ἐν αὐτοῖς K Schwartz.
5 δυνατὸν (**alt.**)] δυνατὸν <ὂν> SVF 2.960; δυνατοῦ
Lond.O.   οὕτως <λεγομένου> Lond.O.   6 μὲν] μὴ a¹
Lond.   9 μένει Usener; μὲν libri.   ἐπειδὰν ἡ Va¹
Lond.; ἐπειδὰν δὲ ἡ Sa²O; *cum autem* lat. (**cf.** Thillet
126); εἰ μὴ ἐπειδὰν ἡ B²; ἐπειδὰν μὴ ἡ Usener.
γένηται ἀληθές a².   10 lege ἐξ ἀνάγκης τὸ (**von Arnim**
+ SVF 2.961); τὸ ἐξ ἀνάγκης cett.   ἀνάγκης]
εἱμαρμένης Heine 35 n.1.   11 ἀνάγκης ἀληθές] lege
ἀνάγκης δέ (**von Arnim** + SVF 2.961; cf. **Comm.**).
13 lege γίνεσθαι (**von Arnim** + SVF 2.961); γένέσθαι
cett.   14 πάντα <λέγοντος> Lond.O.   πάλιν] εἰ
πάντα Ηγρ.ES.   <ὅμοιον τῷ προειρημένῳ> suppl. **Bruns**
Suppl. Ar.; <κένον> id. RhMus 44 (1889) 614.   15 γὰρ
om. a¹² Rodier; μὲν γὰρ B.   παιζόντων ἐστι a¹².
16 γενόμενον O.   17 γίνεσθαι] σθαι in lit. V; exh.
lat.   18 μὴ τὸ Lond.O; τὸ μὴ V lat.a¹; τὸ a²; del.
B².   19 μὴ τοιοῦτον B².   20 εἴ γε μὴν] lege
λέγομεν (**Rodier**); εἴ γε μὴν Va¹; om. a²O; δεῖ λέγειν
(**fort.**) **Bruns**; εἴ γε μὴ[ν οὐ γὰρ] lat.B², **sed cf.**
Donini.   22 ὡς retinendum (**cf. Comm.**); del. **Bruns.**
23 λεγόμενον **Bruns**; γινόμενον libri.   24 λέγοιτο]
lege γίνοιτο (libri); λέγοιτο **Bruns**, γένοιτο KES.
25 τότ'] lege τοῦτ' (libri); τότ' **Bruns.**   27 δὲ] γὰρ
O.

244

p.178.2 δ' om. Va¹; exh. lat. (Thillet 18).

c.XI

p.178.9 lege ἔπεσθαι (Bruns, fort.); ἔσεσθαι cett.
11 <ἂν> a¹²; om. V lat.   14 <τὸ> add. a¹²; confert
Bruns 208.2.   21 τε] τι K; om. ES Euseb.   22 ἢ
lat.B¹ES; εἰ VB²a¹²; καὶ Lond.O.   26 γενομένη(pr.)]
primam lat.   γενομένη (alt.) del. V, om. lat.;
γενομένη B²; γινομένη a¹².

p.179.1 πλέον τι Lond.O; δέοντι Va¹²; opportunum
aliquid lat.   4 lege <τοῦ βουλεύσασθαι>
(Hackforth); <τοῦ βουλεύεσθαι> add. Bruns.
5 punct. post ὡς et post βουλευόμεθα (Hackforth).
6 τὸ corr. ex τοῦ B; τὸῦ sic V; τὸ lat.; τοῦ HESO.
βουλεύσασθαι] βουλεύεσθαι O.   6-7 ἐπ' αὐτό τε] lege
ἐπεὶ αὐτό γε (Apelt, Hackforth); ἐπ' αὐτό τε codd.;
quoniam et tunc lat.; ἐπεὶ αὐτὸ O. <εἰ δέ τι> ἐπ'
αὐτό γε τὸ βουλεύσασθαι περιγίνεται [καὶ] περὶ τῶν
ἄλλων βουλευομένοις περὶ ὧν προειρήκαμεν, τί ποτ' ...
coni. Bruns; ... παρὰ τοῦ βουλεύεσθαι περὶ αὐτῶν ἐπ'
αὐτὸ τὸ βουλεύεσθαι περιγίνεται πλέον coni. Casp.O.
7 βουλεύσασθαι] βουλεύεσθαι O.   καὶ] πλέον ἢ Lond.;
πλέον O (in emendandis).   βουλευομένοις om. lat.
10 ἄλλου V; ἄλλο HB²; ἄλλου B¹a¹²; ἄλλο τι Cas.O.
21 <οὐκ> add. Lond.O.   22 tolle punct.   fort. ὡς
<εἰς> τι, Bruns; respuit Apelt. 23 παρεχομένωι V¹lat.;
παρεχόμενοι v.c.V; παρεχομένων ES; παρεχομένη a¹².
23-180.2 'dubito num haec Alexandri sint', Bruns; cf.
Comm.   ᾧ v.c.V, lat.; ὡς V¹a¹²; οἷς Lond.   τὸ
(alt.) B²; τοῦ libri.   24 ᾧ v.c.V, lat.; ὡς V¹a¹²;
οἷς Lond.   25 τοῦ B²; τὸ libri.   26 ᾧ B²; ὡς V
lat.a¹²; οἷς Lond.

p.180.2 δύνασθαι <πράττειν> O.

cap.XII

p.180.5 οὖ] ᾧ Casp.O.   6 περιισταμένοις B².
7 αὐτοις V; αὐτοῖς a¹²; αὐτοῖς B; αὐτοὺς Lond.O; αὐτοὶ

Adnot. ad text.: c.XII-XIII

ES; αὐτοὺς Cas.   7 ἄγει B²a¹²; ἄγῆ V; ἄγη B¹HES;
ᾗ ἂν ἐκεῖνα ἄγῃ O; ut illa fiant lat.   post ἄγει
gravius interpungendum.   8 περὶ ταὐτό] τοῦτο ES;
περὶ ταὐτεξούσιον Casp.O.   10 μὴ (alt.) V (corr. ex
ἡμιν v.c.) lat. B²H; ἡμῖν a¹²; εἰ μὴ Lond.O.   <δὲ>
add. B²; exhibet lat.   14 ἀγαθόν lat.B²H Cas.;
αγαθῶν sic V; ἀγαθῶν a¹².   15 ἐντύχῃ Bruns lat.
(Thillet 17) Donini; τύχῃ V; τύχοι a¹²; ἐντύχοι Cas.
τοῦ] κἂν Lond.   16 μένει B²Lond.O; εἰ V lat.a¹².
19 αὐτό delendum (Donini; vel ἐπὶ τοῦτο legendum,
idem); ad id quod est lat., sim. Bag., Lond. transl.;
ἐφ᾽ αὐτὸ (sic) O. Cf. Comm.   21 καθ᾽ sic V.
23 γίνεσθαι] ι in lit. V; fieri lat.
27 διαιρεῖσθαι] lege αἱρεῖσθαι (Bruns coni. in app.,
et lat.; Thillet 17, cf. indicem s.vv. eligere,
διαιρεῖσθαι).

p.181.1 ὡς B(in lit.) Schulthess O; οἷς Va¹²; om. lat.
2 δὲ] τε Euseb.   lege τοιούσδε (Bruns, fort., et
Apelt); τοῖσδε Euseb.; τοιοῖσδε libri; ἐν τοῖς
μεγάλοις, cf. Arist. Eth. Nic. 3.3 1112 b 10, coni.
Donini.   3 lege αὐτοῖς συμβουλεύσοντας (Bruns,
fort., et Apelt).   τοὺς] lege καὶ τὸ (Bruns, fort.);
τοὺς Va¹²; τῷ B²; τοῦ ES Cas.; ὡς Lond.O. ... ἢ μή,
παραλαμβάνοντας δὲ πρᾶξαι ... Apelt; tanquam habentes
potestatem lat. (= ὡς ἔχοντες ἐξουσίαν τοῦ, Thillet
18; sed cf. Donini 306f.).   4 ἄλλα [καὶ] τινὰ]
lege καὶ ἄλλα τινὰ (Donini, ex lat.(GO)); [καὶ] del.
V¹y, exh. a¹².   6f. αὐτοῦ] lege αὐτοῦ (Donini, ex
lat.).

cap.XIII

p.181.9 γὰρ <ἂν> Schwartz.   lege ἐγχειρήσοντες
(B²); ἐγχειρήσαντες V lat.; ἐπιχειρήσοντες O.
11 σώζεσθαι καὶ αὐτοῖς Ηγρ.ES.   14 τὸ lat.B²Lond.;
τό τε Cas.; τε V; τε a¹².   καὶ delendum (B² Gercke
112 Donini (1974,1) 33 n.1; om. lat.); <καθ᾽ ὁρμὴν>
δι᾽ ἡμῶν SVF 2.979. ἴσως δεῖ λέγειν: λέγουσιν ἐφ᾽ ἡμῖν
εἶναι τὸ ὑπό τε τῆς εἱμαρμένης γινόμενον καὶ δι᾽ ἡμῶν,

246

B² in marg.   15 ἐπεὶ] ἐπὶ Lond.; ἐπὶ vel εἰσι Gercke
112.   16 διάφοράι V.   21 ὑπὸ om. lat. Cas. Oy.
μὲν] δὲ S.   23 τὴν] fort. μὴν Gercke 112.   fort.
ἀλλ<ὰ τὴν> Bruns.   24 μὴ] lege δὴ (Gercke 112); μὴ,
s.v., v.c.(?)V; om. lat. ES Rodier SVF 2.979.
οὕτως] fort. ὅλως Gercke 112.   <ὡς> add. Lond.O;
<ἃ> SVF 2.979.   25 μὴ (pr.) sic V; om. lat.
περιεστάναι καὶ ἀδύνατον τότε a¹².   τότε om. lat.
27 lege ἐμποδίζοντος· τῷ <γὰρ> (SVF 2.979).
28 <τὴν> add. Bruns; om. SVF 2.979.   κατὰ del. O;
κάτω Casp.O.   <αἰτίαν> add. B².   ὅταν] ὥστ᾽ ἂν
Schwartz, quod approbat Bruns in adnot.   29-30 παρῇ
ὡς ἐξ Lond.O.   30-182.1 πάντως - τότε in parenthesi
(SVF 2.979).

p.182.2 δυνάμενον a¹²; δυναμένων V(supr. ν: ι V¹)B¹ES;
δυναμένου B²; δυναμένῳ H ut vid., Gercke 112; potente
lat.   μὴ (alt.) om. a¹Lond., secl. O Bruns. Cf.
Comm.   5 δὲ om. lat.O; δὴ ES.   7 <τὴν> add. B².
10 πυρός, <τῶν δὲ δι᾽ ὕδατος,> coni. O, quod respuit
Gercke 112.   13 δὲ] lege μὲν (SVF 2.979); δὲ cett.
14 γινομένοις y Schwartz.   τοῖς] lege τούτοις
(Donini (1974,1) 35 n.1); τὰ SVF 2.979; τοῖς cett.;
καὶ delendum vel ὡς scribendum, Gercke 112.
15 αὐτὰ] κατὰ y.   16 post ἐνεργεῖν levius interpungendum.   σὺγκαταθέσεως a¹²; νυὺθέσεως V;
σὺνθέσεως HBES¹; ad placitum lat. (= σὺν καταθέσεως?
Thillet 141).   18 lege τινὰ <αἰτίαν> (Rodier, Donini
(1974,1) 35 n.2); aliam quemdam naturam lat.
λέγοντες] lege λέγουσιν (Rodier, Donini loc. cit.).

cap.XIV

p.182.21 περὶ B ; ἐπὶ libri.   22 αὐτοὺς] αὐτοὺς
lat.? (cf. Thillet 147 s. se ipsum).   26 λέγοντες
ES Lond.   lege οἱ δέ, δέον.   οἱ δέ] εἰ δὲ lat.
ὅτε ante δέον add. Lond.O.   αὐτόθεν] αὐτοῖς Lond.
28 τε] lege τι (Hackforth).   28-29. Lege πόλλ᾽ ἂν
τῶν κατ᾽ αὐτοὺς τῷ ἐφ᾽ ἡμῖν πάσχοντα ταὐτό, <τοῦτο>
ἐδείκνυσαν (Hackforth); πόλλα τῶν καὶ αὐτοῖς τοῦ (τῷ

Adnot. ad text.: c.XIV

ES) ἐφ' ἡμῖν πᾶσάν τε ταὐτὸ δεικνὺς codd.; *multa et ipsis eius quod in nobis esse* (esse G, omne E, om.0) *idem ostendens lat.*; ... αὐτοῖς περὶ τοῦ ἐφ' ἡμῖν <δοκούντων ἀναιρετικόν>... B²; καὶ πόλλα τῶν παρ' αὐτοὺς λεγόμενα περὶ τοῦ ἐφ' ἡμῖν ὡς ἄν τε ταὐτὸ δεικνύναι Lond.: καὶ πόλλα τῶν παρ' αὐτοὺς λεγομένων περὶ τοῦ ἐφ' ἡμῖν, omissis ceteris, Schulthess attrib. 0; ... αὐτοῖς <δοκούντων ἀναιρετικόν>, τὸ ἐφ' ἡμῖν ἐπειράσαντο δεικνύναι Rodier; πόλλα τῶν κατ' αὐτούς, τοῦ ἐφ' ἡμῖν ἀπάσαντα, τοῦτο δεἰκνυσι Apelt. 29 μὴ συνοδεύοντα (vel συνᾴδοντα) Schulthess attribuit 0. <τῷ> Schwartz; λόγῳ, <πειρώμενοί τε> B²; λόγῳ, διὰ <δὲ> τῆς Rodier. 30 ἡγοῦνται] lege ἡγούμενοι (Hackforth). φεύγειν <τε> Lond.0. 32 ἄλλου] lege ἄλλων (lat. Donini); ἄλλως v.c.V; ἄλλου cett.

p.183.1 γινομένου ES Lond. 4 lege τῷ ζῴῳ (coni. Bruns in app.). 5 lege ἄλλως <ἂν> (SVF 2.980). 6 μὴ] lege ἢ (Bruns, coni. in app., SVF 2.980). 7 fort. ὁρμῆσαν, Bruns. ταῦτα] διὰ τοῦτο B². 10 τούτου] ου in lit. V; *propter hoc* (cum sequentibus) lat. (= διὰ τοῦτο?). τὸ B² in lit.; τῷ libri. 17 οὖν] γὰρ Hγρ.ESO (et lat.? - nisi γοῦν; cf. Thillet 44 et n.3, 128 s. enim). 20 τοῦτ' αὐτὸ] τοῦτ' αὐτοῖς H; τοῦτο ES; *et in hoc causandum* (ipsos, sed = αὐτοῖς (pr.)?) lat. 21 <οὐ> κοινωνίαν vel ἀκοινωνίαν Hackforth; sed cf. Comm. τοῦ (alt.)] lege τὸ (Bruns, coni. in app., Hackforth); τοῦ Va¹²;τοὺς KESO. *volentibus ipsis seducere alios* lat. 31 <ποιεῖ> add. Schwartz. 32 τι εἶναι Hγρ.ESO; τιθέναι V lat.a¹². 33 τῷ] lege τὸ (VHa¹² Apelt, cf. 184.15); τῷ Lond.0 Bruns; τὸ corr. ex τῷ B. ἐν αὐτῷ V.

p.184.1 ἄλλα] ἄλογα H. 1-2 κατ' αὐτὰς] καὶ ταύτας Hγρ.ES. 2 πράξεις v.c.V lat.a¹²; τάξεις v¹ES. 9 ἔχων post ὄρεξιν B²HES lat., ante ὄρεξιν a¹²; om. V. 13 ὅτι περ B². 14 <ὅτι> add. Bruns; ante ῥᾳθυμότερον (13) add., vel λέγουσιν (15) del., Casp.0. 16 ἄλλῳ ἐν Cas. 0; ἀπλῶς ἐν Casp.0; ἄλλως libri.

Adnot. ad text.: c.XIV-XV

18 τῷ (tert.)] huic lat.   αὐτῷ Bruns; αὐτῷ Lond.O;
τῷ V lat. a¹².   19 ἐλέσθαι Bruns; ἔχεσθαι libri;
ἐνεργεῖν B².   24 μὴ HSB(in lit.)lat.Lond.O; μὴν V;
μὴν a¹².   32 τὸ (alt.) om. O (in emendandis)?
p.185.1 <οὐκ> ἐπὶ Schulthess.   τῷ ἀνθρώπῳ Lond.O;
τῶν ἀνθρώπων Va¹²; τοῖς ἀνθρώποις B²; in hominibus
lat.   5 τι <καὶ τοῦ μὴ βουλεθσάμενοι> Schwartz.
6 <ἂν> add. Bruns.   τοῦ <μὴ> βουλεύεσθαι
Schulthess O ('ferenda tamen et vulgata lectio', O
adnot.).   7 lege <μὴ> βουλευσάμενοι (Schwartz,
Apelt).   βουλευσάμενοι <ἂν ἐπράξαμεν> Schwartz, sed
hoc subaudiri potest; cf. Apelt.   ἤν ἂν] lege
<μάτ>ην <γὰρ> ἂν (Schwartz); ην αν V; ην ἂν B; ἤν ἂν
K; ἤν ἂν a¹². βουλευσαμένων ἤν, ἂν Cas.O;
βουλευσάμενοι. τί γὰρ ἂν Apelt.   βουλευώμεθα a²Cas.
O. ὃ καὶ - βουλευοίμεθα] quod consiliati volebamus
tantum lat.

cap.XV

p.185.7 ἐποχουμένους Bruns, cf. 196.15; ἐποχουμένων
libri.   8 τῷ εἰ δὴ Schwartz; τωιειδει V, sim. lat.;
τῷ εἴδει a¹²; τῷ εἰ Casp.O.   9 νομίζειν κίνησιν
B².   7-9 τὸ δ' - εἰσάγεσθαι] inducere autem motum
sine causa propterea quia in hiis que ejusdem speciei
eisdem circunstantibus, aliquando quidem sic,aliquando
autem aliter operabitur aliquis lat.; cf. Thillet 36
et n.3.   9 καὶ διὰ B² lat.Cas.Gercke 75(fort.).
14 <οὐκ> add. Schulthess O; ἀναιτίως <τῶν ἔξωθεν> Cas.
15 αὐτοῦ Lond.O; αὐτοῦ Va¹².   17 lacunam post ὡς
statuit Bruns, sed τὸ εἶναι subaudiendum (Rodier;
Valgiglio Riv.Stud.Class. 15 (1967) 312 n.12). ὡς <οὐκ
ἔχει ἐν αὐτῇ> ἡ σφαῖρα τοῦ κατὰ Hackforth; sed cf.
Comm.   20 <ὡς> μὴ Bruns lat. Donini; μὴ Va¹²; τὸ μὴ
H; τῷ μὴ SO; τοῦ μὴ E.   21 καὶ] εἰ O.   21 <εἰ>,
22 <ἂν> add. Bruns.   22 εἶχε Lond.O; εἰ δὲ V lat.
a¹².   26 lege ἡμᾶς τάδε τῶν περιεστώτων προκρίνειν
(Hackforth). <αἱρεῖσθαι> post ἄλλα (27) add.
Schulthess O, post ἡμᾶς (26) Valgiglio loc. cit.; sed

Adnot. ad text.: c.XV-XVI

cf. Donini (1974,2) 177 n.85.   28 κατὰ τὴν B².
30 fort. τῷ <διὰ> ταύτην Bruns.

p.186.1 ἄλλοις] lege αὐτοῖς (fort., Bruns in app.; cf.
Comm.).   3 γὰρ del. yO.   5 τῇ φαντασίᾳ Schwartz;
τὴν φαντασίαν codd.   6 ἁπλῆ] fort. ἁπλῶς, Bruns in
app.   11 παρ' αὐτοις sic V; om. lat.; παρ' αὐτῷ
Lond.O.

cap.XVI

p.186.14 <γίνεσθαι> add.O.   σώζεται lat.a²; σώζεσθαι
Va¹.   15 εἴ γε E; fort. οἷς γε, Bruns in app.
19 συγχεῖν a¹²; συνεχεῖν V; συνεγχεῖν H; συνέχειν ES
lat.; τυχεῖν K.   20 εἰ] καὶ O.   21 ἔχοντες Bruns;
ἔχοντα Lond.O; ἔχοντας libri. μὴ πράττειν ἃ
πράττουσιν, ὡς ἔχοντας Rodier; sed cf. Comm.   24 δὴ]
δὲ Lond.O et fort. lat (Thillet, 22 n.2).   ἡ] ἢ a¹².
δόξα lat.B²Lond.O; δόξαὺ V; δόξαν a¹².   λαβεῖν H;
λαβόντων a².   27 τῷ B²a¹²; τὰ V; que (i.e. quae)
lat.   ταῦτα a¹²; ταυτη V¹; sic lat.; ταυτην v.c.V;
ταῦτα corr. ex ταύτη B; ταύτην E; τοῦτο O.   30 ἢ
συμβήσεται] συμβήσεται ἢ coni.O.   πάντας HE lat.;
πάνταν V; ἃν πάντας a¹².

p.187.1 χαιρεῖ λεγεῖ sic V; dicere gaudere lat.
noli interpungere post ὡς.   2 lege <κἂν> μηδὲν αὐτοὶ
περὶ αὐτῶν <ποι>ῶσιν καλόν. κἂν add. B²; pro μηδὲν
habet lat. ut. <ποι>ωσιν καλόν Amand 150 n.1 (et ὡς,
187.1, cum ποιῶσιν copulandum); ὦσιν καλόν codd. et lat.
(Thillet, app.); πονῶσιν B²; οἴσωσι vel ἔχωσι καλόν O;
μηδὲν αὐτοὶ παρ' αὐτῶν ὦσιν καλοί Apelt; μηδὲν αὐτοῖς
περὶ αὐτῶν οὖσιν καλὸν ὄν Rodier; μηδὲν αὐτοῖς περιάψον
ἀξιῶσιν ὡς εἰσιν καλοί, vel ὡς οὖσιν καλοῖς,
Hackforth.   3 πραττομένων] rebus lat. (? =
πραγμάτων, Thillet 17, 50).   5 <ἢ> add. a².
8 πρὸς οὓς τίς ἂν ὁ Bruns; προσουτισινό V; προσου
τησιν (ὁ) lat.(cod.O). cf. Thillet 58, 84); πρὸς οὖσιν
ὁ E; πρὸς οὓς τίς ὁ a²(τις)Cas.; πρὸς οὓς τίς ἂν Lond.
12 οἱ B²; εὖ V; εὖ a¹²; om. lat.

250

Adnot. ad text.: c.XVI-XVIII

13 ἐπιτίμησις ... κόλασις γρ·HE; *increpationes* ...
punitio lat.   14 τούτων HB²E lat.Cas.Lond.; τούτῳ
Va¹².   16 <ἂν> add. B.   20 ἢ - ἐπαιρόντων del.
Bruns.   21 ἂν ἁμαρτήσας **Bruns**; ἀναμάρτητος V¹lat.;
ἀναμαρτήσας (sive -ιας) v.c.V; ἐναμάρτητος **Casp.**O.
24 αὐτοῦ Hγρ.EO.   26 lege εἰ γὰρ οὕτως ἐχόντων ἡμῶν
(coni. Amand, 151 n.8); εἰ γὰρ οὕτως ἔτι δι' ἡμῶν
Va¹Lond.Rodier; ἐπεί γε οὕτως ὄντων ἡμῶν a² Vict.(ut
vid.) Cas.O; ἐπεί γε οὕτως ἐχόντων ἡμῶν a¹ et Lond.
attrib. O, sed falso; nec tamen ipse vel coniecit,
ut dicit Bruns, vel approbavit; εἴγε οὕτως ὄντων δι'
ἡμῶν Vict. et Cas. falso attrib. O; εἰ γὰρ οὕτως ὡς τὰ
δι' ἡμῶν coni. Bruns in app.; εἴ γε οὕτως ἐστίν, ἡμῶν
πῶς Apelt. Cf. Comm.   28 γοῦν] γὰρ HE.   τῶν] ὄντων
lat.

cap.XVII

p.188.8 διότι] fort. ἀλλ' ὅτι, Bruns; sed cf. Apelt,
Donini ad loc.   10 πλέον <κατηναγκασμένως τὰ δῶρα>
Donini, ut demonstrativo τούτων antecedens suppeditet;
nonne tamen τούτων 'harum rerum' lato sensu
significat?   τούτους] *tales* lat.; αὐτοὺς Donini.
11 ἀναιροῖεν ἂν (vel ἀναιροῦτ' ἂν καὶ μαντική) Casp.O;
ἀναιροῖαν V; ἂν ἀναιρεῖ ἂν KB¹; ἂν ἀναιροῖ ἂν B²;
ἀναιροῖ ἂν HO; ἀναιρεῖ ἂν a¹²; *interiment* (om. ἂν)
lat.   12 μαθεῖν (pr.)] lege μάθοι (Schwartz); μαθεῖν
<δέοι> B²Rodier; μαθὼν <ποιήσειε>, cf. 188.14, Donini.
Cf. Comm.   13 εἰ K Cas.Lond.; ἢ V; ἢ lat.a¹².
14 τοῦ] lege τὸ (Bruns in app., Donini).   τι del.
Schwartz.   15 πρὸ lat.a¹; πρὸς Va².
κατηναγκασμένον] *prefixum* lat. (= προκαταβεβλημένον,
Thillet 17).   τοῦ τε a²; τοῦτο Va¹; τούτοις E.
17 punct. interrog. post αἰτίας (Donini).

cap.XVIII

p.188.18 παντί που] *omnino* lat. (Thillet, 139 s.v.).
22 μὲν v.c.V infra vers.; δὲ V¹lat.(Thillet 43 n.2)
a¹².

251

Adnot. ad text.: c.XVIII-XIX

p.189.1 ἔχοντας αὐτοὺς B². τῶν προτρεπομένων lat.
Cas.Lond.O; τῷ προτρεπομένῳ Va¹²; τὸ προτρεπομένω E.
τοὺς παρ' αὐτῶν λόγους Lond.O; τῶν παρ' αὐτῶν λόγους
Va¹; τῶν παρ' αὐτοῖς λόγων a²; τῶν παρ' αὐτῶν λόγων
Gercke 128.   2 <ὧν> add. Cas.Lond.O.   αὐτῶν O; τῶν
libri.   4 πλεΐω] fort. πλεῖστα, Bruns in app.
6 lege <μὴ> συγγράφειν (Bruns, coni. in app.); tanquam
qui non prohibentur ista scribere   (= ὡς οὐ
κεκωλυμένοι τοῦτο συγγράφειν?) Grotius.

cap.XIX

p.189.9 συγχωρησάντων] lege συνεχώρησαν τῷ (Bruns
coni. in app.); συγχωρήσαιντο Lond.O; συνεχάρησαν τῷ
Hackforth (sed hoc Bruns quoque attribuit Hackforth;
typorum error?).   11 lege πράξεως ἐπὶ περιεστῶσιν
<τοῖς αὐτοῖς, εἰ τοῖς παρὰ πάντων ὡμολογημένοις
προσέσχον. ἔστι γὰρ νόμος> ἀνθρώποις   (coni.
Hackforth).   περιεστῶσιν] περιεστώτων coni. O (sed
περιεστῶσιν Casp.O).   ἀνθρώποις] ἄνθρωποι Lond.;
ἄνθρωπος, vel ἄνθρωποι δίκαιοι ... πεπιστευμένοι,
coni.O, sed ἀνθρώποις Casp.O.   δίκαιος] om. K;
δίκαιοι Lond., Casp.O.   12 πεπιστευμένος]
πεπιστευμένοις H; πεπιστευμένοι Lond., Casp.O.
16 οὐ καλῶς lat.a¹²; ουκαλλῶς sic V; οὐκ ἄλλως HE.
τί] aliquid lat.   lege ἄγνοιαν <τῶν> πραττομένων
(coni. Casp.O); ἀπατωμένων pro πραττομένων coni.O;
πραττομένων del. Bruns. Cf. Aristot. Eth. Nic. 3.1
1110 b 33ff.   17 ἢ lat.Cas.Lond.O; ἡ V; ᾖ H; οἱ in
lit. B²; ἡ a¹². <οἱ> add. Bruns.   20 <πράττειν>
add. y Bruns; post τι (19) lat. (Thillet 18) B²O.
πράττουσιν (τῷ ... ἀφεθεῖεν) ἀφ' αὐτῶν κινεῖσθαι (23)
Rodier.   23 ἀφ' αὐτῶν B²Rodier.   τὸ [τοῦ]] lege
τούτῳ (lat. (Thillet 17) Donini); [τοῦ] del. B²Bruns.
25 τύχης] ψυχῆς a²; ψύχης Lond.O.   27 εὔλογοι a²;
εὔλογον V lat.a¹; τὸ κολάσαι εὔλογον coni.O.

p.190.1 καταλείποντες (supr. ει: ι m¹)V; delinquunt
lat.   2 αὐτῶν a²Cas.O; αὐτοῦ Va¹; ὑπ' αὐτῶν Lond.
τῶν - αὐτῶν] eorum que debent lat.   2f. τὸ νόμιμον

252

coni. O.   5 ὅρα] lege ὥρα (lat.E Cas. Casp.O
Donini).   6 *docereque* lat.   7 ἄξιοι lat. (Thillet
18)a²; add. post ἁμαρτανόντων (8) Β²; om. V.
8 καταναγκάζοντος lat.a²Cas.; καταναγκάζοντας Va¹;
καταναγκάζοντες Lond.   9 ὧν] lege οἷον (Hackforth).
ὑπὸ] lege ἀπὸ (Hackforth).   10 λαθόντας] lege
λυθέντας (Hackforth); ἄλλως Grotius, O in adnot.;
ἑκόντας Casp.O; λαχόντας Gercke 134; fort. <ἦν> οὐδὲν
... λαθόντας, Bruns in app.   10-11 καὶ τίς οὐκ ἂν]
lege καὶ αἰτίας οὐδὲν οὐδ᾽ ἐν (Hackforth); καὶ τίς οὐκ
ἂν V; καί τις οὐκ ἂν a¹²; ἥτις οὖν Lond.O; ἥτις οὖν ἐν
Gercke.   11 τῶν ἁμαρτανομένων coni.O.   αἴτιον]
lege ἄξιον (Hackforth); αἴτιον Va¹; αἴτιος a²Lond.O.
οὔτ᾽ (alt.)] lege οὐδ᾽; οὔτ᾽ Bruns, οὐδ᾽ libri.
οἱ τοῦ Β² in lit.; οὗτοι V(supr. οι: ος ut vid. m¹)
lat.a¹².   12 ταύτην v.c.(?)V, lat.O; ταύτῃ ·V¹a¹².
13 *ferentes ... dicentes* lat.(?).   τι] τε Β²; om.
lat.   καὶ ψευδεῖ V, del. Bruns; καὶ ψευδῆ a¹²; ὡς
ψῦθός τι καὶ ψευδῆ λέγοντι coni. Casp.O.   16 [δεῖ]
del. Bruns; δεῖν Lond. (typorum errore, O 296 n.20).

cap.XX

p.190.19 τι lat.a²O; τις Va¹.   ὀνόμασαι] ἐξουσία
Lond.   22 ἀνεπείσθησαν V; *etiam persuadent* lat.
25 τινος O Bruns; τινων libri, Gercke 107.
26 ἔχοντες lat.(Thillet 17)a² Gercke 107.
πεπιστευκότι Schwartz; πεπιστευμένῳ libri; πεπεισμένῳ
Apelt.   *Ei enim qui crediderit hoc, r e s t a t
non increpare aliquem* lat.   29 lege τοῦ <μὴ> ποιεῖν
(Long *Class. Quart.* n.s. 25 (1975) 158f.).

p.191.1 lege ἐξουσίαν <ἔχειν>; ita, vel τῇ ἐξουσίᾳ
lègendum, Long loc. cit.; ποιοῦσιν <ἢ μὴ ποιεῖν ἔχειν>
τὴν ἐξουσίαν coni. Bruns.   2 <βίος> a²; om. Vlat.a¹.

cap.XXI

p.191.5 ἔχειν] *videtur* lat.   μαρτυρεῖ a¹²; μαρτυρεῖν
VH lat.   6 αὐτό] lege αὐτῶν (Bruns coni. in app.).
8 πάντως γινόμενον Ηγρ.Ε.   [ἢ] del. Β².   11 τὸ]

Adnot. ad text.: c.XXI-XXII

fort. τῷ, Bruns. πραττόμενα] 'exspectes πράττεσθαι δοκοῦντα καὶ', Bruns; sed verba τὰ ὑφ' ἡμῶν - ἐξουσίαν ad ea quae re vera sunt, non quae nos per errorem esse credamus, recte referuntur. 12 γίνεσθαι Cas.Lond.O; γίνεται libri. 18 lege πείθεσθαι <μέλλο>μεν (Hackforth); πείθεσθαι μὲν libri; persuadeatur quidem lat.; πεισθείημεν Β²; διὰ τὸ πείθεσθαι, vel πειθόμενοι, coni. O. 19 παραλείψομεν lat.B²Bruns; παραλίπομεν V; παραλείπομεν a¹²; παραλείποιμεν Lond.O. 20 τὸ (alt.) lat.(? cf. Thillet 159 s. διά, et infra de 208.10)Cas.Lond.O; τοῦ libri. 21 γευόμενοι (υ et μ litura obscurae) V; γινόμενοι E; efficimur lat. αὐτῶν V. 23 <ἂν> add. Schwartz. 24 τε αἱρεῖσθαι a²; ἐπαίρεσθαι V lat.a¹; τε ἑλέσθαι Β². 25 post ἄλλους: διὰ τοιαύτην lat. (Thillet 18).

cap.XXII

p.191.31 αὐτῷ Va¹²Lond.O; αὐτῷ Gercke 72 in app. (fort.), Bruns; in se Bag.Grotius Lond(tr.).

p.192.6 παντί lat.B²O; πάντη V; πάντη a¹². 7 ἠρτημένον] ortum lat. <ἐξ> add.O; ex ipso lat. 8 πρὸ] ἐξ H (in mg. πρὸ). 12 αἱεί cum sequentibus coniungit SVF 2.945. 15 ἴωι sic, s.v., v.c.V; om. EH. ἀναιτίως <γίνεσθαί τι, ὥσπερ τὸ> γίνεσθαι lat. (Thillet 18); quae tamen subaudire poterat lat., sicut O 299 n.5. 16 ἐναργῶς V lat.; ἐνεργῶς Grotius Usener Gercke 72 SVF 2.945 Rodier. 17 super ἀκαταστρόφως: μετὰ Β². 18 ἐκτίθενται Ηγρ.E. σμῆνος E Cas.O; μῆνος V lat.(cf. Thillet 58)a¹²; μηδὲν Lond. γὰρ delendum (von Arnim + SVF 2.945); post τὰ μὲν transtulit Rodier. αἰτίων E Cas.O; αἴτιον V lat.a¹². γὰρ αἰτίων] ἀναίτιον Lond. Parenthesis ab οὐδὲν (19) incipere debet (ita Lond., von Arnim + SVF 2.945), non a σμῆνος (Bruns) neque a τὰ μὲν (Rodier). 19 ἑκτικά K Cas.Lond.; ἀκτικά V lat.; ἀρκτικά E; ἐκτικά a¹². 20 εἰς πάντα Lond.O; ἢ σύμπαντα Usener; διὰ vel εἰς τὸ πάντα Gercke 72. παρατιθέμενα] lege παρατιθέμεν<ον, ἀλλ>ὰ (von Arnim + SVF 2.945); παρατιθέμενα Va¹; παρατιθεμένους ΗΚΕ Cas.

Adnot. ad text.: c.XXII-XXIV

Lond.O; παρατιθεμένους a²; παρατιθέντας in lit. B
(s.v. βουλομένους B²); παρατιθέμενον Gercke 72;
παρατιθεμένοις Rodier; *proponendo* lat. 21 δὴ] δὲ O;
δ' ἤδη E. 23f. ὁτὲ μὲν δὴ μὴ O; ὁτὲ δε μὴ ἢ (sed ᵓ
del.) ὅτε (sed ᶜ del.) | δε μη V; ὅτε δὲ μὴ ηοτεδεμη
B¹; ὅτε μὲν B²; ὁτὲ μὲν ὁτὲ δὲ μὴ H(μή)Ea²; ὅτε μὲν
καὶ ᾧ ὅτε δὲ μὴ K; ὁτὲ μὲν δὲ μὴ a¹Lond.; ὅτε μὲν μὴ
Cas. 24 οὑτωσί πως B²Usener; οὕτως εἴπως V(sed ᵓ
del.),H; οὕτως πως B¹E; οὕτω Ka²Cas.O; οὕτως a¹Lond.
συμβαίνειν EKB²a¹²Cas.Lond.O; συμβαίνει VB¹H. Post
οὕτως (alt.) <εἴ πως συμβαίνει> add. coni. O in adnot.
27 χρωμένην lat.a¹²; χρωμένης V.

cap.XXIII

p.193.3-4 φανερώτερος] γνωριμώτερος, in mg.
φανερώτερος, H. 4 τούτοις a¹²; τοῦτο V (supr. alt.
o: ν v.c.V)lat.; τούτω τούτω B¹E. 5 ὡς πάντων τῶν
V lat.; ὥσπερ τῶν τῶν a¹; ὥσπερ τῶν a²; ὡς τῶν B².
11 τὴν del. B². 12 τὸ ποσὸν] τόπον a¹.
13 ἐλλείψεως lat.(cf. Thillet ad loc.)a¹²Lond.
14 [τῷ] del. B²O, om. lat. ὑπάρχουσαν] *inexistentem*
lat.(? = ἐνυπάρχουσαν; cf. Thillet 133, 173 s.vv.).
16-17 εἰ δ' ὁ μὲν a¹²Lond.; εἴδομεν εἰ V; εἴδομεν εἰ
H; *videmus ... si* lat. 19 Num ἄλλ'?
20 ξηρανθέντα lat. Hmg.EO. 23 πᾶν τὸ Schwartz;
πάντα libri. lege ἐνεργεῖ[ν] (Rodier); ἐνεργεῖν
<ἐνεργεῖ> Bruns. 25 lege <αἴτια> μὲν (von Arnim +
SVF 2.947, Hackforth); λέγειν μὲν καὶ ταῦτα εἶναι
αἴτια B²Bag.¹(sed non Bag.²). ὁμόσε χωροῦντας] cf.
Plato *Resp.* X 610c, *Euthyd.* 294d; Aristot. *Metaph.* N 2
1089 a 3. 26 lege εἶναι, τίνος (interrog.: ita VHO
Gercke 68 von Arnim + *SVF* 2.947 Hackforth); εἶναί
τινος a¹²Lond.(sed *transl.* tanquam τίνος; ita quoque
Bag. Grotius) Bruns. αἴτιον coni. Heine 45 n.1,
αἰτίαν coni. Bruns; sed supervacuo ut manifestum est.

cap.XXIV

p.193.31 <ἢ> ἀναιτίως Schulthess O.

Adnot. ad text.: c.XXIV-XXV

p.194.3 ἀλύσεως Schulthess O; ἀναλύσεως libri.
αἰτιων sic V.   ante λέγει (corr. ex λέγειν v.c.)
lit. 4 litt. V.   4 φύσει ὀφείλειν γίνεσθαι B²Cas.;
φησὶν (ν vel υ supra η, ει supra ἴν v.c.) ὀφείλειν γ.
V; φησὶν ὁ. γ. a¹²; φησὶν ὁ. φύσιν γ. H; φησὶ γ. ὁ. E;
τισιν ὄφειλον γ. Lond.O. et ab hoc quod dicitur quod
primis factis causis scilicet ex necessitate sequatur
aliquid debere fieri lat.   6 κυρίας Lond.O.   8 πᾶν
τὸ B², ?lat.; παντόθεν libri.   μὲν om. lat.a¹².
9 ἔσται O.   10 punct. post εἴη, non post ἀνάγκης
(Donini).   10-11 ἐξ ἀνάγκης delendum (Donini); cf.
Comm.   11 αἴτιος ante Σωφρονίσκος (10) colloc. B²;
causa Sophroniscus ex necessitate causa lat.
12 punct. post ἀνάγκη, non post θεμέλιον (ita Va¹²
Lond.O Rodier; post θεμέλιον Bruns, typorum errore
solum?)   13 ἐξ ἀνάγκης del. B² Schulthess (cf. O 303
n.6); fort. <τὰ> ἐξ ἀνάγκης, Bruns in app. Cf. Comm.
13 οὐ τοῖς v.c.V; αὐτοῖς V¹Ea¹; οὐκ αὐτοῖς a².
14 πρώτοις corr. V¹ ex πρώτης; ἠρώτησεν E.   οὐ τοῖς
(13) - τινων] non quod consequens sit quod prima sint
ex necessitate causa aliquorum lat.   19 ἀλλ' οὐκ] οὐ
μὴν HO.   19 fort. αὐτό, Bruns; hoc lat.Bag.Grotius.
20 μόνον] lege <ἐπό>μενον (ita, vel <ἐσό>μενον,
Hackforth).   καὶ ὡς] lege <ἢ> καὶ ὡς (Hackforth);
καὶ ὡς codd.; et ut lat.(GO); aut lat.(E); fort. ἢ ὡς
Bruns.   ἑπόμενον (in fine versus) delendum
(Hackforth).   21 τὸ αἴτιον]lege τὸ αὐτι<ατ>όν (B²Bag.
Hackforth; cf. fort. Alex. in metaph., CAG 1, 153.7);
τὸ αἴτιον V lat.a¹²; τοιοῦτον Lond.; fort. τὸ <οὗ>
αἴτια Bruns.   24 αὐτομάτου O.   τινα lat.B²Lond.O;
τινας V; τινας a¹².

cap.XXV

p.194.25f. lege ψεῦδος τὸ λέγειν (HB²O SVF 2.948); τὸ
λέγειν ψεῦδος vulg.; τὸ λέγειν τὸ ψεῦδος Cas.

p.195.2 αἰτίων B²Bag.Cas.O; ἰσθμίων V lat.a¹².
3 ποιεῖ V¹, corr. v.c.; faciunt lat.   4 lege φέροντας
(Hackforth, cf.190.13); φέρονται V lat.a¹²; φέρεσθαι

Adnot. ad text.: c.XXV-XXVI

B² *SVF* 2.948. 5 τὸ αὐτὸ B²; τὸ E; αὐτὸ cett. (*id
ipsum lat.*, 91.62). 6 τὸ ante αὐτὸ add. v.c.V; *idem
ipsum* lat. (91.63). 9 ἐχουσῶν B²Lond.0; ἔχουσιν
Va¹²; *habent* lat. 11 lege ἐκείνων τε καὶ τούτων
(lat.); ἐκείνων τε καὶ τούτω V¹; ἐκείνων τε καὶ τούτου
v.c.V a¹²; ἐκείνου τε καὶ τούτου Grotius 0. <ἢ>
add. B². 12 ἔγκλισις lat.a¹²; ἔγκλησις V.
13 αἴτιον KEa². lege καὶ <οὐ μὴν> ὅτι (*SVF* 2.948);
ὅτι del.0. <ἢ> add. Bruns. 15 δίκην <οὐ διὰ
τοῦτ'> coni. Bruns in app. ἂν ἔως] lege ἀναιτίως
(Bruns, coni, in app., *SVF* 2.948); αν ἔως V; ἂν ἔως
lat.a¹²Lond.; ἔως ἂν Cas.0; <οὐκ> ἂν, ἔως <οὕτως>
Hackforth. γίνεται, <εἴη> (sc. ἡ τοῦ κόσμου -
ἕνωσις), ἢ, εἰ μὴ κτλ. Hackforth; cf. Comm. γένοιτο
Lond.0. 19 οὐχ οὕτως] lege οὐχ ὁ τῶν (B², 'fort.
recte' Bruns, *SVF* 2.948); οὐχ οὕτως V(υχ del. v.c.)
a¹²Lond.; ? ὁ τούτων lat.(0), cf. Thillet ad loc. et
p.135 s. *iste*. αὐτῶν v.c.V, lat.; αὐτοῦ V¹a¹².
26 <μὴ> add. B². παραλαβεῖν Cas.0. ὡς HEB²lat.0;
ἔως Va¹²Lond.; ὥστ' Casp.0. 29 ἔχουσαν a¹²; ἔχουσα
V. οὐ γὰρ εἰ] *si enim* lat.(GO), *sed enim* lat.(E).
[πάντα] del.V; om. lat.Bag.¹; exh. a¹²Bag.²Lond.0.
30 πάντα om. EO.

p.196.1 πάντα om. lat. 2 ὡς μήτε v.c.V; ὡς μήτε
lat.; ὡς V¹a¹²Lond. 3 τι μὴ a¹²Lond. 5 δ' ἂν]
γὰρ lat.(Thillet 17, 38 n.1). 7 τε] lege δὲ
(Thillet, 122 s. *autem*, Donini); *autem* lat.; τε cett.
10 λύει] *dissip a b i t* lat.

cap.XXVI

p.196.14 πεπίστευκεν a¹²; πεπιστευκεναί V;
πεπιστευκέναι E; *credit* lat. 16 ἃ Va¹²; τὰ B²HE
Cas.0. 17 καθ' αὐτῶν om. lat. 18 πῶς V¹ (corr.
ex ὡς)a¹yO; ὡς a²Lond. οὐ B² Emg. yO; οὖν VHa¹²
Lond. πῶς οὐ] *est utique velut* lat. ἄλογον Emg.
Lond.0; ὀλίγον V lat.a¹²; ὀλίγωρον B². οὐδὲ VHB²
lat.a¹²; οὐδὲν KB¹; οὐ 0. τῷ μὴ V¹(transpos. ex μὴ
τῷ)HB²lat.0; μὴ τῷ KB¹a¹². 20 ἐνάργεια Lond.0;

Adnot. ad text.: c.XXVI-XXVII

ἐνέργεια libri. 23 οὐδὲ V¹lat.; οὐδὲν v.c.V a¹². εἰς αὐτά] lege δύσλυτα (Bruns, fort., in app.). neque difficultas apparebit in ipsis lat. 25 τοιούτοις] fort. αὐτοῖς Gercke 129. 27 εἶναι <ἐπὶ τοῖς φρονίμοις> Gercke 129. μηκέτ' εἰσιν] μὴ δὲ τισὶ V¹; μηκετεῖσι v.c.V; μηκέτισι B¹; μηκέτεισι B²; μηκέτι εἰσὶ H lat.Casp.O; μὴ δέ τισι a¹²; μηδέ εἰσι Lond.O. 28 κακιῶν V(corr. m¹ vel v.c. ex κάκεινῶν)H lat.O; κάκεινων a¹². δεκτικοῦ v.c.V B(οι in lit.) lat. Schulthess O; δεκτικαὶ V¹a¹². 29 οὐδὲ γὰρ ἐπὶ v.c.V lat.B²; οὐδὲ γὰρ ἐπεὶ μὴ V¹a¹²; οὐδ' ἐπὶ Hmg.; οὐδὲ γὰρ οὐδ' ἐπὶ E; οὐδὲ γὰρ ἐπὶ μὲν Cas.Lond.O.

cap.XXVII

p.197.3 οἱ] lege οἷς (EO); οἱ V; om. B; ἡμεῖς δὲ supr. lit. 2 litt. B²; ὃ vel οὐ vel del. Gercke 129; fort. ἢ, Bruns in app. 4 ἴσως habet O in textu, om. in adnot.; typorum errore? λαμβανόμενοι λέγοιμεν Gercke; λαμβάνοντες λέγοιεν Grot.Lond.; sed ista concedentes dicunt lat.(Thillet, 18). Cf. Comm. ἕξεις] κακίας O in emendandis. 5 ἐπ' Cas.O; ἔτι Va¹²; ἔτι ἐπ' lat.B²Lond. O(fort.). 6 καὶ] lege ἀντὶ (Donini); <ἔξον> καὶ Cas.O. τοῦ τῶν E Bruns; τούτωι V; τούτω a¹; τούτων a²; τὸ τῶν Lond.O; τῶν Cas. Casp.O. et de melioribus eligentes meliora, om. τοῦ et ἀμελεῖν, lat.; cf. Donini ad loc. 13 τὸ μὲν ὃν Hγρ.O; μόνον V¹; μένον v.c.V a ; μὲν ὃν Lond.; ὃν a²; manens quidem lat. 17 ἦν om. lat.BO. ἐγγενετὴς sic, accentu deleto, V; a nativitate lat. 18 καὶ μὴ a² Grotius. 22 ὑγιαινόντων B²Emg.Lond.O; ἐπαινούντων Va¹²; om. lat., cf. Donini 300. 23 post τοιοῦτοι add. lat. scilicet sani; glossema, cf. Donini loc. cit. 25 lege καὶ οὐ νοσοῦντας (non delenda), cum Rodier. τοὺς V lat. a¹²; τοὺς μὴ E Lond.O; μὴ vel διὰ τοῦτο μὴ Gercke 129. νοσουντας V; εὐεκτοῦντας B². καὶ - νοσοῦντας del. Bruns. 26 ἄνευ ... φροντίδων] sine occasione lat. 27 καὶ (alt.) del. B², om.O. 28 ἢ Casp.O; εἰ libri; om. lat.

258

Adnot. ad text.: c.XXVII

p.198.1 [ἡ] del. Schwartz. 3 <ἔχοντα> add. Β²; τῷ
ἀνθρώπῳ συμφῦναι Lond.Ο; virtutem ... hominem a natura
habere lat.; lectionem codicum retinet, et non possunt
homines virtutem gignere (cf. 198.10) vertit, Gercke
129 (φῦναι transit.?). 4 αυτῆς sic V; virtutis lat.
(ἀρετῆς; Thillet 17). 5 αυτῆς sic V; ipsius lat.
7 πολλῶν] τῶν ἄλλων Ο. 8 εἴχομεν Cas.Ο; ἔχομεν
libri. 12 δὲ μὴ V¹(sic coll. quod scr. μὴ δὲ), H;
μηδὲ lat.a¹². εἰ γὰρ ἦν lat.Lond.Ο; οὐ γὰρ ἦν Va¹;
οὕτω ἦν a²; ἢ γὰρ ἂν ἦν Β²; εἰ μὲν γὰρ ἦν Cas.
13 καὶ πάντες Β². 14 lege <τῶν> κατὰ (Apelt,
Hackforth). lege αὐτοῖς τυγχανόντων (Hackforth);
αὐτοῖς τυγχάνουσιν libri; ἂν αὐτῶν ἐτύγχανον καὶ Β²;
αὐτῶν τυγχάνοιεν Lond.Ο; αὕτως (= αὐτομάτως)
τυγχάνουσιν Gercke 129. sicut alia que conveniunt
ipsis secundum naturam adipiscuntur lat. (i.e. αὐτοῖς
προσηκόντων τυγχάνουσιν, Thillet 18). 14-15 οὕτως
οὐ τὴν Β²Ε; οὕτως οὖν τὴν V lat.a¹²; οὕτως οὖν καὶ τὴν
K; οὕτως οὖν οὐ τὴν Cas.; οὐδὲ τὴν Lond.; οὕτως οὖν
οὐδὲ τὴν Ο in adnot. 15 ante μόνην add. habemus
lat. 16 ἂν εἴχομεν Β(εἴ et o in lit.), Cas.; ἂν
ἔχοιμεν Va¹; si habeamus lat.; ἂν ἔχομεν Ε; ἀνέχομεν
a². 17 [δὲ] del. Bruns, exhib. lat. Post κακίαις
add. ἔπαινοί τε καὶ ψόγοι γίνονται Β². 18 οὐσίαν]
ὁσίαν Casp.Ο; αἰτίαν Gercke 129. Cf. Comm. ἔχουσιν]
εἴχομεν Cas.Ο. δὴ Bruns; δ' libri; οὖν Β² in
lit. 22 αὐτοῦ Lond.Ο; αὐτοῦ Va¹²Cyr.; se ipsum lat.
23 lege ἀναγκαίως (Cyr., ?lat.); ἀναγκαῖον VO Bruns.
Cf. 197.30-198.3. 24 μάτην] μάταιοι Cyr. 25 οὔτε
αἱ Β²HE Cyr.; οὐ V¹; οὔτε v.c.V a¹²Cas.Lond.; neque
lat. βελτίω lat.Β²Vict.Cas.Ο(adnot.); τὰ βελτίω
Cyr.; βελτίων Va¹²; βέλτιον HE Lond. ἡ διὰ] iam
lat. (ἤδη?). 25-26 αἱ ... ἀγωγαί Cyr. 27 οὐχ']
οὐδ' vel οὐ γὰρ Gercke 129. 28 κατὰ] παρὰ Grotius y
Nourrisson Gercke(adnot.); sed cf. Valgiglio Riv.Stud.
Class. 15 (1967) 309 n.7. αὐτοῦ coni. Gercke
129; αὐτοῦ libri.

p.199.6 Post γὰρ add. τὰ δίκαια γινόμεθα δίκαιοι Β².

Adnot. ad text.: c.XXVIII-XXIX

cap.XXVIII

p.199.9 ταῦτα] *hoc* lat. 10 γενομένοις Cas.Lond.O;
qui facti sunt lat. 13 συντελέσοντα Η Casp.O *SVF*
3.658; *conferentia* lat. 16-17 μὲν εἶς ἢ om. lat.
17 δεύτερος transcr. corrupte lat.(O), cf. Thillet ad
loc. et 58; om., spatio relicto, lat.(EG). fort.
δεύτερός <τις>, Bruns in app. 21 εἴη] *est ... erit*
lat.(GO); *erit* om. lat.(E). 22 παρὰ | τὰς δοξολογίας
m[1] corr. in τὰς παραδοξολογίας V; τὰς παραδοξολογίας
ΗΒ[2]O; παρὰ τὰς δοξολογίας a[12] Schulthess (sed πάρα, =
πάρεστι, Schulthess; O adnot.); *de opinionibus* lat.
24 τοῦ νῦν] τοίνυν E; τὰ (ᾃ in lit.) νῦν B. *amplius
studium quam sic presens expostulat* lat.

cap.XXIX

p.199.25 οὕτως del. B[2]; exhib. lat. <ἐστὶ> τὸ B[2].
ὅτι] fort. ὡς Bruns. ἔξεως V(m[1] corr. ex ἐξετάσεως)
ΗΕΒ[2]lat.O; ἐξετάσεως B[1]Ka[12]Cas.Lond. 26 τοῦ Ha[1]O;
τὸ Va[2]. τῷ - ἐξουσίαν] *eo quod prius habeat
potestatem q u o d non fiat talis* lat. 27 ἔχειν]
σχεῖν Gercke 131. μηκέτ' ἔχει Bruns; μηκέτ' ἔχειν
libri; *non obtinere* lat. ὡς ἐπ' V lat.a[12]; ἐπ'
Lond.O; οὐκ ἐπ' B[2](οὐκ in lit.)O(coni.) *SVF* 3.242;
μηκέτ' ἐπ' Casp.O. 28 fort. οὐδ' <ἐπὶ> τῷ Gercke
131. ῥίψ///αι V; *proicienti* lat. 29 ἐπ' αὐτῷ
Bruns; ἐπ' αὐτῶν libri, *SVF* 3.242. 30 ἐνεργεῖ ἐπ'
αὐτῷ καὶ B[2] *SVF* 3.242. 31 <τὰς> add. B[2].

p.200.1 κατὰ τοῦτον ΗΟ. τὸ παρὰ μικρὸν]
derelinquere modicum lat. 4 ποτὲ et καὶ om. lat.
5-6 γινόμενον Lond.O; λεγόμενον libri. 7 οἱ Casp.O;
οἱ libri. γε Bruns; τε libri; del. B[2]Casp.O
Valgiglio (*Riv.Stud.Class.* 15 (1967) 315 n.20); om.
lat. 7-8 ὑφορώμενοί τε καὶ φεύγοντες B[2] Valgiglio
(loc. cit.). ὑφορώμενοι - ἐλέγχους] *qui videntur
velle vitare redargutiones* lat. 9 ὥσπερ om. lat.
11 προλέγειν O (qui H attrib., sed falso).

Adnot. ad text.: c.XXX

cap. XXX

p.200.13 ἐκείνους] *illo* lat.   16 χωρούσης lat.a²;
χωροῦσιν Va¹.   οὐδένα a²; οὐδενας V; οὐδένας lat.a¹;
οὐδὲν Lond.   [μᾶλλον] del. B²Lond.O; om. lat.
17 μᾶλλον del. ES Cas.   ἀδυνάτου δ᾽ οὔσης <τῆς
φύσεως> suppl. lat.; subaudiendum, O 310 n.3.
18 πρόρρησιν ES Cas.O; πρόσρησιν Va¹²;
determinationem lat. (cf. infra de 201.4).   19 [τὸ]
del. Bruns.   23 ἐπὶ τῶν V; ἐπὶ τὴν B¹a¹²; τι τῶν
B²O; τὴν ἐπὶ τῶν Cas.; ἐπεὶ τῶν Diels.   ἐπὶ τῶν
ἀδυνάτων] *impossibilia* lat.(E); *impossibilibus*
lat.(GO).   lege οὕτως. <αὐτοῖς>(Hackforth); οὕτως
libri; αὐτοῖς Diels.   γὰρ ἦν] γὰρ ἡ SE; παρῆν <ἡ>
Diels.   βούλονται. ἐπὶ τῶν ἀδυνάτων οὕτως (sc. τῇ
αὐτῶν φύσει) γὰρ ἦν ἂν τοῖς Apelt.   δυσχέρεια B².
25 *v e l ut ... vel ut* lat.(add.? cf. Thillet 152 s.
vel).   οὕτως] *omnino sic* lat.; cf. Comm.   26 ἡ sic
add. v.c.V.   πρὸς B².   28 [εἰ] del. B², om. ES
lat.; exh. V(o s.v. m¹) a¹².   28-29 ἐκ τοῦ ...
κατασκευάζειν] *quod ... astruere volunt* lat.
30 αὐτὰ v.c.V lat.a¹²; αὐτῷ V¹; fort. πάντα Bruns.
ἂν suspectum, Bruns.   31 τε καὶ προσαγορεύσει om.
lat. (cf. Donini 311).   32 post ἕπεται non interpungendum.   καὶ om. lat. (Thillet, 17) Donini Bruns
(fort.); cf. Comm.   οὐκ ἂν] lege οὐδ᾽ ἂν (Donini);
οὐκ ἂν Lond.O; *neque* lat.; οὐ γὰρ Va¹²; οὐδὲ B².

p.201.2 γε] fort. γοῦν Bruns; *autem* lat. (? = δὲ;
Thillet 122 s.v.).   3 δύνασθαι] γίνεσθαι B¹; *quod
d i i non possunt* lat.   4 προρρήσεως] *scientiam*
lat. (cf. supra de 200.18).   4-5 lege προλαμβάνειν
(vulg.); προσλαμβάνειν Bruns.   7 <δυνατὰ> add. O
(sed post δεικνύναι) Casp.O.   8 γὰρ lat.a²; εἰ γὰρ
Va¹.   9-10 μέτρων, θέμενος Casp.O; θέμενος μέτρων
libri; μέτρων lat.O Schwartz.   10 τούτῳ a²Schwartz.
10 et 11 δυνατὸν] ἀδύνατον a².   12 ἦν οὕτως οὐδ᾽ a².
13 εἰ delendum (Hackforth; vel ἔπειτα εἰ legendum,
idem). εἰ τὸ corr. ex εἰ τὰ V; ///τὸ B.   τὸ (alt.)]
καὶ a².   15 <ὁ> add. Bruns.   τἀδ sic V.

Adnot. ad text.: c.XXX-XXXI

16 τὸ τὸ] τὸ lat.   ὡς ἐνδεχόμενον ἐσόμενον
Hackforth; sed ἀναγκαίως cum ἐσόμενον, ἔσεσθαι cum
τὸ ἐνδεχόμενον iungendum; ita lat.   λέγειν] λέγει
lat.   17 ἂν post ὡς ἐνδεχόμενα coll. a¹²; om. lat.
(librarii socordia, cf. Thillet 38).   20 ὧν] οὗ
Cas.; αὐτῶν coni. O.   20-21 προλέγουσιν λέγουσιν
Bruns; λέγουσι προλέγουσιν lat.(Thillet 18) Casp.O;
λέγουσιν V; προλέγουσιν a¹².   21 τοῖς ES Cas.O; τὰ
τοῖς V lat.; τὰ δυνατὰ τοῖς a¹².   22 τῆς s.v. V; om.
ES.   23 τῆς τῶν ESa² Cas.   28 neque (G, om. EO)
interimus neque divinationes neque (om. E)
prescientiam lat.   29 φύσεως τὰ πράγματα] rerum
natura lat.

cap.XXXI

p.201.31 τι] aliquid a l i u d lat.   32 τοῦ θεοῦ·
οἱ δὲ S(δ') Lond.(οὔδε) O; τοῦ θεοῦ δ' VBHEa¹; του
(= τινος). θεοῦ δ' lat. (cf. Thillet 18); τοῦ θεοῦ
δι' a²; τοῦ θεοῦ διυμνοῦντες Cas.; τοῦ θεοῦ. εἰ δ'
Hmg.

p.202.1 αὐτῶν SE Lond.O; αὐτοῦ V Cas.; ipsius lat.
1-2 καὶ ταύτῃ H Lond.O; καὶ ταύτην V lat.a¹²Cas.; καίτοι
Casp.O; καὶ διὰ ταύτην vel καὶ δι' αὐτὴν coni. Gercke
94.   2 <τῇ> non addendum; add. Bruns, resp.
Rodier qui confert Aristot. part. an. 681 a 9, de an.
427 a 13.   χρώμενοι lat.a¹²; χρώμενος V (supra ς: ι
m¹) H.   3 πέρι] lege περὶ (vulg.); πέρι Bruns, sed
περὶ Apelt qui θεῶν cum ἀλλότρια iungit, cf. Alex.
quaest. 68.22, 69.30.   4 ἄτοπα] α in lit. V.   τὰ
add. v.c.V, exhib. lat.   τούτων V lat.; αὐτῶν a²O;
τὰ περὶ τούτων om. a¹.   6 μαντεῖαι] divinatores lat.
(= μάντεις, Thillet 50; cf. infra de mantissa 182.28).
μὲν del. B², SVF 2.941.   7 ἐοικυίαι] assimilare
(infin.) lat.   δι' ὃ lat. Gercke 94 Bruns; διὸ Va¹²;
δι' ἃ HO.   post ἤκουσαν add. responsum lat.
8-9 παραδεχομένων a¹², 'fort. recte' Gercke 94; cf.
Comm.   9 διὸ οὐ K; δι' ὃ O.   10 φυτεύσεις]
τεκνώσεις Euripides.   σ' ὁ φῦς] eum serpens

Adnot. ad text.: c.XXXI

(= ὄφις!) lat.; cf. Thillet 59 et n.1. 12 <οὐ> add.
Bruns; <οὐχ> ante οὕτως add. Usener, *SVF* 2.941.
ὡς] *quod* lat.(GO); -*que* lat.(E). κηρύττει B²O;
κηρύττειν V lat.a¹². αὐτῶν a¹²O; αὐτων (supr. ν: ι)
V; αὐτῷ H lat. 13 οὐχ ὡς οὐκ B²Cas.; μὴ ὡς οὐκ
Lond.O. παντὸς lat.a¹²Casp.O; πάντος (supr. ος: ως
m¹)V; πάντως Lond.O; τὸ SE. ἤδι V¹(corr. m¹);
transcr. corrupte lat.(O), cf. Thillet 58. ἀλλ'οτι
sic V. 14 fort. μηδὲ ἓν αὐτοῦ Gercke 94. τῶν
lat.B Lond.O; τῷ Va¹². 16 ἀνέθηκεν V¹; ἀν ἐξέθηκεν
v.c.V; *reposuit* lat.(et ita pro alt. ἐξέθηκεν), om. ἂν
(Thillet 38). αὐτῷ Va¹²; αὐτῷ lat.(?) Bag.Lond.O Gercke
94. γενόμενον αὐτῷ om. H. 17 ἀναιρεθεὶς]
interemptus lat.; ἤγουν ἀναληφθεύς B². 18 καὶ add.
v.c.V; exh. lat. .20 αὐτῶν Schwartz; αὐτὸν libri;
αὐτοῖς *SVF* 2.941; αὐτῷ O Gercke 94. 20-21 τὴν δὲ-
om. lat. 22 δρᾶμα] *cursus* lat. (cf. supra, Introd.
n.212). 24 διαφερων (supra φ: θ v.c.)V; διαφέρον
ES; διαφθερῶν a¹²; *moriturum* lat. 25 τίς lat.B².
πῶς] πως lat.; del. B². 26 ἢ περὶ V; *qu(a)e de*
lat. εὐσεβεῖς SE; εὐσεβέας O; εὐσεβείας cett.
πρόληψις V¹lat.; προλήψεις v.c.V.

p.203.1 ὦν om. lat. codd., sed cf. Thillet ad loc.
2 εἰ γὰρ B²; ἃ γὰρ Rodier. 3 καὶ <ἃ> διὰ O. τὰ
ἐπ' αὐτοῖς γενόμενα] *que a b ipsis f i u n t* lat.
Fort. (καὶ ... γενόμενα), πως οὐκ Rodier. 4 ἀλλ'
οὐ a¹²Lond.O; ἀλλου V lat.; ἀλλὰ ES; om. K. 6 lege
γίνεσθαι <τὸ ἀγαθὸν αὐτοῖς> (Donini).
συνεργούμενον] lege συνεργεῖν εὔλογον (Donini);
συνεργούμενον libri (supra: τοῖς ἀγαθοῖς αὐτοὺς δεῖ
συνεργεῖν B²); συνεργοῦντας lat. Casp.O; συνεργοὺς
(vel συνεργοῦντας) τὸ ἄμεινον Hackforth. 7 ἄρα V;
forte lat. γε] lege δὲ (libri lat. Donini); γε
Bruns. 8-9 συντελεῖ Cas.; συντέλει Va²; συνετέλει
a¹; *profuit* lat.; συνεργεῖ Ηγρ.O. 9 δὲ om. a¹²;
γὰρ Lond.O. 10 τίς in lit. ante ἀκούσας, et post
ἀκούσας lit. 3 litt., B; τις lat. 10-11
εὐσεβεστέραν] *m i n u s piam* lat. 12 *tali*

Adnot. ad text.: c.XXXI-XXXII

providentiam lat.   15 *assumantur* lat.   18 παίδων]
puer (sing.)lat.   ἀδελφων(supr.ω: ι m¹)V; ἀδελφῶν a¹²;
ἀδελφῶ/// B; ἀδελφῷ H lat.O.   καὶ del. y Casp.O.
19 τῆς v.c.V a¹²; τῶν V¹ lat.; fort. τῆς τῶν **Bruns.**
20 τούτων B²Hγρ.ES Lond.O; τούτῳ V lat.a¹²; τοῦτο K.
21 ἐμποδιεῖ Hγρ.ES.   νομοὺς Lond.O.   23 τίνι]
alicui lat.   25-26 *talia plasmata f i n g e r e*
lat.   26 ἐπιβουλευσαμένην O.   28 παιδίων O.
αὐτοῦ V lat.; αὐτοῦ BHSa¹²Lond.O; *propriorum* Bag.¹;
suorum Bag.²Grotius.   29 πιστεύσουσι **Schwartz.**
τε v.c.V lat. B²; δε V¹; δὲ a¹²; δὴ HO.
30 κατασκευάσουσι **Schwartz.**

p.204.1 ἀναιρεῖν] ἂν add. v.c.V; *interimentes* lat.
2 <ἂν> add. **Bruns.**   εὐγνωμονέστερον] *condonabilibus*
lat.(O); *conditionalibus* lat.(G); *condomalibus* lat.
(E); *condonabilius* lat. ut vid. (Thillet 124 s.v.).
3 ἢ lat.Lond.O; οὐ V; οὐ rel.   4-5 τοῦ - τινὰς]
causas aliquas secundum rationem ipsa fiant lat.

cap.XXXII

p.204.7-8 τὸ - εἶναι τὸ φρονεῖν] ἐν μηδένι ὂν (ὂν
φύσει ES) τὸ φρονεῖν φύσει Hγρ.ES.   8 φρονεῖν
καίτοι] ρονεῖν καίτοι in mg. V¹.   μὴ (pr.) om. O in
adnot.   δυναμένῳ Cas.Lond.O lat.Donini; δυναμένων
Va¹²; δυναμένου B².   μὴ (alt.) Bruns lat. Donini; τὸ
Va¹²; τὸ μὴ B²; τὸ οὐ Lond.; οὐ Cas. Gercke 132; τότε
οὐ coni.O, Casp.O.   ὅτι del. B²; fort. ἔτι Gercke
132.   10 δὲ τοῦ V; //// τοῦ B; τοῦ ES lat.; δὲ τοῦ
a¹²; γὰρ τοῦ Hmg.; δὴ τοῦ Casp.O.   11 lege δι' ἣν
<δὲ> (δὲ transpos. Rodier ex 10); καὶ δι' ἣν Lond.O;
et propter ... quam lat.   12 αὐτῷ lat.(?) Bag.
Grotius O; αὐτῷ VHBSa¹²Lond.   12-13 τοῖς θεοῖς von
Arnim + *SVF* 2.985.   13 οὐκ εἴη ἂν] lege οὐκέτ' ἂν
<εἴη> (von Arnim + *SVF* 2.985, Hackforth); οὐκέτ' ἂν
vulg.; οὐκ ἔστ' ἂν ES; fort. οὐκ ἔστιν Gercke 132;
οὐκ εἴη ἂν **Bruns.**   lege <ἐπ' αὐτοῖς> τὸ εἶναι
(Hackforth).   ὑπ' ἐκείνων O.   14 γάρ ἐστιν] lege
πάρεστιν (von Arnim + *SVF* 2.985, Donini).   <τὸ>

264

add. HO Bruns; respuit Hackforth. 15 ἐπ' αὐτῶν
Gercke 132. 17 lege αὐτῶν <τοῦ χείρονος> (0; cf.
Comm.). ἀνεπίδεκτος ὢν ἐναντίων Β². 18-19 *melioris*
et peioris lat. 19 καὶ] καίτοι Gercke 132, 'fort.
recte' Bruns. 19-20 ἀνιδρωτὶ καὶ om. lat.
20 παραγίνεσθαι Casp.O. 22 lege ἐξουσίαν, <ἔχουσι
δὲ καὶ οἱ θεοὶ ταύτην τὴν ἐξουσίαν> εἴποτε (add.
Donini exempli gratia; cf. γὰρ, 24 init.). εἴποτε
v.c.V; εἴτε V¹; ? εἴ γε lat.(Thillet 145 s. *si*
quidem). 24 τοῦ τῷ a¹²; τοῦ τῶ V; τούτῳ ES; του τῷ
Cas. τῷ αὐτῷ om. lat. χρῆσαί τε καὶ Grotius
Schwartz; χρῆσθαί τε καὶ v.c.V; χρήσεται καὶ V¹; *et*
respondendi et lat. 25 παρίστασθαι coni.O;
προίστασθαι libri; *precedendi* lat. Fort. παρίστασθαι
<τε καὶ μή>, Bruns. 27 οὐ v.c.V lat.a¹²; ὡς V¹.
28 αὐτόν Bag.Lond.O; αὐτὸν Va¹².

cap.XXXIII

p.205.1 ἡγεῖσθαι]lege ἐφεῦσθαι (Hackforth); ἡγεῖσθαι
codd.; *itaque* lat.(O); om. lat.(EG); πλανᾶσθαι Β² von
Arnim + *SVF* 2.1001; <οὐχ> ἡγεῖσθαι Casp.O; <ἄτοπα>
ἡγεῖσθαι Heine 43 n.2; ληρεῖν sive νηπιάζεσθαι Gercke
101; ἐλέγχεσθαι Apelt; παράγεσθαι Rodier. οὐχ sic
V; del. Casp.O; exh. lat.(O), cf. Thillet ad loc. et
p.58. 2 τῷ] τὸ Lond., Casp.O (a¹² attrib. O, sed
falso). μὴ sic V; om. lat.; del. Gercke 101, Bruns,
Apelt; retinuit SVF 2.1001. Cf. Comm. 3 ἐπὶ τοῖς
ὁρμῶσιν] *in sic agentibus* lat. 4 ἐνεργήμάτι sic V;
ἐνερωτήματι ES. τὸ om. lat.; τῶν coni. O.
6 τούτῳ] ῳ in lit. B. μὴ Bruns; μήτε libri; μηδὲν
Β²; del. Heine 43 n.2; fort. μή τι Gercke 101; μηδὲ
Usener; μὴ τὸ Apelt. 7 δὲ <μηδὲ> Heine 43 n.2.
τι del. Β²; τε a²; τὸ Gercke Apelt. οὖ καὶ αὐτοῦ
(καὶ in lit.)B; οὐκ αὐτοῦ V(ὐ in lit. 3 litt.) lat.
a¹²; καὶ αὐτοῦ Lond.O. 11 εἶναι δή] lege ἐπειδὴ
(von Arnim + SVF 2.1001). 12 ἔστι retinendum (von
Arnim + SVF 2.1001); del. Bruns; post παντάπασιν coll.
Β². πῶς οὐ] πῶς οὖν V¹, corr. v.c.; *quidem* lat.
ἀγνοοῦντες Β². 14 lege <τούτου> τοῦ λόγου (Long).

Adnot. ad text.: c.XXXIII-XXXIV

τοῦ λόγου] τοῦτο γοῦν Apelt. 17 <ἢ> add. Bruns.

cap. XXXIV

p. 205.22 γινόμενα] λεγόμενα Casp.O. 23-24 lege αὐτῇ
προσκεχρῆσθαι (Hackforth); αὐτην (supr.ν: ι) πρόστὸ
κεχρῆσθαι V; αὐτῇ κεχρῆσθαι Lond.O; αὐτὴν πρὸς τὸ
κεχρῆσθαι KB (αὐτὴν πρὸς τὸ del. B²)a¹²Cas.; αὐτῇ πρὸς
τὸ κεχρῆσθαι HES; uti, tantum, lat.; αὐτῇ χρῆσθαι
coni. Bruns. 30 μέν, ὄντων] lege μενόντων (von
Arnim + SVF 2.1002); μενόντων τῶν a²; μὲν ὄντων cett.;
κατὰ φύσιν, <κατὰ φύσιν> μὲν <οὖν> ὄντων [δὲ] καὶ
(fort.) coni. Bruns.

p. 206.1 ἀγνοουμένων] lege ἀναιρουμένων (von Arnim +
SVF 2.1002). ἔπαινοι] lege ἔπαινοι μένου<σι> (von
Arnim + SVF 2.1002); ἔπαινοι corr. ex ἐπαινουμένου
V¹; ἔπαινοι μὲν Gercke 54. 5 τὸ καὶ] consequitur
lat. 7 μὴν τοῖς V lat.a¹; μέντοι γε τοῖς a²; μέντοι
γε ES; μέντοι γε ὅτι Lond.O. 8 πάντα] pr. α in lit.
V; exhib. lat.; πάντα <ποιεῖν> Schwartz. ἔπεται
Bruns; ἔπειτα libri. 9 τῶν] et lat. 11 τὰ] fort.
ταῦτα, Bruns; hec lat.; ἡμᾶς τάδε, ἐξ ἀνάγκης Apelt.
12 ταῦτα suspectum, Bruns; exhib. lat. lege χαρίεν
<τι> ποιοῦντα (lat. Donini). 13 ἁμαρτάνειν sic V;
exhib. lat. 14 εἰ v.c.V, lat.; om. a¹². 15 τὰ
βελτίω HES lat. yO; /////βελτίω B; ἢ τὰ βελτίων V; ἢ
τὰ βελτίω a¹²Lond. τὸν γοῦν] et eum cui lat.
19 ὧν H lat.; ἡμῶν V; ἡμῶν a¹²; εἰ γὰρ (del. δὲ)B²;
οἷς Lond.O. 19-20 πράττομεν B². 20 lege <καὶ>
οὐδὲν (Hackforth). αὐτοὺς V; αὐτοῖς lat. a¹².
[τὰ]] lege <ταῦ>τα (lat. y Diels (qui confert 206.12)
Hackforth); τὰ libri (om. ES), del. Bruns.
21 <περιιστάμενα> περιεστάναι B . πράττουσιν, πῶς]
ita interpungendum (Hackforth). 22 τῶνδε] talibus
lat. 23 ἢ ὁρμὴ K; ὁρμὴν a¹². 26 μηδενὸς] lege
μηδὲ ὧν (lat. Donini). 28 οὔ τε corr. ex οὔτε
v.c.V. 30 δὲ] γὰρ O.

p. 207.1-2 [ἐν τούτοις]] del. V¹, om. a¹²; est autem

266

Adnot. ad text.: c.XXXIV-XXXVI

lat.   3 ἣ B²HES lat.; οὐ (η superscr. v.c.)V; οὖ
a¹²; οὐ B¹Cas.; τοῦ y.

cap.XXXV

p.207.4 lege παραλύπωμεν (V, SVF 2.1003); παραλεύπωμεν
KE Cas.O Bruns.   5 δυναμένου Va¹²; δυνάμενον ES;
δυναμένῳ Lond.O; om. K.   5-6 οὐ γὰρ ἐστι] οὐκ ἔστι
Lond.O; confert Bruns 208.19.   6 οὐκ ἔστι δὲ (pr.)
V¹a¹²O; οὐδέ ἐστι v.c.V, lat.; οὐκ ἔστι ES.   Post
πεπρωμένη lege <οὐδέ ἔστι μὲν πεπρωμένη> (ita suppl.
B² Lond.(sed μὲν om.) O Bruns(app.) SVF 2.1003).
οὐκ (alt.)] neque lat.   7 οὐδὲ ἔστι μὲν (alt.)
v.c.V, lat.; οὐδὲ ἔστι V¹Ha¹²; οὐδὲ Lond.; οὐκ ἔστι μὲν
O.   8 δὲ (pr.) v.c.V a¹²O; μὲν V¹H lat.; om. ES.
μὲν v.c.V a¹²O; δὲ V¹H lat.; om. ES.   οὐδ' (alt.)]
lege οὐκ (a¹²O von Arnim + SVF 2.1003); οὐδ' VH lat.
Bruns.   δὲ (alt.) a¹²O; μὲν V(post ras.) HB¹; om.
ES lat.   18 <δὲ> B²S Casp.O.   19 εἰ V¹lat.a¹²;
οὐ v.c.V.   <οὐκ> ἀπείρηται] lege ἅπερ εὔρηται (ES
Hackforth); ἀπεύρηται VH Cas.; <οὐκ> ἀπεύρηται B²
Bruns; ablata sunt lat. (ἀπῆρηται? cf. Thillet 119
s.v.); ἀπῆρηται a¹²; ἀφῆρηται Lond.O; <μὴ> ἀνῆρηται
von Arnim + SVF 2.1003; ἀπαραίτητα Apelt (Kritische
Bemerkungen, Jena 1906, 8).   μὲν εἶναι] lege μένει
πάντα (Hackforth); μὴ εἶναι B²; μένει καὶ von Arnim,
Apelt locc. citt.

cap.XXXVI

p.207.25 δοξαζομένων αἰτία Schwartz; δοξάντων αἰτία
Lond.O; δοξαζόντων αἰτία καὶ B²; δοξαζόντων τινὰ
libri.   28 αὐτοῖς] αὐτὴν a¹²; αὐτοὺς O.   ἐν add.
v.c.V; exh. lat.a¹²; om. KHES.   29 αὐτοῖς] seipsis
lat.

p.208.1 ὡς περίττην O; ὡς ἂν περίττην lat. (Thillet
17); ὡς ἀπέραντον Casp.O.   2 τὸ μὴ δεῖν ὧν ἦν τὸ
ἄρα] lege <ἦ> τὸ μηδὲν ὤνηντο ἄρα (von Arnim; <ἦ>
add. SVF 2.1003); τὸ (του B²?) μὴ δεῖν ὧν ἦν τὸ ἄρα
codd.; quorum erat quod igitur (om. τὸ μὴ δεῖν) lat.;

267

Adnot. ad text.: c.XXXVI

τὸ μὴ δέον, οἷον ἦν τὸ ἀπόρημα Diels; τὸ μηδὲν (die
Nichtigkeit) ὧν ἦν τὸ ἄρα (der Schlusssatz) Apelt; τὸ
μὴ δεῖν ὧν ἦν ἡ τήρησις, vel τὸ τηρεῖν Rodier (fort.).
3 punct. interrogationis post μακρᾶς. 5 post
οὕτως non interpungendum (ante οὕτως punct. O Gercke
109 SVF 2.1003). 6 ἔχει] ἔχων lat. 7 <ὡς> add.
Bruns, om. Apelt; καὶ del. Gercke 109 (fort.).
ὁρμητικη (sic, supra η: ω)V; fort. ὁρμητικῷ <καὶ>
Bruns. 8 ὑφ' αὐτῶν] lege ὑπ' αὐτῆς (sc. τῆς
εἱμαρμένης; Grotius, Gercke 109, SVF 2.1003; cf. supra
182.7, 12); ὑφ' αὐτῶν Va²Bruns, cf. Apelt ad loc. (et
idem Kritische Bemerkungen, Jena 1906, 10); ὑφ' αὐτῶν
a¹O; ab ipsis lat. διὰ τῶν ζῴων del. Heine 40 n.1.
9-10 ἑπομένων - ἂν <ἤ> in parenthesi legendum (SVF
2.1003). 9 τούτων τῶν] lege τούτων τοῖς (Gercke
109, SVF 2.1003); ταῖς τῶν Heine 40 n.1.
10 περιεστώτων] lege περιεστῶσιν (Gercke, SVF
2.1003). αἰτίοις a¹² Gercke SVF 2.1003); αἰτίοις
(supra οις: ων m¹)V; αἰτίων HK; αἰτίαις Lond.O Heine
40 n.1. Post ἂν legendum <ἤ> (Apelt, von Arnim +
SVF 2.1003); <πράττῃ> Heine 40 n.1.
9-10 sequentibus et hiis causas que ... circumstant
lat. τοῦ τὸ] τοῦτο HKES lat.; τοῦ Gercke 109.
12 καὶ τὸ a¹²; τὸ καὶ V. [οὖς] del. Bruns; ·οὖς· V;
om. lat.; οὖς a¹²; οὖν Lond.O. 13 ὡς οὐκ] lege οὐχ
ὡς (von Arnim + SVF 2.1003). 14-15 παρέξειν E;
ταράξειν Lond. 15 δι' αὐτοῦ V(αὐ s.v. m¹); δουτου
transcr. corrupte lat.(cod. O), cf. Thillet ad loc et
58); διὰ τοῦ a¹²; καὶ διὰ τοῦ Lond.; καὶ διὰ τούτων
περὶ Cas.; καὶ, vel καὶ διὰ τοῦτο O. 19 τῆς (alt.)]
ταύτης lat.Cas.yO; om.ES. 20 δὲ B²S Lond.O; γὰρ VH
lat.(cf. Thillet 21 n.2, 41 n.3)a¹². 22 <καὶ> τὴν
αἰτίαν Cas.O. 22-23 αὐτοῦ Gercke 103.
23 συνάπτοντα B²Lond.; συνάπτον V B¹(ο in lit.) lat.
a¹²; συνάπτειν E Cas.O; συνάπτων S. ὡς H lat.; ὥστε
V; ὥστε a¹²; ὥσπερ B². ἀφεθέντα Gercke 103; ἀφέντα
libri; dimissum lat. (dimissis = ἀφεθεῖσιν, 189.22;
cf. quoque 181.26). 27 ουτος|ηδὲ V¹, corr. v.c.;
sic neque lat.

268

Adnot. ad text.: c.XXXVI

p.209.1 *nobis persuadebit utique aliquis, ratione* ...
iubente lat.   7 τὸ HB¹(ex corr.)O; τὰ cett.; *non*
sequitur secundum impetum nos operari lat.   ὅταν τὰ
περιεστῶτα])ὺ illegibile supra αν et τὰ supra π add.
V¹.   10 <οἱ> add. a¹².   13 πραττομένων] lege
πραττόντων (ES Cas.Lond.O); *illi qui agere debent* lat.
13-14 δυνάμεων K.   14 αὐτῷ corr. ex αὐτῶν V; *ipsi*
lat.   15 τῇ δὲ εἱμαρμένῃ, 16 φασι coni.O.
16-17 τῶν ... γινομένων lat.Lond.O; τῷ ... γινομένῳ
libri.   20 πράσσουσιν] προσουσιν V¹; corr. v.c.   κατ᾽
αὐτὸν Lond.O; καθ᾽ αὐτοῖς Va¹²; καθ᾽ αὐτοὺς HES Cas.;
κατ᾽ αὐτοὺς B² lat.(Thillet 17).   21 κατηναγκασμένως
KES; κατηναγκασμένως (supra ω: ο m¹)V; κατηναγκασμένος
lat.(Thillet 17)a¹².   22 αὐτόν Lond.O; αὐτούς libri.
23 τὸ γοῦν] lege ψόγου, εἰ et punct. interrog. post
κεκωλυμένη (26) (Hackforth); *igitur* (om. τὸ) lat. (cf.
Thillet 41 et n.1); ὅτι γοῦν Lond. Casp.O; fort. τότε
γοῦν Bruns in app.   25 fort. ἤν <ἡ> ἐκ Bruns.
26 κεκωλυμένη Lond.O; κεκωλυμένην V; κεκωλυμένης
(supra η: οι)ES; *prohibitum* lat.   ἔχων] ἐξὸν Casp.O
(qui λέγειν cum ἐξὸν, πείθεσθαι cum χρὴ coniungit).
26-27 lege καὶ <τοὺς> πειθομένους (Hackforth); καὶ
πειθομένους Ηγρ.S²Cas.Casp.O; καίπερ θεμένους VHa¹;
καὶ περιθεμένους a²; *ponentes* lat.   27 αὐτῷ Bruns;
αὐτῷ Ηγρ.Cas; αὐτῶν Va¹²; αὐτὸν B²Lond.O; *ipsam* lat.
τούτῳ] τοῦτο (supra ο: ω m¹)V; om. lat.   punct. post
λέγειν, non post ἑπομένους (Hackforth).   29 lege
συν[ειλ]ημμένον; συ|νει|λημμένον V; *consequens* lat.
(= συνημμένον, Thillet 124 s.v.).

p.210.3 τοῦ] lege τῶν (*SVF* 2.1004, Hackforth).
4 lege κατεσκευασμένων (*SVF* 2.1004, Hackforth); κατα-
σκευασμένου V(scr. κ ᵀσκ- ; sed cf. 203.30, *mantissa*
153.19); *probata* lat.; καὶ κατεσκευασμένου B²Smg.;
κατεσκευασμένον Cas. Casp.O.   τε] lege δὲ (coni.
Thillet 122); *autem* lat.; τὸ a². Cf. 196.7.
ἀρξαμένων libri Bruns Apelt (*Kritische Bemerkungen,*
Jena 1906, 9); ἀρξαμένοις B²lat.*SVF* 2.1004.   5 lege
<ἡ> ἀκολουθία (*SVF* 2.1004, Apelt loc. cit.); fort.

Adnot. ad text.: c.XXXVI-XXXVII

<τῆς> ἀκολουθίας Bruns.   6 lege <τι> εἶναι (SVF
2.1004, Hackforth).   εἶναι om. lat.   ὡς corr. ex
πως V¹; πῶς Ha¹²; ὡς lat.Lond.O; τι, ὡς Apelt loc.
cit.   τοῦ προλαβόντας] lege τοῦ προλαβόντες (Rodier
Hackforth); τοῦ προλαβόντας Va¹²Bruns Apelt (loc.
cit.); τοῦ προλαβόντος KES; τὸ προβάλλειν Lond.O.
7 ἄλλους Lond.   ἐφέρειν a¹; ἀφαιρεῖν Lond.O.   αὐτὰ]
lege αἰτίαν (Hackforth); αὐτὸ Lond.O Apelt (loc.
cit.); αὐτὴν (sc. τὴν ἀκολουθίαν) Rodier.   τὸ μὴ]
lege τῷ μὴ (Hmg E Lond.O Rodier Hackforth); τὸ μὴ
Va¹² Bruns Apelt (loc. cit.); τὸ (supra o: ω) μὴ S.
τῷ μὴ δοκεῖν] quod non videatur lat.   ἔχεσθαι V
lat.a¹² Lond.O Bruns Hackforth; ἔπεσθαι KES Hmg.
Rodier Apelt (loc. cit.).   τὸ καὶ τοῖς] lege καὶ
αὐτοῦ (Hackforth); τὸ καὶ τοῖς VKESa¹²; καὶ τοῖς Hmg.
lat. Rodier; ὃ καὶ Lond.O; αὐτὸ καὶ τοῖς Apelt (loc.
cit.).   7-8 lege ἡγούμενοι (Hackforth); ἡγουμένοις
codd. Rodier Apelt (loc. cit.); ἡγοῦνται Lond.O.
6-8 διὰ - ἡγουμένοις] totum hunc locum ita constituit
SVF 2.1004, de cuius licentia novandi in eo cf.
Pohlenz, Berl. Philol. Wochenschrift 23 (1903) 969:
<τὸ> διὰ τοῦ πρώ<του> λαβόντας ἄλλο ἐπιφέρειν αὖ τὰ
τούτῳ δοκοῦντα ἔπεσθαι ἄτοπα καὶ <τού>τοις διαβάλλειν
<τὸ> ἡγούμενον. 10 post φασίν non interpungendum;
cf. O et Gercke 53.   11 τὸ μὴ HB²E lat.Cas.O; μὴ τὸ
Va¹²; τὸ μηδὲ S.   12 <καὶ> add. B².   13 ἀναιρεῖται
HES.   <ἄρα> add. B².

cap.XXXVII

p.210.14 <τὸν> add. Bruns.   15 οὗτος corr. in οὕτως
V¹; οὗτος ES, 'fort. recte' Bruns; οὕτως cett.
17 μὲν •τοῦτο• sic V; exhib. lat.   18 εἰ τοῦτο
v.c.V lat.a¹²; εἰ το V¹; ἀεὶ τὸ εἴ S; εἰ το ει (supra
το ει: θεοίδε)E; τοῦτο K.   ἔστιν v.c.Va¹²; ἔστι V¹K;
ἐστιν S; ἐστὶν E; om. lat.   ἀρετὴ v.c.V lat. E(sine
accentu) Ka¹²; ἀρα V¹; ἄρα S.   19 ἡ delendum
(Gercke 51, SVF 2.1005).   23 κακὰ] αἰσχρὰ SVF
2.1005.   25 τοῦτο] hec lat.   εἰσιν] οὐκ εἰσιν O;

Adnot. ad text.: c.XXXVII-XXXIX

οὐκ ἂν Lond.   29 ἂν delendum (om. lat. - sed cf.
Thillet 38 - et O); cf. Comm.   lege τίς (V Grotius
O Nourrisson Boussoulas) et punct. interrog. post
αὐτομάτως (211.4); τις lat.Lond. Bruns; τὶς a¹².
29-30 lege συγχωρήσει (Va¹²O); συγχωρήσῃ ES;
συγχωρήσειε B²Bruns.   30 τὸ Cas.Lond.O. μὲν om. lat.

p.211.1 [ἐν] del. Bruns.   4 δὲ] γὰρ B².   τὰ ἄλλα]
τὰ αὐτὰ H Lond.; ταῦτα coni. yO. Cf. Comm.   5 <οὐκ>
add. a¹²; <οὐκ ἂν> add. Diels. Cf. Comm.
ἀνεμπόδιστος a¹²Lond.O.   μένει Cas.   6 τε καὶ]
scilicet lat. (? = τὸ καὶ; Thillet 21 n.4).   τὸ
κόσμον H Cas. Casp.O; τὸν κόσμον Lond.O.   ὄντος]
ἐντος Diels.   7 αὐτοῦ O.   12 τῶν θεῶν] ἀνθρώπων
Lond.   13 ἀνθρώπων οὖσα ἀρετή om.O.   17 οὖθ'
εὔλογον Lond.O.   αὐτοῖς V.   δὲ] enim lat. (cf.
Thillet 21 n.2, 41 n.3).   18 <μὴ> non addendum; add.
Lond.O Bruns, resp. Valgiglio Riv.Stud.Class. 15
(1967) 317 n.22, cf. infr.   19 καὶ <μὴ> τῶν
Schwartz, cf. Gercke 51.   Lege τῶν <οὐ> ποιητέων
(lat., Valgiglio loc. cit.).   20 μὴν v.c.V, lat.;
μὴ V¹.   25 τοῦτον B²H lat.Cas.; τοῦτο Va¹²; τούτῳ K.
26 <ἢ> add. K.

cap.XXXVIII

p.211.28 οἱ del. B², ret. SVF 2.1006 (= λόγοι).
30 ὑπὸ] ἀπὸ SVF 2.1006.   31 παρεισάγων H.   32 διὰ
suspectum, Bruns.   33 πρώτων] fort. προτέρων Apelt.

p.212.1-2 ὅσοις ἄλλοις ... λόγοις O.   2 ἐπιπόλαιον
Schwartz; 'bene' Bruns.   ἐπὶ - ἔχοντες] hiis magis
frivole existentes tantum lat.   3 καὶ del.SVF 2.1005.

cap.XXXIX

p.212.5 ὑμῖν HB(ῖν in lit. B); ὑμεῖς V lat.a¹²; μὲν
ὑμεῖς K; ἡμῖν ES.   6 δοξάντες O.   9 κυρίων B²lat.
Cas.Lond.O; κυρίους Va¹²; δοῦναι κυρίοις ES (κυρίων
s.v. S).   lege <καὶ περὶ ὑμᾶς> καὶ περὶ (add.

Adnot. ad text.: *de fato* c.XXXIX, *mantissa* XXII

Hackforth); <περί τε ὑμας> add.Cas.O.   ἡμῖν] lege
ὑμῖν (Cas.Lond.O Hackforth).   ὁμοίως E.
10 εὐχάριστοι] οὐκ ἀχάριστοι Cas.   Lege <οἷ> ταῦτα
(Hackforth); <ὅτι> ταῦτα Apelt.   ταῦτα] τοιαῦτα
Cas.; fort. πάντα Hackforth.   πράττεται] lege
πράττετε (Hackforth); πράττεται codd. Apelt; πράττεται
ὑφ' ὑμῶν Cas.; πράττοντας Lond.; ita quoque, vel
<γὰρ> πράττεται O.   τε καὶ ἡ περὶ ὑμῶν] lege
καθάπερ ἡ ὑμῶν (Hackforth); τε καὶ ἡ περὶ ὑμῶν codd.
(τε om. ES); καὶ ἡ περὶ ἡμῶν Cas.; ἃ ποιεῖ ὑμῶν Lond.
O.   Ante ταῦτα haec B² in mg.: νομίζοντες ἃ περὶ
ἡμῶν τε καὶ τὴν ἡμετέραν πρό (supr. ὅ: ν) ποιεῖτε.
11 πράττειν ὑμᾶς] lege ἄγει ὑμᾶς (ὑμ. ἄγ. Hackforth);
πράττειν ἡμεῖς K; πράττειν ἡμᾶς a²; πράττει ὑμᾶς
Apelt.   αἱρέσει] αἵρεσις ES.   τοῦ (alt.)] lege
τῷ (O Hackforth).   αὐτοῦ] αὐτῶν B².   12 φροντίζειν
V.   ποιοῦντες ES.   ποιεῖτε v.c.V; ποιεῖται V¹.
10-12 ταῦτα - ποιεῖτε] qui in nos b e n e agunt,
propria electione melioris tantum lat.
12 καταπροκαταβεβλημένοις VH.   13 ἄγεσθαι Hγρ.ES.
15 μόνον Cas.Casp.O.   ὧν O; ὧν libri.   αὐτός] αὐτὰ
Lond.O.   16 post ἐξουσίαν lacunam statuit Bruns;
recte tamen negaverunt Apelt, et Rodier qui ὅτι (16)
cum παραστῆσαι (18) copulandum censuit. Cf. Comm.
ὅτι] οὕτω B².   17f. αὐτῆς (sc. τῆς εἱμαρμένης? O
324 n.10)a¹².   18 post ἀποδιδοίημεν: vobis lat.
<ἃς> non addendum (cf. supra ad 16); add. HB²ES Bruns
Apelt; quam (sc. opinionem) lat.   δια sic V.
V(ὑ in lit.) lat.Vict.Cas.Lond.; ἡμῖν a¹².

Mantissa XXII

p.169.35 πάντως c?   Parenthesis cum ἀφυεῖς terminari
debet (ita Gercke 111), non cum γίνεται (37).

p.170.1 τε καὶ ἐφ' ἡμῖν suspectum, cf. 171.28, Bruns.
2 [ὁποῖον - ἀξιοῦμεν] del. Bruns.   3 lege <ὃ> καὶ
(Bruns, fort., et Donini (1974,2) 167 n.70).   ἅπασιν
ἐδόκει V²Pa¹; υπεσιν εδουει V¹; πασιν ἐδοκει v.c.V;

272

fort. τισιν ἐδόϰει Bruns, sed cf. Donini loc. cit. et
Sharples *BICS* 22 (1975) 41 et nn. 6 δὴ V; δὲ Pa[1].
9 τύχῃ v.c.V V²Pa[1]; εὐχῇ V . 11 τοῦ Va[1]; τῶν P.
τὸ V²Pa[1]; om. V[1]. 13 lege ἐν τοῖς οὖσίν (<ἔστι δὲ,
ἐπεὶ ἐν τοῖς οὖσίν> ἐστὶ ... τι ὄν), εἴη ἂν (14); ἔστι
- οὖσίν suppl. ex. gr. et parenthesim constituit
Bruns. συμβεβηϰος ὄν v.c.V; συμβεβηϰοσιν sic V[1];
συμβεβηϰός τι ὄν P; συμβεβηϰὸς ὄν a[1]. μὴ ὄν v.c.V;
δι' ὄν ὄν V[1]; μὴ ὄν ὄν P; μὴ ὄν ὄν a[1]. Lege εἴ τινι
συμβέβηϰεν (Bruns); ꟽ συμβέβη|ϰε (βη in mg. m[1])V[1];
τινι vel γινι in mg. v.c.V; συμβέβηϰεν P; ϰαὶ
συμβέβηϰεν a[1]. 15 ὄντος v.c.V V²Pa[1]; πάντος V[1].
πως V²Pa[1]; πω V[1]. 17 ἐστιν ἀίδια· sic V[1]. ἄλλα
δὲ φθειρόμενα V²Pa[1]; αλλα αειρομεν V[1]; ἄλλα
φθειρόμενα v.c.V. 18 αἰτίαν Pa[1]; αιτιαν v.c.V;
αιτια V[1]. 20 ἀτονία V²Pa[1]; ἀτοπία V[1].

p.171.2 ἐγίγνετο] lege ἐφίετο (Bruns, fort.); *nihil
bene gigneretur* c. 7 γενέσει Vc; γενέσι Pa[1].
8 αὐτὰ corr. ex αὖ τὰ V. 9 τι τοῦ V²Pa[1]; του V[1].
11 τοῦ V²Pa[1]; om. V[1]. 13 Lege αἴτιον. <τὸ> ἄρα;
<τὸ> add. Bruns (fort.), c (ut vid.); om. codd.
17 εἶναι om. Pa[1]. 19 προϰαταβέβληται] προϰ in lit.
V. 20 ἐϰινούμεθα] ϰι in lit. V. 21 punct. *ante*
ταῦτα (ita Va[1]c). ταῦτα] τοῦτο coni. Bruns. 22 ϰατ'
αὐτὰ P. 28 πολλῷ P. 29 ὀλίγον V²Pa[1]; οὐϰ ὀλίγον:V[1].
34 οὐϰέτι] lege οὐϰ ἐπί; *et non ut plurimum* c.

p.172.4-5 οὐδὲ τὸ ἐν τοῖς] lege οὔτε ἐν οἷς τὸ (Bruns,
fort.). 9 ἀναίτιοι] lege αἱ <δ>ὲ <γίγνονται>
ἀναιτίως (coni. Bruns); αἱ ἐάναίτιοι(post αἱ spat. 2
litt,)V; ἀναιτιος P; αι ἀναίτιοι (post αι spat.)a[1];
αἱ <δὲ> ἀναίτιοι c. Ad lacunam in V refert Bruns
litteram φ 'quam in margine posuit v.c.', sed haec
littera in microfilmo quidem non apparet (scholium
quod ad finem paginae legitur in V, φύσις ἐστὶν ἡ
ἐγγιγνομένη τῷ θνητῷ σώματι θεία δύναμις ὑπὸ τῆς πρὸς
τὸ θεῖον γειτνίασος (?) τῶν γεννητῶν, ad 172.17-19
referenda est). ἅς] lege ϰαὶ (Bruns); αἱ c?
δεῖ] lege δὲ (Bruns); δεὶ V; δε?P; δεῖ a[1]; om. c.

Adnot. ad text.: *mantissa* XXII-XXIII

11 τοῦτο (pr.)] οὕτω P (in mg. τοῦτο). τοῦτο
(alt.)] τοῦτον P. 13 τῶν (alt.) om. P. 14 ἔχειν
P.

Mantissa XXIII

p.172.18 γεννητῷ Pa¹. αὐτῷ] ἢ μὴ arab. 27 οἷόν
τε Pa¹. 29 καὶ ὁπότερον in mg. V¹; om. arab.
προέκρινεν om. arab.? 30 ἔρχεται (supra ἔ: α m¹)V;
ἄρχεται Pa¹; ἔρχεται (sc. αὐτῷ) arab.?(Zimmermann).
lege ἔρχεται <ἐπὶ τοῦτο> (Bruns, fort.).

p.173.1 τὸ αὐτὸ τῷ Bruns; τὸ αὐτὸ V¹; τῷ αὐτὸ V².
5 γενέσθαι (pr.) V²arab.; om. V¹Pa¹. καὶ μὴ γενέσθαι
om. arab. 12 ἀεὶ ζητεῖν arab. (sed om. τε καὶ
λέγειν). 14 βουλεύσεως arab. κρίσεως] φύσεως
arab. τε (alt.) om. arab. 20 lege αὐτῷ,
τουτέστι; τουτέστιν αὐτῷ codd.; fort. τουτέστιν αὐτὸ
Bruns. καὶ - τουτέστιν] *denn das bedeutet* tantum
arab. 21 ἔχει P. αὐτῷ arab., cf. *de fato* XIV
184.18, XV 185.17; αὐτῷ codd. Post αὐτῷ lacunam
statuit Bruns, suppl. Ruland (cf. transl.); in arab.
apodosis incipit ab οὐκ ἔστιν, 173.18, cf. Ruland ad
loc. 31 τὸ V arab.; τοῦ Pa¹. 32 τὸ om. P.
τισιν Va¹ arab.; αὐτοῖς P. 33 τοῦ (alt.) Bruns
arab.; عن (فى in lit.)V; τὸ Pa¹. *that in us there is
a cause for the r e f r a i n i n g from doing*
arab.

p.174.1 τῷ] τὸ arab.? (cf. Ruland). 2 ἐκ τῆς βουλῆς
Va¹; ἐν ταῖς βουλαῖς P. 3 τῶν κακῶν P. 4 ἢ (alt.)
del. Gercke 73. ἢ δὴ Gercke 73 (vel δὴ del.),
Bruns; ἤδη codd. 15 γε om. P. 20 πρὸς τούτων
ἕκαστον cum sequentibus iungit arab. 21 ποτὲ δὲ
om. P. 22 καὶ delendum (nos; exhib. arab.).
27 ὅτι] lege ἔτι (ita arab.; cf. Comm.). 28 οὐδ'
εἰ Va¹ arab.; οὐδεὶς P. 29 ταῦτα] lege ταὐτὰ (ita
arab.). 39 ὄντα Va¹ arab.; ἀεὶ ὄντα P. ὅμοιος]
ante ος lit. 1 litt. V; exhib. arab. αὐτῷ Bruns;
αὐτῷ VPa¹.

274

p.175.7 ὅλως Bruns; ὅλως (supra ω: οι)V¹; ὅλοις Pa¹
?arab. (cf. Ruland ad loc.). γὰρ τούτοις Pa¹;
τούτοις γὰρ V. 9 τὸ (pr.)] τι Pa¹. ἦθος] ἔθος
arab. (cf. Ruland ad loc.). 14 ἀ|νεννόητος (ν pr.
in mg.)V; ἀνόητος P; ἀνένοητος a¹. τὰ δίκαια Pa¹.
15 τὰ ἄδικα Pa¹. 18 αὐτοὺς Bruns; αὐτοὺς VPa¹.
21 lege καλὰ <μήτε τὰ αἰσχρὰ> (exhib. arab.).
22 διὰ κακίαν om. arab. πεπηρωμένοις] τετηρημένοις
arab. οὐκ delendum (nos). ἤ] εἰ c. γε] lege
τε (nos). ὁδὸς ἐστιν ἡ P. ἐπ᾽ αὐτὰ Bruns
(coni.), arab.; ἐφ᾽ αὐτὰ codd. πεπηρωμένοις
<ἀγνοεῖται μήτε τὰ αἰσχρὰ (ἀμφότερα γὰρ> οὐκ
ἀγνοεῖται, εἴ γε ὁδὸς ἡ ἐπ᾽ αὐτὰ ἐφ᾽ ἡμῖν τε καὶ
γνωριμός coni. Bruns ex. gr.; Wenn aber der zum Guten
und zum Schlechten führende Weg dem, der unter den
Menschen im Naturzustand ist und noch nicht Gut und
Böse geschaut hat, bekannt ist, so dass es bei ihn und
an ihn (liegt) ihn zu beschreiten, so liegt es also an
uns arab. 23 ποιοῖ a¹; ποιοὶ Gercke 130. ἤθη]
ἔθη arab. (cf. supra de 175.9). 24 <ἢ τάδε> add.
Bruns; etwas vor etwas arab. 25 εὐφυΐαι] αι in lit.
V. τε πρός τινα καὶ V (α s.v., καὶ s.v. et in
lit.); τε καὶ πρός τινας P; τε πρός τινας a¹.
26 τηρῶσιν] fort. μὴ πηρῶσιν Bruns; solange der Mensch
in der ihm eigenen Natur verteilt arab. 28 lege
ἀδιαστρόφοις (cf. Comm.); ἀστρόφοις V; freihalten arab.;
ἀστροφόροις Pa¹. αὐτοῦ Bruns, arab.(sed pl.);αὐτοῦ VPa¹.

Mantissa XXIV

p.176.2 καὶ Va¹; δὲ καὶ HP. 4 τῆς om. P. τῶν
δεδογμένων HPa¹; τῶνδε δειγμενων (supra ι: ο)V.
6 αὐτῶν om. PO. 8 αὐτοῖς VH; om. Pa¹.
12 κἀκείνων VP; καὶ τούτων H. 15 αὕτη Bruns; αὐτὴ
VHPa¹. 16 αὐτῆς VH; αὐτῶν Pc. 18 lege
ἐνυπάρχοντα· οὐ γὰρ (Bruns, fort.). τοῦτο] lege
τὸ (Bruns, fort.). οὐκ ἔχει cO. 19 αὐτῷ Bruns;
αὐτῷ VHPa¹O. 20 αὐτά HPa¹; αὐτό (supra ό: α)V.
22 τε om. Pa¹. 24 ὁ σκοπὸς ὡρισμένος Pa¹.
26 ποιεῖν P. 27 φύσει a¹. 28 τέχνη] τύχη H.

Adnot. ad text.: *mantissa* XXIV-XXV

30 ἄστατον VH; ἄτακτον Pa¹.

p.177.5 τρόπος coni.O.   τῶν αἰτίων H.   οὖν] ἦν a¹.
ἐπεὶ V Hmg. Bloch; ἐπὶ HPa¹c.   7 αὐτω καὶ κυρίῳ P.
8 τοῦτο H; τούτου Va¹c. (8 κατὰ - 10 συμβεβηκός (pr.)
om.P).   9 αἴτι (supra ι: ο)H; αἴτιον Bloch O.
10 τούτῳ P.   11 ἔτι γὰρ O.   12 αἴτιον om.O.
15 τὴν om.P.   19 ἀλλ᾽ ἃ κατὰ P.   21 φασὶ O.
24 ὡρισμένα HO.   26 τὰ HPa¹; om. V.   28 φασιν O.
30 τυχεῖν VHa¹; τυχεῖν αὐτῶν ἐφ᾽ P; πρᾶξαι O.
35 δέλεγομεν V.   δὲ (alt.) om. Pa¹.   γεγονέναι
VHa¹; εἶναι P.   [τε] om.P, secl. Bruns.

p.178.4 ἂν om. Pa¹.   7 ἀόριστον (cf. Aristot. *phys.*
2.5 196 b 28) Bruns; ἀορίστω (supr. ω: ο)V; ἀορίστῳ
ΚΡΟ; ἀορίστου c; ἀορίστως Bloch.   12 τὸ] fort.τι Bruns.
14 γένηται O.   τῇ delendum (Bruns, in app.).
21 τούτων Pa¹c.   23 εἴωθεν μὲν] εἰώθαμεν H.   ἐπὶ
in mg. suppl. H; exhib. VP.   24 γενομένῳ O.   25 τὸ
Pa¹c; τοῦ VH; om.O.   26 γεγονέναι καὶ τὸ
ἐπακολουθῆσαν ὥσπερ P.   26-27 γίγνεται Bloch O;
γίγνηται VHPa¹; *fiebat* c.   29 ἔσται H.

p.179.1 ὁ HPc; οὐ Va¹.   2 τήνδε τὴν θέσιν Va¹c; τὴν
θέσιν P; τήνδε τὴν φύσεως θέσιν H; τήνδε τῆς φύσεως
θέσιν O.   3 καὶ ὁ μὲν] δὲ καὶ ὁ O.   5 τούτῳ om.
Pa¹; *ille* (nom.) c.   8 τῶν ἀνθρώπων om.O.   10 ἐπεὶ
πλείω VHc; ἐπὶ πλείου P; ἐπὶ πλείω a¹.   11 τινας om.
cO.   12 ἔσται Bloch O; εἶναι VHPa¹.   16 συγχωροῦν
ἂν τὸ τυχεν P.   19 τὰς om. P.

Mantissa XXV

p.179.25 τίσι O.   26 τι] τε O.   27 φύσις]
sententia lat.   ἄστατον(supra ατ: οχ)V¹; ἄστοχον H
lat.; ἄστατον Pc; ἄστρατον a¹.   29 γε H; τε VPa¹;
om. lat.   31 αὐτοῖς lat. Bruns; αὐτοῖς VHPa¹.

p.180.3 ὁτὲ] ποτὲ Bloch O Gercke 108; *quando* lat. (? =
ὅτε, Thillet 144 s.v.).   4 καὶ - μοῖραν om. lat.;

276

Adnot. ad text.: *mantissa* XXV

cf. 186.5, *de fato* II 166.7; Thillet 57 n.3.

5-6 μήτε τὰ τῆς τύχης - ἔρρωται] *videtur quod non dominatur super ea que fortune; nec adhuc magis super ea que ex sententia ... prevalent* lat. 6 τε om. lat.; fort. τε <καὶ μοῖραν> Bruns. κρησφύγετόν] *malignum* lat. τι om. P. 8 ἐκείνοις P. γε (supra γ: τ)V; γε HP; *autem* lat.; καὶ a¹. 9 αὐτοῖς VH lat.a¹; αὐτῆς P; om. Q. 10-11 οἷς - δεξία] *quidam autem, quantum ad pospera iuxta votum* lat. 12 αὖ τῶν VPa¹; αὐτῶν H; αὖ om. lat., cf. Thillet 40. 14 γοῆτες] *insensati* lat. 17 αὐτοῖς lat. Bruns; αὐτοῖς VPHa¹. συνειδέναι VP lat.a¹; συνεῖναι HO. 20 οἷον P lat.a¹. an ὁτῳοῦν? Bruns *Interp. Var.* (cf. *Bibliogr.*) 17 n.1. 20-21 τὰ ὁπωσοῦν ἐσόμενα] *qualitercumque tantum* lat.; *librariorum negligentia*, fort., Thillet 50 n.3. 22 αὐτοῖς VH lat.; αὐτῆς Pa¹; αὐτῶν O. 22-23 ἀναπείθουσιν] *consolantur* lat. (cf. *infra de* 180.31). 24 μόνον om. lat. εὐχομένοις] ἐχομένοις lat. (Thillet 50 n.3). 24-25 ἔχον φανῆναι, κατὰ] ἔχουσι φάναι καὶ κατὰ lat. (Thillet 50 n.3); ἔχον φανῆναι καὶ κατὰ P. 25 τὰς τοιαύτας H. 28 ἔχειν om. O; del., vel λέγοντες ἔχειν *legendum*, Bruns *Interp. Var.*17 n.2. μισθοὺς] μύθους lat. 29 πειθομένων *coni.*O. 31 ἀναπεπείκασιν] *dissuaserunt* lat.; cf. *supra de* 180.22-23.

p.181.1 αὐτοῖς Bruns; αὐτοῖς codd.; αὐτοὺς O. 1-2 τοὺς - λέγειν] *mendacia credentes dicere* lat. 2 λέγω P. 4 τίνα VPW lat.a¹; ποῖα H. 6 τὰ (alt.) VH; om. WPa¹. 8 ἄλλως] ὅλως lat. (Thillet 151 s. *totaliter*). 10 τ' αἴδια Wa¹. τὴν τοιαύτην WPa¹. 18 καὶ κατὰ P. 19 οὐσίας O (per errorem?), corr. Casp.O. 21 ἐν] καὶ ἐν P; om. lat. 22 τῆς VWa¹; οἷ? P; τὸ τῆς H. 23 προκείμενα (supra προ: ἀντι)P. 25 ἔχοι Bruns; ἔχειν codd.; ἔχει Bloch O; *haberent* lat. (= ἔχειν vel εἶχεν Thillet 39 n.4). 28 δὲ] μὲν O. 36 ἀλλ' VW lat.a¹; καὶ P?; καὶ (in mg. ἀλλ')H.

p.182.1 ταὐτά Va¹; ταῦτα HW lat.; τὰ αὐτὰ P.

Adnot. ad text.: *mantissa* XXV

3-4 τέχνην τε om. P; τε om. Wa¹.   5 δὴ] δὲ O.
5-6 τὸ τῆς εἱμαρμένης] *fatum* tantum lat.; ita quoque
182.19, 183.7(τὰ), 184.9, 185.11, 13, 186.3.   8 ἀλλ᾽
VHWa¹; καὶ P.   9 τῶν ἐν delenda, vel φύσει post
γενέσει subaudiendum (quod tamen contortum et minime
naturale existimat) Donini, cf. Comm.   12 μετὰ
τούτου O.   16 ἐπ᾽ ἦν V; *sub quo* lat.   18 αὐτῇ O;
αὐτῇ codd.   τοῦδε] τάδε O.   20 αὐτῆς] lege αὐτὴν
(VHWa¹); αὐτῆς P Bruns; *ipsam* lat.(EG); *illam ipsam*
lat.(O).   24 ἄλλην] ἄδηλον coni. Gercke 124 in app.,
cf. *de fato* VIII 174.2 et *mantissa* 179.7.   26 καὶ
(pr.) om. HO.   28 μαντείαις] *divinatoribus* lat.
(cf. *de fato* XXXI 202.6).   ἐνδὸν HWP lat.a¹; ἐμὸν V.
29 δὲ] *igitur* lat. (= δὴ vel οὖν Thillet 41 et n.4).
30 αὐτοῖς V lat.; αὐτοῖς HWPa¹.   32 ἐν (alt.) om. P.
34 ὁραθεισα (supr. α pr.: ισ)V¹; ὁρισθεῖσα WH lat.a¹;
ὁραισθεῖσα P.   35 τὰ μέγιστα O.

p.183.1 καὶ om. O.   fort. ἐνδεχομένου (cf. 184.32)
Bruns.   3 τὸν om. O.   6 τύχης] *natura* c.
πεπίστευται] *persuasum habent* lat. (*persuasus* =
πεπιστευμένος, *de fato* XIX 189.12).   8 προηρημένους
Vmg. Hmg.   9 ταὐτὰ (cf. 182.1) lat. Bruns; ταῦτα
cett.   13 ταὐτὰ Bruns; ταῦτα cett.   14 λέγοιμεν O.
16 εἶναι om. Wa¹; P?   16 τὸ] τὰ O.   17 καὶ om. O.
20 ἀνάγκη] *necessarie* lat.   23 ὅτι γὰρ om.P.
25 <τῶν> add. Bloch O.   τῆς om. WPa¹.   27 ὃν δὲ VH
lat.; οὐδὲ WPa¹.   γε] τε lat. (Thillet 41).
28 γίγνεται Bloch (qui lacunam ante ἐν δὲ τοῖς (26)
statuit), ?lat.   [γεγονότος κενῶς] del. Bloch; exh.
lat.   *certe frustra et temere facta erit* c.
30 τοῦδε WPa¹; τούτου H; *huius* lat.(EG); *huiusmodi*
lat.(O).   31 τοῖς] lege ταῖς; *herentes fantasiis
irrationalibus similiter aliis animalibus* lat. Cf.
Comm.   33 ἡμῶν O; ἡμῖν codd.; om. lat.

p.184.1 συναίρασθαι V; *valere* lat.   3 lege συμβουλῶν
(cf. *de fato* XXXI 202.7), Bruns, *Interp. Var.* 15 n.2;
συμβουλιῶν fort. (cf. 185.21) Bruns in ed.; συμβόλων

278

Adnot. ad text.: *mantissa* XXV

Kontos, Ἀθηνᾶ 3 (1893) 523ff.; συμβούλων codd. et lat.
ὀνείρων] *divinationes* lat.   4 τινῶν om. H.
5 συστῆσαι om. H.   Lege διδασκαλίαι (Bruns, fort.);
doctrina c; διδασκαλίαις cett.   τέ τινων] *honorari*
lat.   κελεύεται cO.   8 *si quidem in nobis e s s e
est* lat.   τι om. H.   10 αἱ om. Wa[1].   15 post
οὐδεμίαν: *vero* lat.(EO), om. lat.(G); secl. Thillet.
16 ἀνεπιτηδειότητα] *ydoneitatem* lat.
18 ἐπιτηδειότητα ante δύναμιν del. W.   19 αὐτῷ] *se
ipso* lat.   20 <ἃ> add. Bloch; ταυτα sic V; ταῦτά
Wa ; τὰυτά H; *hec* lat.; τοιαῦτα P.   ἔστιν] ἔτι lat.
<τι> add.O; *sicut* τὰ ἀίδια *vertit* lat.   οἷς lat.
Bruns; τοῖς cett.   21 ὑποκείμενον, in mg.
ἀντικείμενον H.   22 ἔχει Bruns; ἔχειν libri.
24 τε del. O in adnot.   25 πάσχει O.   τοῦτ'·]
lege τουτ<έστι> (coni. Casp.O, Bruns in app.); *e t hoc*
lat.   ἐνδέχεται VH lat.; ἐνδέχεσθαι WPa[1].   *lacunam*
ante τοῦτο statuit Bloch.   27 ἀνάγκην V.   30 καὶ
(alt.) om. P lat.   32 ἡ om. P.

p.185.3 αὐτοῖς c Bruns; αὐτοῖς codd.   6 τῷ VHP lat.;
τῶν Wa[1].   6-8 διακόπτεται vel potius πολλάκις
<πέφυκε> coni. O.   8 γεννητοῖς PWa[1].   9 συνιστᾶσαν
Wa[1]; συστᾶσαν VH; συνιστωσαν P; *constituentem* lat.
10 τὸ] τὰ lat.   13 lege ζῴῳ, ἀνθρώπῳ (Bruns, fort.,
et Donini (1974,2) 163 n.65); ζῴων, ἀνθρώπων codd.;
animalibus aut hominibus lat., sim. c.   15 οὖσα V
lat.; οὔσης HWPa[1].   lege κατὰ ταύτην (Donini,
loc. cit.); κατὰ ταῦτα H lat.; ταυτά Va[1]; κατ' αὐτὰ W;
κατὰ ταὐτὰ c.   19 ἱκανῶς Wa[1]; *sufficiunt* lat.
20 πρόσταξις VH lat.; προστάξις a[1]; προστάξεις W,
'fort. recte, cf. *de fato* VI 170.15' Bruns.   Post
ἰατρῶν non interpungendum.   24 τὸ om. O.
26 ἀφιμάχων καὶ om. lat.   τῷ ... ἀφιμάχῳ καὶ
φιλοκινδύνῳ coni. Bloch, cf. infra et *de fato* VI
170.21f.   28 αὐτῶν H; αὐτοῦ VWP Hmg. lat.a[1]O.
29 καὶ τῷ καρτερικῷ] *et perseveratio* lat.   καὶ
(alt.) om. Wa[1].   31 καὶ (pr.) om.O.   αὐτῶν WHa[1].
αὐτῶν ὀλιγωροῦσιν] *vilificantur* lat.   31-33 διὰ -

Adnot. ad text.: *mantissa* XXV, *quaest.* II.4

θανάτου **in mg. H.** **32** γοῦν] *et* lat. (= τε? **Thillet**
41). αὐτῷ **Wa¹.** **33** τοῦ καθ' εἱμαρμένην] *fato*
tantum lat.; cf. **supra ad 182.5.** **35** τε om. **P.**

p.186.1 ἕξει] *erit* lat. αἰτίαν **Bloch;** αἰτίων **codd.**
συμπίπτει **cO (et** ἕξει = *habitu).* *causa coincidens*
lat. **2** αἱ **WHa¹;** ὡς **P;** om. **V.** **3** τοῦ] τῶν **P.**
5 καὶ παρὰ μοῖραν καὶ om. lat.; cf. **supra de 180.4.**
τὴν om. **HO.** **6** λέγων om. **HO.** **7** *neque sub fato*
domum Philomena dimittit lat. **8** συνίσται **Wa¹.**
Lege ὑπὸ <τοῦ> τοὺς **(Bruns in app., fort.);** ὑπὸ τῶν
μάντεων **coni.O.** **9** ἐπιτυγχάνειν] *pro certo evenire*
lat. **(qui in** *de fato* **VI 171.8** *per verum dicere*
vertit). τήνδε om. **P.** **10** θαυμαστὸν οὐδέν om.
lat. **11** τοῖς] τῷ **WPa¹.** **15** ὑπολείπεται **O.**
17 μέγας **Aristoteles et** lat.; μέγα **H;** μέρος **VPWa¹.**
τῆς εἱμαρμένες **K.** **19** ἀνταποδόσεις] *causas* lat.
οὐκ ἔχοντες **P.** αὐτοὺς **WPa¹.** τε καὶ **O.**
20 κατηναγκασμένας] *necessario causantes* lat. **(cf.**
necessitatem habere, **183.12 supra).** **22 Punct.**
interrog. post φύσιν **requiritur.** [ἢ] **del. O, om.**
lat. τῷ om. **H.** **24** μὴ τῷ] **lege** τῷ μὴ; *vel 'ei*
quod non fatatum' lat.(cod.O) **in mg.; sim. c.**
26 μὴ om. lat. **28** μὴ ἄλλο **cO, sed hoc loco**
exponitur impossibile (cf. 26).

Quaestio II.4

p.50.28 εἰ τοῦ ἐφ' ἡμῖν τὸ **tabula ad init. libr. II**
Quaestionum; εἰ ἐφ' ἡμῖν οὗ τὸ **H;** εἰ τοῦτο ἐφ' ἡμῖν οὗ
τὸ **vulg.** οὐδὲ τὸ αὐτὸ **eadem tabula.** **29** [ἐφ' ἡμῖν
οὐδὲ] **del. Bruns.** **30** [μὴ] **del.** V²S², om. a²Sp. το
(tert.) **sic V.** **31** μὴ] οὐκ **SVF 2.1007.** τοῦ V²S²B;
τοῦτο V¹S¹EHa²Sp. τὸ **VH;** οὗ τὸ **SHa²Sp.**

p.51.2 οὐδὲ αὐτὸ τὸ **E;** οὐδὲ τὸ αὐτὸ (αὐτὸ **s.v.)F.**
Lege οὐδὲ τὸ ἐφ' ἡμῖν <ἄρα> **(V²B¹H Vict.);** <ἄρα ἐφ'
ἡμῖν> B²S²a²Sp.*SVF* **2.1007; om.** V¹FS **Bruns.** **3** ὃ]
lege οὓς **(V²FHB²S²a²Sp.*SVF*);** ὃ V¹E **Bruns.**
Post οὓς **adde** <ἄρα> **(V²HEB²S²a²Sp.*SVF*); om.** V¹**Bruns;**

280

Adnot. ad text.: *quaest.* II.4-5

οὖν ἄρα F. 3-4 τὸ ἀντικείμενον μὴ ἐφ' ἡμῖν Vict.
4 τοῦτο Diels. <ἢ> add. V²S²BHa²Sp. 5 [τὸ] (pr.)
non delendum; exh. VB¹S¹H Vict.Sp.; del. B²S²a²Bruns.
τὸ εἶναι] lege τι εἶναι (Sp.). 10 ẍαὶ τὸ μὴ B²S²a²
Sp.; μὴ ẍαὶ τὸ VHB¹FS¹. ἴδιον] lege εἰ δι' οὖ
(Bruns, fort.); ἴδιον libri (= *in seiner einen*,
eigenthümlichen Bedeutung Apelt). οὐẍ delendum
(Bruns, fort.). 11 post τούτου non interpungendum
(ita Bruns, fort., in app.). τὸ δὲ] lege τόδε
(Bruns, fort.). ἐφ' ἡμῖν (alt.) V(μ in lit.)HB; ἐφ'
ἡμῖν ἐφ' ἡμῖν Hγρ.EFSa²Vict.Sp. δῆλον] δίττον
Apelt. ὡς οὖν] lege ὡς ὧν (Bruns, fort.); ὡς οὖν
codd.; οὖν ὧν Vict.Sp.; ὧν οὖν Apelt. 12 ὅτι μὴ]
lege ὅτι τὰ ('ὅτι τὰ exspectes', Bruns in app.); ὅτι
μὴ libri; ὃ δ' ἂν ἦ Apelt. 13 [τὸ] del. Sp.
fort. <οὐδ'> ἐν Bruns. 14 τοῦ Sp.; τὸ libri.
15 <ἃ> add. Vict.

Quaestio II.5

p.51.20 Lege τὸ μηδὲν εἶναι ἐφ' ἡμῖν. <τὸ δὲ μηδὲν
εἶναι ἐφ' ἡμῖν> ἀδύνατον. τὸ οὖν (add. *SVF* 2.1007).
ἀδύναΤὸν sic V; ἀδύνατον HFS¹B¹; om. B²S²a²Sp.; fort.
ẍαὶ δύνατον Bruns. Cf. Comm. 21 τὸ.(pr.) del.
Apelt. [τὸ] (alt.) del. Sp.Bruns Apelt. 24 τῷ
Bruns; τὸ libri. 25 σῴζοιτο] σῴζοι τὸ V; σῴζοι ἂν
τοὺς Sp. ẍατὰ τοὺς ἅπαντα Bruns; ẍατ ὑσίαν (supra
τ: α m¹) πάντα V; ẍατὰ οὐσίαν πάντα libri. 27 τὸ]
τῷ H. τῷ VB Vict.Sp.; τὸ HSa²; τὸ οὐ F. 28 <ἦν>
add. Sp. τὸ ᾧ τὸ HB Vict.Sp.; ·τὸ ᾧ τὸ· V; τῶ τὸ
FSa².

p.52.5 Lege ἀντιστρέψει (B²Sp. Bruns in app.);
ἐπιστρέψει codd. 5-6 οὐ δεῖται] lege οὐδ' ἀεὶ ẍαὶ
(Bruns, fort.); οὐ δεῖται codd.; οὐ δεῖται γοῦν Vict.;
οὐ δ' εἴ τι B²; οὐ δεῖ γοῦν εἶναι Sp. 7 οὖ Vict.;
οὐ libri. 9 ὑπάρχει] ει in lit. V. εἱρμὸν
Vict.; εἱμαρμένην libri. αἰτιῶν a²Sp.

Adnot. ad text.: *quaest.* III.13, etc.

Quaestio III.13

p.107.7 μόνῳ **Sp.**; μὲν **libri.**   μόνος **Sp.**; μόνῶν **V;**
μόνων **libri.**   **16** αὐτῇ **Bruns;** αὐτῷ **libri.**   **17** τῷ
(pr.) delendum (Bruns, fort.); τὸ a²**Sp.**   **19 an** ἐκ
τοῦ **delendum?**   [τε] **non delendum (del. Schwartz).**
21 ἡ **Schwartz;** ἥν **libri.**   **23** λεγοίμεθα **Sp.**; λεγόμεθα
libri.   **24** μηδὲ] **lege** δὲ μὴ **(Bruns, fort.);** ἔτι εἰ
μηδὲ **vel** ἐπεὶ <εἰ> μηδὲ **Apelt.**   **26** μὲν **F Vict. Sp.**;
μὴ **Va².**   τὸ **Sp.**; τοῦ **libri.**   **34** αὐτῇ **Sp.**; αὐτῆς
libri; αὐτοῖς **Vict.**   **37** φαντασία **Sp.**; φαντασίαν
libri.   **37-108.1** ἄλλο τεθείη **Vict.**; ἀλλοιωθείη
libri.

p.108.6 το// **V.**   **11** ἐπεὶ **Vict.**; ἐπὶ **libri.**   τοῦδε]
lege τούσδε **(Bruns, fort.).**   **12 fort.** ἢ **delendum,**
Bruns.

In top. 566.18-23

p.566.18 post λόγοις **add.** εὐλόγως **cod. Paris. 1843,**
εὐλόγους **cod. Vatic. 270.**   **20** τοῦτο] ταῦτα **Wallies.**
21 ἁμαρτάνειν συμβαίνει, καὶ ταῦτα **Wallies.**
23 ἐνδεχόμενα **Wallies;** ἔνδοξα **vel** ἔνδοξον **vel om.**
codd.

In top. 570.4-11

p.570.5 μάτην <ἂν> **vel** μάτην **delendum, Wallies.**
10 ὡς - βουλεύεσθαι **huc transpos. Wallies (in app.);**
in codicibus post ἀναιρεῖται **(11) leguntur.**

Select Bibliography

(i) *Editions of ancient works cited* (listed only where there might be doubt as to the system of reference used)

Albinus (Alcinous) *Didascalicus* ed. C.F. Hermann in *Platonis Dialogi* vol. VI 152-189 (Leipzig, Teubner, 1902)

Atticus *Fragments*, ed. E. des Places (Paris 1977)

Augustine *de civitate dei*, ed. B. Dombart (Leipzig, Teubner, 1902)

Boethius *in de int.*[1][2] *Anicii Manlii Severini Boethii commentaria in librum Aristotelis* peri heimarmenes, *editio prima* and *editio secunda*, ed. C. Meiser (Leipzig, Teubner, 1877 and 1880)

Calcidius *in Platonis Timaeum Commentarius*, ed. J.H. Waszink (*Plato Latinus*, IV; London and Leiden, 1962)

Critolaus *Die Schule des Aristoteles*, ed. F. Wehrli, vol. 10 (Basel, 1959)

Diogenes of Oenoanda *Diogenes Oenoandensis fragmenta*, ed. C.W. Chilton (Leipzig, Teubner, 1967)

Epicurus (*On Nature*): G. Arrighetti (ed.), *Epicuro: Opere* (Turin 1960)

(other works) C. Bailey (ed.), *Epicurus: the Extant Remains* (Oxford 1926)

Galen (*quod animi mores*): *C. Galeni Pergameni scripta minora*, ed. I. Marquardt, I. Mueller, C. Helmreich (Leipzig, Teubner, 1884-1893)

(other works): *C. Galeni opera omnia*, ed. C.G. Kühn, repr. Hildesheim, 1964 etc.

Proclus (*Elements of Thelogy*) ed. E.R. Dodds[2] (Oxford 1963)

(*in Platonis Timaeum*) ed. E. Diehl (Leipzig, Teubner, 1903-1906)

(*de providentia, de decem dubitationibus circa providentiam*): H. Boese (ed.), *Procli Diadochi tria opuscula* (Berlin 1960)

Theon of Smyrna *expositio rerum mathematicarum*, ed. E. Hiller (Leipzig, Teubner, 1878)

Theophrastus *Metaphysics*, ed. W.D. Ross and F.H. Fobes (Oxford, 1929)

(ii) *Determinism*

There is as yet no general survey covering all aspects of the treatment of the issues of free-will and determinism in post-Aristotelian philosophy, but general guides to the material are provided by:

G.L. Fonsegrive *Libre arbitre* (Paris 1887)
W.C. Greene *Moira: Fate, Good and Evil in Greek Thought* (Cambridge, Mass., 1944) ch. XI
R. Taylor art. 'Determinism', in *Encyclopedia of Philosophy* (ed. P. Edwards, etc.; New York and London, 1967) II. 359-373
E. Valgiglio (1967) 'Il fato nel pensiero classico antico', *Rivista di studi classici* 15 (1967) 305-330, 16 (1968) 56-84

Particular aspects of the subject are surveyed by:

D. Amand (E. Amand de Mendieta) *Fatalisme et liberté dans l'antiquité grecque* (Louvain 1945, reprinted Amsterdam 1973; references are to the reprint)
V. Cioffari *Fortune and Fate from Democritus to St Thomas Aquinas* (New York 1935)
P.-M. Schuhl *Le Dominateur et les possibles* (Paris, 1960)

Also of general importance is:

W. Theiler 'Tacitus und die antike Schicksalslehre', in *Phyllobolia für P. von der Mühll* (Basel 1946) 35-90; reprinted in Theiler's *Forschungen zur Neuplatonismus* (Berlin, 1966) 46-103. (References are to the 1946 edition)

For modern discussion of the problem, cf.:

D.J. O'Connor *Free Will* (London 1972)
R. Taylor op. cit. above

Aristotle

D.M. Balme (1939), (1941) 'Greek science and mechanism I, Aristotle on nature and chance', *Class. Quart.* 33 (1939) 129-138 (and cf. id. "II, the Atomists', ibid. 35 (1941) 23-28)

D.M. Balme (1972) (tr.) *Aristotle's de part. animal. I and de gen. animal. I* (Oxford, Clarendon Aristotle series, 1972) 76-84

D.J. Furley *Two Studies in the Greek Atomists* (Princeton, 1967) 184-195, 215-225

W.F.R. Hardie *Aristotle's Ethical Theory* (Oxford 1968) 152-180

J. Hintikka (1973) *Time and Necessity* (Oxford 1973) 62-113, 147-213

J. Hintikka (1977) 'Aristotle on Modality and Determinism', *Acta Philosophica Fennica* 29 (1977) no. 1.

R.W. Sharples (1975,1) 'Aristotelian and Stoic conceptions of necessity in the *de fato* of Alexander of Aphrodisias', *Phronesis* 20 (1975), 259-267

R.R.K. Sorabji (1980, 1) *Necessity, Cause and Blame: Perspectives on Aristotle's Theory* (London 1980). (Cf. above p. x)

Sarah Waterlow *Passage and Possibility; a Study of Aristotle's Modal Concepts*, Oxford 1982.

Epicurus

C. Bailey *The Greek Atomists and Epicurus* (Oxford 1928) 316-327, 433-437

M. Bollack '*Momen mutatum* (La déviation et le plaisir, Lucrèce II. 184-293)' in *Cahiers de Philologie I, Etudes sur l'Epicurisme antique* (Lille, 1976) 161-201

D.J. Furley op. cit. above, 161-237

A.A. Long (1974) *Hellenistic Philosophy* (London 1974) 56-61

A.A. Long (1977) 'Chance and natural law in Epicureanism', *Phronesis* 22 (1977) 63-88

P.M. Huby 'The first discovery of the freewill problem', *Philosophy* 42 (1967) 353-362

The Stoics
(for A. Gercke cf. above, p. 233).

(1) *Responsibility*

V. Bréhier *Chrysippe et l'ancien stoïcisme*[2] (Paris 1951) 170-184

P.L. Donini (1974,1) 'Fato e voluntà umana in Crisippo', *Atti dell' Accademia delle Scienze di Torino* 109 (1974-5) 1-44

J.B. Gould (1970) *The Philosophy of Chrysippus* (Leiden 1970) 107-152
(1974) 'The Stoic conception of fate', Journal of the History of
Ideas 35 (1974) 17-32

A.A. Long 'Freedom and determinism in the Stoic theory of human
action', in A.A. Long (ed.) *Problems in Stoicism* (London 1971) 173-
199
(1974) *Hellenistic Philosophy* (London 1974) 163-170
(1976) 'The early Stoic concept of moral choice', in *Images of Man
in Ancient and Medieval Thought, studia Gerardo Verbeke ... dicata*
(Leuven 1976) 77-92

M. Pohlenz *La Stoa, storia di un movimento spirituale*, translated and
revised, V.W. Alfieri etc. (Florence 1967) I. 201-213

A.C. Lloyd 'Emotion and Decision in Stoic Psychology', in J.M.
Rist (ed.), *The Stoics* (Berkeley 1978) 187-202

J.M. Rist *Stoic Philosophy* (Cambridge 1969) 112-132

F.H. Sandbach *The Stoics* (London 1975) 101-104

C. Stough 'Stoic determinism and moral responsibility', in J.M. Rist
(ed.), *The Stoics* (Berkeley 1978) 203-232

M. van Straaten 'Menschliche Freiheit in der stoischen
Philosophie', *Gymnasium* 84 (1977) 501-518

A.-J. Voelke *L'idée de volonté dans le Stoïcisme* (Paris 1973)

(b) *Possibility*

P.L. Donini (1973) 'Crisippo e la nozione del possibile', *Rivista di
filologia* 101 (1973) 333-351

M. Frede *Der Stoische Logik* (Göttingen 1974) 107-117

W. and M. Kneale *The Development of Logic* (Oxford 1963) 117-128

B. Mates *Stoic Logic*[2] (Berkeley 1961)

M. Mignucci 'Sur la logique modale des Stoïciens', in *Les Stoiciens et
leur logique, Actes du colloque de Chantilly* (Paris 1978) 317-346

J. Moreau 'Immutabilité du vrai, nécessité logique et lien causal',
ibid. 347-360

M.E. Reesor (1965) 'Fate and Possibility in Early Stoic Philosophy',
Phoenix 19 (1965) 285-297

S. Sambursky *Physics of the Stoics* (London 1959) 49-80

R.W. Sharples 'Necessity in the Stoic doctrine of fate', *Symbolae
Osloenses* 56 (1981) 81-97

R.R.K. Sorabji (1980, 2) 'Causation, Laws and Necessity', in *Doubt
and Dogmatism: Studies in Hellenistic Epistemology*, eds. M. Schofield,
M. Burnyeat, J. Barnes, Oxford 1980, 250-282

Cicero

M.Y. Henry 'Cicero's treatment of the free will problem', *Trans.*
Amer. Philol. Assoc. 58 (1927) 32-42

A. Yon (ed.) *Cicéron: traité du destin* (Paris, Budé, 1950).

Middle Platonists

J. den Boeft *Calcidius on Fate: his doctrine and sources* (Leiden 1970)

J.M. Dillon *The Middle Platonists* (London 1977) especially 294-298;
320-326; 401-408

P.H. de Lacy (and B. Einarson, ed.) *Plutarch, Moralia* vol. VII (Loeb,
1959). (Includes [Plutarch] *de fato*.)

E. Valgiglio (1964) (ed.) *ps.- Plutarco De Fato* (Rome 1964)

(iii) *Alexander of Aphrodisias*

(a) *General*. Only a few works are listed here; I am myself currently
compiling a *Bericht* on Alexander studies for *Aufstieg und Niedergang der*
Römischen Welt, eds. H. Temporini and W. Haase, Teil II, *Principat*,
section *Philosophie und Wissenschaften*. Meanwhile for a fuller survey cf.
Todd 261-263. Vol. III of P. Moraux' *Der Aristotelismus bei den*
Griechen (Berlin, de Gruyter) will be devoted to Alexander.

A. Badawí *La transmission de la philosophie grecque en monde arabe* (Paris,
1968) 94-99, 121-165

F.E. Cranz arts. 'Alexander of Aphrodisias' in *Catalogus*
Translationum et Commentariorum, ed. P.O. Kristeller (Washington,
D.C.) I (1960) 77-135, II (1971) 411-422

P.L. Donini (1974,2) *Tre studi sull' Aristotelismo nel II secolo d.C.*
(Turin 1974)

J. Freudenthal 'Die durch Averroes erhaltenen Fragmente
Alexanders zur Metaphysik des Aristoteles', *Abhandl. der Berliner*
Akademie 1884, 1

R.M. Grant (Greek fragments of *de prov.*). Op. cit., above p. 232

P. Moraux *Alexandre d'Aphrodise: Exégète de la noétique d'Aristote* (Liège
and Paris 1942)

H.-J. Ruland *Die arabischen Fassungen zwei Schriften des Alexander von*
Aphrodisias, diss. Saarbrücken, 1976

R.B. Todd *Alexander of Aphrodisias on Stoic Physics* (Leiden 1976).
(Includes text and translation of the *de mixtione*)

M. Wallies (ed.) Alexandri Aphrodisiensis in Aristotelis Topicorum libros octo commentaria (CAG 2.2), Berlin 1891

E. Zeller *Die Philosophie der griechen* 3.1³ (Leipzig, 1880) 789-800; tr. S.F. Alleyne ('E. Zeller, *A History of Eclecticism in Greek Philosophy*', London 1883) 318-331

(b) *De Fato and related works*
(Cf. also above, pp. 231-4)

I. Bruns (1889) 'Studien zu Alexander von Aphrodisias – I. Der Begriff des Möglichen und die Stoa', *Rheinisches Museum* 44 (1889) 613-630

(1893) *Interpretationes Variae* (Kiel 1893) 14-17

P.L. Donini (1977) 'Stoici e Megarici nel *de fato* di Alessandro di Afrodisia?' in *Scuole socratiche minori e filosofia ellenistica*, ed. G. Giannantoni (Bologna, 1977) 174-194

F.P. Hager 'Proklos und Alexander von Aphrodisias über ein Problem der Vorsehung', in *Kephalaion: Studies in Greek philosophy and its continuation presented to C.J. de Vogel* (Assen 1975) 171-182

A.A. Long (1970) 'Stoic determinism and Alexander of Aphrodisias *de fato* (I-XIV)', *Arch. Gesch. Philos.* 52 (1970) 247-268

P. Merlan 'Zwei Untersuchungen zu Alexander von Aphrodisias', *Philologus* 113 (1969) 253-256

R.A. Pack 'A passage in Alexander of Aphrodisias relating to the study of tragedy', *American Journal of Philology* 58 (1937) 418-436

R.W. Sharples (1975,1) 'Aristotelian and Stoic conceptions of necessity in the *de fato* of Alexander of Aphrodisias', *Phronesis* 20 (1975) 247-274

(1975, 2) 'Responsibility, chance, and not-being (Alexander of Aphrodisias *mantissa* 169-172)', *Bull. Inst. Classical Studies* (London) 22 (1975) 37-63

(1978) 'Alexander of Aphrodisias *De Fato*: some parallels', *Class. Quart.* 28 (1978) 243-266

'Alexander of Aphrodisias' second treatment of fate? (*de anima libri mantissa* pp. 179-186 Bruns)', *Bull. Inst. Classical Studies* (London) 27 (1980) 76-84

(1982, 1) 'An ancient dialogue on possibility; Alexander of Aphrodisias. *Quaestio* 1.4', *Arch. Gesch. Philos.* 64 (1982) 23-38

(1982, 2) and (1983) 'Alexander of Aphrodisias; Problems about possibility I', *Bull. Inst. Classical Studies* (London) 29 (1982) 91-108, and id II, forthcoming ibid. 30 (1983)

E. Valgiglio (1967) 'Il fato nel pensiero classico antico', *Rivista di studi classici* 15 (1967) (see above), 309-319

G. Verbeke 'Aristotélisme et Stoïcisme dans le *de fato* d'Alexandre d'Aphrodise', *Arch. Gesch. Philos.* 50 (1968) 73-100

Index of Passages Cited

All references both here and in the General Index are by page numbers of this book.

Passages from ancient authors included in *SVF* (see p. x) have been cited both by author's name and by *SVF* number, depending on context. They are therefore given under both in the index, the *SVF* number also being indicated in the author entry to assist the reader in locating the reference in the body of the book if that is by *SVF* number alone; it should be noted, however, that where an *SVF* reference is given after a chapter number, the *SVF* reference may not apply to the whole of that chapter.

General Index

(Under names of ancient authors see also the Index of passages cited.)

Index

cyclical recurrence, 153, 158
cylinder, 9, 56, 143, 153
Cyril of Alexandria, 30, 232

De Lacy, P.H., 141, 163, 286
deliberation, 55-8, 62-4, 70, 85, 97-100, 109, 111, 116, 118-21, 139-42, 145-6, 173-4, 178
Democritus, 4
what depends on us, *see* responsibility
determinism, 3-14, 147. *See next entry*
determinism, hard and soft, 9-11, 21 n.144, 126, 128, 146, 150, 153, 160, 166, 169, 171. *See* libertarianism
diagonal, 81, 108, 165
dialectical argument, 21, 27, 151-2, 177
Diehl, E., 282
Diels, H., x, 125, 130, 172, 233
Dietrich, A., 16 n.98
Dillon, J.M., 13 n.69, 14 n.80, n.84, n.86, 286
Diodorus Cronus, 12, 136-7
Diogenes of Oenoanda, 282
dispositions, 47, 76, 78-9, 86-8, 100-1, 113, 160-1, 163, 169
divination, *see* prophecy
divine, divine body, *see* gods, heavenly body
doctors, 47, 51, 103, 113
Dodds, E.R., 4 n.6, 30 n.208, 282
Donini, P.L., 10 n.47, 11 n.53, 20 n.136, 21, 23, 24 n.159, n.163, 25 n.173, 26 n.175, 31 n.211, 130, 135, 142, 151, 156, 159-61, 163, 166, 170, 173, 176, 233, 284-7
Dover, K.J., 11 n.53

earth, 59, 63-4. *See* heavy bodies
Earth, the 96
Edmunds, L., 4 n.8
education, 67, 94, 152, 173. *See* teaching
effects, 70-4, 152-7. *See* causation
efficient cause, 43-5, 102, 126, 155
Einarson, B., 141, 286
elements, 83, 109. *See* earth, fire, etc.
end, final cause, 43-5, 49, 102-3, 110-11, 133, 139-40, 148-9, 155, 178
Epicurus, Epicureans, 4, 7-9, 11-13, 22, 83, 91, 141, 147, 159, 282
van Ess, J., 16 n.98
eternal things, 56, 95-6, 107-8, 112. *See* heavenly bodies
Euripides, 82

Eusebius, 29-31, 129, 232
evil, problem of, 26. *See* rarity of good men
exceptions, 2-3, 23, 25, 27-8, 46-8, 71-2, 75, 113-15, 129-31, 158-9, 176
excuses, 48, 65-8, 106-7, 131
exhortation, persuasion, 65, 67, 69, 76, 98, 100, 173
explanation, 5-6, 126, 131
external and internal causes, 9, 20-1, 59, 63, 68, 88-9, 95, 100, 108, 127, 134, 143, 148, 152. *See* circumstances

falsity, 95
fatalism, 10, 141, 150-1, 162, 166, 171, 173
fate, 117, 120-1. *See* necessity
  Alexander on, 23-8, 42-8, 106-15, 128-30, 176
  Peripatetics on, 24-5, 114-15
  Stoics on, 8, 20, 59-60, 68, 77, 82-4, 86, 88-91, 128-9, 152, 154, 170
Fell, J., 232
Festugière, A.-J., 25 n.172
final cause, *see* end
fine, noble, 64-5, 87, 90-1, 99-101, 149
fire, 52, 56, 59-63, 112
first cause, 74-5, 157-8. *See* principle
fitness, *see* capacity
FitzGerald, A., 139, 233
Foerster, P.R., 130
Foley, R., 7 n.26
Fonsegrive, G.L., 142, 283
force, 52, 59, 68, 114. *See* compulsion
foreknowledge, 19, 27-9, 80-1, 163-7
form, formal cause, 43-4, 102
Fortenbaugh, W.W., 24 n.162
fortuitous, 50, 104-5, 127, 131, 175. *See* chance
foundation and house, 73
Frede, D., 139, 163
Frede, M., 137, 153, 170-1, 285
freedom of action, 141
freedom, free will, 9, 22, 27, 158-9. *See* responsibility, libertarianism
Freudenthal, J., 286
fruit, 72, 154-5
Furley, D.J., 7 nn.27-8, 8 n.34, 9 n.46, 147, 284
future truth, 11-12, 54-5, 66, 138, 141, 161-2

phoenix, the, 78
Physiognomists, 48, 130
piety, 66, 93
Pines, S., 15 n.93
des Places, E., 282
plants, 72, 154-5
Plato, 4, 13
pleasure, pleasant, 62, 64-5, 68, 99, 149
Plotinus, 16 n.93, 28
[Plutarch], xiii, 14, 286
pneuma, 8, 156
poets, 43, 83, 109, 114
Pohlenz, M., 23 n.156, 153-4, 285
Polybus, 82
Polyzelus, 24, 115
Porphyry, 28-9
Posidonius, 153
possibility, 12, 52-5, 77, 80-1, 134-7, 141, 161-2, 164. *See* capacity, contingency
practical consequences of determinism, 13, 17-18, 41, 64-70, 100, 109, 150-2
practice (*askēsis*), 77-8, 101, 161. *See* habituation, training
praise and blame, 10-11, 65-6, 69, 76-8, 84, 87-8, 90-1, 100, 119, 121, 150, 161-2, 164, 170-1, 173
prayer, 69, 93, 100, 109, 111, 114, 151
prediction, 11-12, 66, 107, 141. *See* prophecy, foreknowledge, future truth
present, necessity or possibility of, 141
Preus, A., 140, 145
Priam, 66
'primary' causes, 49-52, 73, 132-3
principle (*archē*, beginning), 6, 57, 62-4, 74-5, 97-8, 127, 142, 146-8, 157-8
Prior, A.N., 12 n.64
Proclus, 28, 282
proēgoumenos, see primary causes
prophecy, oracles, 19, 47-8, 54, 67, 79, 82-4, 100, 105-7, 109, 111, 113-14, 130, 137, 151, 164-8, 170, 176
providence, divine
  Alexander on, 25-7, 66, 151
  Epicurus, denial of, 22, 83
  Stoics on, 8, 20, 72, 83-4, 142, 159, 162-3, 166
punishment and reward, 10-11, 65, 67-8, 76, 87-91, 100, 111, 119, 150, 171, 173
purpose in nature, 19, 42, 55, 57, 106, 111-12, 139, 142, 154-5

rarity of good men, 19, 78, 162-3
reason, rational, reasonable, 44-6, 61-2, 64, 76, 79, 85-6, 91, 97-8, 100, 116-20, 127-8, 139, 144-6, 148-9, 163-4, 170, 177
Reesor, M.E., 10 n.48, 135, 154, 160, 166, 285
regress, infinite, 157-8, 160
regret, repentance, 58, 98-100
regularity, 2-3, 23 n.155, 137. *See* 133-4, exceptions
reproach, 47, 58, 67, 69, 113, 171
residues, superfluities, 72, 154-5
responsibility, 6-11, 21-2, 45-6, 55-67, 69-70, 76-9, 84-5, 88, 90, 94-101, 106, 108-12, 116-19, 121, 126, 131, 140-6, 150, 156-7, 159-64, 166-9, 171, 177-8
Rieth, O., 144, 153-4, 170
right and wrong action, 85-91, 177. *See* virtue and vice
Rist, J.M., 16 n.93, 135, 137, 140, 145, 165, 285
Rodier, G., 148, 150-1, 173, 233
Rose, H.J., 168
Rosetti, L., 130
Ross, W.D., 5 n.15, 127, 282
Ruland, H.-J., x, 25 nn.170-1, 30, 156, 158, 174-5, 232, 286

Sambursky, S., 5 n.11, 8 n.37, 129, 147, 157, 170, 285
Sandbach, F.H., 8 n.40, 140, 285
Schofield, M., 136, 139, 153
Schuhl, P.-M., 137, 283
Schulthess, J.G., 233
Schwartz, E., 146, 151, 233
Sea-Battle (paradox), 11-12, 54-5, 137-9
seasons, 73-4, 114
Sedley, D.N., 12 nn.63-4, 171
self-contradictions, *see* inconsistencies
seminal reasons, 158
Septimius Severus, 15, 19 n.118, 41
sequence of causes, *see* chain of causes
serpents, 104
Sharples, R.W., bibliography: 159, 162, 232, 283, 285, 287-8
skill, 76, 103-6, 108-9, 113, 161, 175. *See* craft
snow, 52, 112
Socrates, 22 n.148, 48, 73, 113, 130, 156
soft determinism, *see* determinism, hard and soft
Sophroniscus, 73, 156